HANDBOOK OF MIDDLE AMERICAN INDIANS, VOLUME 12
Guide to Ethnohistorical Sources, Part I

HANDBOOK OF MIDDLE AMERICAN INDIANS

EDITED AT MIDDLE AMERICAN RESEARCH INSTITUTE, TULANE UNIVERSITY, BY

ROBERT WAUCHOPE, *General Editor*
MARGARET A. L. HARRISON, *Associate Editor*
JOSEPHITA N. BODDIE, *Administrative Assistant*
JOSEPH C. WIEDEL, *Cartographical Consultant*

ASSEMBLED WITH THE AID OF A GRANT FROM THE NATIONAL SCIENCE FOUNDATION, AND UNDER THE SPONSORSHIP OF THE NATIONAL RESEARCH COUNCIL COMMITTEE ON LATIN AMERICAN ANTHROPOLOGY

HANDBOOK OF MIDDLE AMERICAN INDIANS

ROBERT WAUCHOPE, General Editor

VOLUME TWELVE

Guide to Ethnohistorical Sources

PART ONE

HOWARD F. CLINE, Volume Editor

UNIVERSITY OF TEXAS PRESS · AUSTIN

Published in Great Britain by the
University of Texas Press, Ltd., London

International Standard Book Number 0-292-70152-7
Library of Congress Catalog Card No. 64–10316
Copyright © 1972 by the University of Texas Press
All rights reserved

The preparation and publication of the
Handbook of Middle American Indians
has been assisted by grants from
the National Science Foundation.

Typesetting by G&S Typesetters, Austin, Texas
Printing by The Meriden Gravure Company, Meriden, Connecticut
Binding by Universal Bookbindery, Inc., San Antonio, Texas

CONTENTS

FOREWORD

The Introduction provides details on the purposes of this "Guide to Ethnohistorical Sources," how it was conceived, and remarks on concepts of ethnohistory. This Foreword gives readers information about some of the usages and practices they will encounter, and makes general acknowledgments.

CITATIONS, REFERENCES, AND BIBLIOGRAPHIES

These volumes conform in general to practices developed for previous volumes of the *Handbook of Middle American Indians*. The nature of the material and its handling, however, have imposed some variations. Published materials follow earlier usage by citation of author(s) and date(s) of publication in parentheses throughout the text. Unpublished manuscript sources are cited in footnotes with appropriate archival indicia, and do not figure in the list of references at the end of the article.

As elsewhere in the *Handbook*, each article carries at the end a list of references cited in it. These references appear in full bibliographical form at the end of each volume. However, as some articles are themselves annotated bibliographies, and others carry extensive bibliographical appendices, the reference section at the end of an article may instead direct the reader to a bibliographical article or appendix, most of whose titles will not be repeated in the consolidated bibliography at the close of the volume.

PLACE NAMES AND PERSONAL NAMES

Colonial Mexican writers were anarchistic, and highly individualistic in their orthography, especially of native personal and place names. To some degree the contributors to these volumes display the same traits. Editorial policy has not attempted to impose an essentially false uniformity throughout the Guide for these names, in the text or on maps. We expect that through an index or perhaps a synonymy in the final volume of the Guide readers will learn that Tlacopan, Tlacuba, and Tacuba are one and the same. We have, so far as possible, retained consistency in any one article.

MAPS

The Volume Editor is primarily and ultimately responsible for most of the maps in the Guide. Purposefully, several styles are permitted, but for the most part they have fitted the general framework outlined in Article 1.

The whole enterprise was much aided by Peter Gerhard. Early in it he provided maps of the 16th-century civil jurisdictions that he summarizes in Article 2. We have used these as the bases for maps in other articles. Robert C. West prepared the maps accompanying his treatment of 18th-century relaciones (Article 10). Herbert R. Harvey provided drafts for Article 7.

With the exception of the Gerhard and West maps, the Volume Editor drew or redrew all original maps. In a number of cases, these are reproduced as he prepared them. However, he is grateful to Joseph C. Wiedel of the Department of Geography, University of Maryland, who acted as cartographical consultant. Wiedel and his students reviewed all maps, and in numerous instances produced a final version from Cline's drafts.

ACKNOWLEDGMENTS

Literally dozens of specialists have aided the Volume Editor and the contributors, and without such willing scholarly cooperation our tasks would have been more difficult, if not impossible. So far as possible, appropriate credit appears in footnotes to articles. It would be redundant to attempt to provide a total listing here, especially as the Guide is still in progress and later helping hands would thus be inadvertently omitted.

It is an especially pleasant obligation to record substantial help given by the General Editor, Robert Wauchope. Beyond the unfailing professional and technical assistance he furnished in that capacity, he authorized expenditure of National Science Foundation grant funds for the development of the Collection of Mexican Indian Pictorial Documents (presently housed at the Hispanic Foundation in the Library of Congress) to make available to the contributors and others photocopies of many unpublished such items.

Gratitude is also expressed to the Ford Foundation. On grant funds it furnished the Library of Congress for several programs of the Hispanic Foundation, it was possible at various points to enlist the services of John B. Glass as consultant, and to provide his travel in Mexico and the United States to clarify many mystifying points on sources in the native traditions.

Needless to say, the Volume Editor could not have brought the Guide to publishable shape without the dedicated and largely anonymous aid and support from his coeditors. He also undertook after initial consultation with them and the General Editor some often protracted negotiations with contributors, and is grateful for their good-humored tolerance of his editorial foibles.

HOWARD F. CLINE
Volume Editor

ABBREVIATIONS

ACLS	—	American Council of Learned Societies, New York.
ACM	—	Archivo de la Marina, Museo Naval, Madrid.
AGG	—	Archivo General del Gobierno, Guatemala.
AGI	—	Archivo General de Indias, Seville.
AGN	—	Archivo General de la Nación, Mexico.
AHN	—	Archivo Histórico Nacional (Documentos de Indias), Madrid.
AM	—	Alcaldía Mayor or alcalde mayor.
AMNA	—	Archivo Histórico, Museo Nacional de Antropología, Mexico.
ANCR	—	Archivos Nacionales de Costa Rica, San Jose.
BAGN	—	Boletín del Archivo General de la Nación, Mexico.
BAH	—	Biblioteca de Aportación Histórica, Luis Vargas Rea, ed.; subseries, 1944–47.
BCE	—	*See* Latorre, 1920a (Art. 9).
BHM	—	Biblioteca de Historiadores Mexicanos, 1948–, Vargas Rea, ed.
Bish	—	Bishopric.
BNMA	—	Biblioteca Nacional, Madrid.
BNMex	—	Biblioteca Nacional, México.
BNP	—	Bibliothèque Nationale, Paris.
BPEJ	—	Biblioteca Pública del Estado de Jalisco, Guadalajara.
C	—	Corregimiento or corregidor.
CDG	—	*See* Castañeda and Dabbs, 1939 (Art. 9).
DGMH	—	Dirección de Geografía, Meteorología e Hidrología, Mexico.
DHY	—	Documentos para la historia de Yucatán. *See* Scholes, Menéndez, Rubio Mañé, and Adams, 1936–38 (volume References.)
DII	—	*See* Pacheco, Cárdenas, and Torres de Mendoza, 1864–84 (Art. 9).
DIU	—	*See* Asensio, 1898, 1900 (Art. 9).
DyP	—	Descripción y Población, Sala de Indias, SIM.
ENE	—	Epistolario de Nueva España. *See* volume References.
EP	—	European paper (on which a pintura is painted).
FGO	—	Federico Gómez de Orozco.
FPT	—	Francisco Paso y Troncoso.
G	—	Gobierno.
HAHR	—	Hispanic American Historical Review.
HFC	—	Howard F. Cline.
HMAI	—	Handbook of Middle American Indians.
HSA	—	Hispanic Society of America, New York.
IG	—	Indiferente General, AGI.
INAH	—	Instituto Nacional de Antropología e Historia, Mexico.
Int	—	Intendancy.
JDE	—	*See* Jiménez de la Espada, 1881 (Art. 9).

JGI   — Joaquín García Icazbalceta.
JLV   — *See* López de Velasco, 1583 (Art. 9).
LdeT   — El libro de tasaciones. *See* volume References.
LPM   — Larrañaga . . . Papeles . . . Muñoz. *See* Larrañaga, 1783 (Art. 9).
M   — Municipio.
MNA   — Museo Nacional de Antropología [and predecessor institutions, with varying names], Mexico.
MP   — Memoria by Pinelo, reproduced as Appendix E, Art. 5.
NLA   — Newberry Library, Ayer Collection, Chicago.
NP   — Native paper (on which a pintura is painted).
NV   — *See* Anonymous, 1878 (Art. 9).
NYPL   — New York Public Library, New York.
OBBORE   — Obispado de Cuernavaca, *Boletín Oficial y Revista Eclesiástica*, edited by Francisco Plancarte y Navarrete (1856–1920).
OyB   — Orozco y Berra.
P   — Province.
PAIGH   — Pan American Institute of Geography and History, Mexico.
PNE   — Papeles de Nueva España. *See* Paso y Troncoso (Art. 9).
PR   — Patronato Real, AGI.
RAH   — Real Academia de la Historia, Madrid.
RC   — Royal cédula.
RG   — Relación Geográfica, based on May 25, 1577, questionnaire.
RGM   — Relaciones Geográficas de Michoacán. *See* Corona Núñez, 1958 (Art. 9).
RM   — Relación . . . Muñoz, 1783. *See* Muñoz, 1783 (Art. 9).
RMEH   — Revista Mexicana de Estudios Históricos. *See* Art. 9.
RNE   — *See* Latorre, 1920b (Art. 9).
RT   — Relaciones de Tabasco, DIU, vol. 13.
RY   — Relaciones de Yucatan, DIU, vol. 13.
SEP   — Secretaria de Educación Pública, Mexico.
SIM   — Simancas. *See* Larrañaga, 1783 (Art. 9).
SMGE   — Sociedad Mexicana de Geografía e Estadística.
TL   — *See* Torres Lanzas, 1900, item number, vol. 1 (Art. 9).
UNAM   — Universidad Nacional Autónoma de México.
UTX   — University of Texas Library, Latin American Collection, Austin.
V   — Villa.
VR   — Vargas Rea.

HANDBOOK OF MIDDLE AMERICAN INDIANS, VOLUME 12

Guide to Ethnohistorical Sources, Part I

GENERAL EDITOR'S NOTE

The manuscripts for the following articles were submitted at various dates over a period of several years. Because of revisions and minor updatings made from time to time, it is difficult to assign a date to each article. In some cases, an indication of when an article was completed can be had by noting the latest dates in the list of references at the end of each contribution.

Introduction: Reflections on Ethnohistory

HOWARD F. CLINE

THE *Handbook of Middle American Indians* devotes this and the three following volumes to a "Guide to Ethnohistorical Sources." Both the term "ethnohistory" and its concepts in the sense they are used here have entered the literature rather recently, and as yet are not fully agreed upon. This Introduction provides some information on how the Volume Editor and those who aided him in creating this Guide groped toward definitions and limits of ethnohistory and how the structure of its contents evolved, often more in practical than in ideal or theoretical terms. Given the embryonic state of ethnohistory, perhaps this case history will be illuminating. A second section of the Introduction discusses the varieties of studies which are included under the single term "ethnohistory," noting their likenesses and differences.

HISTORICAL NOTES ON THE
"GUIDE TO ETHNOHISTORICAL SOURCES"

One striking feature of the *Handbook of Middle American Indians* is the substantial space allotted to ethnohistory. The model on which this *Handbook* was generally based, the *Handbook of South American Indians* (1946–59), contained no such large ethnohistorical component. It did include some extremely able substantive articles which now would be labeled ethnohistorical, especially those by Rowe (1946) and by Kubler (1946). Those articles which parallel Rowe's treatment of Incas at Contact are found in the archaeological volumes of the *Handbook of Middle American Indians* (2, 3, 4, and 10), generally prepared by archaeologists who in addition to archaeological evidence have used documentary sources where available and relevant. Kubler's treatment of the Quechua in the colonial world, however, finds no counterpart in this Guide. Such absence is purposeful, the result of an early and important policy decision concerning what these volumes should contain.

Here a preliminary word must be said about the background and planning of the whole *Handbook of Middle American Indians*, to help explain the particular form and content of this Guide to Ethnohistorical Sources. Some brief reports on the genesis

3

and changing plan of the HMAI have been published (Cline, 1960a, 1966a). In summary, before 1956 two distinct groups of specialists, one in Washington, another in New York, had been discussing among themselves the obvious need for volumes on Middle America that would fill the gap between Hodge's *Handbook of American Indians North of Mexico* (1907–10) and the one then recently published on South America. At the third International Congress of Anthropological and Ethnological Sciences (Philadelphia, 1956) the two informal groups merged their plans, which were then taken up by a committee named by the National Research Council.[1]

The committee was to plan the HMAI, secure the necessary scholarly support, and seek the substantial funding required. A smaller subcommittee made the necessary fiscal and administrative arrangements. They enlisted the services of Robert Wauchope as General Editor, and the cooperation of the Middle American Research Institute at Tulane University to assume administrative responsibility. On formal application in 1959 from the latter, the National Science Foundation has provided funds to assemble the HMAI. The General Editor named various specialists as Volume Editors; collectively they have acted as an Editorial Advisory Board, replacing the earlier NRC Commitee (Wauchope, 1968, pp. 40–44). The Board's first task was to agree on an outline of the HMAI and to approve the proposed tables of contents for each volume. It was understood that these might be modified in detail by the General Editor as circumstances later changed. The Editorial Advisory Board did not have sufficient information at that stage to outline the volumes on ethnohistory.

Throughout this early planning process,

[1] Committee members included G. R. Willey, chairman; H. E. D. Pollock; Clyde Kluckhohn, ex officio; N. A. McQuown; T. D. Stewart; M. W. Stirling; J. B. Griffin; G. M. Foster; E. Z. Vogt; G. F. Ekholm; Angel Palerm; H. F. Cline; Glenn Finch, ex officio.

all specialists on Middle American Indians stressed the need for adequate coverage of ethnohistorical materials, but tended to differ widely on what such coverage should be. At length the Editorial Advisory Board decided in 1959 that to attempt to commission the writing of substantive articles on Indian groups of Middle America in the colonial period (like the Kubler one mentioned above) would be premature, given the thin monographic base, the disarray and lack of knowledge about necessary sources, the reduced number of trained ethnohistorical specialists, and conflicting views about the scope and nature of ethnohistory.

Hence the present Volume Editor was broadly charged with producing a guide to the sources, primarily for study of the post-Contact period. This would permit later studies to close the gap between the summaries by archaeologists of Contact Indian societies and cultures and the ethnological and social anthropological summaries of Middle America scheduled for other parts of the HMAI. In short, the volumes allotted to ethnohistory were, by common consent, precluded from attempting to present historiographical syntheses, but were specifically aimed to inventory and discuss documentary and published materials which later hands could utilize to produce professionally acceptable ethnohistory.

Anthropologists have been the chief producers and consumers of ethnohistory. In 1959 the Editorial Advisory Board agreed that however else defined, one of its characteristics was application of historiographical techniques to written sources. Hence they recommended that an historian rather than an anthropologist attempt to develop the basic scholarly infrastructure needed for ethnohistory. Because of relative lack of precedents and the known complexity but unknown magnitude of that task, the Advisory Editorial Board (all anthropologists but the writer) also indicated that the Guide to Ethnohistorical Sources should probably be the final volumes in the HMAI, as indeed they have turned out to be. Their gestation has been long, often troubled.

Again without attempting to define or delimit ethnohistory, these anthropologists who outlined the proposed structure of the HMAI did pose some specific problems and suggested certain guidelines concerning the contents of what in 1958–59 was estimated would be a two-volume guide. Unlike the South American areas covered by the earlier *Handbook*, one of the unique features of Middle America is a substantial body of written materials produced by the Indians themselves, nearly all in the post-Contact era, and more especially in the 16th century. The fact that the corpus exists, and is a differentiating feature for studies of Middle American Indian cultures, is of course, a given datum. The Advisory Editorial Board specifically wanted the corpus explored.

Until the various specialists who have contributed to this Guide undertook nearly a decade of research, it was not even tentatively established how large was the body of native documentation, either in its prose or in larger pictorial components. Little was known about state of publication or about repositories in which the native documents might be found. Similarly for better than half a century since some of them became available in print, the *Relaciones Geográficas* brought together in Middle America by orders from Philip II during the years 1578–85 have been widely used by archaeologists, historians, and others who find the historic, ethnographic, and other data in them of high value for reconstruction of earlier societies and cultures. Yet that body of prime sources lay unanalyzed, uninventoried, partially unpublished. The Board suggested at the outset that these, and other materials primarily in the European traditions, be discussed in the Guide.

The general problem, then, was to provide anthropologically minded historians and historically inclined anthropologists with reliable information about materials that they, their students, and colleagues could utilize to fill what had been shown to be a major gap in Middle American culture history. Increasingly sophisticated archaeological undertakings, finally fused at lower time depths with Paleo-Indian studies, had been moving toward more reliable generalizations about changes over a long time continuum, one which was rather abruptly terminated in many basic ways when Middle America fell under Spanish domination early in the 16th century. Many earlier native ways persisted into and beyond the early 19th century when the erstwhile colonial Viceroyalty of New Spain (which included all of present-day Mexico and Central America, and more) split into national states. But the ethnographic and ethnological reports on the functioning native cultures or quasi-native cultures as seen by scientists in the late 19th and 20th centuries seemingly lacked continuity with those discussed by archaeologists.

Archaeologists and ethnologists have, of course, long been aware that helpful data for their studies may be found in written records. Bernal (1962), Nicholson (1955, 1962), and others have called on archaeologists to make wider use of them. Certain studies, like that of Wauchope (1949), have systematically tried to utilize native sources to solve specific archaeological problems. As early as 1951 Lewis had amply illustrated that recourse to its known history enriched the study of a Mexican community; historians were quick to note that his placing such historically connected microstudies in the macro context of national setting illuminated general Mexican history and aided understanding of social dynamics (Cline, 1952, pp. 215–16, 220–21). The culling of historical data from written records as a relatively minor additional technique of archaeology or ethnology might legitimately be viewed as a variety or subvariety of ethnohistory. Its chief ef-

5

fect, however, is to improve archaeology or ethnology, not join or link them. The colonial period in Middle America, usually with an added century of national life, still separates them.

Nor is this preoccupation with time perspectives and continuities of aboriginal American cultures a novel anthropological topic. Sapir, a linguist, in 1916 devoted an 86-page monograph to exposition and criticism of various then standard methods to provide perspectives (Sapir, 1916). Several later anthropologists, among the first self-consciously to call themselves ethnohistorians, have noted that only five pages of Sapir's treatment discussed use of direct historical evidence, and within these only one page dealt specifically with use of documentary evidence for studies of native culture growth and change, a chief characteristic of what is now called ethnohistory (Lewis, 1942, p. 2; Fenton, 1952, pp. 328–29; Vogelin, 1954, p. 167).

To close that gap in continuity between findings of archaeology and ethnology becomes the task of future ethnohistory. Its techniques may well also continue to serve as auxiliaries both to archaeology and to ethnology (and its variants concerned with recent and contemporary cultures). The written records of the colonial period do contain bits of data which occasionally illume the pre-Hispanic period, some with fair reliability to as early as the 7th century A.D. in the case of certain Mixtecan pictorials, and generally back to the 15th century A.D. for selected other parts of Mesoamerica. On the upper time levels, the same documents, or others from the colonial and national period, provide important diachronic data for reconstruction of remote and immediate backgrounds and contexts for essentially synchronic ethnographic and similar investigations. But ideally conceived and thoughtfully written ethnohistory has an independent mission, quite as valid as that of archaeology or ethnology, in laying bare social dynamics, processes, adapta-

tions, rejections, syncretisms, and other topics in the 400-year colonial and national periods that have been of professional concern to both anthropologists and historians ever since their respective scholarly disciplines developed their unique academic doctrines, value systems, and approved practices for study of man in society.

Thus the mandate for these volumes of the Guide was clear in intent, but far from precise in formulation of specific expectations. In effect the anthropologists asked the historian to tell them, so far as possible, what documentary materials were available for the post-Contact period to answer the questions which anthropologists pose about archaeological or functioning societies and cultures. The historian does not always even know the questions, let alone their answers, but agreed that his own discipline would be much enriched by bringing to the attention of all students an organized series of articles which described, inventoried, and, where possible, evaluated, various groups of documentary research materials.

No one man would have the temerity to undertake such a charge alone. The Volume Editor early stipulated that he would be aided by an anthropologist with some feel for history and bibliography, and an historian similarly sympathetic and knowledgeable about some of the questions that anthropologists ask, plus a firm grasp of the immense historical literature related to colonial Middle America. Fortunately the services of Henry B. Nicholson were enlisted for the one, and those of Charles Gibson for the other. As Co-Editors they formed an editorial planning group with the Volume Editor.

Sailing what amounted to uncharted seas, this editorial trio developed one outline after another, gradually narrowing their goals from the ideal to the feasible coverage. Early and basic, however, was their agreement that the obvious and meaningful distinction between sources primarily produced by natives, or clearly in the native traditions, and those produced by Europeans, or in predominantly European traditions, would govern the final product. The latter, because of continuing interest in the New World since the 15th century and especially New Spain, encompasses a much larger body of materials, but also has the advantage of cumulative bibliographical and much critical scrutiny over many centuries. No such bibliographical reservoir existed for the native products.

Here the prose documents were distinguished from the pictorial, with due allowance for those which contain both prose and pictorial elements. When editorial attention turned to the pictorials, Donald Robertson and John B. Glass joined the planning deliberations. In general the prose items were fewer, and better known as a corpus, hence priorities of effort were assigned to remedying the chaotic, contradictory, and inadequate state of knowledge about the pictorial documents, uniquely Mesoamerican.

To obtain many of the prime data which the pictorials trio (Nicholson, Glass, Robertson) specified as essential to adequate descriptions, Nicholson and Robertson independently visited European and Mexican repositories for relatively brief periods in each; Glass catalogued the codex collection of the National Museum of Anthropology in Mexico (Glass, 1964) as a prerequisite to a census, and visited selected repositories in the United States. Despite these efforts, several collections in Europe and the United States were not searched in detail.

The Volume Editor, aided by funds from the General Editor, was able from the command post in the Hispanic Foundation of the Library of Congress to obtain from cooperative scholars and institutions numerous photocopies of pictorial documents which various circumstances precluded these specialists from seeing *in situ*. These photos form the nucleus of a Collection of Mexican Indian Pictorial Documents, presently housed in the Hispanic Foundation,

organized according to the numbers assigned in the census of such documents herein published (Article 23), itself a cooperative venture in which the editorial and specialist groups pooled data for final presentation by Glass. Thus with the materials on native prose sources prepared by Gibson and Glass, Volume 15 of the *Handbook* fulfills one major requirement placed on the editorial group at the outset: to provide reliable descriptive information on native tradition sources, a major key to unlocking Mesoamerican ethnohistory in the post-Contact period.

When Cline and Gibson, the historians of the team, undertook their share of the enterprise—organization of discussions on European tradition sources—its sheer bulk loomed alarmingly. Nor was it clear what ethnohistorical questions future investigators might be asking. Coverage, therefore, necessarily had to be selective, but relatively broad and general within such selected limits. Hence the first three articles of Volume 13 discuss at some combined length the published collections of documents which contain varying amounts of information of possible utility to ethnohistory (Article 11), followed by biobibliographical sketches of more than 150 writers in the colonial period whose works definitely have such data (Article 12). A pioneering summary of religious chroniclers and historians forms Article 13. These religious were often the nearest to fieldworkers that we have for colonial times. Many reported poorly, but others were surprisingly perceptive and acute. Only Sahagún surpasses Landa (treated in Article 12) as a systematic ethnographer.

To provide benchmarks in the development of what we shall later discuss as ethnohistory, a series of bibliographies of key figures was agreed upon. Towering at the beginning is Sahagún (Article 14), study of whose skein of writings related to his *General History* has recently almost emerged as a subspecialty of its own. This outpour-

7

ing of Sahaguntine studies since 1948 is discussed in Article 14C. Self-conscious early efforts at major synthesis are represented by Torquemada and Herrera (Articles 15, 16). Relying heavily on Torquemada, but important in his own right is one of the first "modern" students, Clavigero (Article 17).

The following articles deal with 19th-century scholars whose works are often considered landmarks. Brasseur de Bourbourg (Article 18) represents an early French tradition, whose works are far from "scientific" in content because of his obsession with the Atlantis theory; such theories, including Kingsborough's about the seven lost tribes, were characteristic of the times. For the English-speaking world the volumes by Bancroft (Article 19), titled *Native Races*, summarized the available materials written before modern archaeology and textual studies revised many of the views. At the forefront of pioneering modern studies are those by Seler, treated in Article 20. Finally, Article 21 synthesizes biobibliographical data on selected writers who firmly established and developed an important Mexican national tradition in ethnohistorical inquiries: Bustamante, Ramírez, Orozco y Berra, Chavero, García Icazbalceta, and Paso y Troncoso, with sidelights on others.

This Volume 12 came into being as something of a surprise to all concerned, an unexpected outgrowth of inquiries primarily associated with the sources discussed in Volumes 13–15. As Articles 1 and 4 note, to provide some organizing principle for the masses of material, the editorial group chose a regional scheme which could be kept relatively constant throughout the Guide. That this would be of small help to the uninitiated unless the tyro ethnohistorian had some notion of where his study area would fit into the complex of Middle American colonial jurisdictions, itself then a largely unstudied maze, soon became evident. These matters are treated very generally in Article 1, to which is appended a

gazetteer-atlas of Mexico by states and their municipios, the basic ethnohistorical unit. Article 2 carries original investigations of these colonial jurisdictions to a major reorganization of the Middle American area in 1786, from whence similar analysis is carried down to modern times by Article 3.

Transitional between essentially historical geographical matters and the historiographical data required for ethnohistory are the *relaciones geográficas*, which are generally discussed at length (Article 5), inventoried (Article 8), and for which as comprehensive a bibliography as possible is provided (Article 9). Two aspects of them are especially relevant to ethnohistory. The *pinturas* accompanying many of them form a recognized subgroup of pictorial sources for the years 1578–85; these are analyzed and inventoried in Article 6. At the time the relaciones were composed cultural and linguistic groups were generally synonymous, hence Article 7 has extracted language data from the corpus, hopefully of interest and importance to linguists as well as to ethnohistorians. Finally, because they contain similar, if less extensive, data, the heretofore puzzling series of 18th-century relaciones in the earlier 16th-century traditions have been rather definitively unraveled in Article 10.

Such, in bare outline, is the background and structure of this Guide to Ethnohistorical Sources. As seen, one constantly uncertain and variable element in its slow development has been the concept of ethnohistory itself. We shall discuss that briefly.

NATURE AND VARIETIES OF ETHNOHISTORY[2]

Some specialists early rejected the term "ethnohistory." Seemingly for them it smacked of some of the earlier European, especially German, writings about "Volk" which eventually had unsavory political

[2] The author appreciatively acknowledges critical comments on earlier versions of this part by William C. Sturtevant and Richard N. Adams.

implications. In the free universe of scholarship they may coin and use whatever substitute they wish.

However, as we shall note below, ethnohistory is a term which entered both United States historiographical and anthropological published literature in the 1950's, based on teaching usages of the term in the 1940's, and whose use has been more frequent since then. It seems here to stay. Possibly the term is now sanctified for Middle America by the title of these HMAI volumes. As the "Overview" by Nicholson (Article 30) suggests, many persons, even in the colonial period as well as in the national, wrote what now we might call ethnohistory. It is on this basis that biobibliographies of Sahagún, Torquemada, Herrera, Clavigero, Brasseur, Bancroft, Seler, and the Mexicans appear in Volume 13.

Even in the short time since "ethnohistory" has been self-consciously used to describe an approach and its product, it seems wholly clear that scholars in the two disciplines primarily concerned, anthropology and history, define the term slightly differently. They also go at the business of producing it on somewhat distinct bases. It saves much confusion and meaningless quibbling to assume at the outset that there is more than one variety of ethnohistory. Under that common label are subsumed several quite discrete classes of writings, all termed "ethnohistory." Let us examine the semantics.

In each instance, within anthropology and within history, a subspecialization called ethnohistory is now a legitimate professional activity. It is one of the numerous subspecializations into which each of these major scholarly disciplines is presently subdivided. Once their basic general training in their major discipline has been completed, students in each are often encouraged to learn enough about the concepts and techniques of the other to publish studies on ethnohistory that meet the canons of their own guild. In short, we are dealing not with a single internally closed and autonomous specialty with a discrete body of theory and practice, but rather with adjacent, sometimes overlapping, branches of anthropology and history which may share common characteristics, but which for vitality and support remain firmly attached to the main trunks of the parent disciplines.

In general, the anthropologists have articulated their notions about what their brand of ethnohistory is and should be, much more consistently and frequently than have historians. In a sense a cachet of legitimacy for anthropologists to undertake documentary research on a par with the then more favored field studies was provided in an important article by William N. Fenton (1952), who with John R. Swanton and others had long employed an historical approach in studies of North American Indians. The prevailing and preferred modes among United States anthropologists, however, had to then been overwhelmingly ahistorical, with emphasis placed on salvage ethnology, functionalism, and other synchronic approaches.

Fenton, however, made a plea for enriched and more mature cultural anthropology by training at least some ethnologists to carry the outlook of fieldwork into the library and archives to provide depth and perspective. "We must," he wrote, "enlist the help of historians to train some ethnologists in historical methods so that our students will be equally at home in the field and in the library and so that they may use the materials and methods of one research to enrich the other" (Fenton, 1952, p. 328). His paper was entitled "The training of historical ethnologists in America," but more widespread use of the term ethnohistory to include this view was just over the horizon. In fact, it had been used at least once in 1946 (S. J. Tucker, 1946).

Fenton's paper, re-examining relations between anthropology and history, brought into the open scattered covert discussions just at a time when other currents were converging to direct anthropological and other professional attention to the same matters. As Nicholson notes below, the Indian Claims Commission Act of 1946 gave major impetus to a movement already slowly getting under way. By the Act, Indian groups in the United States were permitted from 1946 until 1952 to file suits against the United States for recovery of damages allegedly done them by the U.S. Government; most claims were generally concerned with former tribal territories taken since 1789 under one or another guise. More than 400 such Indian suits were filed. Both Indian plaintiffs and the defendant Department of Justice began to employ in large numbers historical and anthropological specialists to support or rebut the claims, on the basis of historical documents and studies that would stand up in open court as legal evidence. A reflex to that situation was formation in 1954 of the Ohio Valley Historic Indian Conference, later renamed American Ethnohistorical Conference, whose bulletin was a journal called *Ethnohistory*. Here it might be noted that ethnohistory had been baptized, but for most intents and purposes, it was narrowly circumscribed by current interest in North American Indians. In fairness it must also be stated that ethnohistory did not become a recognizable and expanding subspecialty of anthropology dedicated exclusively to arguing land claims before the Indian Claims Commission, but the initial sums of money poured into these matters did open anthropological eyes to a large documentary resource that had not previously been exploited for scholarly purposes.

A series of important papers since Fenton's (1952) have recorded the developing views of anthropologists concerning ethnohistory. Early in the sequence was that by Vogelin (1954), "An ethnohistorian's view," followed shortly by Sturtevant's probe (1957) into problems of historical ethnology, and then a long discussion by Gunnerson (1958) which attempted also to inventory for United States anthropologists the major collections of published and unpublished ethnohistorical records, as well as maps and other graphic materials. Adding to the growing stream were remarks at the Viking Fund Seminar (1949), the proceedings of which appeared under the editorship of Sol Tax (1952). They were published very shortly after Lewis' restudy of Tepoztlan, with its substantial historical component, was issued (1951). An historian, in an extended review of these two volumes, indicated to his colleagues that for the moment the Lewis volume had greater importance for them, but also noted that "Almost to a man, the otherwise contentious members of the Seminar agreed that perhaps the single largest gap was suitable historical studies; it is evident, too, from the discussions that by and large none of the [anthropological] technicians seemed fully qualified to fill that particular need adequately" (Cline, 1952, p. 214).

By about 1960, ethnohistory was no longer on trial, but had become an accepted fact of anthropologists' scholarly life. Much attention, for instance, was paid ethnohistory by the University of Chicago anthropologists undertaking their Man-in-Nature program in Chiapas (Barroco, 1960; Calnek, 1961a, 1961b). Adams (1962) summarized for the anthropological guild the state of the art for the Mesoamerican and Andean regions, with a discussion of the disparate views and definitions of ethnohistory as it then stood.

Sufficient specialized literature of an ethnohistorical nature was being regularly produced to warrant creation of a continuing subsection in 1960 to review it for Middle American anthropology in the standard *Handbook of Latin American Studies* (Nicholson, 1960-67). In 1967 a parallel subsection was added in anthropology for South America, initially covering materials from 1960 (Murra, 1967). In each instance the Contributing Editor provided an important opening statement on his view of the nature and scope of ethnohistory; for Mesoamerica, Nicholson's following Introductions define new trends and concepts.

A decade after he had first discussed the subject in public, Sturtevant (1966) summarized much current thinking in perhaps the single best general theoretical statement on "Anthropology, history, and ethnohistory." Two short but important views on Mesoamerican ethnohistory were also published in 1966 by Carrasco and by Kirchhoff. The broadening horizons of ethnohistory were also signalized in 1966 by a significant change in name of the previous American Indian Ethnohistorical Conference, originally Ohio Valley (as noted). By a narrow vote its membership, rather than renaming themselves "Society for American Ethnohistory," elected to be known as "American Society for Ethnohistory," to emphasize the now generalized and broadened scope of ethnohistorical studies (Sturtevant, personal communication).

At the risk of distortion through simplification, it can be said that usually ethnohistory for anthropologists is essentially historical ethnography created from documents rather than from direct informants. Sturtevant (1966) paraphrases by stating that for anthropologists ethnohistory "is (the study of) the history of the peoples normally studied by anthropologists" and runs counter to the historian's usage. He says historians use the label "only for studies of the past of societies wherein written records are lacking or scanty." As we see below, this is not wholly correct. Anthropologists, in his view, consider ethnohistory as a field using nonanthropological evidence (historical documents) for anthropologists' purposes, where historians see it as using nonhistorical (i.e., anthropological findings) for historiographical purposes. Thus there are at least two principal interests covered by anthropological ethnohistory: historical ethnography and historiography of essentially nonliterate cultures. The former is the reconstruction of a synchronic ethnographic

description of a past stage of culture, usually based on written records contemporary with that stage. The latter tends to be an attempt to reconstruct a diachronic account of a past society or culture (even a presently functioning one) from documents not necessarily from that society or culture, which itself may have produced few such written records. In this dichotomy, Roys's (1943) reconstruction of the historical ethnography of the Maya at Contact, and the volumes he and the historian Scholes prepared (1948) on the Maya Chontal Indians of Acalan-Tixchel, would be prototypes of the first variety of ethnohistory.

For very important reasons there are no single equally clear examples of the second type for Middle America. In addition to the European tradition sources normally used for North American diachronic ethnohistorical accounts, fortunately there is for Middle America the nearly unique supplementary material produced by Indians themselves and by Mestizos during the colonial period. Thus the pioneering studies by Gibson on Tlaxcala (1952) and of the Aztec in the Valley of Mexico (1964) approach being prototypes of the second kind of ethnohistory defined by Sturtevant. In the latter study Gibson traces growth and changes from Contact to 1810, utilizing European, Mestizo, and native tradition sources, both prose and pictorial, for his reconstruction.

Historians, like anthropologists, have written ethnohistory of both sorts before that label became common. They were slower than their anthropological colleagues to adopt the term. Seemingly an article by Cline in 1957 was its first use in the principal United States specialized historical journal, the *Hispanic American Historical Review*. But in that same year and earlier the HAHR had carried articles by Gibson, Kubler, Rowe, and others, which now would be classed as "ethnohistory." Phelan, another historian, noted Cline's 1957 use of the term, and labeled his own work on Spanish aims and Philippine responses, 1565–1700, as ethnohistory. This meant, in his view, an "effort to combine sound historical practices with some anthropological techniques" (Phelan, 1959, pp. viii–ix).

Cline reported to a small audience in Paris during 1960 that ethnohistory was even by then respectably recognized among the wide array of approved approaches to historiography (Cline, 1960b). His statements were echoed, expanded, and refined by Gibson (1961). After distinguishing pre-Hispanic from post-Contact ethnohistory of Mexico, Gibson outlined many of the practical and methodological problems facing the investigator. A main block is the European rather than the native point of view of traditional historiography. He noted the very limited, wholly secondary place the direct study of the Indian and his culture in colonial and independent Latin America has had. But as these writings by historians demonstrate, ethnohistory is clearly an accepted subfield of history.[3]

In some ways nearer to works on ethnohistory by historians than to those by anthropologists are certain writings on ethnogeography, a term covering various studies.[4] Relationships between geography and history have long been close (Sparks, 1908).

[3] Significantly, a substantial section on ethnohistory, covering the various regions of the area (including Middle America) is scheduled for inclusion in Charles C. Griffin's forthcoming *Latin America: a guide to the historical literature*, co-sponsored by the Conference on Latin American History (the professional association of historians for the area) and the Hispanic Foundation of the Library of Congress.

[4] In addition to the meaning primarily denoted here, "historical geography," with connotations of the historical geography of native peoples, the term "ethnogeography" also is used to cover "folk geography," i.e., how native peoples organize geographical knowledge, as well as studies of native toponymy, and aspects of cultural ecology. The "ethno-" prefix is tending to be equated with "folk" (Sturtevant, 1964, pp. 99–100). Thus one anthropological usage of "ethnohistory," rather than denoting "history of natives and their culture" (historian's approach), covers study of how natives organize and transmit their knowledge of their own past.

Geographers have reconstructed the earlier phases of the human geography of parts of Middle America, primarily through critical use of documents, generally with considerable attention to previous native patterns and their later changes under varying conditions. Examples would be works by Brand (1944, 1951, 1960) on western central Mexico, also treated by Sauer (1948). In a recent synthesis, West provides a general framework of historical geography for Mexico and Guatemala (West and Augelli, 1966, ch. 8), adding the historical cultural regions to the natural ones he has already outlined in this *Handbook* (Volume 1, Article 10). Some nongeographers have also undertaken studies of geographical topics of the late pre-Hispanic and colonial period. These are typified by Roys's investigations of the political geography of the Maya (1957), and Cook's publications on historical ecology (1949a, 1949b, 1958), as adjuncts to historical demographical research that he, Simpson, and Borah have undertaken. As in the case of anthropologists, these writings on historical geography or ethnogeography employ historical sources and techniques, but the syntheses generally are dictated by conceptual lines of their primary disciplinary concerns (Hartshorne, 1939, pp. 184–88).

The basic theoretical construct underlying such approaches has been called "sequent occupance" by geographers, a term coined by Whittlesey. It is a study of how one group following another, with varying cultural backgrounds, outlooks, and needs, changes utilization of the same habitat. In an important part of his presidential address to the Association of American Geographers in 1944 Whittlesey noted the growing need for such studies, as an aid to a full comprehension of both geography and history. He indicated that most such studies of historical geography probably would be made by geographers rather than by historians. He stated that historical geography was being redefined by geographers to add time depth to their traditional concerns, and summarized the approach as "the geography of chosen periods of the past. The investigation cannot be made in the field with the usual techniques of the geographer; records of observations made at the time selected for study are substituted for field data" (Whittlesey, 1945, p. 31). The parallelism with the anthropologist's brand of ethnohistory seems obvious.

There is yet another class of writings, primarily by historians, which occasionally (as in the Nicholson "Overview") is grouped under ethnohistory. These are investigations of matters directly related to colonial Indians, but nearly always primarily from European tradition sources. The techniques of reconstruction owe little or nothing to anthropological viewpoints or practices, although the subject matter is the colonial Indian. Studies of *encomienda* by Zavala, Simpson, and others, Borah and Cook's demographic researches, Cline's work on 17th-century Indian land suits (1946), congregations (1949, 1955), and the 19th-century background of the Caste War in Yucatan (1947) all would be representative. The purposes, sources, and historiographical techniques for these are nearly exactly the same as for study of other New World institutions involving only colonial Spaniards. Selection of Indians as subject is the distinguishing criterion.

Closely paralleling these latter studies, but perhaps analytically distinct, is the large body of writings on Conquest and its implications for previously wholly aboriginal societies and cultures. From the 16th century to the present the confrontation of European and native has been a dramatic theme that has drawn continued attention. More of these, as with Padden (1967), now take into larger account native sources and outlook.

The Conquest theme raises an interesting and basic question related to selection and synthesis for ethnohistory, common to Latin American historiography but especially important in Middle America where native populations were and remain large and important. The question concerns the nature and place of aboriginal American cultures on a universal scale of all known societies and cultures. It implies the question of whether transculturation of Middle American Indians by 16th-century Europeans was a justifiable improvement of them. It is as much an emotional as a scientific issue, but wide differences of view separate historians (Rico González, 1953). With an ingrained professional dedication to cultural relativism, which tries to eschew such value judgments, anthropologists seldom enter the debate.

Traditionally, writers who consider native civilizations as less advanced than European, meaning Spanish, tout Conquest and Hispanization of the previously aboriginal areas as a major gain. That school of interpretation is loosely tagged Hispanist. Opposed on many scores are *indigenistas*, into which group most anthropological and many historical ethnohistorians fall. Sometimes going even beyond calm cultural relativism, the indigenistas implicitly assume or openly aver that the native societies and cultures were equal, even superior, to the European and mixed ones which displaced them and that rather than viewing Conquest and Europeanization as a boon, they view it as an unfortunate interruption in a native New World cultural evolution that might have produced further but now unknowable wonders.

For complex historical reasons, the indigenista approach has most often characterized works by writers who are politically liberal, often anticlerical, and includes many "progressives" and Marxists of the present. Political conservatives, frequently with a personal fondness for political and religious systems approximating the regalistic, on the other hand, have generally espoused Hispanist interpretations. These basic biases, although seldom absent from historiographical work anywhere, tend to show through more clearly and strongly in Middle American, particularly Mexican, writings of the national period related to ethnohistory than comparable ones from Western Europe (except Spain) or the United States, partly because until very recent times professional training in historiography was nearly nonexistent in Mexico. There has also been a long-standing cultural rejection of such professionalism by many Mexicans who write on historical themes (Cosío Villegas, 1967). The tendency to fight current political and ideological battles through depictions of the Indian and colonial past recently has lessened, but has by no means disappeared as modern concepts of "scientific" historiography have gradually penetrated the Mexican intellectual atmosphere.

In the early part of the 19th century, the use of history as political polemic was open and unabashed in and about Middle America, with noisy clashes between indigenistas and Hispanists quite commonplace. Toward and after midcentury both groups took on slightly more sophisticated façades. Weight of numbers favored Hispanists under the reigning official doctrines of Positivism that characterized the later years of the Porfirio Díaz regime, but a vocal minority of indigenistas kept Indian problems alive. After its partial eclipse the indigenista school took on new life during and after the Mexican Revolution of 1910, many of whose programs and views it incorporated (Powell, 1968). The indigenistas reversed the earlier official view of the precolonial Indian past as a lower stage of cultural and social development, and living Indians as obstacles to Mexico's march toward progress. The Revolution thus had a marked indigenista bias. Part of its credo and mystique called for betterment of living Indians and exaltation of native contributions to Mexican nationality. Numerous official Mexican programs, in the name of the Revolution, are now dedicated to these ends (Comas, 1953; Cline, 1953, 1962), permanently symbolized

in the modern and magnificent Museo Nacional de Antropología in Mexico City.

As in the earlier days of the Mexican republic, there again has been a gradual divorce between works on Indians directly related to their political, social, and economic betterment, and writings more dispassionately concerned with scientific study of Indian past, from pre-Hispanic times to the present. The rise in such scientific studies since about 1940 is notable both in Mexico and elsewhere (L. Manrique and Lesur, 1966). The lead for them was taken primarily by anthropologists like Manuel Gamio rather than by academic historians (Potash, 1960, pp. 400–01; Comas, 1950, 1956). The historian can thus count, as can the anthropologist, on a growing stream of ethnohistorical works by counterparts in Middle America, especially in Mexico, where the burgeoning of such works forms part of a recognized quantum growth since 1940 in the number, scope, and maturity of writings on Mexican history, of which ethnohistory is a well-recognized portion (Potash, 1960; J. A. Manrique, 1966).

Thus in a pluralistic academic universe, various co-traditions of ethnohistory currently flourish, more often as allies than as adversaries. Modes preferred by anthropologists and geographers are not disdained by historians, nor is the reverse any less true. But it is still worth stressing that parallelism, not absolute congruence, is involved. There are many overlapping spheres, noted briefly below, but there are also some important differences.

Perhaps surer of their comparative methods than are historians as yet, anthropologists writing ethnohistory can engage in some guild-approved practices which might still bring censure on the young historian. One of these appears in the anthropological literature as "upstreaming" (Fenton, 1952, p. 335; Gunnerson, 1958, p. 56; Sturtevant, 1966, p. 14). This means in part proceeding from the known to the unknown, usually

14

relying more heavily on recent sources. When they thin out, a main element of "upstreaming" is to begin to fill in ethnographic and other data from comparable groups whose history is better known for that area and period. Quite distinct from earlier "conjectural history," "upstreaming" is thought to be a methodological necessity, based on standard techniques, when no written sources of any sort are available. In some cases "upstreaming" pits an actual earlier contemporary account against the anthropologist's present ethnographic and linguistic knowledge of a later stage of the same culture, or what his comparative study indicates should have existed. Anthropologists state that "upstreaming" can be used to correct bias or error in an historical account.

At present historians probably do not feel that their own comparative techniques are sufficiently developed and tested to engage extensively in "upstreaming." A recent student notes that "historians are concerned and committed to offer the best and most likely account of the past that can be sustained by the relevant extrinsic evidence" (Hexter, 1968). Few are yet prepared to venture more than a short cautious distance beyond verified documentation, and even in those cases they are still inclined to label the effort "tentative hypothesis." In recent days writings about history and its relation to allied disciplines have stressed its differences from the natural and certain of the behavioral sciences, whose premises, techniques, presentation, and results are distinct from other ways of increasing knowledge (Hexter, 1968; Mink, 1968; Passmore, 1958).

The differences could be multiplied, but perhaps here the more important aspects of the varieties of ethnohistory are those where the interests of anthropologists, geographers, and historians (including historians of art) coincide, and are mutually reinforcing. The historian generally thinks of his task as broken into three stages, whatever the historiographical goal. The first is identification and location of the relevant sources, often an arduous bibliographical undertaking but at the heart of his chore. His second step is to subject them to a standardized battery of critical tests, first to validate the authenticity of the material, then to evaluate its reliability by examining the person and circumstances involved in the production of the document. His final step is synthesis: to state his problem, and bring the extrinsic evidence to bear in solving it.

At this latter, final state anthropologists, geographers, and historians may well have a friendly parting of the ways, implicit from the outset. The historian is unlikely to have as much professional urge to write a comprehensive historical ethnography, or painfully to reconstruct the annals or ecology of a single Indian village as an anthropologist or geographer might properly have. But to the extent where the guild-oriented goals of each point in different directions and emphasis in the final product, all share common concerns about sources, their names, numbers, locations, and especially their reliability and relations to one another.

It is precisely and obviously to such areas of shared concerns that this Guide directs its attention. Perhaps it is also now clearer why it has made no attempt to reconstruct Indian history, given the differences in aims among anthropologists, geographers, and historians and what each would expect of such a synthesis.

REFERENCES

Adams, 1962
Barroco, 1960
Beer, 1967
Bernal, 1962
Brand, 1944, 1951
—— and others, 1960
Calnek, 1961a, 1961b
Carrasco, 1966
Cline, 1946, 1947, 1949, 1952a, 1953, 1955, 1957,
    1960a, 1960b, 1962, 1966a
Comas, 1950, 1953, 1956
Cook, 1949a, 1949b, 1958
Cosío Villegas, 1967
Fenton, 1952
Gibson, 1952, 1961, 1964
Glass, 1964
Griffin, 1969
Gunnerson, 1958
Handbook of American Indians
    North of Mexico
Handbook of Latin American Studies
Handbook of South American Indians
Hartshorne, 1939
Hexeter, 1968
Kirchhoff, 1966
Kubler, 1946
León-Portilla and Garibay K., 1959

Lewis, 1942, 1951
Manrique, J. A., 1966
Manrique, L., and Lesur, 1966
Mink, 1969
Murra, 1967
Nicholson, 1955, 1960–67, 1962
Padden, 1967
Passmore, 1958
Phelan, 1959
Pompa y Pompa, 1966
Potash, 1960
Powell, 1968
Rico González, 1953
Rowe, 1946
Roys, 1954, 1957
Sapir, 1916
Sauer, 1948
Scholes and Roys, 1948
Sparks, 1908
Stabb, 1959
Sturtevant, 1957, 1964, 1966
Tax, 1952
Tucker, S. J., 1946
Vogelin, 1954
Wauchope, 1949, 1968
West and Augelli, 1966
Whittlesey, 1945

1. Introductory Notes on Territorial Divisions of Middle America

HOWARD F. CLINE

THROUGHOUT THIS "Guide to Ethnohistorical Sources" we attempt to maintain a single scheme for describing and depicting cartographically many disparate types of information. One consistent device is grouping by area and region, discussed at length in Article 4. The following paragraphs provide notes on some of the main features, historical subdivisions, and relations of various parts of Middle America as we use them.

AREAS AND SUBDIVISIONS

As in other volumes of the *Handbook of Middle American Indians*, the total area involved in this Guide is the modern Republic of Mexico, plus the Central American republics (fig. 1). In general, United States Borderland areas, which formerly were Spanish or Mexican territories, have here been excluded. Hence untouched in detail are California, Arizona, New Mexico, Texas, southeastern United States, Florida, Louisiana, and related areas. The Philippines and the Caribbean Islands were nominally administered from colonial Mexico City but they likewise do not enter serious consideration here.

Many of the significant groups of sources and historical developments covered in these volumes date from the 16th and 17th centuries. Therefore, our emphasis has been placed on areas most important in those periods rather than in pre-Contact or more recent times. Such purposeful focus has further limited the depth and range of cartographic and textual coverage.

Most attention has been placed on Meso-

FIG. 1—AREAS OF MIDDLE AMERICA

america, an area unit first outlined by Kirchhoff (1943). Now fully accepted, that term encompasses the areas, peoples, and native Indian cultures of principal historical importance in Middle America. On the northern periphery of Mesoamerica is present-day northern Mexico; below its southern boundary lie the disparate Central American areas. In neither instance do northern and southern limits of Mesoamerica fit neatly with recent political jurisdictions. For purposes here, areas to the north of the Mesoamerican line, in northern Mexico, and south of it, in Central America, are generally omitted from the modular scheme.

Much printed source material for the ethnohistory of Middle America is presently arranged and catalogued by modern political subdivision, rather than by their earlier colonial jurisdiction. We therefore decided to employ such modern political subdivisions as the base for a general geographical scheme, and to provide their correlation with earlier units as particular problems arise in the articles that follow.

A first main division of modern Middle America is into countries of Mexico, Guatemala, Honduras, El Salvador, Nicaragua, Costa Rica, Panama, and a dependency without sovereign status, British Honduras. Apart from Mexico—and to a lesser degree, Guatemala—the ethnohistorical bibliography covering each of these latter units tends to be fragmentary and much of the extant literature is generally irrelevant to purposes here.

Principal Area

The area with which we are chiefly concerned, labeled "Principal Area," is shown in figure 1, which also shows other divisions and their relations to each other: Middle America (Mexico plus Central America), Mesoamerica ("High Culture Areas"), and the Republics of Mexico and Guatemala. To the north are Borderlands, largely in the United States.

The Principal Area includes all jurisdictions south of a line from the Gulf of California eastward to about Matamoros on the Gulf of Mexico. Its southern terminus and its western limits are the Pacific Ocean. On the east the Mexican state of Yucatan, British Honduras, and Guatemala bound it as they terminate at the Caribbean Sea.

The Principal Area thus embraces various states of the Republic of Mexico and the Republic of Guatemala. For descriptive ends, the Mexican Territory of Quintana Roo and the Federal District are considered state units. British Honduras is shown within the Principal Area, but it figures only slightly in ethnohistorical coverage. Lying outside the Principal Area, and therefore treated only very occasionally, is most of Central America: Honduras, El Salvador, Nicaragua, Costa Rica, and occasionally Panama. In similar fashion the tier of northern Mexican states and the Peninsula of Lower California are generally excluded from detailed consideration, as Mexican Borderlands.

Figure 2 is a general map of the Principal Area, showing state capitals for Mexico and the national capitals of Mexico, Guatemala, El Salvador, and Honduras. It also provides the basic set of coordinates used consistently on maps throughout the volumes of this Guide. Numbers across the top and letters down the left side combine to give a reference point on the maps near which will be found the place in question. Thus for Mexico City the coordinate is always L-14.

The Mexican states within the Principal Area are listed in alphabetical order in Table 1, and assigned a number. Where appropriate these numbers appear on later maps, as well as in figure 2.

The Mexican states and other units are grouped into regions (Table 1). Before we discuss and delimit the regions, however, a word needs to be said about the relationships between modern and colonial jurisdictions. Many sources relate to colonial areas and places, often difficult to correlate with present-day political units. The fol-

18

TABLE 1—MEXICO: STATES AND CAPITALS

No.	State	Capital	Ethnohistorical Region*
1	Aguascalientes	Aguascalientes	Northern Mexico
2	Baja California, Norte	Mexicali	Outside Principal Area
3	Baja California, Sur	La Paz	Outside Principal Area
4	Campeche	Campeche	Southeastern Mexico
5	Chiapas	Tuxtla Gutierrez	Southeastern Mexico
6	Chihuahua	Chihuahua	Outside Principal Area
7	Coahuila	Saltillo	Northern Mexico
8	Colima	Colima	Western Mexico
9	Distrito Federal	Mexico City	Central Mexico
10	Durango	Durango	Northern Mexico
11	Guanajuato	Guanajuato	Western Mexico
12	Guerrero	Chilpancingo	Central Mexico
13	Hidalgo	Pachuca	Central Mexico
14	Jalisco	Guadalajara	Western Mexico
15	Mexico	Toluca	Central Mexico
16	Michoacan	Morelia	Western Mexico
17	Morelos	Cuernavaca	Central Mexico
18	Nayarit	Tepic	Western Mexico
19	Nuevo Leon	Monterrey	Northern Mexico
20	Oaxaca	Oaxaca	Oaxaca
21	Puebla	Puebla	Central Mexico
22	Queretaro	Puebla	Central Mexico
23	Quintana Roo	Chetumal	Southeastern Mexico
24	San Luis Potosi	San Luis Potosi	Northern Mexico
25	Sinaloa	Culiacan	Western Mexico
26	Sonora	Hermosillo	Outside Principal Area
27	Tabasco	Villahermosa	Southeastern Mexico
28	Tamaulipas	Ciudad Victoria	Northern Mexico
29	Tlaxcala	Tlaxcala	Central Mexico
30	Veracruz	Jalapa	Central Mexico
31	Yucatan	Merida	Southeastern Mexico
32	Zacatecas	Zacatecas	Northern Mexico

*See Article 4.

lowing discussion cannot resolve all such problems, but it does try to summarize the principal ways in which modern Mexico was subdivided during its many years as an overseas dependency of Spain, from conquest in 1519 to independence in 1821.

MODERN AND COLONIAL JURISDICTIONS

The present division of Mexico into states, territories, and a Federal District came late in a long historical evolution. Its beginnings lie in pre-Conquest Mexico, when Indian principalities and other governing units were developing. The influences of these preexistent units and their persistence in Spanish, and then in Mexican, eras are topics of vast complexity that we reluctantly exclude from discussion here. Very broadly speaking, such survivals usually remain at local levels, rather than in the larger superstructures which Spaniards imposed for governance on the lands of New Spain, and which underwent successive modifications during the colonial period and after. Thus the modern divisions we treat date only from emergence of Mexico and Central America as republics, but they have deep colonial, even precolonial, roots.

Various helpful summary volumes discuss the general administrative organization and

19

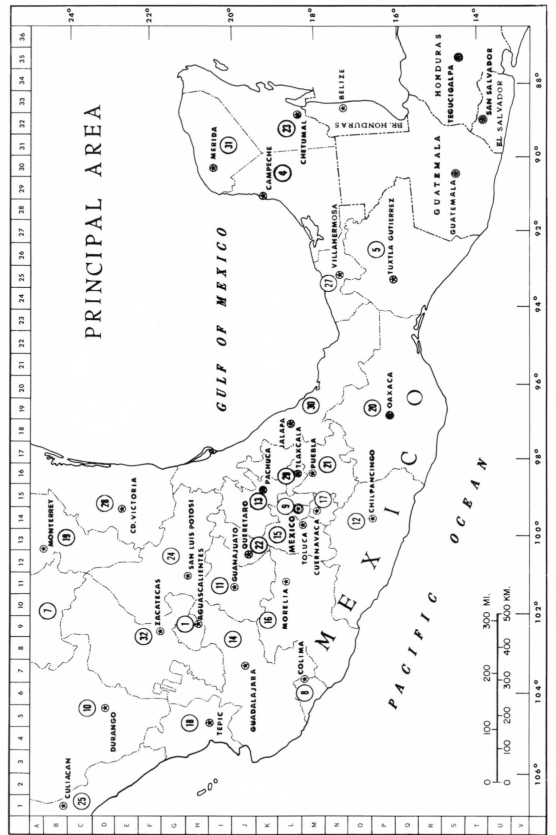

Fig. 2—PRINCIPAL AREA (see Table 1)

functioning of the Spanish empire (Haring, 1963; Gibson, 1966). In them the quite abbreviated sketch below is expanded to encompass the complexities of a system which cannot be directly compared with modern political organizations with which most readers might be familiar. Purposely the overseas Crown in Spain, ultimate sovereign, created in the New World overlapping jurisdictions and offices with parallel duties and powers which checked and balanced one another. Despite its cumbersome and often inefficient structure, however, the Spanish imperial apparatus had at least one overwhelming virtue and strength: it endured. From the late 15th century to the beginning of the 19th, major parts of the New World were governed and administered by such a Spanish system. Part of its durability is explicable by its ability to respond, often slowly but generally surely, to changing demographic and territorial situations.

As European settlements multiplied in Middle America, there was a steady extension of royal authority over newly won or recently populated areas. Content at the outset to remain in highland areas where native populations had clustered, in the first century after securing Mexico (1519), Europeans carried their governing institutions great distances from the heartland in the Valley of Mexico: to the Philippines on the west, to the Isthmus of Panama to the south, and to New Mexico, California, and Florida on the northern peripheries. The northern movement of the Spanish frontier of New Spain provides a dynamic element in Mexican colonial history equal in historical significance to the later western movement in the history of the United States (Cline, 1962). Within the various realms, provinces, and lesser areas subject to the Spanish Crown were wide diversities of practice, but still within a general single theory of government that unified these disparate administrative landscapes.

Here we can only touch major aspects of the general scheme. We can say that Mid-

dle America was governed through several overlapping but related systems. One was political. Another was politico-judicial. Yet another was ecclesiastical. Each has tended to generate its own types of source materials, all of which relate to native matters in varying degrees.

Political Jurisdiction

To end or abate earlier abuses, once major military conquests were behind, Spanish authorities provided a viable system of governance through a viceregal approach. Earlier Iberian practice was adapted in 1535 to regroup and relate earlier organs under a "vice-king" with nearly plenary powers, subject to control by a royal Council of the Indies, acting for the king in Madrid. Thus the first main political unit, the viceroyalty of New Spain, came into being, with Antonio de Mendoza as first viceroy (Aiton, 1927). In 1542 a second viceroyalty of Peru for administration of South America was created, with its seat in Lima.

Placed within the viceroyalty of New Spain were the earlier constituted bodies, the audiencias: Santo Domingo (1511), within whose jurisdiction fell most of the Caribbean (later Florida), and Mexico (1527). As they were created, the later audiencias also formed parts of the viceroyalty: Guatemala (1543), Guadalajara (1548), and Manila (1583). Falling entirely outside our Principal Area are the audiencia areas of Santo Domingo and the Philippines, as well as substantial portions of the audiencias of Guadalajara and of Guatemala. Lying wholly within it was the audiencia of Mexico and parts of Guadalajara and Guatemala. These relationships appear in figure 3.

As the appointed deputy of the king, serving about a five-year (but variable) term, the viceroy held supreme political authority, subject only to limitations placed on him by the Council of the Indies, the audiencias, and bureaucratic procedures

21

Fig. 3—NEW SPAIN: VICEROYALTY ABOUT 1700

Table 2—GOBIERNOS: VICEROYALTY OF NEW SPAIN, 1519–1785

Gobierno	Established	Derived from Earlier Gobierno	Text Section in Article 2
Nueva España	1519	. . .	I
Honduras	1526	Nueva España	XIX
Panuco	1527	Nueva España	XII
Yucatan	1527	Nueva España	XV
Nicaragua	1527	Castilla de Oro	XX
Guatemala	1530	Nueva España	XVI
Nueva Galicia	1531	Nueva España	II
Chiapa	1540	Guatemala	XVII
Soconusco	1561	Guatemala	XVIII
Nueva Vizcaya	1562	Nueva Galicia	III
Nuevo Leon	1596	Nueva España	X
Nuevo Mexico	1598	Nueva Vizcaya	VII
Coahuila	1687	Nueva Vizcaya	VIII
Californias	1697	Nueva Vizcaya	VI
Isla de Carmen	1718	Yucatan	XIV
Costa Rica	1719	Guatemala	XXI
Texas	1722	Coahuila	IX
Sinaloa	1734	Nueva Vizcaya	V
Nuevo Santander	1748	Nuevo Leon	XI
Tabasco	1782	Yucatan	XIII
San Salvador	1785	Guatemala	XXII

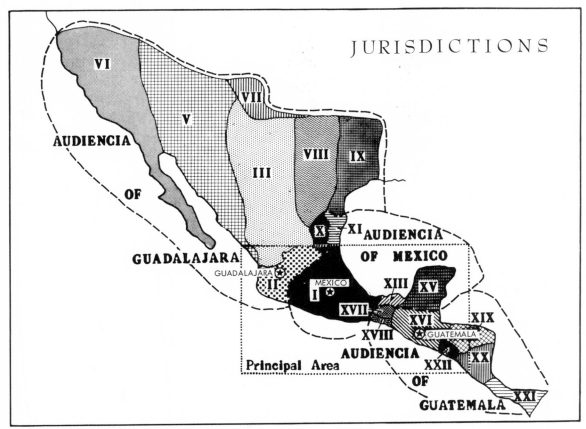

FIG. 4—NEW SPAIN: COLONIAL JURISDICTIONS, 1519–1785

Key:

I NUEVA ESPAÑA	IX TEXAS	XVII CHIAPA
II NUEVA GALICIA	X NUEVO LEON	XVIII SOCONUSCO
III NUEVA VIZCAYA	XI NUEVO SANTANDER	XXX HONDURAS
IV NAYARIT [not shown]	XII PANUCO [not shown]	XX NICARAGUA
V SINALOA	XIII TABASCO	XXI COSTA RICA
VI CALIFORNIAS	XIV ISLA DE CARMEN [not shown]	XXII SAN SALVADOR
VII NUEVO MEXICO	XV YUCATAN	
VIII COAHUILA	XVI GUATEMALA	

hallowed by custom. Like other royal officials, he faced a public accounting (*residencia*) on completion of his term, as well as possibly a special and infrequent but prolonged investigation authorized by the council (*visita*). The viceroy's office also headed up all other systems: judicial (as he was *ex officio* president of the audiencia), fiscal, military, even social. As vice-patron the viceroy had considerable administrative if no spiritual authority over ecclesiastical matters.

As head of the political hierarchy, the viceroy was generally responsible for lesser jurisdictions, through subordinates, usually appointed by him or the Crown but in given cases holding purchasable offices. Subordinate political jurisdictions were *gobiernos*, headed by governors; gobiernos also in the literature are called realms (*reinos*), or provinces (*provincias*). At lower, local levels were smaller units, political and judicial, headed by an alcalde mayor (*alcaldía mayor*), or a corregidor (*corregimiento*), responsible to a governor, ultimately to the viceroy and an audiencia. The smallest con-

Fig. 5—GOBIERNOS IN PRINCIPAL AREA

sequential administrative unit was the *municipio*, a township-sized area governed by a conciliar *cabildo* or *ayuntamiento*. The latter sat in the main community (often flanked by dependent settlements), known as the head town, *cabecera*, which was often the residence of the alcalde mayor, corregidor, or one of their lieutenants.

Thus the viceroyalty was the largest unit, followed in size by the gobiernos. Originally in 1519 the viceroyalty of New Spain and the gobierno of Nueva España covered the same area. As European settlement expanded, the gobierno was more and more subdivided; among his other duties, the viceroy remained the active governor of Nueva España, as well as having general administrative responsibility over governors of the later and lesser gobiernos derived successively from that of Nueva España. Table 2 lists such derivative jurisdictions, important details on each of which are provided by

Peter Gerhard (Article 2). Figure 4 shows these in general terms.

Figure 5 provides a more specific view of the gobiernos within the Principal Area, and indicates in outline which modern states lay within them. For historical reasons two small enclaves that logically would belong to Nueva Vizcaya were assigned to other gobiernos: Culiacan formed a separated portion of Nueva Galicia, and Nombre de Dios a detached segment of Nueva España.

Audiencias: Politico-Judicial Jurisdiction

The Spanish administrative system intertwined rather than separated political and judicial functions, under a common concept of the day that the highest duties of royal officials were to dispense the king's justice. The audiencia was the highest royal court of appeal within the area assigned to it; major cases could be appealed from it to the

FIG. 6—AUDIENCIAS IN PRINCIPAL AREA

Council of the Indies in Spain. The audiencia also acted as council to the viceroy, and in his absence ruled for him until a replacement appointment was made. The judges who comprised the audiencia, of which for Nueva España the viceroy *ex-officio* was president, also inspected the realms and nominally supervised actions of the governors, alcaldes mayores, and corregidores, the local representatives of the king's law. When they sat and listened as judges, they were *oidores*, "listeners"; when reviewing administration afield in the realms, they were *veedores*, "those who see."

Audiencias, the first administrative organs developed for administration of the Spanish Indies, tended to be the heart of the regional bureaucracies, hence their establishment reflects successive stabilized Europeanization of the areas within their immediate purview. In our Principal Area, the audiencia of Mexico was founded in 1527, basically to replace the one-man rule of Fernando Cortés. Excesses of the first au-

diencia caused its replacement and spurred development of the viceregal system sketched above, beginning in 1535. As Guatemala was pacified and organized, its audiencia was established in 1543, with somewhat parallel developments noted for Nueva Galicia, whose audiencia began to function in 1548.

Because of the pervasive nature of audiencia concerns, the areas under its control tend to form a constant and significant colonial jurisdictional unit. Many colonial archives, in Spain and Middle America, are organized by audiencias. Thus because in the earlier period the present Mexican state of Chiapas formed part of the audiencia of Guatemala, the bulk of documents relating to local Indian affairs are located in Guatemala City rather than Mexico City. In general there were no subordinate courts in smaller areas, hence the papers involved in litigations even of small places are usually lodged in the audiencia centers, with attached materials by corregidores and other local officials exercising judicial functions. Especially relevant to ethnohistorical studies are records of special audiencia tribunals created to handle Indian cases, claims of Indian nobility, and surviving land records. The boundaries of the three audiencias which primarily concern us are shown in figure 6.

Archdiocese and Dioceses: Ecclesiastical Jurisdiction

For historical reasons the Catholic Church was considered an arm of Spanish government, supreme in spiritual matters but subordinated to other organs for administrative concerns. Ecclesiastical jurisdictions and units, however, often bore no necessary spatial relationship to civil governmental units. As vice-patron the viceroy had no spiritual authority, but his powers of nomination gave him strong patronage controls over the churches.

At the top of the hierarchical structure was the single archdiocese of Mexico, with its seat in Mexico City. Nominally, all other bishoprics were suffragan, or dependent on it. In most instances the local bishop wielded considerable autonomous power.

Within the gobierno of New Spain fell the archdiocese of Mexico, and the suffragan sees of Michoacan, Tlaxcala, and Antequera. Yucatan and its dependencies formed a suffragan see, although parts of Tabasco came under the jurisdiction of the bishop of Chiapa. Much of Nueva Galicia and, in the 16th century, all of Nueva Vizcaya and Nuevo Leon belonged to the vast diocese of Guadalajara. The see of Guadiana (Durango) was carved from it in 1620; much later Linares (Nuevo Leon, 1777) and Sonora (1780) were similarly detached as separate dioceses. The gobiernos of Chiapa and Soconusco both came within the bishopric of Chiapa.

The diocese of Guatemala, suffragan to Mexico until 1546, contained only part of the gobierno of Guatemala. Between 1561 and 1607 there existed the separate see of

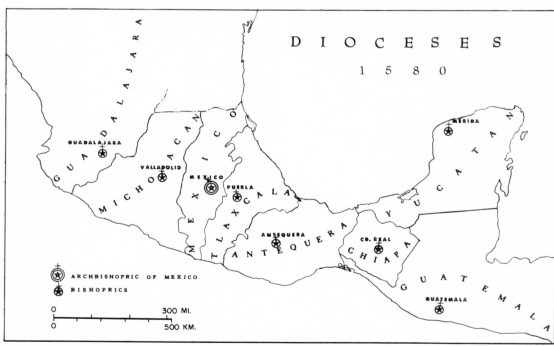

FIG. 7—DIOCESES IN PRINCIPAL AREA

TABLE 3—ECCLESIASTICAL DIVISIONS, 1525–1780

Order of Establishment	Archdiocese Diocese	Date	Previous See
I	Tlaxcala (Puebla)	1525	. . .
II	Mexico	1530	Sevilla
III	Leon	1531	. . .
IV	Guatemala	1534	Sevilla
V	Antequera	1535	. . .
VI	Michoacan	1536	. . .
VII	Chiapa	1539	Guatemala
VIII	Trujillo	1545	Guatemala
IX	Nueva Galicia	1548	. . .
X	Verapaz	1561	Guatemala
XI	Yucatan	1561	. . .
XII	Guadiana	1620	Nueva Galicia
XIII	Linares	1777	Nueva Galicia
XIV	Sonora	1780	Nueva Galicia

Verapaz. Both the bishoprics of Trujillo (Honduras, 1545) and Leon (Nicaragua, 1531) were independently suffragan directly to Mexico, as was Guatemala itself until 1745, when it was elevated to archdiocese status.

Figure 7 sketches the boundaries of the ecclesiastical units. Table 3 lists them in order of establishment.

Within each of the episcopal units were lesser units, parishes, of varying size. The town in which the curate lived, usually with the principal church of the district, was a *cabecera de doctrina*, from which he visited lesser places within the parish. Such curacies formed part of the secular, as distinct from the regular, ecclesiastical establishment. Secular clergy were (and are) in the hierarchical order of apostolic succession, hence can perform Sacraments; the top of the hierarchy is the Pope, whose vicars are the archbishops and bishops.

The mendicant Orders (and the Society of Jesus) generally formed a separate group of religious, each with its own hierarchical structure. Collectively they lived by the *regula* or rule, which included vows of poverty, chastity, and obedience, and hence were generically termed "regulars." Theirs was primarily a missionary mandate. They were encouraged (especially in early days) to establish residence in Indian areas, within a *doctrina* or a main mission, possibly with dependent *visitas*, smaller missions. Many of the important chroniclers discussed by Ernest Burrus in Article 13 had served as religious in Indian areas. By special permission regulars might serve as parish priests, in which case in addition to the superiors of their Order they were theoretically subject to orders from the bishop.

Summary

Purposely the Spanish administrative system checked and balanced the authority of its overseas officials by employing various overlapping subsystems which shared or held concurrent powers. At the top, in Spain, the Council of the Indies directed and coordinated these matters in the name of the king, relying on recommendations from viceroys and audiencias for major policy matters. In our Principal Area, the viceroy of New Spain in Mexico City, and the audiencias in Mexico City, Guadalajara, and Guatemala City, furnished such views, and were responsible to the council for carrying out royal mandates. These were transmitted

27

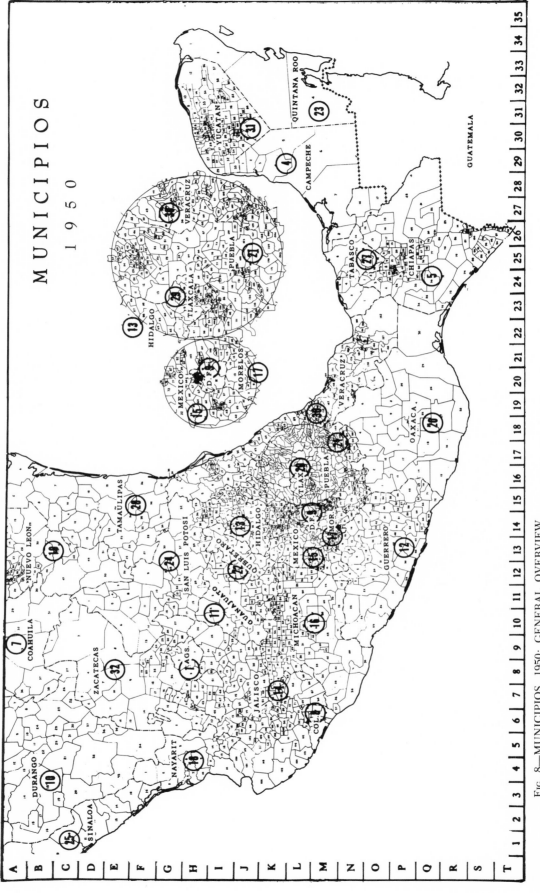

MUNICIPIOS
1950

Fig. 8—MUNICIPIOS, 1950: GENERAL OVERVIEW

No.*	Modern Unit	Colonial			Ethnohistorical Region†
		Gobierno	Audiencia	Diocese	
1	Aguascalientes	Nueva Galicia	Guadalajara	Guadalajara	Northern Mexico
4	Campeche	Yucatan	Nueva España	Yucatan	Southeastern Mexico
5	Chiapas	Chiapa Soconusco	Guatemala	Chiapa	Southeastern Mexico
7	Coahuila	Coahuila	Guadalajara	Guadalajara	Northern Mexico
8	Colima	Nueva España	Mexico	Michoacan	Western Mexico
9	Distrito Federal	Nueva España	Mexico	Mexico	Central Mexico
10	Durango	Nueva Vizcaya	Guadalajara	Guadalajara	Northern Mexico
11	Guanajuato	Nueva España	Mexico	Michoacan	Western Mexico
12	Guerrero	Nueva España	Mexico	Tlaxcala Antequera	Central Mexico
13	Hidalgo	Nueva España	Mexico	Mexico	Central Mexico
14	Jalisco	Nueva Galicia Nueva España	Guadalajara Mexico	Guadalajara	Western Mexico
15	Mexico	Nueva España	Mexico	Mexico	Central Mexico
16	Michoacan	Nueva España	Mexico	Michoacan	Western Mexico
17	Morelos	Nueva España	Mexico	Mexico	Central Mexico
18	Nayarit	Nayarit Nueva Galicia	Guadalajara	Guadalajara	Western Mexico
19	Nuevo Leon	Nuevo Leon	Mexico	Linares	Northern Mexico
20	Oaxaca	Nueva España	Mexico	Antequera	Oaxaca
21	Puebla	Nueva España	Mexico	Tlaxcala	Central Mexico
22	Queretaro	Nueva España	Mexico	Mexico Michoacan	Central Mexico
23	Quintana Roo	Yucatan	Mexico	Yucatan	Southeastern Mexico
24	San Luis Potosi	Nueva Galicia Nuevo Leon Nueva España	Guadalajara Mexico	Guadalajara	Northern Mexico
25	Sinaloa	Sinaloa	Guadalajara	Guadalajara	Western Mexico
27	Tabasco	Tabasco	Mexico	Yucatan	Southeastern Mexico
28	Tamaulipas	Nuevo Santander	Mexico	Linares?	Northern Mexico
29	Tlaxcala	Nueva España	Mexico	Tlaxcala	Central Mexico
30	Veracruz	Nueva España	Mexico	Mexico Tlaxcala Antequera	Central Mexico
31	Yucatan	Yucatan	Mexico	Yucatan	Southeastern Mexico
32	Zacatecas	Nueva Galicia	Guadalajara	Guadalajara	Northern Mexico
	Guatemala	Guatemala	Guatemala	Guatemala	Southeastern Mexico & Guatemala
	Honduras	Honduras	Guatemala	Trujillo	Central America
	El Salvador	San Salvador	Guatemala	Guatemala	Central America
	Nicaragua	Nicaragua	Guatemala	Leon	Central America

*See Table 1.　　　†See Article 4.

for execution to the several subordinate levels of command: gobiernos, alcaldías mayores and corregimientos, town councils.

Paralleling the civil, secular structures were ecclesiastical ones. With the parish as its base unit, lines of command reached upward via Mexico to Madrid and Rome for priest and friar.

MEXICAN STATES AND THEIR MUNICIPIOS

Table 4 summarizes data on states in the Principal Area with colonial jurisdiction through 1785. Again the reader is referred to later, more detailed, coverage of individual places within the modern states.

Article 115 of the Mexican Constitution

TABLE 5—MEXICAN STATES AND THEIR MUNICIPIOS

No. *	State (or Territory)	Total Municipios		Principal Area, 1950	Figure in Appendix
		1940†	1950‡		
1	Aguascalientes	7	7	7	9
2	Baja California, Norte	3	4	. . .	. . .
3	Baja California, Sur	7	7	. . .	. . .
4	Campeche	8	8	8	10
5	Chiapas	109	111	111	11
6	Chihuahua	64	65	. . .	. . .
7	Coahuila	38	38	10	12
8	Colima	9	9	9	13
9	Distrito Federal	13	13	13	14
10	Durango	37	37	30	15
11	Guanajuato	44	46	46	16
12	Guerrero	71	72	72	17
13	Hidalgo	80	82	82	18
14	Jalisco	119	124	124	19
15	Mexico	119	119	119	14
16	Michoacan	102	104	104	20
17	Morelos	32	32	32	21
18	Nayarit	18	19	19	22
19	Nuevo Leon	52	52	52	23
20	Oaxaca	572	571	571	24, 25
21	Puebla	215	220	220	26
22	Queretaro	11	18	18	27
23	Quintana Roo	4	4	4	28
24	San Luis Potosi	58	52	52	29
25	Sinaloa	16	16	9	30
26	Sonora	68	67	. . .	. . .
27	Tabasco	17	17	17	31
28	Tamaulipas	39	39	35	32
29	Tlaxcala	39	42	42	33
30	Veracruz	197	197	197	34
31	Yucatan	105	105	105	35
32	Zacatecas	52	52	52	36
	TOTALS	2,325	2,349	2,160	

*See Tables 1 and 4.   †Whetten, 1948, Table 89, p. 526.   ‡Durán Ochoa, 1955, pp. 11–12.

of 1917 requires that the individual states organize themselves territorially and administratively on the basis of municipios, whose local governments shall be directly and popularly elected. However, each state constitution is free to determine what constitutes a "municipio," and there is wide variety of practice. Similarly, considerable latitude prevails in grouping of various categories of settled places, some 90,603 localities in 1950, within municipal units. These in fact more nearly approximate county-size

jurisdictions in the Anglo-American traditions. Figure 8 provides a panoramic view of Mexican municipios within the Principal Area as of 1950.

It is, however, at this local level that modern interview techniques can most effectively elicit the Indian past, and into it fit data from many of the documents of ethnohistory that also illuminate it. Meaningful ethnohistorical work necessarily means fixing place, as well as time, for which Mexican state units or other regional groupings may often be too large. Various community studies, made chiefly by anthropologists, sometimes contain smatterings of ethnohistory. However, seldom are the communities related to the principal municipio structure of Mexico as a whole, and they tend to be atypical samples, even of our Principal Area (Cline, 1952b).

Table 5 gives the general context by listing for Mexico as a whole comparative data on municipios by states. The wide variation in state practice is quickly evident. Average areas of municipios range from around 50 square miles for ancient Indian areas like Oaxaca, Tlaxcala, and Morelos, to well over 1,000 square miles for northern municipios in Sinaloa, Sonora, and Durango, or peripheral regions like Quintana Roo. Average population varies from 2,000 or so in Oaxaca to over 20,000 in a number of states, with a national average figure (1940) of 8,453 for the 2,325 then recognized municipios (Whetten, 1948, p. 526). In 1950 the number was slightly higher: 10,980 (Durán Ochoa, 1955, p. 11).

Given the diversity of municipal organization within states, and the wide variety of studies for which data are related to the municipio units, an appendix to this article provides summary data on those within the Principal Area. It is a gazetteer and atlas, specifically designed to give a reference base for locating places mentioned later in these volumes. The most usual form will be the figure number, with the coordinates at which the municipio is found, keyed to its number on the accompanying table. Thus, Hecelchakan, Campeche, can always be precisely fixed as "Fig. 2. J/29-30-2."

The following three articles provide historical detail on these and related geohistorical matters. Peter Gerhard's essay (Article 2) gives the investigator, for the first time, detailed statements on evolution and changes of the major divisions of the colonial area, as well as data on the more local units—corregimientos and alcaldías mayores —of basic importance to all historical inquiries. He brings such developments to 1785, a year preceding a fundamental change of administration known as the intendancy system. That change, and the subsequent evolution of the modern Mexican states and territories, plus the separate sovereignties of Central America, are outlined by Cline (Article 3), who also contributes Article 4, which intermingles the historico-geographical traditions by division of Middle America into ethnohistorical regions, with discussion of each of these.

REFERENCES

Aiton, 1927
Cline, 1952b, 1962
Durán Ochoa, 1955
Gibson, 1966

Haring, 1963
Kirchhoff, 1943
Lemoine Villicaña, 1954
Whetten, 1948

APPENDIX. GAZETTEER AND ATLAS OF MEXICAN MUNICIPIOS IN THE PRINCIPAL AREA, 1950

1.° Aguascalientes

ETHNOHISTORICAL REGION: Northern Mexico

COLONIAL PERIOD

Gobierno: Nueva Galicia
Diocese: Guadalajara
Audiencia: Guadalajara
Intendancy: Zacatecas

NATIONAL PERIOD:

Territorial or dependency status: Territory, May 23, 1835; 1847
Statehood: 1836–46; 1853

SPECIAL NOTES

From Zacatecas, the Territory of Aguascalientes was created May 23, 1835. After statehood from 1836 to 1846, the Constitution of 1847 reduced Aguascalientes to a Territory. It was given statehood again by the Constitution of 1853.

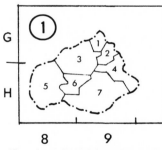

Key:

1. Cosio
2. Tepezala
3. Rincon de Romos
4. Asientos
5. Calvillo
6. Jesus Maria
7. Aguascalientes

FIG. 9—AGUASCALIENTES: MUNICIPIOS

4. Campeche

ETHNOHISTORICAL REGION: Southeastern Mexico

COLONIAL PERIOD
Gobierno: Yucatan
Diocese: Yucatan

°This and subsequent initial numbers refer to those listed in Tables 1 and 4.

Audiencia: Mexico
Intendancy: Merida

NATIONAL PERIOD:

Territorial or dependency status: District became provisional state, Feb. 19, 1862
Statehood: Apr. 29, 1863

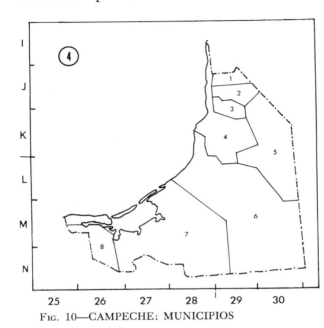

Key:
1. Calkini
2. Hecelchakan
3. Tenabo
4. Campeche
5. Hopelchen
6. Champoton
7. Carmen
8. Palizada

FIG. 10—CAMPECHE: MUNICIPIOS

5. Chiapas

ETHNOHISTORICAL REGION: Southeastern Mexico

COLONIAL PERIOD

Gobierno: Chiapa; Soconusco
Diocese: Chiapa
Audiencia: Guatemala
Intendancy: Chiapa

NATIONAL PERIOD

Territorial or dependency status: None
Statehood: 1824 (exclusive of Soconusco); Sept. 11, 1842, including Soconusco

SPECIAL NOTES

The Intendancy of Chiapa was under jurisdiction of the captain-general of Guatemala. In the Constitution of 1824, Chiapas (exclusive of Soconusco) became part of the Republic of Mexico, following a plebiscite during 1823. On Sept. 11, 1842, Mexicans won Soconusco from Guatemala and added it to Chiapas.

33

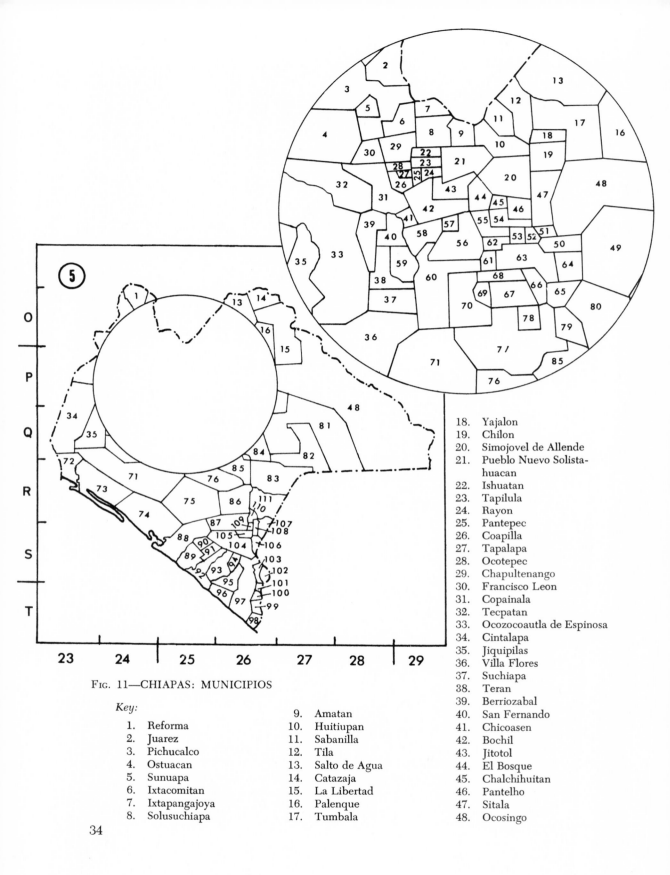

Fig. 11—CHIAPAS: MUNICIPIOS

Key:

1. Reforma
2. Juarez
3. Pichucalco
4. Ostuacan
5. Sunuapa
6. Ixtacomitan
7. Ixtapangajoya
8. Solusuchiapa
9. Amatan
10. Huitiupan
11. Sabanilla
12. Tila
13. Salto de Agua
14. Catazaja
15. La Libertad
16. Palenque
17. Tumbala
18. Yajalon
19. Chilon
20. Simojovel de Allende
21. Pueblo Nuevo Solistahuacan
22. Ishuatan
23. Tapilula
24. Rayon
25. Pantepec
26. Coapilla
27. Tapalapa
28. Ocotepec
29. Chapultenango
30. Francisco Leon
31. Copainala
32. Tecpatan
33. Ocozocoautla de Espinosa
34. Cintalapa
35. Jiquipilas
36. Villa Flores
37. Suchiapa
38. Teran
39. Berriozabal
40. San Fernando
41. Chicoasen
42. Bochil
43. Jitotol
44. El Bosque
45. Chalchihuitan
46. Pantelho
47. Sitala
48. Ocosingo

49. Altamirano	71. Villa Corzo	93. Huixtla
50. Huistan	72. Arriaga	94. Tuzantan
51. Oxchuc	73. Tonala	95. Huehuetan
52. Tenejapa	74. Pijijiapan	96. Mazatan
53. Mitontic	75. Angel Albino Corzo	97. Tapachula
54. Chenalho	76. La Concordia	98. Suchiate
55. Larrainzar	77. Venustiano Carranza	99. Frontera Hidalgo
56. Ixtapa	78. Nicolas Ruiz	100. Metapa
57. Soyalo	79. Las Rosas	101. Tuxtla Chico
58. Osumacinta	80. Comitan de Dominguez	102. Union Juarez
59. Tuxtla	81. Las Margaritas	103. Cacahoatan
60. Chiapa de Corzo	82. La Independencia	104. Motozintla de Mendoza
61. Zinacantan	83. La Trinitaria	105. El Porvenir
62. Chamula	84. Tzimol	106. Mazapa de Madero
63. San Cristobal de las Casas	85. Socoltenango	107. Amatenango de la Frontera
64. Chanal	86. Chicomucelo	108. Bejucal de Ocampo
65. Amantenango del Valle	87. Siltepec	109. La Grandeza
66. Teopisca	88. Mapastepec	110. Bella Vista
67. Totolapa	89. Acapetagua	111. Frontera Comalapa
68. El Zapotal	90. Acacoyagua	
69. Chiapilla	91. Escuintla	
70. Acala	92. Pueblo Nuevo Comaltitlan	

7. Coahuila

ETHNOHISTORICAL REGION: Northern Mexico

COLONIAL PERIOD

> Gobierno: Coahuila
> Diocese: Guadalajara
> Audiencia: Guadalajara
> Intendancy: San Luis Potosi

NATIONAL PERIOD

> Territorial or dependency status: None; combined with Nuevo Leon, 1857
> Statehood: 1824; 1864

SPECIAL NOTES

The comandante of the Gobierno de la Provincia de Coahuila, in the Provincias Internas de Oriente, acted as intendant. In the Constitution of 1824 Coahuila and Texas became a state of the Mexican Republic. The Constitution of 1864 combined as one the state of Coahuila and Nuevo Leon; both again became separate states Feb. 26, 1864.

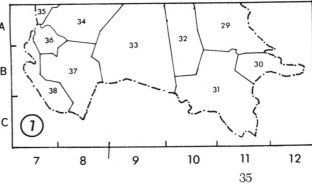

FIG. 12—COAHUILA: MUNICIPIOS

Key:

29. Ramos Arizpe	34. San Pedro
30. Arteaga	35. Francisco I. Madero
31. Saltillo	36. Matamoros
32. General Cepeda	37. Viesca
33. Parras	38. Torreon

8. Colima

ETHNOHISTORICAL REGION: Western Mexico

COLONIAL PERIOD

Gobierno: Nueva España
Diocese: Michoacan
Audiencia: Mexico
Intendancy: Guadalajara

NATIONAL PERIOD

Territorial or dependency status: 1824; 1849
Statehood: 1857

SPECIAL NOTES

With Alta and Baja California, and Santa Fe de Nuevo Mexico, Colima was given territorial status in the Constitution of 1824. From 1835 to 1846, this territorial status was nullified, with the area returned to the Departamento of Michoacan. State status was restored in 1849.

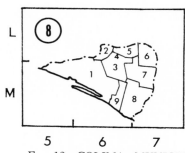

Key:
1. Manzanillo
2. Minatitlan
3. Coquimatlan
4. Villa de Alvarez
5. Comala
6. Cuauhtemoc
7. Colima
8. Ixtlahuacan
9. Tecoman

FIG. 13—COLIMA: MUNICIPIOS

9. Distrito Federal

ETHNOHISTORICAL REGION: Central Mexico

COLONIAL PERIOD

Gobierno: Nueva España
Diocese: Mexico
Audiencia: Mexico
Intendancy: Mexico

NATIONAL PERIOD

Territorial or dependency status: See Special Notes.

SPECIAL NOTES

The Federal District was first created Nov. 18, 1824, from the State of Mexico. From 1836 to 1846, the Distrito was suppressed and its territory returned to the Departamento of Mexico. Its status was restored in 1849. By decree of Feb. 16, 1854, the limits of the District were enlarged. They were further enlarged June 7, 1863. In 1946 the District was reorganized to form a single municipality, divided into delegaciones, eliminating surviving colonial municipios within the area.

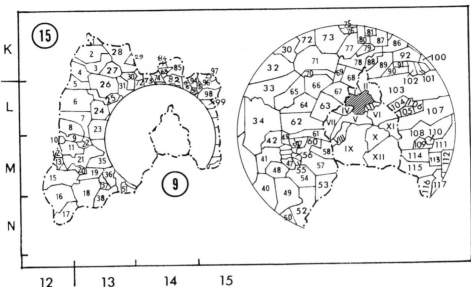

FIG. 14—DISTRITO FEDERAL: DELEGACIONES, AND STATE OF MEXICO: MUNI-CIPIOS

Key to delegaciones (municipios in the state of Mexico are given in No. 15):

I.	Azcapotzalco	VII.	Cuajimalpa
II.	Villa Gustavo A. Madero	VIII.	La Magdalena Contreras
III.	Ixtacalco	IX.	Tlalpan
IV.	Obregon	X.	Xochimilco
V.	Coyoacan	XI.	Tlahuac
VI.	Ixtapalapa	XII.	Milpa Alta

10. Durango

ETHNOHISTORICAL REGION: Northern Mexico

COLONIAL PERIOD

Gobierno: Nueva Vizcaya, Nueva España
Diocese: Guadalajara
Audiencia: Guadalajara
Intendancy: Durango

NATIONAL PERIOD

Territorial or dependency status: None
Statehood: 1824

SPECIAL NOTES

Colonial Nombre de Dios area formed part of Gobierno of Nueva España. In the Provincias Internas de Occidente, the comandante was intendant of Durango

37

and of Arizpe, these two forming Gobierno de la Nueva Vizcaya. By the Constitution of 1824, Durango became a state.

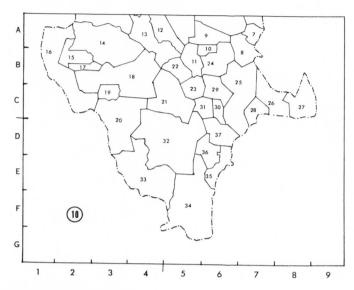

Fig. 15—DURANGO: MUNICIPIOS

Key:

7.	Gomez Palacio	18.	Santiago Papasquiaro	29.	Peñon Blanco
8.	Lerdo	19.	Otaez	30.	Guadalupe Victoria
9.	San Pedro del Gallo	20.	San Dimas	31.	Panuco de Coronado
10.	San Luis del Cordero	21.	Canatlan	32.	Durango
11.	Rodeo	22.	Coneto de Comonfort	33.	Pueblo Nuevo
12.	Inde	23.	San Juan del Rio	34.	Mezquital
13.	El Oro	24.	Nazas	35.	Suchil
14.	Tepehuanes	25.	Cuencame	36.	Nombre de Dios
15.	Tapia	26.	General Simon Bolivar	37.	Poanas
16.	Tamazula	27.	San Juan de Guadalupe		
17.	Canelas	28.	Santa Clara		

11. Guanajuato

Ethnohistorical Region: Western Mexico

Colonial Period

Gobierno: Nueva España
Diocese: Michoacan
Audiencia: Mexico
Intendancy: Guanajuato

National Period

Territorial or dependency status: None
Statehood: 1824

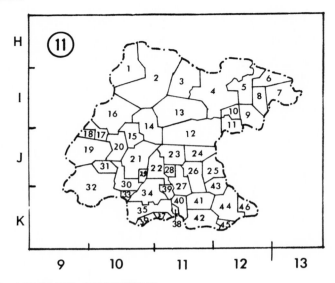

FIG. 16—GUANAJUATO: MUNICIPIOS

Key:

1. Ocampo
2. San Felipe
3. San Diego de la Union
4. San Luis de la Paz
5. Victoria
6. Xichu
7. Atarjea
8. Santa Catarina
9. Tierrablanca
10. Doctor Mora
11. San Jose Iturbide
12. Allende
13. Dolores Hidalgo
14. Guanajuato
15. Silao
16. Leon
17. San Francisco del Rincon
18. Purisima del Rincon
19. Ciudad Manuel Doblado
20. Romita
21. Irapuato
22. Salamanca
23. Juventino Rosas
24. Comonfort
25. Apaseo
26. Celaya
27. Cortazar
28. Villagran
29. Pueblo Nuevo
30. Abasolo
31. Cueramaro
32. Penjamo
33. Huanimaro
34. Valle de Santiago
35. Yuriria
36. Moroleon
37. Uriangato
38. Santiago Maravatio
39. Jaral del Progreso
40. Salvatierra
41. Tarimoro
42. Acambaro
43. Tres Guerras
44. Jerecuaro
45. Tarandacuao
46. Coroneo

12. Guerrero

ETHNOHISTORICAL REGION: Central Mexico

COLONIAL PERIOD

Gobierno: Nueva España
Diocese: Tlaxcala, Antequera
Audiencia: Mexico
Intendancy: Mexico, Puebla, Oaxaca

NATIONAL PERIOD

Territorial or dependency status: Provisional state, 1847
Statehood: Oct. 27, 1849

SPECIAL NOTES

Created from parts of states of Mexico, Michoacan, Puebla, provisionally agreed in 1846.

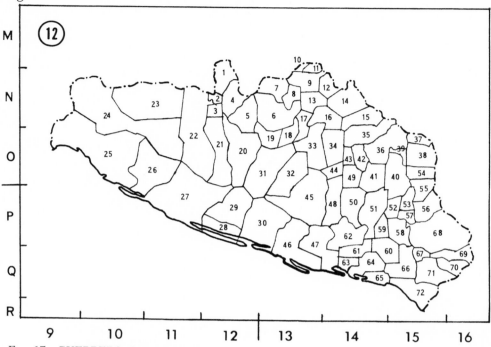

FIG. 17—GUERRERO: MUNICIPIOS

Key:

1. Cutzamala de Pinzon	25. La Union	49. Chilapa
2. Pungarabato	26. Petatlan	50. Quechultenango
3. Tlapehuala	27. Tecpan de Galeana	51. Zapotitlan
4. Tlalchapa	28. Benito Juarez	52. Copanatoyac
5. Arcelia	29. Atoyac de Alvarez	53. Xalpatlahuac
6. Teloloapan	30. Coyuca de Benitez	54. Alpoyeca
7. Pedro Asencio Alquisiras	31. General Heliodoro Castillo	55. Tlalixtaquilla
8. Ixcateopan	32. Leonardo Bravo	56. Alcozauca de Guerrero
9. Taxco de Alarcon	33. Zumpango del Rio	57. Atlamajalcingo del Monte
10. Pilcaya	34. Martir de Cuilapan	58. Malinaltepec
11. Tetipac	35. Copalillo	59. Tlacoapa
12. Buenavista de Cuellar	36. Olinala	60. San Luis Acatlan
13. Iguala	37. Xochihuehuetlan	61. Ayutla de los Libres
14. Huitzuco	38. Huamuxtitlan	62. Tecoanapa
15. Atenango del Rio	39. Cualac	63. Florencio Villareal
16. Tepecoacuilco de Trujano	40. Tlapa	64. Cuautepec
17. Cocula	41. Atlixtac	65. Copala
18. Cuetzala del Progreso	42. Ahuacuotzingo	66. Azoyu
19. Apaxtla	43. Zitlala	67. Igualapa
20. San Miguel Totolapan	44. Tixtla de Guerrero	68. Metlatonoc
21. Ajuchitlan del Progreso	45. Chilpancingo de los Bravos	69. Tlacoachixtlahuaca
22. Coyuca de Catalan	46. Acapulco de Juarez	70. Xochistlahuaca
23. Zirandaro	47. San Marcos	71. Ometepec
24. Coahuayutla de Guerrero	48. Mochitlan	72. Cuajinicuilapa

13. Hidalgo

ETHNOHISTORICAL REGION: Central Mexico

COLONIAL PERIOD

  Gobierno: Nueva España
  Diocese: Mexico
  Audiencia: Mexico
  Intendancy: Mexico

NATIONAL PERIOD

  Territorial or dependency status: Second Military District, Mexico
  Statehood: Jan. 15, 1869

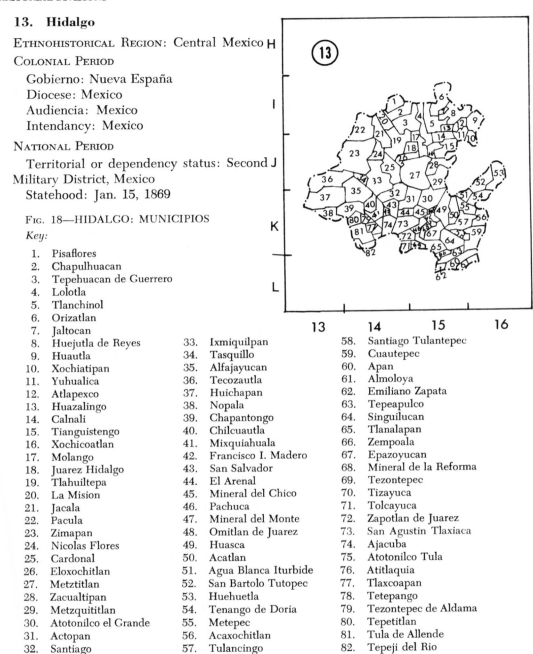

FIG. 18—HIDALGO: MUNICIPIOS

Key:

1. Pisaflores
2. Chapulhuacan
3. Tepehuacan de Guerrero
4. Lolotla
5. Tlanchinol
6. Orizatlan
7. Jaltocan
8. Huejutla de Reyes
9. Huautla
10. Xochiatipan
11. Yuhualica
12. Atlapexco
13. Huazalingo
14. Calnali
15. Tianguistengo
16. Xochicoatlan
17. Molango
18. Juarez Hidalgo
19. Tlahuiltepa
20. La Mision
21. Jacala
22. Pacula
23. Zimapan
24. Nicolas Flores
25. Cardonal
26. Eloxochitlan
27. Metztitlan
28. Zacualtipan
29. Metzquititlan
30. Atotonilco el Grande
31. Actopan
32. Santiago
33. Ixmiquilpan
34. Tasquillo
35. Alfajayucan
36. Tecozautla
37. Huichapan
38. Nopala
39. Chapantongo
40. Chilcuautla
41. Mixquiahuala
42. Francisco I. Madero
43. San Salvador
44. El Arenal
45. Mineral del Chico
46. Pachuca
47. Mineral del Monte
48. Omitlan de Juarez
49. Huasca
50. Acatlan
51. Agua Blanca Iturbide
52. San Bartolo Tutopec
53. Huehuetla
54. Tenango de Doria
55. Metepec
56. Acaxochitlan
57. Tulancingo
58. Santiago Tulantepec
59. Cuautepec
60. Apan
61. Almoloya
62. Emiliano Zapata
63. Tepeapulco
64. Singuilucan
65. Tlanalapan
66. Zempoala
67. Epazoyucan
68. Mineral de la Reforma
69. Tezontepec
70. Tizayuca
71. Tolcayuca
72. Zapotlan de Juarez
73. San Agustin Tlaxiaca
74. Ajacuba
75. Atotonilco Tula
76. Atitlaquia
77. Tlaxcoapan
78. Tetepango
79. Tezontepec de Aldama
80. Tepetitlan
81. Tula de Allende
82. Tepeji del Rio

14. Jalisco

ETHNOHISTORICAL REGION: Western Mexico

COLONIAL PERIOD

  Gobierno: Nueva Galicia, Nueva España

41

Diocese: Guadalajara
Audiencia: Guadalajara, Mexico
Intendancy: Guadalajara

NATIONAL PERIOD

Territorial or dependency status: None
Statehood: 1824

SPECIAL NOTES

Amendment to Article 43 of the 1857 Constitution (Dec. 12, 1884) created the Territory of Tepic from former 7th Cantón.

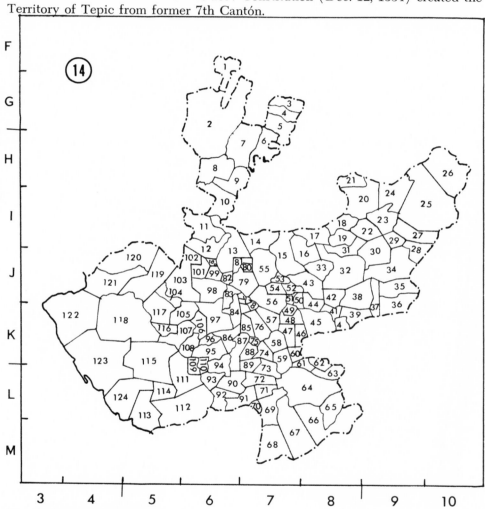

FIG. 19—JALISCO: MUNICIPIOS

Key:

1.	Huejuquilla el Alto	4.	Santa Maria de los Angeles	6.	Totatiche
2.	Mezquitic			7.	Villa Guerrero
3.	Huejucar	5.	Colotlan	8.	Bolaños

9. Chimaltitan
10. San Martin de Bolaños
11. Hostotipaquillo
12. Magdalena
13. Tequila
14. San Cristobal de la Barranca
15. Ixtlahuacan del Rio
16. Cuquio
17. Yahualica
18. Mexticacan
19. Villa Obregon
20. Teocaltiche
21. Villa Hidalgo
22. Jalostotitlan
23. San Juan de los Lagos
24. Encarnacion de Diaz
25. Lagos de Moreno
26. Ojuelos de Jalisco
27. Union de San Antonio
28. San Diego de Alejandria
29. San Julian
30. San Miguel el Alto
31. Valle de Guadalupe
32. Tepatitlan de Morelos
33. Acatic
34. Arandas
35. Jesus Maria
36. Degollado
37. Ayo el Chico
38. Atotonilco el Alto
39. La Barca
40. Jamay
41. Ocotlan
42. Tototlan
43. Zapotlanejo
44. Zapotlan del Rey
45. Poncitlan
46. Tizapan el Alto
47. Tuxcueca
48. Chapala
49. Ixtlahuacan de los Membrillos
50. Juanacatlan
51. El Salto
52. Tonala
53. Guadalajara
54. Tlaquepaque
55. Zapopan
56. Tlajomulco
57. Jocotepec
58. Teocuitatlan de Corona
59. Concepcion de Buenos Aires
60. La Manzanilla
61. Mazamitla
62. Valle de Juarez
63. Quitupan
64. Tamazula de Gordiano
65. Manuel M. Dieguez
66. Jilotlan de los Dolores
67. Tecalitlan
68. Pihuamo
69. Tuxpan
70. Tonila
71. Zapotiltic
72. Ciudad Guzman
73. San Sebastian Ex-9ª Cantón
74. Atoyac
75. Techaluta
76. Zacoalco de Torres
77. Villa Corona
78. Acatlan de Juarez
79. Tala
80. El Arenal
81. Amatitan
82. Teuchitlan
83. San Martin Hidalgo
84. Cocula
85. Atemajac de Brizuela
86. Chiquilistlan
87. Tapalpa
88. Amacueca
89. Sayula
90. Venustiano Carranza
91. Zapotitlan
92. Toliman
93. Tuxcacuesco
94. Tonaya
95. Ejutla
96. Juchitlan
97. Tecolotlan
98. Ameca
99. Ahualulco de Mercado
100. Antonio Escobedo
101. Etzatlan
102. San Marcos
103. Guachinango
104. Mixtlan
105. Atengo
106. Tenamaxtlan
107. Ayutla
108. Union de Tula
109. El Grullo
110. El Limon
111. Autlan
112. Cuautitlan
113. Cihuatlan
114. Casimiro Castillo
115. Purificacion
116. Cuautla
117. Atenguillo
118. Talpa de Allende
119. Mascota
120. San Sebastian ex-10º Cantón
121. Puerto Vallarta
122. Cabo Corrientes
123. Tomatlan
124. La Huerta

15. Mexico (state)

ETHNOHISTORICAL REGION: Central Mexico

COLONIAL PERIOD

Gobierno: Nueva España
Diocese: Mexico
Audiencia: Mexico
Intendancy: Mexico

NATIONAL PERIOD

Territorial or dependency status: None
Statehood: 1824

SPECIAL NOTES

On Nov. 18, 1824, the Federal District was created around Mexico City from the state of Mexico. From 1836 to 1846, the District was suppressed, and its territory returned to the Departamento of Mexico. The same occurred with the Territory of Tlaxcala. In 1846 Mexico agreed to donate territory to form the state of Guerrero. In 1849 the Territory of Tlaxcala and the Federal District were reinstated from state area. Additional territory was taken by decree (Feb. 16, 1854) to enlarge the District. Within the Departamento of Mexico the Distrito of Morelos was created in 1853. From state territory the Federal District was again enlarged June 7, 1863. On Jan. 15, 1869, the Second Military District became the state of Hidalgo; on Apr. 16, 1869, the Third became Morelos.

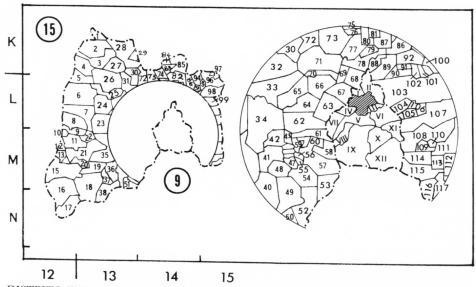

DISTRITO FEDERAL: DELEGACIONES, AND STATE OF MEXICO, MUNICIPIOS

Key:

1.	Polotitlan	16.	Amatepec	31.	Morelos
2.	Aculco	17.	Tlatlaya	32.	Jiquipilco
3.	Acambay	18.	Sultepec	33.	Temoaya
4.	Temascalcingo	19.	Texcaltitlan	34.	Toluca
5.	El Oro	20.	San Simon de Guerrero	35.	Zinacantepec
6.	San Felipe del Progreso	21.	Temascaltepec	36.	Coatepec Harinas
7.	Villa Victoria	22.	Amanalco	37.	Almoloya de Alquisiras
8.	Villa de Allende	23.	Almoloya de Juarez	38.	Zacualpan
9.	Donato Guerra	24.	Ixtlahuaca	39.	Ixtapan de la Sal
10.	Ixtapan del Oro	25.	Jocotitlan	40.	Villa Guerrero
11.	Valle de Bravo	26.	Atlacomulco	41.	Calimaya
12.	Santo Tomas	27.	Timilpan	42.	Metepec
13.	Otzoloapan	28.	Jilotepec	43.	San Mateo Atenco
14.	Zacazonapan	29.	Soyaniquilpan	44.	Mexicalcingo
15.	Tejupilco	30.	Chapa de Mota	45.	Chapultepec

46. San Antonio la Isla
47. Rayon
48. Tenango del Valle
49. Tenancingo
50. Zumpahuacan
51. Tonatico
52. Malinalco
53. Ocuilan
54. Joquicingo
55. Texcalyacac
56. Almoloya del Rio
57. Tianguistenco
58. Jalatlaco
59. Atizapan
60. Capulhuac
61. Ocoyoacac
62. Lerma
63. Huixquilucan
64. Xonacatlan
65. Otzolotepec
66. Jilotzingo
67. Naucalpan
68. Tlalnepantla
69. Zaragoza
70. Iturbide
71. Nicholas Romero

72. Villa del Carbon
73. Tepotzotlan
74. Huehuetoca
75. Coyotepec
76. Teoloyucan
77. Cuautitlan
78. Tultitlan
79. Tultepec
80. Melchor Ocampo
81. Jaltenco
82. Zumpango
83. Tequixquiac
84. Apaxco
85. Hueypoxtla
86. Tecamac de Felipe Villanueva
87. Nextlalpan
88. Coacalco
89. Ecatepec Morelos
90. Atenco
91. Tezoyuca
92. Acolman
93. Teotihuacan
94. Temascalapa
95. San Martin de los Piramides

96. Axopusco
97. Nopaltepec
98. Otumba
99. Tepetlaoxtoc
100. Papalotla
101. Chiautla
102. Chiconcuac
103. Texcoco
104. Chimalhuacan
105. La Paz
106. Chicoloapan
107. Ixtlapaluca
108. Chalco
109. Temamatla
110. Cocotitlan
111. Tlamanalco
112. Amecameca
113. Ayapango
114. Tenango del Aire
115. Juchitepec
116. Tepetlixpa
117. Ozumba
118. Atlautla
119. Ecatzingo

16. Michoacan

ETHNOHISTORICAL REGION: Western Mexico

COLONIAL PERIOD

Gobierno: Nueva España
Diocese: Michoacan
Audiencia: Mexico
Intendancy: Valladolid

NATIONAL PERIOD

Territorial or dependency status: None
Statehood: 1824

SPECIAL NOTES

From 1836 to 1846 the Territory of Colima was temporarily suppressed and added to the Departamento of Michoacan. In 1846 Michoacan agreed to donate territory to form the new state of Guerrero. The Territory of Colima was detached again in 1849.

Key to Figure 20 (p. 46):

1. Regules
2. Jiquilpan
3. Sahuayo
4. Venustiano Carranza
5. Pajacuaran
6. Vistahermosa
7. Tanhuato
8. Ixtlan
9. Chavinda
10. Villamar
11. Cotija
12. Tocumbo

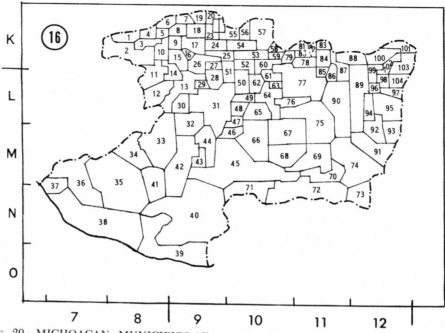

Fig. 20—MICHOACAN: MUNICIPIOS (*Key continued from p. 45*)

13.	Los Reyes	43.	Zaragoza	74.	Tiquicheo
14.	Tingüindin	44.	Paracuaro	75.	Madero
15.	Tangamandapio	45.	La Huacana	76.	Acuitzio
16.	Jacona	46.	Nuevo Urecho	77.	Morelia
17.	Zamora	47.	Taretan	78.	Tarimbaro
18.	Ecuandureo	48.	Ziracuaretiro	79.	Chucandiro
19.	Yurecuaro	49.	Tingambato	80.	Copandaro de Galeana
20.	La Piedad	50.	Nahautzen	81.	Huandacareo
21.	Zinaparo	51.	Cheran	82.	Cuitzeo
22.	Numaran	52.	Zacapu	83.	Santa Ana Maya
23.	Churintzio	53.	Jimenez	84.	Alvaro Obregon
24.	Tlazazalca	54.	Panindicuaro	85.	Charo
25.	Purepero	55.	Penjamillo	86.	Indaparapeo
26.	Tangancicuaro	56.	Angamacutiro	87.	Querendaro
27.	Chilchota	57.	Puruandiro	88.	Zinapecuaro
28.	Paracho	58.	Morelos	89.	Hidalgo
29.	Charapan	59.	Huaniqueo	90.	Tzitzio
30.	Periban	60.	Coeneo	91.	Tuzantla
31.	Uruapan	61.	Quiroga	92.	Juarez
32.	Tancitaro	62.	Erongaricuaro	93.	Susupuato
33.	Buenavista	63.	Tzintzuntzan	94.	Jungapeo
34.	Tepalcatepec	64.	Patzcuaro	95.	Zitacuaro
35.	Coalcoman	65.	Santa Clara	96.	Tuxpan
36.	Chinicuila	66.	Ario	97.	Ocampo
37.	Coahuayana	67.	Tacambaro	98.	Aporo
38.	Aquila	68.	Turicato	99.	Irimbo
39.	Melchor Ocampo del	69.	Nocupetario	100.	Maravatio
	Balsas	70.	Caracuaro	101.	Contepec
40.	Arteaga	71.	Churumuco	102.	Senguio
41.	Aguililla	72.	Huetamo	103.	Tlalpujahua
42.	Apatzingan	73.	San Lucas	104.	Angangueo

17. Morelos

ETHNOHISTORICAL REGION: Central Mexico

COLONIAL PERIOD

Gobierno: Nueva España
Diocese: Mexico
Audiencia: Mexico
Intendancy: Mexico

NATIONAL PERIOD

Territorial or dependency status: District created, 1853
Statehood: Apr. 16, 1869

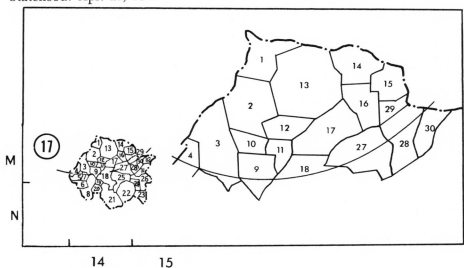

FIG. 21—MORELOS: MUNICIPIOS

Key:

1. Huitzilac
2. Cuernavaca
3. Miacatlan
4. Coatlan
5. Tetecala
6. Amacuzac
7. Mazatepec
8. Puente de Ixtla
9. Xochitepec
10. Temixco
11. Emiliano Zapata
12. Jiutepec
13. Tepoztlan
14. Tlalnepantla
15. Totolopan
16. Tlayacapan
17. Yautepec
18. Tlaltizapan
19. Zacatepec
20. Jojutla
21. Tlaquiltenango
22. Tepalcingo
23. Axochiapan
24. Jonacatepec
25. Ayala
26. Jantetelco
27. Cuautla
28. Yecapiztla
29. Atlatlahuacan
30. Ocuituco
31. Zacualpan
32. Tetela del Volcan

18. Nayarit

ETHNOHISTORICAL REGION: Western Mexico

COLONIAL PERIOD

Gobierno: Nayarit, Nueva Galicia
Diocese: Guadalajara

47

Audiencia: Guadalajara
Intendancy: Guadalajara

NATIONAL PERIOD

Territorial or dependency status: Territory of Tepic, Dec. 12, 1884
Statehood: Constitution of Feb. 5, 1917

SPECIAL NOTES

Territory of Tepic was former 7th Cantón of state of Jalisco.

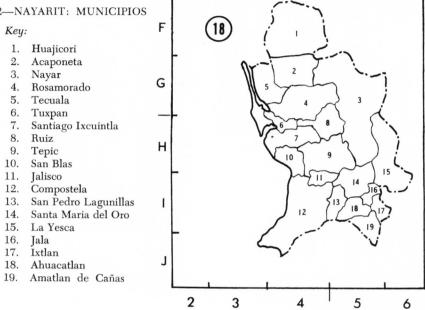

FIG. 22—NAYARIT: MUNICIPIOS

Key:

1. Huajicori
2. Acaponeta
3. Nayar
4. Rosamorado
5. Tecuala
6. Tuxpan
7. Santiago Ixcuintla
8. Ruiz
9. Tepic
10. San Blas
11. Jalisco
12. Compostela
13. San Pedro Lagunillas
14. Santa Maria del Oro
15. La Yesca
16. Jala
17. Ixtlan
18. Ahuacatlan
19. Amatlan de Cañas

19. Nuevo Leon

ETHNOHISTORICAL REGION: Northern Mexico

COLONIAL PERIOD

Gobierno: Nuevo Leon
Diocese: Linares
Audiencia: Mexico
Intendancy: San Luis Potosi

NATIONAL PERIOD

Territorial or dependency status: None. Combined with Coahuila in 1857
Statehood: 1824, 1864

SPECIAL NOTES

In the Provincias Internas de Oriente, the Gobierno del Nuevo Reino de Leon
was subject to the intendant of San Luis Potosi in all but military matters. The

Constitution of 1857 combined Coahuila and Nuevo Leon as a single state of the Republic; they were officially separated Feb. 26, 1864.

FIG. 23—NUEVO LEON: MUNICIPIOS

Key:

11. Los Aldamas
12. Doctor Coss
13. General Bravo
14. Los Herreras
15. Melchor Ocampo
16. Cerralvo
17. Higueras
18. Salinas Victoria
19. Mina
20. Garcia
21. Hidalgo
22. Abasolo
23. Carmen
24. Cienega de Flores
25. General Zuazua
26. Marin
27. Doctor Gonzalez
28. Los Ramones
29. China
30. General Teran
31. Cadereyta Jimenez
32. Pesqueria Chica
33. Apodaca
34. General Escobedo
35. Santa Catarina
36. Garza Garcia
37. Monterrey
38. San Nicholas de los Garzas

39. Guadalupe
40. Juarez
41. Santiago
42. Allende
43. Montemorelos
44. Linares
45. Hualahuises

46. Rayones
47. Galeana
48. Iturbide
49. Aramberri
50. Doctor Arroyo
51. General Zaragoza
52. Mier y Noriega

20. Oaxaca

ETHNOHISTORICAL REGION: Oaxaca

COLONIAL PERIOD

Gobierno: Nueva España
Diocese: Antequera
Audiencia: Mexico
Intendancy: Oaxaca

NATIONAL PERIOD

Territorial or dependency status: None
Statehood: 1824

SPECIAL NOTES

In 1846 Oaxaca agreed to donate territory to form the new state of Guerrero.

49

Oaxaca is the most complex Mexican state, so far as its municipios are concerned. Most Mexican municipio maps (as fig. 8) reproduce only the ex-Distritos, each of which is further subdivided. The ex-Distritos are shown in figure 24. The municipios within each ex-Distrito are shown in figure 25.

Fig. 24—OAXACA: EX-DISTRITOS

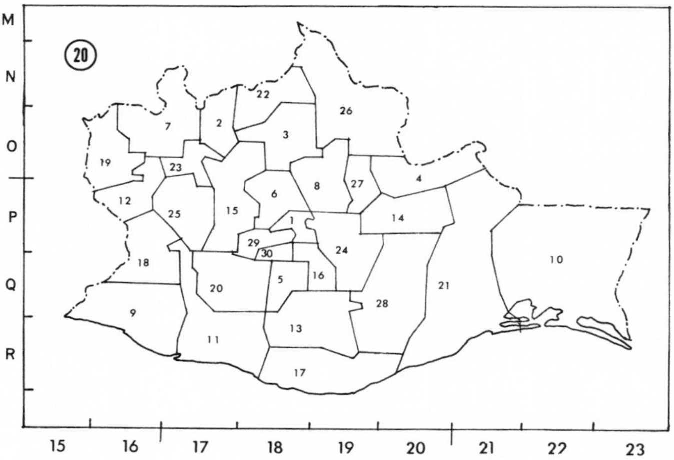

Key to Ex-Distritos:

1. Centro
2. Coixtlahuaca
3. Cuicatlan
4. Choapan
5. Ejutla
6. Etla
7. Huajuapan
8. Ixtlan
9. Jamiltepec
10. Juchitan
11. Juquila
12. Juxtlahuaca
13. Miahuatlan
14. Mixe
15. Nochistlan
16. Ocotlan
17. Pochutla
18. Putla
19. Silacayoapan
20. Sola de Vega
21. Tehuantepec
22. Teotitlan
23. Teposcolula
24. Tlacolula
25. Tlaxiaco
26. Tuxtepec
27. Villa Alta
28. Yautepec
29. Zaachila
30. Zimatlan

(Figure 25 opposite)

21. Puebla

Ethnohistorical Region: Central Mexico

Colonial Period

Gobierno: Nueva España
Diocese: Tlaxcala
Audiencia: Mexico
Intendancy: Puebla

National Period

Territorial or dependency status: None
Statehood: 1824

Special Notes

In 1846 Puebla agreed to donate territory to form the new state of Guerrero. By decree of Dec. 1, 1853, the District of Tuxpan was transferred to the Departamento of Veracruz.

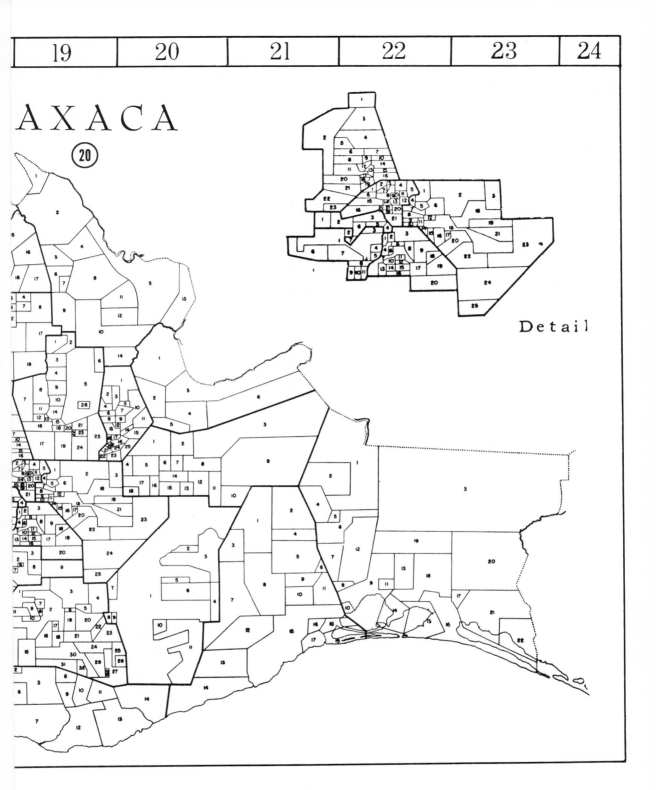

AXACA

20

Detail

andres Sinaxtla
uan Sayultepec
ateo Etlatongo
rancisco Chindua
rancisco Jaltepetongo
ono de Porfirio Diaz
Domingo Nuxaa
iguel Tecomatlan
go Tilantongo

23. San Juan Diuxi
24. Magdalena Jaltepec
25. Asuncion Nochistlan
26. San Mateo Sindihui
27. San Pedro Teozacualco
28. San Miguel Piedras
29. Zaragoza
30. San Andres Nuxiño
31. San Juan Tamazola

32. San Antonio Huitepec

16. OCOTLAN

1. Santa Ana Zegache
2. San Martin Tilcajete
3. Santo Tomas Jalieza
4. Santiago Apostol
5. San Juan Chilateca

(Key continued on reverse side)

Key to Figure 26:

1. Francisco Z. Mena
2. Pantepec
3. Jalpan
4. Tlaxco
5. Tlacuilotepec
6. Villa Juarez
7. Chila Honey
8. Pahuatlan
9. Naupan
10. Huauchinango
11. Ahuazotepec
12. Zacatlan
13. Chignahuapan
14. Aquixtla
15. Ixtacamaxtitlan
16. Tetela de Ocampo
17. Cuautempan
18. Tepetzintla
19. Ahuacatlan
20. Chiconcuautla
21. Tlaola
22. Juan Galindo
23. Zihuateutla
24. Jopala
25. Tlapacoyan
26. San Felipe Tepatlan
27. Amixtlan
28. Tepango de Rodriguez
29. Zongozotla
30. Huitzilan
31. Xochitlan
32. Zapotitlan de Mendez
33. Camocuautla
34. Hueytlalpan
35. Ixtepec
36. Coatepec
37. Hermenegildo Galeana
38. Olintla
39. Huehuetla
40. Ignacio Allende
41. Zoquiapan
42. Nauzontla
43. Jonotla
44. Tuzamapan de Galeana
45. Tenampulco
46. Ayotoxco de Guerrero
47. Hueytamalco
48. Acateno
49. Hueyapan
50. Yaonahuac
51. Tlatlauquitepec
52. Cuetzalan del Progreso
53. Zacapoaxtla
54. Xochiapulco

55. Zautla
56. Zaragoza
57. Atempan
58. Teteles
59. Chignautla
60. Teziutlan
61. Xiutetelco
62. Cuyoaco
63. Ocotepec
64. Libres
65. Tepeyahualco
66. Oriental
67. Guadalupe Victoria
68. Lafragua
69. Chilchotla
70. Quimixtlan
71. Chichiquila
72. Tlachichuca
73. Aljojuca
74. San Nicolas de Buenos Aires
75. San Salvador el Seco
76. Mazapiltepec de Juarez
77. Soltepec
78. San Jose Chiapa
79. Rafael Lara Grajales
80. Nopalucan
81. Acajete
82. Tepatlaxco de Hidalgo
83. Amozoc
84. San Miguel Canoa
85. Resurreccion
86. Puebla
87. San Felipe Hueyotlipan
88. San Jeronimo Caleras
89. Cuautlancingo
90. Coronanco
91. Tlaltenango
92. San Miguel Xoxtla
93. San Martin Texmelucan
94. Chiautzingo
95. San Felipe Teotlalcingo
96. San Matias Tlalancaleca
97. Tlahuapan
98. San Salvador el Verde
99. Huejotzingo
100. Domingo Arenas
101. San Nicolas los Ranchos
102. Calpan
103. Juan C. Bonilla
104. San Pedro Cholula
105. San Andres Cholula
106. San Gregorio Atzompa
107. San Jeronimo Tecuanipan

108. Nealtican
109. Tianguismanalco
110. Tochimilco
111. Atlixco
112. Santa Isabel Cholula
113. Ocoyucan
114. Totimehuacan
115. Cuautinchan
116. Tepeaca
117. Acatzingo
118. General Felipe Angeles
119. San Juan Atenco
120. Chalchicomula
121. Atzitzintla
122. Esperanza
123. Palmar de Bravo
124. Quecholac
125. Tecamachalco
126. San Salvador Huixcolotla
127. Los Reyes
128. Cuapiaxtla de Madero
129. Mixtla
130. Santo Tomas Hueyotilpan
131. Tecali de Herrera
132. Tzicatlacoyan
133. La Magdalena Tlatlauquitepec
134. Santo Domingo Huehuetlan
135. Teopantlan
136. Xochiltepec
137. Epatlan
138. San Martin Totoltepec
139. Tepeojuma
140. San Diego la Mesa Tochimiltzingo
141. Huaquechula
142. Atzitzihuacan
143. Tepemaxalco
144. Acteopan
145. Cohuecan
146. Tepexco
147. Tlapanala
148. Tilapa
149. Atzala
150. Izucar de Matamoros
151. Ahuatlan
152. Coatzingo
153. Santo Catarina Tlaltempan
154. Chigmecatitlan
155. Huatlatlauca
156. San Juan Atzompa
157. Zacapala

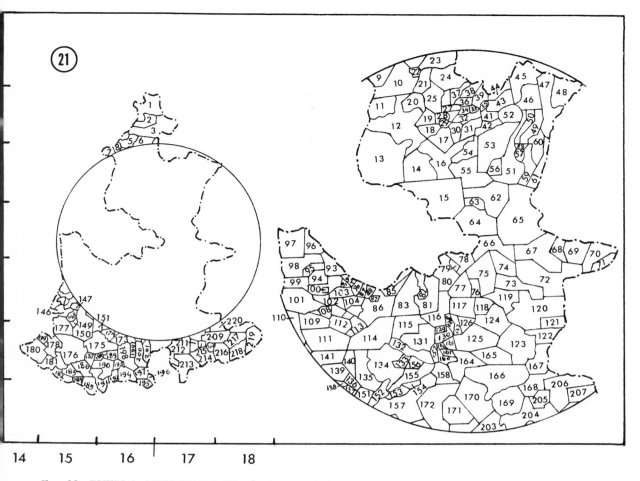

Fig. 26—PUEBLA: MUNICIPIOS (*Key begins opposite*)

158. Molcaxac	179. Teotlalco	201. Totoltepec de Guerrero
159. Atoyatempan	180. Jolalpan	202. Coyotepec
160. Huitziltepec	181. Cohetzala	203. Atexcal
161. Tepeyahualco	182. Ixcamilpa de Guerrero	204. Tehuacan
Cuauhtemoc	183. Xicotlan	205. Santiago Miahuatlan
162. Tlanepantla	184. Albino Zertuche	206. Nicolas Bravo
163. Tochtepec	185. Tulcingo	207. Vicente Guerrero
164. Xochitlan Todos Santos	186. Chila de la Sal	208. San Antonio Cañada
165. Yehualtepec	187. Axutla	209. Ajalpan
166. Tlacotepec	188. Chinantla	210. Altepexi
167. Morelos Cañada	189. Ahuehuetitla	211. San Gabriel Chilac
168. Chapulco	190. Piaxtla	212. Zapotitlan
169. Tepanco de Lopez	191. Tecomatlan	213. Caltepec
170. Juan N. Mendez	192. Guadalupe	214. San Jose Miahuatlan
171. Ixcaquixtla	193. San Pablo Amicano	215. Zinacatepec
172. Tepexi de Rodriguez	194. San Pedro Yeloixtlahuacan	216. Coxcatlan
173. Santa Ines Ahuatempan	195. Chila	217. Zoquitlan
174. Cuayuca	196. San Miguel Ixitlan	218. Coyomeapan
175. Tehuitzingo	197. Petlalcingo	219. San Sebastian Tlacotepec
176. Chiautla	198. Acatlan	220. Eloxochitlan
177. Chietla	199. Xayacatlan de Bravo	
178. Huehuetlan el Chico	200. San Jeronimo Xayacatlan	

22. Queretaro

ETHNOHISTORICAL REGION: Central Mexico

COLONIAL PERIOD

Gobierno: Nueva España
Diocese: Mexico, Michoacan
Audiencia: Mexico
Intendancy: Mexico

NATIONAL PERIOD

Territorial or dependency status: See Special Notes
Statehood: 1824

SPECIAL NOTES

The Partido of Queretaro in 1822 successfully separated itself from the Intendancy of Mexico, with definitive boundaries fixed Aug. 22, 1823, by decree of a Constituent Congress.

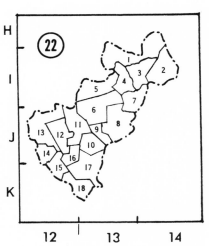

FIG. 27—QUERETARO: MUNICIPIOS

Key:

1.	Arroyo Seco	10.	Tequisquiapan
2.	Landa de Matamoros	11.	Colon
3.	Jalpan	12.	El Marques
4.	Amoles	13.	Queretaro
5.	Peñamiller	14.	Corregidora
6.	Toliman	15.	Huimilpan
7.	San Joaquin	16.	Pedro Escobedo
8.	Cadereyta	17.	San Juan del Rio
9.	Ezequiel Montes	18.	Amealco

23. Quintana Roo

ETHNOHISTORICAL REGION: Southeastern Mexico

COLONIAL PERIOD

Gobierno: Yucatan
Diocese: Yucatan
Audiencia: Mexico
Intendancy: Merida

NATIONAL PERIOD

Territorial or dependency status: Nov. 24, 1902, Territory
Statehood: None

SPECIAL NOTES

Temporarily, 1931–35, territorial status was suspended, and the area reassigned to the state of Yucatan; the *status quo ante* was restored Jan. 16, 1935.

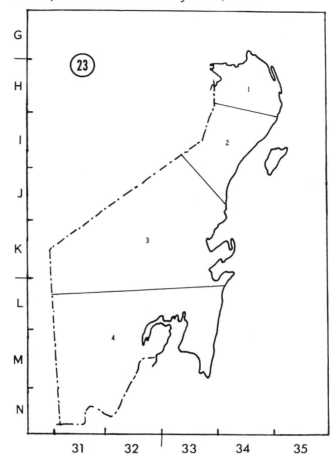

FIG. 28—QUINTANA ROO: MUNICIPIOS

Key:

1. Isla Mujeres
2. Cozumel
3. Felipe Carrillo Puerto
4. Payo Obispo

24. San Luis Potosi

ETHNOHISTORICAL REGION: Northern Mexico

COLONIAL PERIOD

Gobierno: Nueva Galicia, Nuevo Leon, Nueva España
Diocese: Guadalajara
Audiencia: Guadalajara, Mexico
Intendancy: San Luis Potosi

NATIONAL PERIOD

Territorial or dependency status: None
Statehood: 1824

53

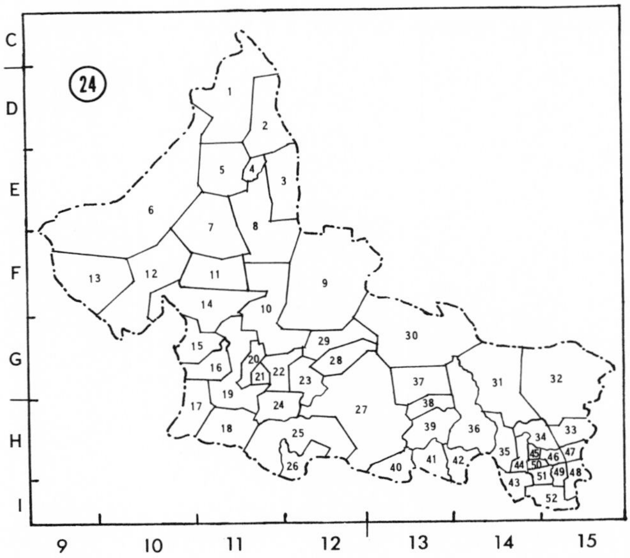

Fig. 29—SAN LUIS POTOSI:
MUNICIPIOS

Key:

1. Vanegas
2. Cedral
3. Matehuala
4. La Paz
5. Catorce
6. Santo Domingo
7. Charcas
8. Guadalupe
9. Guadalcazar
10. Villa de Hidalgo
11. Venado
12. Salinas
13. Ramos
14. Moctezuma
15. Ahualulco
16. Mexquitic de Carmona
17. Villa de Arriaga
18. Villa de Reyes
19. San Luis Potosi
20. Soledad
21. Cerro de San Pedro
22. Villa Morelos
23. San Nicolas Tolentino
24. Zaragoza
25. Santa Maria del Rio
26. Tierranueva
27. Rioverde
28. Villa Juarez
29. Cerritos

30. Ciudad del Maiz
31. Ciudad de Valles
32. Tamuin
33. Tancuayalab
34. Tanlajas
35. Aquismon
36. Temasopo
37. Alaquines
38. Cardenas
39. Rayon
40. Pedro Montoya
41. Lagunillas

42. Santa Catarina
43. Xilitla
44. General Pedro Antonio
    Santos
45. San Antonio
46. Tampamolon
47. Tanquian
48. San Martin
49. Tampacan
50. Coxcatlan
51. Alfredo M. Terrazas
52. Tamazunchale

25. Sinaloa

Ethnohistorical Region: Western Mexico

Colonial Period

> Gobierno: Sinaloa
> Diocese: Guadalajara
> Audiencia: Guadalajara
> Intendancy: Arizpe (Sonora)

National Period

> Territorial or dependency status: Joined with Sonora in 1824
> Statehood: Oct. 13, 1830

Special Notes

In the Provincias Internas de Occidente, the comandante of Arizpe was Intendant for the Gobierno de las Provincias de Sonora y Sinaloa, as well as Durango. Sinaloa was separated from Sonora and raised to statehood Oct. 13, 1830.

54

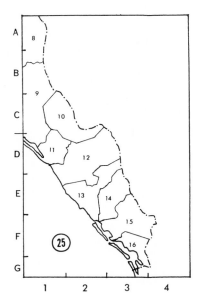

Fig. 30—SINALOA: MUNICIPIOS

Key:

8. Badiraguato
9. Culiacan
10. Cosala
11. Elota
12. San Ignacio
13. Mazatlan
14. Concordia
15. Rosario
16. Escuinapa

27. Tabasco

Ethnohistorical Region: Southeastern Mexico

Colonial Period

Gobierno: Yucatan, Isla de Carmen
Diocese: Yucatan, Chiapa
Audiencia: Mexico
Intendancy: Merida

National Period

Territorial or dependency status: None
Statehood: 1824

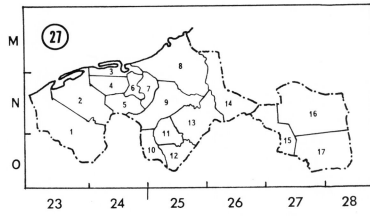

Fig. 31—TABASCO: MUNICIPIOS

Key:

1. Huimanguillo
2. Cardenas
3. Paraiso
4. Comalcalco
5. Cunduacan
6. Jalpa
7. Nacajuca
8. Centla
9. Centro
10. Teapa
11. Jalapa
12. Tacotalpa
13. Macuspana
14. Jonuta
15. Emiliano Zapata
16. Balancan
17. Tenosique

55

28. Tamaulipas

ETHNOHISTORICAL REGION: Northern Mexico

COLONIAL PERIOD

Gobierno: Nuevo Santander
Diocese: Linares
Audiencia: Mexico
Intendancy: San Luis Potosi

NATIONAL PERIOD

Territorial or dependency status: None
Statehood: 1824

SPECIAL NOTES

The Gobierno de Colonia del Nueva Santander was subject to the intendant of San Luis Potosi for all but military matters, for which the Comandante of the Provincias Internas de Oriente was responsible.

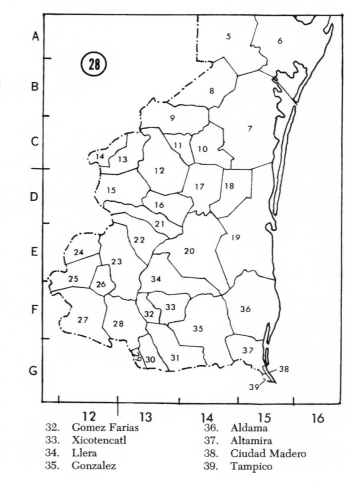

FIG. 32—TAMAULIPAS:
MUNICIPIOS

Key:

5. Reinosa
6. Matamoros
7. San Fernando
8. Mendez
9. Burgos
10. Cruillas
11. San Nicolas
12. San Carlos
13. Villagran
14. Mainero
15. Hidalgo
16. Padilla
17. Jimenez
18. Abasolo
19. Soto la Marina
20. Casas
21. Güemez
22. Victoria
23. Jaumave
24. Miquihuana
25. Bustamante
26. Palmillas
27. Tula
28. Ocampo
29. Nuevo Morelos
30. Antiguo Morelos
31. Mante

32. Gomez Farias
33. Xicotencatl
34. Llera
35. Gonzalez

36. Aldama
37. Altamira
38. Ciudad Madero
39. Tampico

29. Tlaxcala

ETHNOHISTORICAL REGION: Central Mexico

COLONIAL PERIOD

Gobierno: Nueva España
Diocese: Tlaxcala
Audiencia: Mexico
Intendancy: Gobierno of Tlaxcala

NATIONAL PERIOD

Territorial or dependency status: Territory, decree, Nov. 24, 1824
Statehood: Constitution of 1857

SPECIAL NOTES

In 1793 the Gobierno of Tlaxcala was detached from the Intendancy of Mexico, and placed directly under viceroy. From 1836 to 1846 the territorial status was suppressed and the Tlaxcalan area reverted to the Departamento of Mexico. This was restored in 1849.

FIG. 33—TLAXCALA: MUNICIPIOS

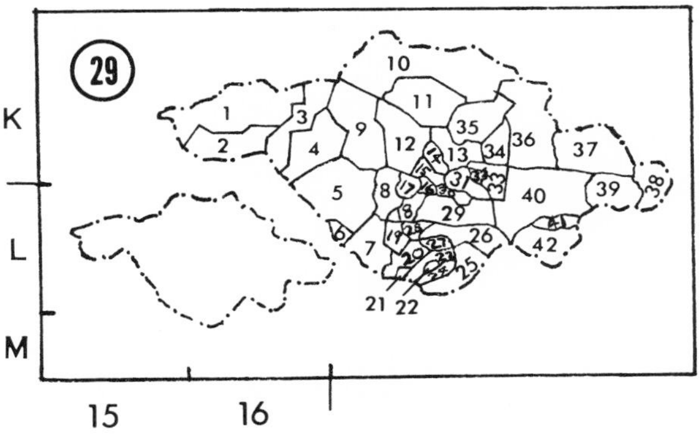

Key:

1. Calpulalpan
2. Mariano Arista
3. Lazaro Cardenas
4. Españita
5. Ixtacuixtla
6. Lardizabal
7. Nativitas
8. Panotla
9. Hueyotlipan
10. Tlaxco
11. Atlangatepec
12. Xaltocan
13. Barron Escandon
14. Yauhquemehcan
15. Amaxac de Guerrero
16. Apetatitlan
17. Totolac
18. Tlaxcala
19. Tetlahuaca
20. Zacatelco
21. Xicohtzinco
22. Xicotencatl
23. Jose Maria Morelos
24. Tenancingo

25. San Pablo del Monte
26. Teolocholco
27. Miguel Hidalgo y Costilla
28. Tepeyanco
29. Chiautempan
30. Juan Cuamatzi
31. Santa Cruz Tlaxcala
32. Cuaxomulco
33. Tzompantepec

34. Xalostoc
35. Tetla
36. Terrenate
37. Actlzayanca
38. El Carmen
39. Cuapiaxtla
40. Huamantla
41. Ixtenco
42. Zitlaltepec

30. Veracruz

ETHNOHISTORICAL REGION: Central Mexico

COLONIAL PERIOD

Gobierno: Nueva España
Diocese: Mexico, Tlaxcala, Antequera

Audiencia: Mexico
Intendancy: Veracruz

NATIONAL PERIOD

Territorial or dependency status: None
Statehood: 1824

SPECIAL NOTES

By decree (Dec. 1, 1853) the District of Tuxpan was transferred from the Departamento of Puebla to that of Veracruz.

Key to Figure 34 (opposite):

1.	Panuco	44.	Gutierrez Zamora	87.	Apazapan
2.	Pueblo Viejo	45.	Tecolutla	88.	Emiliano Zapata
3.	Tampico Alto	46.	Martinez de la Torre	89.	Actopan
4.	Ozuluama	47.	Nautla	90.	Ursulo Galvan
5.	Tempoal	48.	Misantla	91.	La Antigua
6.	Platon Sanchez	49.	Atzalan	92.	Puente Nacional
7.	Chiconamel	50.	Tlapacoyan	93.	Tlacotepec
8.	Chalma	51.	Jalacingo	94.	Totutla
9.	Tantoyuca	52.	Altotonga	95.	Tenampa
10.	Ixcatepec	53.	Las Minas	96.	Sochiapa
11.	Chontla	54.	Tatatila	97.	Huatusco
12.	Citlaltepec	55.	Villa Aldama	98.	Calcahualco
13.	Tantima	56.	Perote	99.	Alpatlahua
14.	Tamalin	57.	Las Vigas	100.	Coscomatepec
15.	Chinampa de Gorostiza	58.	Tlacolulan	101.	La Perla
16.	Amatlan–Tuxpan	59.	Tenochitlan	102.	Atzacan
17.	Tamiahua	60.	Tonayan	103.	Chocaman
18.	Tancoco	61.	Landero y Cos	104.	Tomatlan
19.	Tepetzintla	62.	Miahuatlan	105.	Ixhuatlan–Cordoba
20.	Chicontepec	63.	Acatlan	106.	Tepatlaxco
21.	Benito Juarez	64.	Chiconquiaco	107.	Zentla
22.	Zontecomatlan	65.	Yecuatla	108.	Comapa
23.	Ilamatlan	66.	Colipa	109.	Paso de Ovejas
24.	Huayacocotla	67.	Vega de Alatorre	110.	Veracruz
25.	Zacualpan	68.	Juchique de Ferrer	111.	Manlio Fabio Altamirano
26.	Texcatepec	69.	Alto Lucero	112.	Soledad de Doblado
27.	Tlachichilco	70.	Tepetlan	113.	Temaxcal Camaron
28.	Ixhuatlan de Madero	71.	Naolinco	114.	Paso del Macho
29.	Temapache	72.	Coacoatzintla	115.	Atoyac
30.	Teayo	73.	Jilotepec	116.	Amatlan de los Reyes
31.	Tihuatlan	74.	Banderilla	117.	Cordoba
32.	Tuxpan	75.	Rafael Lucio	118.	Fortin
33.	Cazones	76.	Acajete	119.	Ixtaczoquitlan
34.	Coatzintla	77.	Tlalnelhuayocan	120.	Orizaba
35.	Espinal	78.	Jalapa	121.	Tenango de Rio Blanco
36.	Coyutla	79.	Coatepec	122.	Huiloapan
37.	Coahuitlan	80.	Jico	123.	Camerino Z. Mendoza
38.	Mecatlan	81.	Ayahualulco	124.	Nogales
39.	Filomeno Mata	82.	Ixhuacan	125.	Ixhuatlancillo
40.	Chumatlan	83.	Teocelo	126.	Mariano Escobedo
41.	Coxquihul	84.	Cosautlan	127.	Maltrata
42.	Zozocolco	85.	Axocuapan	128.	Aquila
43.	Papantla	86.	Jalcomulco	129.	Acultzingo

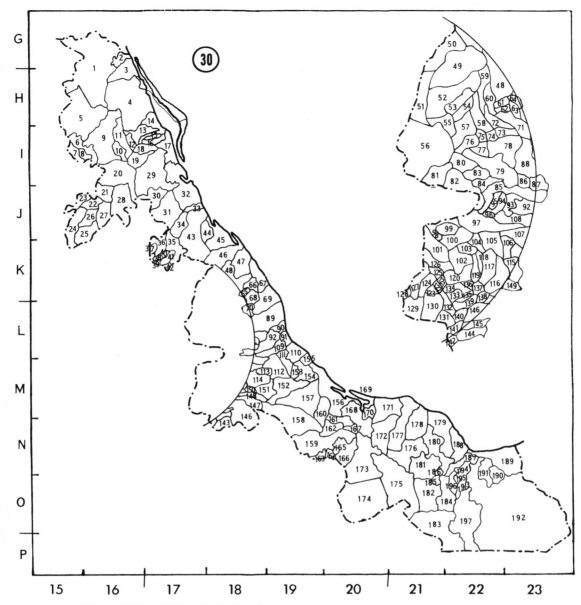

Fig. 34—VERACRUZ: MUNICIPIOS (*Key begins opposite*)

130.	Soledad Atzompa	143.	Tehuipango
131.	Xoxocotla	144.	Mixtla de Altamirano
132.	Atlahuilco	145.	Texhuacan
133.	San Andres Tenejapa	146.	Zongolica
134.	Tlilapan	147.	Tenejapa de Mata
135.	Magdalena	148.	Cuichapa
136.	Rafael Delgado	149.	Yanga
137.	Naranjal	150.	Cuitlahuac
138.	Coetzala	151.	Carrillo Puerto
139.	Tequila	152.	Cotaxtla
140.	Reyes	153.	Jamapa
141.	Tlaquilpa	154.	Medellin
142.	Astacinga	155.	Boca del Rio

156.	Alvarado
157.	Tlalixcoyan
158.	Tierra Blanca
159.	Cosamaloapan
160.	Ignacio de la Llave
161.	Acula
162.	Ixmatlahuacan
163.	Otatitlan
164.	Tlacojalpan
165.	Tuxtilla
166.	Chacaltianguis
167.	Amatitlan
168.	Tlacotalpan

169.	Lerdo de Tejeda	179.	Mecayapan	189.	Coatzacoalcos
170.	Saltabarranca	180.	Soteapan	190.	Moloacan
171.	Angel R. Cabada	181.	Acayucan	191.	Chapopotla
172.	Santiago Tuxtla	182.	Sayula	192.	Minatitlan
173.	Tesechoacan	183.	Jesus Carranza	193.	Cosoleacaque
174.	Playa Vicente	184.	Texistepec	194.	Oteapan
175.	San Juan Evangelista	185.	Oluta	195.	Zaragoza
176.	Hueyapan de Ocampo	186.	Soconusco	196.	Jaltipan
177.	San Andres Tuxtla	187.	Chinameca	197.	Hidalgotitlan
178.	Catemaco	188.	Pajapan		

31. Yucatan

ETHNOHISTORICAL REGION: Southeastern Mexico

COLONIAL PERIOD

> Gobierno: Yucatan
> Diocese: Yucatan
> Audiencia: Mexico
> Intendancy: Merida

NATIONAL PERIOD

> Territorial or dependency status: None
> Statehood: 1824

SPECIAL NOTES

The District of Campeche provisionally became a state Feb. 19, 1862, and finally on Apr. 29, 1863, reducing the area of the state of Yucatan. Creation of the Territory of Quintana Roo (Nov. 24, 1902) further reduced the state area. From 1931 through January 16, 1935, the Territory was suppressed and its area reassigned to Yucatan, but territorial status was restored on latter date.

FIG. 35—YUCATAN: MUNICIPIOS

Key:

1. Progreso
2. Chicxulub
3. Ixil
4. Telcha Puerto
5. Sinanche
6. Yobain
7. Dzidzantun
8. Dzilam de Bravo
9. Dzilam Gonzalez
10. San Felipe
11. Rio Lagartos
12. Tizimin
13. Panaba
14. Sucila
15. Buctzotz
16. Temax
17. Cansahcab

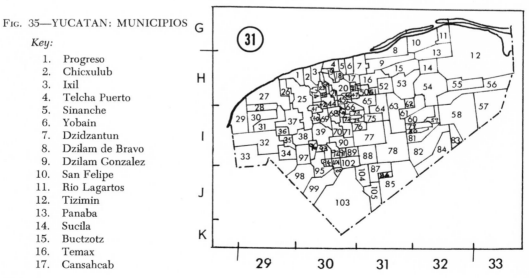

18. Telchac
19. Dzemul
20. Motul
21. Muxupip
22. Baca
23. Mococha
24. Conkal
25. Merida
26. Ucu
27. Hunucma
28. Tetiz
29. Celestin
30. Kinchil
31. Samahil
32. Maxcanu
33. Halacho
34. Opichen
35. Kopoma
36. Chochola
37. Uman
38. Abala
39. Techoh
40. Timucuy
41. Kanasin
42. Tixpeual
43. Yaxkukul
44. Tixkokob
45. Cacalchen
46. Bokoba
47. Tekanto

48. Suma
49. Teya
50. Tepakan
51. Tekal
52. Dzoncauich
53. Cenotillo
54. Espita
55. Calotmul
56. Temozon
57. Chemax
58. Valladolid
59. Uayma
60. Tinum
61. Dzitas
62. Quintana Roo
63. Tunkas
64. Sudzal
65. Izamal
66. Hoctun
67. Tahmek
68. Seye
69. Acanceh
70. Cuzama
71. Homun
72. Hocaba
73. Xocchel
74. Sanahcat
75. Kantunil
76. Huhi
77. Sotuta

78. Yaxcaba
79. Kaua
80. Chan-Kom
81. Cuncunul
82. Tekom
83. Chichimila
84. Tixcacacupul
85. Peto
86. Tahdziu
87. Chaczinkin
88. Cantamayec
89. Mayapan
90. Tekit
91. Chumayel
92. Mama
93. Chapab
94. Dzan
95. Ticul
96. Sacalum
97. Muna
98. Santa Elena
99. Oxkutzcab
100. Akil
101. Mani
102. Teabo
103. Tekax
104. Tixmeuac
105. Tzucacab

32. Zacatecas

ETHNOHISTORICAL REGION: Northern Mexico

COLONIAL PERIOD

Gobierno: Nueva Galicia
Diocese: Guadalajara
Audiencia: Guadalajara
Intendancy: Zacatecas

NATIONAL PERIOD

Territorial or dependency status: None
Statehood: 1824

SPECIAL NOTES

From Zacatecas, the Territory of Aguascalientes was created May 23, 1835.

Key to Figure 36 (p. 62):

1. Melchor Ocampo
2. Concepcion del Oro
3. Mazapil
4. Nieves

5. Juan Aldama
6. Miguel Auza
7. Rio Grande
8. Villa de Cos

9. Fresnillo
10. Sain Alto
11. Sombrerete
12. Chalchihuites

Fig. 36—ZACATECAS: MUNICIPIOS (*Key continued from p. 61*)

13. Jimenez del Tuel
14. Valparaiso
15. Monte Escobedo
16. Tepetongo
17. Susticacan
18. Jerez
19. Calera
20. Morelos
21. Panuco
22. Vetagrande
23. Guadalupe
24. La Blanca
25. Villa Gonzalez Ortega
26. Villa Hidalgo
27. Pinos
28. Villa Garcia
29. Bimbaletes
30. Noria de Angeles
31. Luis Moya
32. Ojocaliente
33. Cuauhtemoc
34. Jose de la Isla
35. Zacatecas
36. Villanueva
37. Tabasco
38. El Plateado
39. Momax
40. Sanchez Roman
41. Huanusco
42. Jalpa
43. Tepechitlan
44. Atolinga
45. Teul de Gonzalez Ortega
46. Garcia de la Cadena
47. Mezquital del Oro
48. Moyahua de Estrada
49. Juchipila
50. Apozol
51. Nochistlan
52. Apulco

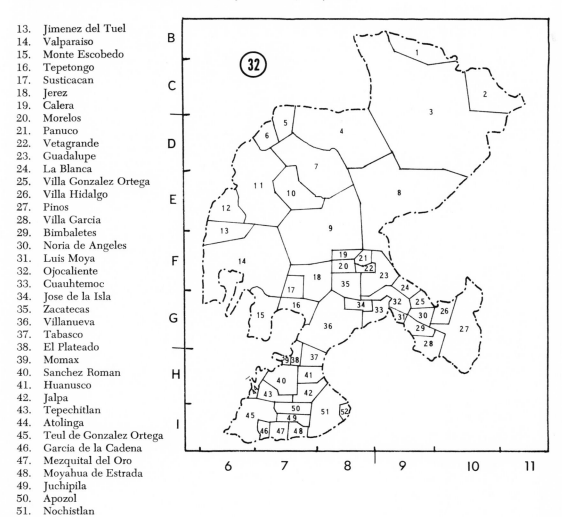

2. Colonial New Spain, 1519-1786: Historical Notes on the Evolution of Minor Political Jurisdictions

PETER GERHARD

THE SPANIARDS who took possession of America imposed on the new lands their own institutions, roots of which can be traced back to the Roman occupation of Iberia. As it had evolved by the late 15th century, the Spanish apparatus of government was divided "horizontally" into five *ramos* or branches: *Gobierno* (civil administration), *Judicial* (judiciary), *Militar* (military), *Hacienda* (exchequer), and *Eclesiástico* (church affairs). While each had its hierarchy, often a single individual would hold parallel positions in two or more ramos. The king headed all the secular branches and, as patron of the church, also had the right to nominate ecclesiastics. Beneath him and delegated with much of his authority was the Council of the Indies, in charge of all matters affecting overseas possessions. Next in the chain of command so far as Middle America is concerned was the viceroy of New Spain, whose relation to the five branches of government was similar to the king's. The viceroy was simultaneously governor of New Spain (gobierno), captain-general (militar) and president of the audiencia of Mexico (judicial). During most of the colonial period he also supervised financial matters, and he nominated lesser ecclesiastical dignitaries.

In practice, the power of the viceroy was limited in many ways, both in geographic area and in the extent to which he controlled subordinates, shared his privileges with others, and was himself watched and controlled. In military and financial matters, the viceroy was responsible in a rather unreal sense for all of North America, northern South America, the Caribbean islands, and the Spanish possessions in southeast Asia. In judicial affairs his power was confined to the jurisdiction of the audiencia of Mexico, a far smaller area; in matters of civil government and ecclesiastical preferment he directly ruled only the gobierno of New Spain, a still more reduced territory. Figure 1 gives a rough idea of the inner workings of this establishment.

Before looking into the geographical division of the viceroyalty, we shall consider briefly the functions of each branch of government.

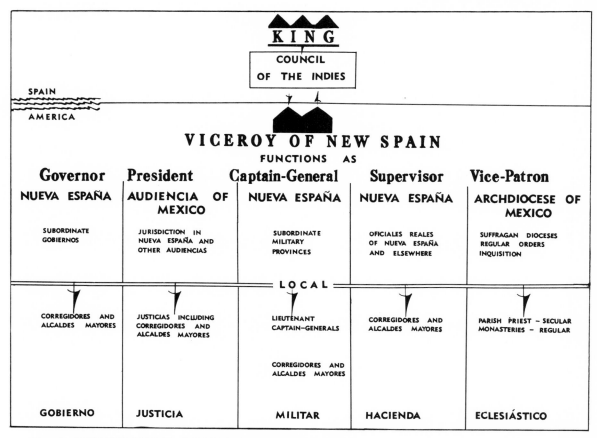

FIG. 1—THE VICEREGAL ADMINISTRATIVE STRUCTURE

Gobierno

A gobierno was a political unit ruled by a *gobernador*, or governor. The latter normally was named by the king on recommendation of the Council of the Indies, although under certain conditions he might receive his appointment from a viceroy. He was the king's representative and administrator in a kingdom (*reino*) or province (*provincia*, a very elastic term), and he might or might not have to do with other branches than that of gobierno. The governor sometimes delegated his powers to one or more lieutenants (*tenientes de gobernador*), but more often he ruled through subordinate officials known as *corregidores* and

alcaldes mayores, who were in effect local "governors" in charge of lesser territorial units called *corregimientos* and *alcaldías mayores*. Since they also exercised judicial power within their jurisdictions, these officials were known collectively as justices (*justicias*). We will have more to say about them later.

The first governor in America was Columbus (1492), whose title covered all lands that he might discover. The area with which we are here concerned, continental Middle America, was invaded and conquered by two groups of Spaniards: the first established itself in the Isthmus of Panama in 1509; the second, headed by Hernando Cortés, landed ten years later at Veracruz.

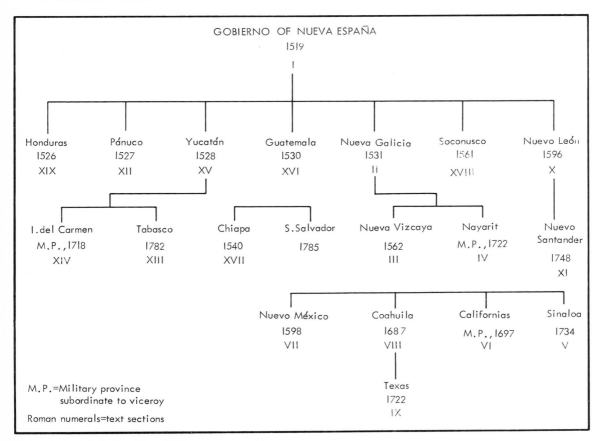

FIG. 2—GOBIERNOS OF NEW SPAIN, 1519–1785

In both cases gobiernos were organized, which soon were split up into other gobiernos. From that of Panama or Castilla del Oro were formed Nicaragua (1527) and Costa Rica (1565). Figure 2 shows chronologically how the original gobierno of New Spain was subdivided.

Justicia

We have mentioned that the viceroy of New Spain was both governor of that realm and president of the royal audiencia, the supreme judicial tribunal of Mexico. The same system of dual function applied down through other governors, who might be presidents of other audiencias and in most cases also had judicial attributes, to the co-

rregidores and alcaldes mayores, who were justices or local magistrates as well as administrators. The audiencia also functioned as a consultative council to the governor purposely as a check on his powers. When there was no viceroy or governor, the judges (*oidores*) of the audiencia collectively assumed responsibility for the civil government in addition to their normal judicial duties.

The first audiencia in America was that of Santo Domingo, established in 1511. Cortés at first held the title of *justicia mayor*, presumably subordinate to that tribunal. At the end of 1528 an audiencia was set up in Mexico City with jurisdiction in all of mainland America north of Nicaragua, although six years later Honduras was transferred back to the audiencia of Santo Domingo. From 1535 the office of president of the audiencia of Mexico was held by the viceroy.

The inconveniences arising from the size of the audiencia of Mexico resulted in a division of its territory, with the establishment of, first, the audiencia of Los Confines (Guatemala) in 1544 and, five years later, the audiencia of Nueva Galicia (finally established at Guadalajara). Thus the area under study here was divided in matters of justice among three supreme tribunals, although for a time (until 1572) the audiencia of Guadalajara was subordinate to that of Mexico. Important suits ruled upon by the audiencias could be appealed to the Council of the Indies for final decision.

Militar

The highest military title in Spanish America was that of captain-general (*capitán general*), an office almost always combined with that of viceroy or governor. The military influence of the viceroy of New Spain at times extended to distant provinces such as Florida and the Philippines, although during much of the colonial period it was in effect confined to the gobierno of New Spain and the northern frontier provinces. A field commander might be known as *teniente de capitán general, teniente general de la costa, capitán comandante*, or *castellano*. Local police matters were handled by the corregidores and alcaldes mayores, with the assistance of *alguaciles*.

Hacienda

Viceroys, governors, and audiencias were constantly enjoined to supervise matters of the royal exchequer, to reduce expenditures, and add to revenues. The actual administration of this ramo, however, was entrusted to special officers (*oficiales reales*), who were stationed in important cities, ports, and mining centers. The extent of each treasury district was carefully defined. In

those areas where there were no treasury officials, taxes and tributes were collected by the corregidores and alcaldes mayores.

Eclesiástico

The church in America was part of the Spanish state, and control of it through the papal concession known as *patronato real* was a privilege jealously guarded by the Spanish kings. The kings nominated (in effect directly appointed) the higher church dignitaries, whereas parish priests were more often nominated or chosen by the viceroys and governors. The church in turn had vast properties, its own judiciary, and considerable political as well as spiritual influence. Ten bishops and archbishops served as viceroys of New Spain.

The ecclesiastical division of America went its own way, with little regard for the other branches of government. Figure 3 shows the proliferation of dioceses in Middle America throughout the colonial period. A large gobierno such as New Spain could have several dioceses within it; a single diocese (e.g., Guadalajara) might include a number of gobiernos. To add to the confusion, the various regular Orders had their own provincias which existed quite independently of the bishoprics, and the tribunals of the Inquisition provided still a third ecclesiastical division of the country. On a local scale, dioceses were subdivided into curacies (*partidos de clérigos*), and regular provinces into monastery and missionary districts (*custodias, guardianías, presidencias*, or *vicarías*), which might or might not coincide with a civil division (corregimiento, alcaldía mayor).

During the first two and a half centuries of Spanish rule, while the governmental organization as described above remained intact, there were many minor changes and adjustments in boundaries and jurisdictions. Early civil and ecclesiastical divisions lost importance and were eliminated; others came into being as a result of conquest,

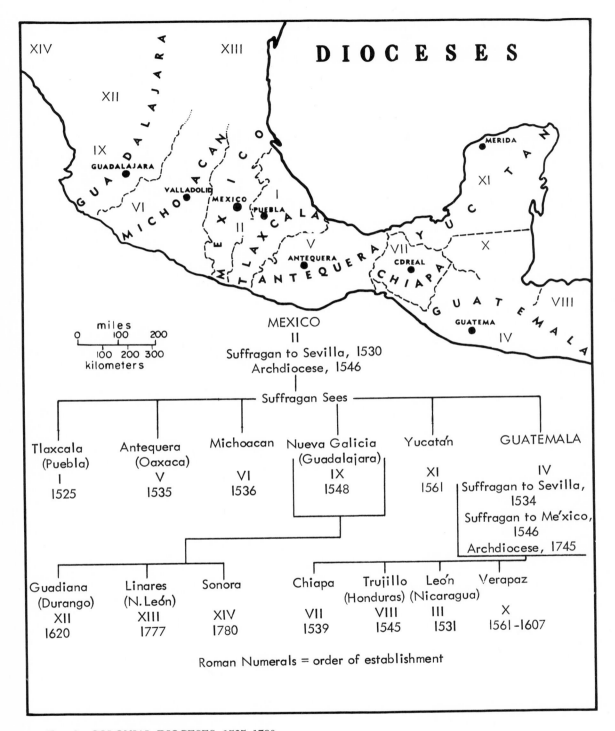

FIG. 3—COLONIAL DIOCESES, 1525–1780

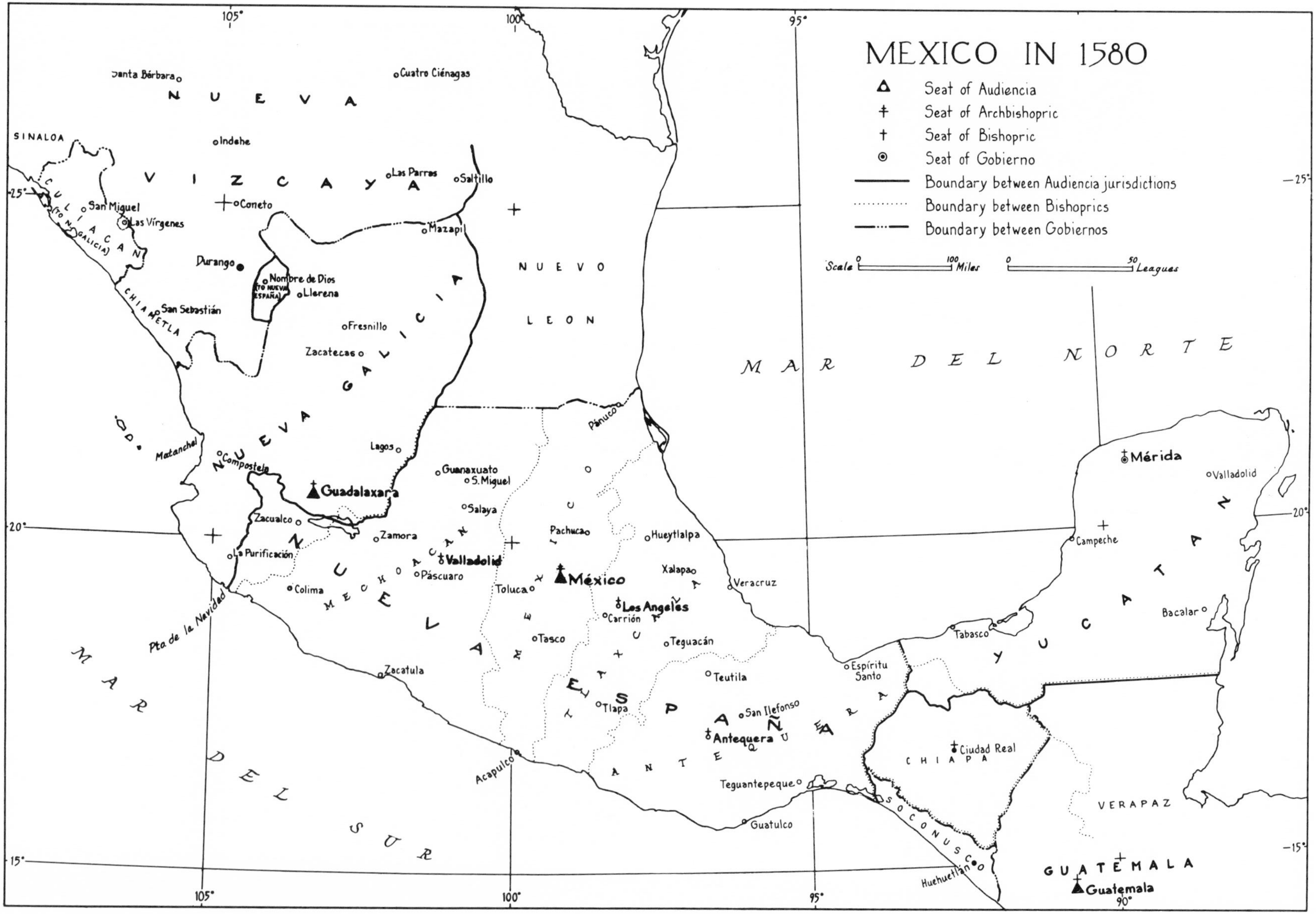
MEXICO IN 1580
Seat of Audiencia
Seat of Archbishopric
Seat of Bishopric
Seat of Gobierno
Boundary between Audiencia jurisdictions
Boundary between Bishoprics
Boundary between Gobiernos
Scale 0 100 Miles
0 50 Leagues
MAR DEL NORTE
MAR DEL SUR
NUEVA VIZCAYA
NUEVA GALICIA
NUEVO LEON
NUEVA ESPAÑA
MECHOACAN
YUCATAN
CHIAPA
VERAPAZ
GUATEMALA
SOCONUSCO
SINALOA
CULIACAN (TO N. GALICIA)
CHIAMETLA
Santa Bárbara
Cuatro Ciénagas
Indehe
Las Parras
Saltillo
San Miguel
Las Vírgenes
Coneto
Mazapil
Durango
Nombre de Dios (TO NUEVA ESPAÑA)
Llerena
San Sebastián
Fresnillo
Zacatecas
Matanchel
Compostela
Lagos
Guadalaxara
Guanaxuato
S. Miguel
Salaya
Zacualco
Zamora
La Purificación
Valladolid
Páscuaro
Colima
Pachuca
Pánuco
Hueytlalpa
Xalapa
Veracruz
México
Toluca
Los Angeles
Carrión
Tasco
Teguacán
Teutila
Tlapa
San Ilefonso
Antequera
Teguantepeque
Guatulco
Pta de la Navidad
Zacatula
Acapulco
Espíritu Santo
Tabasco
Campeche
Mérida
Valladolid
Bacalar
Ciudad Real
Huehuetlán
Guatemala
105°
100°
95°
90°
25°
20°
15°

FIG. 4—MEXICO IN 1580

proselytization, mining activity, and other causes. It was not until 1786 that a supposedly thorough reorganization of the colonial government took place. At this time most of the gobiernos were replaced by intendancies (*intendencias*), generally smaller units, governed by intendants (*intendentes*). These were the final political divisions of Spanish Middle America, which after Independence (1821) became states in the Republic of Mexico and republics in Central America (see Article 3). Under the new system, however, the changes were more apparent than real, and in some cases the only innovation was the title. The least affected, perhaps, was local government. Corregidores and alcaldes mayores were now called *subdelegados*, but they still had much the same functions and behaved in much the same way. The *partidos* into which the intendancies were divided usually coincided in their boundaries with the old alcaldías mayores and corregimientos, and were subject to further subdivisions known as *tenientazgos*.

Thus local government above the municipal level in Spanish America was confided to corregidores and alcaldes mayores and, after 1786, to subdelegados. These, together with the parish priests, were the people most likely to be both literate and cognizant of local affairs, and consequently most often called upon to submit detailed information about their jurisdictions to higher authority. The data of such great value to ethnohistorians contained in the 1579–85 series of *relaciones geográficas* were compiled in nearly all cases by the corregidores and alcaldes mayores (see Article 5). The same is true of the reports in answer to the questionnaire of 1604, and of the valuable series drawn up in New Spain in 1743–45 (see Article 10). The Ovando reports of about 1570, as well as some others of the late 18th century, were written mostly by clerics, but even here the civil division (*jurisdicción*) is usually identified.

The remainder of this article describes in some detail the political geography of Middle America throughout the colonial period. Each gobierno is considered in geographical order, beginning with New Spain (Nueva España), then the areas to the north, and finally those to the south. Within each gobierno, minor civil divisions are listed alphabetically as they existed at the time of their grouping into intendancies. For ease in locating the areas described, two sets of maps have been prepared. The first shows Mexico as it was in 1580, with its audiencias, gobiernos and bishoprics, and the alcaldías mayores and corregimientos (figs. 4–8). The second (figs. 9–14) depicts Mexico and Central America with lesser civil divisions as they were just before the introduction of the intendancy system, in 1785–86.

I. NUEVA ESPAÑA

In 1519, before starting inland to conquer Mexico, Hernando Cortés was chosen by the settlers of Veracruz to be "Governor and Chief Justice of that land." His titles were confirmed and his jurisdiction further defined in a royal cédula of October 15, 1522, as "las tierras e prouinzias de Aculuacan e San Xoan de Olua, llamada la Nueua España" (DII, 26: 59–61; see key to abbreviations at front of volume). By 1524 the new kingdom extended southward to El Salvador and Honduras, northeast to Panuco, and west to Colima. The northwestern boundary was theoretically without limits, restricted only by the degree to which the Spaniards' arms made their authority effective.

The Crown's reluctance to leave too much power in the hands of Cortés resulted first in the creation of additional gobiernos, then (1528) in the establishment of an audiencia, and finally (1535) in the appointment of a viceroy. In 1525 Honduras became a separate gobierno; the first royal governor arrived there in October, 1526 (Chamberlain, 1953, p. 21). Panuco was separated in

69

FIG. 5—NUEVA ESPAÑA: ARCHDIOCESE OF MEXICO IN 1580

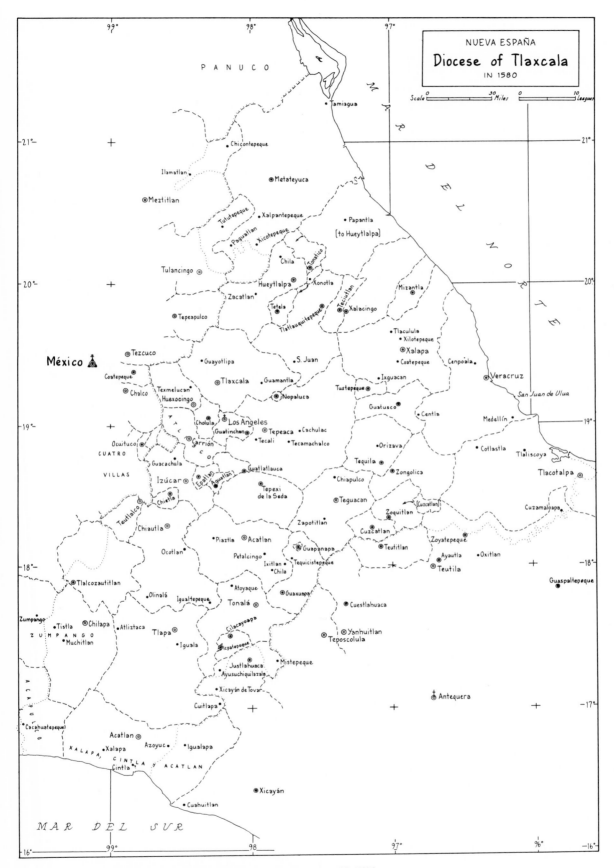

Fig. 6—NUEVA ESPAÑA: DIOCESE OF TLAXCALA IN 1580

FIG. 7—NUEVA ESPAÑA: DIOCESE OF MECHOACAN IN 1580

the same way in 1525 (effective in 1528), and Guatemala, including Chiapa and El Salvador, in 1527 (effective by early 1530; Hackett, 1918, pp. 57–58). The lands to the northwest formed still another gobierno, Nueva Galicia, from 1531. Here a boundary dispute over the Tonala and western Michoacan areas continued until 1533, when Michoacan and Colima (including Amula, Autlan, Izatlan, and the pueblos of Avalos) were assigned to Nueva España, and Tonala (with most of the north shore of Lake Chapala) was appropriated by Nueva Galicia (Bancroft, 1883–86, 2: 366, 372). Within four years Nueva Galicia was made subordinate to the audiencia of Mexico, and on two later occasions (1545–48 and 1572–74) responsibility for the gobierno in that province was invested in the viceroy. But the boundary of 1533, with minor variations, continued in force to the end of the colonial period.

Meanwhile, Panuco was reunited with Nueva España in 1533, Tabasco was removed from the viceroy's governmental jurisdiction in 1544, and Soconusco was likewise lost in 1556 (Puga, 1563, fol. 82, 188; Scholes and Roys, 1948, p. 138). North of the province of Panuco, Nuevo Leon was made a separate government in 1579, although this did not take effect until 1596. From the end of the 16th century the limits of the Gobierno of Nueva España were to remain fairly static. The viceroy, residing in Mexico City, ruled as governor a territory extending from the Isthmus of Tehuantepec to the Panuco River on the Gulf and to Puerto de la Navidad on the Pacific, with a northward extension which came within a few leagues of Guadalajara. It included the modern Federal District and the states of Colima, Guerrero, Guanajuato, Hidalgo, part of Jalisco, Mexico, Michoacan, Morelos, Oaxaca, Puebla, Queretaro, part of San Luis Potosi, Tlaxcala, and Veracruz.

The history of ecclesiastical jurisdictions in Nueva España is complicated and bears little relationship to the political division

(Bravo Ugarte, 1965). The country first came within the bounds of the ephemeral Carolense diocese, erected in theory alone on the island of Cozumel in 1519. In 1525 the seat of a bishopric was established in Tlaxcala, although the first bishop did not arrive there until late 1527. Within a decade three more dioceses had been created: Mexico (the bishop arriving in 1528), Antequera (1535), and Michoacan (1538). In 1546–48 Mexico became an archdiocese to which the aforementioned bishoprics, together with others in Central America, were made suffragan. In early years there was much confusion and bickering between prelates over carelessly drawn diocesan boundaries, but by the end of the 16th century these were relatively well defined. The archbishopric of Mexico and the bishoprics of Tlaxcala and Antequera were entirely within the gobierno of Nueva España. Michoacan fell within the same gobierno, except for the parish of La Barca, which belonged politically to Nueva Galicia. The westernmost jurisdictions of Nueva España north of Colima were attached to the new diocese of Nueva Galicia (Guadalajara). Subsequently there were minor adjustments and a few major changes, such as the transfer of Colima, Zapotlan, and La Barca from Michoacan to Guadalajara in 1795.

The archbishop always resided in Mexico City, and the city of Antequera remained a bishop's seat, but elsewhere the cathedrals were moved about. In 1543 the see of Tlaxcala was officially transferred to Puebla de los Angeles. In Michoacan the cathedral was first (1538) in Tzintzuntzan, then (1538–80) in Patzcuaro, and finally (from 1580) at Valladolid. The bishop of Nueva Galicia officially moved his see from Compostela (where he had never resided) to Guadalajara in 1560.

MINOR CIVIL DIVISIONS IN NUEVA ESPAÑA

The gobierno of Nueva España was subdivided into a great many minor territorial jurisdictions, known during most of the co-

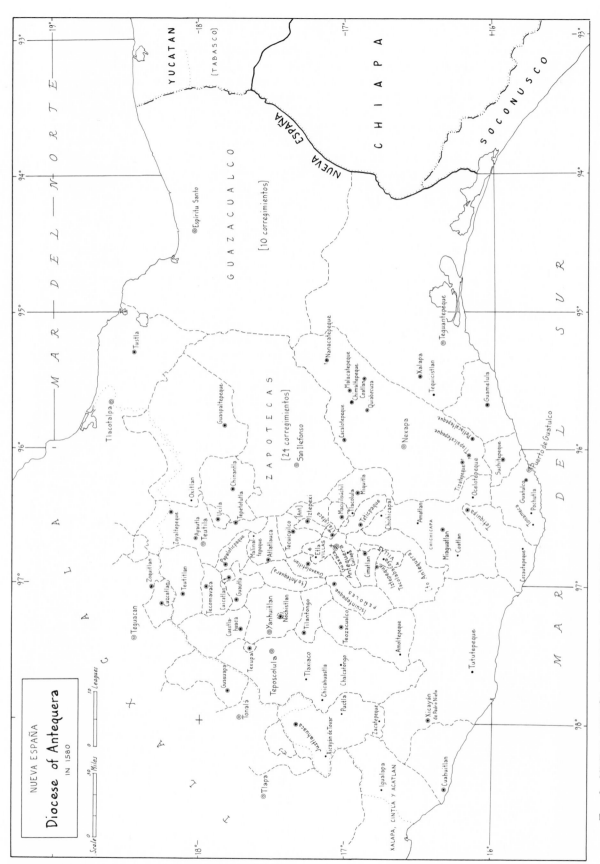

Fig. 8—NUEVA ESPAÑA: DIOCESE OF ANTEQUERA IN 1580

lonial period as corregimientos or alcaldías mayores. These are shown on maps of the bishoprics: the archdiocese of Mexico (fig. 6), Tlaxcala (fig. 7), Mechoacan (fig. 8), and Antequera (fig. 9). They varied in size from a single village to an area of several hundred square leagues. At first these offices (corregidor, alcalde mayor) were given to conquistadors and colonists and their descendants as a means of subsistence, but in later years they were sold at auction to provide revenue for the Crown. Although salaries were low, the prestige and the opportunity for profit that often went with these posts made them much coveted (Castañeda, 1929; Haring, 1949, pp. 138–44; Miranda, 1952, p. 121).

The changing relationship of corregidor to alcalde mayor in Nueva España and the difference between the two titles has not been well understood. When the conquest was in progress in the 1520's, alcaldes mayores were appointed in a few Spanish settlements; others were ruled by their cabildos alone (DII, 26: 59–61, 78, 195, 224; Miranda, 1952, pp. 46–49, 121; Puga, 1563, fols. 6, 47v). An alcalde mayor at this time was in effect a vice-governor, a deputy (teniente) of the governor in a vaguely defined province. Among the first such political divisions were Veracruz, Tenochtitlan (Mexico City), Zacatula, Colima, Guazacualco, Teguantepec, Antequera, Zapotecas, and Panuco. Local government and the administration of justice among Indians in these early years were often left in the hands of the caciques and calpulli councils, important decisions and appeals being handled extra-legally by the encomendero, priest, or an occasional Spanish alguacil or visitador (Gibson, 1952, pp. 62–65; Miranda, 1952, p. 46). Indians' complaints involving Spaniards could generally be referred only to the governor or to the king himself. To fill this gap and establish royal authority on a local level, the first corregimientos came into existence under the second audiencia, which created somewhat

more than a hundred such offices during the years 1531–35.[1] The first corregidores were in charge only of Indian villages belonging to the Crown, although they were supposed to report on conditions in neighboring encomienda towns as well (Puga, 1563, fol. 52v). It was not until 1550 that the order was issued for all Indian settlements in Nueva España, including those in encomienda, to be assigned specifically to one corregimiento or another (Encinas, 1945–46, 3: 19).

Upon the arrival in Mexico of Don Antonio de Mendoza, in 1535, the privilege of appointing magistrates passed from the audiencia to the viceroy. Mendoza, reporting that the corregidores were corrupt and incompetent, advocated replacing them with carefully chosen alcaldes mayores in charge of larger and fewer territorial units (DII, 2: 183–84; ENE, 4: 209–16). His plan was carried out, if only in part, some few years after he left Mexico. In the early 1550's it was remarked that certain encomienda villages had not yet been incorporated into corregimientos, and that many corregidores did not reside within their jurisdictions. Orders were issued to correct these conditions, and in the period from 1550 to 1570 all Nueva España was divided into some 40 provincias, each governed by an alcalde mayor who was expected to supervise a number of "suffragan" corregimientos, making an annual visit to hear appeals and correct abuses. At the same time, an effort was made to raise the quality of administration by appointing letrados (men with legal training) to the provincial alcaldías mayores (ENE, 2: 118; PNE, 4: 88, 163, 207, 232).[2]

[1] AGI, Patronato, leg. 183, doc. 9, ramo 2; Mexico, leg. 91.

[2] AGI, Patronato, leg. 20, doc. 5, ramo 24. AGN, Civil, vol. 1271; General de parte, vol. 1, fols. 95, 106v, 154; vol. 2, fols. 198v, 256v; vol. 3, fols. 20v, 85; Indios, vol. 2, fol. 110; Mercedes, vols. 3–5, passim. RAH, leg. 4662, doc. 6, fol. 1v; leg. 4663, doc. 2, fol. 1.

Thus in the 16th century, although there were exceptions (noted below), it was customary to find an alcalde mayor residing in either a predominantly Spanish settlement (*ciudad, villa, puerto, real de minas*) or a provincial capital, and a corregidor in a subordinate position in an Indian village. Frequently the same individual would hold simultaneously the title of alcalde mayor of a Spanish town or a province, and corregidor of the nearby Indian pueblos.

By 1580 a good many of Mendoza's provincias had in effect ceased to exist, and there the corregidores again enjoyed considerable autonomy.[3] In these jurisdictions, as before, the sole recourse of an Indian with a grievance against the corregidor was to undertake the arduous journey to Mexico City and appeal his case in person to the viceroy. Mendoza's system of intermediate supervisory control survived until the end of the century and even later in certain alcaldías mayores, such as Antequera, Guatulco, Izucar, Michoacan, Meztitlan, Motines, Nexapa, Teutila, and Tezcuco, each of which retained a number of suffragan corregimientos. The older provinces of Colima, Guazacualco, Panuco, Zacatula, and Zapotecas were in a separate category. In them, beginning in the 1530's, corregimientos had been distributed as sinecures to Spanish residents of the capital towns, many of whom rarely or never visited their charges, and in this situation the political authority seems to have belonged in reality to the provincial alcalde mayor (BAGN, 10: 283; Cartas de Indias, 1877, p. 306; Dávila Padilla, 1625, p. 548).[4]

The greatest political fractionization of Nueva España was reached in the decade 1570–80, when there were some 70 alcaldías mayores and over 200 corregimientos, most of the latter falling in the suffragan category. After the epidemic of 1576–81 there was a tendency to abolish minor corregimientos, particularly those in which few Indians survived, and to absorb them into larger units, sometimes replacing the corre-

gidor with a deputy (*teniente*) of the alcalde mayor (Cartas de Indias, 1877, p. 306).[5] The elimination of thousands of minor settlements and the congregation of their Indians in central villages in 1603–05 also detracted from the need for so many magistrates (Cline, 1949, p. 355). By the early 17th century most of the suffragan jurisdictions had been grouped into more realistic divisions and had disappeared. Sometime around 1640 nearly all the surviving corregimientos were redesignated alcaldías mayores, perhaps as a result of Bishop Palafox's recommendations.[6] Thereafter, although there were additional consolidations and adjustments from time to time, jurisdictional boundaries stayed relatively unchanged until the intendancies were set up in 1786–90. In the 18th century two further changes in nomenclature took place. In certain jurisdictions alcaldes mayores were redesignated corregidores, and two provinces (Acapulco, Puebla) within the gobierno of Nueva España achieved the distinction of being themselves called "gobiernos" administered by governors. Tlaxcala and Veracruz Nueva had previously been made gobiernos in this sense. In neither case did the new title apparently alter the character or functions of the royal officer, nor his subordination to viceroy and audiencia. At last count, in 1786, there were 116 civil jurisdictions in Nueva España.[7] We have mentioned that under the intendancies, which supposedly did away with traditional administrative divisions, the outlines of the old alcaldías mayores became those of the *partidos* or *subdelegaciones*. In a way, the intendancy was a revival of Mendoza's proposals adopt-

[3] AGN, General de parte, vol. 1, fol. 140v; vol. 3, fols. 20–21, 56; Indios, vol. 2, fol. 110; vol. 3, fol. 7.
[4] AGN, General de parte, vol. 3, fols. 59v, 85; vol. 4, fol. 137. UTX, leg. 24, doc. 2, fol. 1v; leg. 25, doc. 9, fol. 4v.
[5] Real cédula, June 7, 1582; viceroy to king, Oct. 15, 1581, and Oct. 28, 1582; AGI, Mexico, leg. 20.
[6] AGI, Mexico, leg. 600.
[7] BNMex, MS 1384, fols. 391–411. BNP, Fonds mexicains, MS 258.

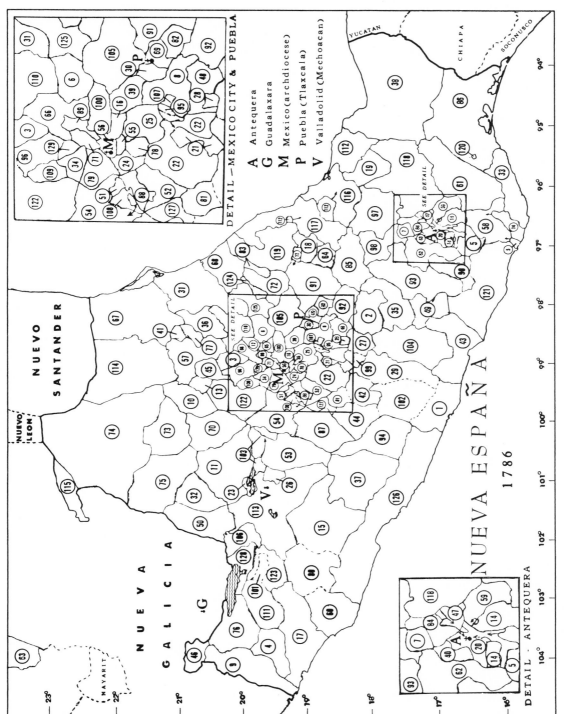

DETAIL—MEXICO CITY & PUEBLA

A Antequera
G Guadalaxara
M Mexico (archdiocese)
P Puebla (Tlaxcala)
V Valladolid (Mechoacan)

NUEVA ESPAÑA
1786

NUEVO SANTANDER

NUEVO LEON

NUEVA GALICIA

NAYARIT

YUCATAN

CHIAPA

SOCONUSCO

DETAIL - ANTEQUERA

Fig. 9—GOBIERNO OF NUEVA ESPAÑA, 1786

ed more than two centuries earlier (Beleña, 1787, 2: iv).[8]

The appointment of justices was for many years a prerogative of the viceroy, but there were several early encroachments on this patronage. A few Spanish settlements, notably Mexico City (1521–74, 1638–48, and later) and Puebla de los Angeles (1538–50), were by special dispensation for a time allowed to govern themselves and administer justice through their *ayuntamientos* (municipal councils) (ENE, 11: 233).[9] The Marqueses del Valle (from 1529) and much later the Duques de Atrisco (from 1706) were permitted to appoint justices in the jurisdictions assigned to them, which thus became in a sense governmental enclaves within Nueva España, a situation which will be further examined below (BAGN, 1: 501; Cortés, 1963, p. 597). A more serious intrusion on the power of the viceroy was the practice of appointing magistrates from Spain, by the king in consultation with the Council of the Indies. A few of the first corregidores of Indians received their posts by being favored with royal cédulas, and the corregidor of Mexico City served through direct royal appointment.[10] During the first sequestration of the estate of the Marqués del Valle the king sent appointees from Spain to Toluca, Cuyoacan, and Cuernavaca to fill posts which since 1570 had been controlled by the viceroy (Cartas de Indias, 1877, p. 302; Encinas, 1945–46, 3: 19; ENE, 11: 63).[11] When the third marquis recovered his seignorial rights, the Crown retained the privilege of appointment in the adjoining jurisdictions of Metepec, Tacuba, and Cuautla Amilpas. In the first half of the 17th century additional jurisdictions (Acapulco, Cholula, Veracruz Nueva, San Luis Potosi, Teguacan, Tlaxcala, Xicayan) were removed from the viceroy's control, and finally from 1678 the right of appointing all magistrates was reserved to the king (Vetancurt, 1698, pp. 59–60; Beleña, 1787, 1: 88; Lohmann, 1957, pp. 125–30).[12] Henceforth the viceroy, although still responsible for matters of gobierno, could only recommend candidates and make ad interim appointments of justices. That this was a drastic blow to the viceroy's power and purse, and a considerable source of new revenue for the Crown, can be gathered from the statement that in 1676 a candidate for the alcaldía mayor of Villa Alta had to pay 24,000 pesos for one year's appointment. We can appreciate from this the extent of venality in public administration which had been reached under the later Hapsburgs (Gibson, 1964, pp. 92–96; Parry, 1953).[13]

The following paragraphs show in abbreviated form the history of each political jurisdiction in Nueva España. These are located by number, with roughly drawn boundaries, in figure 9. Certain jurisdictions of importance which disappeared in the final consolidations of the late 17th and 18th centuries are included, with their names in parentheses. At the beginning of each synopsis is an indication of the bishopric to which the jurisdiction belonged, the intendancy in which it was included, and a suggested 1950 census identification for the final (1786) *cabecera* or chief town. For place names, we have used the spelling most often found in contemporary documents, with certain minor adjustments. The dates given are, in most cases, only approximations. Many details (e.g., boundary changes) not known to me are necessarily lacking. C indicates corregimiento or corregidor, G

[8] NYPL, MS "Ordenanzas de Yntendentes de N. España." Actually the term "corregidor" survived until Independence as an alternate title for certain intendants.

[9] AGI, Mexico, legs. 100, 104. NYPL, MS "Recopilación de todas las consultas y decretos que se hallan en la Sría de Nª Espª," par. 1347.

[10] AGI, Mexico, leg. 104.

[11] Viceroy to king, Feb. 23, 1586, AGI, Mexico, leg. 20. AGN, Hospital de Jesús, leg. 107, doc. 49.

[12] AGN, Reales cédulas, vol. 18, fols. 16, 50. NYPL, "Recopilación . . .," par. 1142. The cédula was nominally revoked two years later, but the Crown in fact controlled all appointments after 1678, and even had a hand in naming magistrates within the marquisate del Valle.

[13] NYPL, "Recopilación . . .," par. 1085.

indicates gobierno, AM stands for alcaldía mayor or alcalde mayor, Bish is bishopric, and Int is intendancy.[14]

POLITICAL JURISDICTIONS: HISTORICAL NOTES

1. ACAPULCO (G)
Bish: Mexico and Tlaxcala
Int: Mexico
1950: Acapulco de Juarez, Gro.

The first royal officer to administer justice in this area was probably the C of Pochotitlan, listed from 1536. Inland was another C, Citlatomagua y Anecuilco (from 1534), at first considered suffragan to Zacatula. Both were ultimately included in the province of Puerto de Acapulco, which appears as an AM from 1550. It extended from the Sierra Madre to the sea and along the coast from Coyuca eastward to Laguna San Marcos. The jurisdiction was divided between the archdiocese of Mexico and the diocese of Tlaxcala. Appointment of the AM, who was also castellan of the Fort of San Diego, passed from viceregal to Crown control in 1628. From about 1710 this magistrate began to be entitled governor. Two adjoining jurisdictions, first Tistla (q.v.) and later Chilapa (q.v.), were annexed and administered by deputies of the governor of Acapulco (BAGN, 10: 271; LdeT, p. 649; PNE, 1: nos. 92, 95, 238, 477, 489, 806; García Pimentel, 1897, pp. 146–53; García Pimentel, 1904, p. 27).[15]

2. ACATLAN Y PIASTLA (AM)
Bish: Tlaxcala
Int: Puebla
1950: Acatlan de Osorio, Pue.

Acatlan and half of Piastla, in the Mixteca Baja, were put under a C in 1532 (LdeT, p. 5). The area was made an AM and province about 1558, and included the suffragan C's of Guapanapa, Guaxuapa y Tequecistepec, and Tonala.[16] By 1579 Tonala had become a separate AM which later absorbed Guapanapa and Guaxuapa, continuing under the latter

name (q.v.).[17] The jurisdiction of Acatlan y Piastla thenceforth included the two villages of its title, plus Chila and Petalcingo.

3. ACTOPAN (AM)
Archbish: Mexico
Int: Mexico
1950: Actopan, Hgo.

This jurisdiction was first called Izcuincuitlapilco, a C from 1531. It came to include a number of villages between Pachuca and Ixmiquilpan in the Mezquital area.[18] In midcentury it was suffragan first to Xilotepec and later to Pachuca, until about 1568, when it became a separate AM. From about 1590 the jurisdic-

---

[14] The principal sources of this information are a number of lists drawn up at various times from about 1534 to 1784, together with two tribute books and the RG's. The lists, with stated or approximate dates, are as follows: About 1534: AGI, Patronato, leg. 183, doc. 9, ramo 2. 1536 and 1545: AGI, Mexico, leg. 91. 1550: AGI, Contaduría, leg. 663-A. 1560: AGI, Patronato, leg. 181, ramo 38. About 1567: AGI, Patronato, leg. 20, doc. 5, ramo 24. 1569: AGI, Contaduría, leg. 663-A. About 1582: BNMA, MS 3048, fols. 137–40. 1590: AGI, Mexico, leg. 22, ramo 2. About 1615: Vázquez de Espinosa, 1948, pp. 264–68. About 1642: BNMA, MSS 3047 (fols. 81–89v) and 18684 (fols. 296–306); published with discrepancies in Díez de la Calle, 1646, pp. 165–68. 1676: AGI, Mexico, leg. 600. 1743: Villaseñor y Sánchez, 1746–48. 1777: NYPL, Phillips MS 15796. 1784: BNMex, MS 1384, fols. 391–411v; BNP, Fonds mexicains, MS 258.

In the notes which follow, reference to the abovementioned sources is omitted. Also omitted are individual citations of the RG's, for which a complete bibliography and geographical correlation are found in Articles 8 and 9. The tribute books are found in AGI, Patronato, leg. 182, ramo 40, and in LdeT. Much additional information has been culled from the following ramos at AGN: General de parte, Indios, Mercedes. The following notes give sources both for information in the text and jurisdictional boundaries as shown on the accompanying maps.

[15] AGN, General de parte, vol. 1, fol. 219v; vol. 2, fols. 54v, 202, 206; Mercedes, vol. 3, fol. 242; vol. 11, fols. 32, 57.

[16] AGN, General de parte, vol. 3, fols. 20v–21; Mercedes, vol. 4, fol. 379; vol. 5, fol. 16.

[17] AGN, General de parte, vol. 2, fol. 89v.

[18] AGI, Patronato, leg. 182, ramo 40, fol. 325v. AGN, General de parte, vol. 1, fol. 207v; vol. 2, fols. 138, 247, 253v; Mercedes, vol. 11, fol. 43v.

tion began to be called Atucpa or Actopan, from the new seat of the AM.[19]

4. AMULA (AM)
Bish: Guadalajara
Int: Guadalajara
1950: Tuxcacuesco, Jal.

The far western province of Amula was taken from its encomendero, Hernando Cortés, and made a C perhaps as early as 1530. It comprised certain villages (Amula, Cuzalapa, Tuscacuesco, Zapotitlan, and others) in the mountains above Colima, to which it was at first suffragan. It was joined with another suffragan C, Xocutla, under an AM with residence in Tuscacuesco about 1570.

5. ANTEQUERA (C)
Bish: Antequera
Int: Oaxaca
1950: Oaxaca de Juarez, Oax.

The Spanish settlement of Antequera, surrounded by possessions of Hernando Cortés (cf. Cuatro Villas), had an AM as early as 1529 (Gay, 1950, 1: 441). Subsequently the office was held by a C, but in 1552 an AM was appointed and given charge of all Crown pueblos and many encomienda villages in the province of Valle de Guaxaca, a vast area extending from Atlatlauca and Cuicatlan to the South Sea at Cozautepec, and from Teozacualco to the limits of Mitla and Ocelotepec.[20] Some of these towns were administered personally by the AM, while others were grouped into suffragan C's: Atlatlauca (q.v.), Cimatlan (q.v.), Cuicatlan (from about 1545), Chichicapa (cf. Cimatlan, Miaguatlan), Huexolotitlan (q.v.), Iztepexi (q.v.), Macuilsuchil (cf. Mitla), Mitla y Tlacolula (q.v.), Ocotlan (1534 to about 1550), Peñoles (from about 1544, cf. Nochistlan), Talistaca (from 1534), Tecuicuilco (q.v.), Teozacualco (q.v.), Teozapotlan e Iztepec (since 1531), Teticpac (cf. Cimatlan), Tetiquipa Rio Hondo (cf. Cimatlan). Soon after 1602 all the suffragan C's became independent except Talistaca and Teozapotlan, which were absorbed by the AM.[21] In the late 17th century the AM was redesignated C. Atlatlauca was annexed around 1750.

6. APA Y TEPEAPULCO (AM)
Archbish: Mexico
Int: Mexico
1950: Apan, Hgo.

Tepeapulco was one of the first C's, created in 1531 (LdeT, p. 400). A nearby village, Tlanalapa, became a C in 1544 but was soon absorbed by Tepeapulco, as were other adjoining towns.[22] The C became an AM around 1640, and later the capital was moved to Apa.

7. (ATLATLAUCA)
Bish: Antequera
Int: Oaxaca
1950: San Juan Bautista Atatlahuca, Oax.

Half of Atlatlauca (the other half belonged to an encomendero), together with the Crown village of Malinaltepec, were made a C in 1532 (LdeT, p. 85). The jurisdiction, comprising several Indian towns in the headwaters of the Alvarado (Grande and Quiotepec rivers), was attached as a suffragan C to Antequera from 1552, but became independent soon after 1600. The C became an AM around 1650, and was absorbed by Antequera in the following century.

8. ATRISCO (AM)
Bish: Tlaxcala
Int: Puebla
1950: Atlixco, Pue.

In 1579 the recently founded Spanish villa of Carrion, in Valle de Atrisco, was made a separate AM with territory taken from the jurisdictions of Huexocingo and Puebla.[23] Later its area was enlarged by

[19] AGN, General de parte, vol. 5, fol. 41; Mercedes, vol. 5, fol. 77.
[20] AGN, Mercedes, vol. 4, fols. 8v, 15, 76v.
[21] AGN, General de parte, vol. 6, fols. 8, 217.
[22] AGN, General de parte, vol. 1, fols. 67v, 96v.
[23] AGN, General de parte, vol. 2, fols. 42v, 48.

the addition of Guaquechula (around 1600) and Zoyatitlanapa. After 1706 the privilege of appointing the AM belonged to the Duques de Atrisco (BAGN, 1: 501).[24]

9. AUTLAN Y PUERTO DE LA NAVIDAD (AM)
Bish: Guadalajara
Int: Guadalajara
1950: Autlan de Navarro, Jal.

Autlan was a C suffragan to Colima from at least 1540. Its magistrate became AM of Puerto de la Navidad around 1560, at which time the suffragan C's of Milpa y Manatlan (=Xiquitlan) and Ispuchimilco y Texuacan were transferred from Colima to the new AM (LdeT, p. 93).[25] Ameca, also a suffragan C from about 1540, became a separate AM about 1550. This last jurisdiction, together with Tenamastlan (a C from 1565), were annexed to Autlan about 1602.[26] This was the westernmost territory in Nueva España.

10. CADEREYTA (AM)
Archbish: Mexico
Int: Mexico
1950: Cadereyta de Montes, Qro.

Mines were discovered in this mountainous area, then belonging to the jurisdiction of Queretaro, toward the end of the 16th century. At first the region was administered by the AM of Sichu (cf. San Luis de la Paz), but by 1615 Minas de Escanela had become a separate AM. About 1650 the seat of government was moved to the recently founded villa of Cadereyta.[27]

11. CELAYA (AM)
Bish: Michoacan
Int: Guanajuato
1950: Celaya, Gto.

Orirapundaro, or Yurirapundaro, was a suffragan C in the province of Michoacan from about 1544. When the villa of Salaya was founded, its AM (from about 1571) became simultaneously C of Yurirapundaro and justice in nearby Acam-

baro. Salamanca was annexed in 1604.[28] It would seem that the city of Salvatierra was a separate C for a time in the 17th century until it was absorbed by Celaya. This AM controlled a large part of the prosperous Bajío region in the Lerma valley.

12. CEMPOALA (AM)
Archbish: Mexico
Int: Mexico
1950: Zempoala, Hgo.

Cempoala y Tlaquilpa and subject villages in the Teutalpa area northeast of Mexico City, together with nearby Tequecistlan, first came under C rule in 1531 (LdeT, p. 627). In the 1550's there was a congregation of *estancias*, and at the same time the encomienda of Epazoyuca was added to the jurisdiction. Tequecistlan (cf. Teotiguacan), however, became a separate C.[29] Cempoala for a time was suffragan to Meztitlan, but by 1580 it was independent. It became an AM about 1640.

13. CIMAPAN (AM)
Archbish: Mexico
Int: Mexico
1950: Zimapan, Hgo.

In the 16th century the mining camp of Çimapan belonged to the province of Xilotepec, although it had its own subordinate magistrate, a *juez repartidor*. It was not until about 1590 that a separate AM was appointed for the mines and surrounding villages.[30]

14. CIMATLAN Y CHICHICAPA (AM)
Bish: Antequera
Int: Oaxaca
1950: Zimatlan de Alvarez, Oax.

This complex of jurisdictions, extend-

[24] AGN, General de parte, vol. 6, fol. 200.
[25] AGN, General de parte, vol. 1, fol. 138v; Mercedes, vol. 11, fols. 7v, 57v, 68v.
[26] AGN, General de parte, vol. 5, fol. 313v.
[27] AGN, General de parte, vol. 5, fol. 45v.
[28] AGN, General de parte, vol. 6, fol. 322.
[29] AGN, General de parte, vol. 1, fol. 115v.
[30] AGN, General de parte, vol. 2, fols. 155, 209.

ing from the valley of Oaxaca to the Pacific, underwent many changes before its final consolidation. Çimatlan y Tepeçimatlan, a short distance south of Antequera, became a C in 1532 (LdeT, p. 636). Nearby to the east, Chichicapa is listed as a C as early as 1534. Far to the south in the mountains were two other C's, Tetiquepaque or Tetiquipa (from 1534) and Amatlan y Cozautepec (from 1535), the latter including a stretch of seacoast west of Tonameca. For a time Chichicapa and Teticquipa were joined under a single magistrate, but in the 1560's they were again separate. By this time Amatlan y Cozautepec had been partitioned between Chichicapa (Amatlan, together with Coatlan, Miaguatlan, and Ocelotepec) and Tetiquipa Rio Hondo (now including Cozautepec). Still another area north of Chichicapa, Teticpac, was a separate C (from 1531), although it and the other jurisdictions named thus far were all suffragan to the AM of Antequera.[31]

At the end of the 16th century mines were discovered near Chichicapa, and in 1600 the northern part of the jurisdiction was made an AM, to which Teticpac was annexed. At the same time, the southern part became a separate C with its capital at Miaguatlan (q.v.).[32] To compensate for this loss, the Rio Hondo area was given to Chichicapa. By 1687 Chichicapa and Çimatlan had been united under a single AM.

15. (Cinagua y la Guacana)
Bish: Michoacan
Int: Valladolid
1950: Sinagua (mun. Churumuco), Mich.

Much of the *tierra caliente* in southern Michoacan was placed under a C with headquarters in Cinagua from about 1534. The jurisdiction, a very large one, was divided about 1544 upon the creation of a new C, Urapa y Guanaxo. In 1554 much of the lower Balsas basin, including Ci-

nagua, was included temporarily in the C of Tiripitio (cf. Valladolid).[33] The C of Cinagua became an AM upon the opening of mines in the vicinity about 1600, at which time the jurisdiction of Guanaxo was abolished and divided between Cinagua and Valladolid. By the early 1700's, Cinagua y la Guacana was being administered as a subordinate C by the AM of Tancitaro (q.v.).[34]

16. Coatepec (AM)
Archbish: Mexico
Int: Mexico
1950: Coatepec (mun. Ixtapaluca), Mex.

Coatepec was one of the first C's in the valley of Mexico, appearing in a list of about 1534, although it reverted to encomienda status from 1538 to 1544. After 1550 the jurisdiction included a number of villages belonging to the Crown and to encomenderos between Lake Tezcuco and Cerro Tlaloc. For a time it was considered suffragan to the AM of Tezcuco. The C became an AM around 1640 (Gibson, 1964, p. 443).

17. Colima (AM)
Bish: Michoacan
Int: Valladolid
1950: Colima, Col.

An AM was assigned to the villa of Colima from 1524, and soon afterward (from around 1532) C's were established in the nearby Crown villages and distributed as sinecures to the Spaniards resident in the villa (Brand and others, 1960, p. 63). Despite the claims of Nuño de Guzmán and subsequent efforts to transfer the province to Nueva Galicia, Colima remained within the gobierno of Nueva España. In early years the area suffragan to Colima was very large, but in 1550–

---

[31] AGN, General de parte, vol. 3, fol. 85.
[32] AGN, General de parte, vol. 5, 148v; vol. 6, fol. 8.
[33] AGN, Mercedes, vol. 4, fol. 78v; vol. 84, fol. 55.
[34] AGN, General de parte, vol. 5, fol. 311v; vol. 9, fol. 200.

60 the C's of Ameca, Amula, Arimao y Borona, Autlan, Motin y Pomaro, Tuspa, Xilotlan, and Xiquilpa were detached. Remaining suffragan C's were Acautlan y Malacatlan, Alima (=Pochotitlan), Caxitlan (=Xocotlan), Ciguatlan y Tlacanaguas, Cinacantepec, Ecatlan y Contla (=Tamala), Iscayamoca, Istlahuacan, Iztapa, Quezalapa, Tecoman (=Chiametla), Tecpa y Tepetlazuneca, Tepetitongo, Tuchimilco, Tustlan, Xuluapa, and Zalagua.[35] All were absorbed by the AM toward the end of the 16th century. At a later date the C of Xilotlan was annexed, whereas the Alima area was lost to the AM of Motines.[36]

18. CORDOBA (AM)
Bish: Tlaxcala
Int: Veracruz
1950: Cordoba, Ver.

The precursor of this jurisdiction on the eastern slopes of Pico de Orizaba was the C of Guatusco e Istayuca, or San Antonio Guatusco, first mentioned in 1536.[37] It later included Tatetetelco, or Tatatetela, which had become a separate C in 1545.[38] In the provincial division of the 1560's Guatusco was made suffragan to Veracruz, but later it was attached to Xalapa. In 1618 Cordoba was founded, and the C of Guatusco became AM of the new villa.

19. COZAMALOAPA (AM)
Bish: Antequera and Tlaxcala
Int: Veracruz
1950: Cosamaloapan de Carpio, Ver.

The first C's in the basin of the Rio Alvarado (Papaloapan) were Guaspaltepec (created in 1531) and Cuzamaluaba (listed from 1534). In 1560 these, together with a number of encomienda villages, were united in one large C, which included all the low country between Chinantla and Tlacotalpa (LdeT, pp. 161, 218, 232, 586; PNE, 1: nos. 232, 441; García Pimentel, 1904, pp. 17, 67).[39] The area was, for a time, suffragan to

Teutila. The C became an AM around 1640, and not long afterward the jurisdiction was renamed Cozamaloapa, after its new capital. The Guaspaltepec area, including Tesechuacan, was transferred to Villa Alta about 1740 while Tuxtepec was annexed to Teutila.[40]

20. CUATRO VILLAS, or GUAXACA (AM)
Bish: Antequera
Int. Oaxaca
1950: Part of Oaxaca de Juarez, Oax.

Cortés may have appointed an AM to govern his possessions in the valley of Oaxaca as early as 1530. The four villas were Guaxaca (adjoining the Spanish settlement of Antequera on the west), Cuilapa, Etla, and Tacolabacoya (modern Santa Ana Tlapacoyan), each with numerous subject pueblos. During the first sequestration of the marquisate (1570–94) the jurisdiction was administered by the AM of Antequera, but from 1594 the appointment of the AM of Las Cuatro Villas del Marquesado del Valle de Guaxaca was again controlled by the descendants of Cortés (Ajofrín, 1959, 2: 88–104).[41] In the 16th century there was another jurisdiction called Cuatro Villas (see next entry).

21. CUAUTLA AMILPAS (AM)
Archbish: Mexico
Int: Puebla
1950: Cuautla, Mor.

The early administrative history of this area, which today occupies the eastern portion of the state of Morelos, is quite

[35] AGN, General de parte, vol. 1, fols. 33, 36v, 135v; vol. 2, fol. 216.

[36] BNMA, MS 2450, fol. 180.

[37] AGN, General de parte, vol. 1, fols. 3v, 93v, 162v.

[38] AGI, Patronato, leg. 182, ramo 40, fol. 353v.

[39] AGI, Indiferente, leg. 187. AGN, General de parte, vol. 2, fols. 229–229v, 272v, 274v; vol. 3, fol. 22v; Indios, vol. 2, fols. 87v, 221; vol. 3, fol. 15; Mercedes, vol. 11, fols. 17–18, 52; vol. 84, fol. 85; Tierras, leg. 70, exp. 1.

[40] AGI, Indiferente, leg. 108, vol. 4, fol. 102. AGN, Padrones, vol. 12, fol. 257.

[41] AGN, Hospital de Jesús, leg. 107, exp. 49.

complicated. Ocuituco became a C in 1534 or earlier, but by March of the following year it was an encomienda of the bishop of Mexico.[42] It reverted to Crown control in 1544, and in the next decade was attached as a suffragan jurisdiction to the province of Chalco. Xumiltepec was a separate C from 1544, but was soon absorbed by Ocuituco, which came to include a number of encomienda villages on the south slope of Popocatepetl (BAGN, 10: 258; ENE, 16: 85–87; PNE, 1: nos. 122–23, 421, 503–04, 800).[43] When the estate of the Marqués del Valle was confiscated in 1570 the eastern half of the jurisdiction of Cuernavaca was attached for administration to Ocuituco, whose C acquired the additional title of AM of Cuatro Villas del Marquesado (Cartas de Indias, 1877, p. 302; Encinas, 1945–46, 3: 21). These villas, not to be confused with those in the last entry, were Acapistla, Guastepec, Tepuztlan, and Yautepec. In 1582–83 the Cuatro Villas were returned to the jurisdiction of Cuernavaca, with the exception of two groups of pueblos which had been lost by the Marquesado to the Crown in a protracted lawsuit: Las Amilpas (formerly subject to Guastepec), with their capital at Cuautla; and the 14 pueblos of Las Tlalnaguas (until then considered subject to Acapistla).[44] The latter group was soon afterward regained in a successful appeal by the third marquis, but Las Amilpas remained Crown property and Cuautla Amilpas became the residence of the

king's C. When mines were discovered in the mountains to the south, they were annexed to the Crown jurisdiction, and an AM was appointed to what was known for a time as Minas de Cuautla or Guautla. This official was appointed by the king from 1609. As it finally evolved, the jurisdiction consisted of three separate areas: Las Amilpas proper, the Real de Guautla, and the former C of Ocuituco. Finally, shortly before the establishment of intendancies, the C of Tetela del Volcan (q.v.) was annexed to Cuautla.[45]

22. Cuernavaca (AM)
Archbish: Mexico
Int: Mexico
1950: Cuernavaca, Mor.

Originally the jurisdiction of Cuernavaca, which had an AM appointed by the Marqués del Valle perhaps as early as 1529, included most of what is now Morelos together with a southern extension into Guerrero. However, important areas were subsequently lost to the Crown, beginning in 1532 when Totolapa (cf. Chalco) was made a C.[46] The vicissitudes of the Cuatro Villas area are traced in the last entry. The AM of Cuernavaca was a royal appointee from 1583 until 1595, when political control was returned to the Marqués del Valle.[47] From the late 16th century the jurisdiction was almost split in two by the intrusion of Cuautla Amilpas (q.v.), with Acapistla and Tlalnaguas forming an eastern appendage.[48]

23. Cuiseo de la Laguna (AM)
Bish: Michoacan
Int: Valladolid
1950: Cuitzeo del Porvenir, Mich.

This jurisdiction, consisting only of the Indian town of Cuiseo and its subject villages around the lake of that name, began as a C about 1555, and was redesignated an AM around 1640. It was suffragan to Michoacan in the 16th century, and attached to Celaya on later occasions.[49]

[42] AGI, Patronato, leg. 180, ramo 65.
[43] AGN, General de parte, vol. 1, fols. 175, 210, 223v.
[44] Viceroy to king, Oct. 15 and 28, 1581, AGI, Mexico, leg. 20. AGN, Indios, vol. 2, fol. 160v. AHN, MS 257.
[45] AGN, Padrones, vol. 8; Mercedes, vol. 84, fol. 379v.
[46] AGI, Patronato, leg. 16, no. 2, ramo 32.
[47] Viceroy to king, Feb. 23, 1586, and Nov. 18, 1586, AGI, Mexico, leg. 20. AGN, Hospital de Jesús, leg. 107, exp. 49.
[48] AGN, Padrones, vol. 8.
[49] AGI, Mexico, leg. 600.

24. CUYOACAN (C)

Archbish: Mexico
Int: Mexico
1950: Coyoacan, D. F.

The possessions of the Marqués del Valle in the vicinity of Mexico City, comprising the villas of Cuyoacan and Tacubaya and their *sujetos*, were governed by a C (sometimes referred to as AM) first appointed around 1530. During the sequestration of the Marquesado, from about 1572 to 1595, the jurisdiction was attached to the adjoining AM of Tenayuca (cf. Tacuba; Gibson, 1964, p. 445).[50]

25. CHALCO (AM)

Archbish: Mexico
Int: Mexico
1950: Tlalmanalco de Velazquez, Mex.

Originally claimed by Hernando Cortés, the important province of Chalco became Crown property with the appointment of a C about 1533. Another early C, Huichilobusco y Mesquique (from about 1534), was broken up in the 1540's, Mesquique being annexed to Chalco. In 1553 the jurisdiction became an AM, to which the suffragan C's of Ocopetlayuca (cf. Tochimilco), Ocuituco (cf. Cuautla), Tetela del Volcan (q.v.), Teutlalco (q.v.), and Totolapa (created in 1532) were attached. Totolapa y Tlayacapa later became an AM and was annexed to Chalco sometime between 1640 and 1676. The residence of the AM of Chalco moved about, from Chalco to Tlayacapa and Tlalmanalco (BAGN, 10: 258; Gibson, 1964, p. 443).

26. CHARO (C)

Bish: Michoacan
Int: Valladolid
1950: Charo, Mich.

Matalcingo, which then included the village of Necotlan (Undameo) and a number of places south and east of Valladolid, is listed as a Crown possession and a C in 1545. At the same time Necotlan was detached and made a separate

C (cf. Valladolid). In 1564 Villa de Matalcingo was added to the estates of the Marqués del Valle in recompense for Valle de Matalcingo (cf. Metepec), which had become a Crown jurisdiction. Subsequently the C was appointed by the marquis, and later Matalcingo came to be called Villa de Charo (García Pimentel, 1904, pp. 42, 154; BAGN, 1: 42–43; LdeT, p. 260).[51]

27. CHIAUTLA DE LA SAL (AM)

Bish: Tlaxcala
Int: Puebla
1950: Chiautla de Tapia, Pue.

One of the first C's (listed in 1534), Chiautla became an important province known also as Minas de Ayoteco, and an AM, from about 1550. It included towns on either side of the Atoyac River, and once extended south almost to Tlapa, but the towns of Igualtepec and Olinala were later transferred to Tonala (cf. Guaxuapa) and Tlapa. Towards 1760 the mining jurisdiction of Teutlalco (q.v.) was annexed to Chiautla (BAGN, 10: 272; García Pimentel, 1904, pp. 109–15).[52]

28. CHIETLA (C)

Bish: Tlaxcala
Int: Puebla
1950: Chietla, Pue.

A C from about 1544, Chietla (consisting of a single cabecera with its estancias) was suffragan to the province of Izucar until about 1575. It was attached to Izucar for a time, but again became a separate C in 1756.[53]

---

[50] AGN, General de parte, vol. 2, fol. 277v; Padrones, vol. 6.

[51] AGN, General de parte, vol. 2, fols. 44v, 57v; Hospital de Jesús, leg. 107, exp. 49; Padrones, vol. 12.

[52] AGN, General de parte, vol. 1, fols. 16v, 18, 21, 23, 221v, 236v; vol. 2, fols. 44v, 106, 175v, 277v; Indios, vol. 2, fol. 151; Mercedes, vol. 3, fol. 277; Padrones, vol. 12, fol. 262v.

[53] AGN, General de parte, vol. 1, fol. 234v; vol. 2, fols. 92, 109v, 213; Indios, vol. 2, fols. 109v, 135v; Padrones, vol. 28.

29. (CHILAPA)
Bish: Tlaxcala and Mexico
Int: Mexico
1950: Chilapa de Alvarez, Gro.

Chilapa was a C from 1534, but soon afterward it was removed from Crown control and given in encomienda. It became the seat of a provincial AM, also known as Minas de Zumpango, from around 1552.[54] The jurisdiction included a great many villages (Chilapa, Huiciltepec, Muchitlan, Tistla, Zumpango, and subject estancias) between the Balsas and the Omitlan rivers. Until 1579 the magistrate of Zumpango was also in charge of the Tlapa (q.v.) area. The region adjoining Chilapa to the north was controlled by encomenderos until around 1560, when the C of Tlalcozautitlan was created.

By 1615 the old AM of Zumpango had been divided into two C's, Chilapa and Tistla (q.v.), the latter administered by a deputy of the AM of Acapulco.[55] The C of Tlalcozautitlan had ceased to exist, and its villages were annexed to Chilapa. The latter in turn became a *tenientazgo* of Acapulco about 1780.

30. CHOLULA (AM)
Bish: Tlaxcala
Int: Puebla
1950: Cholula de Rivadabia, Pue.

This small jurisdiction was at first (from 1531) united with Puebla and Tlaxcala in a single C, but it had its own magistrate after 1545. It became an AM, with the appointment controlled by the king, from 1646 (Gibson, 1952, pp. 67–68).

31. GUACHINANGO (AM)
Bish: Tlaxcala and Mexico
Int: Puebla
1950: Huauchinango, Pue.

Among the first C's were Xicotepec (since 1531) and Metateyuca, Atlan y Teoçapotlan (by 1534), in the mountainous area northeast of Tulancingo. By 1569 Metateyuca y Xicotepec were administered by a single C suffragan to Meztitlan, whose jurisdiction included Guachinango, Paguatlan, Pantepec, Tututepec, and Tamiagua, an extensive region stretching from the sierra to the Gulf coast (LdeT, pp. 76, 229, 474).[56] In 1575 Tututepec was transferred to the neighboring jurisdiction of Tulancingo. Soon afterward, perhaps by 1580, the C had moved to Guachinango and became an AM. In 1609 the jurisdiction contained the suffragan C's of Paguatlan, Tamiagua, Xalpantepec, and Xicotepec, but these disappeared within a few years.[57] Guachinango was one of the AM's where the power of appointment was granted to the Duques de Atrisco from 1706.

32. GUANAJUATO (AM)
Bish: Michoacan
Int: Guanajuato
1950: Guanajuato, Gto.

For several years after the mines of Guanajuato were discovered their jurisdiction was disputed between the AM's of Xilotepec (q.v.) and Mechoacan (cf. Valladolid), until a separate AM of Guanaxuato was created about 1559.[58] Leon (q.v.) was detached in 1579; Irapuato and Silao remained within the jurisdiction.[59]

33. GUATULCO Y GUAMELULA (AM)
Bish: Antequera
Int: Oaxaca
1950: San Pedro Pochutla, Oax.

The first royal officers in this coastal area were the C's of Pochutla y Tunameca and Guamelula (both since 1531)

[54] AGN, Mercedes, vol. 5, fol. 102v. NL, Ayer 1121, fol. 130v.
[55] BNMA, MS 6877, fol. 62.
[56] AGI, Indiferente, leg. 187. AGN, General de parte, vol. 1, fols. 35v, 67, 70, 133v, 190v, 243v; vol. 2, fols. 23, 28, 32, 35, 43, 87v, 88v, 174v, 185, 203; Mercedes, vol. 11, 58v. BNP, Manuscrits mexicains, 113.
[57] BNMA, MS 3064, fols. 15–20v.
[58] AGN, Mercedes, vol. 5, fol. 39v.
[59] AGN, General de parte, vol. 6, fol. 417.

(LdeT, pp. 192, 294). When the port of Guatulco became the northern terminus of trade with Peru, the C of Pochutla was given the additional title of AM of Puerto de Guatulco (from about 1550).[60] At the same time, Guamelula and Suchitepec (cf. Villa Alta) were attached to Guatulco as suffragan C's, continuing as such until 1599 when they were absorbed. The capital of the jurisdiction was moved first in 1616 to a site 3 leagues inland from the port, then to Guamelula, and finally to Pochutla.[61]

34. GUAUTITLAN (AM)

Archbish: Mexico
Int: Mexico
1950: Cuautitlan de Romero Rubio, Mex.

Several towns in the lake region north of Mexico City were joined in a C of Tepozotlan in 1546 (LdeT, p. 149). In the provincial division of the 1560's this jurisdiction became the AM of Guautitlan, to which the suffragan C's of Citlaltepec (cf. Zumpango), Tenayuca (cf. Tacuba), and Tepozotlan (whose C was AM of Guautitlan) were attached. To this group Xaltocan was added in 1566, but by 1580 it had been absorbed, and Tenayuca had become a separate AM. Soon afterward Zumpango became an independent C (García Pimentel, 1897, pp. 81–83, 91, 258–66; Gibson 1964, p. 445).[62]

35. GUAXUAPA (AM)

Bish: Tlaxcala
Int: Oaxaca
1950: Huajuapan de Leon, Oax.

This jurisdiction in the Mixteca Baja began as a group of C's: Guaxuapa y Tequecistepec (from 1534), Guapanapa (from 1534), and Tonala (since 1531, reverting to encomienda in 1537–44) (LdeT, p. 524). From about 1558 they were all suffragan to Acatlan y Piastla. By 1579 Tonala had become a separate AM with its own suffragan C's of Cilacayoapa and Icpatepec.[63] Early in the 17th century Guapanapa was annexed to

Guaxuapa, the AM of Tonala was residing at Minas de Cilacayoapa, and Icpatepec had been joined to the nearby jurisdiction of Justlahuaca (q.v.; LdeT, pp. 422, 524–25; PNE, 1: no. 753).[64] Towards 1690 Tonala and Guaxuapa were united under a single AM with residence in the latter place. Perhaps about the same time, the Igualtepec area was annexed from Chiautla.

36. GUAYACOCOTLA (AM)

Bish: Mexico and Tlaxcala
Int: Puebla
1950: Huayacocotla, Ver.

It would seem that about 1580 Guayacocotla, until then part of the jurisdiction of Meztitlan, was made a separate C, to which the town of Chicontepec was added a few years later. It became an AM about 1630 (García Pimentel, 1897, pp. 248–54).[65]

37. GUAYMEO Y SIRANDARO (AM)

Bish: Michoacan
Int: Valladolid
1950: Huetamo de Núñez, Mich.

This area along the Balsas River was first attached to the C of Tiripitio (cf. Valladolid), from 1554.[66] Twelve years later two C's were created: Cuiseo and Guaymeo y Sirandaro (=Zarandancho), both suffragan to the province of Mechoacan (LdeT, p. 190). These were united in an AM of Minas del Espiritu Santo from about 1575. Toward the end of the century the AM again became a C, Guaymeo y Sirandaro, into which Cuiseo was absorbed. At about the same time

---

[60] AGN, Mercedes, vol. 3, fol. 231v.

[61] Viceroy to king, May 25, 1616, AGI, Mexico, leg. 28.

[62] AGN, Mercedes, vol. 4, fol. 133v.

[63] AGN, General de parte, vol. 2, fol. 89v.

[64] AGN, General de parte, vol. 1, fols. 10v, 44, 58v, 95, 115v, 127v, 139v, 149, 153, 156v, 169, 244; vol. 2, fols. 132v, 274v; vol. 3, fol. 20v.

[65] AGN, General de parte, vol. 2, fol. 45; Indios, vol. 2, fol. 170.

[66] AGN, Mercedes, vol. 4, fol. 78v; vol. 84, fol. 55.

the Pungarabato area was annexed from neighboring Asuchitlan (cf. Tetela del Rio). Redesignated an AM about 1640, the capital was moved from Sirandaro to Huetamo in the 18th century.[67]

38. GUAZACUALCO (AM)
Bish: Antequera
Int: Veracruz
1950: Acayucan, Ver.

The Spanish settlement of Espiritu Santo, near the mouth of the Coatzacoalcos River, may have had an AM as early as 1525. It was capital of the province of Guazacualco, and in the 1530's the Crown villages for many leagues around were made C's and distributed among the Spaniards living in the villa. In 1580 there were 10 of these suffragan C's: Aguataco, Ataco y Ocelotepec, Chicuitlan y Ostuacan, Guazacualco y Agualulcos, Hueytlan y Tilzapoapa, Tapalan, Taquilapas, Tonala, Zacualpa y Cayaco, and Zapotancingo y Miaguatlan (LdeT, pp. 18, 26, 62–63, 203, 207, 346).[68] All of these disappeared, absorbed by the AM, toward the end of the 16th century. For a time the jurisdiction was divided and the eastern part made a separate AM, Agualulcos. In the 18th century Espiritu Santo no longer existed, and the capital had been moved to Acayuca.

39. HUEXOCINGO (AM)
Bish: Tlaxcala
Int: Puebla
1950: Huejotzingo, Pue.

C's were appointed in Guaxocingo and Calpa in 1534 or earlier, although Calpa soon reverted to encomienda. At first the jurisdiction extended south to join that of Izucar, but in 1579 Acapetlahuaca was detached to form the new AM of Atrisco (q.v.).[69] Some time after 1643 the C was redesignated AM.

40. HUEXOLOTITLAN (C)
Bish: Antequera
Int: Oaxaca
1950: San Pablo Huitzo, Oax.

The C of Guaxolotitlan, or Huexolotitlan, was created in 1531. From 1552 it was suffragan to the AM of Antequera, but it became an independent jurisdiction at the beginning of the 17th century.[70]

41. HUEXUTLA (AM)
Archbish: Mexico
Int: Mexico
1950: Huejutla de Reyes, Hgo.

Guaxutla appears as a C from about 1548, first suffragan to the province of Panuco and later to Meztitlan. It was redesignated AM soon after 1640 (García Pimentel, 1904, p. 132; PNE, 1: no. 265).[71]

42. (IGUALA)
Archbish: Mexico
Int: Mexico
1950: Iguala, Gro.

Iguala is listed as a C from 1536. In 1556 the jurisdiction was enlarged to include a great number of villages on either side of the Mexcala or Balsas River. For a time in the 16th century Iguala was considered suffragan first to Chiautla and later to Tasco. It was redesignated AM about 1640, and annexed to Tasco (q.v.) shortly before 1780.[72]

43. IGUALAPA (AM)
Bish: Tlaxcala and Antequera
Int: Mexico
1950: Ometepec, Gro.

Xalapa, Cintla y Acatlan, three villages with many sujetos near the South Sea coast were united under a C about 1534. Farther east, the Igualapa area was first administered by the C of Cuahuitlan, then (1555–58) by that of Xicayan. About 1558 the entire region was made an AM

---

[67] AGN, General de parte, vol. 5, fols. 45v, 108v.
[68] AGN, General de parte, vol. 1, fol. 244v; vol. 3, fol. 175; Indios, vol. 2, fols. 107, 166; Mercedes, vol. 11, fols. 125v, 153v, 157v, 165, 227; Tierras, vol. 2, exp. 11.
[69] BNP, Manuscrits mexicains, 387.
[70] AGI, Patronato, leg. 182, ramo 40, fol. 318v.
[71] AGN, General de parte, vol. 1, fols. 195, 237v, 240v.
[72] AGI, Mexico, leg. 336, fols. 81–91. AGN, Mercedes, vol. 4, fol. 346.

and province of Xalapa, Cintla y Acatlan, including both Crown and encomendero villages. Toward the end of the 16th century the capital was established at Igualapa, and the towns of Xicayan de Tovar and Cuitlapa were annexed. Later (by 1777) the capital was moved to Ometepec.[73]

44. (ISCATEUPA)

Archbish: Mexico
Int: Mexico
1950: Teloloapan, Gro.

Among the first C's created were the villages of Escateupa y Atenango and Tululuava y Tultepec (since 1531), southwest of Tasco. Tululuava, or Teloloapan, was joined to Iscateupa in 1579, and the latter name was applied to the jurisdiction, which by then included many towns both south and north of the Balsas River, although the C (AM from about 1640) lived at Teloloapan. Some of these places were detached about 1602 to form a new AM, Tetela del Rio (q.v.). Iscateupa was annexed to Zacualpa toward the end of the 17th century (García Pimentel, 1897, pp. 242–48; PNE, 1: nos. 7, 162, 420, 545, 675).[74]

45. IXMIQUILPAN (AM)

Archbish: Mexico
Int: Mexico
1950: Ixmiquilpan, Hgo.

One-half of Izmiquilpa y Tlacintla was acquired by the Crown and became a C in 1535. Mines were discovered nearby, and by 1550 Minas de Izmiquilpa had an AM (BAGN, 10: 273; García Pimentel, 1897, pp. 43–44; LdeT, pp. 604–05; PNE, 1: nos. 112, 293).[75]

46. IZATLAN Y LA MAGDALENA (AM)

Bish: Guadalajara
Int: Guadalajara
1950: Etzatlan, Jal.

Izatlan, a northwestern appendage of Nueva España to the west of Guadalajara, is listed as a C from 1536. About 1550 it was made an AM and province with several villages, one of them Agualulco, which in the 18th century was the capital (LdeT, pp. 601–03; PNE, 1: nos. 295, 318, 432).[76]

47. IZTEPEXI (AM)

Bish: Antequera
Int: Oaxaca
1950: Santa Catarina Ixtepeji, Oax.

The jurisdiction of Iztepexi was a small one, in the mountains northeast of Oaxaca. From 1554 it was one of the suffragan C's in Valle de Guaxaca (cf. Antequera).[77] Tecuicuilco (q.v.) was attached to this jurisdiction for a time in the 17th century.[78] In 1706, by which time Iztepexi had become an AM including Calpulalpa and other villages, the right of appointment was given to the Duque de Atrisco.

48. IZUCAR (AM)

Bish: Tlaxcala
Int: Puebla
1950: Izucar de Matamoros, Pue.

Izucar was a Crown possession and C by 1545, and a province and AM from 1560.[79] Suffragan to it were the C's of Aguatlan y Zoyatitlanapa (created in 1532), Chietla (q.v.), and Epatlan y Teupantlan (from 1534). At the beginning of the 17th century Epatlan was absorbed and the other suffragan C's became independent. By 1740 Zoyatitlanapa had been annexed to Atrisco, and Aguatlan to Izucar (LdeT, p. 202).[80]

49. JUSTLAGUACA (AM)

Bish: Antequera and Tlaxcala
Int: Oaxaca
1950: Santiago Juxtlahuaca, Oax.

[73] AGI, Indiferente, leg. 187. AGN, Mercedes, vol. 4, fol. 249v; vol. 5, fols. 18v, 21, 42.
[74] AGI, Patronato, leg. 182, ramo 40, fol. 363v.
[75] AGN, Mercedes, vol. 3, fol. 31v.
[76] AGN, Mercedes, vol. 3, fol. 292v.
[77] AGI, Patronato, leg. 182, ramo 40, fol. 331v.
[78] AGI, Mexico, leg. 600.
[79] AGN, Mercedes, vol. 5, fol. 54.
[80] AGN, General de parte, vol. 1, fols. 23v, 100, 204v; vol. 2, fols. 118, 155, 213v, 276; Mercedes, vol. 11, fol. 1v.

One-half of Xustlaguaca became Crown property and a C in 1548.[81] It included several villages in the Mixteca Baja, and for some years was suffragan to Teposcolula. Toward the end of the 16th century the C of Icpatepec (cf. Guaxuapa) was annexed to it, and Xicayan de Tovar was lost to Igualapa. Later the Zacatepec area was transferred to the AM of Xicayan. By 1740 the C had become an AM.[82]

50. LEON (AM)

Bish: Michoacan
Int: Guanajuato
1950: Leon, Gto.

The villa of Leon first belonged to the jurisdiction of Guanajuato, but had its own AM by 1579. It comprised the southwest corner of what is now the state of Guanajuato as far as the Lerma River. During the 17th and 18th centuries the province of Zacatula (q.v.), on the Pacific coast, was administered by a deputy of the AM of Leon.[83]

51. LERMA (C)

Archbish: Mexico
Int: Mexico
1950: Lerma de Villada, Mex.

The Indian village of Talasco (=Tlalasco, Tlalahco), probably identifiable with the modern San Mateo Atarasquillo, is listed as a C from 1534. During much of the 16th century it was suffragan to Valle de Matalcingo (cf. Metepec). When the city of Lerma was founded within this jurisdiction, appointment of the C was assumed by the Crown (about 1640; LdeT, p. 319; PNE, 1: nos. 561, 782).[84]

52. MALINALCO (AM)

Archbish: Mexico
Int: Mexico
1950: Malinalco, Mex.

Created a C in 1532, Malinalco became a provincial capital and AM about 1558. It had only one suffragan C, Atlatlauca y Suchiaca (cf. Tenango del Valle).[85]

53. MARAVATIO (AM)

Bish: Michoacan
Int: Valladolid
1950: Zitacuaro, Mich.

Maravatio, a suffragan C in the province of Mechoacan, was created in 1550.[86] Toward the end of the 16th century it acquired the Taximaroa area (until then administered from Tlalpuxagua), and somewhat later the C of Tuzantla (which had existed, suffragan to Temascaltepec, since 1546). The jurisdiction was redesignated AM soon after 1600. In the 18th century it was administered jointly with Zamora y Xacona (q.v.).[87]

54. METEPEC (AM)

Archbish: Mexico
Int: Mexico
1950: Metepec, Mex.

In the early 1530's this area, comprising a great many Indian villages in the headwaters of the Matalcingo (Lerma) River, was claimed by the Marqués del Valle as subordinate to his villa of Toluca (q.v.). However, by 1534 the audiencia had taken it in large part for the Crown and had created the C's of Metepec y Tepemachalco, Talasco, Teutenango, and Xiquipilco, and a year later Istlahuaca. All were united about 1550 under a single C, which within a few years was redesignated the AM of Valle de Matalcingo, with its capital at Toluca.[88] The

---

[81] AGI, Patronato, leg. 182, ramo 40, fol. 326v.
[82] AGI, Indiferente, leg. 187. AGN, General de parte, vol. 1, fol. 158v. HSA, MS HC:417/132.
[83] AGN, General de parte, vol. 2, fol. 63v; Mercedes, vol. 11, fol. 68.
[84] AGI, Mexico, leg. 600. AGN, General de parte, vol. 1, fol. 209v; vol. 2, fols. 47, 119v; Mercedes, vol. 4, fol. 198; vol. 11, fol. 71v; vol. 84, fol. 334.
[85] AGI, Patronato, leg. 182, ramo 40, fol. 335v. AGN, General de parte, vol. 1, fols. 94, 191: vol. 2, fols. 36, 231; Indios, vol. 1, fol. 97v.
[86] AGI, Patronato, leg. 182, ramo 40, fol. 336.
[87] AGI, Patronato, leg. 238, no. 2, ramo 1. AGN, General de parte, vol. 1, fols. 31v, 180v; vol. 2, fol. 171v; vol. 10, fol. 32.
[88] AGI, Mexico, leg. 336, fols. 126v–134v. AGN, Mercedes, vol. 3, fols. 305, 336; vol. 4, fols.

latter place was taken from the Marqués del Valle from 1569 to around 1595. Soon after 1580 Teutenango (cf. Tenango del Valle) and Talasco (cf. Lerma) became independent C's; the remaining jurisdiction was renamed Istlahuaca or Metepec, governed by an AM appointed by the king.[89] In the 18th century the AM was for a time divided in two (Istlahuaca and Metepec), and a number of villages were transferred to Tenango del Valle.

55. MEXICALCINGO (C)
Archbish: Mexico
Int: Mexico
1950: Mexicaltzingo, D. F.

The first C's in this area contiguous to Mexico City were Mexicalcingo y Zayula (1531) and Huichilobusco y Mesquique (1534 [LdeT, p. 239]). The latter jurisdiction disappeared about 1540, and Huichilobusco (Churubusco) was annexed to Mexicalcingo, which also included Culhuacan and Ixtapalapa (Gibson, 1964, p. 443). Zayula (cf. Tetepango) became a separate C about 1555. In the 17th century and later the justice of Mexicalcingo was sometimes called AM, but in 1784 he was a C.

56. MEXICO (C)
Archbish: Mexico
Int: Mexico
1950: Mexico, D. F.

At intervals in the 1520's an AM resided in the city of Mexico-Tenochtitlan, but his duties were those of a deputy-governor of Nueva España rather than a local magistrate (DII, 26: 195, 227; ENE, 1: 87). Again in the 1550's the title appears, when there were two AM's, one for

Mexico and the other in Santiago Tlatelolco.[90] However, these officials had jurisdiction only in Indian affairs. Until 1574 the government of the Spanish population in the capital was rotated among the alcaldes ordinarios in the cabildo. In that year the first C, a royal appointee, arrived, and henceforth (with brief interludes) Mexico City and its immediate environs constituted a corregimiento (ENE, 11: 233; Puga, 1563, fol. 86).[91]

57. MEZTITLAN (AM)
Archbish: Mexico
Int: Mexico
1950: Metztitlan, Hgo.

Molango y Malila (from 1531) was the original C in this area. From about 1553 all the surrounding encomienda towns were united in a province and AM of Meztitlan, whose magistrate was also C of Molango Malila (ENE, 7: 90).[92] The AM supervised the suffragan C's of Cempoala (q.v.), Huexutla (q.v.), Otumba (q.v.), Suchicoatlan (q.v.), Tepeapulco (q.v.), Xelitla (a C since 1532), Xicotepec (cf. Guachinango), Yagualica (cf. Suchicoatlan), and Zonguiluca (cf. Tulancingo). By the end of the 16th century all these jurisdictions had become independent except Xelitla, which was annexed to Meztitlan. Meanwhile Guayacocotla (q.v.) had been detached and made a separate C. The Xelitla area was later transferred to Valles.[93]

58. MIAGUATLAN (AM)
Bish: Antequera
Int: Oaxaca
1950: Miahuatlan de Porfirio Diaz, Oax.

The early political history of this area is summarized under Cimatlan y Chichicapa (q.v.). By 1580 the C of Chichicapa was living at Miaguatlan, and by the end of that century, with the separation of Chichicapa, the greater part of the old jurisdiction remained with Miaguatlan. The C was redesignated AM soon after 1640.

106, 125, 159, 257v; vol. 5, fols. 40v, 60.

[89] AGI, Mexico, leg. 20. AGN, Hospital de Jesús, leg. 107, exp. 49.

[90] AGN, Mercedes, vol. 4, fol. 96.

[91] AGI, Mexico, leg. 100, fol. 104.

[92] AGI, Patronato, leg. 182, ramo 40, fol. 336v. AGN, Mercedes, vol. 4, fol. 322v.

[93] AGI, Mexico, leg. 336, fols. 35–52. AGN, General de parte, vol. 1, fols. 195, 220; Indios, vol. 1, fols. 93, 120; vol. 2, fols. 16, 170.

59. MITLA Y TLACOLULA (AM)
Bish: Antequera
Int: Oaxaca
1950: San Pablo Mitla, Oax.

First claimed by Hernando Cortés, Mictla (=Miquitla) y Tlacolula and Macuilsuchil y Teutitlan were created C's in 1531 and 1532 (LdeT, pp. 219, 245). Both were suffragan to the Valle de Guaxaca in the 16th century. They were combined under a single AM soon after 1676, with the capital first in Teutitlan del Valle and finally at Mitla.[94]

60. (MOTINES)
Bish: Michoacan
Int: Valladolid
1950: Coalcoman de Matamoros, Mich.

Three C's, Motin y Pómaro, Aquila, and Cuacoman, all subordinate to the province of Colima, were created in this area in the 1530's. About 1560 an AM was appointed for the entire Motines region, and the above-mentioned C's became suffragan to the new province, together with a new C of Tlatictla y Maquili. By the end of the century the C's had been absorbed into the AM, and the Alima region was transferred from Colima. The jurisdiction was annexed to Tancitaro (q.v.) about 1780 (Brand and others, 1960, pp. 63–80).

61. NEXAPA (AM)
Bish: Antequera
Int: Oaxaca
1950: San Pedro Martir Quiechapa, Oax.

The area corresponding to this jurisdiction was from the 1550's subordinate to the vast province of Zapotecas (cf. Villa Alta).[95] It included the early C's of Nexapa (from about 1546), Cacalotepec, Coatlan, Chimaltepec, Malacatepec, Maxcaltepec (=Peñol de Guelamos), Nanacatepec y Quezalapa, Petlacaltepec, Quiabecuza, Tizatepec, Tlahuitoltepec, and Tlapalcatepec. In 1560, during an Indian uprising, a Spanish villa was founded at Nexapa which became the temporary capital of Zapotecas, and by 1570 an AM and province in its own right (LdeT, pp. 270–72, 497–501; García Pimentel, 1904, pp. 61, 71).[96] Tlahuitoltepec was transferred to Villa Alta in 1579, and within the next two decades the remaining suffragan C's were absorbed by the AM of Nexapa. Sometime before 1742 the capital was moved to Quiechapa. In 1793 a separate partido, Chontales, had recently been formed from part of Nexapa.[97]

62. NOCHISTLAN (AM)
Bish: Antequera
Int: Oaxaca
1950: Asuncion Nochixtlan, Oax.

C's were first appointed in this area at Cuestlahuaca and Yanhuitlan (by 1534), Zoyaltepec y Tonaltepec (1540), and Nochistlan (soon afterwards) (LdeT, p. 526). All these places, with other encomienda towns, were joined under the C of Zoyaltepec in 1553. Within a few years the jurisdiction had been made an AM and province first called Zoyaltepec y Yanhuitlan and finally Yanhuitlan, which in 1565–70 had three suffragan C's, Guautla, Nochistlan, and Zoyaltepec.[98] The latter C soon disappeared, and Guautla was absorbed by Nochistlan in the 1590's, together with another C recently recreated, Cuestlahuaca.

In 1688–89 Yanhuitlan and a few other villages were transferred to the AM of Teposcolula (q.v.), and the capital of the old province was moved to Nochistlan, now an AM.[99] Its area was later increased by the annexation of Peñoles (cf. Antequera).

[94] AGN, General de parte, vol. 6, fol. 217.
[95] AGN, Mercedes, vol. 5, fols. 37, 98, 110v.
[96] AGN, Congregaciones; Indios, vol. 2, fols. 61v, 110, 163; Tierras, vol. 79, exp. 4.
[97] AGN, General de parte, vol. 2, fol. 33; Historia, vol. 523.
[98] AGN, Mercedes, vol. 4, fols. 24, 80v, 157v, 312v; vol. 5, fol. 31.
[99] AGN, General de parte, vol. 2, fol. 48v; Indios, vol. 2, fols. 4v, 103, 231; Tierras, vol. 1520, exp. 2. Letter from Woodrow Borah.

63. NOMBRE DE DIOS (AM)
Bish: Guadalajara (Durango from 1621)
Int: Durango
1950: Nombre de Dios, Dgo.

This place, far beyond the geographical limits of Nueva España, for most of the colonial period was considered to belong to that gobierno. The villa was founded in 1563, and its jurisdiction was disputed at first between Nueva España, Nueva Galicia, and Nueva Vizcaya. In 1569 the audiencia of Nueva Galicia appointed a C of Valles de la Puana in charge of the villa and nearby estancias.[100] Ten years later the viceroy had assumed the right to name an AM of Nombre de Dios; although there were several subsequent attempts to annex the jurisdiction to Nueva Vizcaya, it seems to have remained an enclave of Nueva España until the late 18th century (Tamarón, 1937, p. 183).[101]

In a sense, several other outlying areas might be considered to have fallen within the political limits of Nueva España at one time or another. California, Nayarit, and Isla del Carmen were military provinces, each with a *capitán comandante* subordinate to the viceroy in charge of temporal matters. In a slightly different category were the gobiernos of Nuevo Mexico, Nuevo Santander, and Texas. From 1754 the viceroy appointed the C of Bolaños, with a jurisdiction which somewhat overlapped that of Nayarit. Ultimately this area was included in the military province and gobierno of Colotlan (Mecham, 1927, p. 72). The royal

saltworks of Peñol Blanco and Santa Maria, first in Nueva Galacia, appear in several lists of jurisdictions controlled by the viceroy from the late 16th century and finally were included in the AM of Venado y la Hedionda (q.v.). These cases will be treated in more detail below, under the respective gobiernos.

64. ORIZABA (AM)
Bish: Tlaxcala
Int: Veracruz
1950: Orizaba, Ver.

The C of Tequila y Chichiquila is listed from 1536, and retained that name for many years, although the justice resided almost from the beginning in the nearby settlement of Ahuilizapan, or Orizaba. In the mid-16th century the jurisdiction was suffragan to Teguacan, and included many villages from the valley of Orizaba to *tierra caliente*. It became an AM about 1640.[102]

65. OTUMBA (AM)
Archbish: Mexico
Int: Mexico
1950: Otumba de Gomez Farias, Mex.

First claimed in encomienda by Cortés, this place with subject villages was made a C in 1531 (Gibson, 1964, pp. 422, 444). Nearby Oztoticpac became a separate C in 1544, but soon reverted to encomienda. The jurisdiction was redesignated AM from about 1640.[103]

66. PACHUCA (AM)
Archbish: Mexico
Int: Mexico
1950: Pachuca de Soto, Hgo.

The first C in this mining area was Tezayuca y Zapotlan, created in 1531 (LdeT, p. 471). Minas de Pachuca, one of the provinces of the 1550's, had an AM who was also C of Tezayuca and Tecama (from 1553), although the latter place was transferred in the 1560's to Chiconautla (cf. San Cristobal Ecatepec).[104] Suffragan to Pachuca were the C's of Guaquilpa (from 1560, absorbed about

---

[100] Audiencia to king, Guadalajara, Feb. 15, 1564, leg. 5; same, Dec. 12, 1575, Guadalajara, leg. 34.
[101] AGN, General de parte, vol. 2, fol. 86. BNMA, 2449, fol. 399v.
[102] AGN, General de parte, vol. 1, fols. 10v, 67v, 93v, 214; vol. 2, fols. 99, 106; Mercedes, vol. 11, fols. 28, 48v, 78.
[103] AGN, Congregaciones, fol. 30v; General de parte, vol. 1, fols. 14v, 102v, 192.
[104] AGN, Mercedes, vol. 4, fol. 128v; vol. 5, fol. 90v.

1590) and Izcuincuitlapilco (independent from about 1568, cf. Actopan).[105]

67. PANUCO (AM)
Archbish: Mexico
Int: Veracruz
1950: Tantoyuca, Ver.

One of the original provincias of Nueva España, Panuco had an AM at least part of the time from 1523 to 1526, when it became a separate gobierno outside Cortés's jurisdiction. It was reunited with Nueva España in 1533, and governed at first by alcaldes ordinarios of the villa of San Esteban (Panuco [DII, 26: 78; Puga, 1563, fol. 82]). From 1537 the jurisdiction was ruled by an AM who supervised numerous suffragan C's, most of which disappeared toward the end of that century. Among them were Acececa, Cuzcatan, Chachapala y Tanquian, Huexutla (q.v.), Nanaguatla, Nexpa y Tauzan (since 1555), Piaztla y Ciguala, Tacolula, Tamaol y Tamatlan, Tamintla, Tamohi, Tancuiche y Texupespa, Tancuyname, Tanchinamol, Tanchoy y Mezquitlan, Tanhuis, Tempoal (since 1564), Xelitla (cf. Meztitlan), Xocutla, and Yagualica (cf. Meztitlan). By 1579 Valles (q.v.) had been detached and made a separate AM. In 1581–86 there was a dispute over the northern boundary with Nuevo Leon, and about the same time the seat of government was moved from Panuco to Tantoyuca. In the 17th century this jurisdiction was sometimes referred to as Tampico (ENE, 8: 48–50; LdeT, p. 118).[106]

68. PAPANTLA (AM)
Bish: Tlaxcala
Int: Veracruz
1950: Papantla de Olarte, Ver.

Cetusco was made a C in 1533 and united with Tonatico in 1544 (LdeT, p. 528).[107] Later known as Tonatico y Zozocolco, the jurisdiction was suffragan to Hueytlalpa (cf. Zacatlan) until perhaps the end of the 16th century when it became an independent C. Somewhat later the Papantla area was added, and by 1640 the C had become the AM of Papantla.[108]

69. PUEBLA DE LOS ANGELES (G)
Bish: Tlaxcala
Int: Puebla
1950: Puebla de Zaragoza, Pue.

From the date of its foundation, 1531, until 1538 Los Angeles was administered by a C who also governed Cholula and Tlaxcala. The city was allowed to govern itself by ayuntamiento in 1538–50, after which it had its own C and, from 1555, an AM who was simultaneously C of the nearby village of Guatinchan (Gibson, 1952, p. 68).[109] The Tepeaca area was detached in 1555, and another piece of the jurisdiction was given to Atrisco in 1579 (LdeT, p. 371).[110] After 1755 the magistrate of Puebla was called governor, but remained subordinate to the viceroy.

70. QUERETARO (C)
Bish: First Michoacan, then Mexico
Int: Mexico
1950: Queretaro, Qro.

Queretaro was at first in the province of Xilotepec, but in 1577 or 1578 it became a separate AM. The jurisdiction lost a northeastern slice at the end of the 16th century upon the creation of Minas de Escanela (cf. Cadereyta). By 1662 the AM had been redesignated C.

[105] AGI, Mexico, leg. 336, fol. 13. AGN, General de parte, vol. 2, fols. 61v, 62v. BNMA, MS 3064, fols. 9–97v.

[106] AGI, Mexico, leg. 20. AGN, General de parte, vol. 1, fols. 69v, 108v, 184v, 243; vol. 2, fols. 61, 100v; vol. 6, fol. 362v; vol. 9, fol. 188; Indios, vol. 2, fol. 110; Mercedes, vol. 4, fols. 34v, 71v, 312v; vol. 11, fol. 29v. BNMA, MS 3064, fols. 23–50v.

[107] AGI, Patronato, leg. 182, ramo 40, fols. 352v–353.

[108] AGN, General de parte, vol. 1, fols. 55, 128v; vol. 2, fol. 256v; Mercedes, vol. 11, fol. 40.

[109] AGN, General de parte, vol. 1, fol. 4v.

[110] AGN, General de parte, vol. 1, fol. 130v; vol. 2, fol. 255; Indios, vol. 1, fol. 101v.

71. SAN CRISTOBAL ECATEPEC (AM)
Archbish: Mexico
Int: Mexico
1950: Ecatepec Morelos, Mex.

Chiconautla, made a C in 1532, acquired several other villages in 1550–65, including the C of Tecama which was transferred from Pachuca. It was suffragan to Tezcuco in the 16th century, but later became an independent C which, after 1640, was redesignated the AM of San Cristobal Ecatepec (Gibson, 1964, p. 446).[111]

72. SAN JUAN DE LOS LLANOS (AM)
Bish: Tlaxcala
Int: Puebla
1950: Libres, Pue.

Created in 1535, the C of Tlatlauquitepec at first included nearby Teciutlan y Atempa (q.v.), but the latter was made a separate C about 1553 (LdeT, p. 520).[112] By 1579 the residence of the C had been moved to San Juan de los Llanos (Tlaljocoapa [LdeT, pp. 420, 454]).[113] In 1641 the C became AM, and by 1676 the C of Tustepec y Quimistlan (listed from 1534) had been annexed.

73. SAN LUIS DE LA PAZ (AM)
Bish: Michoacan and Mexico
Int: Guanajuato
1950: San Luis de la Paz, Gto.

The frontier area of Sichu y Pusinquia was made a C in 1552, first suffragan to Xilotepec and later to Michoacan (LdeT, pp. 296–97). In the 1590's the C became AM of Minas de Sichu, or Xichu, and in the following century the capital of the jurisdiction was moved to San Luis de la Paz.[114]

74. SAN LUIS POTOSI (AM)
Bish: Michoacan
Int: San Luis Potosi
1950: San Luis Potosi, S.L.P.

An AM was first sent to the newly discovered Minas de San Luis Potosi in 1592. After 1609 appointment to this post was usually made in Spain by royal order.

The eastern part of the jurisdiction, San Pedro Guadalcazar, was a separate AM from 1618 to about 1745, when it was again joined to San Luis (Borah, 1964; Mecham, 1927, pp. 67–69).

75. SAN MIGUEL EL GRANDE (AM)
Bish: Michoacan
Int: Guanajuato
1950: San Miguel de Allende, Gto.

The AM of Villas de San Miguel y San Felipe was created on the Chichimec frontier from parts of Guanajuato and Xilotepec about 1570. Palmar de Vega was annexed in 1595, but soon was transferred to San Luis de la Paz (q.v.). In later years the jurisdiction was called San Miguel el Grande (Jiménez Moreno, 1958, p. 90).[115]

76. SAYULA (AM)
Bish: Guadalajara
Int: Guadalajara
1950: Sayula, Jal.

By 1545 the Crown had acquired a half-interest in the Pueblos de Avalos, a large encomienda south of Guadalajara, and appointed a C to administer its part, with residence in Atoyac. From about 1551 the jurisdiction was raised to an AM and province called Avalos. The capital was moved first to Zacoalco and finally to Sayula (LdeT, pp. 140–42).[116]

77. SOCHICOATLAN (AM)
Archbish: Mexico
Int: Mexico
1950: Xochicoatlan, Hgo.

---

[111] AGI, Mexico, leg. 336, fols. 8v–9.—HSA, MS HC:N53/29/1.

[112] AGN, Mercedes, vol. 3, fol. 25v.

[113] AGN, General de parte, vol. 1, fols. 140, 146v; vol. 2, fols. 29, 29v, 93, 103, 138v; vol. 8, fols. 90v, 142; Indios, vol. 2, fol. 188; Mercedes, vol. 11, fol. 37. BNMA, MS 6877, fol. 8.

[114] AGN, General de parte, vol. 4, fol. 46; vol. 5, fols. 21, 45v, 111, 210; vol. 6, fol. 166; vol. 8, fol. 87; Mercedes, vol. 4, fol. 179.

[115] AGN, Mercedes, vol. 4, fols. 11v, 165, 282v; vol. 5, fols. 11v, 32v, 44, 57v.

[116] AGN, General de parte, vol. 1, fols. 91v, 94, 153, 229; vol. 2, fols. 52v, 53v, 163, 213v, 228, 252; Mercedes, vol. 11, fols. 3v, 36, 60, 61v.

Suchicuautla and Yagualica became C's in 1531 and 1544, respectively. The latter was first suffragan to Panuco, but in the 1560's and later both were in the province of Meztitlan. They became AM's soon after 1640, and in the late 18th century were united in one AM, Sochicoatlan (LdeT, pp. 302–03).[117]

78. Sochimilco (AM)
Archbish: Mexico
Int: Mexico
1950: Xochimilco, D. F.

Suchimilco and its sujetos became a C on the death of the encomendera in 1541. For years it was suffragan to Tezcuco, but by the 1570's it was an independent jurisdiction governed by an AM. Thereafter both titles, C and AM, were used (Gibson, 1964, p. 443; LdeT, p. 304).

79. Tacuba (AM)
Archbish: Mexico
Int: Mexico
1950: Tacuba (part of Mexico, D. F.)

Tacuba, adjoining Mexico City to the northwest, was long held in encomienda, but there was a C in nearby Tenayuca from 1532 to 1537 and again from 1544. This officer was suffragan to Guautitlan until 1573 when he became an AM. Appointment was made by the Crown after 1583. Toward 1600 the jurisdiction began to be called Tlalnepantla, and finally, Tacuba (Gibson, 1964, p. 445; LdeT, p. 390).[118]

80. Tancitaro (AM)
Bish: Michoacan
Int: Valladolid
1950: Ario de Rosales, Mich.

Tancitaro y Tapalcatepec became a C in 1531. For most of the 16th century it was suffragan to Mechoacan. The C of Arimao (cf. Colima, Zacatula) was absorbed about 1560, and the jurisdiction became an AM about 1640. In the following century, Cinagua y la Guacana and Motines (q.v.) were annexed, and the capital was moved to Ario (García Pi-

mentel, 1904, pp. 38, 40; LdeT, p. 343).

81. Tasco (AM)
Archbish: Mexico
Int: Mexico
1950: Taxco de Alarcon, Gro.

The C of Tasco y Tenango, listed in 1534, had become the AM of Minas de Tasco by 1538 (BAGN, 10: 251).[119] It had at least one suffragan C, Teulistaca (since 1544, absorbed by 1600), and perhaps three more: Capulalcolulco (cf. Tetela del Rio), Iguala (q.v.), and Iscateupa (q.v.). In the late 18th century Iguala was annexed to Tasco.[120]

82. Tecali (AM)
Bish: Tlaxcala
Int: Puebla
1950: Tecali de Herrera, Pue.

This small jurisdiction southeast of Puebla was separated from Tepeaca (q.v.) and made an AM about 1660 (Magdaleno, 1954, pp. 216–18).

83. Teciutlan y Atempa (AM)
Bish: Tlaxcala
Int: Puebla
1950: Teziutlan, Pue.

At first in the jurisdiction of Tlatlauquitepec (cf. San Juan de los Llanos), Teciutlan y Atempa were made a separate C about 1553. Suffragan to Xalapa, it became independent by the end of the 16th century, and was redesignated AM about 1640 (LdeT, p. 448).[121]

84. (Tecuicuilco)
Bish: Antequera
Int: Oaxaca
1950: Teococuilco de Marcos Perez, Oax.

This and several nearby towns claimed

---

[117] AGN, General de parte, vol. 1, fols. 87v, 156, 195; vol. 2, fol. 88v; vol. 6, fols. 174v, 207v; Padrones, vol. 12, fol. 254v.

[118] AGI, Mexico, leg. 20.

[119] AGI, Mexico, leg. 336, fol. 92v. AGN, Mercedes, vol. 1, fol. 7.

[120] AGI, Patronato, leg. 182, ramo 40, fol. 370v.

[121] AGN, General de parte, vol. 1, fols. 190, 206v; vol. 2, fol. 82; Mercedes, vol. 3, fol. 25v; vol. 4, fol. 152v.

by Cortés were made a C in 1531 (LdeT, p. 428). Suffragan to Antequera in the 16th century, and later annexed briefly to Iztepexi, Tecuicuilco was united in one C with Teozacualco (q.v.) soon after 1676.

85. TEGUACAN (AM)

Bish: Tlaxcala
Int: Puebla
1950: Tehuacan, Pue.

Teguacan appears as a C from 1534. It was selected in 1555 to be the seat of an AM and province.[122] Suffragan to it were Cuzcatlan (C since 1534), Teutitlan (q.v.), Tequila (cf. Orizaba), Tustepec y Quimistlan (cf. Xalapa), and Tecomavaca (cf. Teutitlan; LdeT, p. 163). By the end of the 16th century all these C's had become independent, and Zoquitlan (cf. Teutila) had been annexed to Cuzcatlan, which in turn was absorbed by Teguacan about 1650.[123] The AM became a Crown appointee in 1646.

86. TEGUANTEPEC (AM)

Bish: Antequera
Int: Oaxaca
1950: Santo Domingo Tehuantepec, Oax.

The first AM arrived in Teguantepec probably in 1526. Until 1563 this official was appointed by Cortés and his son, the second Marqués del Valle, but after that year the jurisdiction, with the exception of Xalapa del Marques (q.v.), was ruled by an AM named by the viceroy. It was a large province, bounded on the east by Chiapa and Soconusco and extending to the middle of the isthmus.

87. TEMAZCALTEPEC Y ZULTEPEC (AM)

Archbish: Mexico
Int: Mexico
1950: Real de Arriba, Mex.

The first C's in this mining region, sometimes called Provincia de la Plata, were Taxcaltitlan and Amatepec, both listed in 1536. When the silver mines became important, two AM's were created, first (by 1540) Zultepec, and then Te-

mazcaltepec. The AM of Minas de Zultepec was at the same time C of Amatepec y Zultepec, nearby Indian villages, while the magistrate of Minas de Temazcaltepec had jurisdiction in the neighboring C of Tuzantla (cf. Maravatio) until the 17th century. About 1715 the two AM's were united in one, Temazcaltepec y Zultepec.[124]

88. TENANGO DEL VALLE (AM)

Archbish: Mexico
Int: Mexico
1950: Tenango de Arista, Mex.

Teutenango and Atlatlauca y Suchiaca were two small C's south of Toluca, created in 1534 and 1537 respectively (LdeT, p. 81). In the provincial division of the 1550's Teutenango was assigned to Valle de Matalcingo and Atlatlauca to Malinalco. Both are listed as AM's about 1645, and by 1675 they had been combined in one jurisdiction, Tenango del Valle.[125] In the 18th century a number of villages were transferred from Metepec to Tenango.

89. TEOTIGUACAN (AM)

Archbish: Mexico
Int: Mexico
1950: San Juan Teotihuacan, Mex.

Tequecistlan in 1531 was placed under a C who also administered nearby Cempoala, but it became a separate jurisdiction about 1557, suffragan to Tezcuco (LdeT, p. 627).[126] By 1600 it was an independent C called San Juan Teotiguacan, which became an AM soon after 1640. Later, Acolman and its estancias

[122] AGN, Mercedes, vol. 4, fol. 265.
[123] AGN, General de parte, vol. 1, fols. 181v, 188, 244v; vol. 2, fols. 27v, 83; Indios, vol. 2, fols. 33v, 65, 118, 250. BNMA, MS 4476.
[124] AGI, Mexico, leg. 336, fols. 136–137v. AGN, General de parte, vol. 1, fol. 211; Inquisición, fol. 937, fol. 265v; Mercedes, vol. 3, fol. 271v; vol. 5, fol. 54.
[125] AGI, Mexico, leg. 336, fols. 133–134.
[126] AGN, General de parte, vol. 2, fols. 198v–199; Mercedes, vol. 3, fol. 312v.

were transferred from Teotiguacan to Tezcuco (Gibson, 1964, pp. 444–45).

90. TEOZACUALCO (AM)
Bish: Antequera
Int: Oaxaca
1950: San Pedro Teozacoalco, Oax.

Half of Teozacualco was placed under a C in 1532 (LdeT, pp. 39, 462). Adjoining it to the south was Amoltepec, also a C from about 1544. Both were at first suffragan to Teposcolula, but in the late 1560's they were united in a single C subordinate to the AM of Antequera.[127] By 1742 Teozacualco had become an AM to which Tecuicuilco (q.v.) was attached.

91. TEPEACA (AM)
Bish: Tlaxcala
Int: Puebla
1950: Tepeaca, Pue.

Until 1544 in encomienda, Tepeaca then became a C, and from 1555 a large province and AM.[128] Suffragan to it were the C's of Guatlatlauca (cf. Tepexi), Nopaluca (from about 1550), and Tepexi de la Seda (q.v.). Nopaluca was annexed between 1581 and 1609. About 1660 Tecali was detached from this jurisdiction, and what remained of Tepeaca was given in 1710 to the Duque de Atrisco, who henceforth appointed the AM.

92. TEPEXI DE LA SEDA (AM)
Bish: Tlaxcala
Int: Puebla
1950: Tepeji de Rodriguez, Pue.

Both Guatlatlauca (a C from 1535) and Tepexi (from about 1550) were subordinate to the province of Tepeaca from 1555 until about 1580.[129] By 1740 they were AM's and soon afterward they were joined in one jurisdiction, Tepexi de la Seda.

93. TEPOSCOLULA (AM)
Bish: Antequera
Int: Oaxaca
1950: San Pedro y San Pablo Teposcolula, Oax.

The C of Teposcolula (created in 1531) was given charge of a great many villages in the Mixteca Alta, both Crown and encomienda possessions, about 1552, and the resulting province became an AM (LdeT, p. 354).[130] Suffragan to it were the C's of Justlahuaca (q.v.), Texupa (from 1534), and Tilantongo (from about 1565, cf. Nochistlan). These all became independent C's, until in 1688–89 Yanhuitlan (cf. Nochistlan) and probably Texupa were annexed to Teposcolula (LdeT, pp. 13, 221, 248, 336, 467–68, 579).[131]

94. TETELA DEL RIO (AM)
Bish: Michoacan and Mexico
Int: Mexico
1950: Ajuchitlan del Progreso, Gro.

Originally this area along the Balsas River was shared between the C's of Iscateupa (q.v.), Capulalcolulco (from 1534), and Asuchitlan (since 1533). The first two may have been suffragan to Tasco in the 16th century, while Asuchitlan was in the province of Mechoacan (LdeT, pp. 60, 134).[132] In 1602 or soon afterwards a new AM of Minas de Tetela, or Tetela del Rio, was formed, which came to include certain pueblos of Iscateupa, most of Asuchitlan (less the Pungarabato area), and all of Capulalcolulco. By the 18th century the capital had moved to Asuchitlan.

[127] AGN, Mercedes, vol. 4, fol. 81.
[128] AGN, Mercedes, vol. 4, fols. 109v, 117, 132v, 155v.
[129] AGN, General de parte, vol. 1, fol. 150v; vol. 2, fol. 74; Indios, vol. 2, fols. 76, 97v; Mercedes, vol. 11, fol. 42.
[130] AGI, Indiferente, leg. 1530. AGN, Mercedes, vol. 4, fols. 24, 81; vol. 5, fol. 2v.
[131] AGN, Congregaciones; General de parte, vol. 1, fols. 81v, 93, 136v, 154, 231, 249; vol. 2, fols. 9, 131v, 177, 179; vol. 3, fol. 55; vol. 4, fol. 8; Indios, vol. 2, fols. 30, 173, 188, 236v; vol. 3, fol. 40; Mercedes, vol. 11, fol. 122v; Tierras, vol. 39, exp. 1; vol. 44, exp. 2. HSA, MS HC:417/132. Personal communication from Woodrow Borah.
[132] AGN, General de parte, vol. 1, fol. 58; vol. 5, fol. 32; Indios, vol. 2, fols. 7v–8v.

95. (TETELA DEL VOLCAN)
Archbish: Mexico
Int: Puebla
1950: Tetela del Volcan, Mor.

A small village on the southern slope of Popocatepetl, Tetela became a C in 1558 upon the death of its encomendero. It was suffragan to Chalco in the 1570's, and became an AM about 1640. In the 18th century it was subordinate to Cuautla Amilpas (q.v.), to which it was annexed about 1780 (LdeT, pp. 436–41).[133]

96. TETEPANGO HUEYPUSTLA (AM)
Archbish: Mexico
Int: Mexico
1950: Hueypoxtla, Mex.

There were several early C's in this area. Axacuba is listed in 1534, but had become an encomienda by 1543. Tetebanco became a C in 1531, and towards 1560 its magistrate was made AM of a new province, Minas de Tornacustla (LdeT, p. 432).[134] He supervised the suffragan C's of Atitalaquia (created in 1531), Atengo y Misquiaguala (from 1544), Tlagualilpa or Tabaliloca (from 1534), Tula (from 1544), and Yetecomac. Tula (q.v.) became a separate AM about 1563, and had attached to it the C's of Atitalaquia and Tlagualilpa.

By the end of the 16th century, the AM of Minas de Tornacustla had been renamed Hueypustla, and the C's of Tlagualilpa and Yetecomac had been absorbed by the AM. Meanwhile, Atitalaquia and Atengo y Misquiaguala had become independent C's (AM's from about 1640), and the erstwhile C of Zayula (cf. Tula) was annexed to Atengo. About 1700 the jurisdiction of Tetepango Hueypustla, as it was now called, absorbed both Atengo y Misquiaguala and Atitalaquia.

97. TEUTILA (AM)
Bish: Antequera
Int: Oaxaca
1950: San Pedro Teutila, Oax.

Teutila, a C since 1533, was chosen as the center of a large province and AM from about 1555 (LdeT, p. 458).[135] Attached to it were Ayautla y Tepeapa (a C from 1536), Chinantla (from 1533), Guaspaltepec (from 1534), Oxitlan (from 1536), Papaloticpac y Tepeucila (from about 1544), Ucila (from 1534), Zoquitlan (from about 1544), and Zoyaltepec y Zoyatlan (from about 1550). Thus for a time the AM of Teutila governed the entire upper basin of the Alvarado (Papaloapan) River. Toward the end of the 16th century, Chinantla y Ucila, Guaspaltepec (cf. Cozamaloapa), and Papaloticpac (cf. Teutitlan) became independent C's, Zoquitlan was annexed to Cuzcatlan (cf. Teguacan), and the remaining suffragan C's were absorbed by Teutila. In the mid-17th century Chinantla y Ucila was also annexed to Teutila, and Tuxtepec was transferred from Cozamaloapa (Ajofrín, 1959, 2: 54–63; LdeT, pp. 109, 242, 597, 605).[136]

98. TEUTITLAN DEL CAMINO (AM)
Bish: Antequera
Int: Oaxaca
1950: Teotitlan del Camino, Oax.

In 1531 C's were first appointed to Teutitlan and Tecomavaca y Quiotepec (LdeT, pp. 380, 460). For some years, later in the century, both were suffragan to Teguacan. By the early 18th century Tecomavaca, together with Cuicatlan (cf. Antequera) and Papaloticpac (cf. Teutila), had been annexed to Teutitlan del Camino.

99. (TEUTLALCO)
Bish: Tlaxcala

[133] AGI, Patronato, leg. 182, ramo 40, fol. 358. AGN, Padrones, vol. 8.
[134] AGN, Mercedes, vol. 3, fol. 300v; vol. 4, fol. 359; vol. 5, fol. 70.
[135] AGN, Mercedes, vol. 4, fols. 28, 136, 227, 374v. NLA, Ayer 1121, fol. 186.
[136] AGI, Patronato, leg. 182, ramo 40, fol. 340v. AGN, General de parte, vol. 1, fols. 22–22v; vol. 2, fol. 120; Mercedes, vol. 11, fol. 38; Padrones, vol. 12, fol. 257; Tierras, vol. 64, exp. 4.

Int: Puebla
1950: Teotlalco, Pue.

Teutalco y Centeupa became a C in 1531, and for a time was suffragan to Chalco. Mines were discovered, and toward 1570 the jurisdiction became an AM, Minas de Teutlalco y Tlaucingo. By 1770 the area was included in the AM of Chiautla (q.v.; LdeT, pp. 452–53).[137]

100. Tezcuco (AM)
Archbish: Mexico
Int: Mexico
1950: Texcoco de Mora, Mex.

First claimed as an encomienda by Cortés, Tezcuco was made a C in 1531, and an AM and province about 1552 (LdeT, p. 481).[138] Suffragan to it in the 16th century were the C's of Coatepec (q.v.), Chiconautla (cf. San Cristobal Ecatepec), Mexicalcingo y Zayula (q.v.), Sochimilco (q.v.), and Tequecistlan (cf. Teotiguacan). Toward 1690 the town of Acolman and its estancias were annexed from Teotiguacan (Gibson, 1964, pp. 431, 444).

101. (Tinhuindin)
Bish: Michoacan
Int: Valladolid
1950: Tingüindin, Mich.

Tenhuendin y Perivan is listed as a C from 1536, in the province of Mechoacan. An early jurisdictional dispute over Perivan was won by the C of Xiquilpa. Tinhuindin was long considered subordinate to Xiquilpa and was annexed to it about 1740.

102. (Tistla)
Bish: Mexico and Tlaxcala
Int: Mexico
1950: Tixtla de Guerrero, Gro.

The early history of this area is discussed under Chilapa (q.v.). Tistla y Zumpango became a separate C toward the end of the 16th century, but by 1610 it was being administered by a lieutenant of the AM of Acapulco (q.v.).[139]

103. Tlalpuxagua (AM)
Bish: Michoacan
Int: Valladolid
1950: Tlalpujahua, Mich.

The C of Ucareo Cinapecuaro, listed from 1536, became AM of Minas de Tlalpuxagua in 1558. The jurisdiction was split in two by the intrusion of Maravatio. By the early 17th century, Cinapecuaro and Taimeo (cf. Valladolid) had been absorbed by Tlalpuxagua.[140]

104. Tlapa (AM)
Bish: Tlaxcala
Int: Mexico
1950: Tlapa, Gro.

An important cabecera with many subject villages, Tlapa was made a C in 1533, although three-quarters of it was shared between two encomenderos. It was subordinate to Zumpango until 1579, when it became a separate AM (García Pimentel, 1904, pp. 97–107; LdeT, pp. 511–13).[141] Subsequently the Cuitlapa area was lost to Igualapa, and Olinala was annexed from Chiautla.

105. Tlaxcala (G)
Bish: Tlaxcala
Int: Puebla
1950: Tlaxcala de Xicotencatl, Tlax.

The boundaries of this province coincided roughly with those of the modern state of Tlaxcala, less the Calpulalpan area. It was administered with Puebla and Cholula by a single C from 1531 to 1545, when it received its own magistrate. In 1555 the C became an AM, who supervised the suffragan C's of Cholula

[137] AGN, General de parte, vol. 1, fols. 114, 129, 174, 186, 203, 217, 229; vol. 2, fol. 115v; vol. 4, fol. 23; vol. 5, fol. 80.
[138] AGN, Mercedes, vol. 4, fol. 145v.
[139] AGN, General de parte, vol. 6, fol. 135v. BNMA, MS 6877, fol. 62.
[140] AGN, General de parte, vol. 1, fols. 21, 50v, 147, 180v, 226v; vol. 2, fols. 22v, 46, 59v, 166, 199v; Mercedes, vol. 5, fol. 7; vol. 11, fols. 2v, 10v, 28v, 29v; vol. 84, fols. 23v, 42v.
[141] AGN, General de parte, vol. 1, fols. 34, 47v, 141v, 163, 180; vol. 2, fols. 43v, 166, 194, 214, 226v.

100

(q.v.), Guatinchan (cf. Puebla), and Huexocingo (q.v.). In 1587 the magistrate's title was changed to gobernador, an office subject to Crown appointment from 1609 (Gibson, 1952, pp. 66–68, 217).[142]

106. TLAZAZALCA (AM)
Bish: Michoacan
Int: Valladolid
1950: La Piedad, Mich.

Tlazazalca (a C since 1534) and Chilchota (from about 1540) were suffragan to Mechoacan in the 16th century. They became AM's soon after 1640, and toward the end of that century they were joined under a single AM who resided in La Piedad (García Pimentel, 1904, pp. 43–44; LdeT, p. 362).[143]

107. TOCHIMILCO (AM)
Archbish: Mexico
Int: Puebla
1950: Tochimilco, Pue.

Ocopetlayuca, later known as Tochimilco, became a C in 1546.[144] The jurisdiction formed a small intrusion of the archdiocese of Mexico into the valley of Atrisco. During the 17th century Tochimilco and Guaquechula were attached as a subordinate C to the AM of Atrisco, but later Tochimilco (minus Guaquechula) appears as a separate AM.[145]

108. TOLUCA (C)
Archbish: Mexico
Int: Mexico
1950: Toluca de Lerdo, Mex.

A C or AM for the Valle de Matalcingo (cf. Metepec) was appointed by the first Marqués del Valle, Hernando Cortés, in the early 1530's, but his jurisdiction was soon reduced to the villa of Toluca and its immediate estancias. From 1569, during the sequestration of the marquisate, Toluca was administered by the AM of Valle de Matalcingo, a royal appointee; political control was returned to the third marquis about 1595.[146]

109. TULA (AM)
Archbish: Mexico
Int: Mexico
1950: Tula de Allende, Hgo.

Tula and its subjects were taken from their encomendero in 1544 and made a C. In the 1560's it was suffragan to Tornacustla, but seems to have become a separate AM about 1563. Atitalaquia (cf. Tetepango), Tlagualilpa (ibid.), and Zayula (cf. Mexicalcingo) were in turn made suffragan to Tula for some years. From 1706 the Duques de Atrisco had the privilege of appointing the AM (LdeT, pp. 243, 267, 270, 403, 535–37).[147]

110. TULANCINGO (AM)
Bish: Mexico and Tlaxcala
Int: Mexico
1950: Tulancingo, Hgo.

Originally named after its first capital, Zonguiluca or Cinguiluca, this jurisdiction began as a C in 1534. For some years it was suffragan to Meztitlan, but by 1575 it was a separate AM. Tututepec and its sujetos were transferred from Metateyuca in 1575.[148]

111. TUSPA (AM)
Bish: Michoacan
Int: Guadalajara
1950: Ciudad Guzman, Jal.

At first attached to the province of Colima, the towns of Tuspa, Tamazula

[142] AGN, General de parte, vol. 1, fol. 109; vol. 2, fols. 64, 254.

[143] AGN, General de parte, vol. 1, fol. 135v; vol. 2, fol. 69; Indios, vol. 2, fol. 9v; Mercedes, vol. 11, fol. 54.

[144] AGI, Patronato, leg. 182, ramo 40, fol. 341.

[145] AGN, General de parte, vol. 1, fol. 239; vol. 10, fols. 6v, 173v.

[146] AGN, Hospital de Jesús, leg. 107, exp. 49; Mercedes, vol. 3, fol. 310v; vol. 4, fols. 125, 159, 257v; vol. 5, fols. 40v, 60; Padrones, vol. 21.

[147] AGN, General de parte, vol. 1, fols. 40v, 101v, 113, 186v, 199, 224; vol. 2, fol. 265; Mercedes, vol. 11, fol. 70v; vol. 84, fol. 129.

[148] AGI, Indiferente, leg. 187, AGN, General de parte, vol. 1, fols. 35v, 57, 92v, 101, 107–107v, 117v, 138; vol. 2, fols. 40v, 73v, 74v, 145v, 174, 192, 211v.

y Zapotlan are listed as a C in 1534, and became an AM about 1560. A neighboring C, Xilotlan (from 1534), was suffragan to Colima in the 1560's and to Tuspa in the 1580's, but later was absorbed by Colima. In the late 18th century the AM resided in Zapotlan (LdeT, p. 334).[149]

112. TUXTLA Y COTAXTLA (AM)
Bish: Antequera and Tlaxcala
Int: Veracruz
1950: Santiago Tuxtla, Ver.

The first magistrate in this jurisdiction belonging to the Marquesado del Valle may have been appointed as early as 1529. After Cortés's claims were pared down by the second audiencia, the province consisted of three noncontiguous areas—Tuxtla, Cotaxtla, and Ixcalpan (La Rinconada)—generally governed by a single AM or C. During the first sequestration of the marquisate (1570–95) Tuxtla y Cotaxtla was administered by the AM of Tlacotalpa (cf. Veracruz Nueva [LdeT, pp. 581–82; García Pimentel, 1904, pp. 80–81]).

113. VALLADOLID (C)
Bish: Michoacan
Int: Valladolid
1950: Morelia, Mich.

A C was first appointed to the province of Uchichila or Mechoacan in 1531. The capital moved from Tzintzuntzan to Patzcuaro in 1538 and to Valladolid in 1576, although subsequently the justice resided much of the time in Patzcuaro. Mechoacan became an AM about 1550 and had a considerable number of suffragan C's: Asuchitlan (cf. Tetela del Rio), Capula (from 1534), Cinagua (q.v.), Cuiseo (cf. Guaymeo), Cuiseo de la Laguna (q.v.), Chilchota (cf. Tlazazalca), Chocandiro (1597), Guanaxo (cf. Cinagua), Guaniqueo (from 1544), Guaymeo y Sirandaro (q.v.), Jaso y Teremendo (from 1534), Maravatio (q.v.), Necotlan (from about 1549), Sichu y Pusinquia (cf. San Luis de la Paz), Taimeo (from

about 1550), Tancitaro (q.v.), Tinhuindin (q.v.), Tiripitio (from 1550), Tlazazalca (q.v.), Xacona (cf. Zamora), Xiquilpa (q.v.), and Yurirapundaro (cf. Celaya [BAGN, 1: 11–55; García Pimentel, 1904, pp. 32–49; LdeT, pp. 196, 483]).[150] Of these, by the early 17th century Capula, Chocandiro, Guaniqueo, Necotlan, and Tiripitio had been absorbed by the AM, Yurirapundaro had been absorbed by Celaya, and Taimeo had been transferred to Tlalpuxagua. The others had become independent C's. Later Jaso y Teremendo was annexed to Mechoacan or, as it came to be called, Valladolid. From 1775 the magistrate's title was again changed, to corregidor.

114. VALLES (C)
Archbish: Mexico
Int: San Luis Potosi
1950: Ciudad de Valles, S.L.P.

Santiago de los Valles de Oxitipa was first administered with Panuco, but was a separate AM by 1579. The jurisdiction contained a great many villages in the Huasteca, and at least one suffragan C, Tancuilave or Tamaholipa (mentioned from 1547), which seems to have been partitioned between Valles and Panuco in 1602. In the 17th century the Xelitla area was annexed from Meztitlan. The AM of Villa de los Valles became a C about 1695 (LdeT, p. 333; Magdaleno, 1954, p. 213).[151]

115. VENADO Y LA HEDIONDA (AM)
Bish: Guadalajara
Int: San Luis Potosi
1950: Venado, S.L.P.

[149] AGN, Indios, vol. 2, fol. 176.
[150] AGI, Contaduría, leg. 663-A. AGN, General de parte, vol. 1, fols. 8, 15v, 93v, 100v, 134v, 141, 156, 170v, 181v, 222v; vol. 2, fols. 55v, 58v, 67, 72v, 116v, 173v–174, 258; Indios, vol. 1, fol. 138; vol. 2, fol. 191; Mercedes, vol. 3, fols. 253v, 337; vol. 4, fols. 4v, 36.
[151] AGI, Mexico, legs. 103–104, passim. AGN, General de parte, vol. 1, fols. 95v, 125, 195–196, 220, 226v, 237v; vol. 2, fols. 39v, 114, 274; vol. 6, fol. 148v; Indios, vol. 2, fol. 85.

Probably the last AM to be created, San Sebastian del Venado y la Hedionda was formed about 1770 by taking these two villages from the AM of Charcas in Nueva Galicia and adding them to the jurisdiction of the Salinas del Peñol Blanco (cf. Nombre de Dios), controlled by the viceroy.[152]

116. VERACRUZ NUEVA (G)

Bish: Tlaxcala
Int: Veracruz
1950: Veracruz Llave, Ver.

The C of Tezayuca or Taliscoya, first mentioned in 1534, was a small jurisdiction south of Veracruz governed by the AM of that province. It was soon combined with the C of Tlacotalpa (created in 1541), which became an AM about 1570 (LdeT, pp. 312, 468).[153] When the city of Veracruz had been established at its final site, in 1600, a new jurisdiction was organized comprising Veracruz Nueva and the port of San Juan de Ulua, to which Tlacotalpa was added soon afterward. The magistrate was at first a C. In 1629 this became a Crown appointment, and by the end of that century the title of governor was in use (Vetancurt, 1698, 4: 75).[154]

117. VERACRUZ VIEJA (AM)

Bish: Tlaxcala
Int: Veracruz
1950: La Antigua, Ver.

La villa rica de la Vera Cruz, the first Spanish settlement in Mexico, was governed by its ayuntamiento in early years but may have had an AM by 1522. It became the capital of a province which in the 1550's acquired a number of suffragan C's: Cempoala y Chicuacentepec (created about 1544), Guatusco (cf. Cordoba), Mizantla (from 1534), Tezayuca (cf. Veracruz Nueva), Tlapacoya (from 1534), and Zongolica (from 1534 [García Pimentel, 1904, pp. 10–12]).[155] All of these were absorbed into the AM during the 16th century except Guatusco (which became an independent C) and Mizantla (still a C in 1610, but absorbed soon afterward).[156] In 1600 the southern part of the jurisdiction was detached and made a separate C (cf. Veracruz Nueva).

118. VILLA ALTA (AM)

Bish: Antequera
Int: Oaxaca
1950: San Ildefonso Villa Alta, Oax.

Villa alta de San Ildefonso was the center and capital of the province of Zapotecas, an AM as early as 1530. By royal dispensation, the Spanish settlers of the villa, or at any rate those who did not have encomiendas, were given Crown pueblos in corregimiento as a means of subsistence. As the population of Villa Alta increased, so did the number of C's. There were nine in 1533, 19 in 1545, and 34 in 1569 (Dávila Padilla, 1625, pp. 548–49; ENE, 3: 50).[157] About 1570 the southern half of the province was detached and made a separate AM with its capital at Nexapa (q.v.). In the following list of suffragan C's, those which belonged to Nexapa are omitted: Camotlan (from about 1544), Comaltepec (from about 1560), Cuezcomaltepec (from about 1555), Chuapa (from about 1544), El Tagui y Lazagaya (from about 1555), El Tagui y Yalahui (from about 1560), Guaquilpa (in 1545), Guayacatepec y la Hoya (from 1534), Iscuintepec (1534 to about 1550), Lalana y Xaltepec (from 1534), Lalopa (from about 1544), Mazuich y Zapotequillas (from about 1565), Metepec y Alotepec (from 1534), Ocelotepec (from about 1544, cf. Chichicapa), Suchitepec (from 1537, cf. Guatulco), Suchitepec (another, from about 1540), Taba (from about 1560), Tecomatlan (in 1545), Teotlasco (from about 1544), Teu-

[152] AGI, Guadalajara, leg. 348.
[153] AGN, Mercedes, vol. 4, fol. 65v.
[154] AGN, General de parte, vol. 5, fols. 212v, 222.
[155] AGN, Mercedes, vol. 11, fols. 38v, 78.
[156] BNMA, MS 6877, fol. 26.
[157] AGN, General de parte, vol. 3, fol. 59v.

talcingo (from 1534), Tiltepec (from 1534), Tizatepec (from about 1560), Tlahuitoltepec y Huitepec (from 1534; in Nexapa, 1570–79), Toavela (from about 1560), Tonaguia y Tepetitongo (from about 1546), Totontepec (from about 1546), Valachita (in 1545), Yabago (from about 1544), Yacochi (from about 1544), Yagavila y los Guatinicamanes from 1534), Yagayo y Chichitepec (from 1534), Yatobi or Venchinaguia (from about 1544), and Yaxila (from about 1544).[158]

Ocelotepec and Suchitepec were transferred to adjoining jurisdictions about 1550, and all of the Chontal and much of the Mixe area was detached when Nexapa became an AM. Early in the 17th century the remaining suffragan C's were eliminated and absorbed into the AM of Villa Alta. The Guaspaltepec area was acquired from Cozamaloapa about 1740.[159]

119. Xalapa de la Feria (AM)
Bish: Tlaxcala
Int: Veracruz
1950: Jalapa Enriquez, Ver.

Xalapa became the seat of an AM and province about 1558. Suffragan to it were Teciutlan y Atempa (q.v.), Tlatlauquitepec (cf. San Juan de los Llanos), and Xalacingo (a C from 1536). Earlier C's in the area, Chapultepec y Maltrata (from 1538) and Papalote de la Sierra (from about 1544) were soon absorbed; the others became independent. Xalacingo was annexed late in the 17th century.[160]

120. Xalapa del Marques (AM or C)
Bish: Antequera
Int: Oaxaca
1950: Santa Maria Jalapa del Marques, Oax.

One of the villas granted to Cortés, Xalapa was first included in the jurisdiction of Teguantepec. When the latter province was taken by the Crown in 1563, Xalapa remained in the marquisate and

became a small jurisdiction by itself. The justice was henceforth appointed by the Marqueses del Valle, although Xalapa was reannexed to Teguantepec from 1570 to 1595.[161]

121. Xicayan (AM)
Bish: Antequera
Int: Oaxaca
1950: Santiago Jamiltepec, Oax.

The large province of Tututepec was claimed by Cortés, then for a brief period (1932–34) came under Crown control before it was given in encomienda to don Luis de Castilla. Nearby Cuahuitlan became a C in 1535, and half of Xicayan de Pedro Nieto in 1544. In the 1550's the whole coastal area including Tututepec was placed under the jurisdiction of the C of Cuahuitlan, and subsequently that of Xicayan.[162] The latter in 1582 became AM of Xicayan y Tututepec, and Cuahuitlan was added to his jurisdiction. Later the Zacatepec area was annexed from Justlahuaca, and the capital was moved from Xicayan to Xamiltepec.[163]

122. Xilotepec (AM)
Archbish: Mexico
Int: Mexico
1950: Jilotepec de Abasolo, Mex.

The Crown had some difficulty in wresting administrative control of this area from the encomenderos, but from about 1548 there was a justicia of Chichimecas

[158] AGN, General de parte, vol. 1, fols. 2, 4, 6v, 42–43, 195v, 224, 228v; vol. 2, fols. 33, 204, 253, 283v, 285; Mercedes, vol. 3, fols. 241v, 307v, 309v, 314–317v; vol. 4, fols. 9, 362; vol. 5, fols. 37, 98, 110v; vol. 11, fol. 26v.
[159] AGI, Indiferente, leg. 108, vol. 4, fol. 102.
[160] AGN, General de parte, vol. 17, fol. 228.
[161] AGN, General de parte, vol. 3, fol. 218v; Hospital de Jesús, leg. 209; Tierras, leg. 102, exp. 3.
[162] AGN, General de parte, vol. 3, fols. 130–134v; Mercedes, vol. 4, fol. 249v; Tierras, vol. 29, exp. 1.
[163] AGN, General de parte, vol. 1, fols. 26–27v; vol. 2, fols. 23v, 285v; vol. 3, fol. 28v; Indios, vol. 1, fol. 33; vol. 2, fols. 184, 221; vol. 3, fols. 24–26; Mercedes, vol. 11, fols. 41v, 147v; Tierras, vol. 29, exp. 1; vol. 46, exp. 2; vol. 1875, exp. 2; Vínculos, vol. 272, exp. 9.

y provincia de Xilotepec, soon made an AM, with an immense jurisdiction extending westward to the limits of Nueva Galicia and northward to an undefined frontier.[164] From it were formed in the 16th century the jurisdictions of Sichu y Pusinquia (cf. San Luis de la Paz), Guanajuato (q.v.), Tlalpuxagua (q.v.), San Miguel (q.v.), and Queretaro (q.v.), and toward the end of that century a separate AM was appointed for Cimapan (q.v.). The northern part of what remained of the province of Xilotepec is listed as a separate AM, Hueychiapa, in 1640–98 (García Pimentel, 1897, pp. 139–46).[165]

123. XIQUILPA (AM)
Bish: Michoacan
Int: Valladolid
1950: Jiquilpan de Juarez, Mich.

Xiquilpa appears as a C suffragan to Colima in 1545, but was soon transferred to the province of Mechoacan. The C became an AM after 1640, and Tinhuindin (q.v.) was annexed in the following century.

124. XONOTLA Y TETELA (AM)
Bish: Tlaxcala
Int: Puebla
1950: Jonotla, Pue.

A small jurisdiction in the province of Hueytlalpa, Xonotla y Tetela and adjoining villages were made a C in 1533. The C was redesignated AM shortly after 1640 (LdeT, p. 217).

125. ZACATLAN DE LAS MANZANAS (C)
Bish: Tlaxcala
Int: Puebla
1950: Zacatlan, Pue.

First controlled by encomenderos, the province of Hueytlalpa from 1531 had a C, toward 1557 raised to the category of AM, who governed a large region extending from the mountains to the Gulf coast.[166] Suffragan C's were Tonatico y Zozocolco (cf. Papantla) and Xonotla y Tetela (q.v.). By 1600 these had become independent jurisdictions, and the

coastal area centering in Papantla was transferred to Tonatico. Early in the 17th century Zacatlan had become the capital. The AM was redesignated C by 1646 (Magdaleno, 1954, p. 240).[167]

126. (ZACATULA)
Bish: Michoacan
Int: Mexico
1950: Tecpan, Gro.

The Spanish settlement of Zacatula may have had an AM as early as 1524, although for a brief period (1526–28) the province was claimed as an encomienda by Cortés. It included the entire coast and hinterland from Texupan almost to Acapulco, the largest jurisdiction in Nueva España. Suffragan C's mentioned in the 16th century were Arimao y Borona (from the 1530's, disappeared about 1560), Axalo (from about 1578), Ayutla (from 1534), Cacalutla (from 1534), Cayaco (from about 1575), Ciguatanejo (in 1545), Ciguatlan y Tamaluacan (from about 1560), Ciutla Metlapan (from about 1560), Coyuca (from 1534), Cuacuatlan (from about 1544), Mechia (from about 1550), Mexcaluacan (from about 1545), Nexpa (from about 1538), Pantla y Yautepec (from 1534), Petatlan or Ximalcota (from 1545), Pochutla (from about 1560), Tecomatlan (from 1545), Texupan y Topetina (from 1534), Xiguacan y Pichique (from about 1544), Zacualpa y Panutla (from 1536), and Zoyatlan y Atlan (from about 1568). The number of C's had been reduced to 11 in 1580, and these probably were absorbed towards the end of the century, although "Ciutla prouᵃ de Çacatula" appears in a list of 1676. The same document shows

[164] AGN, Mercedes, vol. 3, fols. 297v–298v; vol. 4, fols. 11v, 77, 126v; vol. 5, fols. 11v, 32v, 44, 45v, 77, 113.
[165] AGN, General de parte, vol. 1, fol. 38v, 164v, 179; vol. 2, fols. 25v, 41; vol. 9, fol. 24; vol. 17. fol. 191; Mercedes, vol. 11, fols. 64, 73v.
[166] AGN, Mercedes, vol. 4, fols. 218, 377.
[167] AGN, General de parte, vol. 2, fol. 256v. BNMA, MS 4476.

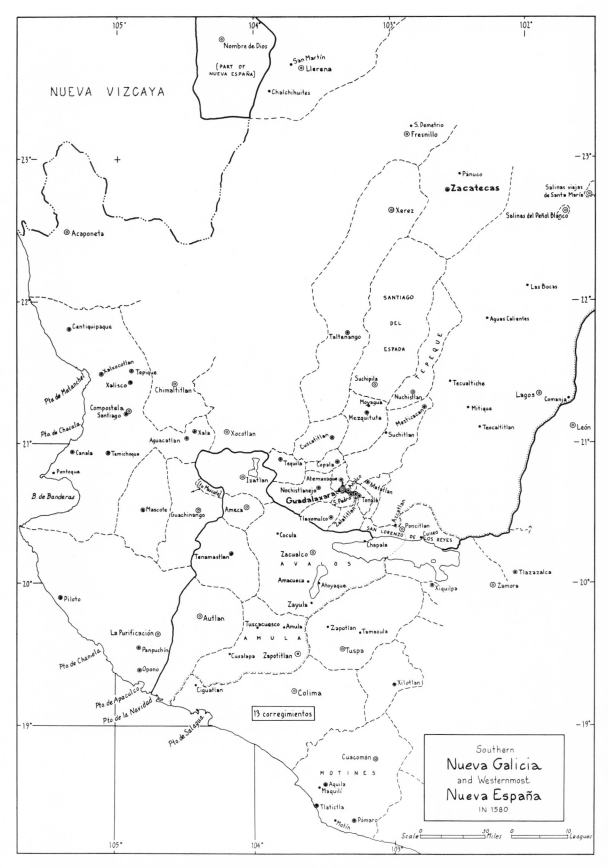

Fig. 10—SOUTHERN NUEVA GALICIA AND WESTERNMOST NUEVA ESPAÑA IN 1580

Zacatula administered jointly with Leon (q.v.), and subsequently the coastal province appears as a *tenientazgo* of that distant jurisdiction, although in the late 18th century it was again a separate partido.

127. ZACUALPA (AM)

Archbish: Mexico
Int: Mexico
1950: Zacualpan, Mex.

The villages of Zacualpa e Iztapa had a C from perhaps 1544. By 1563 the area was under an AM of Minas de Zacualpa. The jurisdiction was enlarged in the 1570's by the transfer of Coatepec and Cuitlapilco from Zultepec, and again about 1680 with the annexation of Iscateupa (q.v.).[168]

128. (ZAMORA Y XACONA)

Bish: Michoacan
Int: Valladolid
1950: Zamora, Mich.

Xacona was an encomienda until 1544, when it was made a C suffragan to Mechoacan (LdeT, pp. 213–16). The jurisdiction became an AM in 1574 after the founding of Villa de Zamora (Rodríguez Zetina, 1956).[169] In the 17th century for a time Jaso y Teremendo (cf. Valladolid) was administered from Zamora, which in turn was attached to Maravatio about 1692.

129. ZUMPANGO DE LA LAGUNA (AM)

Archbish: Mexico
Int: Mexico
1950: Zumpango de Ocampo, Mex.

The village of Citlaltepec became a C suffragan to the province of Guautitlan

about 1560. The capital was moved to Zumpango before 1590, and from about 1640 the C became an AM (Gibson, 1964, p. 446).[170]

II. NUEVA GALICIA

The region northwest of Michoacan extending along the Pacific coast as far as Culiacan was occupied by Spaniards under Nuño de Guzmán in 1530–31. In the latter year this vast territory was made a separate gobierno, but the name bestowed upon it by Guzmán, Mayor España, did not find favor at court, and it was renamed Nueva Galicia. Guzmán proceeded to annex a number of provinces which had been previously occupied by Cortés's adherents and were considered part of Nueva España. A cédula of April 20, 1533, ordered these places returned, which was done except in the case of Tonala, held thenceforth by the Guzmán faction. The capital of Nueva Galicia was established at Compostela, first located at or near Tepic and moved in 1540 to its present site (Bancroft, 1883–86, 2: 341–74; Parry, 1948). Much of the area as it appeared in 1580 is shown on figure 10; its later jurisdictions are shown on figure 11.

In early years (1531–45) Nueva Galicia was ruled by governors commissioned by the Crown. From 1545 to 1549 matters of gobierno were confided to the audiencia of Mexico, which appointed two alcaldes mayores, one for Nueva Galicia and another for the distant province of Culiacan.[171] Early in 1549 a separate but subordinate audiencia established residence at Compostela. It comprised four *oidores alcaldes mayores* who, in addition to their judicial duties, were given charge of the government, a situation which prevailed until 1572. For the next two years the viceroy was made responsible for matters of gobierno in Nueva Galicia, until in December, 1574, a governor (who was also president of the audiencia of Guadalajara) arrived. Henceforth this official was in charge of the government

[168] AGI, Mexico, leg. 336, fol. 138v. AGN, General de parte, vol. 1, fols. 13v, 15, 28, 79v, 131v, 226; vol. 2, fol. 162; Mercedes, vol. 11, fol. 92; vol. 84, fol. 126.

[169] AGN, General de parte, vol. 1, fols. 19v, 25, 55v, 245; vol. 2, fols. 96v, 135v, 149v, 158v, 245; Mercedes, vol. 11, fol. 2.

[170] AGI, Mexico, leg. 336, fol. 10.

[171] Tejada to king, Mar. 11, 1545; audiencia to king, Mar. 17, 1545; AGI, Mexico, leg. 68.

FIG. 11—GOBIERNO OF NUEVA GALICIA, 1786

and had the privilege of naming subordinate justices until it was taken from him in 1678.[172]

Meanwhile, Nueva Galicia suffered territorial losses, although most were of lands that had never been occupied. In 1562 a new gobierno, that of Nueva Vizcaya, was erected to administer the area beyond San Martin and Nombre de Dios. A dispute over the latter place was resolved by annexing it to Nueva España. In 1564–65 the provinces of Chiametla and Sinaloa were claimed by the governor of Nueva Vizcaya, and after 1620 the Avino area was transferred to the new gobierno. The mountain fastness of Nayarit, claimed by both Nueva Galicia and Nueva Vizcaya, was made a separate military province in 1722. The province of Culiacan continued to belong to Nueva Galicia until it was included in the new gobierno of Sinaloa in 1734. As finally constituted, Nueva Galicia covered the area now occupied by the states of Aguascalientes, Zacatecas, and parts of Jalisco, Nayarit, and San Luis Potosi.

Nueva Galicia belonged to the diocese of Michoacan until 1548, when a new bishopric was founded with its seat officially at Compostela. In 1560 both bishop and audiencia were authorized to change their residence to Guadalajara. The diocese of Guadalajara included Nueva Galicia, the westernmost part of Nueva España, Nueva Vizcaya, Nuevo Leon, and Nuevo Mexico. After 1620 it retained jurisdiction in Saltillo, Coahuila, Nuevo Leon, and Texas, but the rest of Nueva Vizcaya and the Sombrerete area were given to the new bishopric of Durango. Nayarit belonged to the diocese of Guadalajara, whereas California was long disputed with Durango. The jurisdiction of La Barca, politically in Nueva Galicia, belonged in part to the diocese of Michoacan until 1795.

At first local government in Nueva Galicia was handled informally by an occasional justicia or lieutenant of the governor. Compostela had a cabildo from 1532, and

Guadalajara from 1538. Most of the Indian villages were held in encomienda, and it was not until the first audiencia was installed that many of these places were taken for the Crown and corregimientos were first established. The decade of the 1550's saw the same conflict that occurred in Nueva España between powerful encomenderos and corregidores, until each Indian village was assigned to a corregimiento. In the period 1560–70 some 16 alcaldías mayores and 54 corregimientos were grouped into four *provincias* (Compostela, Culiacan, Guadalajara, La Purificacion) for intermediate supervision, corresponding to the system which prevailed in Nueva España in those years. By the early 17th century many corregimientos had been abolished and others were redesignated alcaldías mayores. In 1637 there were 23 alcaldías mayores and 26 corregimientos, 15 of the latter in the province of Culiacan. By 1786 the number had been reduced to 19 alcaldías mayores and only eight corregimientos.[173]

In the following section the history of each minor civil division in Nueva Galicia is summarized. Included are one jurisdiction (Juchipila) which had been annexed to another by 1786, and one minor gobierno (Colotlan) which was controlled by the viceroy. All are located by number, with approximate boundaries, in figure 11. The abbreviations and observations explained above under Nueva España apply here.

---

[172] Cédula of May 24, 1678, AGI, Indiferente, leg. 430.

[173] As with Nueva España, the main sources of this information and that in the following summaries are certain lists of jurisdictions, compiled from 1563 to 1793, as follows. 1563: ENE, 9: 196. 1570 and 1575: AGI, Guadalajara, leg. 5. 1582: RAH, MS 4662, doc. 11. About 1606: AGI, Guadalajara, leg. 56. 1621: Arregui, 1946. 1637–40: RAH, MS 4795. 1743: Villaseñor y Sánchez, 1746–48. 1777: NYPL, Phillips MS 15796. 1786; Orozco y Berra, 1881, pp. 333–34. 1793: AGI, Mexico, leg. 1973. The RG's (see Article 9) were also of use in plotting jurisdictional boundaries. In the notes which follow, reference to the above-mentioned sources is omitted.

POLITICAL JURISDICTIONS: HISTORICAL NOTES

1. ACAPONETA (AM)
Bish: Guadalajara
Int: Guadalajara
1950: Acaponeta, Nay.

Acaponeta and its subject villages, first held by an encomendero, became a C suffragan to the province of Compostela about 1565. The Cañas River was the northern boundary and frontier with Nueva Vizcaya. By 1582 the C of Acaponeta had become AM of the royal saltworks nearby. The eastern boundary was undefined until the military province of Nayarit was formed in 1722.

2. AGUACATLAN Y JALA (AM)
Bish: Guadalajara
Int: Guadalajara
1950: Ahuacatlan, Nay.

Originally this jurisdiction was divided among three separate C's all suffragan to Compostela: Aguacatlan, Xala, and Suchipila. They are listed as half Crown property in 1549 (PNE, 1: nos. 57, 824). Suchipila was annexed to Aguacatlan about 1580, and the two remaining C's were united under an AM early in the 17th century.

3. AGUASCALIENTES (AM)
Bish: Guadalajara
Int: Guadalajara
1950: Aguascalientes, Ags.

Aguascalientes, a Spanish settlement, was detached from Lagos and made a separate AM toward the beginning of the 17th century. The jurisdiction of Juchipila (q.v.) was administered jointly with Aguascalientes on several occasions. A nearby mining center, Los Asientos de Ibarra, is listed as an AM in 1740–70, but by 1773 it had been returned to Aguascalientes.

4. LA BARCA (AM)
Bish: Michoacan and Guadalajara
Int: Guadalajara
1950: La Barca, Jal.

Cuiseo and Poncitlan are listed as C's in 1549 (PNE, 1: no. 204). They were at first both in the diocese of Michoacan, but after 1548 most of Poncitlan was attached to the new bishopric of Compostela, the ecclesiastical boundary running through the center of the church. About 1580 the two C's were combined under an AM of Fuerte de San Lorenzo de los Reyes. By 1585 this name was no longer used, but Poncitlan y Cuiseo continued to have an AM. About 1650 La Barca became the capital of the jurisdiction.

5. CAJITITLAN (C)
Bish: Guadalajara
Int: Guadalajara
1950: Cajititlan, Jal.

The villages of Zalatitlan and Cuyutlan were Crown possessions in 1549 (PNE, 1: nos. 202–03). By 1563 they had been combined in a single C which included Cajititlan, which became the capital of the jurisdiction. After 1786 Cajititlan was combined with Tlajomulco.

6. CENTIPAC (AM)
Bish: Guadalajara
Int: Guadalajara
1950: Sentispac, Nay.

Centiquipaque (later shortened to Centipac), with subject villages in the Rio Grande delta, was held by the Crown in 1549 (PNE, 1: no. 184). In 1563–82 it appears as a C suffragan to the province of Compostela, but by 1637 it had become a separate AM. There was an ephemeral AM of Minas de Tenamache (Tinamaque) in this area in 1605–37, eventually divided between Centipac and Tepic.

7. COLOTLAN (G)
Bish: Guadalajara
Int: Guadalajara
1950: Colotlan, Jal.

At first in the jurisdiction of Tlaltenango, this area became important about 1740 when rich silver mines were discovered at Bolaños. A new AM of Colotlan, including both Bolaños and Tlaltenango, was created within a few years by the audiencia of Guadalajara, but in 1754 the viceroy named a C to administer justice in the mines. While the king assumed the right to appoint the C of Bolaños from 1760, the Colotlan area (minus Tlaltenango) was separated from Nueva Galicia and attached for military and administrative purposes to Nueva España. It was called "Gobierno de las Fronteras de San Luis de Colotlán," its governor appointed by the king and subordinate to the viceroy (Lemoine, 1964; Magdaleno, 1954, p. 110; Mecham, 1927, p. 72; Velázquez, 1961).

8. Cuquio (AM or C)
Bish: Guadalajara
Int: Guadalajara
1950: Cuquio, Jal.

The first two sites of Guadalajara were in this area, at or near Nochistlan (1531–33) and Tacotlan (1533–42). Governor Vázquez de Coronado in 1538 organized an ayuntamiento at the Tacotlan site, appointing *alcaldes ordinarios* and *regidores*.[174] In 1542 Guadalajara was moved to its final site, and a few years later the AM of Nueva Galicia appointed a *teniente* at Nochistlan, whose jurisdiction extended to Zacatecas. This official in 1549 became AM of Minas de Tepeque (Parry, 1948, p. 45). About 1570 the villages of Mexticacan y Juchitlan were removed from encomienda and made a C. By 1621 the AM of Tepeque had become AM of Tacotlan, which included Mexticacan; Nochistlan by that time had been transferred to the jurisdiction of Juchipila (q.v.). A century later Tacotlan and Nochistlan were in the AM now called Cuquio, but soon afterward Nochistlan was restored to Juchipila.

9. Charcas (AM)
Bish: Guadalajara
Int: San Luis Potosi
1950: Charcas, S.L.P.

An AM was first appointed to the mines of Las Charcas about 1575. In 1621–37 the magistrate resided at Minas de los Ramos, but soon afterward he returned to Charcas. His jurisdiction went from near Zacatecas northeast to Matehuala, where it met the gobierno of Nuevo Leon. About 1770 the villages of El Venado and La Hedionda were taken from Charcas and combined with the saltworks of Peñol Blanco in a new AM subordinate to Nueva España.

10. Fresnillo (AM)
Bish: Guadalajara
Int: Zacatecas
1950: Fresnillo, Zac.

At first in the jurisdiction of Zacatecas, Fresnillo was being administered by the AM of the royal saltworks of Peñol Blanco in 1570. Five years later it had been made a separate AM, which came to include all the territory from Valparaiso to Pozo Hondo (Lemoine, 1964).

11. Guadalajara (Ayuntamiento)
Bish: Guadalajara
Int: Guadalajara
1950: Guadalajara, Jal.

The first magistrate in this area was a C of Tonala appointed by the audiencia of Mexico in 1531 (ENE, 2: 113).[175] His jurisdiction was soon occupied by the adherents of Nuño de Guzmán. In 1542 Guadalajara was moved to its present site (cf. Cuquio). During the 16th century the surrounding villages of Analco, Atemaxaque, San Pedro Tlacpac, and Tonala were C's suffragan to Guadalajara. The first two became AM's (Analco, Zapopan) which eventually were annexed to the city, while Tonala (with San Pedro) remained an independent C (q.v.). From 1560 Guadalajara was the residence of the audiencia and the bishop.

---

[174] Governor to king, Dec. 16, 1538, AGI, Guadalajara, leg. 5.
[175] Audiencia to king, Aug. 5, 1533, Mexico, leg. 68; Patronato, leg. 183, doc. 9, ramo 2.

12. GUAUCHINANGO (AM)
Bish: Guadalajara
Int: Guadalajara
1950: Guachinango, Jal.

Although mines were discovered in this area perhaps as early as 1540, it is doubtful that there was an AM before 1549. In 1563–82 the AM of Minas de Guauchinango acted simultaneously as C of Atengoychan, and in the latter year he was also C of Tepuzuacan y Zacatlan, previously in the AM of Acuitlapilco (cf. Tequepespan). By 1605 these two C's had been absorbed by Guauchinango, as well as Mascota, which appears as a C in 1575–82.

13. HOSTOTIPAC (AM)
Bish: Guadalajara
Int: Guadalajara
1950: San Sebastian, Jal.

An AM was first appointed in Minas de Ostotiquipaque toward the end of the 16th century. His jurisdiction comprised four mining camps together with nearby Indian villages. By 1743 the AM was living at San Sebastian, by which name the jurisdiction appears in several lists.

14. HOSTOTIPAQUILLO (AM)
Bish: Guadalajara
Int: Guadalajara
1950: Hostotipaquillo, Jal.

The silver mines of Xocotlan y Guaxacatlan were discovered in the 1540's, but no AM seems to have been appointed until about 1565. Before that, justice in this area was administered by the C of Mochitiltique, an office which was absorbed by the AM. Jora, another mining center adjoining Xocotlan to the north, was made a separate AM in 1621, but later the two jurisdictions were combined under a single AM of Hostotipaquillo.

15. JEREZ (AM)
Bish: Guadalajara
Int: Zacatecas
1950: Ciudad Garcia Salinas, Zac.

This jurisdiction came into existence in 1570, when the villa of Xerez de la Frontera was settled and an AM was organized from part of Zacatecas together with the C of Tlaltenango (q.v.). In the 1740's Tlaltenango was transferred to the new jurisdiction of Colotlan, while Jerez continued to have its own AM.

16. (JUCHIPILA)
Bish: Guadalajara
Int: Guadalajara
1950: Juchipila, Zac.

At first exploited by encomenderos, the villages of the Juchipila valley began to come under Crown control about 1560 when the C of Mezquituta y Moyagua was created. By 1575 Suchipila (Juchipila) had also become a C, administered by the AM of Minas de Tepeque. Toward 1610 the two C's were united in a new AM of Juchipila, which also included Nochistlan and its sujetos. Later in the 17th century the jurisdiction was made subordinate to the AM of Aguascalientes (q.v.).

17. LAGOS (AM)
Bish: Guadalajara
Int: Guadalajara
1950: Lagos de Moreno, Jal.

An AM was first appointed by the audiencia in 1549 to govern the Llanos region (now called Los Altos de Jalisco) to the east of Guadalajara (Parry, 1948, p. 45). In 1561–63 this official established residence in the new villa of Santa Maria de los Lagos and acquired the additional title of C of Los Pueblos Llanos de Tecualtiche. At first his jurisdiction was very large, extending from the Rio Grande to Sierra de Pinos, but early in the 17th century parts were detached to form the C of Tecpatitlan and the AM's of Aguascalientes and Sierra de Pinos (q.v.).

The mines of Comanja had an AM appointed by the audiencia of Guadalajara from 1561, but his authority was disputed by the viceroy for some years. Eventually Comanja was annexed by the AM of Lagos. Teocaltiche also had its own AM for a period in the 18th century before being reunited with Lagos.

18. MAZAPIL (AM)
Bish: Guadalajara
Int: Zacatecas
1950: Mazapil, Zac.

The northernmost jurisdiction in Nueva Galicia, Minas de Mazapil became an AM at the time of or soon after its settlement in 1568. It was bounded by Nueva Vizcaya on the north.

19. LA PURIFICACION (AM)
Bish: Guadalajara
Int: Guadalajara
1950: Purificacion, Jal.

The villa of La Purificacion, at first governed by its ayuntamiento, was the southernmost jurisdiction in Nueva Galicia, bounded by Autlan (Nueva España) on the southeast and Cape Corrientes on the northwest. It included many Indian villages which were grouped into three suffragan C's: Opono (from about 1550), Panpuchin (about 1565), and Piloto (about 1565). These were absorbed by the AM toward the end of the 16th century.

20. SAN CRISTOBAL DE LA BARRANCA (C)
Bish: Guadalajara
Int: Guadalajara
1950: San Cristobal de la Barranca, Jal.

The Crown villages near Guadalajara to the northwest were organized in three C's, first (from about 1550) Camotlan and Cuzcatitlan, and somewhat later (by 1563) Copala y Quilitlan. The first two were united before 1570 in a single C, to which Copala was added by 1606. From this time the jurisdiction was called San Cristobal de la Barranca.

21. SIERRA DE PINOS (AM)
Bish: Guadalajara
Int: Zacatecas

1950: Pinos, Zac.

Mines were discovered in the Sierra de Pinos, then part of the jurisdiction of Lagos, in 1603 (Chevalier, 1952, p. 43). Two years later a separate AM had been appointed (Mota y Escobar, 1940, p. 158). At times the area was listed as subordinate to the AM of Charcas.

22. SOMBRERETE (AM)
Bish: Durango
Int: Zacatecas
1950: Sombrerete, Zac.

In 1555 the silver deposits of San Martin began to be exploited by miners from Zacatecas, to which the area was subject until (by 1570) a separate AM was appointed. The new jurisdiction came to be known as Villa de Llerena y minas de Sombrerete, and included the Avino area to the north until this was annexed to Nueva Vizcaya (sometime after 1621).

23. TALA (C)
Bish: Guadalajara
Int: Guadalajara
1950: Tala, Jal.

Nochistlanejo, with its dependencies Ahuesculco and Nexticpac near Guadalajara to the west, was among the first C's created by the audiencia, perhaps in 1549. By 1605 the jurisdiction began to be called Tlala, and later, Tala.

24. TECPATITLAN (C)
Bish: Guadalajara
Int: Guadalajara
1950: Tepatitlan de Morelos, Jal.

Amatatlan (Matatlan), with its estancias of Atengo, Coliman (Colimilla), and San Juan, was a Crown possession by 1549 (PNE, 1: no. 67). In 1621 it appears as a C, Matatlan y Colimilla, whose jurisdiction extended to some of the Llanos villages previously subject to Lagos. The capital of the C was moved first to Jonacatlan and later (by 1740) to Tecpatitlan (González Navarro, 1953, pp. 40, 71).

25. Tepic (AM)
Bish: Guadalajara
Int: Guadalajara
1950: Tepic, Nay.

Compostela, the oldest Spanish settlement in Nueva Galicia, was founded by Nuño de Guzmán at or near the site of modern Tepic probably in late 1531. The residence of the governor, it had an ayuntamiento with alcaldes ordinarios from 1532.[176] The city was moved to its present site about 1540, and its jurisdiction extended from Cape Corrientes northward to join that of Culiacan until 1564–65, when the Cañas River became the boundary with Nueva Vizcaya. The province was first divided among encomenderos, but after the audiencia was organized in Compostela (early 1549) certain villages were taken for the Crown and C's were created. The earliest of these were Centipac, Tepic, Aguacatlan, Suchipil, and Jala. By 1563 additional C's had come into existence at Pontoque, San Juan Ixtapa (Xalxocotlan), Santiago Ixtapa, and Temichoque. Twelve years later the C's of Acaponeta, Xalisco, and San Miguel had been added to the list of jurisdictions suffragan to what was now called the AM of Compostela y las Minas del Espiritu Santo. Each had its own magistrate except Tepic, which was administered by the AM. Early in the 17th century, Acaponeta, Aguacatlan y Jala, and Centipac had become separate AM's, while the remaining C's disappeared, absorbed by the AM of Compostela. Not long afterward the AM moved to Tepic (Páez Brotchie, 1940, p. 40).

26. Tequepespan (AM)
Bish: Guadalajara
Int: Guadalajara
1950: Santa Maria del Oro, Nay.

Probably in the late 1560's an AM was

[176] AGI, Guadalajara, leg. 46, ramo 1.

114

first appointed to the mines of Acuitlapilco and the adjoining C of Tepuzuacan y Zacatlan. By 1582 this official had moved to the newer mining center of Chimaltitlan (at or near Santa Maria del Oro), and ruled a jurisdiction bounded on the east and north by the Rio Grande and on the west by Compostela. Tepuzuacan, to the south, had been transferred to the AM of Guauchinango. Later, in the 18th century, the jurisdiction was called Santa Maria Tequepespan.

27. Tequila (C)
Bish: Guadalajara
Int: Guadalajara
1950: Tequila, Jal.

In 1563 the AM of Minas de Xocotlan was also C of Tequila and its dependencies. Seven years later Tequila was a separate C with its own magistrate, a situation which continued until 1786 and later.

28. Tlajomulco (C)
Bish: Guadalajara
Int: Guadalajara
1950: Tlajomulco de Zuñiga, Jal.

Tlajomulco with subject villages adjoining Guadalajara to the south probably became a C in 1549–50 and continued without change until 1786, after which it was joined with Cajititlan (q.v.) in a single partido.

29. Tlaltenango (AM)
Bish: Guadalajara
Int: Zacatecas
1950: Sanchez Roman, Zac.

Sometime between 1549 and 1563 the Indian town of Tlaltenango and its subject villages were taken from encomienda and made a C. The jurisdiction, which came to include the valley of Teul to the south, was administered by the AM of Xerez from 1570 to about 1740, when it was annexed to the new AM of Colotlan. By 1786 Tlaltenango was again a separate jurisdiction.

30. TONALA (C)

Bish: Guadalajara
Int: Guadalajara
1950: Tonala, Jal.

The early history of this jurisdiction is summarized under Guadalajara (q.v.). The C's of Tonala and San Pedro Tlacpac (Tlaquepaque) were probably created in 1549. Sometime between 1640 and 1700 they were united in a single C (González Navarro, 1953, p. 199).

31. ZACATECAS (C)

Bish: Guadalajara
Int: Zacatecas
1950: Zacatecas, Zac.

The newly settled mining camp of Zacatecas received its first AM, appointed by the audiencia of Nueva Galicia, in 1548 (Parry, 1948, p. 45). From 1580 the AM was replaced by a C appointed by the king on recommendation of the Council of the Indies. After 1786 Zacatecas was the residence of an intendant-corregidor.

III. NUEVA VIZCAYA

In June, 1562, Francisco de Ibarra began the occupation of the northern and hitherto unsettled part of Nueva Galicia, which was made a separate gobierno with the name of Nueva Vizcaya. Durango, also known as Guadiana, became the seat of government in 1563. The new jurisdiction comprised all of the country beyond San Martin and Mazapil, but before it was clearly defined there were several early boundary disputes with Nueva Galicia. Nombre de Dios shifted back and forth between the two gobiernos until, by 1579, it was annexed to Nueva España. At the end of 1563 the Spanish settlements extended northward to Santa Barbara, and in the following year the coastal areas of Chiametla and Sinaloa, both claimed by Nueva Galicia, were occupied by Ibarra and annexed to his jurisdiction. This left the province of Culiacan still part of Nueva Galicia but separated from it by an intrusion of Nueva Vizcaya. By 1580 Parras and Saltillo had been added and there was a settlement even farther north, at Cuatro Cienegas. The latter was soon abandoned, and the region was disputed between Nueva Vizcaya and Nuevo Leon until another gobierno, that of Coahuila, was set up in 1687. In 1598 the gobierno of Nuevo Mexico was organized to the north. Sinaloa and Sonora were gradually occupied in the 16th and 17th centuries by Jesuit missionaries. In 1734 these provinces, together with Culiacan and Chiametla, were made a separate gobierno, Sinaloa. Finally, the jurisdictions of Parras and Saltillo were transferred to Coahuila in 1787. This left Nueva Vizcaya, considerably reduced, with a territory corresponding to that of the modern states of Durango and most of Chihuahua.

After 1573 Nueva Vizcaya came under the judicial authority of the audiencia of Guadalajara (Mecham. 1927, p. 197). Its governor was subordinate in military matters to the viceroy until 1777 when the Provincias Internas were organized. From 1786 the governor of Nueva Vizcaya became governor-intendant of Durango. In the same year the alcaldes mayores who had managed matters of local administration were redesignated subdelegados.

The official capital of Nueva Vizcaya was always Durango, but the governors resided in Parral from 1633 to 1739 (Tamarón, 1937, p. 127).

Nueva Vizcaya fell within the diocese of Guadalajara until 1620, when the see of Durango or Guadiana was constituted. This new bishopric included not only Nueva Vizcaya (with the exception of Parras and Saltillo, which remained under the bishop of Guadalajara), but also Sonora, Sinaloa, New Mexico, and the Sombrerete area of Nueva Galicia. California was claimed by Durango but awarded to the diocese of Guadalajara in 1681.

The alcaldías mayores of Nueva Vizcaya as they were in 1786 are listed below with

115

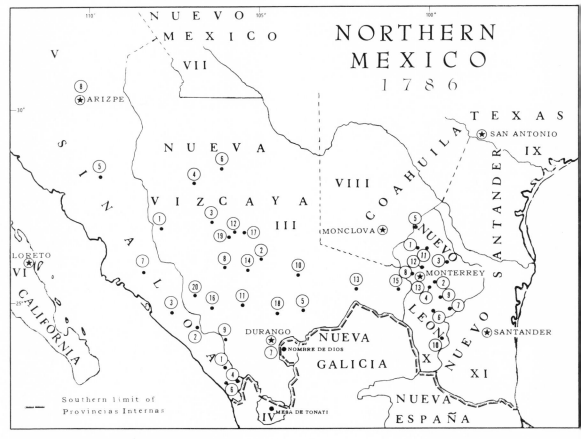

F<small>IG.</small> 12—NORTHERN MEXICO, 1786
Roman and arabic numerals refer to text.

brief historical references. All were in the intendancy of Durango from that year. They are located by number in figure 12.[177]

P<small>OLITICAL</small> J<small>URISDICTIONS</small>: H<small>ISTORICAL</small> N<small>OTES</small>

1. B<small>ATOPILAS</small>
   1950: Batopilas, Chih.

This mining camp in the Chinipas area had a bonanza in the years 1730–50 (Tamarón, 1937, p. 177). The region until then had belonged to Sinaloa, but toward the end of this period it was made an AM within Nueva Vizcaya, called San Pedro Batopilas or San Joaquin de los Arrieros. About 1750 another rich mine

[177] In the following notes, references to the 18th-century RG's (listed in Article 10) are omitted.

116

was discovered nearby, Santisima Trinidad del Oro de Topago, and this was for a time a separate AM, but finally was absorbed by Batopilas.

2. C<small>ERRO</small> G<small>ORDO</small>
   1950: Villa Hidalgo, Dgo.

The presidio of Cerro Gordo, founded in the 17th century, was an AM which included a number of nearby villages and haciendas (Bancroft, 1884–89, 1: 644n.; Lafora, 1958, pp. 8, 64; Tamarón, 1937, pp. 120, 125).

3. C<small>IENEGA DE LOS</small> O<small>LIVOS</small>
   1950: Valle de Olivos, Chih.

At first in the jurisdiction of Santa Barbara, Cienega de los Olivos became a separate AM toward the end of the 18th century (Bancroft, 1884–89, 1: 644, 655n.; Tamarón, 1937, p. 133).

4. COSIHUIRIACHIC
1950: Cosihuiriachic, Chih.

Mines were discovered in this area about 1670, and somewhat later an AM was appointed with a large jurisdiction including many Indian mission villages (Bancroft, 1884–89, 1: 644, 654; Lafora, 1958, p. 132).

5. CUENCAME
1950: Cuencame de Ceniceros, Dgo.

An AM was first appointed here at the beginning of the 17th century. In later years the jurisdiction of Mapimi (q.v.) was annexed (Bancroft, 1884–89, 1: 644; Borah, 1955, p. 401; Mota y Escobar, 1940, p. 195; Vázquez de Espinosa, 1948, p. 179).[178]

6. CHIHUAHUA
1950: Chihuahua, Chih.

An AM may have been appointed at San Felipe el Real de Chihuahua as early as 1703. From 1719 the villa, a fast-growing mining camp, had a C appointed from Spain. The jurisdiction may have included Conchos and Julimes, both listed as separate partidos in 1789 (Bancroft, 1884–89, 1: 599, 644; Magdaleno, 1954, p. 110; Tamarón, 1937, p. 153).

7. DURANGO
1950: Victoria de Durango, Dgo.

Durango (Guadiana), the capital of Nueva Vizcaya, was governed by its ayuntamiento from 1563. The jurisdiction covered a number of villages and extended south to the borders of Nayarit. During the governor's absence (notably in 1633–1739, when he resided in Parral) a *teniente de gobernador* stayed in Durango (Bancroft, 1884–89, 1: 104, 644;

Mota y Escobar, 1940, p. 191; Tamarón, 1937, p. 127).

8. GUANACEVI
1950: Guanacevi, Dgo.

A separate AM was created in this mining center, until then subject to Indehe, toward the beginning of the 17th century (Bancroft, 1884–89, 1: 644; Borah, 1955, p. 401; Mota y Escobar, 1940, pp. 202–03; Vázquez de Espinosa, 1948, p. 260).[179]

9. GUARIZAME
1950: Guarisamey, Dgo.

Rich mines were discovered here in 1784, and an AM was soon appointed (Bancroft, 1884–89, 1: 644; Tamarón, 1937, pp. 64, 73).

10. MAPIMI
1950: Mapimi, Dgo.

The mines of Santiago de Mapimi were first exploited toward the end of the 16th century, and an AM was appointed. On at least one occasion Mapimi was annexed to Cuencame, but it was a separate jurisdiction in 1786 (Bancroft, 1884–89, 1: 597, 644; Borah, 1955, p. 401; Mota y Escobar, 1940, p. 196; Vázquez de Espinosa, 1948, p. 180).[180]

11. PAPASQUIARO
1950: Santiago Papasquiaro, Dgo.

At first in the jurisdiction of San Juan del Rio, Santiago Papasquiaro was an AM after it became a mining camp in the 18th century (Bancroft, 1884–89, 1: 644; Borah, 1955, p. 401; Tamarón, 1937, p. 93).[181]

12. PARRAL
1950: Hidalgo del Parral, Chih.

The important mining center of San Jose del Parral, until then administered from Santa Barbara, had its own AM from 1631. Two years later it became the residence of the governor of Nueva Vizcaya, but after 1739 AM's were again appointed (Bancroft, 1884–89, 1: 644; Ri-

---

[178] AGI, Indiferente, leg. 102. BNMA, MS 3047.
[179] Ibid.
[180] Ibid.
[181] AGI, Indiferente, leg. 102.

117

vera, 1736; Tamarón, 1937, pp. 124, 127; West, 1949, pp. 12–13).[182]

13. PARRAS

1950: Parras de la Fuente, Coah.

Valle del Pirineo, or Santa Maria de las Parras, had an AM from 1578 to 1580, was abandoned until 1598, and thereafter again had an AM. The jurisdiction included the Laguna area and probably Guanabal (Aguanaval), a mining camp listed as an AM in 1632–40. From 1787 Parras belonged to Coahuila (Alessio Robles, 1938, p. 141; Bancroft, 1884–89, 1: 125; Borah, 1955, p. 401; Lafora, 1958, p. 137; Mota y Escobar, 1940, pp. 164–67; Saravia, 1930, p. 262; Tamarón, 1937, pp. 18, 109–10, 213).[183]

14. REAL DEL ORO

1950: Santa Maria del Oro, Dgo.

The first AM was appointed to the mines of Indehe (Inde) in 1567. In the 18th century the capital of the jurisdiction had become the nearby Real del Oro (Bancroft, 1884–89, 1: 106, 644; Borah, 1955, p. 401; Mota y Escobar, 1940, p. 198; Saravia, 1930, p. 199; Tamarón, 1937, p. 119; Vázquez de Espinosa, 1948, p. 260).[184]

15. SALTILLO

1950: Saltillo, Coah.

A Spanish settlement was founded at El Saltillo in 1577, at which time the first AM was appointed. Ojos de Santa Lucia (Monterrey) was considered part of this jurisdiction for a few years until it was annexed to the gobierno of Nuevo Leon. From 1787 Saltillo belonged to Coahuila (Borah, 1955, p. 401; Mota y Escobar, 1940, pp. 162–63; Saravia, 1930, pp. 262–63).[185]

16. SAN ANDRES

1950: San Andres de la Sierra, Dgo.

Mines were opened here in 1581, and an AM was appointed soon afterward. Another AM, that of San Jose de Basis, existed in this area for some years after

1763, and may have been absorbed by San Andres (Bancroft, 1884–89, 1: 644; Borah, 1955, p. 401; Mota y Escobar, 1940, p. 206; Tamarón, 1937, p. 68; Vázquez de Espinosa, 1948, p. 260).[186]

17. SAN BARTOLOME

1950: Allende, Chih.

At first in the jurisdiction of Santa Barbara, Valle de San Bartolome became a separate AM in the 17th century (Bancroft, 1884–89, 1: 644; Lafora, 1958, p. 65; West, 1949, p. 11).[187]

18. SAN JUAN DEL RIO

1950: San Juan del Rio, Dgo.

Two AM's existed in this region in the 16th century and later, San Juan del Rio and Minas de Coneto. Sometime after 1640 Coneto was absorbed by San Juan (Bancroft, 1884–89, 1: 644; Borah, 1955, p. 401; DII, 16: 564–68; Mota y Escobar, 1940, p. 197).[188]

19. SANTA BARBARA

1950: Santa Barbara, Chih.

This mining center acquired its first AM in the 1570's. The jurisdiction at first was very large, and from it were formed the AM's of Parral, Cosihuiriachic, San Bartolome, Chihuahua, and Cienega de los Olivos (Bancroft, 1884–89, 1: 106, 644; Borah, 1955, p. 401; Mota y Escobar, 1940, p. 198; Vázquez de Espinosa, 1948, pp. 179, 260).[189]

20. SIANORI

1950: Sianori, Dgo.

The first AM in this area lived at the mines of Topia, which began to be ex-

[182] Ibid.
[183] AGI, Mexico, leg. 31. BNMA, MSS 3047, 4532.
[184] AGI, Mexico, leg. 216. BNMA, MS 3047.
[185] BNMA, MSS 3047, 4532.
[186] AGI, Indiferente, leg. 102. BNMA, MS 3047.
[187] AGI, Indiferente, leg. 102.
[188] BNMA, MS 3047.
[189] AGI, Guadalajara, leg. 34; Mexico, leg. 216. BNMA, MS 3047.

ploited in the 1580's. Sometime between 1640 and 1740 the capital of the jurisdiction was moved to Sianori (Bancroft, 1884–89, 1: 107, 644; Borah, 1955, p. 401; Mota y Escobar, 1940, p. 205; Ocaranza, 1937–39, 1: 138; Tamarón, 1937, p. 79; Vázquez de Espinosa, 1948, p. 179; West and Parsons, 1941, p. 408).[190]

PROVINCIAS INTERNAS

During the last 45 years of the colony, from 1776 to 1821, the northern frontier provinces were the scene of various experiments in administrative reorganization. The gobiernos of Nueva Vizcaya, Sinaloa, California, Nuevo Mexico, Coahuila, Texas, Nuevo Leon, and Nuevo Santander (some of which were later excluded) formed what were called the Provincias Internas, at times under a single *comandante general*, at others divided into two or three *comandancias*. Originally intended to be independent of the viceroyalty in administrative and military matters, the commandant-generals for most of this period were in fact still subordinate to the viceroy and further shared their powers in a confusing overlapping of jurisdictions with audiencias, governors, and intendants. The southern boundary of Provincias Internas is shown in figure 12; see also Article 3.

IV. NAYARIT

This small inland province, also called Nuevo Reino de Toledo, was an Indian refuge along the border between Nueva Galicia and Nueva Vizcaya, unconquered by the Spaniards until 1722. In that year a military government was established, with a *capitán comandante* (often referred to as governor) appointed by the viceroy. He was subordinate to the viceroy in military matters, to Nueva Galicia in political affairs, and to the audiencia of Guadalajara in matters of justice. The boundary with Nueva Vizcaya on the north passed just south of Huazamota. To the east and south the Atengo

and Santiago rivers separated Nayarit from Nueva Galicia; the limit on the west was the San Pedro River. The capital was the presidio of Mesa del Tonati. By 1784 Nayarit was attached as a subordinate gobierno to Nueva Vizcaya, but two years later it was included in the intendancy of Guadalajara. Ecclesiastically, it belonged to the diocese of Guadalajara. It occupied what is now the northeast corner of the state of Nayarit (Bancroft, 1883–86, 3: 297; 1884–89, 1: 518–19; Lafora, 1958, p. 209; Villaseñor y Sánchez, 1746–48, 2: 268–71).[191]

V. SINALOA

Previous to 1734 this area was shared between the gobiernos of Nueva Vizcaya and Nueva Galicia. In that year a separate gobierno was organized, known as San Felipe y Santiago de Sinaloa. It comprised the New Galician province of Culiacan, plus the alcaldías mayores of El Rosario, Copala, San Benito, Sinaloa, Ostimuri, and Sonora, until then all subordinate to Nueva Vizcaya. The area was more or less equivalent to the modern states of Sonora and Sinaloa, with small portions of Arizona and Chihuahua.

At first the official capital was the villa of Sinaloa, but the governors resided most of the time in the north, at San Juan Bautista, Pitic, Alamos, or San Miguel Horcasitas, until finally the seat of government was fixed at Arizpe. The governor became an intendant from 1768, but it was not until 1788 that the intendancy of Arizpe was formally constituted. From 1777 Sinaloa formed part of the Provincias Internas (see above).

Sinaloa belonged to the bishopric of Guadalajara until 1620, when it was made part of the new diocese of Durango. In 1779 a papal bull authorized the formation of a bishopric of Sonora, with jurisdiction in

[190] BNMA, MS 3047.
[191] AGI, Guadalajara, legs. 144, 401. BNP, Fonds mexicains, MS 201, fols. 1–11; MS 258.

Sinaloa and California. The first bishop arrived at Arizpe on May 1, 1783. Later the episcopal seat was moved to Alamos.

Local government in this area began with the Spanish settlement of San Miguel de Culiacan in 1531. The suffragan corregimientos in that province are mentioned below. Elsewhere alcaldes mayores were appointed by the governor of Nueva Vizcaya until 1734, and afterward by the governor of Sinaloa, except when this privilege was assumed by the king. Below is a list of the minor civil jurisdictions as they were in 1786, just before they were incorporated as subdelegaciones in the intendancy of Arizpe, with brief historical notes on each. They are located by number in figure 13.

POLITICAL JURISDICTIONS: HISTORICAL NOTES

1. COPALA

1950: Copala, Sin.

The villa of San Sebastian (modern Concordia), founded in 1565, at first had jurisdiction over all the country between the Cañas and Elota rivers, an area known as the province of Chiametla. Toward the end of the 16th century a separate AM was created in the south (cf. Maloya). By 1633 a number of AM's are listed in this region: Piastla y Mazatlan, Chiametla y Salinas, Minas de Maloya, Villa de San Sebastian, and Minas de Panico y San Bartolome. After 1655, when a mining settlement was established at El Rosario (q.v.), the AM of Chiametla moved there, and perhaps about the same time Piastla, San Sebastian, and Panico were combined under a single AM with residence in Copala (Bancroft, 1884–89; 1: 206, 547; Ocaranza, 1937–39, 1: 136; Villaseñor y Sánchez, 1746–48, 2: 379–81).[192]

2. COSALA

1950: Cosala, Sin.

A separate AM is listed in 1582–1637 for Minas de las Virgenes, although this area was considered subordinate to Culiacan. Long afterward (between 1750 and 1777) the mining camp of Las Once Mil Virgenes de Cosala, together with other villages, was detached and made a separate AM (López de Velasco, 1894, p. 276).[193]

3. CULIACAN

1950: Culiacan, Sin.

The villa of San Miguel de Culiacan, founded by Nuño de Guzmán, seems to have been ruled by its ayuntamiento until 1545, when an AM was appointed by the audiencia of Mexico. The privilege of naming this official passed to the audiencia of Guadalajara in 1549, was assumed by the king in 1691–1708, returned to the governor of Nueva Galicia, and from 1734 devolved on the governor of Sinaloa. The Indian villages in the province gradually passed from encomienda to Crown control and were given to local settlers as corregimientos, all suffragan to the AM of Culiacan. By 1550 there were six C's: Ayone y Miltotone, Cogota,* Culiacan,* Tecuberito, Tecurimeto,* and Vayla.* By 1582 the number had increased to 20, with the addition of Acalo,* Acatitlan y Natuato, Achiotla, Cosala, Cuatro Barrios, Chilovito,* Hulahuerito,* Navito,* Navolato,* Oguani y Xifa,* Quila y las Flechas, Tacolimbo,* Vizcaino y Mexcaltitlan,* and Yevavito.* Those marked with an asterisk were still in existence as late as 1637, along with three others, Cuspita, El Osso, and Tlaye y Guzmanillo. Eventually all these C's were absorbed by the AM. The mining region of Cosala (q.v.) occupied a special position and eventually was separated from Culiacan (Arregui, 1946, pp. 104–07; Bancroft, 1883–86, 2: 264; López de Velasco, 1894, p. 276; Magdaleno, 1954, p. 113; Ocaranza, 1937–39, 1: 136; PNE, 1:

[192] AGI, Indiferente, leg. 102; leg. 107, vol. 1, fols. 302–309v; Mexico, leg. 1973. BNMA, MS 3047. BNP, Fonds mexicains, MS 201.

[193] AGI, Indiferente, legs. 102, 1526; Mexico, legs. 68, 1973. BNMA, MS 3047. RAH, MS 4662, doc. 11.

nos. 71–81, 211–15, 246–47, 253, 279, 290, 413–14, 469–70, 484, 720–24, 789–90, 830; Villaseñor y Sánchez, 1746–48, 2: 381–83).[194]

4. MALOYA

1950: Maloya, Sin.

Once in the province of Chiametla (cf. Copala), Minas de Maloya appears from 1604 as a separate jurisdiction with its own AM (Borah, 1955, p. 401; Mota y Escobar, 1940, p. 85; Ocaranza, 1937–39, 1: 136; Villaseñor y Sánchez, 1746–48, 2: 379.[195]

5. OSTIMURI

1950: Rio Chico, Son.

The province of San Ildefonso de Ostimuri, at first in the jurisdiction of Sonora, had its own AM from the late 17th century. It was bounded by the Yaqui and Mayo rivers, although at times it seems to have included the Alamos area. The capital was the mining camp of Rio Chico (Villaseñor y Sánchez, 1746–48, 2: 387–90).[196]

6. EL ROSARIO

1950: Rosario, Son.

The history of the province of Chiametla is sketched above (cf. Copala). El Rosario became an important mining center (about 1655) and the residence of the AM of Chiametla (Borah, 1955, p. 401; Magdaleno, 1954, p. 128; Mota y Escobar, 1940, pp. 86–91; Tamarón, 1937, p. 202; Vázquez de Espinosa, 1948, p. 180; Villaseñor y Sánchez, 1746–48, 2: 377–79).[197]

7. SINALOA

1950: Sinaloa de Leyva, Sin.

A settlement called San Juan Bautista de Sinaloa was established by the governor of Nueva Vizcaya in 1564 at the site of what is now El Fuerte. While the outpost had a precarious existence for several years and had to move about because of Indian hostility, it was re-established permanently at its final site (San Felipe y Santiago) in 1583. The com-

mander of the garrison was also AM and was often referred to as "governor," although he did not rightly have this title until 1734. During the 17th century Ostimuri and Sonora were detached and made separate AM's; California for a time was included in the jurisdiction of Sinaloa. After 1734 the town of Sinaloa and its subject territory was ruled in the absence of the governor by a lieutenant who was also justicia mayor. There was a dispute over jurisdiction in the Chinipas region, which was divided about 1750 between Nueva Vizcaya and Sinaloa. Later the administrative center moved to Alamos (Bancroft, 1884–89, 1: 113–14, 207, 255, 272, 520–21; Mota y Escobar, 1940, pp. 108–09; Pompa y Pompa, 1960, pp. 151, 214; Saravia, 1930, pp. 144, 154, 197, 206–07; Sauer, 1932, pp. 39–40; Tamarón, 1937, p. 233; Vázquez de Espinosa, 1948, pp. 180, 260).[198]

8. SONORA

1950: Arizpe, Son.

The province of Nueva Andalucia or Sonora was organized with its capital at San Juan Bautista in 1641 and may have had an AM continuously from that date, although on later occasions it was considered subordinate to the AM of Sinaloa. After 1734 Sonora continued as an AM in the gobierno of Sinaloa, the governor generally residing in the northern province. The capital moved to San Miguel Horcasitas in 1751, and to Arizpe in 1783 (Bancroft, 1884–89, 1: 232–33, 255,

---

[194] AGI, Guadalajara, leg. 5; Indiferente, leg. 102; Mexico, legs. 68, 1973. BNMA, MS 3047. RAH, MSS 4662, doc. 11, and 4795; Muñoz, A/113.

[195] AGI, Indiferente, leg. 102; Mexico, leg. 1973. BNMA, MS 3047.

[196] AGI, Mexico, leg. 1973. BNP, Fonds mexicains, MS 201.

[197] AGI, Guadalajara, leg. 34; Mexico, leg. 1973. BNMA, MS 3047. BNP, Fonds mexicains, MS 201, fol. 69.

[198] AGI, Guadalajara, leg. 117; Mexico, legs. 607, 1973. BNMA, MS 3047. BNP, Fonds mexicains, MS 201, fol. 29.

272, 517, 520–21; Pompa y Pompa, 1960, p. 151).[199]

VI. CALIFORNIAS

By the terms of his 1529 agreement with the Spanish Crown, Hernando Cortés was granted the government of any lands that he might discover in the Pacific. Accordingly, when he arrived at Santa Cruz in Lower California on May 3, 1535, Cortés proclaimed himself governor of the colony. He took the further precaution of leaving an alcalde mayor in the settlement when he returned to New Spain (Bancroft, 1883–86, 2: 312; Cortés, 1963, p. 546; Puga, 1563, fol. 36).[200] Santa Cruz was abandoned in late 1536 or early 1537, and although there were further attempts to establish Spanish control during the next 160 years, none of them had any permanent effect. In 1599 Sebastián Vizcaíno was granted California in encomienda "for three lives," and his grandson still laid claim to the fief as late as 1681 (Portillo, 1947, p. 186).[201] Nicolás de Cardona (in 1634) and Manuel de Sousa (in 1678) offered to colonize the peninsula if the king would entrust them with its government, but their proposals were rejected (Portillo, 1947, p. 238).[202] For a time, beginning in the 1640's and culminating in the voyages of Atondo y Antillón in 1683–89, the still unreduced Californias were placed within the jurisdiction of Sinaloa (Bayle, 1933, p. 96; Pérez de Ribas, 1645, pp. 441–42; Portillo, 1947, p. 277).

In October, 1697, the Jesuits began the permanent occupation of California, founding the first Spanish settlement at Loreto. From then until 1767 the government, both spiritual and temporal, was left to the Jesuit missionaries. During this period there was a *capitán comandante* (sometimes referred to as governor) in charge of police matters, who although subordinate to the viceroy, in fact acted under the orders of the Jesuit father superior. As there were few lay Spaniards in the peninsula, appeal to the audiencia of Guadalajara, in whose jurisdiction California belonged, was rarely if ever resorted to (Chapman, 1939, pp. 174–76).[203] From 1767 California was ruled by governors commissioned by the Crown who at first resided at Loreto. For administrative purposes the peninsula was divided into two *departamentos*, Norte and Sur, with the boundary between San Luis Gonzaga and San Javier. A lieutenant-governor was stationed at Santa Ana, in the southern portion.[204] In 1777 the governor moved to Monterrey, in Upper California, leaving a deputy in Loreto. The boundary between the two Californias, as fixed in 1788, extended from the Pacific coast at Arroyo del Rosarito to the Gulf at the mouth of the Colorado (Meigs, 1935, pp. 111, 113).

From 1776 to 1793 the Californias were subordinate in administrative and military matters to the Provincias Internas, but subsequently they came under the command of the viceroy. Locally, all branches of government were handled by the governor and his deputies. Ayuntamientos were installed in the Spanish settlements in 1794 (Chapman, 1939, pp. 324, 347, 389–95; Haring, 1947, p. 145). The Californias fell first within the diocese of Mexico, then (from 1548) in that of Guadalajara, although ecclesiastical jurisdiction was disputed for many years after 1620 between the latter see and the diocese of Durango. Finally, upon the erection of a bishopric in Sonora in 1781, the Californias were attached to it.

In 1848 most of Upper California was annexed to the United States. Lower California, part of Mexico, is now divided be-

[199] AGI, Guadalajara, leg. 119; Mexico, leg. 1973.
[200] AGI, Patronato, leg. 21, doc. 2, ramo 4.
[201] Bishop of Guadalajara to king, July 27, 1681, AGI, Guadalajara, leg. 38.
[202] AGI, Guadalajara, leg. 1; Mexico, leg. 51.
[203] "Empressas apostólicas . . . por el P. Miguel Venegas," MS in Asociación Histórica Americanista, San Angel, D.F.
[204] AGN, "Archivo del Colegio de San Fernando," tomo 3.

tween a state (Baja California) and a federal territory (Baja California Sur).

VII. NUEVO MEXICO

Nuevo Mexico was taken possession of by the Spaniards and became a gobierno in April, 1598. For most of its history it was a military province, the governor being subordinate to the viceroy. The capital, first at San Juan de los Caballeros, was moved to Santa Fe in 1609. During the Indian uprising of 1680–96 it was at El Paso del Norte. The boundary with Nueva Vizcaya passed midway between Carrizal and Ojo Caliente, and on the southwest followed the Santa Maria River (Tamarón, 1937, p. 327). Most of this area is now in the state of New Mexico, but the southern part is divided between Texas and Chihuahua.

For a while after 1690 Nuevo Mexico was subordinate to the audiencia of Guadalajara, but at other times it belonged to that of Mexico. It was part of the Provincias Internas from 1776. It fell within the diocese of Guadalajara until 1620, after which it was in the bishopric of Durango.

VIII. COAHUILA

This area, also called Nuevo Almaden and Nueva Extremadura, was for many years disputed between rival groups of Spaniards. Claimed by Luis de Carvajal as part of his grant of Nuevo Leon, it had AM's appointed by the governor of Nueva Vizcaya in 1582 (Cuatro Cienagas) and again from 1643; in 1674 the appointment was made by the audiencia of Guadalajara. In 1682 it was decided to form a separate gobierno, the first royal governor arriving in October, 1687, and establishing residence in the town of San Miguel de Luna, later called Monclova. The new province was bounded on the southeast by Nuevo Leon and on the southwest by Nueva Vizcaya (it was not until 1787 that Saltillo and Parras were acquired from Nueva Vizcaya). To the north

the limits were at first undefined and included Texas until a separate governor was appointed for that province in 1722. The boundary between Coahuila and Texas was the Medina (San Antonio) River (Alessio Robles, 1938, pp. 72, 107, 184, 201, 233, 302, 474; Lafora, 1958, pp. 154–56, 190; Villaseñor y Sánchez, 1746–48, 2: 306–10).

From 1776 Coahuila formed part of the Provincias Internas, and from 1786 it was subject to the intendancy of San Luis Potosi, but it continued to have its own governor. There was a long-standing jurisdictional dispute over Coahuila between the audiencias of Mexico and Guadalajara, which was finally settled in favor of the latter. Local government, except for the cabildos of the few Spanish settlements, seems to have been handled directly by the governor, with deputies in the various presidios. Coahuila belonged to the diocese of Guadalajara until 1777, when it was included in the new bishopric of Linares (Alessio Robles, 1938, p. 595; Bancroft, 1884–89, 1: 605). The area today forms the state of Coahuila and part of Texas.

IX. TEXAS

The province of Texas (Tejas), otherwise known as Nuevas Filipinas, belonged to the gobierno of Coahuila until 1722, after which it was administered as a separate jurisdiction with its own governor. The boundary with Coahuila and Nuevo Santander was the Medina River, and that with Louisiana was the Red River. Texas was a military province usually subordinate to the viceroy. From 1776 it was one of the Provincias Internas, and in 1786 Texas was attached to the intendancy of San Luis Potosi, although it remained a gobierno. In judicial affairs it was within the audiencia of Mexico. It belonged first to the diocese of Guadalajara, then (from 1777) to that of Linares. The only municipal government was that of Bejar, or San Antonio, where a cabildo was installed in 1731 (Alessio Robles, 1938, pp. 474, 515–16; Lafora, 1958, pp. 160, 184–86; Villaseñor y Sánchez, 1746–48, 2: 319–36).

X. NUEVO LEON

By royal cédula of May 31, 1579, Luis de Carvajal was commissioned with the title of governor and captain-general to establish a new gobierno on the northern frontier to be called Nuevo Reino de Leon. Its boundary was to run from the mouth of the Panuco River, 200 leagues west and the same distance north (Bancroft, 1883–86, 2: 777).[205] Carvajal probably arrived in the Panuco area in early 1581, and at first confined his activities to the spoliation of nearby Indian settlements, becoming embroiled in jurisdictional disputes with the alcaldes mayores of Panuco and Valles. In 1584 he engaged in a conflict with Nueva Vizcaya over the western boundary of his kingdom. At the end of 1586 the viceroy wrote that Carvajal had founded no permanent settlement and that he had taken more than 2000 Indian slaves. Further, the claim that he and his followers were Jews attracted the attention of the Inquisition. Consequently he was ordered to stop his "conquest" and was recalled to Mexico, where he died in prison in 1590.[206]

Nuevo Leon remained without a government until 1596, when a new governor was sent out to establish a settlement at Monterrey, thenceforth capital of the province. It was to be subordinate to the audiencia of Mexico and to the viceroy in matters of justice and gobierno. The question of boundaries with Nueva Vizcaya was settled in 1687 with the founding of another gobierno in Coahuila. On the east, Nuevo Leon extended to the Gulf shore until 1748, when the gobierno of Nuevo Santander was organized.

From 1785 to 1792, and again after 1804, Nuevo Leon was attached to the Provincias Internas, but its administration remained in the hands of a governor, generally appointed by the king. In 1786 Nuevo Leon was assigned as a single partido to the intendancy of San Luis Potosi.

At first in the diocese of Guadalajara, Nuevo Leon formed part of the newly erected diocese of Linares or Nuevo Leon after 1777. This bishopric also included Coahuila, Texas, Saltillo, and Nuevo Santander (annexed from Guadalajara), Tula, Palmillas, and Jaumave (from Michoacan); and Santa Barbara (from Mexico [Bancroft, 1883–86, 3: 693]).

During the 17th century some 12 or 14 alcaldías mayores were created in Nuevo Leon for local administration. Following is a list of these minor civil divisions as they were about 1750, with modern equivalents (Bancroft, 1883–86, 3: 333, 335; Mota y Escobar, 1940, pp. 31, 208–09; Villaseñor y Sánchez, 1746–48, 2: 294).[207]

MINOR CIVIL DIVISIONS, 1750

1750	1950
1. Boca de Leones	Villaldama, N. L.
2. Cadereyta	Cadereyta Jimenez, N.L.
3. Cerralvo	Cerralvo, N. L.
4. Guajuco	Santiago, N. L.
5. Horcasitas	Lampazos de Naranjo, N. L.
6. Labradores	Galeana, N. L.
7. Linares	Linares, N. L.
8. Pesqueria	Villa de Garcia, N. L.
9. Pilon, El	Montemorelos, N. L.
10. Rio Blanco	Aramberri, N. L.
11. Sabinas, Las	Sabinas Hidalgo, N. L.
12. Salinas, Las	Salinas Victoria, N. L.
13. Santa Catalina	Santa Catarina, N. L.

XI. NUEVO SANTANDER

The region north of the Panuco River between the Sierra Gorda and the Gulf coast was assigned to Nuevo Leon in 1579, but it remained without Spanish settlement until the 18th century. By a royal order of September 3, 1746, the establishment of a new military government to be called Nu-

[205] AGI, Mexico, leg. 104.
[206] AGI, Mexico, legs. 20, 104.
[207] AGI, Indiferente, leg. 108, tomo 5, fols. 207–224v. BNMex., MS 1384.

evo Santander was authorized, to be bounded on the south by Nueva España (Panuco River), on the west by Nueva España, Nuevo Leon, and Coahuila, and on the north by Coahuila and Texas (Espiritu Santo bay). The settlement and organization of the province was effected by José de Escandón, beginning in December, 1748. The town of Santander (Jimenez), founded in February, 1749, was made the seat of government (Bancroft, 1883–86, 3: 342–43).[208]

Perhaps in the 1770's, the Jaumave–Palmillas–Tula region was transferred from Nueva España to Nuevo Santander. Somewhat later the boundary with Texas was moved southward to the Nueces River. This left Nuevo Santander with an area approximately the same as the present state of Tamaulipas and part of southern Texas (Alessio Robles, 1938, p. 9).[209]

Ruled by governors appointed from Spain but subordinate to the viceroy, Nuevo Santander was in the jurisdiction of the audiencia of Mexico. It fell mostly within the diocese of Guadalajara until 1777, when it became part of the new bishopric of Linares. Local government was handled by military officers (*capitanes*) in each settlement. In 1786 the province was attached as a partido to the intendancy of San Luis Potosi, although remaining a separate gobierno. For military purposes it belonged to the Provincias Internas in 1785–92 and after 1804; at other times the viceroy supervised military matters (Bancroft, 1883–86, 3: 346–47; Lafora, 1958, pp. 181–82).[210]

XII. PANUCO

The Huasteca area, along the banks of the Panuco and its tributaries, had a brief existence as a separate gobierno. Late in 1525 Nuño de Guzmán was appointed governor of the province, known as Panuco y Vitoria Garayana, after an earlier (1523) abortive attempt by Francisco de Garay to settle the country. Guzmán arrived in May, 1527, at San Esteban del Puerto, the only Spanish settlement, which until then had been considered part of Nueva España (Hackett, 1918, p. 57). Within a year Guzmán was named president of the audiencia of Mexico and went to that city, leaving a deputy in charge at San Esteban. By a cédula of April 20, 1533, the province of Panuco ceased to be a separate gobierno and was reunited with Nueva España (Puga, 1563, fol. 82).

XIII. TABASCO

The first Spanish settlement in Tabasco, Nuestra Señora de la Victoria, probably had ordinary alcaldes to administer justice from 1525. Francisco de Montejo was appointed AM there in 1529, and four years later Tabasco was included in the territory assigned to him as governor (Hackett, 1918, p. 57; Scholes and Roys, 1948, pp. 124–25). The province was part of Yucatan until 1549, when it was attached to the new audiencia of Los Confines for two years, then reannexed to the audiencia of Mexico (1551), and once more made subject to Guatemala (1552–60). During this period alcaldes mayores were designated in Tabasco by the respective audiencia (Chamberlain, 1953, p. 249; Hackett, 1918, p. 61; Rubio Mañé, 1955, pp. 32–33; Scholes and Roys, 1948, p. 138). After 1561 the province remained in the jurisdiction of the audiencia of Mexico, but was subordinate in matters of gobierno to Yucatan. For some years no alcalde mayor was appointed, local administration being managed by ordinary alcaldes of the villa of Tabasco (Victoria [López de Velasco, 1894, pp. 258–59]).[211] The governor of Yucatan in 1577 appointed an alcalde mayor, but the residents of the villa complained to the audiencia, which ordered the official to be removed (DII, 11:

---

[208] AGI, Indiferente, leg. 108, tomo 5, fols. 114–132v.
[209] AGI, Mexico, leg. 1445.
[210] BNMex, MS 1384, fol. 398.
[211] AHN, MS 254. BNMA, MS 19692.

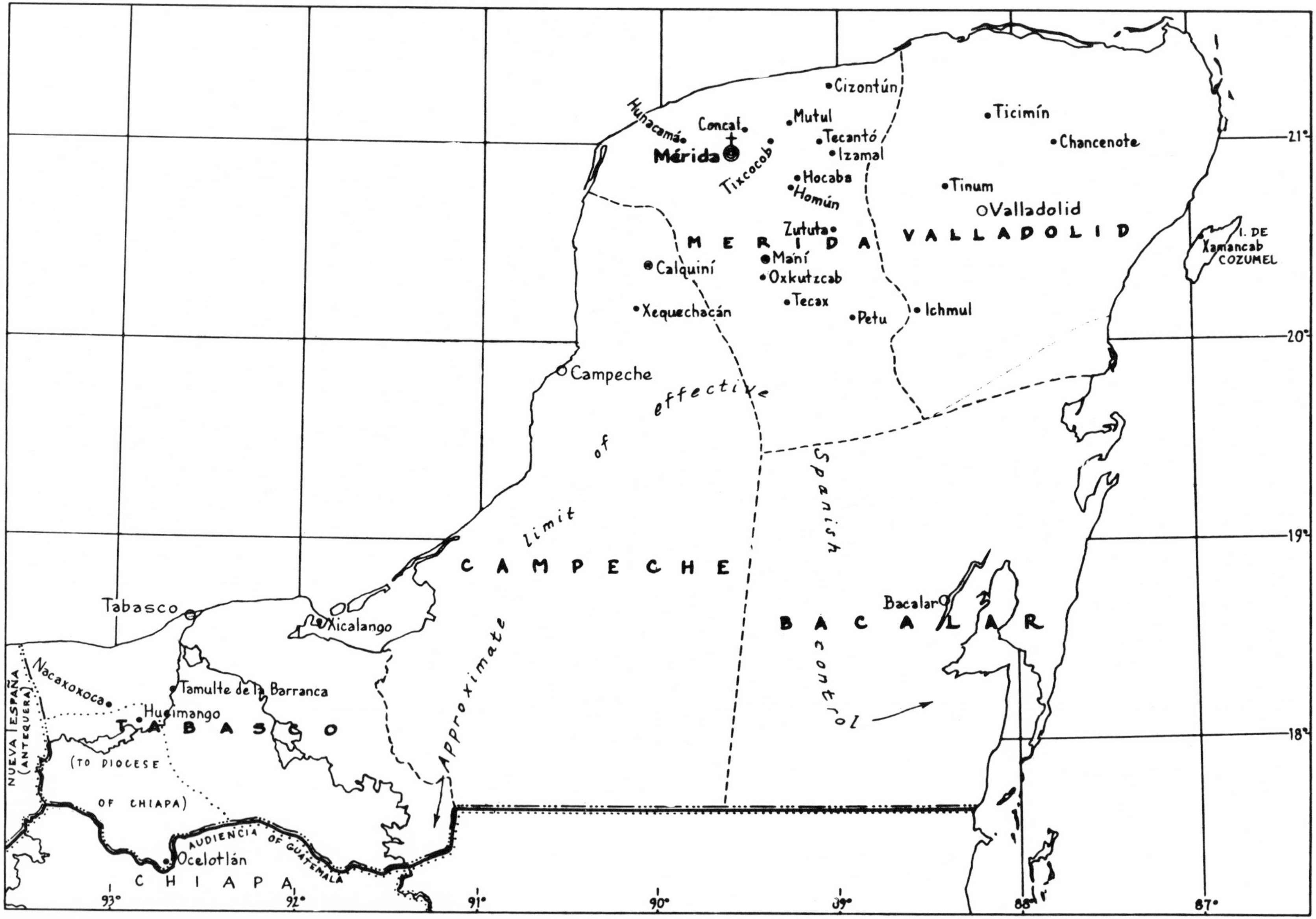

Fig. 13—NUEVA ESPAÑA: DIOCESE OF YUCATAN IN 1580

312). The dispute was referred to Spain, and by 1588 it seems to have been resolved by the appointment by the Council of the Indies of an alcalde mayor, who was subordinate to the governor of Yucatan. This arrangement lasted until 1782, when the magistrate's title was changed to governor. Five years later, Tabasco became a partido in the intendancy of Yucatan, although it continued to have a governor (BAGN, 24: 459; Magdaleno, 1954, p. 214; Ponce, 1873, 2: 453; Vázquez de Espinosa, 1948, p. 264).[212]

By 1607 the alcalde mayor had changed his residence from La Victoria to San Juan Bautista Villa Hermosa, some distance inland. Somewhat later (before 1686) the capital had moved to Tacotalpa, and in 1795 it was returned to Villa Hermosa (Gil y Sáenz, 1872, p. 149).[213]

Tabasco belonged first to the diocese of Tlaxcala (until 1532), then to Guatemala (1536–45), then to Chiapa (1545–61), and finally to the bishopric of Yucatan (fig. 14). The southwest corner of the province, however, remained subject to the diocese of Chiapa for some years (DHY, 2: 84).[214]

XIV. ISLA DEL CARMEN

Laguna de Terminos, on the boundary between Tabasco and Yucatan, was the site of a colony of English dyewood cutters from the mid-17th century until they were driven out by Spanish forces in 1717. At this time a presidio was established on Isla del Carmen, whose commander came to have the title of governor of Laguna de Terminos y Presidio del Carmen. His jurisdiction included several villages on the mainland, formerly subject to Tabasco and Campeche,

[212] BNMA, MS 3047. BNMex, MS 1384, fol. 397v. RAH, MS 4795.
[213] AGI, Indiferente, leg. 108, tomo 3; Mexico, leg. 369.
[214] AGI, Mexico, leg. 369. AHN, MS 254.
[215] AGI, Indiferente, leg. 1527. BNMex, MS 1384, fol. 398.
[216] AHN, MS 254.

in which he appointed "administradores de justicia." The territory belonged to the audiencia of Mexico and the diocese of Yucatan (fig. 14) and from 1786 it was part of the intendancy of Merida.[215]

XV. YUCATAN

Yucatan existed as a gobierno on paper as early as 1526, when Francisco de Montejo received authorization for the conquest of the peninsula together with a commission of "gobernador, adelantado, y capitán general." Begun in 1528, the subjugation of the natives continued with lapses until 1542, when Merida was founded and made the seat of government.

At first within the jurisdiction of the audiencia of Mexico, Yucatan was transferred on two occasions (1549 and 1552–61) to the audiencia of Los Confines. In 1549 Montejo was removed as governor, and for a time the province was governed by alcaldes mayores. Since these officials were appointed by the respective audiencia until 1562, Yucatan might be said to have belonged to the gobiernos of Nueva España and Guatemala during those years (Bancroft, 1883–86, 2: 450, 659; Puga, 1563, fol. 163; Rubio Mañé, 1955, pp. 32–33, 288; Scholes and Roys, 1948, p. 138). In 1562 an alcalde mayor appointed by the king arrived, and from 1565 Yucatan was ruled by a governor who (after 1616) held the additional title of captain-general. In judicial matters the province remained in the audiencia of Mexico, and in military and political affairs it was in a sense subordinate to the viceroy, who had the right to appoint interim governors (Bancroft, 1883–86, 2: 649–50; 3: 153; Scholes and Roys, 1948, p. 138).

Yucatan was divided into five provinces: Merida, Campeche, Valladolid, Bacalar, and Tabasco.[216] These, together with the military gobierno of Isla del Carmen, are located with approximate boundaries in figure 14. For most of the colonial period each

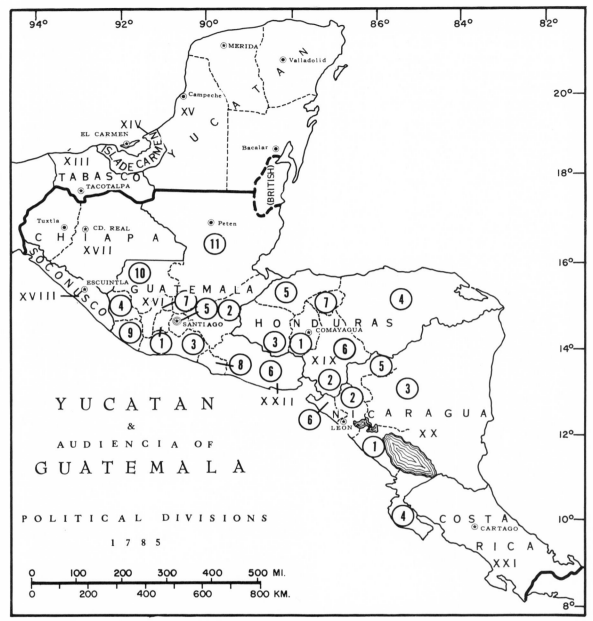

Fig. 14—YUCATAN AND AUDIENCIA OF GUATEMALA, 1785

province, with the exception of Tabasco (q.v.), was ruled by the ayuntamiento of the capital town, justice being administered by ordinary alcaldes; appeals could be referred either to the governor or directly to the audiencia. Beginning in the 1570's efforts were made by the governors to control local affairs through the appointment of corregidores and alcaldes mayores. In 1579–80 Tabasco and Valladolid were alcaldias mayores, and Calquini, Mani, and Tizimin were corregimientos, but within a few years the governor had been forced by the opposition of the ayuntamientos to withdraw his appointments.[217] Subsequent governors, trying to evade the restrictions on their power, appointed other kinds of local justices, but after 1630 it would seem that local government remained undisputed in the hands of the ayuntamientos. In 1786 Yucatan became the intendancy of Merida, still with a governor, divided into partidos (Orozco y Berra, 1881, p. 332). The area corresponded to that of the modern states of Yucatan, Campeche, and Tabasco, with the territory of Quintana Roo.

The boundary between Yucatan and Guatemala was at first ill-defined and of no practical interest since they were separated by many leagues of territory unoccupied by the Spaniards. In 1582 the town of Bacalar had subject villages extending southward into what is now British Honduras to the 18th parallel. Beginning about 1670, English dyewood cutters established themselves at the mouth of the Belize River and gradually expanded their settlement as far as Rio Hondo in the north. The presence of the English colony was recognized by Spain in the Treaty of Versailles (1783), which set the northern boundary at Rio Hondo. The same treaty, however, acknowledged Spanish sovereignty over the area (Bancroft, 1886–87, 2: 623–34; Sepúlveda, 1958, pp. 156–66).[218]

The first diocese in Mexico, the Carolense, was proclaimed on Cozumel Island in 1519, but it was not operative. From 1545 to 1561 Yucatan was claimed by the bishop of Chiapa. In the latter year the diocese of Yucatan y Cozumel, with its seat at Merida, was erected, the first bishop arriving in 1562 (Bancroft, 1883–86, 2: 296–97, 688–89).

XVI. GUATEMALA

As did "Nueva España," the term "Guatemala" had a variety of meanings in the colonial period. The gobierno of Guatemala,

while at times it had a greater or lesser extension, for most of the period corresponded in outline to the modern republics of Guatemala and El Salvador. The audiencia of Guatemala (at first called audiencia of Los Confines) embraced all Central America from Chiapas to Costa Rica. The diocese of Guatemala was approximately equal in extent to the gobierno; the archdiocese (after 1745) corresponded to the audiencia limits.

The political history of this area under Spanish rule can be divided into four periods. In the first (1520–44) the Spaniards conquered most of the country, and royal governors were appointed in Chiapa, Guatemala, Honduras, and Nicaragua. The second (1544–60) saw the establishment of an audiencia distinct from that of Mexico, originally resident at Gracias a Dios but soon (1549) moved to Guatemala City. During these years the audiencia took charge of all branches of government, royal governors being replaced by alcaldes mayores and corregidores appointed and controlled by the audiencia. In the third period (1560–1786) governors were again sent out from Spain, and a long and serious jurisdictional conflict occurred between the audiencia with its president-governor on the one hand, and the governors of the individual provinces on the other. In the final period (1786–1821) the intendancy system was imposed.

In matters of justice, the rule of the audiencia of Guatemala was supreme throughout the area, except for a brief period (1564–70) when its seat was moved to Panama. During those six years, Panama was added to the jurisdiction; Chiapa, Soconusco, part of Honduras, and Guatemala itself were taken from it and attached to the audiencia of Mexico. From 1570 the northern boundary would remain relatively unchanged. To the south, the limit between the audiencias of Guatemala and Panama

[217] Ibid.
[218] Ibid.

was fixed in 1573, running from the Escudo de Veragua in the Caribbean to Golfo Dulce on the Pacific (Chamberlain, 1953, p. 249; Peralta, 1883, p. xv).

The first royal governor of Guatemala, Pedro de Alvarado, was commissioned in 1528 and reached his government two years later. Alvarado acquired in encomienda nearly all the Indian villages and ruled the country as a personal fief. After his death, at the beginning of 1544, the new audiencia took charge and seized all of Alvarado's encomiendas for the Crown. Three years later these villages were apportioned among seven corregimientos, the first in Central America (Molina A., 1960, p. 125).[219] In 1560 the president of the audiencia was given the additional title of governor and was made personally responsible for matters of gobierno, but the size of his jurisdiction was soon diminished on the arrival of royal appointees for the gobiernos of Soconusco, Honduras, and Nicaragua. At the same time the king appointed alcaldes mayores for Sonsonate, Verapaz, and Zapotitlan, further limiting the power of the president-governor. The audiencia and its president in effect ignored these inroads on their authority and proceeded to name corregidores and other magistrates within the surrounding gobiernos. Thus for a number of years (over a century in some cases) many Indian communities of Central America were ruled by two rival governments of Spaniards competing with each other for the privilege of exploiting them. The problem was eventually resolved in 1678, to the dissatisfaction of all parties, when the Crown reserved to itself the right to sell at auction all provincial and local government offices (Molina A., 1960, p. 105).[220]

The history of jurisdictional changes in each gobierno within the audiencia of Guatemala is outlined below, beginning with that of Guatemala proper. As elsewhere, the lesser jurisdictions are listed alphabetically as they were just before the introduction of the intendancy system, in 1785. They are located by number, with roughly drawn boundaries, in figure 14. In the case of the gobierno of Guatemala, all C's (corregimientos) and AM's (alcaldías mayores) belonged to the archdiocese of Guatemala, and all became partidos in the intendancy of that name except San Salvador, which was made a separate intendancy in 1785 (Samayoa G., 1960).[221]

POLITICAL JURISDICTIONS: HISTORICAL NOTES

1. CHIMALTENANGO (AM)
1960: Chimaltenango, Guat.

The villages surrounding the first site of Guatemala City formed a single jurisdiction known as Valle de Guatemala. The C was at times named by the governor, but for many years the area was ruled by the ordinary alcaldes of the city. This situation lasted until 1753, when the valley was divided into two AM's, Chimaltenango and Sacatepeques (q.v.). Chimaltenango was redesignated a C in 1794.

2. CHIQUIMULA (C)
1960: Chiquimula, Guat.

Originally the area east of Guatemala City to the Atlantic coast was shared between several jurisdictions. Some of the mountain villages were held in encomienda, others were administered by the C of Guazacapan (cf. Escuintla), and the lowland area belonged to the province of Verapaz (q.v.). In 1604 the AM of Amatique y Puerto Nuevo de Santo Tomas de Castilla was created, comprising the coastal region between Verapaz and

[219] AGI, Guatemala, leg. 9.
[220] AGI, Guatemala, legs. 39–40. RAH, MS 4663, doc. 43.
[221] For the audiencia of Guatemala and its gobiernos, lists of jurisdictions at various times are found in the following places, not individually cited below. 1558: AGI, Contaduría, leg. 966. 1563: AGI, Guatemala, leg. 9. 1583: AGI, Patronato, leg. 183, doc. 1, ramo 1. About 1620: Vázquez de Espinosa, 1948, pp. 264–65, 268. About 1640: Díez de la Calle, 1646, fols. 118v–132. 1735: AGI, Guadalajara [sic], leg. 144. 1800: Juarros, 1809, 1:9–72, 105–28.

Honduras. By 1620 two C's, Acasaguastlan and Chiquimula de la Sierra, had been created by the audiencia. The first of these somewhat later absorbed the jurisdiction of Santo Tomas, and about 1760 Acasaguastlan in turn was absorbed by the C of Chiquimula (Molina A, 1960, p. 123).[222]

3. ESCUINTLA (AM)
1960: Escuintla, Guat.

The provinces of Escuintepeque and Guazacapan were taken for the crown in 1544 and became C's three years later. In 1678 the two C's, until then controlled by the president-governor, were joined under a single AM of Escuintla appointed from Spain.

4. QUEZALTENANGO (C)
1960: Quezaltenango, Guat.

At first an encomienda of Alvarado, Quezaltenango and subject villages became a C appointed by the audiencia in 1547. In the late 16th century it was suffragan to the AM of Zapotitlan (cf. Suchitepeques). Quezaltenango remained a C until Independence.

5. SACATEPEQUES (AM)
1960: San Pedro Sacatepequez, Guat.

This jurisdiction, which included all three sites of Guatemala City, was part of the C of Valle de Guatemala (cf. Chimaltenango) until 1753, when it became a separate AM, first called Amatitan y Sacatepeques. In 1800 the AM resided in Antigua Guatemala.

6. SAN SALVADOR (AM)
1960: San Salvador, El Salvador

In early years the Spanish settlements of San Salvador and San Miguel were governed by their ayuntamientos, although the audiencia exercised jurisdiction in nearby Indian villages through the appointment of three C's: Guaymoco y Tacachico, Tecolnac y Tecoluchlo, and Ucelutlan. By 1582 the last two of these C's had been absorbed by a new AM appointed by the king, whose jurisdiction included San Salvador, San Miguel, and the province of Choluteca. The C of Guaymoco y Tacachico, still listed in 1583, does not appear thereafter. In 1672 the Choluteca and Nacaome area was transferred to the AM of Tegucigalpa (see below). The territory remaining in the AM of San Salvador, which comprised the modern republic of El Salvador less the departments of Sonsonate and most of Ahuachapan, became the first intendancy in Central America, with its own governor-intendant, in 1785. This official was redesignated corregidor-intendant in 1791 (Molina A., 1960, p. 116).

7. SOLOLA (AM)
1960: Solola, Guat.

The C's of Atitlan and Tecpanatitlan were created by the audiencia in 1547. Although within the AM of Zapotitlan (cf. Suchitepeques), the area was controlled by the president-governor until 1689, when the two C's were combined in a new AM of Solola, subject to royal appointment.[222a]

8. SONSONATE (AM)
1960: Sonsonate, El Salvador

The port of Acajutla with the surrounding Indian villages known as Los Izalcos had an AM before the foundation of the audiencia in 1544.[223] In 1556 this magistrate moved to the recently founded town of La Trinidad (Sonsonate). It would seem that he was always a royal appointee, whose jurisdiction included what are today the departments of Sonsonate and Ahuachapan, less the village of Atiquizaya.

9. SUCHITEPEQUES (AM)
1960: Mazatenango, Guat.

The AM of La Costa de Zapotitlan, controlled by the Crown, was created

[222] AGI, Guatemala, leg. 966.
[222a] AGG, A 1.23, leg. 4591, fol. 135v (data by Murdo MacLeod).
[223] AGI, Guatemala, leg. 9.

131

soon after 1560, and extended along the Pacific coast from Tiquizate to the border of Soconusco and some distance inland. The jurisdiction at first included the suffragan C's of Atitlan, Tecpanatitlan, Quezaltenango, and Totonicapa, but in the 17th century it was reduced to the coastal area of Suchitepeques, with the capital at San Bartolome Mazatenango.

10. TOTONICAPAN (AM)
1960: Totonicapan, Guat.

Totonicapa was an encomienda of Alvarado, then (1544) Crown property, and from 1547 a C controlled by the audiencia. In 1678 the jurisdiction, which included Huehuetenango, became an AM subject to Crown appointment.

11. VERAPAZ (AM)
1960: Coban, Guat.

This extensive province northeast of Guatemala City was partly brought under Spanish control by Dominican missionaries beginning in 1537. The Dominicans ruled Verapaz with little interference from governors and audiencias until November 23, 1561, when an AM was named by the president-governor, to be replaced the following year by a Crown appointee.[223a] At the same time Verapaz was made a separate bishopric, although the diocese was extinguished in 1608.[223b] The capital of the province was Santo Domingo Coban. The northern part of Verapaz was long a refuge for unsubdued Indians. In 1697 a presidio was established at Peten, which later appears as a separate jurisdiction with its own governor-castellan, although it would seem that he was subordinate to the AM of Verapaz.

XVII. CHIAPA

The subjugation of Chiapa was begun by Spaniards from the villa of Espiritu Santo (Coatzacoalcos) in 1523. Perhaps the first magistrate named specifically for Chiapa was an AM sent there by the audiencia

of Mexico in 1529 (Bancroft, 1886–87, 2: 214–15). Meanwhile the province was included in the area assigned to Pedro de Alvarado as governor of Guatemala, and it was not until 1539 that Alvarado gave up his claim in favor of Francisco de Montejo, who resided in Chiapa as governor from 1540 to 1542 (Chamberlain, 1953, pp. 177, 205, 246). Two years later Chiapa was assigned to the new audiencia of Los Confines (Guatemala), and henceforth (except for the years 1564–70 when it was returned to Mexico) it was ruled from Guatemala City. Still, Chiapa occupied a special category in matters of gobierno. Because of the difficulty of communications and perhaps for other reasons, local government was at first left in the hands of the ayuntamiento of the capital, Ciudad Real (López de Velasco, 1894, pp. 303–04). At the same time the president-governor of Guatemala appointed C's for the Indian population. In 1563 there was a single C with jurisdiction in all Crown villages, and 20 years later there were two such officers, one for the Indians near Ciudad Real and another for the rest of the province. On May 18, 1572, it seems that the ayuntamiento of Ciudad Real was replaced as governing body by an AM.[223c]

In 1764 Chiapa was divided into two AM's, Ciudad Real (1950: San Cristobal de las Casas) and Tuxtla (Tuxtla Gutierrez). Finally, in 1786–90 the province became an intendancy, with the addition of Soconusco (q.v.). The boundaries of the intendancy were more or less the same as those of the modern state of Chiapas, in the republic of Mexico.

The diocese of Chiapa, which until then belonged to Tlaxcala (1525–36) and Guatemala (1536–39), was created in 1539, but

[223a] AGG, A 1.23, leg. 1512, fol. 296 (data by Murdo MacLeod).
[223b] AGG, A 1.23, leg. 1514, fol. 197 (data by Murdo MacLeod).
[223c] AGG, A 1.23, leg. 1512, fol. 416 (data by Murdo MacLeod).

its first bishop, Bartolome de las Casas, did not arrive there until 1545. This bishopric included Yucatan and Tabasco until 1561, and Soconusco after 1596 (fig. 14).

XVIII. SOCONUSCO

This erstwhile cacao-rich province, stretching along the Pacific coastal plain from the Isthmus of Tehuantepec to the borders of Guatemala, was conquered by Pedro de Alvarado in 1522–24. Cortés listed it among his encomiendas in 1526, but it was taken from him by the first audiencia (DII, 12: 279; Cortés, 1963, p. 470). In 1531 it became a C (AM from 1550) within the gobierno of Nueva España. Soconusco remained under the control of the viceroy until August 6, 1556, when it was transferred to the audiencia of Guatemala (Puga, 1563, fol. 188).[224] In 1563 it became a separate gobierno, with a governor subject to royal appointment (Molina A., 1960, pp. 115, 123). Again subject to Mexico in 1564–70, it remained within the audiencia of Guatemala after 1570 (Bancroft, 1886–87, 2: 370; ENE, 10: 62; 16: 78; López de Velasco, 1894, pp. 282–83, 301–03; Serrano y Sanz, 1908, pp. 440–41; Vázquez de Espinosa, 1948, p. 192).[225] The province in colonial times was bounded on the northeast by the continental divide, which separated it from Chiapa; on the east by the Tilapa River; and on the west by Rio de las Arenas (Cuevas, 1944, pp. 196–97; Ponce, 1873, 1: 291–305). Thus it occupied the coastal region of the present state of Chiapas, plus a corner of Guatemala.

The capital of Soconusco in the 16th and 17th centuries was Huehuetlan. In 1786 Escuintla was the residence of the governor, and eight years later the capital moved to Tapachula. In 1790 Soconusco became a

---

[224] AGI, Mexico, leg. 91; Patronato, leg. 182, ramo 40; leg. 183, doc. 9, ramo 2. AGN, Mercedes, vol. 3, fols. 281v, 293v; vol. 4, fols. 115, 221, 339, 366v.

[225] AGI, Guatemala, leg. 40.

partido in the intendancy of Chiapa (Alcedo, 1786–89, 4: 563; Juarros, 1809, 1: 11–16). Ecclesiastical jurisdiction was first exercised by the bishop of Tlaxcala, then (1536–48) by that of Guatemala. From 1548 Soconusco belonged to the diocese of Chiapa, except for another period (about 1560 to 1596) when it was returned to the bishopric of Guatemala (fig. 14).

XIX. HONDURAS

After a confusing period of conflicting jurisdictions, the province of Higueras e Cabo de Honduras received its first royal governor in 1526. Two years later, despite an attempt by this official to include Nicaragua in his jurisdiction, the limits of Honduras were fixed at Puerto de Caballos (modern Puerto Cortés) and Cape Gracias a Dios, specifically excluding the Gulf of Fonseca on the south. It was not until 1672 that Honduras acquired an outlet on the Pacific, giving it approximately the limits that the republic of Honduras has today (Barón Castro, 1942, p. 24; Chamberlain, 1953; Molina A., 1960, pp. 113–14).

From 1526 to 1544 much of Honduras was subjugated and colonized by the Spaniards, settlements being made at Comayagua, Gracias a Dios, Olancho, San Pedro Sula, and Trujillo. Each of these places included within its "limits" a number of Indian villages, and thus the country was divided into jurisdictions or lesser provinces, ruled sometimes by the ayuntamientos, occasionally by lieutenants of the governor, and rarely by alcaldes mayores. For a brief period (1539–41) all of Honduras was annexed to the gobierno of Guatemala and ruled by a deputy-governor (Chamberlain, 1953). In judicial affairs, Honduras was subordinate first to the audiencia of Santo Domingo, then (1528–34) to Mexico, then for a second time (1534–44) to Santo Domingo. In 1544 the new audiencia of Los Confines established residence at Gracias a Dios. This body appointed an AM to govern the province, but from 1552 governors were once more sent out from Spain.[226] Honduras had its own bishop from 1545. Five years later the audiencia moved to Guatemala City.

Below is a list of the lesser jurisdictions within Honduras as they were when the intendancy of Comayagua was organized in 1786–87. They are located by number in figure 16, with approximate boundaries.[227]

POLITICAL JURISDICTIONS: HISTORICAL NOTES

1. COMAYAGUA
1963: Comayagua, Honduras
Valladolid del valle de Comayagua, founded in 1539, became the residence of both governor and bishop of Honduras. It first included the region around Tegucigalpa (q.v.), which became a separate jurisdiction in 1579.

2. CHOLUTECA
1963: Choluteca, Honduras
The Spanish settlement of Jerez de la Frontera or Choluteca was founded in 1545 or shortly before. It belonged to the AM of San Salvador in the gobierno of Guatemala until perhaps 1672, when the area, together with Nacaome and Guascoran, was transferred to Honduras. Choluteca is sometimes listed as a separate jurisdiction, but most of the time it was included in the AM of Tegucigalpa (q.v. [Barón Castro, 1942, p. 24]).

3. GRACIAS A DIOS
1963: Gracias, Honduras
Founded in 1536 and moved to its final site three years later, Gracias a Dios had a large jurisdiction covering much of western Honduras. In 1582 it was ruled by a lieutenant-governor, but within the "limits of the city" there was also a corregidor of Tencoa appointed by the president-governor of Guatemala. This C seems to have existed until 1670 and perhaps later,[227a] as Tencoa is mentioned in the 18th century as a separate partido. A more short-lived intrusion was the AM of

San Andrés de Zaragoza, created about 1678. This was a mining camp which soon declined, and the jurisdiction was reunited with that of Gracias a Dios (Molina A., 1960, p. 123).[228]

4. OLANCHO
1963: Pueblo Viejo, Honduras
Trujillo was the first Spanish settlement in Honduras, founded in 1525. Some 20 years later San Jorge de Olancho was settled, inland from Trujillo, and in 1546 an AM was named by the audiencia to administer justice there (Molina A., 1960, p. 122). Each place was the capital of a province in 1582, with a deputy-governor. By 1683 Trujillo had been annexed to Olancho, and the combined province covered the entire eastern half of Honduras. At this time the jurisdiction was divided between the old town of Olancho and the newer Olanchito (Olancho Nuevo). The latter partido included Trujillo and the islands of Roatan and Guanaja.

5. SAN PEDRO SULA
1963: San Pedro Sula, Honduras
In the 16th century this area was first known as the province of Higueras, and was claimed for a time by both Guatemala and Yucatan. After San Pedro was founded in 1536 the region was shared between two jurisdictions, San Pedro and San Juan de Puerto de Caballos, each governed by its ayuntamiento. Not long afterward San Juan was annexed to San Pedro, but by 1733 certain villages had been detached to form a new partido, Yoro (q.v.). Towards 1780 the coastal area, now known as Omoa, seems to have been administered separately.

[226] AGI, Guatemala, leg. 9.
[227] For sources, see note 221. The 1582 list for Honduras is found in RAH, MS 4663, doc. 43. Another list for 1777–79 is found in AGI, Indiferente, leg. 1527.
[227a] Royal cédula, 4 June 1670, inquires if C of Tencoa should be suppressed, AGG, A 1.23, leg. 1519, fol. 233 (data by Murdo MacLeod).
[228] AGI, Guatemala, leg. 39.

6. TEGUCIGALPA (AM)

1963: Tegucigalpa, Honduras

Mines were discovered in this area, until then part of the jurisdiction of Comayagua, and in 1579 an AM was appointed by the president-governor of Guatemala to Minas de Guazucaran, with residence in Tegucigalpa.[229] The governor of Honduras protested this intrusion, and by about 1620 the AM was made subject to Crown appointment. In 1672 Tegucigalpa became a littoral jurisdiction through the acquisition from San Salvador of Choluteca (q.v.).

7. YORO

1963: Yoro, Honduras

Yoro and other nearby villages, first in the jurisdiction of San Pedro Sula, appear from 1733 as a separate partido.

XX. NICARAGUA

Jurisdiction over Nicaragua was claimed by both Cortés and Pedrarias, but it was the latter who sent colonists northward from Panama to found Granada and Leon in 1524. At first the province was part of Castilla del Oro, but in 1527 it was made a separate gobierno with Pedrarias as the first royal governor. The government was taken over by the audiencia of Los Confines in 1548, Nicaragua being ruled by AM's appointed by that body and by the king until 1565, after which governors were again sent out from Spain. Costa Rica (q.v.) was detached and made a separate gobierno in 1565 (Molina A., 1960, p. 122).[230] Nicaragua had its own bishop, with residence in Leon, the capital, from 1531.

As far as local government is concerned, the situation which prevailed in Nicaragua was similar to that in Honduras. The country was first divided into jurisdictions ruled by the ayuntamientos of the Spanish settlements. Beginning in the 1540's, the audiencia began to appoint AM's and C's within the existing provinces, with the inevitable jurisdictional disputes which persisted until some of the C's were eliminated and others made subject to Crown appointment.

After 1786 Nicaragua became the intendancy of Leon, which also included Costa Rica. At that time it had the following political subdivisions, shown in figure 14.[231]

POLITICAL JURISDICTIONS: HISTORICAL NOTES

1. GRANADA

1963: Granada, Nicaragua

The area subject to the city of Granada comprised most of southern Nicaragua, until the C of Monimbo y Masaya was created by the audiencia, superimposing one jurisdiction on the other. This C was eliminated in 1673. Meanwhile another C was appointed (before 1620) to administer the Chontales region east of Lake Nicaragua, but these villages eventually were divided between Granada and and Matagalpa (q.v.).

2. LEON

1963: Leon, Nicaragua

The city of Leon, founded in 1524, was the residence of the governor. Part of Leon's jurisdiction was included in the C of Cazaloaque y Pozoltega (1583), created by the audiencia. This C was later called Subtiava, suppressed in 1673 but restored in 1693; eventually it was annexed to Realejo (q.v.).[232]

3. MATAGALPA (C)

1963: Matagalpa, Nicaragua

Los Chontales appears as a C appointed by the president-governor of Guatemala in 1620–40, within the jurisdiction of Granada. In the latter year another C is listed, Sebaco, which by 1684 had absorbed Los Chontales, and by 1787 had been redesignated Matagalpa.

[229] Ibid.
[230] AGI, Guatemala, leg. 40; Mexico, leg. 68.
[231] Sources are given in note 221. 1583 jurisdictions are listed in AGI, Guatemala, leg. 40.
[232] AGI, Guatemala, legs. 39, 40, 128. AGG, A 1.23, leg. 4852, fol. 265, leg. 4592, fol. 53v (data by Murdo MacLeod).

4. NICOYA (C)

1960: Nicoya, Costa Rica

For most of the colonial period the peninsula of Nicoya was subordinate to the province of Nicaragua, although on occasion it was attached to Costa Rica (Peralta, 1883, p. 480). It was governed at times by a C, at others by an AM, appointed by the audiencia in the 16th century and by the king afterwards, except for a brief period after 1648 when the president named the C.[233]

5. NUEVA SEGOVIA

1963: Ocotal, Nicaragua

Founded in 1536, Nueva Segovia had an AM appointed by the audiencia in 1545, but thereafter the city and its jurisdiction were governed by the ayuntamiento.

6. EL REALEJO (C)

1963: El Realejo, Nicaragua

The seaport of El Realejo by 1583 had become a villa governed by ordinary alcaldes, while the Indian villages nearby were administered by a C of El Viejo, appointed by the president-governor. In 1600 the audiencia took control of the port itself through the appointment of another C, and by 1620 the two had been united in a single jurisdiction, El Viejo y Puerto del Realejo (Molina A., 1960, p.

128). After 1722 the C was appointed from Spain. Sometime between 1741 and 1778 the adjacent C of Subtiava (cf. Leon) was annexed to Realejo.

XXI. COSTA RICA

The valley of Cartago was settled by Spaniards in 1563, and two years later the first royal governor arrived in Costa Rica, until then part of Nicaragua. The province came within the diocese of Leon. As elsewhere, the audiencia attempted to impose its authority in Costa Rica by naming corregidores (there were four such officers in the 1620's and 1630's), but they were finally eliminated in 1661.[233a] In 1719 the governor ruled his province through lieutenants in Barba, Boruca, Esparza, and Matina.[234] After 1786 Costa Rica continued as a gobierno within the intendancy of Leon (fig. 14).

XXII. SAN SALVADOR

In 1785 became a separate intendancy (see above, XVI, GUATEMALA).

[233] Ibid. AGG, A 1.23, leg. 1517, fols. 164v, 166 (6 Nov. 1648) (data by Murdo MacLeod).
[233a] AGG, A 1.23, leg. 4569, exp. 39234 (data by Murdo MacLeod).
[234] AGI, Guadalajara, leg. 144; Guatemala, leg. 39.

REFERENCES

Ajofrín, 1959
Alcedo, 1786–89
Alessio Robles, 1938
Arregui, 1946
Bancroft, 1883–86, 1884–89, 1886–87
Barón Castro, 1942
Bayle, 1933
Beleña, 1787
Borah, 1955, 1964
Brand and others, 1960
Bravo Ugarte, 1965
Cartas de Indias, 1877
Castañeda, 1929
Chamberlain, 1953
Chapman, 1939
Chevalier, 1952
Cline, 1949
Colección de Documentos Inéditos, 1864–84
Cortés, 1963
Cuevas, 1944
Dávila Padilla, 1625
Díez de la Calle, 1646
Documentos para la historia de Yucatán, 1936–38
Encinas, 1945–46
Epistolario de Nueva España, 1939–42
García Pimentel, 1897, 1904
Gay, 1950

Gibson, 1952, 1964
Gil y Sáenz, 1872
González Navarro, 1953
Hackett, 1918
Haring, 1947
Jiménez Moreno, 1958
Juarros, 1809
Lafora, 1958
Lemoine Villicaña, 1964
Libro de Tasaciones, 1952
Lohmann Villena, 1957
López de Velasco, 1894
Magdaleno, 1954
Mecham, 1927
Meigs, 1935
Miranda, 1952
Molina Argüello, 1960
Mota y Escobar, 1940
Ocaranza, 1937–39
Orozco y Berra, 1881
Páez Brotchie, 1940
Papeles de Nueva España, 1905–06
Parry, 1948, 1953

Peralta, 1883
Pérez de Ribas, 1645
Pompa y Pompa, 1960
Ponce, 1873
Portillo y Díez de Sollano, 1947
Puga, 1563
Rivera, 1736
Rodríguez Zetina, 1956
Rubio Mañé, 1955
Samayoa Guevera, 1960
Saravia, 1930
Sauer, 1932
Scholes and Roys, 1948
Sepúlveda, 1958
Serrano y Sanz, 1908
Tamarón y Romeral, 1937
Vázquez de Espinosa, 1948
Velázquez, 1961
Vetancurt, 1698
Villaseñor y Sánchez, 1746–48
West, 1949
———— and Parsons, 1941

3. Viceroyalty to Republics, 1786-1952: Historical Notes on the Evolution of Middle American Political Units

HOWARD F. CLINE

COLONIAL NEW SPAIN was the matrix out of which grew modern Mexico, along with Guatemala and the other republics of Central America. With changes in dynasty in Spain, then a later shift of sovereignty following successful declarations of independence from overseas rule, the ancient viceroyalty of New Spain underwent successive alterations of the colonial territorial units. In summary fashion we shall trace the most important of these.

In general, within a century after the viceroyalty was given reorganized form under the colonial intendant system of 1786 the present configuration of Mexican states and territories, and the small countries of Central America, had emerged and their main territorial outlines had been stabilized. The boundaries often reflect but are by no means always wholly synonymous with earlier colonial units which they replaced.

A striking feature, then, of the period from 1786 to 1952 is the fractionalization of the earlier viceregal territory. Mexico devel-

oped 29 states, each with its own government, and in addition contains two territories and a Federal District under national control. The separate national sovereignties of Guatemala, Honduras, El Salvador, Costa Rica, and Nicaragua likewise came into being; each further subdivided its own national area for purposes of local government. A final remnant of colonial days, British Honduras, precariously continues as a dependency of an overseas crown, British rather than Spanish.

A second feature is the shrinkage of the total area occupied by the national successor states to the viceroyalty. As a result of growth of the United States, former Spanish possessions for which the colonial viceroy in Mexico City was responsible were successively absorbed by it: East and West Florida, Texas, California, New Mexico (all with more territory in colonial times than within bounds of present states), the Philippines, and Puerto Rico.

Finally, in the Republic of Mexico, the initial focus here, we note the internal

138

splitting of larger colonial units into smaller ones from 1786 through 1902. Such process is particularly visible within our Principal Area where, since conquest in 1519, a majority of the population—native, European, and mixed—has always congregated.

Our aim here is limited to outlining and illustrating successive political and administrative arrangements of the Middle American territory from late colonial times to the present. The treatment of Mexico leans heavily on a pioneering sketch first published by O'Gorman in 1937 (rev. ed., 1966), and other related materials. We do not provide the degree of detail furnished in Article 2, on which much reliance is also placed for certain summary statements. Purposely we have not undertaken to enter in the successive internal administrative and territorial divisions of Mexican states in the national period, but rather have restricted coverage to the evolution of such state units. Summaries of the data are in Article 1, appendix, which also provides details on the municipios within each state as of 1950.

I. LATE COLONIAL MEXICO, 1786–1821

Background to important changes in New Spain during the 18th and early 19th centuries is a change of Spanish dynasties. As a result of European wars, Bourbon monarchs in 1700 replaced Habsburgs on the Spanish throne. With strong family ties to France, the Bourbon kings and their revitalized Spanish bureaucracies introduced many practices that had been developed in that latter highly centralized state, and replaced numerous hallowed Habsburg institutions in Spain and its overseas dominions with French adaptions and innovations to halt and reverse what seemed to them an alarming and spreading decadence. Reforms in trade, commerce, military matters, and many other aspects gained increasing momentum under able Spanish ministers and vigorous monarchs of the 18th century. These reforms began earlier and generally

were more effective in Spain itself than in its ultramarine possessions. They, too, were purposefully brought into the reformist streams (Haring, 1963, pp. 314–25; Gibson, 1966, pp. 170–71).

The Council of the Indies, heart of the administrative system of the colonies under the Habsburgs, was shorn of its direct powers by the Bourbons. Many of its functions devolved on a single Minister of Marine and the Indies, a post created in 1714. By decree a second Minister was added in July, 1787. Shortly thereafter (1790) both these special ministries were suppressed, and their numerous responsibilities were partitioned among five cabinet officers in Madrid responsible to the Crown alike in Spain and overseas areas for Foreign Affairs, War, Marine, Justice, Finance (Haring, 1963, p. 107). The regnant Bourbon notion was that the Spanish homeland and overseas areas were comparable and integral parts of a single juridical, political, and economic unit, displacing the older Habsburg theories of the special relationships between the Crown and its several peninsular and overseas provinces and kingdoms. The Bourbons typically did not at first abolish the Council of the Indies, which they retained in an advisory capacity until its usefulness was long past, and then dissolved it by law in March, 1834, when most of the American empire had been long lost.

For New Spain, in somewhat parallel fashion, the Bourbons retained the earlier system of the viceroy and audiencias, but changed it by adding to it and partially replacing it with a special system of intendants (Fisher, 1928, 1929). In Spain itself the Bourbons had early (1718) imported this French device for provincial government, but it was at first unsuccessful; the division of Spain into intendancies was revitalized by Ferdinand VI in 1749 and had taken firm root by the 1750's. Although administrative reformers urged that it be immediately extended to the Indies, it was first tried only in limited form in Havana,

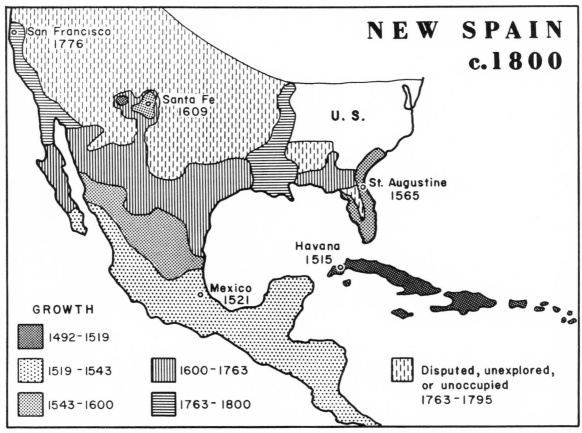

Fig. 1—ETHNOHISTORICAL REGIONS WITHIN PRINCIPAL AREA

where in 1764 an *intendencia* was created to handle related matters of war and finance, with responsibilities to suppress contraband trade, to handle public lands, and to administer fortifications. The Cuban intendant was given a rank equivalent to captain-general.

José de Gálvez, sent to New Spain on an extended *visita* (1765–71) to examine what changes seemed necessary, had strongly recommended that the intendancy system be broadened and extended to New Spain (Priestley, 1916). In 1768 one such experimental intendancy was established, merging the provinces of Sonora and Sinaloa under a single official (Haring, 1963, p. 134, note 7). After his promotion to Minis-

ter of the Indies (1776) Gálvez in 1782 introduced the system entire in the viceroyalty of Buenos Aires, in Peru (1784), and during 1786 in Chile and New Spain. Finally, in 1790, the plan of using intendants was put in general operation throughout the empire, with the exception of certain frontier provinces, which remained under military governments.

The Intendancy System in New Spain

The introduction of the intendancy system in New Spain was designed, there as elsewhere, to end various abuses, notably by corregidores, and more especially to increase royal revenues, badly needed for defense of the realms in the prolonged 18th-

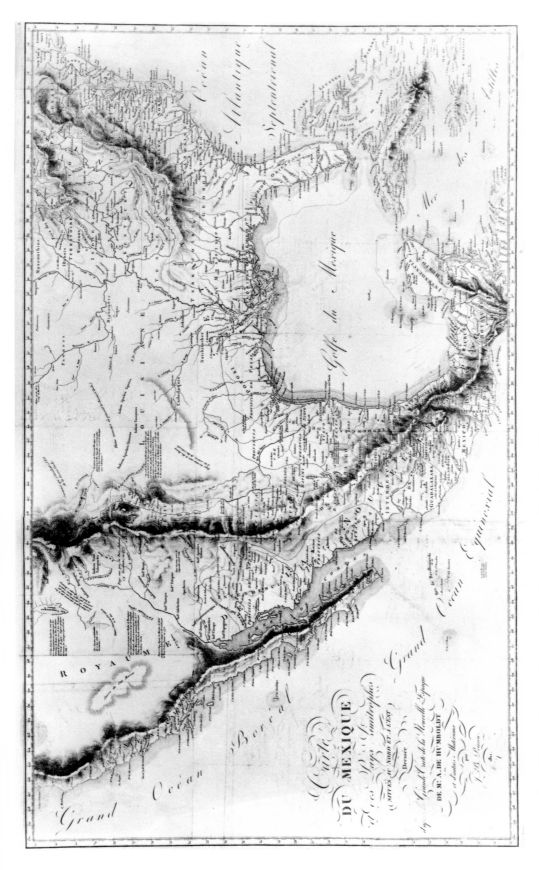

Fig. 2—NEW SPAIN AND RELATED AREAS, 1804 (after Humboldt, 1811)

FIG. 3—INTENDANCIES AND PROVINCIAS INTERNAS

INTENDANCIES
1804

After Humboldt, 1811

INTENDANCY
PROVINCE
Seat of Intendant

TEXAS

NUEVO MEXICO

Santa Fe

NUEVA CALIFORNIA

Monterey

San Diego

VIEJA CALIFORNIA

Loreto

SONORA

Arizpe

Sonora

Sinaloa

Culiacan

SINALOA

DURANGO

Chihuahua

Durango

COAHUILA

Coahuila

Bejar

NUEVO SANTANDER

Santander

NUEVO LEON

Monterrey

Saltillo

ZAC.

Zacatecas

GUADALAJARA

Guadalajara

Colima

SAN LUIS POTOSI

S.L.Potosi

GTO.

Guanajuato

Queretaro

VALLADOLID

Valladolid

MEXICO

Cd. Mexico

PUEBLA

Tlaxcala

Puebla

VERACRUZ

Veracruz

OAXACA

Oaxaca

CHIAPA

Cd. Real

MERIDA

Merida

PROVINCIAS INTERNAS

ORIENTE
OCCIDENTE

POTOSI

SAN LUIS

ZAC.

DURANGO

SONORA

century international struggles between Spain and England in the Old World and the New. It also aimed at simplifying lines of command and responsibilities, blurred in the confusing welter of gobiernos, alcaldías mayores, and corregimientos that had evolved under the Habsburgs, described at length in Article 2.

These older jurisdictions were nominally abolished in 1786. In their stead the viceroyalty was divided into 12 sizable intendancies, apart from Central America (treated below). Each intendancy was further subdivided into districts or *partidos*, usually the former alcaldías or corregimientos. The intendant was to be a Spanish-born officer, named in Spain, and was responsible for the intendancy. Over each partido was a *subdelegado*, who served a five-year term; he was nominated by the intendant, to whom he was responsible, but was appointed by the viceroy. Intendants and subdelegados absorbed the previous functions of the provincial governor, alcalde mayor, and corregidor, whose offices were abolished (Navarro García, 1959).

A detailed "Ordinances for the Intendants of New Spain," consisting of 306 articles and published in Madrid (1786) with over 400 pages, specified their general and specific duties (translated and annotated in Fisher, 1929). They had principal control within their jurisdictions over administration, finance, justice, and war, but remained generally subject to the viceroy and the audiencia in whose district the intendancy lay. They were exhorted to stimulate economic progress by encouraging industry, agriculture, and trade.

Intendants were given full charge of collecting royal revenues within their intendancy. This financial independence, and the fact that intendants communicated directly with the Minister of the Indies (and the successor offices) in Madrid lessened the direct authority over them exercised by the viceroy, to whom they remained subordinate, and by the supervisory audiencia. In

TABLE 1—NEW SPAIN: INTENDANCIES AND GOBIERNOS, 1788–1821*

INTENDANCIES:
 1. Mexico
 2. Guadalajara
 3. Puebla
 4. Veracruz
 5. Merida [Yucatan]
 6. Oaxaca
 7. Guanajuato
 8. Valladolid [Michoacan]
 9. San Luis Potosi
10. Zacatecas
11. Durango
12. Arizpe (Sonora)

GOBIERNOS (no intendant; directly under viceroy):
13. Vieja California
14. Nueva California
15. Tlaxcala (created 1793)

* Source: O'Gorman, 1966, pp. 24–25.

contrast to the average 300–500-peso salary previously given a corregidor, an intendant received 4000–6000; the viceroy received 60,000 pesos. However, the subdelegados continued to be paid only about 600 pesos.

Most of the former corregimientos and alcaldías mayores remained as partidos of intendancies after creation of the new units in New Spain by order of King Charles III on December 4, 1786. This decree provided that a large area around Mexico City was to be an Intendancy-General of Army and Provinces (i.e., ranking) and that the 11 others would be Intendancies of Provinces, named after the capital city of each. Later actions established three jurisdictions, called gobiernos, that had no intendants. These were governed directly by the viceroy: Vieja (Lower) California, Nueva (Upper) California, and Tlaxcala, created from the Intendancy of Puebla in 1793. Table 1 lists the intendancies and gobiernos.

Humboldt, whose five-volume *Essay on New Spain* (1811) gives a minute account of the viceroyalty on the eve of independence, drew a detailed map showing the intendancies (reproduced here as fig. 2). Figure 3 places the approximate intendancy

143

boundaries on a map of modern Mexican states; it also shows limits of the Provincias Internas, as stabilized about 1812.

Provincias Internas

Gerhard (Article 2) has briefly touched on the history of the Provincias Internas ("Internal Provinces"). These were also a Bourbon innovation to protect the frontiers of northern Mexico. Russians, British (Americans), French, and Indians all threatened these bastions during the late 18th century. The meager human and economic resources of the vast northern frontier area were wholly inadequate to support a suggested second viceroyalty to be centered at Guadalajara. On his prolonged *visita* José Gálvez spent much time and effort examining these complex problems of frontier defense (Priestley, 1916; Navarro García, 1964). When in 1776 he became Minister of the Indies he first tried to solve them by creating the office of commandant-general of the Internal Provinces, with jurisdiction over what are now the northern Mexican states of Mexico (Sinaloa, Sonora, Lower California, Durango, Chihuahua), together with California, New Mexico, and Texas, with his capital first at Arizpe (Sonora) but later moved to Chihuahua. The commandant-general was to be the supreme political and military governor, independent of the viceroy and responsible via the Minister of the Indies directly to the king.

The autonomous nature of control over the provinces was changed in 1785, when they were replaced under viceregal control. At the same time the large territory was split into three comandancias, each under a comandante, with the total area slightly expanded. One comandancia included Coahuila, Texas, Nuevo Leon, Nuevo Santander, and the Districts of Parras and Saltillo. Another was formed by Nueva Vizcaya and Nuevo Mexico. The third embraced the two Californias, Sonora, and Sinaloa (O'Gorman, 1966, p. 17).

TABLE 2—NEW SPAIN, PROVINCIAS INTERNAS, 1812–21[*]

A. PROVINCIAS INTERNAS DE Oriente: Intendant	
1. Gobierno del Nuevo Reino de Leon	San Luis Potosi for all except military
2. Gobierno de Colonia del Nuevo Santander	San Luis Potosi for all except military
3. Gobierno de la Provincia de Coahuila	Comandante acted as intendant
4. Gobierno de la Provincia de Texas	Comandante acted as intendant
B. PROVINCIAS INTERNAS DE OCCIDENTE:	
1. Gobierno de la Nueva Vizcaya	Durango; comandante was intendant of both Durango and Arizpe
2. Gobierno de las Provincias de Sonora y Sinaloa	Arizpe; comandante was intendant of Arizpe and also Durango
3. Gobierno de la Provincia del Nuevo Mexico	No intendant; directly under viceroy for all but military

[*] Source: O'Gorman, 1966, p. 24.

Nor did this arrangement prove satisfactory or lasting. In 1787 the area again was reorganized with two comandancias: Eastern and Western. The Western grouped the single province of Sonora-Sinaloa with the single province of both Californias, Nueva Vizcaya, and Nuevo Mexico. Coahuila, Texas, Nuevo Leon, Santander, and the Districts of Parras and Saltillo constituted the Eastern. Other reshufflings occurred, but by orders of 1804, not executed until 1811–12, the 1787 lines remained until independence, except that the Californias were detached and placed directly under the viceroy.

The Provincias Internas were basically, almost exclusively, military jurisdictions. For other matters—political, fiscal, judicial—there were complicated delegations of authority. They are listed in Table 2.

Summary

Final years of Spanish rule in New Spain witnessed important administrative changes, reflected in reorganization of the viceregal territory to carry out policies of the Bourbon monarchs. Perhaps the most important of these was introduction of the intendant system. Experimentally introduced in 1768 (Arizpe), it was extended to the whole viceroyalty on December 4, 1786. That law abolished the former offices of gobernador, alcalde mayor, and corregidor, substituting for them the intendant and subdelegado. Twelve intendancies replaced the 200 or so corregimientos and alcaldías mayores, though many of these lingered on as districts (partidos) into which all intendancies were subdivided.

Paralleling the intendancy system and supplementing it was a set of special military frontier jurisdictions known as the "Internal Provinces," first created in 1776 to solve defense problems of the northern frontiers. When fully evolved, the system divided areas generally north of our Principal Area into two military zones, each under an independent commander who, in the Western Command, also acted as intendant for each of two intendancies (Durango, Arizpe). The greater part of the Eastern Command left all but military matters in the hands of the intendant of San Luis Potosi.

By the early years of the 19th century, when movements for independence from Spain began to develop more strongly in New Spain, the Bourbon intendant system had taken rather firm root. It provided the transitional context out of which crystallized the system of Mexican states within the Republic of Mexico and the development of the independent nations of Central America.

II. THE MEXICAN EMPIRE, 1821–23

A major development in Middle American history was the separation of that area from overseas rule by Spain, replacing it first with an abortive attempt to create a Mexican Empire that would retain the principal features of the Spanish system but be a separate American sovereignty. The ephemeral Mexican Empire was a short intermediate step between the viceregal system under which New Spain had been governed since 1535, strongly modified in 1786, and the republican forms that succeeded it. The outlines of the American independence movements are well known. They form a fascinating and perennially investigated period, over which we must lightly skip.

Briefly stated, independence came when, for quite diverse reasons, earlier republican insurgents and conservative elements in New Spain were for a short time able to make common cause. Faced with this odd but overwhelming coalition, a newly arrived Spanish viceroy signed the Treaty of Cordoba (August 24, 1821) relinquishing Spanish sovereignty over the viceroyalty of New Spain. For many legal and historical purposes the Treaty of 1821 divides the colonial period from the modern or national period.

That treaty provided that until a suitable European monarch, perhaps the King of Spain himself, could be enticed to the throne of Mexico, a junta of the successful revolutionary coalition would name a regency to govern as executive, the junta itself holding legislative powers until a constituent assembly could be called to frame a suitable constitution for the new imperial entity. On November 17, 1821, the junta decreed the "Law of Bases for Convocation of the Constituent Congress." It met in February, 1822, and among other things, voted to form the Mexican Empire on the basis of a "moderate constitutional monarchy." The congress, because of internal differences, never wrote a constitution, but on May 19, 1822, voted to make Agustín Iturbide, a Mexican creole officer, the Mexican emperor. He was crowned in July. By

Fig. 4—THE MEXICAN EMPIRE, 1821-23

October, the congress had proved so recalcitrant that Emperor Agustín I dissolved it, ruling alone as the first of many subsequent Mexican and Central American military dictators.

The Mexican Empire had no recorded formal political divisions. It apparently was considered a single political unit, with administrative divisions, vaguely termed "Provincias Mexicanas" in the convocatory law of 1821, and similar decrees in 1822. These were generally the former intendancies.

The only novelty in listings of provinces which sent representatives to the Constituent Congress is the appearance of Queretaro. During the struggles for independence, the city and its surrounding district had separated itself from the intendancy of Mexico. It sent a deputy to the Constituent Congress. Later, August 22, 1823, its boundaries as a provincial unit were fixed by decree (O'Gorman, 1966, p. 44, note 25).

The territorial situation of the Mexican Empire was further confused by political uncertainties. Areas such as Yucatan, Chiapas, and Guatemala had individually declared their independence of Spain, derivative from the circumstance that after the Treaty of Cordoba the only loyal Spanish soldiers were a handful immured on the island of San Juan de Ulloa, opposite Veracruz. Yucatan, Chiapas, Guatemala (and its provinces of Central America) first agreed to join the empire, and were at first represented in the Constituent Congress. The Mexican Empire of 1822, essentially the mainland areas of the viceroyalty of New Spain (less the Caribbean and Philippine Islands), marks the largest territorial extent of independent Mexico.[1] It is shown in figure 4.

The various causes for the downfall of the empire need not concern us, except to say

[1] Here it may be recalled that through the Louisiana Purchase (1803) and treaties (1819, 1821) former areas of the viceroyalty in Florida and the Mississippi Valley were ceded to the United States.

FIG. 5—MEXICO, 1824 (after Cline, 1962)

that Agustín I was unable to quell an increasing number of revolts and rebellions sparked by republican partisans. With little military support remaining, Iturbide reconvened the Constituent Congress in March, 1823, and abdicated, turning over Mexican national sovereignty to it. The deputies immediately banished him in perpetuity; he was summarily shot later the same year when he returned from European exile. They also voted to change the form of government of Mexico to a federated republic, and in June, 1823, passed an act to convene yet another constituent assembly, a newly elected congress. Its duty was to draft and ratify a basic constitution for the federal republic.

Meantime, the various provinces of Guatemala convened a general congress in that provincial capital June 29, 1823. On July 1 the assembled body proclaimed that the "Provinces which form the Realm of Guatemala are free and independent of ancient Spain, of Mexico, and of any other power, be it in the Old or New World" (O'Gorman, 1966, p. 48). Indirectly the Mexican Constituent Congress recognized this departure from the Mexican Empire—becoming—Republic by allowing the Guatemalan

147

MEXICO
&
CENTRAL AMERICA

1824-1835

NUEVO
MEXICO

COAHUILA & TEXAS

SONORA

CHIHUAHUA

DURANGO

BAJA CALIFORNIA

1830   SINALOA

XALISCO

MICHOACAN

ZACATECAS   1835

GTO.

SAN LUIS
POTOSI

NUEVO LEON

TAMAULIPAS

MEXICO

PUEBLA

VERACRUZ

OAJACA

TBS.

CHIAPAS

YUCATAN

UNITED PROVINCES
Constituted 1824

PRINCIPAL AREA

Disputed

New State

Territory

0   100   200 MI

0   100   200   300 KM

Fig. 6—MEXICO, 1824–35

TABLE 3—MEXICO: STATES AND
TERRITORIES, 1824–35[*]

STATES:
1. Chiapas (exclusive of Soconusco)
2. Chihuahua
3. Coahuila y Texas
4. Durango
5. Guanajuato
6. Mexico
7. Michoacan
8. Nuevo Leon
9. Oajaca
10. Pueblo de los Angeles
11. Queretaro
12. San Luis Potosi
13. Sonora [y Sinaloa]
14. Tabasco
15. Tamaulipas
16. Veracruz
17. Xalisco
18. Yucatan
19. Zacatecas

TERRITORIES:
20. Alta California
21. Baja California
22. Colima
23. Santa Fe de Nuevo Mexico
24. Tlaxcala (Decree, Nov. 24, 1824)

CHANGES:
25. Distrito Federal (Nov. 18, 1824)
26. Sinaloa (separate state, Oct. 13, 1830)
27. Aguascalientes (from Zacatecas, Territory, created May 23, 1835)

[*] Source: O'Gorman, 1966, pp. 73–74.

representatives in its assembly peacefully to withdraw, without their taking further part in formation of the Republic of Mexico. The Guatemalan assembly said that their area would henceforth be known as "The United Provinces of Central America." *De facto* a substantial southern portion of the earlier viceroyalty thus peacefully withdrew from its bounds, determined to guide its own future, which we shall touch on in Section X.

The representatives of the Mexican "provinces" who had been elected to the second Mexican constituent assembly met in November, 1823. On December 3, they began to debate a draft constitution that a special committee had prepared.

III. REPUBLIC OF MEXICO: FEDERALIST CONSTITUTION, 1824–35

On October 4, 1824, the Constituent Congress as a whole adopted the first national Mexican constitution, creating a federal republic modeled in part on the United States. Its Article 5 (Title II) enumerated the states and territories (designated as such) which constituted the national territory. These appear as Table 3; their approximate boundaries are shown in figure 6.

With adoption of a republican constitution, earlier terms—gobiernos, intendancies, provinces—lost legal or administrative meaning, although they lingered in popular speech. Units of somewhat comparable size were called "states," each to have its own elected governors and legislative assemblies. Legally and politically the transition from colonial rule to republicanism had been completed, and was never henceforth reversed. The idea, however, that Mexico might revert to monarchy (like Brazil) did not wholly die until after the unsuccessful attempt to keep Maximilian on a Mexican imperial throne in the 1860's (see Section VII). Perhaps one other feature of the 1824 charter is worth noting. It made all inhabitants, including Indians, citizens of the Republic. It was not for nearly a century, however, that legal and other barriers to their effective participation in suffrage began to crumble (González Navarro, 1954).

Although Mexico officially recognized the "United Provinces of Central America" through congressional action August 20, 1824, a minor problem was left temporarily unresolved. Soconusco had elected to join that Central American entity, despite the claims of Chiapas to it. The small area became a bone of contention whose fate was later settled (see Section IV).

Here also worth noting is that the Federal District (Distrito Federal) officially came into being through a congressional decree

149

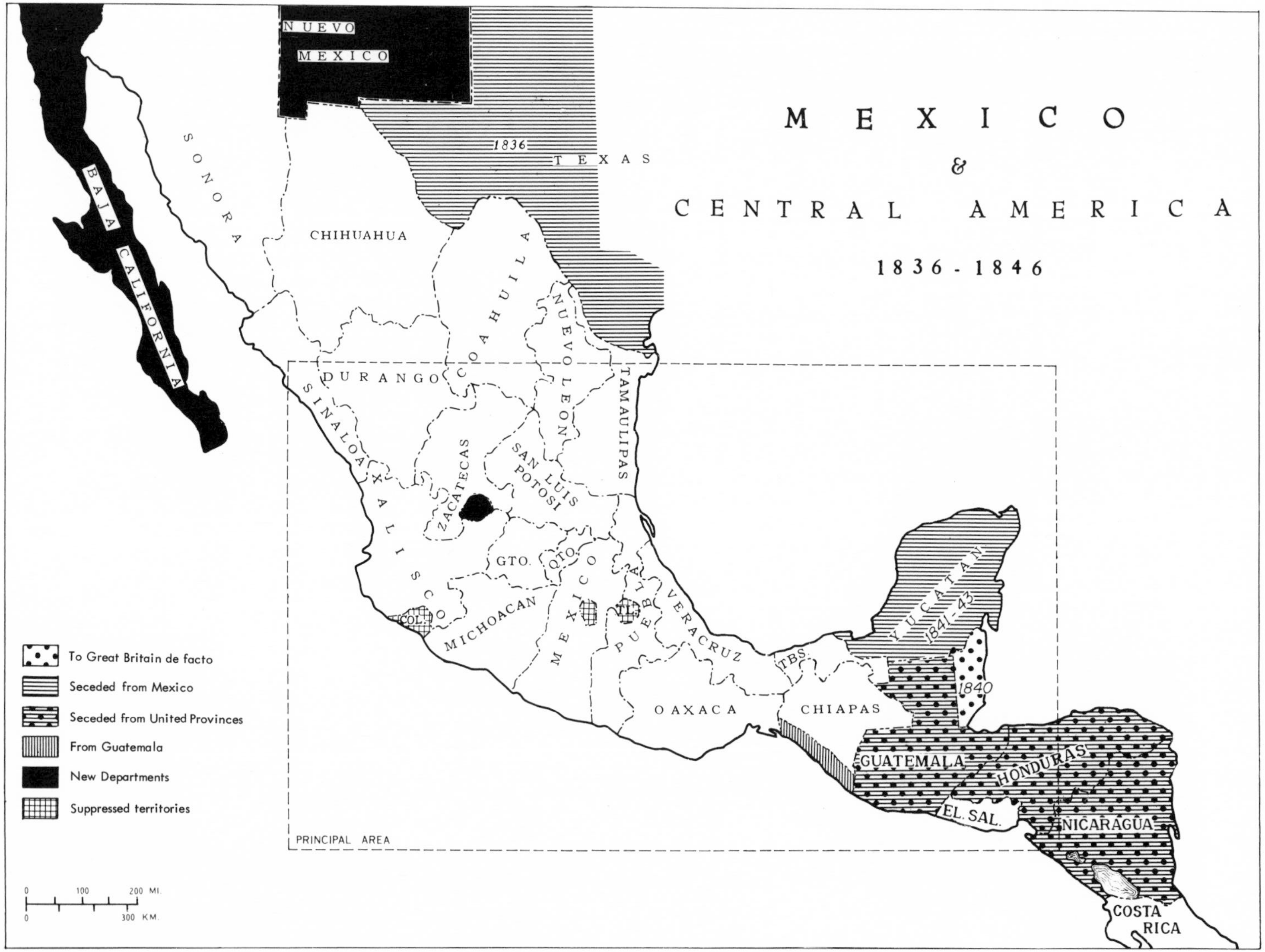

MEXICO
&
CENTRAL AMERICA

1836 - 1846

Fig. 7—MEXICO, 1836–46

Legend:
- To Great Britain de facto
- Seceded from Mexico
- Seceded from United Provinces
- From Guatemala
- New Departments
- Suppressed territories

0   100   200 MI
0   300 KM

of November 18, 1824. Its center was the main plaza (Zócalo), and its extent was a radius of 2 leagues, an area taken from the state of Mexico (O'Gorman, 1966, p. 70).

As Table 3 indicates, two other changes occurred before the Constitution of 1824 was displaced by that of 1836. A decree (October 13, 1830) separated Sinaloa from Sonora and raised it to a state of the Federation. Similarly, a May 23, 1835, decree carved the small Territory of Aguascalientes from Zacatecas (O'Gorman, 1966, pp. 70–72).

During the period following adoption of the Constitution of 1824, political currents in Mexico began to polarize between those who called themselves Federalists and their opponents, the Centralists. At issue were many matters, but fundamentally Federalists believed in limited national government, with political power residing in the states, whereas the opposite, strong central government, weak state powers, was the basic Centralist political position. Centralists tended strongly to be conservative, proclerical, and backed by the professional military. Federalists were "liberal," moderately anticlerical, and relied on militia for force. Struggles between the groups were compounded by deteriorating economic conditions and international controversies. Colonization by Americans in Texas, then in California, created even further tensions. The Federalists had essentially written the Constitution of 1824, so that when the Centralists first gained power in 1835, they decided to make important changes, to be embodied in a new constitution.

IV. REPUBLIC OF MEXICO: CENTRALIST CONSTITUTIONS, 1836–46

The Centralist philosophy of government is symbolized by the fact that when first in power, they changed the name of "states" to "departments" and divided the latter into "partidos" as had the late colonial Spanish government. Chary of "states' rights," the Centralists of the national government usu-

TABLE 4—REPUBLIC OF MEXICO: DEPARTMENTS, 1835–46

1. Aguascalientes
2. Californias
3. Chiapas (including Soconusco)
4. Chihuahua
5. Coahuila
6. Durango
7. Guanajuato
8. Mexico
9. Michoacan
10. Nuevo Leon
11. Nuevo Mexico
12. Oaxaca
13. Puebla
14. Queretaro
15. San Luis Potosi
16. Sinaloa
17. Sonora
18. Tabasco
19. Tamaulipas
20. Texas
21. Veracruz
22. Xalisco
23. Yucatan
24. Zacatecas

SUPPRESSED:

25. Distrito Federal (added to Depto. of Mexico)
26. Territory of Colima (added to Depto. of Michoacan)
27. Territory of Tlaxcala (added to Depto. of Mexico)

* Source: O'Gorman, 1966, p. 44.

ally named the governors of the "departments" rather than relying on departmental elections, and did not view with much favor any rapid increase in the number of such departments or territories. In fact, when partisan politics brought them to national power they issued a new set of "Constitutional Laws" on December 30, 1836, that among other matters entirely suppressed some earlier units created by their foes, the Federalists.

Those Laws erased the status of Colima and Tlaxcala by returning them respectively as parts of the Department of Michoacan and Department of Mexico. The latter had added to its territory the Federal District, also suppressed. The two Territories of Cal-

151

MEXICO
&
CENTRAL AMERICA
1847 - 1853

COSTA RICA
NICARAGUA
HONDURAS
EL SAL.
GUATEMALA
YUCATAN
CHIAPAS
B.C.
VERACRUZ
OAXACA
PUEBLA
MEXICO
TAMAULIPAS
NUEVO LEON
COAHUILA
SAN LUIS POTOSI
QTO.
GTO.
MICHOACAN
1849
ZACATECAS
AG.
COL.
JALISCO
DURANGO
SINALOA
CHIHUAHUA
NUEVO MEXICO
SONORA
BAJA CALIFORNIA

PRINCIPAL AREA

Annexed to United States
New State
Reinstated territories
Reduced to territories

0   100   200 MI.
0   300 KM.

Fig. 8—MEXICO, 1847–53

ifornia were combined, but the new unit was given departmental status. Coahuila and Texas were separated. Until it seceded in 1836, the latter was considered a department. Two other territories, Aguascalientes and Nuevo Mexico, were raised to departments. Under the Centralist revision, Mexico in late 1836 consisted of 24 departments, but without territories or a Federal District. These departments are listed in Table 4 and mapped in figure 7.

Some changes occurred before the Centralists finally rewrote the Constitution in 1843, since the Laws of 1836 did not have full status as a formally adopted constitution. In 1836 the Republic of Texas was declared by its citizens, and hurriedly was recognized as an independent nation by the United States and other governments. Despite the fact, Mexican legislators for some years carried Texas on the books as a "temporarily lost" part of the national territory. Another outlying area, the Peninsula of Yucatan, similarly proclaimed itself a republic, briefly allied itself with Texas, but was brought back into the Mexican Union by force (1841–43).

The status of Soconusco, claimed both by Mexico and Guatemala, was also settled. The Mexican Centralists won most of it by arms from Guatemala and, on September 11, 1842, added it to Chiapas, where it has since remained (O'Gorman, 1966, p. 86).

Technically, the Centralists' "Constitutional Laws" were congressional acts that did not displace but merely suspended various portions of the original Constitution of 1824. The latter remained on the books until June 13, 1843, at which time a new Centralist constitution, based largely on the "Constitutional Laws," was ratified. In debates about the document, some efforts were made to reinstate the territorial status of Colima and Tlaxcala, and to divide and reduce the Californias again to territorial level. Because these efforts failed, the arrangements adopted in 1836 (Table 4) remained in force.

TABLE 5—REPUBLIC OF MEXICO: STATES AND TERRITORIES, 1849*

STATES:
1. Chiapas
2. Chihuahua
3. Coahuila (without Texas)
4. Durango
5. Guanajuato
6. Jalisco
7. Mexico
8. Michoacan
9. Nuevo Leon
10. Oajaca
11. Puebla
12. Queretaro
13. San Luis Potosi
14. Sonora
15. Sinaloa
16. Tabasco
17. Tamaulipas
18. Veracruz
19. Yucatan
20. Zacatecas
21. Guerrero

TERRITORIES:
22. Baja California
23. Colima
24. Tlaxcala
25. Aguascalientes
(New Mexico lost)
(Upper California lost)
26. Federal District (Distrito Federal)

* Source: O'Gorman, 1966, p. 109.

V. REPUBLIC OF MEXICO: RETURN TO FEDERALISM, 1846–53

The swing of the political pendulum brought the Federalists back to national power in 1846. A series of decrees and laws ensued, culminating in the now familiar pattern of rewriting and adopting a new Federalist constitution (May 21, 1847). As might be expected, Federalists immediately renamed the "departments" as "states," recreated the Federal District, and reinstated the Territories of Colima and Tlaxcala.

The Constitution of May 21, 1847, was, with minor exceptions, a repetition of 1824, so far as territorial units were concerned. It reduced Aguascalientes, New Mexico,

153

M E X I C O
&
C E N T R A L   A M E R I C A

1853 - 1856

NEW
MEXICO

SONORA

CHIHUAHUA

COAHUILA

NUEVO LEON

TAMAULIPAS

DURANGO

SINALOA

ZACATECAS

SAN LUIS POTOSI

JALISCO

GTO.

OTO.

QUERETARO

MICHOACAN

MEXICO

GUERRERO

VERACRUZ

PUEBLA

OAXACA

TABASCO

CHIAPAS

YUCATAN

BAJA CALIFORNIA

GUATEMALA

HONDURAS

EL SAL.

NICARAGUA

COSTA RICA

PRINCIPAL AREA

To United States

New department

To Veracruz

Ephemeral territories

Surviving territories

0	100	200 MI.
0		300 KM.

Fig. 9—MEXICO, 1853–59

Upper and Lower California (as separate units) to territories, suppressed its state status and added Texas (now independent for nearly a decade) to the state of Coahuila. The one innovation of 1846 was provisional inclusion of a new state, Guerrero, subject first to approval by the states whose areas had been taken to form it (Mexico, Michoacan, Puebla) and then by other states of the union.

The Federalists encountered the grave misfortune of running Mexico while their national government waged a highly disastrous war with the United States, 1846–48. Whatever its other consequences, the war made important territorial changes for Mexico. In the Treaty of Guadalupe–Hidalgo (1848) which ended the conflict, Mexico recognized the loss of Texas and Upper California, which by annexation and conquest were added to the United States, near the height of its midcentury surge of "Manifest Destiny."

In the post-war year, 1849, other changes occurred in the truncated Republic of Mexico. Lower (Baja) California territory was divided into two districts, North and South (April 12, 1849). The other states agreed to welcome Guerrero as a state; it definitively entered the federation October 27, 1849.

Shorn of its northern borderlands, Mexico in 1849 consisted of 21 states, 4 territories, and the Distrito Federal. These are listed in Table 5 and illustrated in figure 8.

VI. REPUBLIC OF MEXICO: CENTRALIST EPILOGUE, 1853–56

Political instability continued to plague Mexico, as the notorious General Antonio López de Santa Anna made a final appearance on the political scene. Since dissolution of the Mexican Empire, which he helped to foster, this charismatic ex-royalist Mexican officer had been at or near the center of the political and military stage, sometimes as Federalist, sometimes as Centralist, but always involved in running the

government or seeking (often successfully) to overthrow those who were trying to. In 1853 he headed yet another barracks revolt, an insurrection that again brought Centralists to power. They briefly retained it until 1856, when new issues and new faces replaced them.

The territorial changes the Centralists made, via a constitution they proclaimed April 22, 1853, were relatively few and ephemeral. Predictably they renamed territorial units "departments," but unlike their previous actions they neither suppressed the Federal District nor the territories. They not only retained those established by Federalists (Baja California, Colima, Tlaxcala), but in addition created three short-lived ones of their own: Istmo de Tehuantepec, Sierra Gorda, and Isla de Carmen. Again they raised the Territory of Aguascalientes to a full-fledged department.

The Santa Anna regime permanently set larger limits to the Distrito Federal (February 16, 1854), and transferred the District of Tuxpan from the Department of Puebla to that of Veracruz (December 1, 1853). Foreshadowing later developments, the government also created a District of Morelos in the Department of Mexico.

His present compatriots tend more to remember, however, that Santa Anna for ten million dollars brazenly sold a portion of the Mexican national territory to the United States. The transaction is known in the latter's history as the Gadsden Purchase, involving the Valley of Mesilla in what is now southern Arizona, formerly part of Sonora and Chihuahua. That final North American nibble of Mexican territory was the last change of any major consequence in the international border between the two countries. The situation from 1853 through 1856 is shown in figure 9.

VII. REPUBLIC OF MEXICO: STABILIZATION, 1857–1902

A new political generation of young reformers acting as the brain-trust for the aging

155

FIG. 10—MEXICO, 1857–1916

M E X I C O

&

C E N T R A L   A M E R I C A

1857 - 1916

New states
New territories

ARIZONA

NEW MEXICO

TEXAS

SONORA

BAJA CALIFORNIA

CHIHUAHUA

NUEVO LEON

TAMAULIPAS

COAHUILA

DURANGO

SINALOA

1864

SAN LUIS POTOSI

ZACATECAS

AGS.

GTO.

QTO.

1884

JALISCO

COL.

MICHOACAN

MEXICO

1869

1862

PUEBLA

VERACRUZ

GUERRERO

OAXACA

TBS.

CHIAPAS

YUCATAN

1902

1863

BRIT. HON.

GUATEMALA

HONDURAS

EL SAL.

NICARAGUA

COSTA RICA

PRINCIPAL AREA

0   100   200 MI

0   300 KM

Federalist military who finally rid Mexico of Santa Anna became modern Mexican national heroes. Benito Juárez, Melchor O'Campo, and others whose incipient local political careers the Centralists had interrupted by forcing them into prolonged exile in the United States, were repatriated and became leaders of what in Mexican history is called "The Reform" (*La Reforma*). Far from an easy course, their generation managed against large odds to create the major liberal Constitution of 1857, defend it militarily against conservatives, and then uphold its doctrine of Mexican Federal republicanism through the French Intervention (1861–63). That episode for a historical instant (1864–66) put the Emperor Maximilian on the phantom throne of Mexico. Upon re-establishment of the Republic, Juárez' regime was barely able to sketch out an attractive and even possible development of Mexico before he died (1872).

After unseemly and self-serving fratricidal struggles among Liberals, heirs of earlier Federalists, the victory of General Porfirio Díaz ushered in what most historians call a dictatorship. It lasted from 1876 until the revolutionary forces mobilized by Francisco I. Madero forced the resignation of Díaz in May, 1911.

For our avowedly limited purposes, the fecund period from 1857 through 1910 represents the maturity and stabilization of the present Mexican territorial organization. Before Juárez' death, all the present Mexican states but two (Nayarit; Lower California, North) were permanently in the union. The only innovation following it was creation of one additional territory (Quintana Roo). Less than a century after the 1786 establishment of the colonial intendancy system, the present state organization had essentially evolved.

The Constitution of 1857 governed Mexico until most of its main features were incorporated and extended in the present basic charter of 1917. The 1857 document

TABLE 6—REPUBLIC OF MEXICO: 1857–1902[*]

1.	Aguascalientes
26.	Campeche (1862)
2.	Colima
3.	Chiapas
27.	Coahuila (1864)
4.	Chihuahua
5.	Durango
6.	Guanajuato
7.	Guerrero
28.	Hidalgo (1869)
8.	Jalisco
9.	Mexico
10.	Michoacan
29.	Morelos (1869)
11.	Nuevo Leon [y Coahuila]
12.	Oaxaca
13.	Puebla
14.	Queretaro
15.	San Luis Potosi
16.	Sinaloa
17.	Sonora
18.	Tabasco
19.	Tamaulipas
20.	Tlaxcala
21.	[Valle de Mexico]. Distrito Federal
22.	Veracruz
23.	Yucatan
24.	Zacatecas

TERRITORIES:
25.	Baja California
30.	Tepic (1884)

[*] Nos. 1–25 included in Constitution of 1857; nos. 26–30 included in Constitution, Dec. 12, 1884. Source: O'Gorman, 1966, pp. 134, 140–43.

accepted all the "departments" of the Centralists, again reflexively relabeling them "states." However, with the exception of Lower California, the code omitted the Centralists' ephemeral territories. For reasons not wholly clear, the framers in 1857 combined Nuevo Leon and Coahuila as a single state. The only other new departure was their creation of a contingent state, "Valle de Mexico," that was to come into being whenever the Federal government moved its seat from Mexico City. Until such circumstances, the state was to be considered the "Distrito Federal," which therefore did not figure as a separate entity. The Constitution of 1857 organized the Republic of Mexico on the basis of 24 states (Nuevo Leon and Coahuila as one, "Valle de Mexico" as another), and a single territory (Baja California).

Alterations in the scheme were relatively few until the Mexican Revolution of 1910. Five changes occurred in the decade 1860–69. The earlier District of Campeche provisionally became a state February 19, 1862, made final April 29, 1863, thus reducing the area of the State of Yucatan. On June 7 of the same year, the Federal District ["Valle de Mexico"] was further enlarged at the cost of the state of Mexico. The logical division of Coahuila as a separate state from Nuevo Leon took place February 26, 1864. During 1869 two further portions of the state of Mexico became separate Mexican states: on January 15 the Second Military District became Hidalgo, and on April 16 the Third District was henceforth the state of Morelos.

These actions had been decreed by Congress or the Executive. To make them more binding, in 1884 the 1857 Constitution was amended to incorporate the actions (December 12). Article 43 was reworded to add Campeche, Coahuila, Hidalgo, and Morelos as states. At that time also the 7th Cantón of Jalisco was detached, and was given status as the Territory of Tepic.

The final action on territorial matters by the Porfirian regime was to carve from the state of Yucatan yet another territory, named Quintana Roo, November 24, 1902. Much like the Internal Provinces of an earlier day, the latter was essentially a military zone created to permit operations against rebel Maya, lingering remnants of the Caste War in Yucatan, 1848–53.

Thus with the exception of the Territories of Tepic (1884) and Quintana Roo (1902) the state system of Mexico was completed by May, 1869. The units are listed in Table 6 and illustrated in figure 10.

VIII. Republic of Mexico: Twentieth Century

The Mexican Revolution, which Mexicans consider a continuous and continuing process, made many and basic changes in society and politics, but the territorial organization it inherited from the Porfirian regime was left virtually unaltered. Beginning with a small movement against the regime of Porfirio Díaz led by Francisco I. Madero in 1910, the successful political revolution broadened, and developed after Díaz' fall into a series of bloody regional civil wars that wracked the country. By 1917 one group, the Constitutionalists under Venustiano Carranza, exerted sufficient control over most of the area to call a constitutional convention that on February 5, 1917, issued the constitutional charter under which Mexico is currently governed.

In its Article 43, which enumerates the components of national territory, are found few differences from the amended Constitution of 1857. Nayarit was given status as a state. The chimerical state of Valle de Mexico was omitted in Article 43 but included in Article 44, the same area being included in Article 43 as the "Distrito Federal."

The ensuing revolutionary regimes have tampered very little with the arrangements set forth in the Constitution of 1917. In 1931 (February 7) the Territory of Baja California was subdivided into two territories, North and South. By decree of January 16, 1952, Baja California, Norte, entered the Mexican union as a state; Baja California, Sur, remains a territory. For a brief period (1931–35) the Territory of Quintana Roo was eliminated, its area annexed to Yucatan, but the *status quo ante* was restored January 16, 1935, and it, too, remains in territorial status.

One other matter stemming from the Constitution of 1917 warrants notice. Article 115 required that states maintain "the free municipality as the basis of territorial division of their political and administrative organization" (W. P. Tucker, 1957, p. 394), an important difference from the Constitution of 1857, which makes little mention of the municipal unit.

The constitutionalists of 1917 had specifically in mind elimination of the political districts (also called cantóns, partidos, or other local names) into which the states had been subdivided under Díaz, each such intermediary unit in charge of a *jefe político*. Under the state governors, the latter had collectively been major local instruments in maintenance of the repressive political and administrative system that developed under Díaz. In contrast to the system before 1917, the Mexican municipio is now a basic political unit. Municipios vary widely in territorial extent, but all have the same constitutional base. However, this theoretical power is illusory (Padgett, 1966, pp. 150–51).

Each has a municipal council directly elected (formerly indirect). A specific constitutional provision forbids any "intermediate authority between this body and the government of the state" (Tucker, 1957, p. 394). Thus the approximately 2,400 municipios, each often with lesser dependent communities, are the smallest Mexican legal and political territorial entities, followed in size by the states and territories, the whole comprising the Republic. Municipios are also treated in Article 1, appendix.

The Federal District has evolved since its first establishment in 1824 to a present area of about 573 square miles. After various unsatisfactory experiments to maintain municipal autonomy of various ancient communities within its bounds, in 1946 the district was reorganized as a single municipal unit, subdivided into a dozen subordinate and dependent *delegaciones*, headed by delegados appointed by the chief of the district. Unlike the comparable District of Columbia in the United States, citizens of

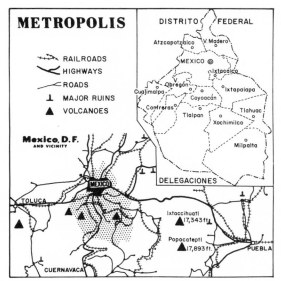

Fig. 11—THE FEDERAL DISTRICT (after Cline, 1962)

the Mexican Federal District elect congressmen and senators to the national congress and have wide autonomy in running local affairs (Tucker, 1957, pp. 409–14). This metropolitan area is shown in figure 11.

The territorial organization of the Republic of Mexico under the Revolution appears in Table 7 and in figure 12, showing the present 29 states, 2 territories, and the Distrito Federal.

TABLE 7—REPUBLIC OF MEXICO: STATES AND TERRITORIES, 1917–52°

STATES:
1. Aguascalientes
2. Baja California, Norte (1952)
3. Campeche
4. Chiapas
5. Chihuahua
6. Coahuila
7. Colima
8. Durango
9. Guanajuato
10. Guerrero
11. Hidalgo
12. Jalisco
13. Mexico
14. Michoacan

159

Fig. 12—MEXICO, 1917–52

(Table 7 continued)

15. Morelos
16. Nayarit
17. Nuevo Leon
18. Oaxaca
19. Puebla
20. Queretaro
21. San Luis Potosi
22. Sinaloa
23. Sonora
24. Tabasco
25. Tamaulipas
26. Tlaxcala
27. Veracruz
28. Yucatan
29. Zacatecas
30. Distrito Federal

TERRITORIES:
31. Baja California, Sur
32. Quintana Roo

* Source: O'Gorman, 1966, pp. 158–59.

IX. LATE COLONIAL CENTRAL AMERICA, 1785–1821

As the intendancy system seems to have spread generally from South America to Middle America, reorganization of Central America preceded the more comprehensive division of the viceroyalty of New Spain (December 4, 1786). In Central America the former gobiernos were regrouped, but the alcaldías mayores and corregimientos remained as much before: partidos within the five intendancies into which the captain-general of Guatemala was split, 1785–86. Nominally subordinate to the viceroy of New Spain, the Central American intendants also were subject to the audiencia of Guatemala, but wielded comparably more power than did their counterparts to the north (Samayoa Guevera, 1960). As no important defense problems existed in the captaincy-general, no Internal Provinces were created.

X. CENTRAL AMERICA AFTER INDEPENDENCE

On September 15, 1821, a group of Central American patriots, including royal officials, ecclesiastics, and creoles, declared that area's independence of Spain, in wake of events in Mexico (touched on above). One of the first questions that then arose was Central America's relationship to the ex-viceroyalty and the proposed Mexican Empire. One Central American group favored separate existence for the ex-captaincy-general, while another proposed continuance within the empire, now Mexican rather than Spanish. A local junta polled the municipal authorities in December, 1821. As a majority voted to join the Mexican Empire, the junta issued a decree January 5, 1822, annexing Central America to Iturbide's empire.

The union was short-lived. Within Central America there occurred the political polarization that also marked Mexico: those who favored monarchy opposed republicans, with the added feature in Central America that the latter espoused independence from Mexico. The intendancies of Central America are listed in Table 8 and are shown in figure 13. An assembly convened in Guatemala City, representing va-

FIG. 13—CENTRAL AMERICAN INTENDANCIES, 1785–1821

TABLE 8—INTENDANCIES OF CENTRAL AMERICA, 1785–1821*

No.	Intendancy	Former Jurisdictions Included	Date of Establishment	Article 2 Section
1.	San Salvador	ex-Guatemala	Dec. 17, 1785	XXII
2.	Chiapa	Chiapa Soconusco	Sept. 20, 1786	XVII XVIII
3.	Leon	Nicaragua Costa Rica	Dec. 25, 1786	XX XXI
4.	Comaguaya	Honduras	Dec. 25, 1786	XIX
5.	Guatemala	Guatemala		XVI

* Source: Navarro, 1959, p. 50.

rious partidos, and on July 1, 1823, declared that the former realm of Guatemala was henceforth free and independent of the sovereignty of Spain, Mexico, or any other power.

The same representatives turned themselves into a Constituent Congress to provide a charter for the provisional republic, "United Province of Central America," which they had declared. On December 17, 1823, a preliminary document, "Bases for the Constitution," was issued. It formally constituted the United Provinces, consisting of Guatemala, El Salvador, Honduras, Nicaragua, and Costa Rica, under a popular, representative, federal republican government. It may be recalled that when Central America declared independence of Mexico, the former gobierno of Chiapa elected to remain in the Mexican union.

On November 22, 1824, the Constitution of the United Provinces of Central America was promulgated. It provided a national government, with seat in Guatemala City, and state governments for the former provinces. It did not establish a Federal District, hence Guatemala City was until 1834 both seat of the national entity and the state of Guatemala, causing much friction. In 1834 the national capital was moved to San Salvador. Although the constitution spoke of a federal system, in fact the new nation

was a confederation, with each state quite jealous of its own power and that of its partners. By decree of Congress, Mexico formally recognized the independence of this former part of the viceroyalty on August 20, 1824 (Bancroft, 1883–86, 5: 23, note 47). Despite constant factional bickering, however, the United Provinces survived as a governmental unit until about 1838.

Endemic political instability was held in brief check by the first presidents and leaders of the Federal Republic. As they died or lost power, latent centrifugal political and regional forces prevailed. One by one the component states seceded from the United Provinces, whose national government disintegrated in the face of constant revolts in the states. In May, 1838, almost as one of its final acts, the national congress granted the separate states the privilege of acting according to their own views in the welter of civil wars, a decree tantamount to dissolution of the United Provinces. No national elections were held to fill the presidential post which fell vacant February 1, 1839.

Although the Federal Republic of five Central American states ceased about 1840, for some years thereafter attempts were made to reconstitute or substitute it by various ephemeral pacts among the small "sovereign states." However, after living in

TABLE 9—CENTRAL AMERICA, 1838–64*

State	Secession from United Provinces	Republic Declared
Guatemala	Apr. 17, 1839	Mar. 21, 1847 (ratified Sept. 14, 1848)
Honduras	Oct. 26, 1838	Oct. 26, 1838
Costa Rica	?	Aug. 30, 1848
Nicaragua	Apr. 30, 1838	Feb. 28, 1854
El Salvador	?	1856 (confirmed Mar. 19, 1864)

* Source: Bancroft, 1886–87, 3: 160–61, 164, 178, 207, 209, 300–01.

something of an international limbo, politically speaking, these small units individually declared themselves republics, and were so recognized by other governments. In the cloudy situation of the day, even such dates of beginnings of national sovereignty are difficult to ascertain. Table 9 is a schematic outline of the dissolution of the United Provinces and the beginnings of recognized national sovereignty of the components of the ex-captaincy-general.

Territorial and Jurisdictional Changes

Despite the tangled partisan politics, invasions, and fratricidal strife, relatively few permanent territorial changes occurred. Briefly, these were:

Sonsonate, 1823. Previously a partido in the intendancy of Guatemala, in 1823 it was annexed, through intrigues, by El Salvador. Although for many years the state of Guatemala did not recognize the jurisdictional change, it seems to have been permanent (Bancroft, 1886–87, 3: 166, note 1).

Chiapa, 1824. During the Mexican Empire and in its wake, Chiapa was relatively aloof from Mexican events. Partisans from Guatemala and from Mexico urged that it join one or another of the two republics when the empire fell. On May 26, 1824, the Mexican Congress indicated that Chiapa should make a free choice. A local junta

took a popular vote, announced publicly on September 12: 96,829 favored Mexico, 60,400 were for Guatemala, and 15,724 eligible voters cast no ballot. On September 14, 1824, the Chiapanecan junta solemnly declared that henceforth the Chiapas (the plural to include Soconusco) were united with Mexico. Although the state constitution, proclaimed November 19, 1825, claimed Soconusco as one of the 12 state departments, that old gobierno was in fact occupied by Guatemalan troops, supporting strong local feelings of basic allegiance to Guatemala (Bancroft, 1883–86, 5: 23–24).

Nicoya (Guanacaste), 1825. For local political reasons, the district of Nicoya, or Guanacaste, that traditionally had belonged to Nicaragua seceded, and asked annexation to Costa Rica. The latter's Congress acceded December 9, 1825. Thenceforth Nicoya formed a fifth department of Costa Rica (Bancroft, 1886–87, 3: 179).

Soconusco, 1842. Although *de jure* part of the Mexican state of Chiapas, *de facto* the small area of Soconusco was Guatemalan until August, 1842. At that time, Mexican Centralist military forces chased out the Guatemalan soldiers and captured it. By Mexican congressional decree of September 11, 1842, Soconusco was added to the Department of Chiapas, where it has since remained (Bancroft, 1883–86, 5: 240–41).

Belize (British Honduras), 1840. Under earlier 18th-century treaties with Spain, Great Britain had colonized the area now known as British Honduras, chiefly to cut logs. The British as early as 1798 had fortified Belize, and administered it as a colony, although the treaties had given only usufructuary rights. What amounted to an official, unilateral annexation to Great Britain occurred when on November 2, 1840, the British superintendent of Belize declared that henceforth all earlier laws and usages were set aside, and that only the law of England would prevail (Bancroft, 1886–87, 3: 315). Both Mexico and Guatemala

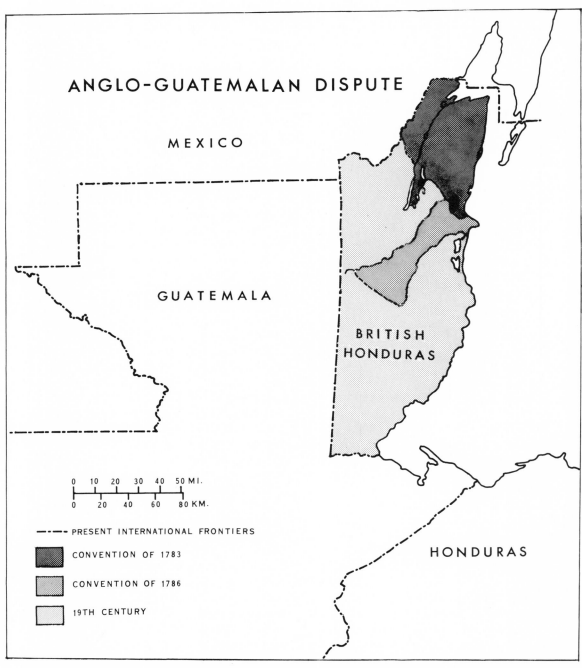

FIG. 14—DISPUTED BOUNDARIES OF BRITISH HONDURAS, 1783–1893
(after Humphreys, 1961, Map II)

had previously laid national claim to the area, as had Great Britain. The matter has never been fully settled. The "Belize Question" has bred a veritable library of tracts and monographs (best summarized in Humphreys, 1961; see also Clegern, 1967). Figure 14 is a useful map by Humphreys, which summarizes the problems of these minor, but troubled, frontiers. For our purposes, it is enough to note that in the disintegration of the viceroyalty of New Spain, British Honduras was effectively detached from either Mexico or Guatemala before mid-19th century.

REFERENCES

Bancroft, 1883–86, 1886–87
Clegern, 1967
Cline, 1952a, 1962
Durán Ochoa, 1955
Fisher, 1928, 1929
Gibson, 1966
González Navarro, 1954
Haring, 1963
Humboldt, 1811

Humphreys, 1961
Navarro García, 1959, 1964
O'Gorman, 1966
Padgett, 1966
Priestley, 1916
Samayoa Guevera, 1960
Tucker, W. P., 1957
Whetten, 1948

4. Ethnohistorical Regions of Middle America

HOWARD F. CLINE

A T ALL TIMES in its past, the Middle American area has been marked by strong local and regional divergences. These persisting traditions have strongly colored and shaped historical developments (fig. 1). Historians and geographers have taken special note of these features (Bernstein, 1944; Cline, 1953, 1962), as have many others. The complex interplay of natural environment and cultural developments to form regions has been summarized by West earlier in the *Handbook* (volume 1, Article 10), and in a later more extended treatment on cultural regions (West and Augelli, 1966). The latter provides subdivisions as seen from a cultural geographer's point of view. As figure 2 we reproduce his map, on which we have superimposed the area that we designated as "Principal Area" (Article 1, this volume).

The regional subdivisions we independently developed for this guide (fig. 1) have a more heuristic, pragmatic base. Arbitrarily we subdivide the Principal Area into regional units, grouping together individual states or portions that seem to have a number of traits and traditions in common, reflected by their ethnohistorical sources.

Necessarily there are compromises between boundaries which would best fit any one single set of such sources better than others. The regions which we use result from an empirical balance between ideal or theoretically correct lines and those imperatively imposed by the way the area and materials which treat it are currently organized. So long as it is initially understood that any regional scheme has inherent, subjective limitations, and that the one employed here is no exception, little further explanation seems requisite or profitable. Our regions are thus explicitly pragmatic, provisional working devices to aid in organization of heterogeneous source materials, and have no other sanctity.

To facilitate later discussion of various classes and types of ethnohistorical sources, we employ the following regional groupings: (1) Northern Mexico, (2) Western Mexico, (3) Central Mexico, (4) Oaxaca, (5) Southeastern Mexico and Guatemala, (6) Central America.

1. NORTHERN MEXICO

A great portion of this vast semi-arid and arid region bordering the United States is

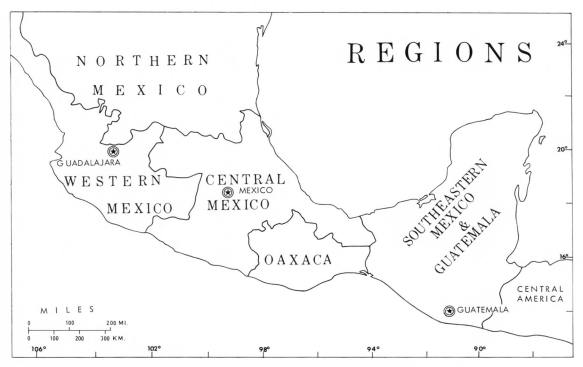

Fig. 1—ETHNOHISTORICAL REGIONS WITHIN PRINCIPAL AREA

Fig. 2—CULTURAL AREAS OF MODERN MEXICO (after West and Augelli, 1966, fig. 12.1 [adapted])

167

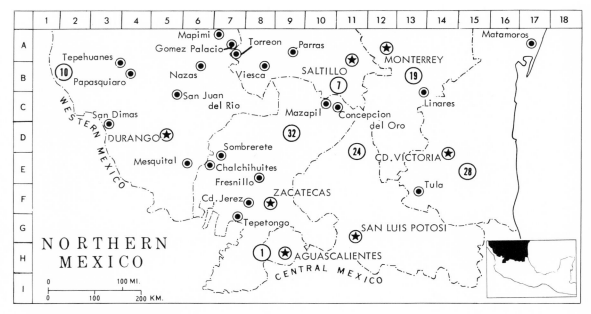

Fɪɢ. 3—NORTHERN MEXICO

peripheral to our main concerns. Much of it in pre-Contact and colonial times was the habitat of nomadic or seminomadic native groups, collectively known to the Aztec and the colonial Spaniards alike as "barbarians," or Chichimec. Northern Mexico rose to its present importance in Mexican history only in the latter half of the 19th century.

Table 1 summarizes the states which form the region of Northern Mexico included in our Principal Area. They extend slightly beyond the northern limit of the Mesoamerican area. Figure 3 provides the location of modern places, many with roots in the colonial past.

Except for the writings of religious chroniclers, who often note at length the missionary efforts of their Orders among the northern Indian groups (treated by Ernest Burrus in volume 13, Article 13), ethnohistorical sources are relatively thin and sparse. Almost no native sources, prose or pictorial, are reported. There is only a handful of Relaciones Geográficas (hereinafter abbreviated to RG's) of the 1577 series, none with contemporary maps.

In the 16th century, most of this region was divided among Nueva Galicia (centered at Guadalajara), Nueva Vizcaya, and Nuevo Leon. The most important permanent settlements were Spanish, chiefly serving as frontier outposts. With mining as a main concern, a characteristic organizational unit was the *real de minas*, or mining camp, a clearly defined lesser civil jurisdictional unit (Mecham, 1927; West, 1949). In the late 16th century and through the colonial period, the mission was similarly a characteristic Spanish institution utilized here as elsewhere to establish and maintain

TABLE 1—MEXICAN STATES IN NORTHERN MEXICO REGION (fig. 3)

A. *Outside Principal Area* (not generally considered):

2. Baja California, North (state)
3. Baja California, South (territory)
6. Chihuahua
26. Sonora

B. *Within Principal Area, Whole or Part:*

1. Aguascalientes (whole)
7. Coahuila (part)
10. Durango (part)
19. Nuevo Leon (part)
24. San Luis Potosi (whole)
32. Zacatecas (whole)

168

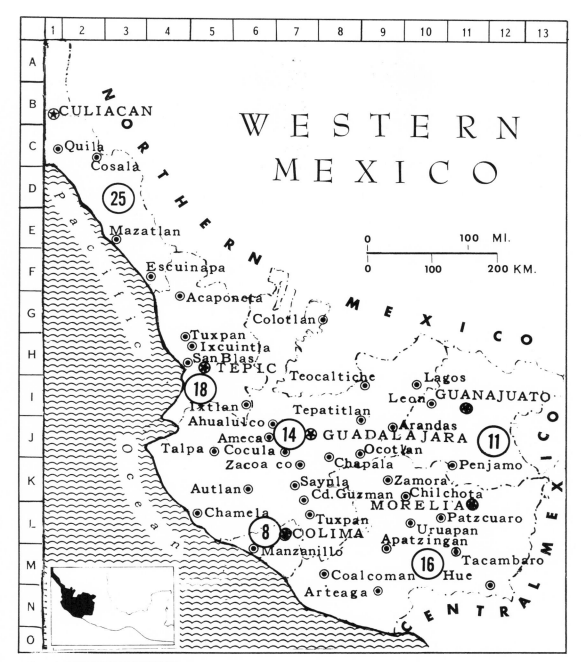

FIG. 4—WESTERN MEXICO

relations with Indians (Bolton, 1917). Missions persisted and expanded in the scantily populated region of Northern Mexico and related areas of the Spanish Borderlands long after their effective life in other parts of New Spain had long ceased.

2. WESTERN MEXICO

All of Western Mexico lies within the Mesoamerican area, bordering the Pacific Ocean. A small portion of northern Sinaloa falls outside our Principal Area, but otherwise

169

TABLE 2—MEXICAN STATES IN WESTERN MEXICO REGION (see fig. 4)

No.	State
8	Colima
11	Guanajuato
14	Jalisco
16	Michoacan
18	Nayarit
25	Sinaloa (part)

TABLE 3—MEXICAN STATES IN THE CENTRAL MEXICAN REGION

No.	State	Relation to Valley of Mexico
9	Distrito Federal	Included
12	Guerrero	Excluded
13	Hidalgo	Partial
15	Mexico	Partial
17	Morelos	Excluded
21	Puebla	Excluded
22	Queretaro	Excluded
29	Tlaxcala	Partial
30	Veracruz	Excluded

the units are complete Mexican states, listed in Table 2. Figure 4 shows selected modern places.

There is a variety of ethnohistorical sources, to some degree concentrated within the areas formerly under Tarascan hegemony and cultural influences. Brand (1944) is a useful introduction to these. For parts of Western Mexico there exist native materials, both prose and pictorial, a rather substantial body of RG's, some religious and secular chronicles, and various printed documents.

In the 16th century, the region belonged partly to the realm of New Spain, centered in Mexico City, and partly to the gobierno of Nueva Galicia, with its seat at Guadalajara. Its two principal bishoprics were those of Guadalajara and of Michoacan. Important non-Aztec native communities survived initial Contact. To them the Spanish added a number of mining camps, ringing the Spanish centers of Guadalajara and Valladolid (present Morelia). The region was thus administratively organized into mining camps, corregimientos, alcaldías mayores, pueblos de indios, and other subdivisions stipulated by the general legislation for the Spanish Indies.

Extreme northern and western portions of the region, the present states of Sinaloa and Nayarit, share many characteristics of Northern Mexico. The eastern borders of Michoacan and Guanajuato likewise share numerous features of Central Mexico, with which they were intimately linked in post-Contact times, less so earlier.

3. CENTRAL MEXICO

Central Mexico is by far the most important single region in our total ethnohistorical treatment. The area reflects continuous human occupance for hundreds, if not thousands, of years. In pre-Hispanic and post-Contact times it has been and remains the heartland of most developments within our Principal Area. It lies entirely within the Mesoamerican area and the Republic of Mexico.

In addition to the Federal District (Distrito Federal) which contains Mexico City and its satellite suburbs, the region has a number of densely populated states, listed in Table 3. The region is shown in figure 5.

Though it contained varied native peoples, most of the region was embraced within the Aztec domains which were directly under the Triple Alliance of Tenochtitlan–Texcoco–Tacuba when the Spaniards arrived in 1519. As would be expected, it has a great wealth of ethnohistorical sources of all kinds. There is a large corpus of native materials, prose and pictorial, for many of the ancient enclaves, with an equal or larger body of sources produced in European traditions following the conquest and pacification of Mexico.

The main seat of government for the viceroyalty of New Spain was established early in Mexico City. Under the viceroy were a number of jurisdictions for which he delegated administrative power (Articles 1 and 2). The viceroy was also local governor of

170

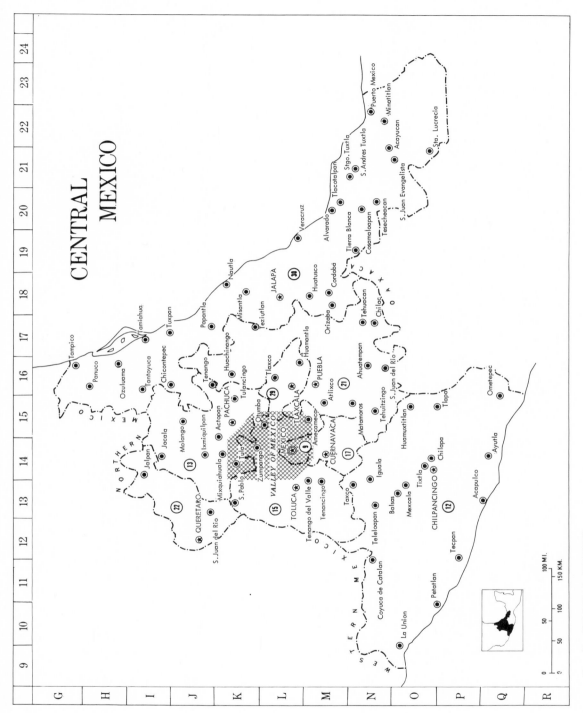

CENTRAL MEXICO

Fig. 5—CENTRAL MEXICO

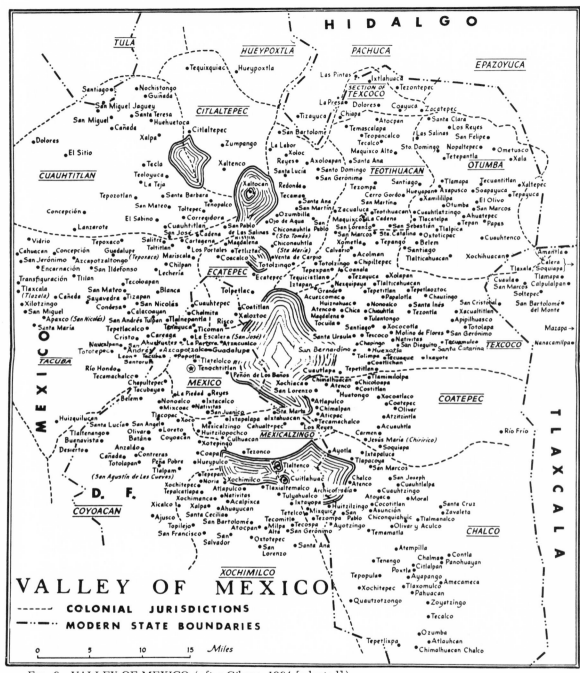

FIG. 6—VALLEY OF MEXICO (after Gibson, 1964 [adapted])

172

the gobierno of New Spain in which much of our region falls and which included the archbishopric of Mexico and the bishoprics of Tlaxcala, Michoacan, and Antequera. The audiencia of Mexico of which the viceroy was president, included these, plus Yucatan. The bishopric of Michoacan has been included above as part of Western Mexico; those of Antequera and of Yucatan are in other regions, discussed below. Hence, for purposes here Central Mexico is principally the combined area of the colonial archbishopric of Mexico, and the bishopric of Tlaxcala, whose cathedral was at Puebla.

With its relatively dense native, European, and mixed populations, Central Mexico developed a wide range of institutions, often an amalgam of indigenous and imported traditions. Research on them has bred a large technical and an even larger popular literature. Their study is by no means exhausted.

Although western Guerrero shares a number of matters with the Oaxaca region, it has been found impractical to split the state unit, originally part of the state of Mexico, Puebla, and Michoacan. Much the same is true of the state of Veracruz; its areas south and east of the present port of Veracruz and the adjoining cities of Cordoba and Orizaba similarly have strong affinities with the Oaxaca region, but for the same reason they arbitrarily remain for us in Central Mexico.

At the heart of Central Mexico is the Valley of Mexico. Relatively small in area, it has been enormous in influence and significance. This fertile valley also has been the subject of many investigations. For ethnohistorical purposes, the study by Gibson (1964) is a model synthesis providing data from Conquest through 1810. The Gibson study furnishes clues and a useful measure of what was possibly happening elsewhere in colonial Middle America but for areas on which no such comparable complete summaries have yet appeared.

The Valley, with its own major traditions and literature, might well have been separated as a distinct region or subregion. It has not. But because of its pre-eminence in the ethnohistory of Middle America, and its dominant position in Central Mexico, its principal communities appear in figure 6, adapted from Gibson (1964).

4. Oaxaca Region

The general Oaxaca Region is shown in figure 7. It consists solely of the present state of that name, the only region so restricted. Its importance in Middle American ethnohistory warrants such special treatment.

The western portion is the Mixteca, rich in pre-Conquest history and afterwards of equal continuing colonial importance. Eastward of the Central Valley of Oaxaca, shared by the Mixtec and Zapotec, were Zapotec areas, flanked by numerous smaller but important native cultural units: Chinantec, Mazatec, Cuicatec, Huave, Mixe, and others. Recent studies edited by Paddock (1966) contain much information on Oaxaca not elsewhere available.

From the Mixteca and other parts of Oaxaca has survived a rather large body of native pictorial documents of great beauty, complexity, and historiographical utility. A long list of studies by Alfonso Caso and others attest to the sustained interest in the pictorially recorded ethnohistory of Oaxaca. Less abundant are native prose sources. Oaxaca is quite remarkable also for its large corpus of RG's, both texts and maps. There is, however, only a small and minor body of colonial chronicles, religious or secular. Official colonial documentation is spotty both for times and for places.

In the 16th century Oaxaca was roughly equivalent to the bishopric of Antequera, which then included a portion in the eastern extremity of the present state of Veracruz. Then Oaxaca (Antequera) was bounded on the north by the Gulf of Mexico, on the south by the Pacific Ocean.

173

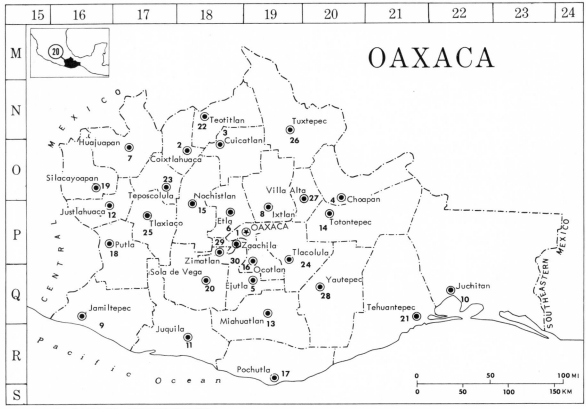

FIG. 7—OAXACA: EX-DISTRITOS

Administratively Oaxaca was part of the realm of New Spain, and within the audiencia of the Mexican judicial district. The cathedral of Antequera was in the city of Oaxaca, the only major European settlement. The area developed a quite full array of Spanish colonial institutions, strongly tinctured by the deep-rooted indigenous practices of its numerous surviving native communities.

Lemoine (1954, p. 69) notes that the great variety of settlements, cultures, and terrain has made Oaxaca one of the most complex state units in the Republic. During much of the 19th century a varying number of districts (from 26 to 30) grouped some 1,128 settlements, many with their own strings of lesser units and dependencies.

The last census which employed such districts was 1940, when there were 30. For the 1950 census the district scheme was abandoned; each of the 571 municipios, the largest number for any Mexican state, then was reported separately.

With much care Lemoine (1954), covering more than a 50-year span, has traced to 1950 the history of the ex-distritos and municipios of Oaxaca from manuscript and printed materials. He notes the contradictions among cartographic and other sources, changes in nomenclature, and emphasizes common hazards of such investigations; he points out that the map he developed from his findings differs in many respects from the "official" ones, often based on inadequate data. His general map has

174

TABLE 4—OAXACA: EX-DISTRITOS AND MUNICIPIOS, 1950 (fig. 7)

No.	Ex-Distrito	Principal Cabecera°	Number of Municipios 1950
1	Centro	Oaxaca de Juarez	21
2	Coixtlahuaca	San Juan Bautista Cuicatlan	13
3	Cuicatlan	San Juan Bautista Cuicatlan	19
4	Choapan	Santiago Choapan	6
5	Ejutla	Ejutla de Crespo	13
6	Etla	San Pedro Etla	23
7	Huajuapan	Huajuapan de Leon	29
8	Ixtlan	Ixtlan de Juarez	26
9	Jamiltepec	Santiago Jamiltepec	19
10	Juchitan	Juchitan de Zaragossa	22
11	Juquila	Santa Catarina Juquila	14
12	Juxtlahuaca	Santiago Juxtlahuaca	9
13	Miahuatlan	Santa Lucia Miahuatlan	32
14	Mixe	Tetontepec	18
15	Nochistlan	Asuncion Nochistlan	32
16	Ocotlan	Asuncion Ocotlan	20
17	Pochutla	San Pedro Pochutla	14
18	Putla	Putla de Guerrero	10
19	Silacayoapan	Silacayoapan	19
20	Sola de Vega	San Miguel Sola de Vega	15
21	Tehuantepec	Santo Domingo Tehuantepec	19
22	Teotitlan	Teotitlan del Camino	24
23	Teposcolula	San Pedro y San Pablo Teposcolula	21
24	Tlacolula	Tlacolula de Matamoros	25
25	Tlaxiaco	Santa Maria Asuncion Tlaxiaco	34
26	Tuxtepec	San Juan Bautista Tuxtepec	14
27	Villa Alta	San Ildefonso Villa Alta	25
28	Yautepec	San Carlos Yautepec	11
29	Zaachila	Trinidad de Zaachila	7
30	Zimatlan [Villa Alvarez]	San Lorenzo Zimatlan	11

Source: Lemoine, 1954.
° Supplied by author.

been reproduced as figure 7, omitting the municipal subdivisions he has shown. These appear in Article 1, figure 25. Table 4 summarizes data which Lemoine provides in more detail.

Modern investigators have grouped the Oaxacan municipios and ex-districts into various subregions for particular purposes (Tamayo, 1950; Cline, 1966b). There is, however, no fully established subregional scheme. In volume 14, Article 23, for instance, John Glass employs one which seems to fit the classification of the native pictorial documents from that region.

5. SOUTHEASTERN MEXICO AND GUATEMALA

Whereas Oaxaca was a single state, the region here called Southeastern Mexico and Guatemala spans the two republics implicit in the name, as well as a dependent British territory. The region embraces part of Mexico, and all of Guatemala and British Honduras, whose territory has recurrently been in dispute between the two republics and Great Britain and currently is moving toward independence.

The main unifying threads of the region are the underlying native Maya co-traditions that formed the principal post-Contact contexts for ethnohistorical developments. These Maya co-traditions subdivide the region (shown in fig. 8) into two subregions: Lowlands and Highlands.

The Maya and their neighbors who share this region have long attracted scholarly attention. From various disciplines and points of view, specialists have created a large technical literature, supplemented by an even larger popular or semischolarly body of writings on the Maya. These peoples—ancient, historic, and modern—have long been recognized as one of the more important native groups in Mesoamerica.

The particular areas they inhabit fall within this region. It is entirely within Mesoamerica, whose extreme eastern and southern limits extend only a short distance beyond the boundaries between Guatemala and its smaller Central American neighbors. The region lies between the Gulf of Mexico and the Pacific Ocean, a relatively short distance apart where separated by the Isthmus of Tehuantepec, and extends eastward to the Caribbean Sea. The ranges of mountains on the Pacific side break the region

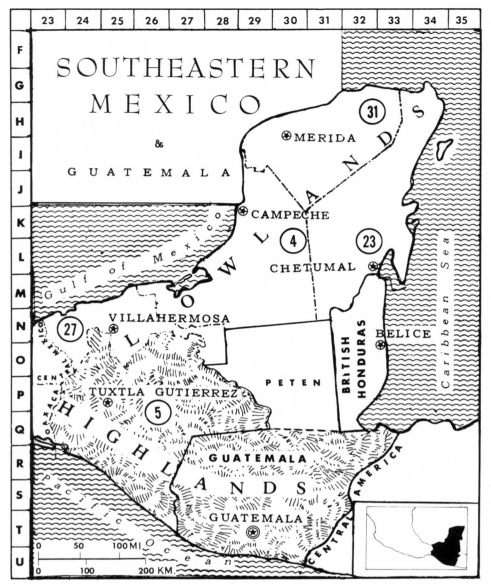

FIG. 8—SOUTHEASTERN MEXICO AND GUATEMALA

into its two subregions, Highlands and Low-lands. Ethnohistorical sources for each, as well as the cultures and subcultures they reflect, differ for the subregions.

Lowlands

Figure 9 provides details on the Low-lands, whose components are outlined in Table 5.

Much of the specialized literature on pre-Hispanic and post-Contact Maya deals pri-

TABLE 5—SOUTHEASTERN MEXICO AND GUATEMALA: LOWLANDS SUBREGION (fig. 9)

No.	Unit	Status
A. *Mexican Components:*		
4	Campeche	State
23	Quintana Roo	Territory
27	Tabasco	State
31	Yucatan	State
B. *Non-Mexican Components:*		
	British Honduras	British dependency
	El Peten	Department of Republic of Guatemala

176

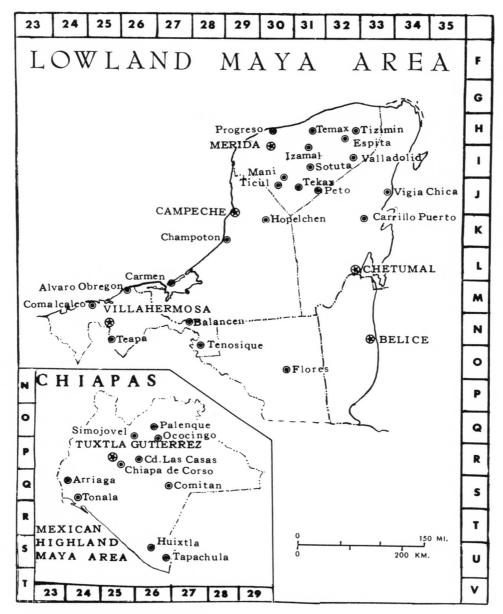

Fig. 9—LOWLAND MAYA REGION
Insert: Mexican Highland Maya Region.

marily with the Lowlands. Documentary sources are conveniently summarized in Roys (1962). In late pre-Conquest times Yucatan was divided into 17 or 18 minor Maya realms, providing the immediate background to the colonial area (Roys, 1957). Undoubtedly these pre-Contact divisions affected later colonial jurisdictions. The present divisions of the Peninsula of Yucatan into three Mexican political states and a territory, plus a British dependency and a department of Guatemala, is largely a 19th-century phenomenon, partially a result of the famous War of the Castes, 1847–53 (Cline, 1952b; Reed, 1964).

Of the native pictorial documents from Lowland Yucatan three major pre-Conquest items, all seemingly calendrical and nonhistorical, are of prime importance for certain studies. Apart from a rather curious cluster known as the Books of Chilam Balam, native prose sources also are relatively few and generally insignificant. Apart from the monumental Landa chronicle, colonial European sources, except for RG's, are thin.

The Lowlands are well represented by RG's. Some 54 texts relate to communities in Yucatan, but only two have map materials. No relaciones are extant for Campeche. Tabasco and Quintana Roo have a few, with one map.

Highlands

The Highlands are basically formed by a single ecological zone, the Sierra de Chiapas, with its narrow Pacific coastal plain. For historical reasons the subregion is now artificially bisected by an international boundary, separating the Mexican state of Chiapas from the Republic of Guatemala (Article 3). In colonial times they formed part of the same audiencia; Chiapa and Soconusco, now combined as the state of Chiapas, were each colonial ecclesiastical units as well as minor political units under the captain-general of Guatemala.

With the exception of a few religious and secular chronicles, usually primarily relating to other areas, Chiapas is nearly bereft of ethnohistorical sources. It lacks native chronicles and pictorials, and no RG's are reported for it.

The subregion of Highlands is, for our purpose, the Mexican state of Chiapas, plus all departments of Guatemala exclusive of El Peten. The latter area, to recent times a barren tract, has generally been marginal both to Lowlands and Highlands; ecologically it belongs with the former.

In colonial times the Peten was little known, and was not fully pacified until 1697, one of the last of the Mesoamerican areas to undergo that process. It tends to be an ethnohistorical enclave, with its own special, local history, even yet not fully told. Cowgill (1963, ch. 5) has reviewed

178

TABLE 6—REPUBLIC OF GUATEMALA: DEPARTMENTS, CAPITALS, AND SECTIONS

No.	Department	Capital	Section
1	El Peten	Flores	North
2	Huehuetenango	Huehuetenango	West
3	San Marcos	San Marcos	West
4	Totonicapan	Totonicapan	West
5	Quetzaltenango	Quetzaltenango	West
6	Retalhuleu	Retalhuleu	West
7	El Quiche	Quiche	North
8	Solola	Solola	West
9	Suchitepequez	Mazatenango	West
10	Chimaltenango	Chimaltenango	Center
11	Sacatepquez	Antigua	Center
12	Escuintla	Escuintla	South
13	Alta Vera Paz	Coban	North
14	Baja Vera Paz	Salama	North
15	Guatemala	Guatemala	Center
16	Santa Rosa	Culiapa	South
17	El Progreso	El Progreso	East
18	Jalapa	Jalapa	East
19	Jutiapa	Jutiapa	East
20	Izabal	Puerto Barrios	North
21	Zacapa	Zacapa	East
22	Chiquimula	Chiquimula	East

and restudied many of the ethnohistorical sources for the Itza of the Peten.

The large Guatemalan segment of the Highlands subregion completely overshadows Chiapas in ethnohistorical sources. Even so, the total Guatemalan numbers are very small. From Highland Guatemala, there are important annals and native writings, but only two RG's and relatively few and unimportant native pictorial documents. It has some major religious chronicles but few secular ones. There is relatively rich official documentation, important for local detail. Much geography has been sketched by Termer (1936).

The present Republic of Guatemala is but a small part of the original audiencia jurisdiction of colonial days. Other parts are treated below under Central America, and in Article 3. The modern organization (in the national period) has been by departments, each of which contains municipio units and their dependencies. In 1961–62 the Guatemalan Government published an excellent *Diccionario Geográfico*, whose

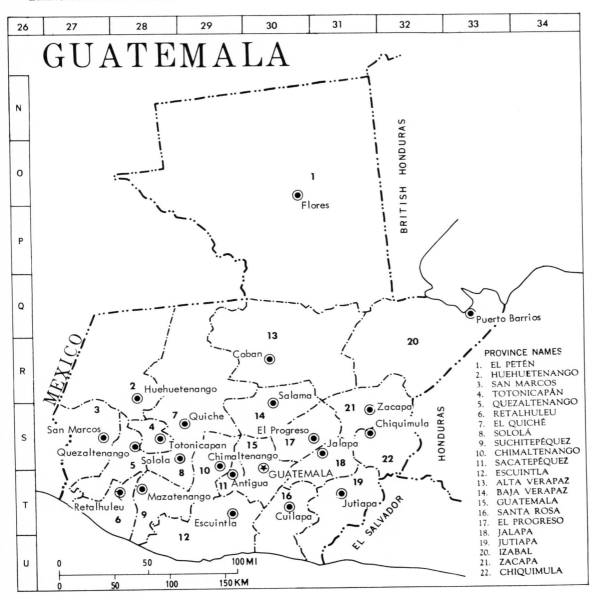

FIG. 10—GUATEMALA

two volumes contain a vast body of data on places, toponyms, historical and administrative changes, and other relevant historical information on these municipios, and related sites and places. (Dirección General, 1961–62). There is also a helpful bibliography on geographical studies since 1547 (Reyes, 1960).

Guatemalan writers occasionally group the 22 departments into five sections: North, South, East, West, and Center (Mejía, 1927; Arévalo, 1936). Table 6 gives the names and capitals of the departments, together with their sections; these are shown in figure 10.

179

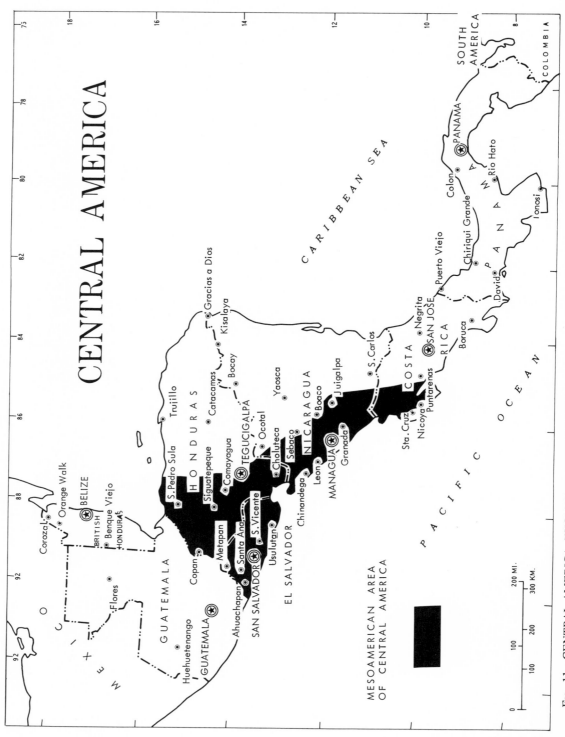

FIG. 11—CENTRAL AMERICA, EXCLUSIVE OF GUATEMALA

TABLE 7—CENTRAL AMERICA (fig. 11)

Republic	Capital	Relation To Mesoamerica
El Salvador	San Salvador	Totally included
Honduras	Tegucigalpa	Western portion included
Nicaragua	Managua	Western portion included
Costa Rica	San Jose	Western portion included
Panama	Panama	Not included

6. CENTRAL AMERICA

Figure 11 shows the region of Central America. It consists of five small republics —El Salvador, Honduras, Nicaragua, Costa Rica, and Panama—collectively occupying a relatively narrow land bridge between Mesoamerica and South America.

Most of Central America lies east and south of the high culture areas of Mesoamerica. El Salvador is wholly contained within the latter, as are western parts of Nicaragua, Honduras, and a very small portion of Costa Rica. Most of the latter, and Panama, lie wholly outside Mesoamerica. Table 7 summarizes data on Central America.

At time of Spanish conquest, Central America contained a congeries of relatively small Indian groups, none particularly advanced. During the colonial period the area was generally dependent on the audiencia at Guatemala, itself a southern periphery of the realm of New Spain. These areas were for a short time part of the Mexican Empire when the latter became independent of Spain, but shortly thereafter the Central American regions declared themselves independent national states (Article 3).

They do not figure largely in our surveys of ethnohistorical sources. From Central America there are no known Indian pictorial documents, or RG's of the 1577–85 series, although a considerable body of comparable material has been published (Peralta, 1883; Serrano y Sanz, 1908). Secular and religious chronicles are infrequent and yield few data. The documentation in European traditions is similarly sparse, spotty, and scattered. Many of the known historical data on two of the more important groups, the Nicarao and the Chorotega, have been extracted and published by A. M. Chapman (1960), with useful bibliography. A major point of departure for the general history of Central America remains the old three-volume work by Bancroft (1886–87).

FINAL NOTE

The first four articles in this volume have underscored the cultural and jurisdictional complexity of Middle America. To reduce that tangle to manageable proportions, we have designated the ethnohistorically most important portion of it as the "Principal Area," whose bounds tend to be anthropologically "Mesoamerica," here translated roughly into modern state and national units. For the ordering and analysis of various sources that we shall now cover in detail, the Principal Area has been further subdivided into the six regions sketched above. Of these, Northern Mexico and Central America remain quite marginal, with Central Mexico and Oaxaca as the regions richest in sources; Western Mexico and Southeastern Mexico (and Guatemala) occupy an intermediate position.

The remainder of this volume is devoted to various aspects of the RG's. They form a corpus transitional between ethnogeography and ethnohistory, contributing to each. Thereafter we shall confine our attention to standard historiographical materials, first those in European traditions, then those in the native traditions.

REFERENCES

Arévalo, 1936
Bancroft, 1886–87
Bernstein, 1944
Bolton, 1917
Brand, 1944
Chapman, A. M., 1960
Cline, 1952b, 1953, 1962, 1966b
Cowgill, 1963
Dirección General, Guatemala, 1961–62
Gibson, 1964
Lemoine Villicaña, 1954
Mecham, 1927

Mejía, 1927
Paddock, 1966
Peralta, 1883
Reed, 1964
Reyes, M., 1960
Roys, 1957, 1962
Sauer, 1948
Serrano y Sanz, 1908
Tamayo, 1950
Termer, 1936
West, 1949, 1964
——— and Augelli, 1966

5. The Relaciones Geográficas of the Spanish Indies, 1577-1648

HOWARD F. CLINE

COMPILED ON THE ORDER of Philip II, the *Relaciones Geográficas* have long been recognized by historians as a major group of sources on the 16th-century Spanish Indies. Surprisingly little, however, is found in the historiographical literature about this body of materials.

The RG's (the abbreviated form used here) are replies by local Spanish officials in Middle and South America to a standard questionnaire developed by imperial bureaucrats in Madrid, making 50 broad queries applicable alike to European, Indian, and maritime communities in the overseas realms. Designed to elicit basic information about diverse regions, the questionnaire, a memoria accompanied by printed instructions, specified in detail how alcaldes mayores, corregidores, and others assigned to answer it were to do so.

The stipulated procedures required a map or *pintura* (picture) of the area as well as the detailed textual report. Hence, in addition to a documentary corpus on the American dominions in the years 1578–85, there is a lesser but quite significant cartographic and pictorial body of material for the same period. It complements and often extends the written statements. These documents are treated in Article 6 by Donald Robertson.

We are thus dealing with a general group of source materials of consequence to historical investigations in the environmental sciences, the social sciences, and the humanities. The RG's have never been systematically exploited, for a number of reasons, chief of which is that these documents are not well known except to a small handful of specialists.

Because of the direct importance of the RG corpus to studies of Middle American ethnohistory, both pre-Contact and 16th century, they are given extensive coverage in this Guide. The present article recapitulates information about their administrative history, major collections, areas for which the documents were prepared, and related data, with documentary appendices. A census of the 1577 series of RG's is detailed in Article 8, collated from data collected by many hands.[1] The separate corpus of

[1] Grateful appreciation is expressed to many colleagues who provided information and aid, among

pictorial materials accompanying the textual reports is analyzed, discussed, and listed in Article 6 by Donald Robertson. Herbert R. Harvey then summarizes in Article 7 material on languages revealed by the 1577 RG's. Supplementary groups of documents in the RG tradition for the 18th century are covered in Article 10 by Robert C. West. A comprehensive bibliography, related not only to the RG materials of Middle America, but to those of Spain and South America, appears in Article 9.

Despite the almost self-evident importance of the RG documents, individually and collectively, there has been relatively little written about them. A major point of departure for learning about their background, nature, and number is still the work of Marcos Jiménez de la Espada, a distinguished Spanish scholar who published four volumes of these RG materials between 1881 and 1897. His erudite introductions to these volumes sum up much of what was then known about such matters. All subsequent treatments rely heavily on his data. Little has been added, since his day, beyond publication of documents.

Exceptions are three very recent publications received after the present summary was written. One is an article by Sylvia Vilar; it appeared as these pages were in galley proof. In 1970 she reviewed the series of questionnaires and the reports they evoked from 1577 through 1812, utilizing unpublished manuscripts and much published literature. She notes especially the changes in types of data requested as evolution of the Spanish overseas realms proceeded and bureaucratic thought altered. More directly related to New Spain is the extended analysis of the RG's from 1579–1585, which Alejandra Moreno de

whom are Ignacio Bernal, Clinton R. Edwards, Alfonso Caso, Peter Gerhard, Henry J. Bruman, John Glass, Nettie Lee Benson, Adele Kibre, Donald Robertson, Donald Brand, H. B. Nicholson, Charles O. Houston, Leoncio Cabrero, Ida K. Langman, Günter Zimmermann, Nancy P. Troike, Murdo MacLeod, and Sylvia Vilar.

184

Florescano published in Mexico (1968). Another noteworthy contribution is Clinton Edwards' 1969 study of the Juan de Velasco questionnaires and their results. These treatments extend and provide additional depth to the present summary.

Besides Jiménez de la Espada, several scholars in the late 19th and early 20th centuries published collections of American RG's. Chief among them was Francisco del Paso y Troncoso, a Mexican savant sent abroad at the close of the last century by his government especially to search for historical documents on colonial Mexico in European archives (Zavala, 1939; Carrera Stampa, 1949, pp. 5–55). As we shall see, a large collection of these RG documents relating to Mexico was obtained independently by Joaquín García Icazbalceta, another well-known 19th-century investigator. Individual RG's have been published in widely scattered places, often obscure journals. Very few RG's, however, escaped initial notice by Jiménez de la Espada in his 1881 preliminary listing of these and similar items (Jiménez de la Espada, 1881).

For this Guide, various scholars have surveyed intensively the RG's covering Middle America. One result of such collective labors is that we have now a relatively firm list of those known to have been prepared. A summary of data of the Census listing appears here as Table 1, excluding "lost" items, which are on Table 5.

ADMINISTRATIVE HISTORY
Juan de Ovando and Juan López de Velasco

For these archival and bibliographical inquiries it has been necessary to reconstruct the general bureaucratic and administrative history of the RG's. In the academic discourse required of those newly elected to the Spanish Academy of History, Fermín Caballero in 1866 first systematically directed scholarly attention to the enormous value of the geographical reports ordered by Philip II on Spanish and American

TABLE 1—RELACIONES GEOGRÁFICAS OF NEW SPAIN, 1579–85: SUMMARY LISTING

Census No.	Principal Cabecera	Bishopric or Archbishopric	Date	Repository	Publication Text	Map	Class of RG
1	ACAPISTLA	Mexico	1580	UTX	Pub	Unpub	Simple
2	ACATLAN	Tlaxcala	1581	RAH	Pub	None	Composite
3	AHUATLAN	Tlaxcala	1581	RAH	Pub	None	Composite
4	AMECA	Guadalajara	1579	UTX	Pub	Pub	Simple
5	AMULA	Guadalajara	1579	UTX	Pub	None	Composite
6	ANTEQUERA	Antequera	1580	UTX	Pub	None	Simple
7	ASUCHITLAN	Michoacan	1579	RAH	Pub	None	Complex
8	ATENGO	Mexico	1579	UTX	Pub	Unpub	Complex
9	ATITLAN	Guatemala	1585	UTX	Unpub	Unpub	Composite
10	ATLATLAUCA	Mexico	1580	UTX	Pub	Pub	Composite
11	ATLATLAUCA	Antequera	1580	RAH	Pub	Pub	Complex
12	ATLITLALQUIA	Mexico	1580	AGI	Pub	Lost	Complex
13	CACALAC (V)	Yucatan	1579	AGI	Pub	None	Complex
14	CACALCHEN (M)	Yucatan	1581	AGI	Pub	None	Composite
15	CAMPOCOLCHE (V)	Yucatan	n.d. [1579]	AGI	Pub	None	Complex
16	CANACHE (M)	Yucatan	1580	AGI	Pub	None	Complex
17	CANZACABO (M)	Yucatan	n.d. [1581]	AGI	Pub	None	Simple
18	CELAYA	Michoacan	1580	RAH	Pub	Pub	Composite
19	CEMPOALA	Mexico	1580	UTX	Pub	Pub (3)	Composite
20	CHANCENOTE (V)	Yucatan	1579	AGI	Pub	None	Composite
21	CHICHICAPA	Antequera	1580	AGI	Pub	None	Composite
22	CHICONAUTLA	Mexico	1580	AGI	Pub	None	Complex
22bis	CHILAPA	Tlaxcala	1582	RAH	Unpub	Lost?	Simple
23	CHILCHOTLA	Michoacan	1579	RAH	Pub	None	Simple
24	CHINANTLA	Antequera	1579	RAH	Pub	None	Simple
25	CHOLULA	Tlaxcala	1581	UTX	Pub	Pub	Simple
26	CHUBULNA (M)	Yucatan	n.d. [1581]	AGI	Pub	None	Composite
27	CHUNCHUCHU (M)	Yucatan	1581	AGI	Pub	None	Complex
28	CITLALTOMAGUA	Mexico	1580	AGI	Pub	None	Complex
29	COATEPEC	Mexico	1579	AGI	Pub	Pub (3)	Composite
30	COATZOCOALCO	Antequera	1580	UTX	Pub	Unpub	Simple
31	COMPOSTELA	Guadalajara	1584	RAH	Pub	Pub	Simple
32	CUAUHQUILPAN	Mexico	1581	AGI	Pub	None	Simple
33	CUAHUITLAN	Antequera	1580	RAH	Pub	Pub	Complex
34	CUAUTLA	Antequera	1580	UTX	Pub	None	Composite
35	CUICATLAN	Antequera	1580	RAH	Pub	None	Simple
36	CUICUIL (V)	Yucatan	1579	AGI	Pub	None	Simple
37	CUILAPA	Antequera	1580	UTX	Pub	None	Simple
38	CUISEO	Michoacan	1579	RAH	Pub	None	Simple
39	CUITELCUM (M)	Yucatan	1581	AGI	Pub	None	Complex
40	CUIZIL (M)	Yucatan	1581	AGI	Pub	None	Complex
41	CULHUACAN	Mexico	1580	UTX	Pub	Pub	Simple
42	CUZCATLAN–1	Tlaxcala	1580	AGI	Pub	Pub	Simple
43	CUZCATLAN–2	Tlaxcala	1580	UTX	Unpub	Pub	Simple
44	FRESNILLO	Guadalajara	1585	RAH	Pub	None	Composite
45	GUATULCO	Antequera	n.d. [1580]	RAH	Pub	None	Composite
46	GUAXOLOTITLAN	Antequera	1581	RAH	Pub	None	Simple
47	GUAXTEPEC	Mexico	1580	UTX	Pub	Unpub	Simple
48	GUAYMA (V)	Yucatan	1597	AGI	Pub	None	Complex
49	GUEYTLALPA	Tlaxcala	1581	UTX	Pub	Unpub	Composite
50	HOCABA (M)	Yucatan	1581	AGI	Pub	None	Simple
51	HUEXOTLA	Mexico	1580	AGI	Pub	Pub	Simple
52	ICHCATEOPAN	Mexico	1579	AGI	Pub	None	Composite

185

(*Table 1, continued*)

Census No.	Principal Cabecera	Bishopric or Archbishopric	Date	Repository	Publication		Class of RG
					Text	Map	
53	IGUALA	Mexico	1579	UTX	Pub	None	Composite
54	IXCATLAN	Antequera	1579	UTX	Unpub	Pub (2)	Composite
55	IXMUL (V)	Yucatan	1579	AGI	Pub	None	Complex
56	IXTAPALAPA	Mexico	1580	UTX	Pub	Unpub	Simple
57	IXTEPEXIC	Antequera	1579	RAH	Pub	Pub	Simple
58	IZAMAL (M)	Yucatan	1581	AGI	Pub	None	Complex
59	IZTEPEC	Antequera	1581	UTX	Pub	None	Complex
60	JILQUILPAN	Michoacan	1579	RAH	Pub	None	Composite
61	JUSTLAVACA	Antequera	1580	UTX	Pub	None	Composite
62	MACUILSUCHIL	Antequera	1580	RAH	Pub	Pub	Composite
63	MAMA (M)	Yucatan	1580	AGI	Pub	None	Composite
64	MERIDA (M)	Yucatan	1579	AGI	Pub	None	Simple
65	MEXICATZINGO	Mexico	1580	AGI	Pub	Lost	Simple
66	MEZTITLAN	Mexico	1579	UTX	Pub	Pub	Complex
67	MIZANTLA	Tlaxcala	1579	UTX	Pub	Pub	Simple
68	MOTINES	Michoacan	1580	RAH	Pub	None	Composite
69	MOTUL (M)	Yucatan	1581	AGI	Pub	Pub	Simple
70	MOXOPIPE (M)	Yucatan	1581	AGI	Pub	None	Simple
71	NABALON (V)	Yucatan	1579	AGI	Pub	None	Complex
72	NECOTLAN	Michoacan	1579	RAH	Pub	None	Simple
73	NEXAPA	Antequera	1580	AGI	Pub	Lost	Simple
74	NOCHIZTLAN	Antequera	1581	RAH	Pub	Pub	Simple
75	NUCHISTLAN	Guadalajara	1584	RAH	Pub	None	Complex
76	OCOPETLAYUCA	Mexico	1580	AGI	Pub	None	Simple
77	OSCUZCAS (M)	Yucatan	1581	AGI	Pub	None	Simple
78	PAPALOTICPAC	Antequera	1579	RAH	Pub	None	Composite
79	PATZCUARO	Michoacan	1581	UTX	Pub	None	Simple
80	PEÑOLES, LOS	Antequera	1579	UTX	Pub	Unpub	Composite
81	PIJOY (V)	Yucatan	1579	AGI	Pub	None	Simple
82	PONCITLAN	Guadalajara	1585	RAH	Pub	None	Composite
83	POPOLA (V)	Yucatan	1579	AGI	Pub	None	Composite
84	PURIFICACION	Guadalajara	1585	RAH	Pub	None	Simple
85	QUATLATLAUCA	Tlaxcala	1579	UTX	Unpub	Unpub (2)	Composite
86	QUERETARO	Michoacan	1582	UTX	Pub	Lost	Complex
87	SAN MARTIN	Guadalajara	1585	RAH	Pub	None	Composite
88	SUCHITEPEC	Antequera	1579	RAH	Pub	Pub (5)	Complex
89	TABASCO (AM)	Yucatan	1579	AGI	Pub	None	Complex
90	TABASCO (P)	Yucatan	1579	AGI	Pub	Pub	Complex
91	TABASCO (V)	Yucatan	1579	AGI	Pub	None	Complex
92	TAHZIB (M)	Yucatan	1581	AGI	Pub	None	Simple
93	TAIMEO	Michoacan	1579	RAH	Pub	None	Simple
94	TALISTACA	Antequera	1580	RAH	Pub	None	Simple
95	TANCITARO	Michoacan	1580	UTX	Pub	None	Composite
96	TAXCO	Mexico	1581	AGI	Pub	None	Complex
97	TEABO (M)	Yucatan	1581	AGI	Pub	None	Complex
98	TECAL (M)	Yucatan	n.d. [1581]	AGI	Pub	None	Simple
99	TECANTO (M)	Yucatan	1581	AGI	Pub	None	Complex
100	TECON (V)	Yucatan	1579	AGI	Pub	None	Composite
101	TECUICUILCO	Antequera	1580	UTX	Pub	Pub	Complex
102	TEHUANTEPEC	Antequera	1580	UTX	Pub	Unpub	Complex
103	TEMAZCALTEPEC	Mexico	1579	AGI	Pub	Pub (5)	Complex
104	TEMUL (V)	Yucatan	1579	AGI	Pub	None	Simple
105	TENAMZTLAN	Guadalajara	1579	UTX	Pub	None	Simple

(*Table 1, continued*)

Census No.	Principal Cabecera	Bishopric or Archbishopric	Date	Repository	Publication Text	Map	Class of RG
106	TENUM (V)	Yucatan	1579	AGI	Pub	None	Complex
107	TEOTITLAN	Antequera	1581	RAH	Pub	Pub	Composite
108	TEOZACOALCO	Antequera	1580	UTX	Pub	Pub	Composite
109	TEOZAPOTLAN	Antequera	1580	RAH	Pub	None	Simple
110	TEPEACA	Tlaxcala	1580	AGI	Pub	None	Complex
111	TEPEAPULCO	Mexico	1581	AGI	Pub	Lost	Simple
112	TEPUZTLAN	Mexico	1580	AGI	Pub	Lost	Simple
113	TEQUALTICHE	Guadalajara	1585	UTX	Pub	Lost	Simple
114	TEQUISQUIAC	Mexico	1579	UTX	Pub	None	Composite
115	TEQUITE (M)	Yucatan	1581	AGI	Pub	None	Simple
116	TEQUIZISTLAN	Mexico	1580	AGI	Pub	Pub	Composite
117	TETELA (VOLCAN)	Mexico	1579	AGI	Pub	None	Composite
118	TETELA (SANTA MARIA ASUNCION)	Antequera	1581	AGI	Pub	Pub (2)	Composite
119	TETICPAC	Antequera	1580	RAH	Pub	None	Simple
120	TETIQUIPA	Antequera	[n.d. 1580?]	UTX	Pub	None	Composite
121	TETZAL (M)	Yucatan	1581	AGI	Pub	None	Complex
122	TEUTENANGO	Mexico	1582	AGI	Pub	Pub	Simple
123	TEXCOCO	Mexico	1582	UTX	Pub	None	Complex
124	TEXUPA	Antequera	1579	RAH	Pub	Pub	Simple
125	TEZEMI (V)	Yucatan	1579	AGI	Pub	None	Complex
126	TEZOCO (V)	Yucatan	1579	AGI	Pub	None	Complex
127	TILANTONGO	Antequera	1579	RAH	Pub	Lost (2)	Composite
128	TINGÜINDIN	Michoacan	1581	RAH	Pub	None	Simple
129	TIQUIBALON (V)	Yucatan	1579	AGI	Pub	None	Simple
130	TIRIPITIO	Michoacan	1580	UTX	Unpub	None	Simple
131	TISHOTZUCO (V)	Yucatan	1579	AGI	Pub	None	Complex
132	TISTLA	Tlaxcala	1582	UTX	Unpub	Unpub	Composite
133	TLACOLUIA	Antequera	1580	RAH	Pub	None	Composite
134	TLACOTLALPA	Tlaxcala	1580	RAH	Pub	Pub	Composite
135	TORNACUSTLA	Mexico	1579	AGI	Pub	None	Composite
136	TOTOLAPA	Mexico	1579	RAH	Pub	None	Complex
137	TUXPAN	Michoacan	1580	RAH	Pub	None	Composite
138	USILA	Antequera	1579	RAH	Pub	Lost	Simple
139	VALLADOLID	Yucatan	1579	AGI	Pub	Pub	Complex
140	VERA CRUZ	Tlaxcala	1580	UTX	Pub	Pub	Complex
141	XALAPA	Tlaxcala	1580	AGI	Pub	Pub	Composite
142	XALAPA-CINTLA	Tlaxcala	1582	RAH	Pub	None	Composite
143	XEREZ	Guadalajara	1584	RAH	Pub	None	Composite
144	XOCOTLAN	Guadalajara	1584	RAH	Pub	None	Simple
145	XOQUEN (V)	Yucatan	1579	AGI	Pub	None	Simple
146	YALCON (V)	Yucatan	n.d. [1579]	AGI	Pub	None	Simple
147	YUCATAN	Yucatan	1582	AGI	Pub	None	Simple
148	ZACATULA	Michoacan	1580	UTX	Pub	None	Simple
149	ZAMA (V)	Yucatan	1579	AGI	Pub	None	Simple
150	ZAMAHIL (M)	Yucatan	1581	AGI	Pub	None	Complex
151	ZAN (M)	Yucatan	1581	AGI	Pub	None	Complex
152	ZAPOTITLAN	Guatemala	1579	UTX	Pub	Unpub	Complex
153	ZAYULA	Mexico	1580	AGI	Pub	None	Simple
154	ZICAL (V)	Yucatan	1579	AGI	Pub	None	Simple
155	ZIMAPAN	Mexico	1579	AGI	Pub	Pub	Simple
156	ZINAGUA	Michoacan	1581	RAH	Pub	None	Simple
157	ZIRANDARO	Michoacan	1579	RAH	Pub	None	Composite

(*Table 1, continued*)

Census No.	Principal Cabecera	Bishopric or Archbishopric	Date	Repository	Publication Text	Map	Class of RG
158	ZISMOPO (V)	Yucatan	1579	AGI	Pub	None	Simple
159	ZIZONTUM (M)	Yucatan	n.d. [1581]	AGI	Pub	None	Simple
160	ZONOT (V)	Yucatan	1579	AGI	Pub	None	Simple
161	ZOTUTA (M)	Yucatan	1581	AGI	Pub	None	Complex
162	ZOZIL (V)	Yucatan	1579	AGI	Pub	None	Complex
163	ZULTEPEC	Mexico	1582	AGI	Pub	None	Complex
164	ZUMPANGO	Mexico	1582	RAH	Pub	Unpub	Simple
165	ZUSOPO (V)	Yucatan	1579	AGI	Pub	None	Simple
166	ZUZAL (M)	Yucatan	n.d.	AGI	Pub	None	Complex

places (Caballero, 1866).[2] Caballero meticulously provided information on the archival history, varied contents, and other aspects of the manuscript reports drawn up in Spain for 636 jurisdictions under the Crown of Castile, deposited in the Escorial. He noted that non-Castilian areas were omitted, and suggested that separate inquiries had been contemplated to cover them at a later date. To substantiate his view, he mentioned in passing (1866, p. 20) similar reports in answer to a 50-chapter questionnaire on the New World which the Academy had recently acquired, different from that employed in Spain itself. From this casual aside a minor academic argument developed.

Jiménez de la Espada inferred that Caballero was giving chronological priority to the Castilian RG's, and thereupon showed the primacy of American ones. He and others demonstrated that from Columbus' time the monarchs had demanded increasingly detailed reports, and that the form and contents of such reports steadily evolved, the procedures becoming more and more standardized. In effect, they argued, the

Castilian program was an offshoot of the American, not vice-versa.

A recent review of the differing views of Caballero and Jiménez de la Espada and their followers concludes that the evolution of the RG's early responded to administrative needs for information about the American overseas realms (Martínez Carreras, 1965, pp. lx–lxi). As noted below, the techniques for such areas were systemized about 1569–73. In 1574 these American questionnaires were adapted for use in Spain; in turn the Peninsular experiences with them in 1575 led to further modifications, so that the 1577 questionnaire which brought into being the RG's of the Indies, with which we are concerned, was influenced by the parallel Spanish documents of 1574 and 1575. There were thus similar but distinct programs for Spain and for the Indies, 1575–85, each of which created an important corpus of sources.

Here we do not propose to enter into details about the 636 documents on places in peninsular Spain. Numerous discussions, listings, and reproductions of the cédulas and texts exist (Academia Real, 1821; Caballero, 1866; Marcel, 1899; Fernández Duro, 1899; Bláquez, 1904, 1909; Becker, 1917; Miguélez, 1917; Ortego Rubio, 1918; Zarco Cuevas, 1927; Melón, 1943; Viñas y Mey, 1951; García-Badell, 1963). Slowly accurate and well-edited versions of the total Spanish corpus are appearing (Viñas y Mey

---

[2] The Caballero pamphlet, issued in a small edition, was a rarity as early as 1899, according to Marcel, 1899, 177, note 1. A brief biography of Caballero (1800–76) is in García–Badell, 1963, pp. 162–64. Data on him appear in "Discurso de D. Cayetano Rosell en contestación al precedente" in Caballero, 1866, pp. 65–84.

and Paz, 1949–63). In 1965 José Urbano Martínez Carreras (1965, pp. xliii–lxvi) summarized much material, including bibliographical notes, on both the RG's of the Indies and those of Spain.

Quite correctly his treatment stresses the key role in these programs played by two highly capable bureaucrats in the government of Philip II: Juan de Ovando y Godoy, and Juan López de Velasco.

The American RG's we treat were outgrowths of administrative reform begun by appointment in 1569 of Juan de Ovando as visitor to the Council of the Indies, familiar to all students as the major administrative organ in Spain for government of the Spanish New World. He was ordered to survey the overseas realms and to reorganize the Council to assure their better administration (Haring, 1947, pp. 102–27; Schäfer, 1935–47, 1: 129–37; Jiménez de la Espada, 1881; Cline, 1964a, p. 344, note 10).

Ovando, a lawyer with strong interests in geography and history, previously had codified much administrative material (Becker, 1917, pp. 101–04). He had also dispatched a number of scientific expeditions to the New World. The most famous of these is perhaps the mission of Dr. Francisco Hernández, who collected botanical, medicinal, and similar data and reported on other natural phenomena (Becker, 1917, p. 113; Schäfer, 1935–47, 1: 118–19; Somolinos d'Ardois, 1960, 1: 44–47, 53–54). Ovando also brought together the well-known set of Ordinances of Discovery and Population, issued by the Crown in 1573 (DII, 8: 484–537 [incorrectly dated]; 16: 484–537; Nuttall, 1921–22). But even more significant were his ordinances to systematize the work of the Council of the Indies, given royal approval in 1571 (DII, 16: 406–60; Muro Orejón, 1957).

An important section of the ordinances created the office of Principal Royal Chronicler-Cosmographer, whose stated tasks were to prepare appropriate histories and geographies of the Indies (DII, 16: 457–60; JDE,

1: lxi–lxii; Schäfer, 1935–47, 1: 129–37, 2: 407–09; Carbia, 1940: 100–17). He was to form a volume or files describing all aspects of the Indies. Apparently the broad outlines of such a body of documents had already existed. But fuller implementation of the Ovandine idea was left mainly to the first Cronista-Cosmógrafo under the new ordinances: Juan López de Velasco, who had been Ovando's secretary for the reorganization of the Council in 1567–68.

Velasco was appointed to the post in October, 1571, only a few days after the Crown had approved the new ordinances of the Council. He served until 1591, when he was promoted to be Secretary to the King (JDE, 1: lxxi–lxxv, xciv; Becker, 1917: 104–06; Schäfer, 1935–47, 1: 119, 2: 406–08; Carbia, 1940: 143–49). However, he is now chiefly remembered as compiler of a massive work entitled *Geografía y descripción universal de las Indias*, completed between 1571 and 1574 but not published until 1894 (from a corrupt copy). The data included in that basic compendium in fact stemmed from 1569 questionnaires created and circulated by Ovando for the overseas American realms to gather systematic information on population, administrative divisions, and related matters (López de Velasco, 1894; Cline, 1964a, pp. 345–46, note 17).

In 1569 Ovando sent a 37-chapter questionnaire to a number of jurisdictions, seeking information on "entradas y descubrimientos," navigation, description of the provinces, and the like. He also drafted, about 1570, a parallel inquiry of some 200 queries sent to heads of civil and ecclesiastical units to obtain more detailed coverage of these specific and allied subjects. López de Velasco and Ovando probably found this inquiry too long and cumbersome; in 1573 a similar one of only 135 questions was also circulated. Apparently the results, a trickle of responses, went into a "Población y Descripción" file in the offices of the Cronista-Cosmógrafo. Until Ovando's death he seems to have aided

189

López de Velasco quite actively in acquiring data about the Indies (JDE, 1: xliv–xlvii, lxx; Carbia, 1940, pp. 81–99; Cline, 1964a, p. 346, notes 18, 19), as well as starting in motion a 1574 questionnaire for like information on places in Spain itself.

Ovando died September 8, 1575 (JDE, 1: lxxi). Ovando's successors on the Council carried on the Ovandine policies. Following Juan López de Velasco's promotion of 1591, the double office of chronicler–cosmographer was split. His successors as Cosmógrafo were first Pedro Ambrosio de Onderiz (1591–96) and then Andrés García Céspedes (1596–1611). The latter was not replaced, duties of the cosmographer's office being transferred to Colegio Superior de la Compañía de Jesús, 1628 (Schäfer, 1935–47, 2: 406–12). Céspedes was ordered to reorganize the files, hence the frequent "Visto, Céspedes," on many RG's (Becker, 1917, pp. 130–32). Antonio de Herrera y Tordesillas became Cronista Mayor in 1596 and produced his *Historia General*, first major official chronicle (Carbia, 1940, pp. 150–81; Schäfer, 1935–47, 2: 413–15; see this *Handbook*, volume 13, Article 16).

In 1577 López de Velasco was awarded a 400-ducat bonus for various achievements. In that year he had completed the geographical compilation mentioned above, and had just initiated two further main inquiries of considerable importance. One was a questionnaire on eclipses of the moon, as seen in various parts of the Indies; he prescribed the procedure for gathering data, which would aid in making accurate maps of the New World and throw light on other scientific inquiries.[3] The other was preparation and circulation of the questionnaire that brought into being the RG's (JDE, 1: lxxii–lxxiii; Schäfer, 1935–47, 2: 407).

The 1577 Questionnaire

This was the famous 50-chapter inquiry, preceded by instructions on how to evoke answers to a wide range of topics. The questions are largely taken from the 200-question and 135-question American documents developed earlier by Ovando, and his shorter Spanish question schedule. The first edition of the printed American questionnaire bears the date of May 25, 1577; a second edition of 1584 was altered in minor detail (JDE, 1: cxiv–cxix).

It was sent, via the two viceroys of Peru and New Spain, to lesser Crown officials responsible for provincial areas in those realms, usually to the governor of a county-size area known as a corregimiento, or a somewhat similar and often larger jurisdiction known as an alcaldía mayor.

In New Spain most replies to the questionnaire indicate that the viceroy transmitted them. Several name him, Martín Enríquez, with one reply noting that he had been transferred to Peru. Others mention his successor as viceroy, Lorenzo Xuárez de Mendoza, Conde de Coruñas, as the commanding official. Several others state they received the instructions from Gordian Cassassano, Contador y Administrador General de la Renta de Alcabala. Characteristically the printed instructions, with questionnaires, are often found still attached to the manuscript replies, despite the stipulation that they should be reissued.

The Instructions and Questionnaire of 1577 have been published several times in Spanish (JDE, 1: cxiv–cxix; PNE, 4: 2–7; Amaya, 1951, pp. 23–75). No adequate English translation has previously been made of them, although Zelia Nuttall (1926) made a version of Questions 1–37; Ida Langman (1955) translated Questions 22–26; and Cline (1964a) translated Questions omitted by Nuttall. Appendices A and B to this article provide Cline's translation of the instructions; Appendix C reproduces

[3] Several versions of "Instrucción para la observación de eclipse de luna . . .," 1577–84, are known. Data were to be used primarily for determining longitude, although the Instruction included a measurement of noonday sun for latitude. Response was poor; known are five (1 for Puerto Rico, 4 for Mexico City). Edwards, 1969

a new and unpublished translation of the questionnaire prepared by Clinton R. Edwards.

From it may be seen that Questions 1–10 were meant primarily for towns with Spanish colonial citizens. Questions 11–15 were especially applicable to Indian places. Questions 16–37 continued to subject these same inland communities to searching scrutiny but on more general topics. Questions 38–50 were designed to gather specific data on ports and other maritime towns.

The questionnaire leaves few overt aspects of colonial life untouched. For the 16th century it comprehensively covers matters still of interest in the 20th (Vivó, 1942; Nichols, 1944). Starting with political geography, the questionnaire progresses to the environment and terrain, with queries on toponymic and related matters. It requires coverage of town bounds and, for Indian places, language affiliation, native governmental structures, modes of war, historical traditions, and comparative demography. Names of plants, both native and imported, are sought, with emphasis on medicinal herbs. Questions on mineral resources are followed by others on defensive arrangements, house types, and economic life. Religious and social welfare institutions close the portion of the questionnaire to be prepared for nonmaritime settlements.

Questions 38–50 sought additional specialized information about tides, depth of bays, offshore islands, landfalls, and other matters of special concern to mariners. Question 42 also again requested a painting or chart of these phenomena.

Replies

Just as there was in the Indies a wide variety of places and conditions to be reported, so the responses themselves are diverse, yet usually within the general framework of the questionnaire. Quite apart from the differences in length and quality of answers to the queries, according to the interest and ability of the local official, priest, or encomendero ordered to make the report, is the variation in their handling of matters not clearly covered by the instructions.

The instructions failed to specify sufficiently how reports on rather complicated jurisdictions were to be divided or subdivided. No problems arose when a single official reported on a single corregimiento; he followed the instructions, listed its dependencies, and submitted a single or simple RG. There are a great number of these, designated "simple" in the Census (Article 8).

However, jurisdictions were not always simple. Especially difficult to describe were alcaldías mayores, which contained two or more corregimientos. Complex in themselves were some corregimientos having large towns dependent on the principal cabecera, yet themselves subordinate cabeceras, each with smaller dependencies or "subjects." In general, officials took one of two approaches, creating further types of RG's: composite and complex.

The more direct and useful is what we term a "composite" RG. At the outset the official usually listed briefly the main places of his jurisdiction, and then in that sequence prepared for each a more or less extensive complete RG, following for each place the questions of the instruction. Thus for Xalapa de la Vera Cruz (Tlaxcala) there are 20 such separate subreports by the alcalde mayor, one after another in geographical order (Census, 141).

The other major mode creates what we call in the census a "complex" RG. In answer to each question of the instruction, the alcalde mayor or corregidor provided information on that topic for each major place in his jurisdiction. Usually he wrote a separate paragraph on each of the subordinate places, following much the same order of presentation under each question. Many of the RG's from Yucatan, prepared by encomenderos on the two or three widely scattered towns entrusted to each of them, are such complex documents.

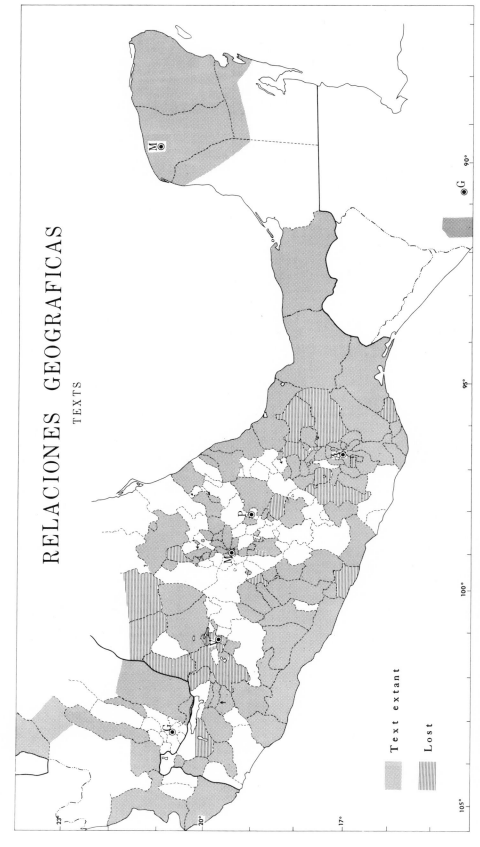

RELACIONES GEOGRAFICAS

TEXTS

Text extant

Lost

Fig. 1—RELACIONES GEOGRÁFICAS: TEXTS

TABLE 2—EXTANT RELACIONES GEOGRÁFICAS OF THE INDIES, 1578–86

	Principal Documents†	Dates From	To
SOUTH AMERICA°		1578	1589
Venezuela	12	1578	1579
Nuevo Reino de Granada	7	1580	1582
Quito	6	1582	1582
Peru	15	1583	1586
Subtotal	40		
CARIBBEAN	1	1582	1582
NEW SPAIN		1579	1585
Mexico	33	1579	1582
Michoacan	17	1579	1582
Guadalajara	13	1579	1585
Antequera	33	1579	1581
Tlaxcala	15	1579	1582
Yucatan	54	1579	1581
Guatemala	2	1579	1585
Subtotal	167		
TOTAL	208	1578	1586

° Jiménez de la Espada, 1881.
† See Table 3.

These disparate responses to a standard questionnaire give the same kind of information in the end, but do complicate generalizations about the number of RG's. One complex RG for a principal region may in fact provide full data on as many as 10 smaller towns (Census, 66, 125).

The Corpus

It would strain credulity to state that each provincial Spanish official complied fully and faithfully with the royal orders. Not all answered the questionnaire or all the questions, but many did. What is perhaps most surprising and important, however, is that we still have so many of these RG's. A central consideration is the quantity of unique data they contain.

The information we now have about the number of RG's is listed in Table 2. Details on the RG's from New Spain are in Table

3. For purposes here only the principal documents of all places in the Indies are so quantified in Table 2. The material on the Caribbean, Central America (apart from Guatemala), and South America is derived wholly from Marcos Jiménez de la Espada's "Catálogo" (1881) and hence is subject to later verification and amendment. Present indications are that no RG's in the 1577-85 series exist for the Philippines, nominally part of the viceroyalty of New Spain. From even this rather crude array in Table 2 certain broad generalizations emerge.

The regions and areas of New Spain contributed most of the RG's. None is recorded, however, for its northern borderlands, none appearing to cover realms above a line approximately from Tampico on the Gulf to Tepic on the Pacific side (fig. 1). Thus omitted are the former Spanish areas of the present United States, notably Florida, Texas, California, and other parts of the present Southwest, and most of northern Mexico. For the Caribbean islands there is in this series only a single surviving RG, that for Puerto Rico. Apart from two Guatemalan items, we have nothing in the series from Central America, although somewhat similar documents exist (Peralta, 1883; Serrano y Sainz, 1908). One Central American item, for the province of Costa Rica, seemingly, was extant in 1783, but its present whereabouts is not known.

In South America coverage is exclusively confined to Andean places. Present Argentina (except for a document from Tucuman), Chile, and Panama record no RG's. Although then recently added temporarily to Spanish possessions, Brazil does not seem to have been included in the surveys of this series.

The scheduling also seems clear. The earliest returns came from Venezuela, 1578-79. The bulk of the RG's from New Spain were prepared 1579-81; a later group supplemented them in 1584-85. Those for Ecuador, all 1582, were followed by the

193

TABLE 3—RELACIONES GEOGRÁFICAS OF NEW SPAIN: PRINCIPAL DOCUMENTS, BY TYPE

Bishopric Archbishopric	Simple	Composite	Complex	Total
Mexico	14	8	11	33
Michoacan	9	6	2	17
Guadalajara	6	6	1	13
Antequera	14	13	6	33
Tlaxcala	5	8	2	15
Yucatan	22	6	26	54
Guatemala	0	1	1	2
TOTAL	70	48	49	167

RG's from Peru, beginning in 1583 but mostly dated 1585–86. Most RG's were thus compiled 1579–86.

A paradoxical and striking feature of the corpus is that after all the efforts which went into planning and then actually having these amazing reports compiled, little or no administrative use was apparently ever made of them. With some few exceptions they seemingly lay untouched in files until they were rediscovered by Juan Bautista Muñoz in the late 18th century. By then they could only be considered important historical source materials for his projected official history of Spanish America. Nearer to their date of compilation the RG's were in small part employed as sources by Antonio Herrera y Tordesillas in the early 17th century for his official chronicle of the Indies. As we shall see, Antonio de León Pinelo obtained some RG documents for projected scholarly work in the 17th century, but it was really not until Caballero's Academy address in 1866 that significant scholarly attention was paid to these remarkable reports.

The Relaciones Geográficas of New Spain

Table 2 shows that the RG's from New Spain are the most numerous. Table 3 reveals that we have record of at least 167 principal documents, less than half of which are "simple." The composite and complex types together actually contain an equal amount of data on another 248 subordinate cabeceras. Collectively the RG documents provide extensive information on at least 414 major towns, plus innumerable smaller hamlets dependent administratively on them.

The lack of cartographic documents accompanying many of the RG's indicates that local officials did not always comply fully with the instructions ordering such depictions. Not every RG, simple, complex, or composite, has a map; some RG's have several. In a few instances the document states that a map was prepared, or it appears on an inventory, but today the map is lost. Apart from one item (Census, 203) we do not have the reverse situation: a known and extant map, whose text is lost. In another case the text of RG of Suchitepec, Oaxaca (Census, 88), is found in the library of the Royal Academy of History in Madrid, but the five maps originally belonging to it are lodged in the Archivo General de Indias in Sevilla, much to the puzzlement of earlier investigators who there sought in vain to attach them to the proper text (Torres Lanzas, 1900, 1, nos. 25–29; PNE, 4: 24, note 1). Partially paralleled is the case of Celaya (Census, 18), whose texts and two maps are in the Academy, but with a third (and fourth) map in the Archivo. Table 4 summarizes quantitative data on extant maps, treated in greater detail by Robertson in Article 6.

TABLE 4—RELACIONES GEOGRÁFICAS OF NEW SPAIN: EXTANT MAPAS*

Bishopric or Archbishopric	Unpublished	Published	Total
Mexico	6	15	21
Michoacan	2	4	6
Guadalajara	. . .	2	2
Antequera	5	17	22
Tlaxcala	3	16	19
Yucatan	2	2	4
Guatemala	2	. . .	2
TOTAL	20	56	76

* Source: Robertson, Article 6.

TABLE 5—RELACIONES GEOGRÁFICAS OF NEW SPAIN: LOST TEXT ITEMS

Census	Principal Document	Source JLV	MP
201	ACAPULCO. Mexico	2/15	...
202	CAPOLA. Michoacan	3/11	...
203	CHICHIMECAS. Michoacan	1/1a	21
204	CHURUBUSCO. Mexico*	...	...
205	GUASPALTEPEC. Antequera	2/25	7
206	HUAMELULA. Antequera	3/2	96
207	ISMIQUILPA. Mexico	3/7	97
208	LEON. Michoacan	3/26	13
209	MEXICO. Mexico	4/1	18
210	OCUITUCO. Mexico	1/4	...
211	SICHU. Michoacan	3/5	105
212	TALASCO. Mexico	1/25	98
213	TAMAZULA. Unidentified	2/3	...
214	TAZAZALCA. Michoacan	3/6	99
215	TEPEZI DE LA SEDA. Tlaxcala	4/36	...
216	TEPOSCOLULA. Antequera	3/1	101
217	TEUTILA. Antequera	3/3	94
218	TLAQUILPA. Mexico	4/31	...
219	VALLADOLID. Michoacan	3/14	95
220	YANGUITLAN. Antequera	...	3
221	YAUTEPEC. Mexico	3/4	103
222	ZACUALPA. Mexico	1/6	...
223	ZAPOTECAS. Antequera	1/7	102
224	ZAYULA. Guadalajara	3/13	92
225	ZIMATLAN. Antequera	3/12	93

* PNE, 6:196.

Lost Items

A group of texts and maps is tantalizingly labeled "lost." Knowledge about them derives from collation of various colonial lists and inventories, discussed below, and from statements in texts of the RG's themselves. Some of the choice morsels to be rediscovered by the modern investigator are these "lost" items: the RG and pintura of Mexico City itself, and several texts and pinturas from the Mixteca. Table 5 lists the missing or lost items. It does not include texts of two published RG's, Xalapa de la Veracruz and Taxco, which Dr. Adele Kibre reports to have disappeared from the Archive of the Indies about 1925.

Summary

From the separate tabulations above, Table 6 summarizes the total corpus of RG's and their maps from New Spain, including the "lost." They total 192 texts, of which 167 survive, and 91 maps, of which 76 are extant. Thus from 283 major items, some 243 or about 85 per cent, remain for current scholarship.

Colonial Lists and Inventories

Of the four important colonial documents which aid in establishing this total of RG materials for New Spain, one is 16th century, another 17th, and two come from the close of the 18th century.

On November 21, 1583, the Cronista-Cosmógrafo López de Velasco signed an inventoried receipt when the Council of the Indies officially turned over to him 121 RG's plus a group of maps and plans from New

195

TABLE 6—RELACIONES GEOGRÁFICAS OF NEW SPAIN:
SUMMARY QUANTITATIVE DATA

Bishopric or Archbishopric	Texts			Maps			Total		
	Lost	Extant	Total	Lost	Extant	Total	Lost	Extant	Total
Mexico	7	33	40	5	21	26	12	54	66
Michoacan	6	17	23	2	6	8	8	23	31
Guadalajara	1	13	14	1	2	3	2	15	17
Antequera	7	33	40	5	22	27	12	55	67
Tlaxcala	1	15	16	1	19	20	2	34	36
Yucatan	0	54	54	0	4	4	0	58	58
Guatemala	0	2	2	0	2	2	0	4	4
Unidentified	3	0	0	1	0	1	4	0	4
TOTAL	25	167	189	15	76	91	40	243	283

Spain (López de Velasco, 1583; Cline, 1964a, p. 354, note 34). The inventory is reproduced as Appendix D. Of the RG texts in the 1583 inventory, 23 are now lost, as are all the maps separately listed. But repositories of the others are known. We also have many RG's from New Spain not included on the 1583 López de Velasco inventory. Those listed by him are noted "JLV" in the Census (Article 8).

About 1624 the Spanish jurist and bibliographer, Antonio León de Pinelo, listed 105 documents in his possession concerning the geography of the New World (León Pinelo, 1624?). Baudot (1968) discusses this listing, given here as Appendix E. Many of these items apparently never were replaced in their proper files, and hence are now accounted "lost." In the Pinelo listing (abbreviated MP) are 17 RG's from Middle America, all but one (Census, 220) previously listed by López de Velasco and all of which are "lost." Their sequence in the Pinelo manuscript suggests that they may have formed a single legajo or file bundle. Researchers hope, of course, that it will some day reappear. He seemingly never used these sources (Schäfer, 1935–47, 2: 416–18; Carbia, 1940: 205–07).

With the exception of the 17 strayed Pinelo items and 7 "lost" that López de Velasco alone records, the main collection of RG's seems to have survived almost intact

until the end of the 18th century. We have for that time two inventories, both dated 1783.

One is a memorandum by the Royal Cosmographer, Juan Bautista Muñoz, noting 255 items that he had set aside in the General Archives of Simancas as sources for a large general history of the Indies that he never completed (Muñoz, 1783). In the Census, the Muñoz listing numbers are abbreviated RM. A correlative document gives the items actually shipped for Muñoz from Simancas to Madrid, by an archivist known to us only by his last name, Larrañaga. Larrañaga (1783) seemingly numbered the documents themselves to correspond to his record of the shipment. This number in Census entries is SIM. They came chiefly from a file generally labeled "Descripción y Población" in the Sala de Indias (Simancas).

Either López de Velasco or Céspedes seems originally to have organized this file. In it documents were placed in one of nine legajos, "Desc. y Pob.," eight of which were consecutively numbered. The legajo number still appears before a slash mark on many documents, after which is the number of that document. These sequences run from 1/1 (leg. 1, doc. 1), a 1537 item, to Document 1051 in a ninth legajo which is unnumbered but labeled "Sobrantes." A partial reconstruction of that old DyP file shows there were at least these 1051 documents in it, including most of the RG's from the Indies. The DyP numbers and the Larrañaga numbers are important aids in tracing the pedigrees and provenance of the RG's, and in keeping track of them in their various wanderings.

Dispersal of the Corpus

For move they did. After their original arrival in Spain from the Indies seemingly the RG's were handed from the Council to the Cosmographer, as we see from the López de Velasco document of 1583. Later, possibly in a general transfer of documents from the Council of the Indies files in Madrid that occurred in 1659 and again in 1718, they were sent to Simancas. We have just seen that Juan Bautista Muñoz in 1783 ordered them returned to Madrid, and that Larrañaga shipped them.

It may here be recalled that Muñoz was also primarily responsible for creating a specialized archive to house the exclusively American papers. After some discussion, on his recommendation, the famous Archivo de Indias in Sevilla was inaugurated in 1785: to it were to come not only papers from Simancas relating to the Indies, but similar and related documents from a wide variety of other Crown administrative offices dealing with overseas matters. The papers actually started to arrive in 1786, the early beginnings of a collection of some 34,000 legajos that now constitute its holdings (Gómez Canedo, 1961, 1: 6–13, 139–49; Burrus, 1955).

We now enter a realm of drama and mystery, where facts are few and detective work still lies ahead. Between 1783 and 1853 better than half of the RG's disappeared, only to reappear later in widely separated places.

REPOSITORIES

Archivo General de Indias (AGI)

With thousands and thousands of other papers, 80 RG texts and 22 maps did go from Madrid to Sevilla, presumably around 1787. All but two texts are in two legajos of Papeles de Simancas in Indiferente General (Legajos 1529–30); the maps are now kept in a separate section. All the AGI materials have been published.

The Library of Congress was given microfilmed copies of the AGI RG's by the Carnegie Institution of Washington. They offer few problems of provenance or of accessibility. Table 7 lists the documents in the AGI collections.

TABLE 7—RELACIONES GEOGRÁFICAS: REPOSITORY LISTINGS—AGI

Census No.	Principal Cabecera	Bishopric Archbishopric	Documents		Publication	
			Text	Maps	Text	Maps
12	ATLATLAQUIA	Mexico	X	Missing	X	None
13	CACALAC	Yucatan	X	None	X	None
14	CACALCHEN	Yucatan	X	None	X	None
15	CAMPOCOLCHE	Yucatan	X	None	X	None
16	CANACHE	Yucatan	X	None	X	None
17	CANZACABO	Yucatan	X	None	X	None
20	CHANCENOTE	Yucatan	X	None	X	None
21	CHICHICAPA	Oaxaca	X	None	X	None
22	CHICONAUTLA	Mexico	X	None	X	None
26	CHUBULNA	Yucatan	X	None	X	None
27	CHUNCHUCHU	Yucatan	X	None	X	None
28	CITLALTOMAGUA	Mexico	X	None	X	None
29	COATEPEC	Mexico	X	1	X	X
32	CUAUHQUILPAN	Mexico	X	None	X	None

(*Table 7, continued*)

Census No.	Principal Cabecera	Bishopric Archbishopric	Documents Text	Documents Maps	Publication Text	Publication Maps
36	CUICUIL	Yucatan	X	None	X	None
39	CUITELCUM	Yucatan	X	None	X	None
40	CUIZIL	Yucatan	X	None	X	None
42	CUZCATLAN–1	Tlaxcala	X	1	X	X
48	GUAYMA	Yucatan	X	None	X	None
50	HOCABA	Yucatan	X	None	X	None
51	HUEXOTLA	Mexico	X	1	X	X
52	ICHCATEOPAN	Mexico	X	None	X	None
55	IXMUL	Yucatan	X	None	X	None
58	IZAMAL	Yucatan	X	None	X	None
63	MAMA	Yucatan	X	None	X	None
64	MERIDA	Yucatan	X	None	X	None
65	MEXICATZINGO	Mexico	X	Missing	X	None
69	MOTUL	Yucatan	X	1	X	X
70	MOXOPIPE	Yucatan	X	None	X	None
71	NABALON	Yucatan	X	None	X	None
73	NEXAPA	Oaxaca	X	Missing	X	None
76	OCOPETLAYUCA	Mexico	X	None	X	None
77	OXCUZCAS	Yucatan	X	None	X	None
81	PIJOY	Yucatan	X	None	X	None
83	POPOLA	Yucatan	X	None	X	None
89	TABASCO (AM)	Yucatan	X	None	X	None
90	TABASCO (P)	Yucatan	X	1	X	X
91	TABASCO (V)	Yucatan	X	None	X	None
92	TAHZIB	Yucatan	X	None	X	None
96	TAXCO	Mexico	X	None	X	None
97	TEABO	Yucatan	X	None	X	None
98	TECAL	Yucatan	X	None	X	None
99	TECAUTO	Yucatan	X	None	X	None
100	TECON	Yucatan	X	None	X	None
103	TEMAZCALTEPEC	Mexico	X	4	X	X
103D	TUZANTLA	Michoacan	X	1	X	X
104	TEMUL	Yucatan	X	None	X	None
106	TENUM	Yucatan	X	None	X	None
110	TEPEAC	Tlaxcala	X	None	X	None
111	TEPEAPULCO	Mexico	X	Lost	X	None
112	TEPUZTLAN	Mexico	X	Lost	X	None
115	TEQUITE	Yucatan	X	None	X	None
116	TEQUIZISTLAN	Mexico	X	1	X	X
117	TETELA (VOLCAN)	Mexico	X	None	X	None
118	TETELA (SANTA MARIA ASUNCION)	Tlaxcala	X	1	X	X
121	TETZAL	Yucatan	X	None	X	None
122	TEUTENANGO	Mexico	X	1	X	X
125	TEZEMI	Yucatan	X	None	X	None
126	TEZOCO	Yucatan	X	None	X	None
129	TIQUIBALON	Yucatan	X	None	X	None
131	TISHOTZUCO	Yucatan	X	None	X	None
135	TORNACUSTLA	Mexico	X	None	X	None
139	VALLADOLID	Yucatan	X	2	X	X
141	XALAPA VERACRUZ	Tlaxcala	X	1	X	X
145	XOQUEN	Yucatan	X	None	X	None
146	YALCON	Yucatan	X	None	X	None

(*Table 7, continued*)

Census No.	Principal Cabecera	Bishopric Archbishopric	Documents Text	Maps	Publication Text	Maps
147	YUCATAN (P)	Yucatan	X	None	X	None
149	ZAMA	Yucatan	X	None	X	None
150	ZAMAHIL	Yucatan	X	None	X	None
151	ZAN	Yucatan	X	None	X	None
153	ZAYULA	Mexico	X	None	X	None
154	ZICAB	Yucatan	X	None	X	None
155	ZIMAPAN	Mexico	X	1	X	X
158	ZISMOPO	Yucatan	X	None	X	None
159	ZIZONTUM	Yucatan	X	None	X	None
160	ZONOT	Yucatan	X	None	X	None
161	ZOTUTA	Yucatan	X	None	X	None
162	ZOZIL	Yucatan	X	None	X	None
163	ZULTEPEC	Mexico	X	None	X	None
165	ZUSOPO	Yucatan	X	None	X	None
166	ZUZAL	Yucatan	X	None	X	None

University of Texas (UTX), Ex-Icazbalceta

From 1783, when Larrañaga shipped the materials to Muñoz, until mid-19th century, we lose track of 86 RG texts on New Spain, together with 49 maps. Where they remained hidden during the Napoleonic invasions and civil wars in Spain is now unknown. One possibility, not yet fully explored, is that they formed part of a famous book and manuscript collection formed by the Spanish writer, bibliographer, and politician, Bartolomé José Gallardo. The date of his death, 1853, coincides with the reappearance of one of two groups of the RG's that did not go to Sevilla (Cline, 1964a, p. 356, note 40). This may be mere coincidence, as we have no firm information on how one large group of RG's left Spain.

The lot with which we are now concerned was purchased in Spain by Joaquín García Icazbalceta. Details of this private sale are completely unknown; his published correspondence furnishes no clues. These original documents became Volumes XX, XXIII, XXIV, and XXV of his manuscript "Collection of Documents for the History of America," started in 1849 and to 1853 largely made up of transcripts or copies of colonial materials, several furnished by William Hickling Prescott. At García Icazbalceta's death in 1894, his son, Luis García Pimentel, inherited the manuscripts and books collected by his father. They remained in the family until 1937, when the heirs sold the bulk of the manuscripts to the University of Texas, where they now remain (Martínez, 1947, 1951; Teixidor, 1937; Cline, 1964a, p. 357, note 41).

From their acquisition by García Icazbalceta in 1853, when the RG's passed from Spain to Mexico, until 1937, when they migrated to the United States, various lists of them were made, some published. García Icazbalceta himself prepared one such list of his manuscripts, including the RG originals, for his friend Nicolás León. Later it was published in 1927 by Federico Gómez de Orozco. In comparing these inventories with one made after the materials reached Texas, it appears that no original RG's were lost in the 1937 transfer (Gómez de Orozco, 1927a–c; Orozco y Berra, 1864, pp. viii, 240–55; 1871: Items 5–23, 3043–44; 1881; JDE, 2: xxxviii–xlvi; Anonymous, 1936?; Castañeda and Dabbs, 1939).

The Texas collection contains 41 text

documents and 35 RG maps. Various individual investigators for private research have occasionally obtained copies of some texts and maps but no microfilms are commonly available. The question of how many texts are published is complicated by circumstances, although it is quite clear that 20 of the 35 maps still remain unpublished.

When García Icazbalceta obtained the original documents in 1853, he followed a system somewhat at variance with modern practice. He twice copied all the texts, by hand, to form separate but unnumbered volumes of his manuscript collection. Generally such handcopies of original documents subsequently served him as printer's copy for the several published collection materials he issued during his lifetime. In case of the RG's, however, he published neither originals nor copies of them, with very minor exceptions (García Icazbalceta, 1875, 1891). He allowed both originals and copies to be used freely by contemporary investigators, such as Manuel Orozco y Berra and Nicolás León, and even made further special handcopies for the latter's use (Cline, 1964a, p. 358, note 45).

It is not clear whether a few of the RG's from his collection, published by his son after don Joaquín's death, were from the originals or the handcopies (Census, 1, 47, 112, 117). We do know, however, that the son, Luis García Pimentel, made available to Gómez de Orozco and to Alfonso Caso the JGI handcopies, some of which they published in 1927–28 (Gómez de Orozco, 1923, 1924, 1927a–c, 1928a,b; Caso, 1928a–e, 1949a). Robert Barlow, Ignacio Bernal, and Luis Vargas Rea later also published some of the JGI handcopies (Barlow, 1945, 1946, 1947; Bernal, 1952, 1957; Vargas Rea, 1956j, 1957b,c). All these publications omit the maps; the texts are unreliable because of copyist's errors and omissions.

One two-volume set of JGI handcopies did not pass to Texas in the 1937 sale. Seemingly they were acquired by Vicente

de Paúl Andrade (Zavala, 1939, p. 45), then by Federico Gómez de Orozco; currently they are volumes 9–10 of the Colección Gómez de Orozco in the Archivo Histórico of the Instituto Nacional de Antropología e Historia (Mexico), where they continue to be utilized by investigators who are often unaware of their deficiencies (Barlow, 1949a). A duplicate set of JGI handcopies is in the private library of his grandson, Dr. Ignacio Bernal; these, too, lack maps.

Hence many of the Texas RG's have been published from the JGI handcopies. To date the Texas group is the largest unpublished group of RG texts and maps. During 1965 a cooperative program between the Conference on Latin American History (the professional association of these area specialists) and the University of Texas was initiated to prepare them for publication, the maps to be in color. Table 8 lists the items in the UTX collection, with publication status as of early 1966, before the projected publication had appeared.

Royal Academy of History (RAH)

The final lot of strayed RG's reappeared in Spain about a decade after those which García Icazbalceta purchased and brought to Mexico in 1853. I know nothing about arrangements by which the Spanish government in 1863 purchased for the Royal Academy of History three volumes of these RG documents. Search of the published material of the time has yielded no details about the transaction. About the only clue we now have is a statement, twice repeated on the cover and a sheet of folded paper at the beginning of the third volume, to the effect that the documents were for the use of Juan Bautista Muñoz, and had been turned over to the Royal Academy on March 8, 1863, by one Don José Arias y Miranda, otherwise unidentified (Robertson, *in litt.*).

Documents for South America fill one volume. The RG's for New Spain are found,

TABLE 8—RELACIONES GEOGRÁFICAS: REPOSITORY LISTINGS—UTX

Census No.	Principal Cabecera	Bishopric Archbishopric	Documents Text	Maps	Publication Text	Maps
1	ACAPISTLA	Mexico	X	1	X	Unpub
4	AMECA	Guadalajara	X	1	X	X
5	AMULA	Guadalajara	X	None	X	None
6	ANTEQUERA	Oaxaca	X	None	X	None
8	ATENGO	Mexico	X	1	X	Unpub
9	ATITLAN	Guatemala	X	1	Unpub	Unpub
10	ATLATLAUCA	Mexico	X	1	X	X
19	CEMPOALA	Mexico	X	3	X	X
25	CHOLULA	Tlaxcala	X	1	X	X
30	COATZCOALCOS	Oaxaca	X	1	X	Unpub
34	CUAUTLA	Oaxaca	X	None	X	None
37	CUILAPA	Oaxaca	X	None	X	None
41	CULHUACAN	Mexico	X	1	X	X
43	CUZCATLAN–2	Tlaxcala	X	1	Unpub	X
47	GUAXTEPEC	Mexico	X	1	X	Unpub
49	GUEYTLALPA	Tlaxcala	X	7	Unpub	Unpub
53	IGUALA	Mexico	X	None	X	None
54	IXCATLAN	Oaxaca	X	2	Unpub	X
56	IXTAPALAPA	Mexico	X	1	X	Unpub
59	IZTEPEC	Oaxaca	X	None	X	None
61	JUSTLAVACA	Oaxaca	X	None	X	None
66	MEZTITLAN	Mexico	X	1	X	Unpub
67	MIZANTLA	Tlaxcala	X	1	X	X
79	PATZCUARO	Michoacan	X	Lost	X	None
80	PEÑOLES	Oaxaca	X	1	X	Unpub
85	QUATLATLAUCA	Tlaxcala	X	2	X	None
86	QUERETARO	Michoacan	X	Lost	X	None
95	TANCITARO	Michoacan	X	None	X	None
101	TECUICUILCO	Oaxaca	X	1	X	Unpub
102	TEHUANTEPEC	Oaxaca	X	2	X	1 pub, 1 unpub
105	TENAMAZTLAN	Guadalajara	X	None	X	None
108	TEOZACOALCO	Oaxaca	X	2	X	X
113	TEQUALTICHE	Guadalajara	X	Lost	X	None
114	TEQUISQUIAC	Mexico	X	None	X	None
120	TETIQUIPA	Oaxaca	X	None	X	None
130	TIRIPITIO	Michoacan	X	None	Unpub	None
132	TISTLA	Tlaxcala	X	1	Unpub	Unpub
140	VERA CRUZ	Tlaxcala	X	2	X	X
148	ZACATULA	Michoacan	X	None	X	None
152	ZAPOTITLAN	Guatemala	X	1	Unpub	Unpub

with other materials, in the remaining two. A survey by Peter Gerhard, supplemented by Donald Robertson, indicates that there are in the RAH 45 principal RG documents, with maps, and one additional unattached map (Robertson, Catalogue, 48; Census, 203). Nearly all the RAH items have been published, primarily by Paso y Troncoso, or by Vargas Rea from transcripts made by Paso y Troncoso. There are no readily accessible microfilms of these RAH originals in the United States, nor is there a previously published listing of the RG holdings, apart from partial notes about eight maps (Ballesteros-Gaibrois, 1955). Table 9 summarizes the RAH holdings.

TABLE 9—RELACIONES GEOGRÁFICAS: REPOSITORY LISTINGS—RAH

Census No.	Principal Cabecera	Bishopric Archbishopric	Documents		Publication	
			Text	Maps	Text	Maps
2	ACATLAN	Tlaxcala	X	None	X	None
3	AHUATLAN	Tlaxcala	X	None	X	None
7	ASUCHITLAN	Michoacan	X	None	X	None
11	ATLATLAUCA	Oaxaca	X	1	X	X
18	CELAYA	Michoacan	X	2	X	X
22bis	CHILAPA	Tlaxcala	X	Lost	X	None
23	CHILCHOTLA	Michoacan	X	None	X	None
24	CHINANTLA	Oaxaca	X	None	X	None
31	COMPOSTELA	Guadalajara	X	1	X	X
33	CUAHUITLAN	Oaxaca	X	1	X	X
35	CUICATLAN	Oaxaca	X	None	X	None
38	CUISEO-LAGUNA	Michoacan	X	None	X	None
44	FRESNILLO	Guadalajara	X	None	X	None
45	GUATULCO	Oaxaca	X	None	X	None
46	GUAXILOTITLAN	Oaxaca	X	None	X	None
57	IXTEPEXIC	Oaxaca	X	1	X	X
60	JILQUIPAN	Michoacan	X	None	X	None
62	MACUILSUCHIL	Oaxaca	X	1	X	X
68	MOTINES	Michoacan	X	None		None
68d	POMARO	Michoacan	X	None	Unpub	None
72	NECOTLAN	Michoacan	X	None	X	None
74	NOCHIZTLAN	Oaxaca	X	1	X	X
75	NUCHISTLAN	Guadalajara	X	None	X	None
78	PAPALOTICPAC	Oaxaca	X	None	X	None
82	PONCITLAN	Guadalajara	X	None	X	None
84	PURIFICACION	Guadalajara	X	None	X	None
87	SAN MARTIN	Guadalajara	X	None	X	None
88	SUCHITEPEC	Oaxaca	X	5 (AGI)	X	X
93	TAIMEO	Michoacan	X	None	X	None
94	TALIZTACA	Oaxaca	X	None	X	None
107	TEOTITLAN	Oaxaca	X	1	X	X
109	TEOZAPOTLAN	Oaxaca	X	None	X	None
119	TETICPAC	Oaxaca	X	None	X	None
124	TEXUPA	Oaxaca	X	1	X	X
127	TILANTONGO	Oaxaca	X	Lost	X	None
128	TINGUINDIN	Michoacan	X	None	X	None
133	TLACOLULA	Oaxaca	X	None	X	None
134	TLACOTLAPA	Tlaxcala	X	1	X	X
136	TOTOLAPA	Mexico	X	None	X	None
137	TUXPAN	Michoacan	X	None	X	None
138	USILA	Oaxaca	X	Lost	X	None
142	XALAPA-CINTLA-ACTLAN	Oaxaca-Tlaxcala	X	None	X	None
143	XEREZ	Guadalajara	X	None	X	None
144	XOCOTLAN	Guadalajara	X	None	X	None
156	ZINAGUA	Michoacan	X	None	X	None
157	ZIRANDARO	Michoacan	X	None	X	None
164	ZUMPANGO	Mexico	X	1	X	Unpub

TABLE 10—RELACIONES GEOGRÁFICAS: REPOSITORY LISTINGS—LOST

Census No.	Principal Cabecera	Bishopric Archbishopric	Documents Text	Documents Maps	Publication Text	Publication Maps
123	TEXCOCO	Mexico	X UTX	Illus copy	X	Lost
201	ACAPULCO	Mexico	X	None		
202	CAPOLA	Michoacan	X	None		
203	CHICHEMECAS	Michoacan	X	RAH		X
204	CHURUBUSCO	Mexico	X	None		
205	GUASPALTEPEC	Oaxaca	X	None		
206	HUAMELULA	Oaxaca	X	None		
207	ISQUIMILPA	Mexico	X	None		
208	LEON	Michoacan	X	None		
209	MEXICO CITY	Mexico	X	Lost		
210	OCUITUCO	Mexico	X	None		
211	SICHU	Michoacan	X	None		
212	TALASCO	Mexico	X	None		
213	TAMAZULA	Unidentified	X	Lost		
214	TAZAZALCA	Michoacan	X	None		
215	TEPEXI DE LA SEDA	Tlaxcala	X	None		
216	TEPOSCOLULA	Oaxaca	X	None		
217	TEUTILA	Oaxaca	X	None		
218	TLALQUILPA	Unidentified	X	None		
219	VALLADOLID	Michoacan	X	Lost		
220	YANGUITLAN	Oaxaca	X	None		
221	YAUTEPEC	Mexico	X	None		
222	ZACUALPA	Mexico	X	None		
223	ZAPOTECAS	Oaxaca	X	None		
224	ZAYULA	Guadalajara	X	None		
225	ZIMATLAN	Oaxaca	X	None		

Lost Items

The group of documents accounted "lost" is not presently available in any public or private collection. Table 10 recapitulates what is now known about them.

Summary

The surviving corpus of RG's is divided among three repositories. No RG's are known to be in private hands. With 80 text documents in the AGI, and another 45 in the RAH, the Spanish holdings in each outranks the Texas collection of 41 documents. Nearly all these texts are in print, but often in substandard form. Only two or three of the magnificent maps accompanying the RG's appear in full color, doing them proper justice.

Table 11 recapitulates information on the extant RG's, by repositories. It must be used with some caution. In noting the published status of documents, the table does not reveal that such publication may be the questionable texts issued by Vargas Rea, or that their appearance in serials is often more inaccessible than the manuscript RG's.

GEOGRAPHICAL COVERAGE

Many colonial civil jurisdictions of New Spain lack RG's. The latter cover slightly less than half the identifiable units of about 1580, and their coverage is reduced by the fact that "lost" documents would embrace

TABLE 11—RELACIONES GEOGRÁFICAS OF NEW SPAIN: REPOSITORIES

		AGI	RAH	UTX	Total
TEXTS:					
Published		80	46	33	159
Unpublished		0	0	8	8
	Total	*80*	*46*	*41*	*167*
MAPS:					
Published		21	13	15	49
Unpublished		1	1	20	22
	Total	*22*	*14*	*35*	*71*
MAPS & TEXTS:					
Published		101	59	49	209
Unpublished		1	1	27	29
	Total	*102*	*60*	*76*	*238*

substantial areas. Yet where the RG texts and/or maps describe areas, they provide highly important local ethnohistorical data.

Here we shall try to indicate such Middle American areas for which the investigator can count on RG materials, or lack of them. In 1580 the most general territorial subdivision used to identify areas from which these documents emerged was the archdiocese or archbishopric of Mexico, and the dioceses of Guadalajara, Michoacan, Tlaxcala, Yucatan, and Guatemala. Figure 1 is a reduced summary of the individual dioceses (figs. 2, 4, 9, 10, 18, 20) which provide colonial details. Other figures show modern municipios within states of our principal area, outside of which no Middle American RG's exist. Using as bases the maps prepared by Peter Gerhard showing Mexico in 1580, we have indicated on them the colonial areas for which RG's were prepared.

The following paragraphs attempt to correlate in some degree the 16th-century jurisdictions with the geographical scheme utilized generally in this Guide by analyzing the coverage of the RG's by modern regions and states. The 167 extant texts, plus the 25 lost, are thus regrouped by regions. No RG's are reported for Central America, so it drops from consideration. Table 12 shows that coverage is far from uniform, by regions or by states.

Northern Mexico (fig. 2)

ZACATECAS (fig. 3). The sparse population of Northern Mexico from 1579 to 1585 is reflected in the few RG's from that region. The four documents come from mining centers in the present state of Zacatecas, then part of Nueva Galicia in the diocese of Guadalajara. Extraneous notes to the RG's, one a petition to have Tlaxcalan Indians settled nearby to protect settlers against marauding bands, attest to the frontier nature of the area. (See Table 13.)

Western Mexico (figs. 2, 4)

As we use the term, this region comprises the bishoprics of Guadalajara and of Michoacan. The latter lay within the realm of Nueva España; the former included Nueva Galicia and Nueva Vizcaya. From Nueva Vizcaya there are no RG documents; nor are there any from the present state of Colima, within Michoacan. The area immediately surrounding the main Spanish center of Guadalajara is similarly bare of reports.

GUANAJUATO (fig. 5). The present state of Guanajuato has a single (fig. 5) extant RG. In the bishopric of Michoacan (fig. 4) it covers the area around Celaya. Three other documents are "lost." For San Miguel (Census, 202) the map but not its text survives. (See Table 14.)

Table 12—Relaciones Geográficas: Coverage of Modern Mexico and Guatemala

Section/Region State[°]	Diocese Archdiocese 1580 Name	Figure	Texts Extant	Total	Lost	Modern Map Figure
Northern Mexico:						
32 Zacatecas	Guadalajara	2	4	0	4	3
Western Mexico:						
11 Guanajuato	Michoacan	4	1	3	4	5
14 Jalisco	Guadalajara	2	8	1	9	6
16 Michoacan	Michoacan	4	12	3	15	7
18 Nayarit	Guadalajara	2	1	0	1	8
Subtotal			22	7	29	
Central Mexico:						
9 Distrito Federal	Mexico	9	3	2	5	11
12 Guerrero	Michoacan	4				
	Mexico	9				
	Tlaxcala	10	10	1	11	12
13 Hidalgo	Mexico	9	10	1	11	13
15 Mexico	Mexico	9	9	2	11	11
17 Morelos	Mexico	9	5	2	7	14
21 Puebla	Mexico	9				
	Tlaxcala	10	10	1	11	15
22 Queretaro	Mexico	9	1	0	1	16
30 Veracruz	Tlaxcala	10				
	Antequera	18	5	1	6	17
Subtotal			52	10	62	
Oaxaca:						
20 Oaxaca	Antequera	18	32	6	38	19
Southeastern Mexico & Guatemala:						
23 Quintana Roo	Yucatan	20	5	0	5	21
27 Tabasco	Yucatan	20	3	0	3	22
31 Yucatan	Yucatan	20	46	0	46	23
— Guatemala	Guatemala		2	0	2	24
Subtotal			56	0	56	
Unidentified:						
			0	2	2	
			167	25	192	

[°] Numbers refer to those assigned to Mexican states, Article 1, Table 1.

Table 13—Relaciones Geográficas of Northern Mexico: Zacatecas (fig. 3)

Census No.	Principal Document	Diocese	Modern Place
44	FRESNILLO	Guadalajara	Fresnillo de Gonzalez Echeverria
75	NOCHISTLAN	Guadalajara	Nochistlan
87	SAN MARTIN	Guadalajara	San Martin, M. Sombrete
143	XEREZ	Guadalajara	Garcia Salinas, M. Jerez

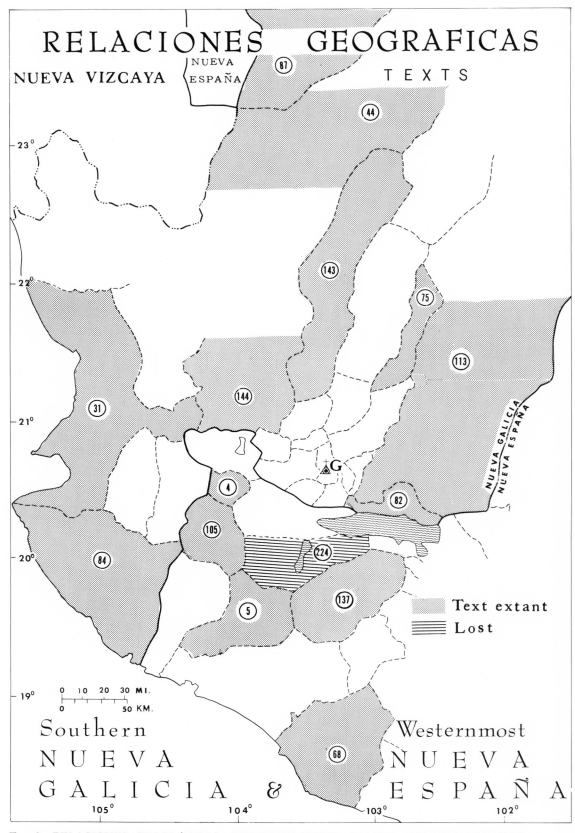

FIG. 2—RELACIONES GEOGRÁFICAS: SOUTHERN NUEVA GALICIA AND WESTERNMOST
NUEVA ESPAÑA, 1580

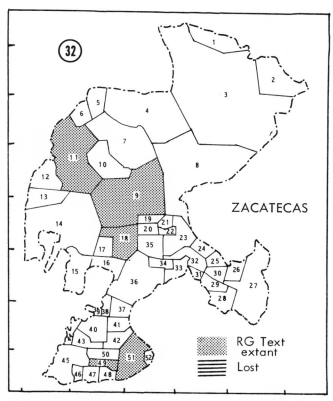

FIG. 3—RELACIONES GEOGRÁFICAS: ZACATECAS

TABLE 14—RELACIONES GEOGRÁFICAS OF WESTERN MEXICO:
GUANAJUATO (fig. 5)

Census No.	Principal Document	Diocese	Modern Place
18	CELAYA	Michoacan	Celaya
	Lost:		
203	CHICHIMECAS	Michoacan	San Miguel de Allende
208	LEON	Michoacan	Leon
211	SICHU	Michoacan	Xichu

TABLE 15—RELACIONES GEOGRÁFICAS OF WESTERN MEXICO: JALISCO (fig. 6)

Census No.	Principal Document	Diocese	Modern Place
4	AMECA	Guadalajara	Ameca
5	AMULA	Guadalajara	*see sub-cabeceras*
82	PONCITLAN	Guadalajara	Poncitlan
84	PURIFICACION	Guadalajara	Villa Vieja, M. Purificacion
105	TENAMAZTLAN	Guadalajara	Tenamaxtlan
113	TEQUALTICHE	Guadalajara	Teocaltiche
137	TUXPAN	Michoacan	Tuxpan
144	XOCOTLAN	Guadalajara	Joctlan, M. Hostotipaquillo
	Lost:		
224	ZAYULA	Guadalajara	Sayula

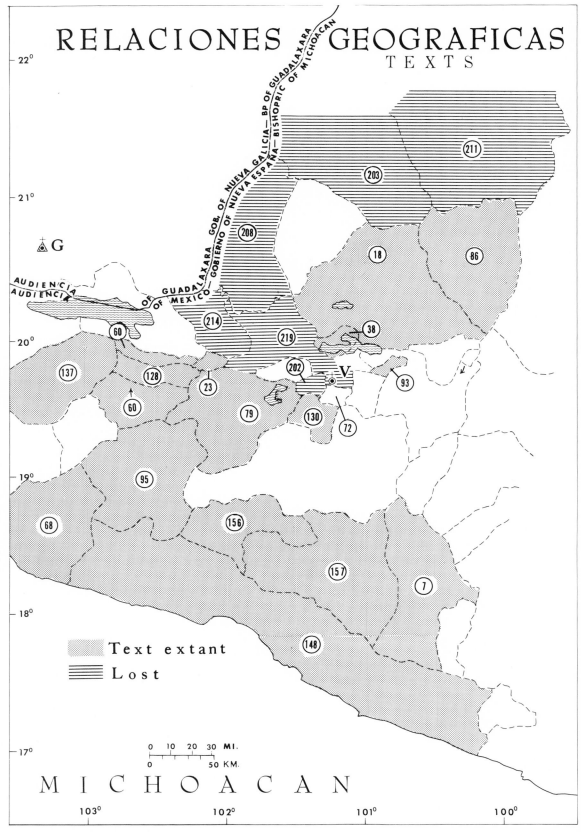

FIG. 4—RELACIONES GEOGRÁFICAS: DIOCESE OF MICHOACAN, 1580

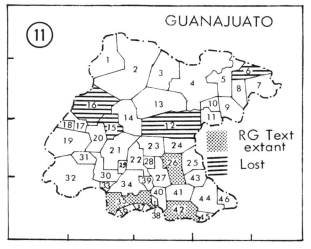

Fig. 5—RELACIONES GEOGRÁFICAS:
GUANAJUATO

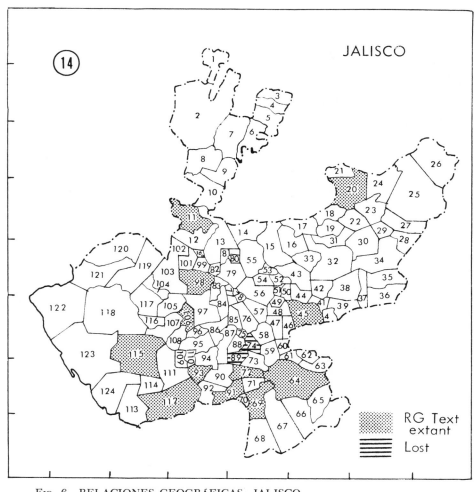

Fig. 6—RELACIONES GEOGRÁFICAS: JALISCO

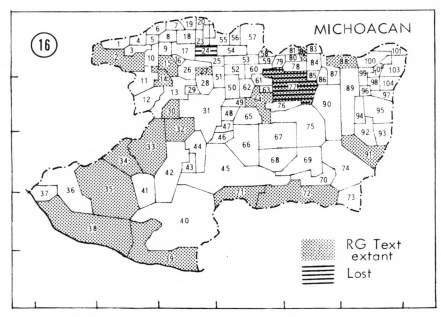

Fig. 7—RELACIONES GEOGRÁFICAS: MICHOACAN

TABLE 16—RELACIONES GEOGRÁFICAS OF WESTERN MEXICO: MICHOACAN (fig. 7)

Census No.	Principal Document	Diocese	Modern Place
23	CHILCHOTLA	Michoacan	Chilchota
38	CUISEO	Michoacan	Cuitzeo del Porvenir
60	JILQUILPAN	Michoacan	Jilquilpan de Juarez
68	MOTINES	Michoacan	*see sub-cabeceras*
72	NECOTLAN	Michoacan	Stgo. Undameo, M. Morelia
79	PAZCUARO	Michoacan	Patzcuaro
93	TAIMEO	Michoacan	Taimeo, M. Zinepecuaro
95	TANCITARO	Michoacan	Tancitaro
128	TINGUINDIN	Michoacan	Tingindin
130	TIRIPITIO	Michoacan	Tiripetio, M. Morelia
148	ZACATULA	Michoacan	Nr. Melchor Ocampo de Balsas
156	ZINAGUA	Michoacan	Sinagua, M. Churusuco
	Lost:		
202	CAPOLA	Michoacan	Capula, M. Morelia
214	TAZAZALCA	Michoacan	Tlazazalca
219	VALLADOLID	Michoacan	Morelia

JALISCO (fig. 6). The most settled portion of Nueva Galicia in the period around 1580, Jalisco records 9 RG's, of which one is considered "lost." Only the document for Ameca (Census, 4) is now accompanied by map materials. (See Table 15.)

MICHOACAN (fig. 7). The present state of Michoacan formed a large part of the 16th-century bishopric of that name, in the realm of Nueva España, subject to Mexico City (fig. 4). Notable is the lack of accompanying maps to the 15 known RG's, one of

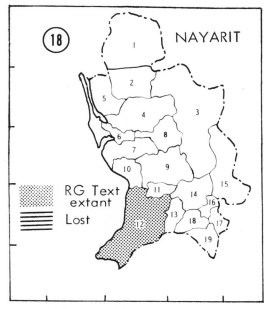

FIG. 8—RELACIONES GEOGRÁFICAS: NAYARIT

which is "lost." Such a map is found only for Tuzantla (Census, 103D), a community subordinated to a cabecera in the archbishopric of Mexico. (See Table 16.)

NAYARIT (fig. 8). From Nayarit comes the single RG for Compostela (Census, 31). For consistency's sake, the sole item is tabulated as Table 17.

Central Mexico (figs. 9, 9A, 10)

At the heart of the viceroyalty and center of Nueva España the Central Mexican region has RG's from all modern states except Tlaxcala. A large number of the numerous jurisdictions within the bishopric of Tlaxcala and the archbishopric of Mexico are represented by RG documents and maps. For the region as a whole, there are 62 principal documents, of which 10, including that for Mexico City, are "lost."

DISTRITO FEDERAL (fig. 11). The Distrito Federal, modern Mexico City and suburbs, is covered by five RG's, the extant three of which relate to parts of the ex-municipio of Ixtapalapa. (See Table 18.)

GUERRERO (fig. 12). In colonial times, the present municipal jurisdictions of Guerrero fell within one of two bishoprics (Michoacan, fig. 4; Tlaxcala, fig. 10) or the archbishopric of Mexico (fig. 9). Of the 11 RG's for Guerrero, the important one for the port of Acapulco (Census, 200) is "lost." The others often cover considerable areas, es-

TABLE 17—RELACIONES GEOGRÁFICAS OF WESTERN MEXICO: NAYARIT (fig. 8)

Census No.	Principal Document	Diocese	Modern Place
31	COMPOSTELA	Guadalajara	Compostela

TABLE 18—RELACIONES GEOGRÁFICAS OF CENTRAL MEXICO: DISTRITO FEDERAL (fig. 11)

Census No.	Principal Document	Diocese	Modern Place
41	CULHUACAN	Mexico	Culhuacan, M. Ixtapalapa
56	IXTAPALAPA	Mexico	Ixtapalapa
65	MEXICATZINGO	Mexico	Mexicaltzingo, M. Ixtapalapa
	Lost:		
204	CHURUBUSCO	Mexico	Churubusco
209	MEXICO	Mexico	Mexico City

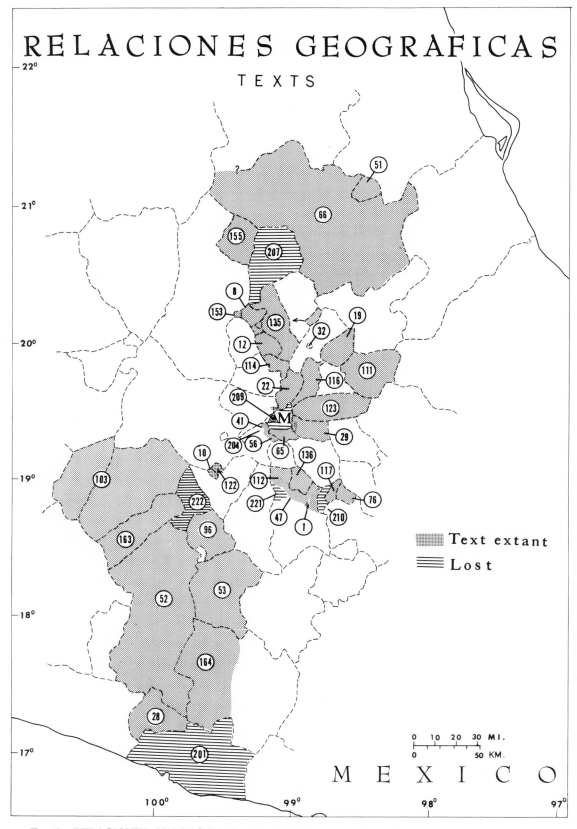

RELACIONES GEOGRÁFICAS
TEXTS

Text extant
Lost

Fig. 9—RELACIONES GEOGRÁFICAS: ARCHDIOCESE OF MEXICO, 1580

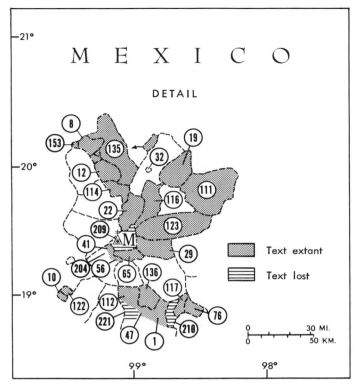

Fig. 10—RELACIONES GEOGRÁFICAS: CENTRAL
MEXICO, 1580

TABLE 19—RELACIONES GEOGRÁFICAS OF CENTRAL MEXICO: GUERRERO (fig. 12)

Census No.	Principal Document	Diocese	Modern Place
7	ASUCHITLAN	Michoacan	Ajuchitlan de Progreso
22bis	CHILAPA	Tlaxcala	Chilapa de Alvarez
28	CITLALTOMAGUA	Mexico	Zitlala?
52	ICHCATEOPAN	Mexico	Ixcateopan
53	IGUALA	Mexico	Iguala
96	TAXCO	Mexico	Taxco de Alarcon
132	TISTLA	Tlaxcala	Tixtla de Guerrero
142	XALAPA-CINTLA	Tlaxcala-Antequera	*see sub-cabeceras*
157	ZIRANDARO	Michoacan	Zirandaro
164	ZUMPANGO	Mexico	Zumpango del Rio
	Lost:		
200	ACAPULCO	Mexico	Acapulco de Juarez

213

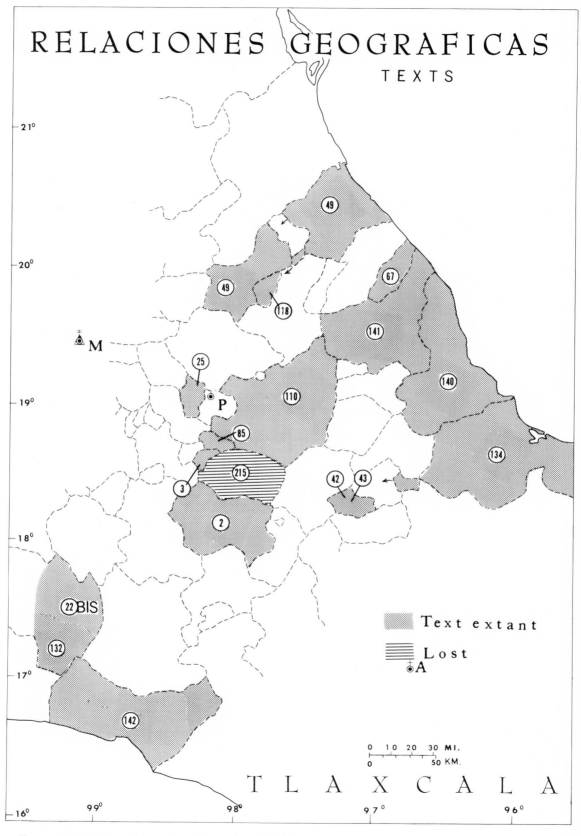

RELACIONES GEOGRAFICAS
TEXTS

Text extant
Lost
A

FIG. 11—RELACIONES GEOGRÁFICAS: DIOCESE OF TLAXCALA, 1580

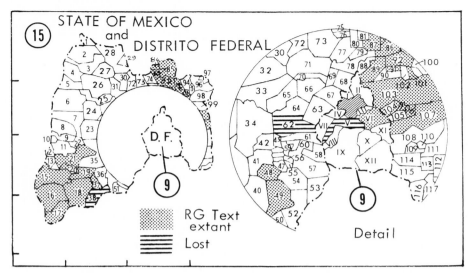

FIG. 12—RELACIONES GEOGRÁFICAS: DISTRITO FEDERAL AND STATE OF MEXICO

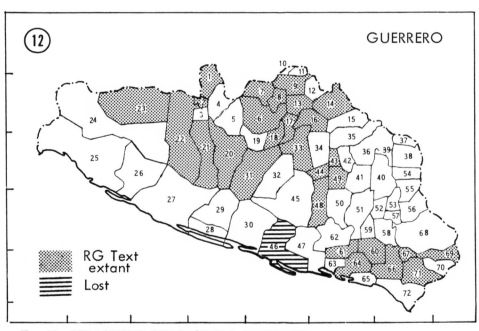

FIG. 13—RELACIONES GEOGRÁFICAS: GUERRERO

pecially along the Pacific coast. (See Table 19.)

HIDALGO (fig. 13). The colonial Hidalgo area fell wholly within the archbishopric of Mexico, at the edge of the Valley of Mexi-co. There are 10 extant documents, with mention of one "lost," for a total of 11. All have at least one map; in the case of Mezti-tlan (Census, 66) there is, in addition, a native calendrical drawing. (See Table 20.)

215

TABLE 20—RELACIONES GEOGRÁFICAS OF CENTRAL MEXICO: HIDALGO (fig. 13)

Census No.	Principal Document	Diocese	Modern Place
8	ATENGO	Mexico	Atengo, M. Tezontepec de Aldama
12	ATLITALQUIA	Mexico	Atitalaquia
19	CEMPOALA	Mexico	Zempoala
32	CUAUHQUILPAN	Mexico	S. Pedro Huauquilpan, M. Zapotlan de Juarez
51	HUEXOTLA	Mexico	Huejutla de Reyes
66	MEZTITLAN	Mexico	Metztitlan
111	TEPEAPULCO	Mexico	Tepeapulco
135	TORNACUSTLA	Mexico	Tornacustla, M. S. Agustin Tlaxiaca
153	ZAYULA	Mexico	Sayula, M. Tepeitlan
155	ZIMAPAN	Mexico	Zimapan
	Lost:		
207	ISMIQUILPA	Mexico	Ixmiquilpa

TABLE 21—RELACIONES GEOGRÁFICAS OF CENTRAL MEXICO: MEXICO (fig. 11)

Census No.	Principal Document	Diocese	Modern Place
10	ATLATLAUCA	Mexico	Atlatlahuca, M. Tenango del Valle
22	CHICONAUTLA	Mexico	Sta. Maria Chiconautla, M. Ecatepec
29	COATEPEC	Mexico	Coatepec, M. Ixtapaluca
103	TEMAZCALTEPEC	Mexico	Real de Arriba, M. Temascaltepec
114	TEQUISQUIAC	Mexico	Tequixquiac
116	TEQUIZISTLAN	Mexico	Tequisistlan, M. Tezoyuca
122	TEUTENANGO	Mexico	Tenango de Arista, M. Tenango del Valle
123	TEXCOCO	Mexico	Texcoco de Mora
163	ZULTEPEC	Mexico	Sultepec de Pedro Asencio
	Lost:		
212	TALASCO	Mexico	M. Lerma
222	ZACUALPA	Mexico	Zacualpan

TABLE 22—RELACIONES GEOGRÁFICAS OF CENTRAL MEXICO: MORELOS (fig. 14)

Census No.	Principal Document	Diocese	Modern Place
1	ACAPISTLA	Mexico	Yecapixtla
47	GUAXTEPEC	Mexico	Oaxtepec, M. Yautepec
112	TEPUZTLAN	Mexico	Tepoztlan
117	TETELA	Mexico	Tetela del Volcan
136	TOTOLAPA	Mexico	Totolapan
	Lost		
210	OCUITUCO	Mexico	Ocuituco
221	YAUTEPEC	Mexico	Yautepec

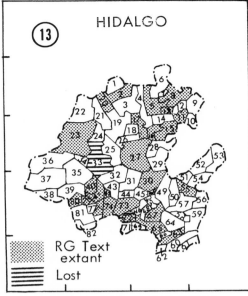

FIG. 14—RELACIONES GEOGRÁFICAS: HIDALGO

STATE OF MEXICO (fig. 11). Containing a majority of the precolonial Indian communities of the Valley of Mexico, the state of Mexico has a reported 11 RG documents, two of which are "lost." Missing, too, are the important drawings which accompanied the description of Texcoco (Census, 123), a matter discussed in volume 14, Articles 23 and 24. All RG's are in the archbishopric of Mexico (fig. 4). (See Table 21.)

MORELOS (fig. 14). The small state of Morelos, lying within the archbishopric of Mexico, in colonial years was occupied by various estates and holdings of Fernando Cortés as Marqués del Valle. Two RG's for such jurisdictions are "lost" but five for Morelos areas survive, none with maps. (See Table 22.)

PUEBLA (fig. 15). The state of Puebla lay almost entirely within the diocese of Tlaxcala, of which the main city, Puebla de los Angeles, was seat of the bishop. Through the area passed major trade routes from Mexico City to the Atlantic and Pacific ports and to Guatemala. Only one small community, Ocopetlayuca (Census, 76), within the present state of Puebla was in the colonial archbishopric of Mexico. (See Table 23.)

QUERETARO (fig. 16). Queretaro, with its capital of the same name, is almost wholly included in the single RG for that state. The cabecera itself lay within the diocese of

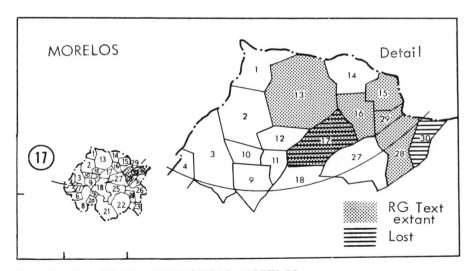

FIG. 15—RELACIONES GEOGRÁFICAS: MORELOS

TABLE 23—RELACIONES GEOGRÁFICAS OF CENTRAL MEXICO: PUEBLA (fig. 15)

Census No.	Principal Document	Diocese	Modern Place
2	ACATLAN	Tlaxcala	Acatlan de Osorio
3	AHUATLAN	Tlaxcala	Ahuatlan
25	CHOLULA	Tlaxcala	Cholula de Rivadabia, M. S. Pedro Cholula
42	CUZCATLAN–1	Tlaxcala	Coxcatlan
43	CUZCATLAN–2	Tlaxcala	Coxcatlan
49	GUEYTLALPA	Tlaxcala	Hueytlalpan
76	OCOPETLAYUCA	Mexico	Tochimilco
85	QUATLATLAUCA	Tlaxcala	Huatlatlauca
110	TEPEACA	Tlaxcala	Tepeaca
118	TETELA	Tlaxcala	Tetela de Ocampo
	Lost:		
215	TEPEXI DE LA SEDA	Tlaxcala	Tepexi de Rodriguez

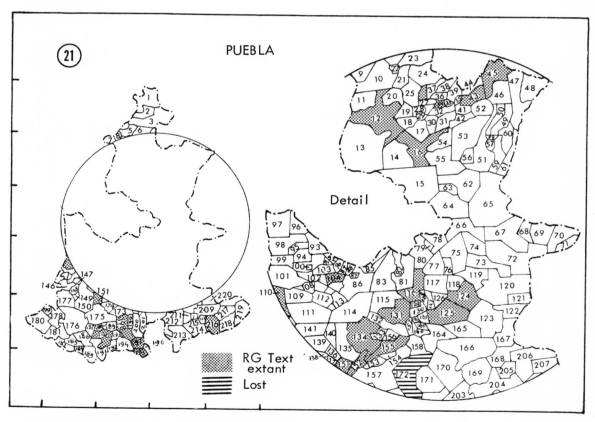

FIG. 16—RELACIONES GEOGRÁFICAS: PUEBLA

TABLE 24—RELACIONES GEOGRÁFICAS OF CENTRAL MEXICO: QUERETARO (fig. 16)

Census No.	Principal Document	Diocese	Modern Place
86	QUERETARO	Michoacan	Queretaro

TABLE 25—RELACIONES GEOGRÁFICAS OF CENTRAL MEXICO: VERACRUZ (fig. 17)

Census No.	Principal Document	Diocese	Modern Place
30	COATZOCOALCO	Antequera	Nr. Tuzandepetl, M. Chapoptla
67	MIZANTLA	Tlaxcala	Mizantla
134	TLACOTLALPA	Tlaxcala	Tlacotalpan
140	VERA CRUZ	Tlaxcala	Antigua Veracruz, M. M. La Antigua
141	XALAPA	Tlaxcala	Jalapa Enriquez
	Lost:		
205	GUASPALTEPEC	Antequera	Guaxpala, M. Playa Vicente

FIG. 17—RELACIONES GEOGRÁFICAS: QUERETARO

Michoacan, but its main dependency, San Juan del Rio, was in the archdiocese of Mexico. (See Table 24.)

VERACRUZ (fig. 17). The final state in the Central Mexican region, Veracruz, during colonial days occupied the Atlantic coast littoral of the bishoprics of Tlaxcala and Antequera (fig. 18). The areas covered in five extant RG's tend to be rather large, as is the jurisdiction for which one "lost" document is reported. (See Table 25.)

Oaxaca Region (figs. 18, 18A, and 19)

OAXACA. The state of Oaxaca (fig. 19) lay wholly within the diocese of Antequera (figs. 18, 18A) named for the principal Spanish city, seat of the bishop. With 38 RG's, six of them "lost," Oaxaca ranks second only to Yucatan as the modern state with the most such documents. Unfortunately the "lost" items cover areas of major concern to ethnohistory, notably an apparently extended coverage of the Mixteca in a volume compiled for the Yanhuitlan area, and including Teposcolula. As especially in the case of Teozacoalco, the map materials accompanying the RG's are often important native pictorial documents (see Articles 23, 24). (See Table 26.)

Southeastern Mexico and Guatemala

There are a number of unusual features about the RG's from this region. Within it, the coverage by modern units is quite disparate. No documents exist for Chiapas, Campeche, or British Honduras, leaving the

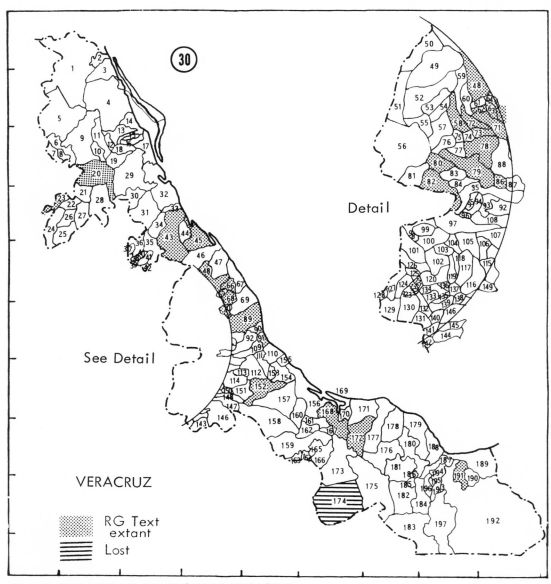

Fɪɢ. 18—RELACIONES GEOGRÁFICAS: VERACRUZ

concentration for the Mexican states of Yucatan and Tabasco, with two RG's known for all Guatemala. For the region as a whole, there are 56 documents, only five of which have maps. The bishopric of Yucatan, which included much of the region, is shown in figure 20.

Because nearly all the Yucatan RG's have deviant features, it has proven difficult to provide precise cartographical depiction. Rather than subdivisions in alcaldías mayores and corregimientos, the Peninsula of Yucatan used the holdings of encomenderos as the units for the reports; the same man could draw tributes from various Maya settlements, not necessarily contiguous. In the

220

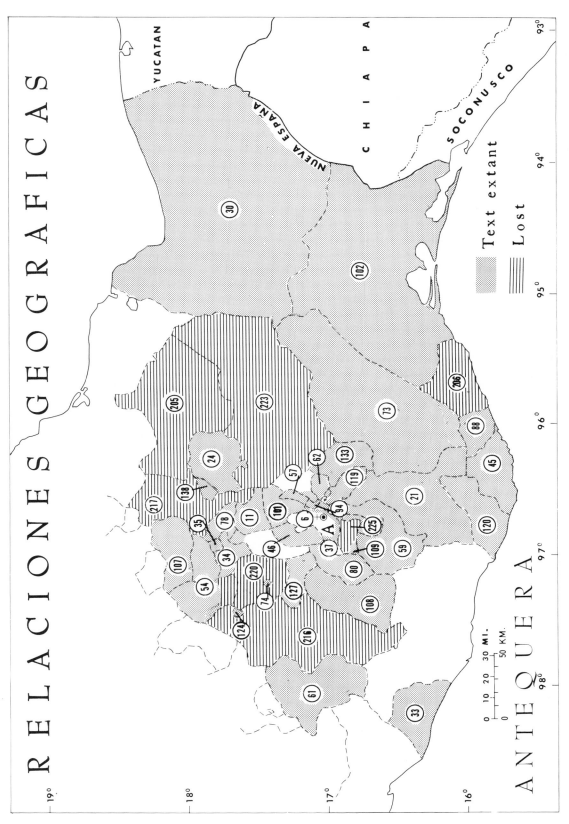

RELACIONES GEOGRÁFICAS

Text extant

Lost

Fig. 19—RELACIONES GEOGRÁFICAS: DIOCESE OF ANTEQUERA, 1580

TABLE 26—RELACIONES GEOGRÁFICAS OF OAXACA REGION:
STATE OF OAXACA (fig. 19)

Census No.	Principal Document	Diocese	Modern Place
6	ANTEQUERA	Antequera	Oaxaca de Juarez
11	ATLATLAUCA	Antequera	S. Juan Bautista Atlatlahuca
21	CHICHICAPA	Antequera	S. Baltasar Chichicapan
24	CHINANTLA	Antequera	S. Juan Bautista Valle Nacional
33	CUAHUITLAN	Antequera	Cahuitan, M. Stgo. Tapextla
34	CUAUTLA	Antequera	S. Miguel Huautla Nochixtlan
35	CUICATLAN	Antequera	S. Juan Bautista Cuicatlan
37	CUILAPA	Antequera	Cuilapan de Guerrero
45	GUATULCO	Antequera	*see sub-cabeceras*
46	GUAXOLOTITLAN	Antequera	S. Pablo Huitzo
54	IXCATLAN	Antequera	Sta. Maria Ixcatlan
57	IXTEPEXIC	Antequera	Sta. Catarina Ixtepeji
59	IZTEPEC	Antequera	Sta. Cruz Mixtepec
61	JUSTLAVACA	Antequera	Stgo. Juxtlahuaca
62	MACUILSUCHIL	Antequera	S. Mateo Macuilxochitl, M. Tlacochahuya
73	NEXAPA	Antequera	Nejapa de Madero
74	NOCHIZTLAN	Antequera	Asuncion Nochixtlan
78	PAPALOTICPAC	Antequera	Stos. Reyes Papalo
80	PEÑOLES	Antequera	Sta. Maria Peñoles
88	SUCHITEPEC	Antequera	Sta. Maria Xadan, M.S. Miguel del Puerto
94	TALISTACA	Antequera	Tlalixtac de Cabrera
101	TECUICUILCO	Antequera	Teococuilco
102	TEHUANTEPEC	Antequera	Sto. Domingo Tehuantepec
107	TEOTITLAN	Antequera	Teotitlan del Camino
108	TEOZACOALCO	Antequera	S. Pedro Teozacoalco
109	TEOZAPOTLAN	Antequera	Zaachila
119	TETICPAC	Antequera	S. Sebastian Teitipac
120	TETIQUIPA	Antequera	S. Sebastian Rio Hondo
124	TEXUPA	Antequera	Stgo. Tejupan
127	TILANTONGO	Antequera	Stgo. Tilantongo
133	TLACOLULA	Antequera	Tlacolula de Matamoros
138	USILA	Antequera	S. Felipe Usila
	Lost:		
206	HUAMELULA	Antequera	S. Pedro Huamelula
216	TEPOSCOLULA	Antequera	S. Pedro y S. Pablo Teposcolula
217	TEUTILA	Antequera	S. Pedro Teutila
220	YANGUITLAN	Antequera	Sto. Domingo Yanhuitlan
223	ZAPOTECAS	Antequera	S. Ildefonso Villa Alta
225	ZIMATLAN	Antequera	Zimatlan de Alvarez

case of Tabasco, one document merely lists numerous communities, without providing many data on any. Nominally all settlements except Guatemala lay in the general jurisdiction either of Merida, seat of the bishopric of Yucatan, or Valladolid, hence the structure of jurisdictions differed markedly from other parts of the viceroyalty, even within the realm of New Spain, on which the two main divisions of the peninsula of Yucatan were nominally dependent. These and other peculiarities appear as we analyze the documents by modern jurisdictional units.

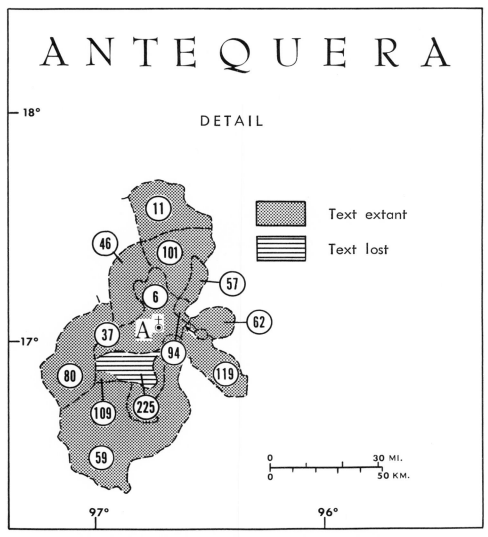

Fig. 20—RELACIONES GEOGRÁFICAS: ANTEQUERA, 1580, DETAIL

TABLE 27—RELACIONES GEOGRÁFICAS OF SOUTHEASTERN MEXICO:
QUINTANA ROO (fig. 21)

Census No.	Principal Document	Diocese	Modern Place
13	CACALAC	Yucatan	Sacalaca, M. Felipe Carrillo Puerto
15	CAMPOCOLCHE	Yucatan	Kampokolche, M. Felipe Carrillo Puerto
27	CHUNCHUCHU	Yucatan	Chunkuku, M. Felipe Carrillo Puerto
55	IXMUL	Yucatan	Ichmul, M. Felipe Carrillo Puerto
149	ZAMA	Yucatan	Tulum, M. Cozumel

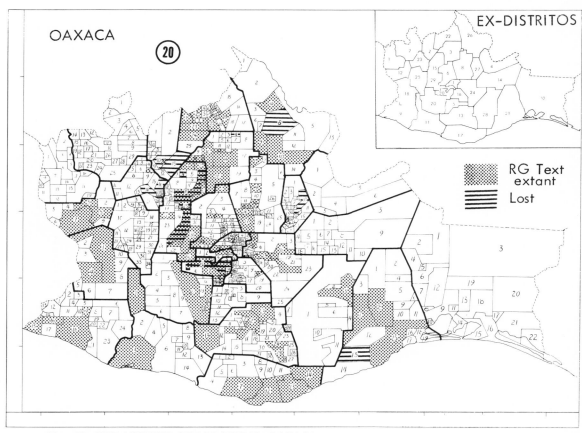

Fig. 21—RELACIONES GEOGRÁFICAS: OAXACA

TABLE 28—RELACIONES GEOGRÁFICAS OF SOUTHEASTERN MEXICO:
TABASCO (fig. 22)

Census No.	Principal Document	Diocese	Modern Place
89	TABASCO (AM)	Yucatan	*see sub-cabeceras*
90	TABASCO (P)	Yucatan	*see sub-cabeceras*
91	TABASCO, Sta. Maria de la Victoria (V)	Yucatan	La Victoria, M. Centla

QUINTANA ROO (fig. 21). Quintana Roo, a Mexican territory, in colonial times lay within the bishopric of Yucatan, and was subject to authorities at Valladolid. For it are reported five RG's, none with maps. (See Table 27.)

TABASCO (fig. 22). Tabasco records three RG's, one of which has an elaborate map.

Spanning the whole jurisdiction, an alcaldía mayor, is a complex listing of known settlements (Census, 89). A more descriptive document is a summary of the province as a whole, with a map (Census, 90). Finally, the town council of the main town provided further information on the territory for which they were collectively responsible, nearly the same as the previous two areas. (See Table 28.)

STATE OF YUCATAN (fig. 23). The state of Yucatan records more RG's than any other modern Mexican unit, a total of 46, two of which have maps. Sewed in a single volume, with those for Tabasco and Quintana Roo, presumably none has been lost.

One of the oddities of these documents is that, unlike other parts of the viceroyalty, they were compiled by civilian holders of encomiendas rather than by royal officials, often aided by ecclesiastical persons. A second and important feature of the compilers is that many of them leaned on a single individual to help them comply with their obligation of providing the captain-general with answers to the 1577 questionnaire.

Gaspar Antonio Chi, also known as Gaspar Antonio Xiu, or Gaspar Antonio Herrera, was a Maya Indian who had been Christianized at the age of fifteen (about 1546) and who performed various clerical and other chores until his death in 1610. He aided Bishop Landa in gathering information. Tozzer (1941, pp. 44–46, note 219) has summarized much information on him, and others have discussed him. Purporting to be descended from the Xiu rulers, he generally exalted their importance in the RG documents on which he assisted. He was the sole author of a general RG for the province of Yucatan (Census, 147), the only one of the corpus not found in the same manuscript volume. He was primarily responsible for a number of others, whose similarity on historical matters thus derives from the single source; these include Census, 39, 40, 64, 70, 97, 98, 99, 151, 166. (See Table 29.)

GUATEMALA (fig. 24). In this complicated Maya area, Guatemala forms part of the same region of which the peninsula of Yucatan is the major component. The bishopric of Guatemala extended over all of Central America, and included the present Mexican state of Chiapas, but within these large confines, only two RG's are known,

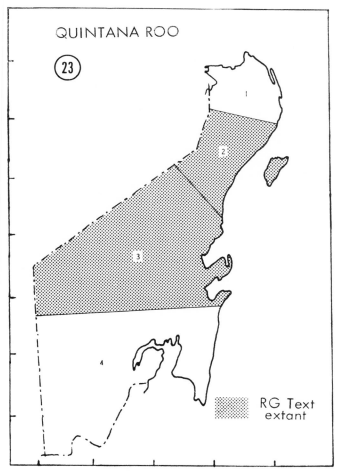

FIG. 22—RELACIONES GEOGRÁFICAS: QUINTANA ROO

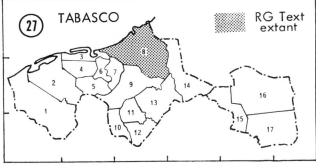

FIG. 23—RELACIONES GEOGRÁFICAS: TABASCO

225

TABLE 29—RELACIONES GEOGRÁFICAS OF SOUTHEASTERN MEXICO:
STATE OF YUCATAN (fig. 23)

Census No.	Principal Document	Diocese	Modern Place
14	CACALCHEN	Yucatan	Cacalchen
16	CINANCHE	Yucatan	Sinanche
17	CANZACABO	Yucatan	Cansahcab
20	CHANCENOTE	Yucatan	Chan Cenote, M. Tizimin
26	CHUBULNA	Yucatan	Chuburna de Hidalgo, M. Merida
36	CUICUIL [QUIQUIL]	Yucatan	Kikil, M. Tizimin
39	CUITELCUM [QUITELCUM]	Yucatan	Citilcun, M. Izamal
40	CUIZIL [QUIZIL]	Yucatan	*unlocated*
48	GUAYMA	Yucatan	Uayma
50	HOCABA	Yucatan	Hocaba
58	IZAMAL	Yucatan	Izamal
63	MAMA	Yucatan	Mama
64	MERIDA	Yucatan	Merida
69	MOTUL	Yucatan	Motul de Felipe Carrillo Puerto
70	MOXOPIPE	Yucatan	Muxupip
71	NABALON	Yucatan	Nabalam, M. Tizimin
77	OSCUZCAS	Yucatan	Okutzcab
81	PIJOY	Yucatan	Pixoy, M. Valladolid
83	POPOLA	Yucatan	Popola, M. Valladolid
92	TAHZIB	Yucatan	Tahdziu
97	TEABO	Yucatan	Teabo
98	TECAL	Yucatan	Tekal de Venegas
99	TECANTO	Yucatan	Tekanto
100	TECON	Yucatan	Tekom
104	TEMUL	Yucatan	Panaba
106	TENUM	Yucatan	Tinum
115	TEQUITE	Yucatan	Tekit
121	TETZAL	Yucatan	*unlocated*
125	TEZEMI	Yucatan	Tizimin
126	TEZOCO	Yucatan	Tescoco, M. Valladolid
129	TIQUIBALON	Yucatan	*unlocated*
131	TISHOTZUCO	Yucatan	Chikindzonot, M. Tekom
139	VALLADOLID	Yucatan	Valladolid
145	XOQUEN	Yucatan	Xocen
146	YALCON	Yucatan	Yalcon, M. Valladolid
147	YUCATAN (P)	Yucatan	
150	ZAMAHIL	Yucatan	Samahil
151	ZAN	Yucatan	Dzan
154	ZICAL	Yucatan	*part of Valladolid*
158	ZISMOPO	Yucatan	Dzitnup, M. Valladolid
159	ZIZONTUM	Yucatan	Dzidzantun
160	ZONOT	Yucatan	Tizimin
161	ZOTUTA	Yucatan	Sotuta
162	ZOZIL	Yucatan	*unlocated*
165	ZUSOPO	Yucatan	Sucopo, M. Tizimin
166	ZUZAL	Yucatan	Sudzal

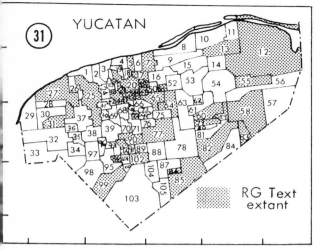

Fig. 24—RELACIONES GEOGRÁFICAS: STATE OF YUCATAN

for areas within the present republic of Guatemala. Both have handsome maps, generally covering territory from around Lake Atitlan to the Pacific Ocean. In addition, the RG of Zapotitlan (Census, 152) has a native genealogy of rulers of the area, which has been published; the maps have not. (See Table 30.)

Summary Conclusions

The *Relaciones Geográficas*, 1578–86, compiled under orders of Philip II for the Spanish Indies, form an unusual and important group of sources, providing data not obtainable elsewhere on a wide variety of topics, at the local and regional level. The fact that they are modular or standardized in their topical coverage gives them particu-lar significance for comparative studies of topics or of regions. This value is enhanced by their virtual contemporaneous compilation, falling four years either side of 1582, a single moment of colonial historical time. To these attributes are added the graphic and cartographical elements. Most RG's are still capable of revealing important new information of surprising variety.

The more detailed knowledge we have recently begun to accumulate about the *Relaciones* supports and extends the judgment passed on them in 1947 by Clarence H. Haring. He stated that they represented "one of our richest sources of information regarding both Spanish and Indian communities in the New World before 1600" (Haring, 1947, p. 104). Even though Ovando and López de Velasco were unable to fulfill their ambitious dream of preparing a comprehensive volume on the places and people of the 16th-century overseas Spanish dominions, modern students can thank them for their broadly conceived and ably executed program that brought into being the *Relaciones*, a legacy that continues to yield important scholarly returns.

Epilogues

Collectively the RG's prepared in response to the 1577 questionnaire form the most extensive and important single corpus of such materials. But that series is not wholly unique. Other and later but smaller bodies of information in the same tradition were developed by Spanish colonial officials, extending and adapting the established questionnaire technique.

TABLE 30—RELACIONES GEOGRÁFICAS OF SOUTHEASTERN MEXICO AND GUATEMALA (fig. 24)

Census No.	Principal Document	Diocese	Modern Place
9	ATITLAN, Santiago	Guatemala	Stgo. Atitlan, Dept. Solola
152	ZAPOTITLAN (AM)	Guatemala	Zapotitlan

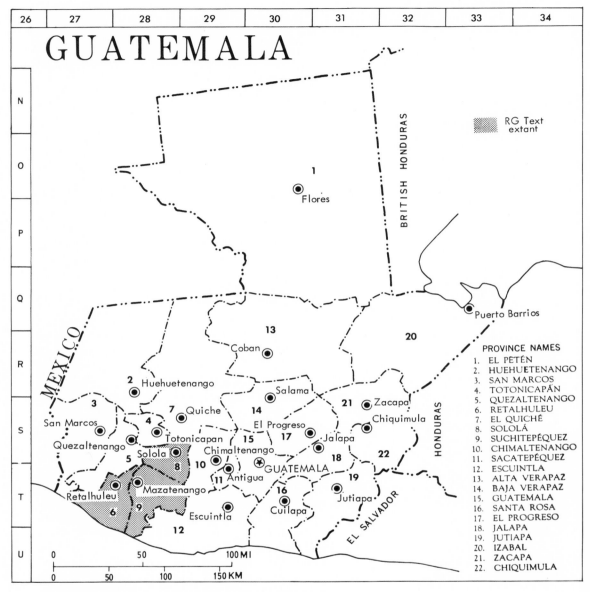

FIG. 25—RELACIONES GEOGRÁFICAS: GUATEMALA

During the 17th century, at least two further efforts were made to compile data similar to those appearing in the 1578–86 RG's. Brief treatment of these attempts is provided here. In the 18th century, other major programs were undertaken, apparently primarily for New Spain. They are discussed by West in Article 10.

The 1604 Program

The Conde de Lemus, President of the Council of Indies (1603–09), in collaboration with the Cosmographer Andrés García de Céspedes (1596–1611), in 1604 attempted to emulate earlier efforts to obtain data about the overseas realms by formulating

TABLE 31—RELACIONES GEOGRÁFICAS OF THE 1604 SERIES: NEW SPAIN

Census No.	Principal Document	Date	Status
301	AMATLAN, PUEBLO	March, 1609	Pub
302	COATLAN, PUEBLO	April, 1609	Pub
303	COLIMA, VILLA	1608	Lost
304	GUACHINANGO & TAMIAGUA	1612	Pub
305	GUAXUAPA	1608	Lost
306	MIAGUATLAN	February, 1609	Pub
307	NOMBRE DE DIOS, VILLA	May, 1608	Pub
308	OCELOTEPEQUE, PUEBLO	March, 1609	Pub
309	PACHUCA, MINAS	1608	Pub
310	PANUCO	1612	Pub
311	SULTEPEQUE, MINAS	1609	Lost
312	TAMPICO, VILLA	1612	Pub
313	TEPEXI DE LA SEDA, PUEBLO	1608	Lost
314	TEPOZCOLULA, ALCALDÍA MAYOR	1608	Lost
315	ZACATECAS, CIUDAD	1608	Pub
316	ZAGUALPA, MINAS	1608	Lost
317	ZUMPANGO, PARTIDO	1608	Lost

and circulating in the Indies a lengthy questionnaire (Becker, 1917, pp. 144–45). Paso y Troncoso suggested that Céspedes, who had reviewed many if not all the returns from the 1577 schedule, sought to remedy some of the defects in topical coverage (JDE, 1: lxxv, xcvii; PNE, 4: 269). Possibly also involved was the need for up-to-date information on various areas, especially in New Spain, that recently had been subject to a major regrouping of Indian towns, the civil congregations of 1603–05 (Cline, 1949).

Céspedes' 1604 questionnaire utilized most of the queries of the 1577 schedule, but simplified, split, and augmented them. Each 1604 question was simple, uncomplicated, direct; they total 355 items. Apparently on receipt of completed questionnaires, bureaucratic hands in Madrid then regrouped the answers under four general headings: Environment [Lo Natural]; Culture, Economics, and Administration [Lo Moral y Lo Político]; military matters [Lo Militar]; and Church [Lo Eclesiástico]. No maps seem to have been required, although we do not know what precise instructions accompanied the questionnaire. Only one copy of the latter is presently known: Manuscript 3035, Biblioteca Nacional (Madrid), folios 46–53, published in 1905 by Paso y Troncoso (PNE, 4: 273–88). Paso y Troncoso noted that the interrogation was drawn up by persons who utilized localisms of the Andean areas; terms like "yanaconas," "guacas," "tambos," "chacaras," are examples.

The questionnaire was expected to apply to "all cities, villas, and Spanish places, and native communities of the Indies." After personal investigation authorities were supposed, "with punctuality and care," to answer each of the 355 queries. These were overwhelming in the detail required from already overburdened local officials.

The program was generally a failure. Few completed questionnaires seem to have been transmitted to Madrid for bureaucratic recompilation. In fact, no original such documents are known to survive.[4] The little we know about these documents derives directly and indirectly almost exclusively from Antonio de León Pinelo. In his

[4] The one exception may be a document prepared by Baltasar Murial de Valdivieso, Gobernador de Soconusco, May 4, 1613, an unpublished report in AGI, Guatemala, 40 (4 fols.), covering modern Huehuetan, Chiapas. Data from Peter Gerhard.

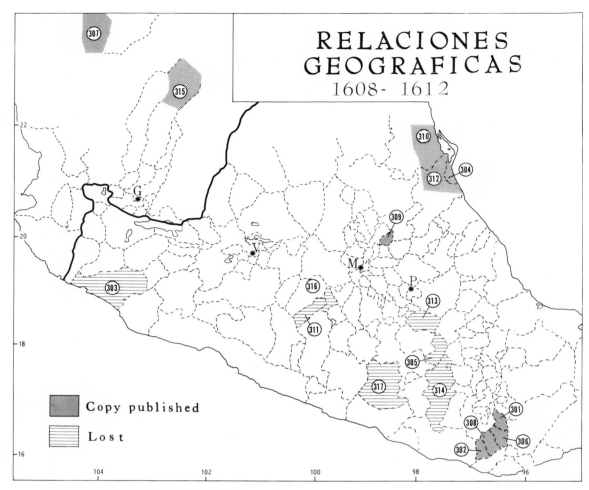

FIG. 26—RELACIONES GEOGRÁFICAS: 1608–12

"Memoria" (Appendix E) he lists various of these manuscripts then in his possession; as with many other documents on the Pinelo list, these items are lost. In addition, however, he either copied or extracted large segments, which now form Manuscript 3064 in the Biblioteca Nacional (Madrid), a document previously designated J-42, some 240 closely written folios. The whole group of these was published (1868) in volume 9 of *Documentos Inéditos . . . de Indias* (DII).

Paso y Troncoso republished four (Census 301, 302, 306, 308) from the same copy (PNE, 4: 289–319). He also reproduced the questionnaire.

In response to the 1604 questionnaire, we have record of 31 documents, several known bibliographically only through mention of them by León Pinelo. Of the total, seemingly 14 relate to South America, 17 to New Spain, 1608–12. As six of the latter are "lost" we have, in fact, only 11 extant published items. The documents for New Spain, extant and lost, are listed in Table 31 and shown in figure 26.

Interrogation of 1648

Following earlier RG traditions, a royal cédula dated April 26, 1648, was sent to bishops ordering transmittal of data on towns, communicants, and related matters.

230

TABLE 32—DEMOGRAPHIC REPORTS: CENTRAL AMERICA, 1683–84
(AGI, Contaduría, leg. 815)

Place	Date	Compiler	Notes
Escuintla	1684?	Corregidor	
Chiapa	May 20, 1683	Teniente de oficial real	Ciudad Real & 97 Indian towns; no. of tributaries
Verapaz (Coban)	Mar. 20, 1683	Alcalde Mayor	List of towns; no. of tributaries
Atitlan	Feb. 26, 1683	Corregidor	
Puerto de Sto. Tomas de Castilla	Mar. 5, 1683	Alcalde Mayor	
Guazacapan	Feb. 21, 1683	Corregidor	
Totonicapa	Mar. 17, 1683		
Tecpananitlan	Mar. 20, 1683	Corregidor	
Honduras	Apr. 24, 1683	Gobernador & Capt. General	Each jurisdiction; names of towns & citizens
Sonsonate	Apr. 20, 1683	Alcalde Mayor	Census by names
Chiquimula de la Sierra	Apr. 3, 1683	Corregidor	
Quesaltenango	Aug. 19, 1683	Corregidor	
Nicoya	June 30, 1683	Alcalde Mayor Diego de Partoja	Complete census
Suchitepeques			Census
Valle de Guatemala		Corregidor	
Acazaguastlan		Corregidor	
Soconusco (Gueguetlan)	Dec. 15, 1684	Gobernador Juan Ramírez y Valdés	No town list
Costa Rica		Gobernador	
Tegucigalpa	Oct. 7, 1684	Alcalde Mayor	
Leon	Nov. 15, 1684		
Sevaco y Chontales		Corregidor	
Granada	Sept. 23, 1684		
Nueva Segovia	Oct. 20, 1684		
El Realejo	Oct. 1, 1684	Corregidor	Complete census

A similar cédula, November 8, 1648, was sent to civil officials; it has been published (Salcedo y Herrera, 1958, pp. 11–14). It requested information to be used by Gil González Dávila, Royal Chronicler of the Indies and the Two Castiles (Becker, 1917, p. 145). His published work, *Teatro eclesiástico*, does not fully reflect whatever information the latter cédula may have generated. The *Teatro* contains a history of the Church, biographies of bishops, notes on art and literature, and native vocabularies. The first of two volumes appeared in Madrid in 1649, and is said to contain many errors (Bancroft, *Works*, 10: 190).

For New Spain, apparently only two replies to the 1648 inquiries survive. One is a manuscript in the Archivo Arquiepiscopal de Guadalajara. Prepared by Francisco

231

Manuel de Salcedo y Herrera, curate, it reports on the parish of Tlaltenango (bishopric of Guadalajara), dated July 16, 1650. It has been published (López, 1958). The other is an unpublished document dated April 25, 1649, in the Ayer Collection (MS 1106A), Newberry Library.[5]

Demographic Survey, 1679–83

Although clearly not RG's in the 16th-century tradition, a group of documents compiled in Central America to comply with royal cédulas of April 21, 1679, and August 5, 1681, warrant mention.[6] The earlier order was directed to archbishops and bishops in New Spain and the Philippines, whereas the second was sent to secular officials: audiencias, governors, and treasury officials in the same areas. They were commanded to give information about all cities, villas, and other settlements, and particularly to provide population figures for the whole, by social groupings among non-native, and Indians.

At present only one body of replies is known. These come from Central America, otherwise sparsely represented by RG's. In AGI, Contaduría, legajo 815, is a long (about 240 folios) "Razón" prepared by the audiencia of Guatemala, together with copies of more or less complete replies from subordinate officials of lesser jurisdictions (except San Salvador) giving detailed information on population for the years 1683–84. These materials are unpublished.

Table 32 lists the contents of the legajo, based on notes by Peter Gerhard. He reports that the entire group of papers was prepared by one scribe in Santiago de Guatemala. Because the legajo has been badly damaged by fire, it is difficult to use.

Summary

The 1577 questionnaire was emulated at least twice in the 17th century, but various official inquiries produced only a small crop of surviving documents. Replies from 1608 through 1612 to queries formulated in 1604 are the most numerous, but even these are relatively few and are known only in copies. For New Spain we have only a single response to a 1648 interrogation. A damaged manuscript for 1683–84 provides population data for Central America (except San Salvador). None of these is as replete as the RG's of the 1580 period.

As the Habsburg regime in Spain waned and gave way to the Bourbon monarchs at the beginning of the 18th century, and as the Enlightenment began to stress useful, statistical knowledge, there were numerous revivals of the RG tradition. This complex development is summarized by West in Article 10. Here we shall terminate this discussion by providing documents, a census, and bibliography of the 16th- and 17th-century *Relaciones Geográficas*.

[5] Information furnished by Peter Gerhard (personal communication). He also states that still another manuscript reply, for Puerto Rico (April, 1649), is in the same Collection (MSS 1106L,3; L,5).

[6] Information furnished by Peter Gerhard (personal communication).

REFERENCES

Note: Text references not listed here will be found in Article 9.

Burrus, 1955
Carbia, 1940
Cline, 1949
Edwards, 1969
Gómez Canedo, 1961
Haring, 1947

López de Velasco, 1894
Martínez, 1947, 1951
Muro Orejón, 1957
Nuttall, 1921–22
Schäfer, 1935–47
Somolinos d'Ardois, 1960

APPENDIX A. CEDULA

THE KING:

Know ye, our Governor of . . .

Those of our Council of the Indies having at various times discussed the procedure that should be established in order that within it there can be certain and detailed information about the things of the said Indies, so that the Council can attend to their good government, it has seemed a proper thing to decree that a general description be made of the whole condition of our Indies, islands, and their provinces, the most accurate and certain possible.

In order that you properly aid in forming such description, you will comply with the Instructions that have been drawn up for it, in printed form. They are herewith being sent to you. Because it is our will that such descriptions be made specifically in each province, we command you to make a description of that city in which you reside and of the places within its jurisdiction as soon as you receive this, our Cedula.

You shall send to each of the governors, *corregidores*, and *alcaldes mayores* of the districts within your jurisdiction the number of the said Instructions which you deem necessary for them to distribute among the towns of Spaniards and of Indians within the scope of their *gobernación, corregimiento*, or *alcaldía mayor*. You shall despatch them under command that as promptly as possible they shall comply and do what they are ordered to do by the said Instructions.

You shall collect the reports which may be made in each place. You shall send them, together with those you yourself have prepared, as promptly as possible to our Council of the Indies, for review. It will advise us if there are faults in them, and for what cause, and make appropriate recommendations.

Signed,
San Lorenzo el Real, 25 May 1577.
I, THE KING.
By Command of His Majesty, Antonio de Eraso.

APPENDIX B. INSTRUCTION AND MEMORANDUM FOR PREPARING THE REPORTS WHICH ARE TO BE MADE FOR THE DESCRIPTION OF THE INDIES THAT HIS MAJESTY COMMANDS TO BE MADE, FOR THEIR GOOD GOVERNMENT AND ENNOBLEMENT

Firstly, the Governors, Corregidors, or Alcaldes Mayores to whom the Viceroys, Audiencias, or other governmental or administrative officials may send the printed Instruction and Memorandum are, before everything, to make a list and statement of the town inhabited by Spaniards and by Indians within their jurisdictions, on which only the names of these towns are to appear, written clearly and legibly. This list is to be sent immediately to the officials of government, so that they may return it to His Majesty and the Council of the Indies, together with the reports prepared in each town.

They shall distribute this printed Instruction and Memorandum throughout their jurisdiction to all towns of Spaniards and Indians, sending them to the municipal councils of towns in which there are Spaniards, or, if these are lacking, to the parish priests or monks charged with religious instruction. They shall directly order the councils or recommend from his Majesty to the ecclesiastics, that within a short time they satisfactorily respond to the queries, as specified. The reports they make, together with this Instruction, are to be sent to the above official of government who ordered them. The latter shall redistribute the Instructions and Memoranda to other towns, to which none have been sent previously.

In the towns and cities where the Governors, Corregidores, or other administrative officials reside they are to write the reports themselves. Or they may encharge them to intelligent persons with knowledge of matters of the area, requiring them to follow the specifications of the Memorandum.

Persons in the towns to whom responsibility for each of them is given for preparing the particular report shall respond to the chapters of the Memorandum, in the following order and form:

Firstly, on a separate paper, as a cover sheet for their report, they are to write the date—day, month, year—with the name of the person or persons who were found to prepare it. Also the name of the Governor or other person who sent them the Instruction shall appear.

After carefully reading each paragraph of the Memorandum, they are to write down separately what they have to say, answering each one of the questions it contains, one after the other. Those questions to which they have nothing to answer are to be omitted without comment, passing on to the following ones, until all are read. The answers are to be short and clear. That which is certain shall be stated as such, and that which is not shall be declared doubtful, in such a way that the reports shall be valid, and in conformance with the following queries:

APPENDIX C. MEMORANDUM OF THE ITEMS TO WHICH RESPONSES SHALL BE MADE, AND WHAT THE REPORTS ARE TO CONTAIN [1577][7]

1. Firstly: For each Spanish town, state the name of the district or province in which it is situated, what this name means in the language of the Indians, and why it is so called.

2. Who was the discoverer and conqueror of this province; by whose command was it discovered; in what year was it discovered and conquered; as far as can readily be determined?

3. Describe generally the climate and quality of the province or district: whether it is very cold or hot, humid or arid; with much or scanty rainfall and when it is greater or lesser; how violently and from which directions the wind blows, and at what times of the year.

4. State whether the land is level or rough, open or wooded; with many or few rivers or springs; abundant or lacking in water; fertile or lacking in pasture; abundant or lacking in fruits, and in means of sustenance.

5. State whether there are many or few Indians; whether there have been more or fewer in former times, and any reasons for this that may be known; whether or not they are presently settled in regular and permanent towns; the degree and quality of their intelligence, inclinations, and way of life; and whether there are different languages throughout the province or some general language that they all speak.

6. Give the latitude, or the altitude of the pole star, at each Spanish town, if it has been observed and determined, or if there is anyone who knows how to observe it; or, state on which days of the year the sun

---

[7] Translation prepared by Dr. Clinton R. Edwards. He indicates that for New Spain a slightly variant questionnaire, probably issued in 1584, was also used. Notes to these variations were also made by Dr. Edwards.

234

does not cast a shadow exactly at noon.

7. Note the distance in leagues and the direction of each Spanish city or town from the city where the audiencia in whose district it falls is established, or from the town where the governor to whom it is subject resides.

8. Likewise, note the distance in leagues and the direction of each Spanish city or town from the others with which they have boundaries, and whether the leagues are long or short, through level or hilly land, and whether over straight or winding roads, easy or difficult of travel.

9. Give the present or former name and surname for each city or town. Why was it called thus, if known; who assigned the name; who was its founder; by whose order did he settle it; in what year was it founded; with how many residents was the settlement begun, and how many does it have at present?

10. Describe the site upon which each town is established: whether it is on a height, or low-lying, or on a plain. Make a plan in color of the streets, plazas, and other significant features such as monasteries, as well as can be sketched easily on paper, indicating which part of the town faces south or north.

[*Variant 1584*]
10. Describe the site upon which each town is established: whether it is on a height, or low-lying, or on a plain. Make a plan of each [*remainder omitted*].

11. For Indian towns, state only how far they are from the town in whose corregimiento or jurisdiction they fall, and from that which is their center for doctrine [*following is added in handwriting to many copies of the 1577 version, but is not found in the 1584 version*], listing by name all of the centers for doctrine that lie in this jurisdiction, and all of their subject towns.

12. Likewise, state how far they are from other Indian or Spanish towns that lie around them, noting in each case their direction from them, and whether the leagues are long or short, the roads through level or hilly land, and straight or winding.

13. What does the name of this Indian town mean in the language of the Indians; why is it so called, if known; and what is the name of the language spoken by the Indians of this town?

14. To whom were they subject when they were heathens; what power did their rulers have over them; what did they pay in tribute; what forms of worship, rites [*omitted in 1584*], and good or evil customs did they have?

15. Describe how they were governed; with whom they fought wars, and their manner of fighting; their former and present manner of dressing; their former and present means of subsistence; and whether they were more or less healthy than at present, giving any insight you may have as to the cause.

16. For each Spanish and Indian town, describe the site on which it is settled: whether it is in the mountains, in a valley, or in open level land; give the name of the mountain or valley, and district; and for each, state what the name means in the local language [*final phrase concerning local language omitted in 1584*].

17. Also state whether it is in a healthy or unhealthy situation; if unhealthy, for what reason (if it is known); the illnesses that commonly occur, and the remedies that they commonly use for them.

18. State how far or near and in what direction each lies from some nearby prominent mountain or range, giving its name.

19. Note any major river or rivers that flow nearby, with their distance and direction; the magnitude of their flow; and anything notable that might be determined about their sources, water, plantings and

235

other developments along their banks; and whether there are or could be irrigated lands of value.

20. Note any lakes, lagoons, or significant springs within the town lands, and anything remarkable about them.

21. Note any volcanoes, caves, and all other notable and remarkable aspects of the natural scene worthy of being known that occur in the district. [*Here and elsewhere were minor orthographical changes in 1584: "cuevas" for "grutas," for instance.*]

22. Note the common wild trees of the district, with their fruits, the use made of them and their wood, and for what purposes they are or could be beneficial.

23. Note the cultivated trees and fruit orchards native to the region; and those that have been brought from Spain and elsewhere, and whether or not they bear well in that land.

24. Note the grains and seed plants, and other garden vegetables and greens that serve or have served as sustenance for the natives.

25. Note also those that have been brought from Spain; if the land yields wheat, barley, wine, and olive oil; the quantities harvested; if there is silk or cochineal in the region, and in what quantities.

26. Note the herbs or aromatic plants with which the Indians cure themselves, and their medicinal or poisonous properties.

27. Note the wild and domestic animals and birds native to the region; and those that have been brought from Spain, and how well they breed and multiply in that land.

28. Note any gold and silver mines and other sources of metals, or black mineral or other dyes, that occur in the district and in the town lands.

29. Note any quarries of precious stone,

236

jasper, marble, and others of significance and value that may occur.

30. Note whether there are sources of salt in the town or nearby, or whence they procure their salt and all other things they may lack for sustenance or clothing.

31. Describe the form and construction of the houses, and the building materials that occur in the towns, or elsewhere whence they may be brought.

32. Describe the towns' fortifications, posts, and any strong and impregnable places that occur within their bounds and district.

33. Describe the dealings, trade, and profits by which they live and sustain themselves, Spaniards as well as the native Indians; the items involved; and with what they pay their tribute.

34. Note the diocese of the archbishopric, bishopric, or abbey in which each town lies; the district to which it is assigned; how many leagues and in which direction it lies from the town where the cathedral and center for doctrine of the district are located; whether the leagues are long or short, along straight or winding roads, and through level or hilly land.

35. Note the cathedral and parish church or churches that there may be in each town, with the number of endowed church offices and allotments for clergymen's salaries for each; whether they have a chapel or significant endowment, and, if so, whose it is and who founded it.

36. Note any monasteries or convents of each Order that the town may have; by whom and when they were founded; any remarkable items they may contain; and the number of religious.

37. Note also any hospitals, schools, and charitable institutions in the towns, and by whom and when they were founded.

38. If the towns are on the seacoast, describe in the report, in addition to the fore-

going, the nature of the sea in their vicinity: whether it is calm or stormy, the nature of the storms and other dangers, and in which seasons they are more or less frequent.

39. Note whether the coast has a beach or is lined by cliffs; and the prominent reefs and other dangers to navigation that occur along it.

40. How great are the tides and tidal ranges; on which days and at which hours do they occur; and at which seasons are they greater or lesser?

41. Note any prominent capes, points, bights, and bays that occur in the district, with their names and sizes, as well as can be stated accurately.

42. Note the ports and landings that occur on the coast, making a plan of each in color, as can be drawn on a sheet of paper, by which their form and shape can be seen.

43. Note the size and capacity, with their approximate width and length in leagues and paces, as well as can be determined; and note how many ships they will accommodate.

44. Note their depths in fathoms; whether the bottom is clean; any shallows and shoals, indicating their locations; and whether they are free of shipworm and other disadvantages.

45. Note the directions faced by their entrances and exits, and the winds with which one must enter and depart.

46. Note their accommodations or lack of them in the way of firewood, water, and provisions, and other favorable or unfavorable considerations for entering and remaining.

47. Note the names of the islands along the coast; why they are so called; their form and shape in color, if possible; their length, width, and area; the soil, pastures, trees, and resources they may have; the birds and animals; and the significant rivers and springs.

48. Note generally the locations of abandoned Spanish towns; when they were settled and abandoned; and anything known about the reasons for abandonment.

49. Include anything else notable about the natural scene, and any effects worth knowing of the soil, air, and sky of whatever region.

50. Once the report is completed, the persons who have composed it will sign it and without delay will send it, with this Instruction, to the person from whom they received the Instruction.

APPENDIX D. RELACION DE LAS DESCRIPCIONES Y PINTURAS DE PUEBLOS DE LAS PROVINCIAS DEL DISTRITO DE NUEVA ESPAÑA QUE SE AN TRAYDO AL CONSEJO Y SE ENTREGAN A JUAN LOPEZ DE VELASCO [21 NOVEMBER 1583][8] [fol. 11]

[1] – Una pintura de la ciudad de Mexico. [Catalog, 36]

[2] – Otra pintura de Chilapa. [Catalog, 12]

[3] – Otra de Tepenpulco [Tepeapulco]. [Catalog, 61]

[4] – Otra de Atitalaquia. [Catalog, 8]

[5] – Otra de Huizila [Ucila]. (Catalog, 77]

[6–7]– Otra de Tilantongo, *digo dos.* [Catalog, 71, 72]

[8] – Otra de Queretaro. [Catalog, 47]

[8] AGI (Sevilla), Patronato Real, leg. 171 (2-1-2/19), doc. 1, ramo 16 (fols. 11–14v). Transcribed by Dr. Adele Kibre, Consultant to the Hispanic Foundation, Library of Congress. Citations to catalogue refer to Robertson, Article 6. Census references are to entries in Article 8.

[9] – Otra de la ciudad de Valladolid de Michoacan. [Catalog, 78]

[10] – Otra de Totoltepec. [Catalog, 75]

[11] – Otra de Nixapa [Nexapa]. [Catalog, 42]

[12] – Otra de Tamazula. [Catalog, 52]

Legajo Numero [fol. 11v]

[1] – Una descripción y pintura de las villas de Sant Miguel y Sant Philipe de los Chichimecas. [Census, 203]

[2] – Otra del pueblo de Uzila. [Census, 138]

[3] – Otra del de Totolapa. [Census, 136]

[4] – Otra de Ocuytuco. [Census, 210]

[5] – Otra de Guazacualco. [Census, 30]

[6] – Otra de Zacualpa. [Census, 222]

[7] – Otra de la provincia de los Zapotecas. [Census, 223]

[8] – Otra de las minas de Tornacustla. [Census, 135]

[9] – Otra de Atitalaquia. [Census, 12]

[10] – Otra de Xiquilpa. [Census, 60]

[11] – Otra de Acapistla. [Census, 1]

[12] – Otra de Teutitlan. [Census, 107]

[13] – Otra de Tancitaro. [Census, 95]

[14] – Otra de Amula. [Census, 5]

[15] – Otra de Talistaca. [Census, 94]

[16] – Otra de Tista y Mohitanis [Tistla y Muchitlan (Mochitlan)] [Census, 132]

[17] – Otra de Chinantla. [Census, 24]

[18] – Otra de Aguatlan. [Census, 3] [Fol. 12]

[19] – Otra de Chichicapa y Amatlan. [Census, 21]

[20] – Otra de Cholula. [Census, 25]

[21] – Otra de Mexicalcingo. [Census, 65]

[22] – Otra de Tlacotlalpa y Tustla. [Census, 134]

[23] – Otra de Zumpango y subjetos. [Census, 164]

[24] – Otra de Temazcaltepec. [Census, 103]

[25] – Otra de Talasco. [Census, 212]

[26] – Otra de Atengo y Mizquiaguala. [Census, 8]

[27] – Otra de Asuchitlan. [Census, 7]

Legajo Numero II

[1] – Otra descripción de Guaxutla. [Census, 51]

[2] – Otra de Suchitepeque. [Census, 88]

[3] – Otra de Tamazula. [Census, 213]

[4] – Otra de Xalapa. [Census, 142; see also 141]

[5] – Otra de Guaymeo y minas del Spiritu Santo. [Census, 157]

[6] – Otra de Guatulco. [Census, 45]

[7] – Otra de Miquitla y Tlacolula. [Census, 133]

[8] – Otra Teutalpa. [Census, 49]

[9] – Otra de Tetiquepac [Tetiquipac]. [Census, 119]

[10] – Otra de Zultepeque. [Census, 163]

[11] – Otra de Cinagua. [Census, 156]

[12] – Otra de Atatlan [Acatlan] y Piaztla. [Census, 32]

[fol. 12v]

[13] – Otra de Tecomavaca y Quiotepeque. [Census, 54]

[14] – Otra de Cuycatlan. [Census, 35]

[15] – Otra de Acapulco. [Census, 201]

[16] – Otra de Teguantepeque. [Census, 102]

[17] – Otra de Maquilsuchile [Macuilsuchil]. [Census, 62]

[18] – Otra de Teutenango. [Census, 122]

[19] – Otra de Jonotla [Jonotla] y Tetela. [Census, 118]

[20] – Otra de Teozacualco. [Census, 108]

[21] – Otra de Amoltepeque. [Census, 108A]

[22] – Otra de Coatepeque. [Census, 29]

[23] – Otra de Tepeaca. [Census, 110]

[24] – Otra de Guauquilpa. [Census, 32]

[25] – Otra de Guazpaltepeque. [Census, 205]

[26] – Otra de Cimapan. [Census, 155]

[27] – Otra de Chiconautlla [Chiconautla]. [Census, 22]

[28] – Otra de Tepuztlan. [Census, 112]

[29] – Otra de Queretaro. [Census, 86]

Legajo Tercero

[1] – Otra descripción de Tepuzculula. [Census, 216]

[2] – Otra de Guamelula. [Census, 206]
[3] – Otra de Teutila. [Census, 217]
[4] – Otra de Yautepeque. [Census, 221]
[fol. 13]
[5] – Otra de Sichu i Puzinquia. [Census, 211]
[6] – Otra de Tezazalca. [Census, 214]
[7] – Otra de Yzmiquilpa. [Census, 207]
[8] – Otra de Tonaltepeque. [Census, 220]
[9] – Otra de Cuzcatlan. [Census, 41, 42]
[10] – Otra de Cozautepeque y Tetipeque [Tetiquipa]. [Census, 120]
[11] – Otra de Capula. [Census, 202]
[12] – Otra de Zimatlan. [Census, 225]
[13] – Otra de Zayula, Atoyaque. [Census, 224]
[14] – Otra de la ciudad de Valladolid. [Census, 219]
[15] – Otra de Justlavaca. [Census, 61]
[16] – Otra de la ciudad de Mechoacan. [Census, 79]
[17] – Otra de Tequecastlan [Tequecistlan] y Totolcingo. [Census, 116]
[18] – Otra de Atlatlauca y Malinaltepeque. [Census, 11]
[19] – Otra de Mizantla. [Census, 67]
[20] – Otra de Nochistlan. [Census, 74]
[21] – Otra de Ocopetlayuca. [Census, 76]
[22] – Otra de Zacatula. [Census, 148]
[23] – Otra de Taymeo. [Census, 93]
[24] – Otra de Tamaztlan [Tenamaztlan]. [Census, 105]
[25] – Otra de la ciudad de la Veracruz. [Census, 140]
[26] – Otra de la villa de Leon. [Census, 208]

LEGAJO NUMERO IIII [fol. 13v]

[1] – Otra descripción de la ciudad de Mexico. [Census, 209]
[2] – Otra de Xalapa. [Census, 141; see also 142]
[3] – Otra de Guaxtepec. [Census, 47]
[4] – Otra de Zayula. [Census, 153]
[5] – Otra de Tlatlauca [Atlatlauca] y Suchiaca. [Census, 10]
[6] – Otra de Necotlan. [Census, 72]

[7] – Otra de Nixapa. [Nexapa.] [Census, 73]
[8] – Otra de Teozapotlan. [Census, 109]
[9] – Otra de Santa Cruz. [Census, 59]
[10] – Otra de Texupa. [Census, 124]
[11] – Otra de Cuylapa. [Census, 37]
[12] – Otra de la ciudad de Antequera. [Census, 6]
[13] – Otra de Tiripitio. [Census, 130]
[14] – Otra de Guacoman. [Census, 68]
[15] – Otra de Papalotiquipaque y Tepeuzila. [Census, 78]
[16] – Otra de Tilantongo. [Census, 127]
[17] – Otra de Molango y subjetos. [Census, 66]
[18] – Otra de Ameta [Ameca]. [Census, 4]
[19] – Otra de Yguala. [Census, 53]
[20] – Otra de Guaxolotitlan. [Census, 46]
[21] – Otra de Tepeapulco. [Census, 111]
[fol. 14]
[22] – Otra de Chilchota. [Census, 23]
[23] – Otra de Zalaya. [Census, 18]
[24] – Otra de Tasco. [Census, 96]
[25] – Otra de Tenguenden [Tingüindin, Chocandiran]. [Census, 128]
[26] – Otra de Teoquilco [Tecoquilco]. [Census, 101]
[27] – Otra de Yzquintepeque. [Census, 80]
[28] – Otra de Yztepex [Yztepexi]. [Census, 57]
[29] – Otra de Yzcateupa. [Census, 52]
[30] – Otra de Cuiseo. [Census, 38]
[31] – Otra de Tlaquilpa. [Census, 218]
[32] – Otra de Citlaltepeque. [Census, 114]
[33] – Otra de Zitaltomagua. [Census, 28]
[34] – Otra de Goautla [Guautla]. [Census, 34]
[35] – Otra de Tetela y Guayapa. [Census, 117]
[36] – Otra de Tepex de la Seda. [Census, 215]
[37] – Otra de Coauitlan [Cuahuitlan] e Ycpatepeque. [Census, 33]

239

[38] – Otra de Hilapa [Chilapa]. [Census, 164]

[39] – Otra de Guatlatlauca. [Census, 85] Recebilos en 21 de noviembre 1583. JUAN LÓPEZ DE VELASCO. [*Rubric*].

APPENDIX E. [ANTONIO DE LEON PINELO] MEMORIA DE LOS PAPELES QUE TENGO PARA LA DESCRIPCION DE LAS INDIAS[9]

[fol. 7]

1. Descubrimiento de la California año de 1533.
2. Papeles tocantes a la Nueva Galicia.
3. Relación de los pueblos do Yanguitlan en la Misteca alta, Tenaltepeque, Coyaltepeque, Cuextlavaca, Tequicistepeque, Apoala, Istactepec, Chichahuaztepec, Nochistlan, otros en la Nueva España del año de 1579. [Census, 220]
4. Descripción del Perú desde Chile a Tierra firme por Martín de Ocampo.
5. Descripción de la Prov[inci]a del santo Evangelio de la Orden de S. Fran[cisc]o en N. España.
6. Doctrinas del Arzobispado de la Plata.
7. Descripción del distrito de Oxitlan i Guaspaltepeque Rio de Alvarado por el Correg[ido]r Alonso de Piñeda, año de 1580. [Census, 205]
8. Relación de los pueblos donde pone clerigos el obispo de Guaxaca.
9. Relación de las cosas notables de la Provincia de Chiapa por el Lic. Palacio.
10. Razones porq[ue] de mudo a Guadalaxara la Aud[ienci]a de la [Nueva] Galicia.
11. Relación de la [Nueva] Galicia por el Lic. Xpal. de Pedraza.

[fol. 14v]

Ynventario de los papeles de descripciones que se an entregado a Juan López de Velasco.

12. Relación del Río de la Plata i Paraguay, por Fr[ancis]co Ortiz De Vergara.
13. Descripción de la Villa de Leon i Llanos de Silao en N. España año 1582. [Census, 208]
14. Relación de lo q[ue] descubrio Juan Rodriguez por la mar del Sur año de 1542.
15. Descripción de Honduras i Nicaragua. 1572.
16. Relación de los monasterios de S. D[oming]o en las Provincias Mexicana 710, Misteca i Zapoteca.
17. Relación de Honduras i costumbres de sus naturales.
18. Descripción de Mexico de 1580 por el L[icencia]do Avilas. [Census, 209]
19. Relación de lo q[ue] descubrio Alvaro de Saavedra año de 1529, por la mar del Sur i costa de N. España.
20. Descripción de la [Nueva] Galicia. 1572.
21. Relación de los Chichimecas. [Census, 203]
22. Pueblos de Indios de N. Esp[añ]a de 1570.
23. Descripción del pueblo de Laxa prov[inci]a de Humasuye en el Perú con otros del distrito, por d. Ger[ónim]o de Marañon.
24. Modelo de Tierra firme por el Lic. Diego Garcia.
25. Descripción de la isla Española i otras.
26. Descripción del correg[imient]o de los Yahuyos en el Perú de 1536, por Lazaro Pérez de Idiaquez.
27. Descripción de la Ciudad de N. S[eñor]a de la Palma en el N. R[ei]no por Diego Pérez de Bejar año de 1533. [fol. 7v]

⁹ Biblioteca Nacional (Madrid), MS 3064, fols. 7–8v. Transcribed by Howard F. Cline. See also same list in Baudot, 1968, pp. 230–34 (Item 56 omitted; Item 57 misnumbered 56).

240

28. Descripción de la Ciudad de la Palma del N. R[ei]no año de 1588.
29. Otra descripción desta Ciudad de 1588.
30. Relación de S. Cruz de la Sierra por el Gov[ernad]or don Lor[enz]o Suárez de Figueroa. 1533.
31. Descripción de las Provincias de Parinacocha Pomatambo i Guaynacota por su Corregidor Pedro de los Rios. 1586.
32. Relación de las Indias por fray Francisco de Mena Religioso de S. Fr[ancis]co. 1559.
33. Relación de viage de Nueva España a Filipinas i su buelta.
34. Relación de Alonso de Grado de su ida a N. España. 1524.
35. Descripción de Guatimala por Francisco de Castellanos. 1530.
36. Relación de las tierras de México por B[artolo]me de Zárate.
37. Descripción de la isla Española. 1559.
38. Relación de la Ciudad de Tunja i pueblos comarcanos por d. Fr[ancis]co Guillen Chaparo. 1583.
39. Relación de la Ciudad de S. Fe del N. R[ei]no.
40. Relación de la Ciudad de la Trinidad de los Musos en el N[uev]o R[ei]no por Al[ons]o Luis Langero. 1582.
41. Relación de las tierras de Guatimala por el Lic. Palacios.
42. Relación de la N[uev]a Andalusia.
43. Relación de la Florida.
44. Fundación de Venezuela.
45. Relación de S. Marta por el Cap. don Lope de Orozco, su gov[ernad]or. 1530.
46. Descripción de La Española por Luis Gómez. 1559.
47. Relación del piloto Joan Ruiz de Noriega año de 1562 de lo q[ue] navegó por cerca de la Española.
48. Sobre la navegación de la Carrera por Vicente de Soto. 1593.
49. Descripción del puerto de Nombre de Dios i Panama por el Lic. Diego Garcia.
50. Descripción de la governación de S. Marta por don Lope de Orozco.
51. Relación de Venezuela hecha por el cabildo de Coro. 1579.
52. Población de Veragua.
53. Cuaderno tocante a la descripción de las Indias.
54. Descripción de la China.
55. Del Arzobispado de los Charcas.
56. Descripción de la Mina en Guinea.
57. Descripción de la Baia de Todos Santos.
58. Relación de lo q[ue] se descubrío cerca de Quito por Fr. Ant[oni]o Vasquez de Espinoza.

[fol. 8r]
59. Relación del cerca del Rio de la Plata por Simon de Valdés.
60. Relación de las Pro[vinci]as de Tipuana i Paytite por Juan Recio de León.
61. Relación de la Ciudad de Quito de don Alvaro de Figueroa.
62. Parte de una historia antigua de costumbres de Indios de N. Esp[aña].
63. Descripción de la prov[inci] de Guauchinango i Tamiagua en N[uev]a España. 1612. [Census, 304]
64. Descripción de la prov[inci]a i pueblo de Guaxuapa en N[uev]a España. 1608. [Census, 305]
65. Descripción del pueblo de Tepexi de la Seda en N[uev]a España. 608. [Census, 313]
66. Descripción de Pánuco i Tampico por P[edr]o Martínez de Gayia. 612. [Census, 310]
67. Descripción de la Alcaldia M[ay]or de Tepozcolula por Fr[ancis]co Ruano. 608. [Census, 314]
68. Descripción del partido de Zumpango. 608. [Census, 317]
69. Descripción de la Villa de Colima i su distrito por Melchor de Colindres Puerta. 608. [Census, 303]

70. Descripción de la ciudad de Zacatecas. 608. [Census, 315]
71. Descripción de las Minas de Pachuca por d Diego de Ovalle i Guzman. 608. [Census, 309]
72. Descripción del partido de Miaguatlan por Estevan Gutierrez. 608. [Census, 301]
73. Descripción de las Minas de Sultepeque 609 por G[erónim]o de Salinas Salazar. [Census, 311]
74. Descripción de la Villa de Nombre de Dios en la [Nueva] Vizcaya. 608. [Census, 307]
75. Descripción de las Minas de Zagualpa. 608. [Census, 316]
76. Descripción de Puertovelo. 608.
77. Descripción de Guayaquil. 608.
78. De la Ciudad de Mérida en el N. R[ei]no. 620.
79. De la Ciudad de Altamira de Cáceres del N. R[ei]no. 610.
80. De la Villa de Santiago de la Frontera de Tomina. 608.
81. De la Ciudad de Jaén de Pacamoras. 606.
82. De la Ciudad de Baeca de los Cuixos. 605.
83. De Panamá por el g[obernad]or Fr[ancis]co Guidi. 605.
84. De la Villa de S. X[Cristo]bal en el N. R[ei]no. 609.
85. De la Ciudad de N[uest]ra S[eñor]a de Pedraza del N[uev]o R[ein]o. 620.
86. De la Ciudad del Espiritu Santo de la Grita. 609.
87. De la Ciudad de Sant[iag]o de Puertoviejo. 605.
88. Descripción i noticia de los Chirihuanaes.
89. De la Villa del Vilar don Pardo. 605.
90. De la Ciudad de Tunja en el N[uev]o R[ei]no. 610.
91. Descubrimiento del puerto de Amatigue de S. Tomas de Castilla. (fol. 8v).
92. De los Pueblos de Avalos de 1580. [Census, 224]
93. De Zamatlan i Tepuimatlan. 1580. [Census, 225]
94. De la Alcaldía de Teutila. 1580. [Census, 217]
95. De la Ciudad de Valladolid de Mechoacán. 1581. [Census, 219]
96. Del Corregimiento de Guamelula. 1580. [Census, 206]
97. Del pueblo de Izmiquilpa. 1579. [Census, 207]
98. Del pueblo de Talasco. 1580. [Census, 212]
99. Del pueblo de Tazazalca. 1580. [Census, 214]
100. Algunas cosas del Río de la Plata.
101. Del pueblo de Teposcolula. 1580. [Census, 216]
102. De la Villa de S. Ildefonso en los Zapotecas. [Census, 223]
103. De Yautepeque. 1580. [Census, 221]
104. Mapa del Río Orinoco.
105. De los pueblos de Sichu i Puzcinquias. [Census, 211]

6. The Pinturas (Maps) of the Relaciones Geográficas, With a Catalog

DONALD ROBERTSON

A POIGNANT QUALITY marks the works of art which document the domination of one civilization over another. This is especially so in the New World, where the autochthonous styles of American art were superseded by the imported arts of Renaissance Spain. The process is clearly demonstrated for the history of painting in Middle America by 92 pinturas accompanying the written texts of the *Relaciones Geo-gráficas* of 1579–86 (hereafter abbreviated as RG's), making up the largest single group of interrelated early colonial pictorial manuscripts which has come down to us.[1] These paintings and their texts were both called forth by the Real Cédula and associated documents issued by Philip II, May 25, 1577.[2] Answers to its 50 questions were requested of important officials in the cabeceras or principal places, and the question-

[1] Often called "maps" in the modern literature, they are spoken of as *"pinturas"* or paintings in the original 16th-century documents. In 1949, when I was on the faculty of the Art Department of the University of Texas, Austin, Dr. George Kubler first proposed the pinturas of the Relaciones Geográficas as a group worth studying. I take this opportunity to express thanks for this fruitful suggestion. Dr. Howard F. Cline, Director of the Hispanic Foundation, Library of Congress, has given of his knowledge and shared information in the Foundation's files. The three major repositories have been most helpful in making their collections freely accessible: in Austin, Dr. Nettie Lee Benson, Librarian of the Latin American Collection of the University of Texas; in Sevilla, Don José María de la Peña y Cámara, Director of the Archivo General de Indias; and in Madrid, Father José López de Toro and Srta. María-África Ibarra y Orez, Librarians of the Real Academia de la Historia. In addition, Dr. Adele Kibre was most helpful in the

Archivo General de Indias; John B. Glass and Henry B. Nicholson have given additional aid. Research for continuing investigation of the pinturas has been supported over a period of years by the American Council of Learned Societies, Guggenheim Foundation, Social Science Research Council, Tulane University Council on Research, Tulane University Center for Latin American Studies, and the U.S. Department of Health, Education and Welfare (NDEA-Related Fulbright-Hays Award). A seminar class of the Art Department of the Tulane University Graduate School, composed of J. W. B. De Blois, B. Foster, A. G. P. Orenstein, P. Schmidt, and M. Zengel, studied the pinturas during the spring of 1964. The results of this seminar are incorporated into this article.

[2] See Article 5, Appendix, for English translation of texts of these documents: "Cédula, Instruction, and Memorandum, for the Formation of the Relations and Descriptions of the Places of the Indies."

243

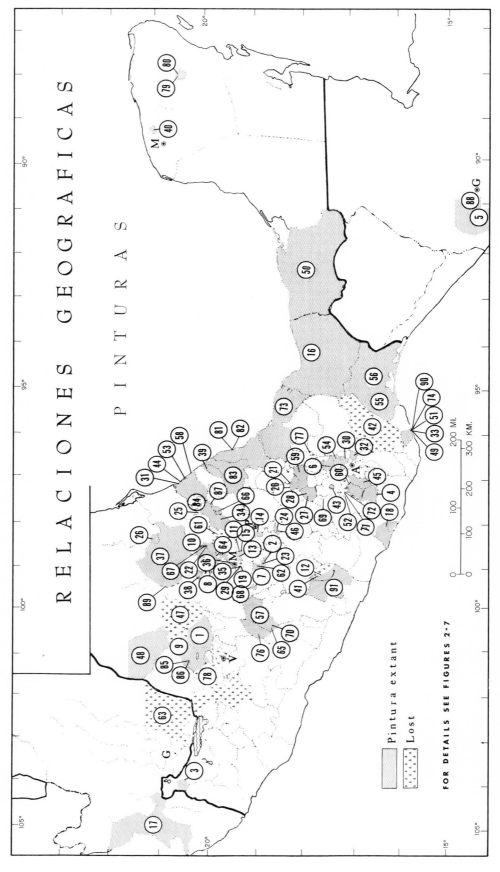

FIG. 1—PINTURAS OF THE RELACIONES GEOGRÁFICAS, NEW SPAIN, 1579–85.
Areas shown are civil jurisdictions (after Gerhard, Article 2), not necessarily the precise areas recorded on the individual pinturas.

naire was often forwarded to the heads of the sub-cabeceras or dependent towns.[3] The geographical distribution of the pinturas is so wide as to cover the areas of dense population south from "Chichimecas" in northern Michoacan to Lake Atitlan in the captaincy-general of Guatemala (see fig. 1).[4]

Many facets of life in Philip's colonies were touched upon in the written answers as well as in the paintings paralleling them. There is a basic underlying similarity among the pinturas coming from the patterns imposed by the questionnaire and the fact that they were all made within a period of seven years.[5] Major differences lie in dissimilarity of graphic style, indicating that the artists ranged from relatively faithful followers of the premises of pre-Conquest artistic style to painters in the manner of Spanish 16th-century painting.

The combination of wide geographic distribution, narrow limits in time, and diversity of style, makes the pinturas primary sources for the study of the acculturation of native artists during the first 60 years after the Conquest. They constitute a "horizon marker," although their differences are so clear that they cannot constitute a single "horizon style." It is an almost ideal pattern and contrasts with more usual patterns of long sequences in time, often with unsatisfactory relations among places of wide geographic separation. The pinturas are thus a measure of the strength of European penetration into the native life of even small and remote villages of their time. Their range of content is great, and, as a corpus of data, they give a remarkably detailed picture of life in the Spanish colonies in the late 16th century.

HISTORY

The story of how the pinturas and texts arrived at their present repositories, the Archivo General de Indias, Sevilla (AGI), the Real Academia de la Historia, Madrid (RAH), and the Latin American Library of the University of Texas, Austin (UTX),

is recounted by Cline in Article 5. Many of the pinturas with their accompanying texts had arrived in Spain in late 1583 and were available to the 16th-century officials and historians such as López de Velasco, Céspedes, and Herrera. Antonio León Pinelo and the 18th-century historian Juan Bautista Muñoz also had access to them. They all seem to have made little if any use of them in their studies of New World history and geography.

A large number (27) of the pinturas went to the new Archivo de Indias set up in Sevilla in 1785 for documents dealing with America. An even larger number (37) turned up in 1853 when Joaquín García Icazbalceta bought those now at UTX from an unknown private source. The rest (12) came from an equally unknown source in 1863 to the Library of the RAH. Thus all the currently known pinturas are at present in three public repositories, except for the 16 now lost.[6]

---

[3] Cline, 1964a, pp. 347–49. Not all administrative officials of the Spanish colonial bureaucracy answered all the questions; all answering with a text did not submit a pintura. Some seem never to have answered (received?) the questionnaire.

[4] See figs. 1–7 for information on the geographical distribution of the pinturas; areas shown are civil jurisdictions and not necessarily the areas recorded in the pinturas. For individual pinturas, see Catalog of Pinturas at the end of this article, where main cabeceras are in capital letters, sub-cabeceras in lowercase letters. This pattern is followed throughout this article.

[5] The known pinturas are related to texts dated between 1579 and 1585. Only two pinturas are specifically dated: COATZOCOALCO, 1579; and TLACOTALPA, Feb. 5, 1580.

[6] See Table 2. Exceptions include:

a. *Pintura and text separated*: SUCHITEPEC text in RAH, its five pinturas in AGI: CELAYA text in RAH, pinturas of Yurirpundaro belonging to it in AGI.

b. *Pintura preserved, text lost*: San Miguel y San Felipe de los CHICHIMECAS in RAH, printed Instruction and empty folder in AGI.

c. *Pinturas lost, texts preserved*: CELAYA text in RAH; MEXICATZINGO and TEPUZTLAN texts in AGI; TEQUALTICHE text in UTX (this pintura is possibly in private hands, see Catalog, 63).

d. In addition, 12 pinturas listed at the beginning of the JLV, 1583, inventory are missing:

Modern research depends on the publication of most of the pinturas of the Spanish collections by Francisco del Paso y Troncoso with good quality of black and white photographs.[7] Two Maya pinturas (TABASCO and MOTUL) have appeared only in nonphotographic versions (DIU). The unpublished UTX pinturas present bibliographic difficulties, as few have been published except from 19th-century copies in Mexico.[8] The reader is referred to individual items in the Catalog at the end of this article.

The major publications of the pinturas as source documents in recent times have been Caso (1949a), using the "Mapa de TEOZACOALCO" for deciphering the genealogical documents from the Mixteca; Cline (1959, 1961a, 1961b, 1966a, 1966b) in his studies of 16th-century geography; Kubler (1948) and McAndrew (1965) for studies in the history of architecture and city planning; Robertson (1959a, 1959b) for the study of early colonial painting; and Chevalier (1956) and Amaya (1951) for the study of the latifundio and colonial economy, especially stock-raising and agriculture.

Figures 2–7 give a cartographic view of the civil jurisdictions in New Spain for which pinturas have been reported or are extant. The coverage is obviously uneven. In some cases the pinturas cover a smaller area, in some cases a larger area, than the map indicates.

ANALYSIS

Analysis of the pinturas can proceed from several points of view, but fundamentally they break down into four major divisions: content, written glosses, materials, and artistic style.

Content

Content in this article refers to the information conveyed through graphic devices and reflects that part of the traditional history of art concerned with iconography, or the study of meaning in the visual arts. The Instruction and Memorandum of 1577 with its 50 questions called forth a pictorial answer directly in Question 10, asking for a "plan or colored painting showing the streets, squares, and other places" (a city plan). It also asked for "the site and . . . the situation of said town" (a map or landscape). Question 42 asked for "a chart and map" of "the ports and places of disembarkation . . . on the . . . coast," and Question 47 for "the names of islands belonging to the coast . . . their shapes and forms, and show them on the map" (a mariner's chart).[9] Other questions could be answered, and sometimes were, in the text, or with a pintura, or by both.[10]

The pinturas resulting from Questions 10, 42, and 47 can be divided into four groups: (1) the city plan showing the gridiron pattern of streets, selected important public buildings (church, jail, monas-

---

ATLITLALAQUIA, Chilapa, MEXICO, NEXAPA, QUERETARO, Tamazula, TEPEAPULCO, TILANTONGO (two), Totoltepec, USILA, and VALLADOLID of Michoacan. Of these 12, the following texts are also lost: MEXICO, VALLADOLID of Michoacan, Totoltepec (text unidentified), and Tamazula (unless it is the sub-cabecera of the relación of TILANTONGO, see Catalog, 52). For further discussion, see section Lost Pinturas.

[7] Twenty-eight pinturas were published in PNE; six others were printed for PNE but not published. See Zavala, 1938, pp. 311, 603–04.

[8] These copies, since they are *drawings* or *paintings* after the originals and not *photographs*, are not wholly reliable. The pintura of MEZTITLAN, for instance, has a moon on a hillside behind the town, described in the relación text as part of the place sign for the town, but the copyist has left it out. A notable exception is the very carefully made and often published copy of CHOLULA.

[9] See Cline, 1964a, pp. 365–71 and this volume, Article 5, Appendix C, for the complete text of the questionnaire.

[10] The text for TLACOTALPA specifically states that Questions 11, 20, 38, 41–45, and 47 are answered on the pintura (PNE, 5: 1–4). The text for NEXAPA specifically says that Questions 10, 11, 19, and 29 are answered on the (lost) pintura (PNE, 4: 32, 33, 38, 42). In TEPUZTLAN, Questions 11, 16, 18, and 19 are answered on the pintura (PNE, 6: 238, 244, 246).

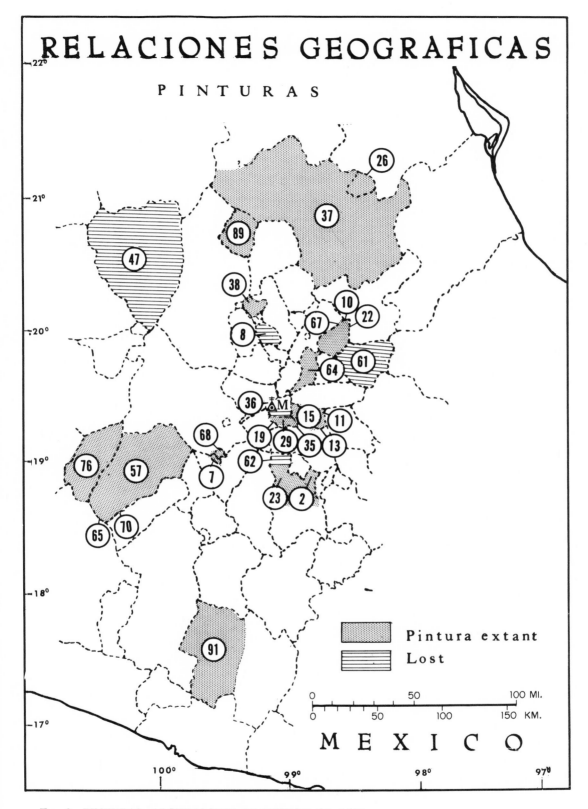

RELACIONES GEOGRAFICAS

PINTURAS

▨	Pintura extant
☰	Lost

0   50   100 MI.

0   50   100   150 KM.

MEXICO

FIG. 2—PINTURAS: ARCHDIOCESE OF MEXICO, CA. 1580

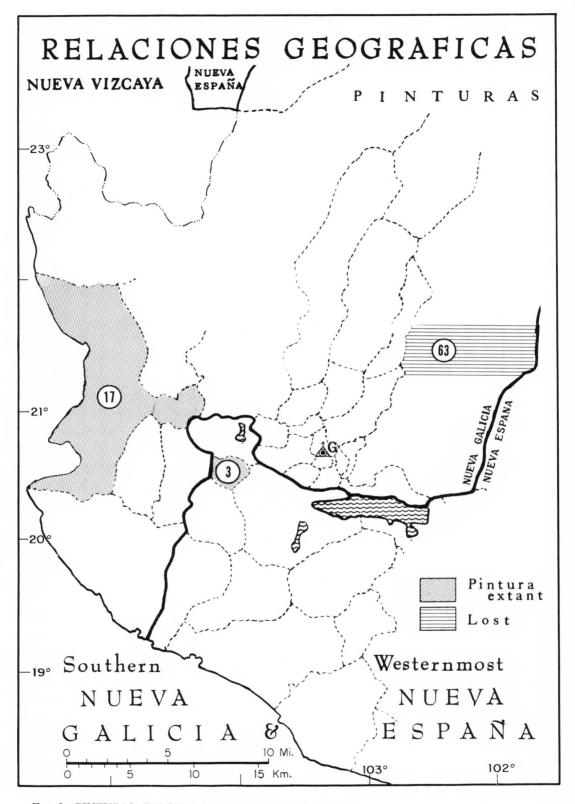

FIG. 3—PINTURAS: DIOCESE OF GUADALAJARA, CA. 1580

teries, "casas reales"), and sometimes the roads from the countryside leading into the gridiron pattern of city streets (CHOLULA, NOCHIZTLAN, and QUATLATLAUCA); (2) a landscape or map showing the area surrounding the city making the report (MEZTITLAN, IXCATLAN, Gueguetlan, TEQUIZISTLAN); (3) a combination of a somewhat detailed city plan at one scale with a map or landscape of the surrounding area at another, less detailed scale (TEXUPA, COATEPEC CHALCO, Culhuacan); and (4) a mariner's chart of the type familiar to students of European marine cartography (COATZOCOALCO, TLACOTALPA, TEHUANTEPEC–2).

It is interesting to note the existence in the native tradition of city plans (Plano en Papel de Maguey) and maps of larger areas (Historia Tolteca-Chichimeca). Few significant examples of the combination of a city plan and a map of the surrounding areas now exist in the native tradition earlier than the pinturas of the RG's.[11] However, it is quite possible that they did or that they could have within the framework of what we know from preserved examples of pre-Conquest and early colonial manuscript painting (for example, the Maps of Cuauhtinchan). Paintings in the form of landscape were not part of the pre-Hispanic native tradition and thus represent the introduction of a new mode of vision.[12] Spain and pre-Spanish Mexico did have in common the making of plans and maps; only landscape painting was missing from the native modes of representing environment.

Other questions were answered in the pinturas or even in text drawings separate from the main pintura.[13] Divided into groups, these questions with their pictorial answers give us an idea both of what Spain wanted to know of the colony and of what the inhabitants thought were adequate and interesting answers. Just as the answers in the written responses vary, so do the pictorial responses.

History of the pre-Conquest period was called for directly or indirectly in Questions 2, 9, 14, and 15. The most famous set of depictions of native rulers survives in the pintura or map accompanying the Relación of TEOZACOALCO. Using the text and the pinturas as a "Rosetta Stone," Caso (1949a) deciphered the genealogical significance of the pintura, and by careful attention to detail projected historical continuity from this document into the pre-Conquest genealogical data of the Mixtec history manuscripts. Usually unnoticed on the pintura of SUCHITEPEC is a column of heads of rulers without name signs in a similar genealogical columnar relationship, pretty much painted out. The pintura of Misquiahuala shows three major towns and their current rulers in native garb. MACUILSUCHIL shows members of the native nobility seated in a cave.

Political boundaries (Question 8) are shown often, but an extension of land formerly held is also given in the pintura of TEOZACOALCO. Dependent villages recorded pictorially by signs commonly document these data in landscapes or on maps. Native place signs defining boundaries may refer to named natural phenomena and not necessarily to villages or inhabited places. It is also to be noted that the area recorded in the pintura may be significantly larger than the political unit returning the written text. The pintura of ATLATLAUCA and Suchiaca, for instance, includes Toluca which was not a sub-cabecera of ATLATLAUCA.

Warfare and weapons appear in the pintura of San Miguel y San Felipe de los CHICHIMECAS, where Spaniards in armor on horses with blankets have firearms and

[11] The Mapa de Santa Cruz is so Europeanized in this sense that it is not in the native tradition.

[12] For a discussion of these categories in terms of early colonial manuscript painting in a larger sense than the pinturas of the RG's, see Robertson, 1959a, passim. For an extended discussion of these differences and an indication of their importance in assessing the paintings, see section Artistic Style.

[13] See note 10. See also Catalog, appendix: "Other Drawings and Paintings."

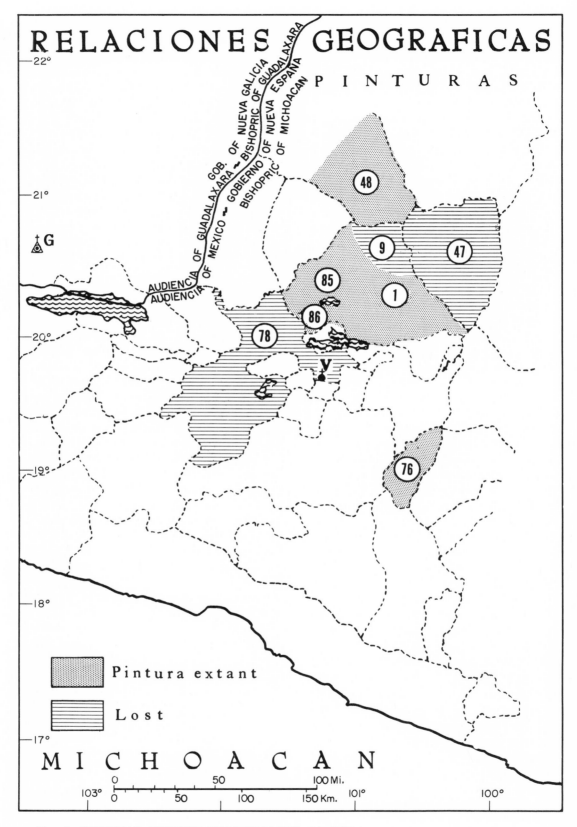

FIG. 4—PINTURAS: DIOCESE OF MICHOACAN, CA. 1580

Chichimecs have bows and arrows (Question 15).

Population statistics (Questions 5 and 9) on the pinturas need not agree with those given in the written text.[14]

The pinturas also show natural geographic phenomena such as waterways (Question 19) and springs (Question 20). On the pintura of Guaxtepec are four springs and a well; one flows into the garden of Montezuma, another starts in a grove of trees surrounded by a wall. Volcanoes and caves were called for in Question 21 (ATITLAN with the volcanoes by the lake; XONOTLA with a waterfall and a cave). The mountains asked for in Questions 16 and 18 are common to most of the pinturas. Geographical data on seacoasts of significance for Spanish commerce are requested in Questions 38, 39, 41, 42, 45 and 47, and resulted in the mariner's charts of TEHUANTEPEC–2, COATZOCOALCO, and TLACOTALPA.

The colonial economy is touched on in terms of both European and indigenous plants (Questions 22–26), which appear often in the pinturas. The patterns of field boundaries are delineated in careful detail on the pintura of CEMPOALA. Livestock (Question 27) is shown in pictorial answer on the pinturas of GUEYTLALPA, AMECA, MACUILSUCHIL, and San Miguel y San Felipe de los CHICHIMECAS. The last has some charming genre scenes of cattle copulating, pulling oxcarts, and cows nursing calves.

Commerce and communications—roads and the qualities of the countryside they traverse, whether flat, rough or mountainous, and distances asked for in Questions 7, 8, 11, 12, 33, and 34—are commonly answered in landscapes or maps. That of TEXUPA shows roads still in use and some formerly of importance but now abandoned, attesting to its accuracy.[15]

Architecture, both native and post-Hispanic, appears in many of the pinturas. Native temples or ruins appear in TEXUPA and TEOTITLAN DEL CAMINO. In the pintura of TEQUIZISTLAN the ruins of Teotihuacan are shown. Christian churches and monasteries (Questions 10, 35, 36) documenting the material spread of the "spiritual conquest" appear on many maps (Kubler, 1948; McAndrew, 1965). Elaborate 16th-century religious establishments are shown on the pinturas of TEUTENANGO (open chapel, atrium, steps, battlements); HUEXOTLA (posas and atrium with fountain in front of church); Yurirpundaro, no. 85 (church with atrium); VALLADOLID, Yucatan–1 (iglesia mayor with three-tiered tower); and Guaxtepec (the most elaborate church of all). Even the crude pinturas of the SUCHITEPEC group depict the church with an atrium. The city plan of QUATLATLAUCA has the "seldas" of the monastery carefully drawn. The monastery of Teotitlan del Valle appears as an addition in another hand on the pintura of MACUILSUCHIL. Indeed the richness of architectural detail on some of these pinturas makes them important sources for the study of 16th-century architecture.

In addition to churches and monastic foundations there are hospitals (Question 37) on VALLADOLID, Yucatan–1, and government buildings; QUATLATLAUCA and TEUTENANGO both show elaborate "casas reales" with arcades on the second story. Common house types (Question 31) of specific areas returning the pintura ap-

[14] Notice of population data on several of the pinturas has been made in an unpublished study by A. G. Orenstein from published and unpublished pinturas. This survey lists IXTEPEXIC, Tetela, XONOTLA, and ZUMPANGO, to which can now be added Muchitlan, Tamagazcatepec, Tlacotepec, ZAPOTITLAN and Suchitepec, and Zozopastepec.

[15] See the unpublished M. A. thesis of De Blois (1963) for a detailed study of the pintura of Texupa based on the relevant documents, supplemented by photographs by Ross Parmenter and his field notes of visits to the site. Subsequently, kodachromes of TEXUPA, taken by Dr. and Mrs. William Smither, made the demonstration of the accuracy of this pintura even more clear.

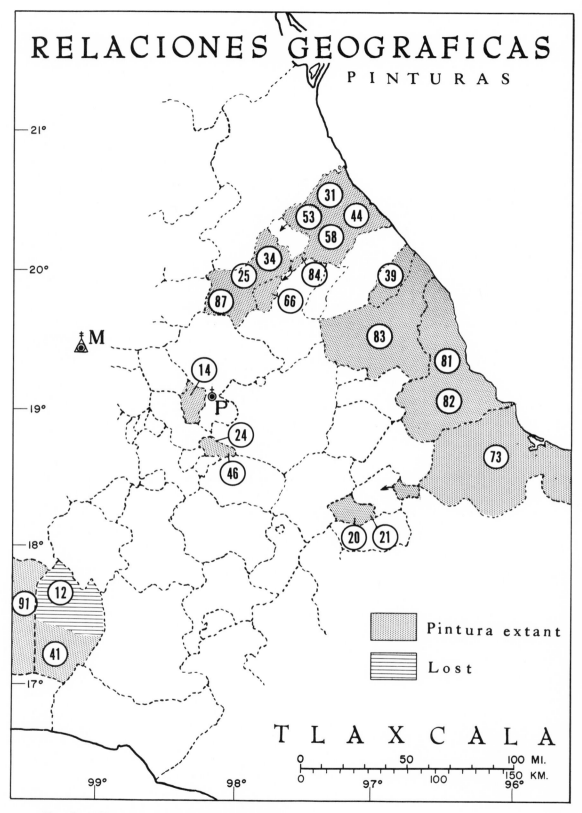

FIG. 5—PINTURAS: DIOCESE OF TLAXCALA, CA. 1580

pear; XALAPA DE VERA CRUZ and MI-
ZANTLA have a type of thatched-roof
house different from that of CUZCATLAN,
which is in a different region, and in QUA-
TLATLAUCA there is a flat-roof type.
Fortifications asked for in Question 32 are
shown on the pintura of TEXUPA, which
has a fortified hill with defenders inside the
wall. TEUTENANGO, which means fortified place, has a native place sign for fortified hill; MEZTITLAN shows "el fuerte de
Xalapa." Among other public works and
buildings is the water mill on San Miguel
y San Felipe de los CHICHIMECAS and
the reservoir, paper mill, and bridges of
Culhuacan.[16] There was even a slaughter-
house at TEUTENANGO!

These pictorial answers can be easily
overlooked as part of the content of the
RG and appear as mere embellishment of
the pintura. However, they are valuable
documents in themselves and should not be
considered as being merely supplements to
the written texts.[17] To now, no systematic
study of the complementary information
given on the pinturas and their related texts
has been made of the group as a whole, or
even of small groups of related ones.

Glosses

Glosses on the pinturas in European writing, usually in Spanish, are frequent addenda to the pictorial forms.[18] Sometimes
native languages are also used, Nahuatl
being the most frequent even though the
text of the RG may indicate that another
language was more commonly spoken in
the pueblo.[19] This makes concrete the implicit dominance of Nahuatl over other
Indian languages as the one used in dealing with the Spanish bureaucracy. Even
the highly polished pintura of CHOLULA
glosses the Mexico City road as "Mexico
ohtli," another road as "Uexotzinco ohtli,"
the market square as "Tianquizco," and the
residence of the corregidor as "Gorregidor
ychã."

Other languages appearing in the glosses

include Mixtec (place names only) on the
pintura of TEOZACOALCO and an unidentified language, probably Tarascan or
Otomi, on the two pinturas of Yurirpundaro. Native pictorial conventions for expressing numbers (population statistics)
glossing the pintura of Muchitlan are translated into Spanish.

Materials

Four materials of support were used in
the pinturas. Amatl or native paper (NP

16 A "molina de papel" and an "estanque," both
described in the reply to Question 20 of the text of
Culhuacan, were added to the pintura in the European faded brown ink of the written glosses and
are undoubtedly additions to the original painting,
contrasting sharply with the other forms, such as
bridges, painted with a dense black line. These
bridges are reminiscent of those on the Plano en
Papel de Maguey.

17 See note 10 for examples of texts which specifically state that certain questions are answered
on the pintura. See also notes 37 and 39, indicating
that at least some of the pinturas were the primary
documents, the texts secondary.

18 Written glosses, in this article, are any words
written on the pintura proper. In the appended
Catalog, where the text of an RG and the pintura
share parts of the same page, the text is not considered a gloss. Where only place names appear,
they are considered glosses but noted as place
names only. Where words such as "plaza," "iglesia," "estancia" appear in addition to place names,
they are considered glosses in Spanish. Words like
"ohtli" (road), "tecpan" (temple), "tianquizco"
(marketplace) are considered Nahuatl words and
are recorded as Nahuatl glosses. Sometimes long
texts or descriptive labelings in Nahuatl appear;
the five pinturas of the SUCHITEPEC RG and the
pintura of MACUILSUCHIL are examples. These
are not differentiated in Catalog annotations from
glosses consisting of only single isolated words.

19 Twelve extant pinturas and one lost lienzo
have Nahuatl glosses. The five pinturas belonging
to the text of SUCHITEPEC are glossed in Nahuatl, although the language of SUCHITEPEC was
Zapotec and its four sub-cabeceras spoke Chontal;
the same is true of the pintura of MACUILSU-
CHIL, a Zapotec community, which has a long
Nahuatl gloss. It is especially interesting to note
that the last sentence of the RG for QUERETARO
tells us that the place names on the pintura (a lost
lienzo) are given in Nahuatl, but in Otomi in the
text (Velásquez, 1897, 1: 48), an explanation given
no doubt to avoid confusion. One doubts that it
would have helped the royal cosmographers in
Madrid!

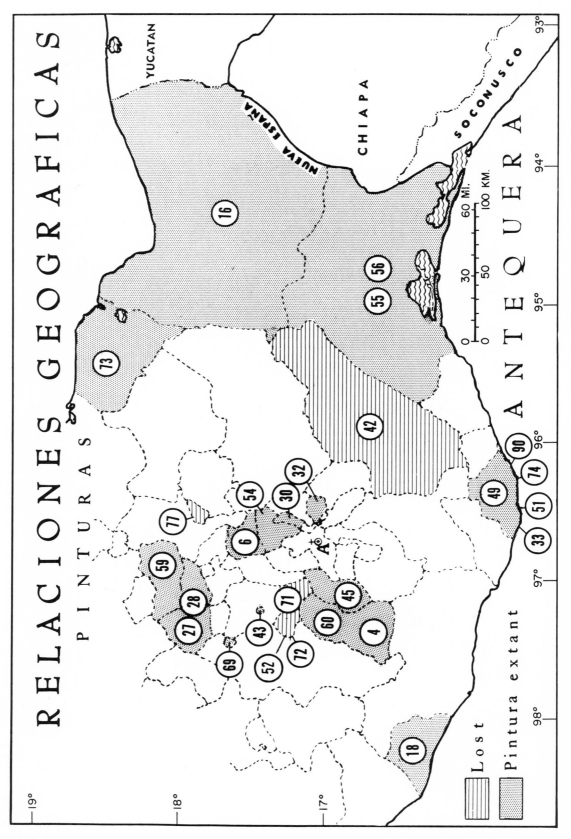

FIG. 6—PINTURAS: DIOCESE OF ANTEQUERA, CA. 1580

in the Catalog), made from the bark of the fig tree, is a native material with pre-Hispanic antecedents. Five pinturas are on amatl paper: Acambaro, Culhuacan, Muchitlan, TEUTENANGO, and ZUMPANGO. "Amatl" is used in Nahuatl for both our word "book" and our word "paper." Cloth lienzos, also native, have no counterpart in the European tradition, for the cloth is a loose-weave cotton, quite unlike European canvas. Lienzos were used for the three lost pinturas of NEXAPA, QUERETARO, and USILA; it is quite possible that others on the missing list were also lienzos.[20] Tanned animal skins with a layer of plaster size, used in the Mixtec and adjacent areas in the pre-Hispanic period, are lacking among the extant pinturas.[21] Most of the RG paintings are on 16th-century European rag paper with watermarks (EP in the Catalog), made in sheets of 31 by 44 cm., folded into folios of 31 by 22 cm. One pintura, Misquiahuala, is painted on parchment (or vellum), a European support material, which may also have been used in the pre-Conquest period.

Materials to a certain extent conditioned the format of the pintura. Single folios of European rag paper are common, and two or more glued together make up larger sheets, usually in multiples of the standard dimensions. Lienzos and amatl paper, not having such standardized sizes and shapes, could be more varied in size and proportion. One of the major pre-Conquest formats, the tira or long strip rolled or folded, like sized tanned leather, is missing from the group of RG pinturas.

Pigments and inks permit less clear-cut statements, since less is known about them. It is probable that the native colors were all earth colors or vegetable or animal dyes and that European artists, at least in the early days of colonial life, used the native colors. Pigments seem to have been applied as water color or gouache and thus give the pintura a lightness and delicacy in contrast with contemporary European oil or

tempera painting. European ink, now a distinctive faded brown color, is easily identifiable when used for written glosses or, more importantly, for pictorial addenda to the pinturas which otherwise used the native black paint, today still clear and dark.[22]

Artistic Style

Artistic style in this article consists of the systems of graphic conventions used in the pinturas. These are recorded in the Catalog as ranging from *European*, through a *Mixed* category, to *Native*. Table 1 lists the salient characteristics for the two extremes. Various combinations make up the group we call "Mixed." In establishing this vocabulary, we make no reference to the artist *per se*, to his racial antecedents, or the cultural ambient in which he lived. "European" means, thus, a painting in the European tradition showing no evidence of the inheritance or persistence of traits of pre-Hispanic manuscript painting. In similar fashion, "Native" refers only to the characteristics of graphic style and not to the person using it. "Mixed" indicates a pintura with traits from both the European and the Native traditions.[23]

European art in the late 16th century was transmitted to the colonies through easel or fresco paintings done in the colonies by European artists such as Simón Peréyns.[24] The other main source of contact with European art for the colonial painter was through easel paintings and prints imported from Spain or through Spain from the Netherlands and Germany. These prints were sometimes single leaves, usually of

[20] See Catalog.
[21] See Robertson, 1963, p. 162, where the pintura of Amoltepec is erroneously said to be painted on skin.
[22] See note 16 regarding additions to the pintura of Culhuacan.
[23] For an earlier statement of the principle and the distinctions here presented, see Robertson, 1959a, 1959b.
[24] Toussaint, 1936, 1948a, 1962, 1965, 1967, for the major studies of 16th-century colonial painting.

TABLE 1—GRAPHIC STYLE

	Native	European
General comments:[1]	Conceptual Unitary Horror vacui	Perceptual Unified Focused composition
Line:[2]	"Frame line," unvarying width, used as cloisons for areas of flat color	Varied in width to indicate lost edges of rounded shapes
	Used in patterns to qualify forms symbolically	Broken to show modeling of plastic form, as hatching to indicate shading
Color:[3]	Applied in unvarying flat areas	Modulated to show light and shade (chiaroscuro) and to model three-dimensional form
Forms:[4]	Signs Qualifying signs	Images (Written glosses)
Geographic:	Place signs	Views of specific features in nature
Architectural:	Native temples in "T-elevation"[5]	Christian churches in elevation, perspective, plan, or "plan-view," a combination of these[6]
Human:[7]	Unitary construction	Unified construction
Space:[8]	Two-dimensional	Three-dimensional
	Place signs of linderos as frame	Landscape
	Maps and plans	Maps and plans

[1] *Native* and *European* are established as poles of contrast, with the understanding that they represent extreme statements. I point out (p. 260) that in the "folk art" phase of both European and Native draughtsmanship, the phenomenon of convergence can be seen. An example of folk art may be so far from its source that one can only with difficulty postulate from which source it ultimately derives, or it may even have within itself traits coming from both styles (*Mixed*).

Native style is essentially *conceptual* in contrast with the *perceptual* nature of European art. The Native artist paints conventional forms to represent classes of objects rather than painting the individual appearance of objects as they exist in nature. The conventional forms of the Native tradition are *unitary*, composed of separable parts. European style is *unified*, where the parts are subordinated to the whole.

What is true of individual forms is true also of principles of composition linking them. The pure Native tradition composes in terms of the *horror vacui*, forms distributed evenly on the page. European art unifies the whole by subordinating the individual forms to a single *focused composition*.

See notes 2–8 to this table and also Robertson, 1959a, passim, for a more extended discussion of graphic style.

[2] *Line* performs two differing functions in the two styles. In Native painting it is a cloison surrounding areas of color, or it makes symbolic or meaningful patterns on areas of color. "*Frame line*" is varied in width only through the artist's stroke or trait, not consistently for illusionistic purposes. In European painting it is essentially an adjunct of color when it is used

(*Notes continued opposite*)

to impart mass to objects through variations in width, broken to show lost contours of rounded shapes, or when used as hatching.

³ The Native artist uses *color* as a concept and constant quality of objects, applying it in flat unvarying two-dimensional washes. The European artist uses color as it is perceived in nature, changing with light and shade (chiaroscuro) and modeling three-dimensional form. Where variations in areas of color appear in Native-style paintings, it is due to the artist's touch rather than the purposefulness of variation as in European style.

⁴ The Native vocabulary of *form* is essentially a restricted series of shapes, each with its own iconographic meaning; these we call *signs*. In pre-Conquest art the painter does not indulge himself with added details for the sake of the enjoyment they might give him or the observer. All that one sees is there as a concentrated vehicle carrying a burden of conceptual meaning. Meaning is not so concentrated and restrictive for the European artist, and so he can add landscape, light and shade, the images one perceives in nature, and a myriad of details for their own sake. It is interesting to note that in some of the relaciones pinturas, where the precision of Native signs has been eroded, long written glosses are used to supplement what remains, to replace what is missing (see the SUCHITEPEC pinturas).

The Native *place sign* is constructed on the base of a bell-shaped form ending in volutes connected by a horizontal bar at the bottom. *Qualifying signs*, indicating the particular name, are surcharged upon this basic shape to distinguish one place from another. The surcharge may be the name or descriptive characteristics of the place. Similar qualifying signs were used to indicate the gods to whom temples were dedicated, and a row of disks in a horizontal frieze indicated a public building. This use of qualifying signs made it a simple thing for the natives to record Christian churches. In some instances the church is a building whose qualifying sign is the Christian cross, in others an "espadaña" or open belfry.

Qualifying signs are, then, the Native device for rendering the general form specific. They are equivalent, in the Native pictorial writing systems, to labels on European maps, for the European map-maker, like the Native artist, deals with stylized forms or signs standing for classes of objects which he must make specific.

⁵ The *"T-elevation"* of the Native tradition is used in the representation of native temples (TEXUPA). It shows front and side elevations at the same time in a continuous drawing reduced to a single plane, avoiding the three-dimensionality implicit in European perspective rendering of buildings.

⁶ *Christian churches* can be shown in elevation, or in perspective with façade, one wall, and sometimes a flat roof. They also appear in more unorthodox fashion with façade and both side walls, making buildings built on a rectangular plan seem as though constructed on an octagon (Guaxtepec), or they can be shown combining plan and elevations in a single drawing.

⁷ Examples of a completely *unitary human form* are rare in the pinturas of the relaciones, but in pre-Hispanic manuscript painting are diagnostic for painting in Mexico proper (Maya painting such as the frescoes of Bonampak are clear-cut exceptions). The unitary figure is composed of a series of parts—head, trunk, arms, legs—each maintaining its own integrity so that the composition is essentially by the juxtaposition of isolatable units. The great change in drawing the human figure after Spanish contact is in the *unification* of the parts; their subordination to the conception of the whole is clear. The human figure appears more rarely in the pinturas of the RG's than other forms, but when it does appear, it becomes an important diagnostic trait. One can say, the more *unified* and less *unitary*, the more European the style of the pintura.

⁸ The *map or plan* is a schematic representation of a geographical area shown in terms of the abstract symbols of the cartographer. A single repeating sign standardized according to a convention can represent each individual city: the native temple or the Christian church. *Landscape*, on the other hand, shows the specific representation of the individual phenomena of nature as perceived. Each individual mountain or hill will be drawn differently from all others, since they are unique forms in nature. In map-making mountains may follow the patterns of European *or* Native stylizations, recording what is known as an intellectual conception, while landscape representations of mountains in the pinturas can be so close to natural appearance that present-day visitors are still able to identify them (see note 15 re TEXUPA).

The landscapist uses a single limited point of view from which he observes the area to be painted (or he may use an imaginary single point of view from which it might have been seen, i.e., the bird's-eye view), but essentially, the whole of the contents of the pintura is determined by this single viewpoint. The map-maker, on the other hand, makes no assumption of a viewpoint; rather, he reduces the world to a flat two-dimensionality in which measurable distances take precedence over perceived relationships. The landscapist gives us, in short, a perceptual view of the world, and the map-maker gives us a conceptually constructed version of nature. The pintura of TEXUPA is instructive, for it combines landscape showing the whole valley and the map *cum* city plan drawn in a different scale. (It answers both parts of Question 10, as it shows both the city plan and the setting.)

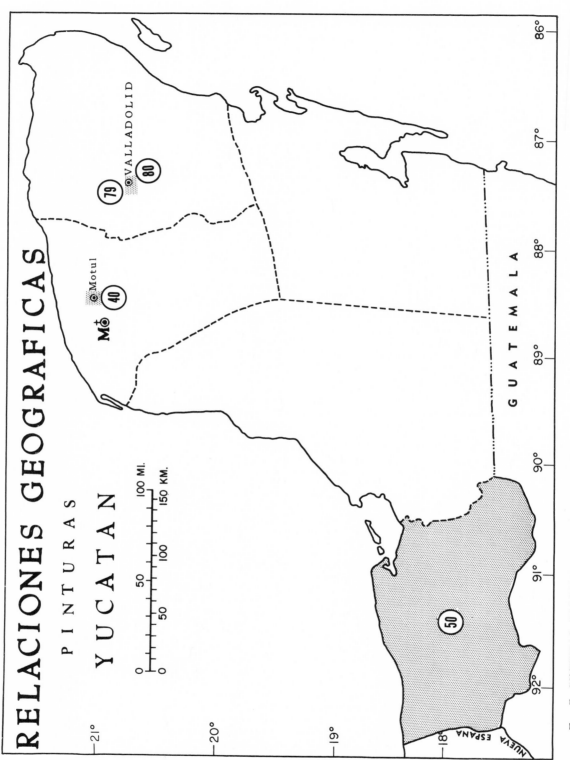

RELACIONES GEOGRAFICAS

P I N T U R A S
Y U C A T A N

Fig. 7—PINTURAS: DIOCESE OF YUCATAN, CA. 1580

devotional subject matter, or book illustrations.[25] European paintings and prints demonstrate for us the forms and usages of landscape as the background and setting for devotional subjects and portraits.[26] The landscape pinturas of the RG's are different, however, in that the landscape is not merely an adjunct to another subject but an end in itself. Landscape painting as an independent genre is a late development in the history of European painting, and thus the pinturas of the RG's, when they portray landscape alone, are abreast of trends then current in the Old World.[27]

Native style and its local traditions as yet have not had adequate and serious study.[28] Study of the mixing of the two traditions in the early colonial period has just begun.[29]

If one removes from consideration those paintings having no trace of Native style, essentially the mariner's charts (TLACO-TALPA, COATZOCOALCO, and TE-HUANTEPEC–2) and those from mining towns founded by Spaniards with no previous Native traditions (TEMAZCALTE-PEC MINAS and associated villages, clearly derived from the European woodcut tradition of book illustration [Robertson, 1959a, pp. 187–88] and ZIMAPAN), one is left with a large and valuable body of material to document the variation of style among the Mixed paintings and paintings with an essentially Native background. This material documents the rate and degree of acceptance of the new European style by Native artists—how much was retained from the old and how much taken from the new in a period of approximately 60 years or about three generations after the Spanish conquest. These two aspects of this group of maps still await adequate study. A start has been made on the basis of published versions of the maps now in Spain and kodachromes of a certain number in UTX. In the one case, color had to be left out of consideration; in the other, not all examples were available.[30]

The levels of artistic production and achievement are other elements that enrich the study of the pinturas.[31] Remnants of the high style of the Native tradition exist in manuscripts such as the pintura of Culhuacan, giving every indication of having been drawn by an artist with a strong Native orientation in his depiction of individual forms, use of native black ink (paint), and native paper. However, he painted a passage of true landscape in the foothills beyond the town, most expressively showing his acquaintance with this aspect of European painting. In such cases landscape is limited to parts or details; the pinturas of ATLATLAUCA and Suchiaca, Chicoalapa, and TEHUANTEPEC–1 all have superimposed passages of landscape. XONOTLA and MEZTITLAN are continuous landscapes, closer to the backgrounds of contemporary painting in Spain.

Examples of the two "high styles" are, by their very nature, clearly definable, because they are distinct. It is in the area of pinturas whose graphic style represents the slovening of either of the high styles that problems of analysis become more acute. The paintings, whose styles are born

[25] Kubler and Soria, 1959, chap. 17, passim, have a discussion of colonial painting derived from prints. The pinturas belonging to the TEMAZCAL-TEPEC RG text are quite obviously based on woodcuts (Robertson, 1959a, pp. 187–88).

[26] Useful general handbooks on Spanish painting include Angulo Iñíguez, 1954; Kubler and Soria, 1959; Lafuente Ferrari, 1953; and Mayer, 1949.

[27] Benesch, 1945, chap. 3: "The New Attitude Toward Nature, The Discoverers of Landscape in Painting and Science."

[28] Robertson, 1959a, 1963, 1964, and 1966.

[29] Robertson, 1959a, 1959b.

[30] See note 14.

[31] The RG text of ATENGO, referring to the pintura of Misquiahuala, says in answer to Question 10 that the painting will answer this question splendidly and in more detail. "A la desima rresponde que la pintura . . . lo dira mas en particular y esplendidamente" (fol. 4r). This gives us a qualitative judgment in the text, referring to the pintura, and most probably written by a Spanish official. This is a rare example of a Spanish secular person admiring Native art.

of the repetition of forms until their meaning is blurred or almost lost in the mind of the artist, represent examples of the convergence of the two traditions.[32] The use of forms no longer completely understood but preserved through successive copying, whether deriving from Europe or pre-Conquest America, leads to the "folk art" versions of both styles, and these, deriving from two such diverse and sophisticated styles, can be remarkably alike as they converge and their distinctive features are being eroded away. This problem has only been touched upon but presents important areas for future analysis, which one hopes will bear fruit in subsequent studies and perhaps even sharpen the distinction between the two "folk arts."

ARTISTS

Solutions to the problems posed by the pinturas could come from knowledge of the artists and their antecedents. Why did some artists preserve Native ways so faithfully, while others absorbed so much of the new modes imported from Europe? Distance from Mexico City, the main center for the diffusion of Spanish culture, does not seem to be a decisive factor, nor does the language of the reporting town. It is thus unfortunate that we know so little about the specific artists of these pinturas. Few names of artists are preserved—and one of them is for a missing pintura.

The names of the artists of the pinturas of MEXICATZINGO (lost) and its two sub-cabeceras, Culhuacan and Ixtapalapa, are all known. "Domingo Bonifaçio, yndio pintor" painted the lost pintura of MEXICA-TZINGO, according to the RG text (PNE, 6:197). The text of Ixtapalapa states at the end of the RG that M[a]r[tí]n (?) Cano was the painter. Pedro de St. Augustin is named painter on the verso of the pintura of Culhuacan.[33] The TABASCO pintura was painted by Melchor de Alfaro Santa Cruz (DIU, 13:317). The two mariner's

charts of TLACOTALPA and COATZO-COALCO are signed by Capitán Francisco Stroza Gali, presumed to be a European.

For other knowledge of the painters, we are turned back to the paintings and the texts and what can be deduced from them. One can assume that the person in the pueblo or cabecera most capable of drawing up a map was commissioned to make the pintura.[34] Some texts say that no one in the town was able to make a pintura.[35] This can record either that there never was a manuscript tradition in the town or that the manuscript tradition had died out by 1579–86.

The pinturas of TEQUIZISTLAN and TEOTITLAN DEL CAMINO are so much alike that they must have come from the same school. The first, in the style of Texcoco, was probably made by the same person as the second, although it came from a pueblo at a considerable distance. The explanation here is that the two pueblos were both under the same corregidor,[36] and thus no deduction about the present or previous state of the art of manuscript painting in TEOTITLAN DEL CA-MINO can be made from the evidence of these two pinturas.

[32] Kubler, 1961, has an extended discussion of this process.

[33] Domingo Bonifaçio we know to have been an Indian. It is possible that M[a]r[tí]n (?) Cano and Pedro de St. Augustin also were.

[34] The text of ZAPOTITLAN strongly suggests that the scribe, Fernando de Niebla, also made the pintura. Question 42 asked that "a chart" be made "as best possible." See note 31.

[35] The RG of GUATULCO says that there is no one in that pueblo or in all of its jurisdiction who can paint the land and coast, that mariner's coast charts would have to be relied upon (PNE, 4: 238, 242, 247, 251), although there is no mariner's chart accompanying this RG. The text of COATZO-COALCO says also that there is no painter in the province (Caso, 1928c, p. 180), but the mariner's chart of Capitán Francisco Stroza Gali is appended to the RG.

[36] Robertson (1959a, pp. 151–53) has a fuller demonstration of this example of the spread of a native style under the stimulus of a Spanish administrator.

Chronological and Other Relationships

Relationship to Texts

One usually thinks of the pinturas as documents supplementary to the texts, but at least two texts say that the painting was made first, making it the *urtext*, and that the written text was then drawn up based on the pintura. The lost lienzo of NEXAPA and the lost pintura of TEQUALTICHE are examples.[37] This recalls a pre-Hispanic tradition described in European writings of the time of the Conquest telling of oral explanations accompanying pictorial documents.[38] In certain of the RG's the written text has taken the place of the earlier oral explanation as a device for explaining the pintura. The text of TILANTONGO says that it is based on statements of old Indian informants who had paintings;[39] it is not specified whether they were old paintings or the pinturas prepared especially to accompany the text.

A significant question not raised until now is the chronological relationship of the pinturas to the written texts. We have already noted that only two of the pinturas are dated (see note 5); dates assigned to the others are the dates of the accompanying texts. In many cases, on the basis of the texts themselves, we know the pinturas were made especially to accompany the texts. In others, where written text and pintura share a common sheet of European paper, the supposition of a pintura made especially for the RG is well founded. Where the pintura is clearly drawn up to supply pictorial answers to the questionnaire, likewise, there is little or no question of contemporaneity. It is possible, however, that in other instances an already existing pintura was used and sent with the newly drawn up written answers.[40] Any examples where a significantly prior date for the pintura can be established, or the indication of a prior date can be reasonably defended, will be exceptions to our previous statements that the pinturas represent a series linked by closeness in time.

Relationship to Prototypes

Still another element enters into the analysis of the existing pinturas: their relationship to prototypes. In several instances the text tells that paintings by the Indians were used in preparing the written texts.[41] It is to be assumed that older paintings were also available for preparing the painted answers which appeared in the pinturas. The pintura of Misquiahuala, for instance, strongly suggests a lienzo copied at reduced scale, with the historical content omitted. In these instances of a new pintura deriving from older painted documents, the question of the degree of fidelity to the model in the process of making or compiling the copy is of key importance in assessing the development of style.

The pintura of TEOZACOALCO, for instance, is much more consistently Native in the painted genealogical lists than in the portrayal of elements of landscape which makes it Mixed. It has been pointed out that in the early colonial period faithful copying of the model by the Indians was remarked upon by the Spaniards; it was also pointed out that they did not copy without making changes (Robertson, 1959a, pp. 41–42). This apparent contradiction is resolved if we say that they could and did

---

[37] The text for NEXAPA states: "la qual pintura va en un lienço de la tierra . . . y sobre ello hizieron y respondieron a los capitulos de la dicha ynstruyçion. . . ." (PNE, 4: 29). The TEQUAL-TICHE pintura was apparently so Native in style that "yndios antiguos" had to interpret the pintura for the scribe writing the text of the RG (NV, 1878, pp. 359–60).

[38] Robertson, 1959a, pp. 28–29.

[39] "E lo que a podido saber y aberiguar con los naturales deste pueblo biejos y ançianos . . . y por las pinturas que los dichos yndios tienen es lo siguiente" (PNE, 4: 70).

[40] We know that this was true in the mariner's chart COATZOCOALCO, dated 1579; the text is dated Apr. 29, 1580. See note 35.

[41] See notes 37 and 39.

copy with startling fidelity when they wanted to, but that when not limited, they were prone to make variations on the theme established by the models. The pintura of TEOZACOALCO may represent almost direct copying of the pre-Hispanic or early colonial genealogical manuscript, while the map cum landscape, drawn up especially for the pintura, allowed the artist to indulge in the delineation of the geographical ambient, an ambient not recorded in his genealogical models. The genealogical model was adhered to with fidelity because it was a legal document establishing claims of a ruling family. Significant variations from its model would invalidate its juridical correctness and thus its value. The linderos or boundaries likewise constituted a legal document, a land claim as it were, and tended to maintain the old forms (place signs), correct because they are drawn traditionally. Mountains within the area of the jurisdiction, however, having less significance for maintaining older rights and privileges, could be shown in a new more European fashion without jeopardizing any legal rights. It is in the central area of the pintura of TEOZACOALCO then that some new elements of landscape painting appear.

Lost Pinturas

The group of lost pinturas may very well include examples of paintings of disparate date. A receipt signed for documents turned over to Juan López de Velasco in 1583 is our main source of information on the group. This receipt clearly shows the first 12 items on the list are pinturas separated from their texts.[42] They are as listed: MEXICO, Chilapa, TEPEAPULCO, ATLI-TLALAQUIA, USILA, TILANTONGO (two), QUERETARO, VALLADOLID of Michoacan, Totoltepec, NEXAPA, and Tamazula. The texts of NEXAPA, QUERE-TARO, and USILA say the pinturas were lienzos. The texts of TEPEAPULCO, Chilapa, and TILANTONGO all indicate large amounts of information on the pinturas,

suggesting a large size. From this data we can conclude with some degree of certainty that, since all 12 of the missing pinturas were separate from their texts, they were probably large and possibly all were lienzos.[43] The lienzo of NEXAPA, according to the text, was made especially to accompany the text.[44] There is no such assurance about other missing pinturas on the López de Velasco inventory, some of which may very well have been old documents submitted with the later text. Either way, they are more likely to have been Native in style than were pinturas done on European paper, if they used a native material of support.

Four other paintings are lost in addition to the 12 of the López de Velasco list. The text for TEPUZTLAN gives a long description of the lost pintura; the text for TE-QUALTICHE says it is based on interpretations of the pintura by old Indians (see note 37), and the text of MEXICATZINGO says it was painted by "Domingo Boni-façio, yndio pintor" (see Catalog references for all three). These pinturas are more likely to have been Native than European in their styles, leaving us with the interesting possibility that at least 15 of the missing pinturas were among the most Indian in style. A sixteenth missing pintura seems to be a city plan of CELAYA. There is no indication that any of them are in the AGI, RAH, Archivo General de Si-

---

[42] See note 6,d. See also Article 5, Appendix D, for transcription of the JLV, 1583, inventory by Dr. Adele Kibre. Also see Catalog for individual lost pinturas.

[43] The pintura of TEOZACOALCO, although large and containing much information, did not appear in the list of separate pinturas of the JLV, 1583, inventory, because it was, until recently, not kept separate from its text. It is on European paper and was folded and filed with the text, in contrast with the lienzos which could not be handled so easily. Its absence from the list of separated pinturas is another indication that the ones on the list were lienzos, or at least not on European paper.

[44] See note 37; possibly also TILANTONGO, note 39.

TABLE 2—DISTRIBUTION OF PINTURAS BY REPOSITORIES

Archivo General de Indias (AGI)	Royal Academy of History (RAH)	University of Texas (UTX)
1. COATEPEC CHALCO	1. Acambaro (CELAYA)	1. AMECA
2. Chicoalapa	2. ATLATLAUCA & Malinaltepec	2. ATITLAN
3. Chimalhuacan Atengo	3. COMPOSTELA, MINAS DE	3. ATLATLAUCA & Suchiaca
4. CUZCATLAN–1	4. CUAHUITLAN	4. CEMPOALA
5. HUEXOTLA	5. IXTEPEXIC	5. Epazoyuca
6. MOTUL	6. MACUILSUCHIL	6. Tetlistaca
7. SUCHITEPEC (text in RAH)	7. NOCHIZTLAN	7. CHOLULA
8. Macupilco	8. San Miguel y San Felipe de los CHICHIMECAS (text lost)	8. COATZOCOALCO
9. Tamagazcatepec	9. TEOTITLAN DEL CAMINO	9. CUZCATLAN–2
10. Tlacotepec	10. TEXUPA	10. GUEYTLALPA
11. Zozopastepec	11. TLACOTALPA	11. Jujupango
12. TABASCO	12. ZUMPANGO, MINAS DE	12. Matlatlan & Chila
13. TEMAZCALTEPEC, MINAS DE	[Chilapa (lost)]	13. Papantla
14. Cacaloztoc	[Muchitlan (UTX)]	14. Tecolutla
15. Tescaltitlan		15. Tenanpulco & Matlactonatico
16. Texupilco		16. Zacatlan
17. Tuzantla		17. IXCATLAN–1
18. TEQUIZISTLAN		18. IXCATLAN–2 [MEXICATZINGO–lost]
19. TEUTENANGO		19. Culhuacan
20. VALLADOLID, Yuc.–1		20. Ixtapalapa
21. VALLADOLID, Yuc.–2		21. MEZTITLAN
22. XALAPA DE VERA CRUZ		22. Misquiahuala (ATENGO)
23. XONOTLA		23. MIZANTLA
24. Tetela		24. PEÑOLES
25. Yurirpundaro (CELAYA) (text in RAH)		25. QUATLATLAUCA
26. Yurirpundaro, verso (CELAYA) (text in RAH)		26. Gueguetlan
27. ZIMAPAN, MINAS DE		27. TECUICUILCO
		28. TEHUANTEPEC–1
		29. TEHUANTEPEC–2
		30. TEOZACOALCO
		31. Amoltepec [TEPUZTLAN—lost]
		32. Acapistla
		33. Guaxtepec
		34. VERACRUZ–1
		35. VERACRUZ–2
		36. ZAPOTITLAN & Suchitepec [ZUMPANGO, MINAS (RAH)] [Chilapa–lost]
		37. Muchitlan

mancas, Escorial, or Biblioteca Nacional or Biblioteca del Real Palacio, Madrid. If they still exist, they may very well still be in private hands.[45] It can be noted here that the UTX RG pinturas and texts were bought in the middle of the last century by García Icazbalceta, apparently from a private owner in Spain. It is possible that

[45] The pintura of TEQUALTICHE is probably in private hands; see Catalog, 63.

TABLE 3—LOST PINTURAS

	Pintura	Text
1.	ATLITLALAQUIA	AGI
2.	CELAYA	RAH
3.	MEXICATZINGO	AGI
	[Culhuacan (UTX)]	UTX
	[Ixtapalapa (UTX)]	UTX
4.	MEXICO	Lost
5.	NEXAPA	AGI
6.	QUERETARO	UTX
7.	TEPEAPULCO	AGI
8.	TEPUZTLAN	AGI
	[Acapistla (UTX)]	UTX
	[Guaxtepec (UTX)]	UTX
9.	TEQUALTICHE	UTX
10.	TILANTONGO	RAH
11.	TILANTONGO (Mitlantongo?)	RAH
12.	Tamazula	RAH
13.	Totoltepec	Unidentified
14.	USILA	RAH
15.	VALLADOLID, Michoacan	Lost
16.	[ZUMPANGO, MINAS (RAH)]	RAH
	Chilapa	RAH
	[Muchitlan (UTX)]	UTX

sometime in the future the remaining 16 pinturas will emerge from a private collection to appear on the art market.

PROBLEMS AND SUMMARY

Certain problems arise in connection with pinturas from related cabeceras. For instance, the pintura of CEMPOALA is a sophisticated example of the early colonial manuscript School of Texcoco (Robertson, 1959a, pp. 188–89; chap. 7), whereas the pinturas of Tetlistaca and Epazoyuca, its sub-cabeceras, show a remarkable difference of style and inferior artistic quality. A similar question arises in the study of the pintura of Amoltepec, a fine example of a Native-style pintura from a sub-cabecera,

REFERENCES

Note: Text references not listed here have been incorporated into Article 9.

Angulo Iñíguez, 1954
Benesch, 1945
Kubler, 1961
—— and Soria, 1959

Lafuente Ferrari, 1953
Mayer, 1949
Robertson, 1964, 1966
Toussaint, 1936, 1965

whereas TEOZACOALCO, the main cabecera, presented a painting in a Mixed style. There are two pinturas of IXCATLAN for the same text, each slightly different from the other. There are also two different pinturas *and* texts for CUZCATLAN (one in the AGI, the other at UTX), both texts dated October 26, 1580.[46]

Future research on other aspects of acculturation can be based on the solid foundation of the regional distribution of the pinturas of the Relaciones Geográficas in a limited time range. The pinturas themselves still present formidable problems to the investigator, but the solutions to these problems will have significance beyond the pinturas alone. If a principle underlying the respective geographic distributions of the more Native and the more Europeanizing pinturas can be formulated, this principle can be used in assessing other aspects of acculturation in Middle America.

Table 2 provides a summary of extant pinturas by the repositories in which they are found. Table 3 lists those presently considered "lost."

[46] The two pinturas have slightly different contents. The AGI pintura has a gallows to the right of the main church and a fountain to the left; the UTX version has the fountain to the right and no gallows. Only UTX has a calendrical sign in the lower center (rabbit, "tochtli") in a rectangular frame but without its numerical coefficient. Three parallel streams of water, right center on both maps, are probably irrigation ditches; only the UTX pintura shows a row of corn growing between two of them. The positions of the place signs bounding the area are different; there are 20 in the Spanish and only 11 in the UTX pintura (in this count we exclude stars and suns indicating directions and the market symbol at bottom center of the page). The CUZCATLAN relaciones are the only known examples of duplicate 16th-century texts.

CATALOG OF PINTURAS (MAPS) OF THE RELACIONES GEOGRÁFICAS

Donald Robertson and
Martha Barton Robertson

KEY:

MAIN CABECERA (in capital letters) or Sub-Cabecera (lowercase) followed by (MAIN CABECERA) Diocese. Pintura style.[47]

(MAIN CABECERA).

Date [of RG text]. Glosses (see note 18).

Repository.[48] Physical description: colors (b/w unless color indicated); NP (native paper); EP (European paper); height x width.

Publication data (b/w unless color indicated).

Copy, if any. Repository. Physical description. Publication data.

References (catalogs, etc.).

Bibliography (study of document).

Comments.

See also, related documents.

1. Acambaro (CELAYA). Michoacan. European.

> June 15, 1580. Glosses: Spanish.
> RAH. Colors. NP. 113 x 110 cm.
> Published: VR/PNE, 7/4: opp. p. 115 (very reduced, from map printed for PNE, 7, but not published).
> Refs: Zavala, 1938, pp. 311, no. XVII; 604.
> *See also* CELAYA, 9; Yurirpundaro, 85, 86.
> Census, 18A.

2. Acapistla [Yecapistla] (TEPUZTLAN). Mexico. Mixed.

> Oct. 10, 1580. Glosses: Spanish.
> UTX. Colors. EP. 62 x 85 cm.
> Unpublished.
> Copy: DGMH, no. 1195. (Pencil on brownish-yellow paper. 61.5 x 82 cm. Dated Jan. 28, 1888.)
> *See also* Guaxtepec, 23; TEPUZTLAN, 62.

[47] See section Artistic Style and notes to Table 1.
[48] AGI pinturas are separate from texts; call no. is same as TL no. For RAH and UTX call nos., see RG Text Census, Article 8, under MAIN CABECERA.

Census, 1.

3. AMECA. Guadalajara. European.

> Oct. 2–Dec. 15, 1579. Glosses: Spanish.
> UTX. Colors. EP. 43 x 31.5 cm.
> Published: Amaya, 1951, opp. p. 76 (with added caption dated 1948 by Jesús Amaya). Chevalier, 1956, p. 114 (after Amaya); 1963, opp. p. 114 (after Amaya).
> Copy: DGMH, no. 1182. (Pale watercolors; paper on cloth. 44 x 34 cm. Dated Jan. 19, 1858.) Published: Amaya, 1944, p. 7 (retraced); Palomino y Cañedo, 1947, 2: (after Amaya, 1944, retracing).
> *See also* Appendix, 1 (house drawing).
> Census, 4.

4. Amoltepec (TEOZACOALCO). Antequera. Native.

> Jan. 9–21, 1580. Glosses: Spanish.
> UTX. Colors. EP. 85 x 92 cm.
> Published: Robertson, 1959b, p. 544, fig. 3 (very reduced).
> Copy: DGMH, no. 1193. (Watercolor. 90 x 95 cm. Dated Feb. 17, 1858.)

Published: Tamayo, 1949, 1:50; 1950, p. 11; 1962, 1:54.
Census, 108A.

5. ATITLAN, SANTIAGO. Guatemala. European.
Feb. 8/9–27, 1585. Glosses: Spanish.
UTX. Colors. EP. 61.5 x 81 cm.
Unpublished.
Census, 9.

6. ATLATLAUCA and Malinaltepec. Antequera. Mixed.
Sept. 8, 1580. Glosses: Spanish.
RAH. Colors. EP. 31 x 21 cm.
Published: PNE, 4: 163; Cline, 1961b, pl. 6b (after PNE).
Census, 11.

7. ATLATLAUCA and Suchiaca [Suchiata]. Mexico. European.
Sept. 17, 1580. Glosses: Spanish.
UTX. Colors. EP. 42 x 31 cm.
Published: Robertson, 1959b, p. 544, fig. 4 (very reduced).
Census, 10.

8. ATLITLALAQUIA [ATITALAQUIA]. Mexico. Native (?).
Feb. 22, 1580.
Pintura lost. Text in AGI.
Physical details unknown; probably large.
Refs: JLV, 1583, P-4. PNE, 6: 199, n.1; 207.
Census, 12.

Cacaloztoc, Asiento de. See TEMAZCALTEPEC, MINAS, 57.

9. CELAYA, VILLA DE. Michoacan. Style unknown.
June 15, 1580.
Pintura lost. Text in RAH.
Physical details unknown.
Refs: VR/PNE, 7/4: 155; RGM, 2: 70.
Comment: Alcalde Mayor signed RG and said: "con ella [la relación] van las pinturas de las dichas provincias de Acambaro y Yurirapundaro e Villa de Salaya. . . ." This text implies that *three* pinturas accompanied the relación, includ-

ing a city plan of Celaya. Previously the pintura of Acambaro was thought to be also for Celaya.
See also Acambaro, 1; Yurirpundaro, 85, 86.
Census, 18.

10. CEMPOALA [ZEMPOALA]. Mexico. Mixed.
Nov. 1, 1580. Glosses: Nahuatl.
UTX. Colors. EP. 83 x 66 cm.
Published: Barlow, 1949b, opp. p. 40, pl. VI; Robertson, 1959a, pl. 88.
Copy: DGMH, no. 1189. (Watercolor on heavy paper. 82 x 68 cm. Dated Dec. 13, 1857.) Published: Olvera, 1964, cover (color); pl.; p. 15 (vignette of "Santa yglesia").
See also Epazoyuca, 22; Tetlistaca, 67.
Census, 19.

CHICHIMECAS. *See* San Miguel y San Felipe de los CHICHIMECAS, 48.

11. Chicoalapa (COATEPEC CHALCO). Mexico. Mixed.
Dec. 3, 1579. Glosses: Spanish.
AGI, 12 (TL). Colors. EP. 43 x 60 cm.
Published: PNE, 6: 86; Kubler, 1948, vol. 1, opp. p. 93, fig. 25, after PNE.
Census, 29B.

12. Chilapa (ZUMPANGO, MINAS). Tlaxcala. Native (?).
Jan. [i.e., Feb.] 21, 1582.
Pintura lost. Text in RAH.
Physical details unknown; probably large.
Refs: JLV, 1583, P-2; PNE, 5: 174, 176, 177.
Comment: Reply to Question 11: "Esta cabeçera tiene quarenta y cuatro estançuelas . . . en la pintura va puesto el numero y nombre de ellas y lo que distan un pueblo a otro" (PNE, 5: 177).
See also Muchitlan, 41; ZUMPANGO, MINAS, 91.
Census, 22bis.

13. Chimalhuacan Atengo (COATEPEC CHALCO). Mexico. Mixed.
   Dec. 1, 1579. Glosses: Spanish.
   AGI, 11 (TL). Colors. EP. 55 x 52 cm.
   Published: PNE, 6: 69; Kubler, 1948, vol. 1, opp. p. 73, fig. 20, after PNE.
   Census, 29A.

14. CHOLULA. Tlaxcala. Mixed.
   1581. Glosses: Nahuatl and Spanish.
   UTX. Colors. EP. 31 x 44 cm.
   Published: Bandelier, 1884, between pp. 230 and 231, pl. xv (color facsimile).
   Copy: MNA 36–23. (Colors. Modern paper. 47 x 65 cm.) Made by Rafael Aguirre for Madrid, 1892, Exposición. Published: Gómez de Orozco, 1927a, p. 170, 1927d, p. 150; Kubler, 1948, vol. 1, opp. p. 92, fig. 22; Chevalier, 1956, p. 151; Maza, 1959, pl. 5; Glass, 1964, pl. 24; McAndrew, 1965, p. 403, fig. 194. Ref: Paso y Troncoso, 1892–93, 1: 53, no. VI.
   Census, 25.

15. COATEPEC CHALCO. Mexico. Mixed.
   Nov. 16, 1579. Glosses: Spanish.
   AGI, 10 (TL). Colors. EP. 43 x 60 cm.
   Published: PNE, 6: 48; Kubler, 1948, vol. 1, opp. p. 93, fig. 26, after PNE.
   See also Chicoalapa, 11; Chimalhuacan Atengo, 13.
   Census, 29.

16. [COATZOCOALCO]. ESPIRITU SANTO, VILLA DE. Antequera. European.
   Apr. 29, 1580. Glosses: Spanish.
   UTX. Colors. EP. 31 x 85 cm.
   Unpublished.
   Comment: Mariner's chart signed by Francisco Stroza Gali and dated 1579 [sic] submitted with the text, because there was no painter in the province

("... de no aber. pintor en esta probinçia." Caso, 1928c, p. 180).
   Census, 30.

17. COMPOSTELA, MINAS. Guadalajara. European.
   Nov. 26, 1584. Glosses: Spanish.
   RAH. B/w. EP. 43 x 36 cm.
   Published: Ramírez Cabañas, 1930, opp. p. 80; 1940, opp. p. 80 (from map printed for PNE, 8, but not published).
   Ref: Zavala, 1938, p. 604.
   Census, 31.

18. CUAHUITLAN [CUAUHUITLAN]. Antequera. Mixed.
   Aug. 14, 1580. Glosses: Spanish.
   RAH. Colors. EP. 21 x 31 cm.
   Published: PNE, 4: 155.
   Census, 33.

19. Culhuacan (MEXICATZINGO). Mexico. Mixed.
   Jan. 17, 1580. Glosses: Spanish.
   UTX. Colors. NP. 70 x 54 cm.
   Unpublished.
   Copy: DGMH, no. 1187. (Pale watercolor on heavy paper. 75 x 55 cm.) Published: Gorbea Trueba, 1959, p. 8.
   Comment: Inscription on verso says: "Fue el pintor Pedro de St. Augustin."
   See also Ixtapalapa, 29; MEXICATZINGO, 35.
   Census, 41.

20. CUZCATLAN. Version 1 (AGI). Tlaxcala. Mixed.
   Oct. 26, 1580. Glosses: Spanish.
   AGI, 19 (TL). Colors. EP. 43 x 32 cm.
   Published: PNE, 5: 46, BCE, 1920, p. 9 (nos. 32–33), repeated in RNE, 1920, 4: 13 (tipped in); Gómez de Orozco, 1927d, opp. p. 148; Pérez Bustamente, 1928a & 1928b, opp. p. 20, pl. III; McAndrew, 1965, p. 28, fig. 7 (all after PNE). Vázquez Vázquez, 1965, cover.
   Comment: There was also a chromolithographic edition by Poulat (23.9 x 16.9

cm.) sold by MNA in 1933, *Anales*, IV, 8: wraps. Nicolas León's 1906 edition of *Codex Sierra* is by the same lithographer, same size and type of printing; possibly this edition was printed for León about the same time but not published.
Census, 42.

21. CUZCATLAN. *Version 2* (UTX). Tlaxcala. Mixed.
Oct. 26, 1580. Glosses: Spanish.
UTX. Colors. EP. 43 x 30 cm.
Published: Robertson, 1959b, p. 541, fig. 1. (very reduced).
Copy: DGMH, no. 1192.
Census, 43

22. Epazoyuca (CEMPOALA). Mexico. Mixed.
Nov. 1, 1580. Glosses: Place name only.
UTX. Colors. EP. 31 x 21.5 cm.
Published: Barlow, 1949b, opp. p. 40, pl. V.
Copy: DGMH, no. 1190. (Watercolor on heavy paper. Dated Dec. 18, 1857.) Published: Olvera, 1964, plate (bottom of pintura cut off).
Census, 19A.

ESPIRITU SANTO, VILLA DE. *See* [COATZOCOALCO], 16.

23. Guaxtepec (TEPUZTLAN). Mexico. Mixed.
Sept. 24, 1580. Glosses: Spanish.
UTX. Colors. EP. 62 x 85 cm.
Unpublished.
Ref: Robertson, 1959b, p. 544.
See also Acapistla, 2; TEPUZTLAN, 62.
Census, 47.

24. Gueguetlan (QUATLATLAUCA). Tlaxcala. European.
Sept. 15, 1579. Glosses: Spanish and Nahuatl.
UTX. Colors. EP. 31 x 43 cm. Fols. 9v, 10r.
Unpublished.
Census, 85A.

25. GUEYTLALPA. Tlaxcala. Mixed.
May 30–July 20, 1581. Glosses: Spanish.
UTX. Colors. EP. 24.5 x 22 cm. Fol. 4r.
Published: García Payón, 1965, p. 35, pl. 2.
See also Jujupango, 31; Matlatlan and Chila, 34; Papantla, 44; Tecolutla, 53; Tenanpulco and Matlactonatico, 58; Zacatlan, 87.
Census, 49.

26. HUEXOTLA. Mexico. European.
Feb. 3–4, 1580. Glosses: Nahuatl.
AGI, 16 (TL). B/w. EP. 90 x 77 cm.
Published: PNE, 6:183; Kubler, 1948, vol. 1, opp. p. 102, fig. 27; McAndrew, 1965, p. 289, fig. 134, line drawing (both after PNE).
Census, 51.

27. IXCATLAN, STA. MARIA. *Pintura 1.* Antequera. European.
Oct. 13, 1579. Glosses: Spanish.
UTX. Colors. EP. 22.3 x 21.5 cm.
Published: Robertson, 1959b, p. 541, fig. 2a (very reduced).
Census, 54.

28. IXCATLAN, STA. MARIA. *Pintura 2.* Antequera. European.
Oct. 13, 1579. Glosses: Spanish.
UTX. Colors. EP. 33 x 31 cm.
Published: Robertson, 1959b, p. 541, fig. 2b (very reduced).
Census, 54.

29. Ixtapalapa (MEXICATZINGO). Mexico. Mixed.
Jan. 31, 1580. Glosses: Spanish.
UTX. Colors. EP. 42 x 31 cm.
Unpublished.
Comment: Artist is named at end of relación text: M[a]r[tí]n (?) Cano.
See also Culhuacan, 19; MEXICATZINGO, 35.
Census, 56.

30. IXTEPEXIC. Antequera. Mixed.
Aug. 27–30, 1579. Glosses: Spanish.

HRA. Colors. EP. 43 x 60 cm.
Published: PNE, 4: 10.
Census, 57.

31. Jujupango [Xuxupango] (GUEYTLAL-PA). Tlaxcala. Mixed.
May 30–July 20, 1581. Glosses: Spanish.
UTX. Colors. EP. 18 x 21 cm. Fol. 8v.
Published: García Payón, 1965, p. 51, pl. 4.
Census, 49B.

32. MACUILSUCHIL. Antequera. Mixed.
Apr. 9–11, 1580. Glosses: Nahuatl.
RAH. Colors. EP. 84 x 61 cm.
Published: PNE, 4: 100; Alba, Duque de, 1951, pl. 33 (color).
Census, 62.

33. Macupilco, S. Miguel. (SUCHITE-PEC). Antequera. Mixed.
Aug. 23–29, 1579. Glosses: Nahuatl with some Spanish words.
AGI, 25 (TL). Colors. EP. 43 x 62 cm.
Published: PNE: 4: 27.
Comment: Text in RAH; pintura in AGI.
Census, 88D.

34. Matlatlan and Chila (GUEYTLALPA). Tlaxcala. Mixed.
May 30–July 20, 1581. Glosses: Spanish.
UTX. Colors. EP. 31 x 22 cm. Fol. 11r.
Published: García Payón, 1965, p. 57, pl. 5.
Census, 49C.

35. MEXICATZINGO. Mexico. Native (?)
Feb. 7, 1580.
Pintura lost. Text in AGI.
Physical details unknown.
Comment: Text states that "Domingo Bonifaçio, yndio pintor" made pintura (PNE, 6: 197).
See also Culhuacan, 19; Ixtapalapa, 29.
Census, 65.

36. MEXICO, CIUDAD DE. Mexico. Native (?)
1580.
Pintura lost. Text lost.
Physical details unknown; probably large.
Ref: JLV, 1583, P-1.
Census, 209.

37. MEZTITLAN. Mexico. European.
Oct. 1, 1579. Glosses: Spanish.
UTX. Colors. EP. 42 x 58 cm.
Unpublished.
Copy: DGMH, no. 975? (44 x 60 cm. Dated Dec. 23, 1857.) Published: Cantú Treviño, 1953, opp. p. 248.
See also Appendix, 2 (calendrical drawing).
Census, 66.

38. Misquiahuala (ATENGO). Mexico. Native.
Oct. 8, 1579. Glosses: Spanish.
UTX. Colors. Parchment or vellum. 77 x 56 cm.
Unpublished.
Copy: MNA 35–15. (Colors. Paper mounted on cardboard. 77 x 56 cm.) Made by Rafael Aguirre for Exposición histórico-americana (Paso y Troncoso, 1892–93, 1: 62, no. XVIII). Published: Glass, 1964, pl. 17;
MNA 35–15A. Modern copy (before 1934) of MNA 35–15 (cardboard);
DGMH, no. 1185.
Census, 8B.

Mitlantongo. See TILANTONGO, 72.

39. MIZANTLA. Tlaxcala. Mixed.
Oct. 1, 1579. Glosses: Spanish.
UTX. Black ink. EP. 44 x 31 cm. Fols. 3v, 4r.
Published: Ramírez Lavoignet, 1962, opp. p. 16 (tracing).
Copy: DGMH, no. 1188. (Ink on heavy paper. 44 x 32 cm. Dated Dec. 13, 1857.)
Census, 67.

40. MOTUL [MUTUL]. Yucatan. European.
Feb. 20, 1581. Glosses: Spanish.
AGI, 30 (TL). Brown ink. EP. 22 x 25 cm.
Published: DIU, 11, between pp. 74 and 75.
Census, 69.

41. Muchitlan (ZUMPANGO, MINAS). Tlaxcala. Native.
Mar. 7, 1582. Glosses: Spanish, Nahuatl, and Native Pictorial.
UTX. Colors. NP. 56.5 x 76 cm.
Unpublished.
Ref: Robertson, 1959b, p. 543.
Comment: Pintura accompanies complex relación text for Tistla and Muchitlan, sub-cabeceras of MINAS DE ZUMPANGO. Tistla does not appear on the pintura. The Spanish glosses are in large part translations of population statistics given in the native pictorial system.
See also Chilapa, 12; ZUMPANGO, MINAS, 91.
Census, 132A.

42. NEXAPA, STGO. DEL VALLE DE. Antequera. Native (?)
Sept. 12, 1579–Apr. 20, 1580.
Pintura lost. Text in AGI.
Lienzo; probably large.
Refs: JLV, 1583, P-11; PNE, 4: 29, 32, 33, 38, 42.
Comment: Text refers to lienzo "de la tierra y en el todos los pueblos y estançias, rios, çerros, grutas y otras cosas . . ." (PNE, 4: 29).
Census, 73.

43. NOCHIZTLAN. Antequera. Mixed.
Apr. 9–11, 1581. Glosses: Spanish (cardinal points only).
RAH. B/w, with blue shading. EP. 30 x 41 cm.
Published: PNE 4: 206; Kubler, 1948, vol. 1, opp. p. 92, fig. 24 (after PNE).
Census, 74.

44. Papantla (GUEYTLALPA). Tlaxcala. Mixed.
May 30–July 20, 1581. Glosses: Spanish.
UTX. Colors. EP. 31 x 22 cm. Fol. 15r.
Published: García Payón, 1965, p. 68, pl. 9.
Census, 49D.

45. PEÑOLES, LOS. Antequera. European.
Aug. 20–Oct. 3, 1579. Glosses: Spanish.
UTX. Black ink. EP. 44 x 31 cm. Fols. 7v, 8r.
Unpublished.
Census, 80.

46. QUATLATLAUCA. Tlaxcala. European.
Sept. 2–5, 1579. Glosses: Spanish.
UTX. Colors. EP. 21.5 x 31 cm. Fol. 4r.
Unpublished.
Ref: Robertson, 1959b, p. 542, 545.
See also Gueguetlan, 24.
Census, 85.

47. QUERETARO. Michoacan. Native (?)
Jan. 20–Mar. 30, 1582.
Pintura lost. Text in UTX.
Lienzo; probably large.
Refs: JLV, 1583, P-8; Velásquez, 1897, 1: 30, 48; Frías, 1906, pp. 39–40, 60.
Comment: Reply to Question 10 and final sentence of text indicate that a lienzo was prepared. Last sentence also states that place names in the pintura were glossed in Nahuatl, although text gives them in Otomi.
Census, 86.

Real de los Rios. See TEMAZCALTEPEC, MINAS, 57.

48. San Miguel y San Felipe de los CHICHIMECAS. Michoacan. European.
1582? Glosses: Spanish.
RAH. Colors. EP. 61 x 83 cm.
Published: PNE, 7 (printed but not distributed with volume); Jiménez More-

no, 1944, opp. p. 144; 1958, opp. p. 90 (larger than 1944)*; Powell, 1952, line drawings in end papers; Alba, Duque de, 1951, pl. 32 (color).

Ref: JVL, 1583, 1/1 (text and pintura). Text lost but printed Instruction found in AGI.

Census, 203.

49. SUCHITEPEC [XUCHITEPEC]. Antequera. Mixed.

Aug. 23–29, 1579. Glosses: Nahuatl with some Spanish words.

AGI, 29 (TL). Colors. EP. 83 x 60 cm.

Published: PNE, 4: 26.

Ref: TL, 29 (attributes to incorrect place).

Comment: One of five pinturas in AGI covering area. Text in RAH.

See also Macupilco, 33; Tamagazcatepec, 51; Tlacotepec, 74; Zozopastepec, 90.

Census, 88.

50. TABASCO, PROVINCE. Yucatan. European.

May 2, 1579. Glosses: Spanish.

AGI, 14 (TL). Colors. EP. 60 x 57 cm.

Published: DIU, 11, opp. p. 436 (color facsimile, full scale); Maudslay, 1916, vol. 5: end pocket (color); BCE, 1920, p. 25 (nos. 36–37), repeated RNE, 1920, 4: 77 (both after PNE, tipped in): Scholes and Roys, 1948 and 1968, opp. p. 16 (drawing with English trans.).

Comment: Artist, Melchor de Alfaro Santa Cruz (DIU, 11: 317).

Census, 90.

51. Tamagazcatepec [Tlamacazcatepec], S.

Bartolome (SUCHITEPEC). Antequera. Mixed.

Aug. 23–29, 1579. Glosses: Nahuatl with some Spanish words.

AGI, 26 (TL). Colors. EP. 60 x 43.5 cm.

Published: PNE, 4: 27.

Comment: Text in RAH; pintura in AGI.

Census, 88C.

52. Tamazula (TILANTONGO). Antequera. Native (?).

Nov. 16, 1579.

Pintura lost. Text in RAH.

Physical details unknown; probably large.

Ref: JLV, 1583, P-12.

Comment: This identification is tentative but highly probable, as text response to Question 20 refers to a "pintura" (PNE, 4: 85). A text for Tamazula listed in JLV, 1583, 2/3, may refer to this cabecera. (There is also a Tamazula, subject to TUXPAN.)

See also TILANTONGO, 71, 72

Census, 127B, 213.

53. Tecolutla (GUEYTLALPA). Tlaxcala. Mixed.

May 30–July 20, 1581. Glosses: Spanish.

UTX. Colors. EP. 31 x 22 cm. Fol. 15v.

Published: García Payón, 1965, p. 67, pl. 8.

Comment: Also includes area around mouth of Rio San Pedro y San Pablo.

Census, 49E.

54. TECUICUILCO. Antequera. European.

Oct. 2, 1580. Glosses: Spanish.

UTX. B/w. EP. 31 x 22 cm.

Published: Cline, 1966b, p. 113, fig. 5.

Census, 101.

55. TEHUANTEPEC. *Pintura 1*. Antequera. Mixed.

Sept. 20–Oct. 5, 1580. Glosses: Spanish.

UTX. Colors. EP. 22 x 31 cm.

Published: Covarrubias, 1946, p. 212 (very reduced, line drawing of lower

---

* Both possibly reproduced from "exemplar" (photograph from which PNE, 7, was printed?) in AGN (Mexico), leg. 9, exp. 509, no. 1, Año 1908; see Zavala, 1938, p. 311. No. XV (Mapa de una parte del territorio de Zacatecas" [sic]), 604, and Carrera Stampa, 1949, pp. 42–43.

central part) and titlepage (line drawing, place glyph).

Copy: DGMH, no. 1184. (Pale watercolor on paper mounted on cloth. 48 x 63 cm. Dated Jan. 12, 1858.)

Census, 102.

56. TEHUANTEPEC. *Pintura* 2. Antequera. European.

Sept. 20–Oct. 5, 1580. Glosses: Spanish.

UTX. Colors. EP. 42.5 x 58 cm.
Unpublished.

Comment: Mariner's coastal chart.

Census, 102.

57. TEMAZCALTEPEC, MINAS. Mexico. European.

Synonym: Asiento de Cacaloztoc; Real de los Rios.

Dec. 1, 1579–Jan. 1, 1580. Glosses: Spanish.

AGI, 20 (TL). B/w. EP. 25 x 40.5 cm.

Published: PNE, 7: 18.

See also Temazcaltepec, 57bis; Tescaltitlan, 65; Texupilco, 70; Tuzantla, 76.

See also Appendix, 3 (animal drawings).

Census, 103.

57bis. Temazcaltepec (TEMAZCALTEPEC, MINAS). Mexico. European.

Dec. 1, 1579–Jan. 1, 1580. Glosses: Place names only.

AGI, 23 (TL). B/w. EP. 23 x 27 cm.

Published: PNE, 7: 19; Robertson, 1959a, pl. 85.

Census, 103C.

58. Tenanpulco and Matlactonatico (GUEYTLALPA). Tlaxcala. Mixed.

May 30–July 20, 1581. Glosses: Spanish.

UTX. Colors. EP. 31 x 22 cm. Fol. 16r.

Published: García Payón, 1965, p. 59, pl. 7 (also in color on cover).

Census, 49F.

59. TEOTITLAN DEL CAMINO. Antequera. Mixed.

Sept. 15–22, 1581. Glosses: Spanish.

272

RAH. B/w. EP. 85 x 42 cm.

Published: PNE, 4: 213; Robertson, 1959a, pl. 53.

Bibliog: Cline, 1964b, figs. 4, 5; 1966a, Maps 4, 5, and 9 provide reoriented diagram and locations.

Census, 107.

60. TEOZACOALCO. Antequera. Mixed.

Jan. 9–21, 1580. Glosses: Spanish; Mixtec (place names only).

UTX. Colors. EP. 138 x 176 cm. Bad condition.

Published: Benítez, 1967, pl. xi, opp. p. 320 (color).

Copy: DGMH, no. 1186. (Watercolor on heavy paper. 130 x 180 cm. Dated Feb. 17, 1858. 19th-century glosses. Copy does not record corrections in the drawing of the original.) Published: Caso, 1949a, opp. p. 176 (color), opp. p. 174 (detail), and various line drawings; 1949b (reprint of 1949a), opp. p. 40 (color), opp. p. 34 (detail), and various line drawings. Tamayo, 1949, 1: 48; 1950, p. 11; 1962, 1: 52.

Bibliog: Caso, 1949a, 1949b.

See also Amoltepec, 4.

Census, 108.

61. TEPEAPULCO [TEPENPULCO]. Mexico. Native (?).

Apr. 15, 1581.

Pintura lost. Text in AGI.

Physical details unknown; probably large.

Refs: JLV, 1583, P–3; PNE, 6: 291, n. 1, 295–96, 303–05.

Comment: Reply to Question 37 is a long description of the "pintura" (PNE, 6: 303–05).

Census, 111.

62. TEPUZTLAN. Mexico. Style unknown.

Sept. 19, 1580.

Pintura lost. Text in AGI.

Physical details unknown.

Refs: PNE, 6: 237, 238, 244, 246.

Comment: Glossed in margin at beginning of the text: "La villa de Tepuztlan y sus estancias con la pintura" (PNE, 6: 237, n. 2).

See also Acapistla, 2; Guaxtepec, 23.

Census, 112.

63. TEQUALTICHE.   Guadalajara

Native (?).

Dec. 30, 1585.

Pintura lost.   Text in UTX.

Physical details unknown.

Ref: NV, 359–60.

Comment: Text mentions "de lo contenido en la dicha pintura medyante ynterpretes . . . yndios antiguos" (NV, 360). "Un mapa de los alrededores de Tequaltiche en la Nueva España," belonging to the José Sancho Rayón Collection, Madrid, may be the missing pintura (Madrid, 1892a, p. 129, no. 883).

Census, 113.

64. TEQUIZISTLAN, Tepechpan, Acolman and San Juan Teotihuacan.   Mexico.

Mixed.

Feb. 22–Mar. 1, 1580.   Glosses: Spanish.

AGI, 17 (TL).   B/w.   EP.   61 x 145 cm.   Upper right corner missing (30 x 17.5 cm.).

Published: PNE, 6: 209 (all), 222 (detail upper central section); Gamio, 1922, vol. 1, pl. 138 (after PNE); Nuttall, 1926, pl. 1.

Census, 116.

65. Tescaltitlan [Texcaltitlan] (TEMAZCALTEPEC MINAS).   Mexico.   European.

Dec. 1, 1579–Jan. 1, 1580.   Glosses: Spanish.

AGI, 21 (TL).   B/w.   EP.   24 x 39 cm.

Published: PNE, 7: 19; Brandon, 1961, pp. 106–07.

Census, 103A.

66. Tetela, Sta. Maria Asuncion (XONOTLA).   Tlaxcala.   European.

Oct. 29, 1581.   Glosses: Spanish.

AGI, 31 (TL).   Colors.   EP.   70 x 42 cm.

Published: PNE, 5: 146; BCE, 1920, p. 29 (nos. 32–33), repeated in RNE, 1920, 4: 33 (tipped in); Pérez Bustamente, 1928a & 1929b, opp. p. 50, pl. VII (both after PNE); Blacker, 1965, p. 53 (margins cropped); García Payón, 1965, p. 86, pl. 15 (after PNE).

Ref: TL, 31, incorrectly assigns to TETELA Y UEYAPAN (TETELA DEL VOLCAN).

Census, 118.

67. Tetlistaca (CEMPOALA).   Mexico.

Mixed.

Nov. 15, 1581.   Glosses: Nahuatl.

UTX.   Colors.   EP.   31 x 43 cm.

Published: Barlow, 1949b, opp. p. 41, pl. VII.

Copy: DGMH, no. 1191.   (Watercolor on heavy paper.   EP.   33 x 45 cm.   Dated Dec. 15, 1857.) Published: Olvera, 1964, [p. 44] (line drawing of main church).

Census, 19B.

TETZAL.   Yucatan.   *See* Appendix, 4 (house drawing).

68. TEUTENANGO.   Mexico.   Mixed.

Mar. 12, 1582.   Glosses: Spanish.

AGI, 33 (TL).   Colors.   NP.   73 x 68 cm.

Published: PNE, 7: 1; BCE, 1920, p. 21 (nos. 32–33), repeated in RNE, 1920, 4: 25 (tipped in); Gómez de Orozco, 1923, p. 87; Pérez Bustamente, 1928a & 1928b, opp. p. 28, pl. IV; Toussaint, 1948a, p. 13, fig. 10; 1962, pl. 11, 1967, p. 13, pl. 4, after PNE?; Kubler, 1948, vol. 1, opp. p. 102, fig. 28; McAndrew, 1965, p. 597, fig. 320, line drawing, upper half (all after PNE).

Census, 122.

TEXCOCO.   Mexico (Pomar's Relación).   *See* Appendix, 5 (portraits of Indian rulers, etc.).

273

69. TEXUPA. Antequera. Mixed.
Oct. 20, 1579. Glosses: Spanish.
RAH. Colors. EP. 56 x 41 cm.
Published: PNE, 4: 53; León, 1933, p. 10;
Kubler, 1948, vol. 1, opp. p. 92, fig. 23;
McAndrew, 1965, p. 95, fig. 18, line
drawing, lower center (all after PNE).
Bibliog: De Blois, 1963, pl. 12.
Census, 124.

70. Texupilco (TEMACALTEPEC, MI-
NAS). Mexico. European.
Dec. 1, 1579–Jan. 1, 1580. Glosses: Place
names only.
AGI, 22 (TL). B/w. EP. 22.5 x 38
cm.
Published: PNE, 7: 19.
Census, 103B.

71. TILANTONGO. Antequera. Native
(?).
Nov. 5, 1579.
Pintura lost. Text in RAH.
Physical details unknown; probably large.
Ref: JLV, 1583, P-6, P-7, "Tilantongo,
digo dos."
Comment: Text responses to Questions 18
and 20 refer to a "pintura" (PNE, 4:
75, 76).
See also TILANTONGO (Mitlantongo?),
72; Tamazula, 52.
Census, 127.

72. TILANTONGO (Mitlantongo?). An-
tequera. Native (?).
Nov. 5 and 12, 1579.
Pintura lost. Text in RAH.
Physical details unknown; probably large.
Ref: JLV, 1583, P-6, P-7, "Tilantongo,
digo dos."
Comment: Text response to Question 20
refers to a "pintura" (PNE, 4: 81).
See also TILANTONGO, 71; Tamazula,
52.
Census, 127A.

TIRIPITIO. Michoacan. *See* Appendix, 6.

73. TLACOTALPA [TLACOTALPAN].
Tlaxcala. European.
Feb. 18–22, 1580. Glosses: Spanish.

RAH. Colors. EP. 31 x 42 cm. Up-
per right corner cut off.
Published: PNE, 5: 1; Cline, 1959, fig. 4
(after PNE); fig. 5 (diagram detail by
Cline).
Comment: Signed by Capitán Francisco
Stroza Gali and dated Feb. 5, 1580.
Mariner's coastal chart.
Census, 134.

74. Tlacotepec, San Sebastian (SUCHITE-
PEC). Antequera. Mixed.
Aug. 23–29, 1579. Glosses: Nahuatl with
some Spanish words.
AGI, 28 (TL). Colors. EP. 44 x 62
cm.
Published: PNE, 4: 26.
Comment: Text in RAH; pintura in AGI.
Census, 88A.

75. Totoltepec. Unidentified. Native (?)
Date unknown (before 1583).
Pintura lost. No known text.
Physical details unknown; probably large.
Ref: JLV, 1583, P-10.
Comment: Possibly refers to Tutultepec
in ICHCATEOPAN (Census, 52M), or
to Tototepec in XALAPA-CINTLA-
ACATLAN (Census, 142N), although
neither text mentions a pintura. A relación text for the Mixtec Tututepec
is not known to exist. Possibly it was
a sub-cabecera of one of the lost relaciones (see Cline, 1964, p. 352), and
this was its pintura.
Census (not identified).

76. Tuzantla (TEMAZCALTEPEC, MI-
NAS). Michoacan. European.
Oct. 20, 1579. Glosses: Spanish.
AGI, 23bis. B/w. EP. 23 x 38 cm.
Published: Cline, 1965, opp. p. 68.
Comment: Printed for PNE, 7, but not
distributed (Zavala, 1938, pp. 269; 311,
no. XIV; 604). *See also* PNE, 7: 15–16,
note 1. Not listed in TL.
Census, 103D.

77. USILA. Antequera. Native(?).
Oct. 2, 1579.

Pintura lost. Text in RAH.

Lienzo; probably large.

Refs: JLV, 1583, P-5; PNE, 4: 47, 52.

Comment: Glossed on the printed questionnaire: "La pintura esta aparte en vn lienço grande" (PNE, 4: 52).

Census, 138.

78. VALLADOLID. Michoacan. Native (?).

1581.

Pintura lost. Text lost.

Physical details unknown; probably large.

Ref: JLV, 1583, P-9.

Census, 219.

79. VALLADOLID. *Pintura 1.* Yucatan. European.

Apr. 8–9, 1579. Glosses: Spanish.

AGI, 15 (TL), fol. 4v/93v. B/w. EP. 25 x 21 cm.

Published: Cline, 1967, pl. 1, opp. p. 220 (top).

Comment: Plaza and main church with surrounding buildings.

Census, 139.

80. VALLADOLID. *Pintura 2.* Yucatan. European.

Apr. 8-9, 1579. Glosses: Spanish.

AGI, 15, fol. 5r/94r. B/w. EP. 16 x 21 cm.

Published: Cline, 1967, pl. 1, opp. p. 220 (bottom).

Comment: Allée of ceiba trees leading to Franciscan monastery. Not in TL. *See* DIU, 13: 20.

Census, 139.

81. VERACRUZ. *Pintura 1.* Tlaxcala. European.

Mar. 15, 1580. Glosses: Spanish.

UTX. Colors. EP. 29 x 43 cm.

Published: Wagner, 1944, p. 101, pl. 6 (line drawing); Cline, 1959, fig. 1, fig. 3 (diagram by Cline).

Copy: DGMH, no. 57.

Bibliog: Cline, 1959.

Census, 140.

82. VERACRUZ. *Pintura 2.* Tlaxcala. European.

Mar. 15, 1580. Glosses: Spanish.

UTX. Colors. EP. 29 x 43 cm.

Published: Cline, 1959, fig. 2.

Copy: DGMH (colors). Published: Ramírez Cabañas, 1943, opp. p. 18 (color); Trens, 1947, unnumbered plate (after Ramírez Cabañas, 1943).

Bibliog: Cline, 1959.

Census, 140.

83. XALAPA DE VERA CRUZ. Tlaxcala. European.

Oct. 20, 1580. Glosses: Spanish.

AGI, 18 (TL). Colors. EP. 122 x 122 cm.

Published: PNE: 5: 99; Kubler, 1948, vol. 1, opp. p. 73, fig. 19 (detail); Cline, 1959, fig. 6, fig 7 (reoriented drawing by Cline; both after PNE). Real, 1959a & 1959b pl. 1 (detail upper center) opp. p. 14/180.

Census, 141.

84. XONOTLA, SAN JUAN. Tlaxcala. European.

Oct. 20, 1581. Glosses: Spanish.

AGI, 32 (TL). Black ink with gray washes. EP. 31 x 41 cm.

Published: PNE, 5: 127; Blacker, 1965, p. 46 (margins slightly cropped); García Payón, 1965, p. 85, pl. 14 (after PNE).

See also Tetela, 66.

Census, 118A.

85. Yurirpundaro [Yuririapundaro] (CELAYA). Michoacan. European.

June 15, 1580. Glosses: Tarascan or Otomi (?).

AGI, 24 (TL). Text in RAH. Colors. EP. 83 x 89 cm.

Published: VR/PNE, 7/4, opp. p. 146 (very reduced from map printed for PNE, 7, but not published); Chevalier, 1956, p. 81 (cuts out area around edges).

Refs: Zavala, 1938, pp. 311, no. XIX; 604.

See also Acambaro, 1; CELAYA, 9; Yurirpundaro, 86.
Census, 18B.

86. Yurirpundaro [Yuririapundaro] (CELAYA). *Verso.* Michoacan. European.
June 15, 1580. Glosses: Tarascan or Otomi (?).
AGI, 24 (verso). Text in RAH. B/w (very faint). EP. 83 x 89 cm.
Unpublished.
Comment: Not formerly in literature. Main place is obscured by mending tape and cannot be identified. Glosses include: "Hancuparo/ Japinaio/ Caheriaiuo/ Ciasio/ Hirepineato (?)/ Capapentiro/ Ururiro (?)" and also "Canpielio/vilansino/ ruhut/ pa (?)."
See also Acambaro, 1; CELAYA, 9; Yurirpundaro, 85.
Census, 18B.

87. Zacatlan (GUEYTLALPA). Tlaxcala. Mixed.
May 30–July 20, 1581. Glosses: Spanish.
UTX. Colors. EP. 31 x 22 cm. Fol. 6v.
Published: García Payón, 1965, p. 45, pl. 3.
Census, 49A.

88. ZAPOTITLAN and Suchitepec [Suchitepequez]. Guatemala. European.
Nov. 22, 1579. Glosses: Spanish.
UTX. Colors. EP. 55 x 57 cm.
Published: Mapa, 1966, [p. 97].
Comment: Probably made by Fernando de Niebla, scribe; long text at foot of map explaining geography of the area.

Map includes population figures, some not in text.
See also Appendix, 7 (genealogical tree or chart of rulers).
Census, 152.

89. ZIMAPAN, MINAS. Mexico. European.
Aug. 11, 1579. Glosses: Spanish.
AGI, 13 (TL). Faded brown ink with touches of pink wash. EP. 34.5 x⁻31 cm.
Published: PNE, 6: 1; BCE, 1920, p. 17 (nos. 32–33), repeated in RNE, 1920, 4: 21 (tipped in); Pérez Bustamente, 1928a & 1928b, opp. p. 62, pl. VIII; Kubler, 1948, vol. 1, opp. p. 73, fig. 21 (all after PNE).
Census, 155.

90. Zozopastepec, Sta. Maria (SUCHITEPEC). Antequera. Mixed.
Aug. 23–29, 1579. Glosses: Nahuatl with some Spanish words.
AGI, 27 (TL). Colors. EP. 60.5 x 43 cm.
Published: PNE, 4: 27.
Comment: Text in RAH; pintura in AGI.
Census, 88B.

91. ZUMPANGO, MINAS [ZUMPANGO DEL RIO]. Mexico. Mixed.
Mar. 10, 1582. Glosses: Spanish.
RAH. Colors. NP. 70 x 71 cm.
Printed for PNE, 6, but not distributed (Zavala, 1938, pp. 311, no. XVI, "Mapa de Qualotitlan" [*sic*]; 603).
See also Chilapa, 12; Muchitlan, 41.
Census, 164.

APPENDIX. OTHER DRAWINGS AND PAINTINGS

1. AMECA. Guadalajara. UTX. Simple b/w house sketch.
   Unpublished.
   See also Catalog, 3; Census, 4.

2. MEZTITLAN. Mexico. UTX. Calendrical drawing, in description of native calendar appended to relación text.
   B/w. EP. 31 x 22 cm. Fol. 1r. European style with shading in rabbit and perspective in house.
   Unpublished.
   Copy: RAH, Col. de Muñoz, vol. XXXIX. Ms. copy fol. 1r [*sic*] by Buckingham Smith, Mar. 29, 1857, of Muñoz copy. Location unknown. Gates photocopy of Smith copy, Tulane University, Latin American Library. See Gates cats. 1924, no. 622; 1937, no. 506; 1940, p. 15. (Comment: Clearly derives from UTX original.
   Published: DII, 1865, 4: 553 (b/w diagram based on Muñoz copy with names instead of figures).
   Gómez de Orozco, 1924, p. 118. Footnote says text from DII and b/w drawing from Muñoz copy, but drawing is different: pre-Conquest-style glyphs for the figures, i.e., T-elevation temple for house, and glyphs for flint and cane. The bibliographic problem here is the source of Gómez de Orozco's drawing. Since he published his catalogue of the JGI collection just 3 years later (1927), he probably had access to the *original* MEZTITLAN relación, which is different and more Europeanized in style. Cantú Treviño, 1953, p. 260 (after DII).

Bibliog: Carrasco Pizana, 1950, 193–95 (discussion of day and month names). *See* Article 23, no. 212. *See also* Catalog, 37.
Census, 66.

3. TEMAZCALTEPEC, MINAS. Mexico. AGI.
   Two b/w drawings in text answer to Question 27:
   a. Armadillo (published: PNE, 7: 25).
   b. *Tlaquátzin* (published: PNE, 7: 26).
   See Catalog, 57.
   Census, 103.

4. TETZAL. Yucatan. AGI.
   Black ink drawing of a Maya house in text answer to Question 31.
   Published: DIU, 11: 304.
   Census, 121.

5. TEXCOCO, Pomar's Relación of. Mexico.
   Six paintings (Colors. EP. 31 x 21 cm.) now identified as Codex Ixtlilxochitl, part 2, fols. 105–112, with 2 leaves missing.
   BNP, 65–71. 4 full-length portraits of Indian nobles including Nezahualcoyotl and Nezahualpilli, rulers of Texcoco; Tlaloc; and double pyramid-temple of Texcoco (?).
   Published: Boban, 1891, 2: 114–139, pls. 66–71.
   Two missing leaves (Huitzilopochtli and Nezahualpilli seated on throne) survive through copies published various places.
   See Article 23, no. 172, for bibliographic data.
   Studies: Thompson, 1941a; Robertson, 1959a, pp. 130–33, 149–51, 201–02, pl. 52.
   Census, 123.

6. TIRIPITIO. Michoacan. UTX. Two colored drawings in text:
   a. Priest or sacerdote. Fol. 3r (unpublished).
   b. Small circular building with ladder going up base to building on top with straw roof. Fol. 14v (unpublished).
Census, 130.

7. ZAPOTITLAN. Guatemala. UTX. Genealogical tree or chart of rulers of "esta tierra," illustrating textual addendum to RG text in answer to Questions 14 and 15.
B/w. EP. 31 x 22 cm.
Published: Descripción, 1955, p. 84.
See also Catalog, 88; Census, 152.

7. The Relaciones Geográficas, 1579–1586: Native Languages

H. R. HARVEY

ONE OF THE most important bodies of source material on the native languages of Middle America for the 16th century is the *Relaciones Geográficas* (hereinafter cited as RG.) Compiled between 1578 and 1586, the RG's were responses to a comprehensive questionnaire of 1577 ordered by the Crown, soliciting basic geographic facts on the peoples and places of its American overseas possessions. There were 191 responses from Middle America, of which 167 are presently known. Of these extant documents, all but eight have been published (Cline, Article 5).

Information on native languages is explicitly requested in the questionnaire. Question 5, for example, calls for a statement as to "whether different languages are spoken throughout the whole province or whether they have one which is spoken by all" (Cline, 1964a, pp. 365–66). Questions 1 and 13 call for native place names and their meanings. Many other questions, although not directly requesting language information, allow for responses likely to contain linguistic data. Most linguistic information tends to cluster in Questions 1, 5, and 13, but relevant information may

occur virtually anywhere in the report. Most respondents followed the royal instructions, at least to the extent of naming the native language or languages within their respective jurisdictions.

The compilers were various civil officials and clerics: alcaldes, corregidores, regidores, alguaciles, judges, and priests, as well as private encomenderos. As a group, they seem to have been conscientious in their efforts to describe the situation within their jurisdictions. For example, not infrequently a language or dialect will be compared with a well-known referent such as Nahuatl of the Mexicans. Occasionally, a comment on pronunciation is made, or vocabulary is included for illustration. As with any questionnaire response, modern or ancient, the reliability of the information varies according to the integrity and knowledge of the person making the response. Clearly, some of the individual RG's not only are more informative, but are also more reliable than others.

There was among the Spaniards, moreover, a considerable familiarity with the more important Indian languages. Missionary-priests were regularly administering to

279

their congregations in native dialects. Courts of law were accepting testimony in Indian languages and appointing official interpreters. Even legal documents, when they concerned Indians, were often translated from Spanish into native languages. In fact, Nahuatl had virtually become the second language of the courts in Central Mexico. Dictionaries and grammars, together with catechisms, *doctrinas*, and confessionals were published in or related to Indian languages, and some, like Molina's *Vocabulario*, had by 1580 undergone several editions. A listing of those items relating to native languages known to have been published in New Spain through the 1580's appears as Appendix A to this article.

For the Spaniard, the great drama of the 16th century was the conquest; for the Indian, it was the decades that followed. When the Spaniards arrived in 1519, there were by a recent estimate 25 million people in Central Mexico (Borah and Cook, 1963). Six decades later, the native population in the area had declined to an estimated 1,900,000 (Cook and Borah, 1960). By this time, whole societies had become extinct; others were already in their twilight. Greedy as they seem to have been for facts —the Crown, the church, the chroniclers —some Indian groups escaped their attention before much was recorded. For some of them, however, the countless unexploited manuscripts that are part of the historical legacy of 16th-century Mexico still hold promise.

While the RG's are the most extensive series of reports covering native languages in the 16th century, they cover approximately only half of the region between Nueva Galicia and Central America. From this substantial sample, however, it is apparent that Middle America was an area of extraordinary linguistic complexity.

CLASSIFICATIONS

The first systematic modern effort to clarify both the historical and the contemporary situation was published in 1864 by Orozco y Berra (1864). In his classification, Orozco y Berra arranged 35 subgroups into 11 families, left 16 languages unclassified, and listed 62 others as extinct. Since that day a century ago numerous classifications have appeared. The general trend has been in the direction of establishing fewer, but more inclusive, groupings—toward the recognition of more remote relationships.

The task of classification has always been fraught with problems. Until recently, there has been a paucity of modern descriptive and comparative linguistic studies. Only 25 years ago, Mason noted (1940, p. 55) that for most Middle American languages ". . . we have only vocabularies made long ago by men without training in phonetics or linguistics, on many not even that much." Even given good material, the problem of establishing affinity between languages is one thing; the problem of determining the degree and order of relationship is quite another.

All the languages reported in the RG's are tabulated in the "Language Index" (Tables 1–3). The lists include 39 languages which are classifiable, 30 which are not. Of those classifiable, 30 are still spoken today. The remaining nine are extinct, but are known from descriptions in the literature. Most of the unclassifiable languages are those for which inadequate information exists to establish linguistic affinities. The majority of these appear to have been of extremely limited distribution and to have disappeared early.

For present purposes, the languages reported in the RG's are divided into six main groups (represented by roman numerals in Tables 1–3). To a large extent, these reflect the linguistic groups at the stock, superstock, or phylum level, the "macro" groupings, which have long been in use. The subdivisions are represented by arabic numerals, and refer to the "micro" groupings

280

Table 1—LANGUAGE INDEX TO
RELACIONES GEOGRÁFICAS

I.	**UTO-AZTECAN**	
	Related:	Coca
		Guachichil
		Tecoxquin
	1. Nahua	Cazcan (?)
		Cuisca
		Mexicano
		Pipil
		Sayultec (?)
		Zacatec (?)
II.	**MACRO-OTOMANGUEAN**	
	Related:	Pinoles (?)
	1. Pame-Otomian	Matlatzinca
		Mazahua
		Otomi
	2. Mixtecan	Amusgo
		Cuicatec
		(Quiotec)
		Mixtec
	3. Popolocan	Chocho
		Mazatec
		Popoloca
	4. Zapotecan	Zapotec
	5. Chinantecan	Chinantec
III.	**MACRO-MAYAN**	
	1. Mayan	Achi
		Chontal
		Mam
		Maya (Yucatec)
		Tzeltal (?)
		Tzotzil (?)
		Uhtlatec
		Zutuhil
	2. Totonacan	Tepehua
		Totonac
	3. Mixe-Zoquean	Mixe
		Popoluca
		Zoque
	4. Huave	Guazontec (Huave)
IV.	**TARASCAN**	Tarascan
V.	**HOKALTECAN**	
	1. Tlapanecan	Tlapanec
	2. Tequistlatecan	Chontal (Oaxaca)
VI.	**UNCLASSIFIED**	
		Apanec
		Ayacastec
		Cintec
		Chichimec
		Chontal de Guerrero
		Chunbia
		Cochin
		Cuacumanes
		Cuitlatec
		Culiaretes
		Huehuetec
		Iscuca
		Izteca
		Mazatec de Guerrero
		Mazatec de Jalisco
		Melagueses
		Otomi de Jalisco
		Pantec
		Pocotec
		Quacomec
		Quahutec
		Tamazultec
		Tepuztec
		Tiam
		Tolimec
		Tomatec
		Totonac de Jalisco
		Tuztec
		Xocotec
		Zapotec de Jalisco

—the language or family level. When it is reasonably certain that a language pertains to a particular microgroup, it is represented in Tables 1–3 by the appropriate combination of roman and arabic numerals, e.g., II.3 or III.1. In those instances where the microaffiliation is not certain, but the macroaffiliation is reasonably so, it is simply assigned a roman numeral.

The groupings included in Table 1 are as follows: Group I consists of Uto-Aztecan languages. Its only identifiable subgroup mentioned in this body of documents is Nahua, which is represented as I.1. Group II contains: 1. Pame-Otomian; 2. Mixtecan; 3. Popolocan; 4. Zapotecan; 5. Chinantecan. These were included by Mason in his Macro-Otomangue Phylum.[1] Group III in-

[1] There has been extensive comparative linguistic work among the languages included in this phylum since Mason's classification appeared (Mason, 1940). For present purposes, however, Mason's classification is still the most useful benchmark for a comprehensive classification of the languages of Mexico, and for this group of languages in particular. See also Longacre, 1957; Gudschinsky, 1959; Fernández de Miranda and Weitlaner, 1961; Swadesh, 1960; Longacre, 1961.

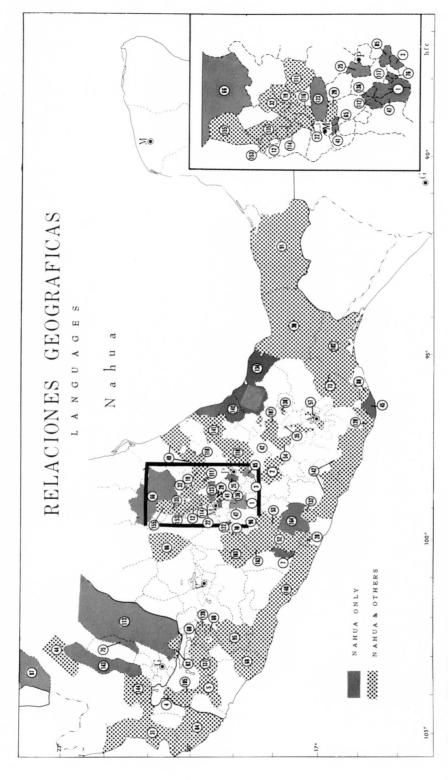

RELACIONES GEOGRAFICAS

LANGUAGES

N a h u a

NAHUA ONLY

NAHUA & OTHERS

Fɪɢ. 1—DISTRIBUTION OF NAHUA, CA. 1580
Numbers refer to Table 2.

TABLE 2—LANGUAGE INDEX TO RELACIONES GEOGRÁFICAS,
BY PRINCIPAL DOCUMENTS

Census No.[*]	Communities	Diocese	Languages	Group and Subgroup
1	ACAPISTLA	MX	Mexicano	I.1
2	ACATLAN	T	Mixtec	II.2
	A. Chila		Mixtec	II.2
	B. Petlaltzingo		Mixtec	II.2
	C. Icxitlan		Mixtec	II.2
	D. Piastla		Mexicano	I.1
3	AHUATLAN	T	Mexicano	I.1
	A. Texaluca		Mexicano	I.1
	B. Zoyatitlanapa		Mexicano	I.1
	C. Coatzinco		Mexicano	I.1
4	AMECA	NG	Mexicano	I.1
			Cazcan	I.1 (?)
			Totonac (de Jalisco)	VI
5	AMULA	NG		
	A. Cusalapa		Mexicano	I.1
			Otomi (de Jalisco)	VI
	B. Tuscaquesco		Mexicano	I.1
			Otomi (de Jalisco)	VI
	C. Zapotitlan		Mexicano	I.1
			Otomi (de Jalisco)	VI
6	ANTEQUERA	A	Mexicano	I.1
			Mixtec	II.2
			Zapotec	II.4
7	ASUCHITLAN	MN	Cuitlatec	VI
	A. Coyuca		?	
	B. Pungaravato		Tarascan	IV
	C. Cuzamala		Tarascan	IV
	X - Tetela		Mexicano	I.1
	X - Capulalcoculco		Mexicano	I.1
8	ATENGO	MX	Otomi	II.1
9	ATITLAN	G	Zutuhil	III.1
			Achi	III.1
			Uhtlatec	III.1
			Mexicano	I.1
	A. Aguatepec		Pipil	I.1
10	ATLATLAUCA	MX	Mexicano	I.1
			Matlatzinca	II.1
11	ATLATLAUCA	A	Cuicatec	II.2
	A. Malinaltepec		Chinantec	II.5
12	ATITLALQUIA	MX	Otomi	II.1
			Mexicano	I.1
13	CACALAC & TAMUY	Y	?[Maya]	III.1
14	CACALCHEN	Y	?[Maya]	III.1
15	CAMPOCOLCHE	Y	?[Maya]	III.1
16	CANACHE (Cinanche)	Y	?[Maya]	III.1
17	CANZACABO	Y	Maya	III.1

[*]Diocese and archdiocese abbreviations: A, Antequera; G, Guatemala; MN, Michoacan; MX, Mexico; NG, Guadalajara (Nueva Galicia); T, Tlaxcala; Y, Yucatan. Census numbers are from Article 8. Communities with prefix "X" are not in the Census; they were added by the author.

(*Table 2, continued*)

Census No.*	Communities	Diocese	Languages	Group and Subgroup
18	CELAYA	MN	Spanish	
	A. Acambaro		Tarascan	IV
			Otomi	II.1
			Mazahua	II.1
			Chichimec	VI
	B. Yurirpundaro		Tarascan	IV
			Chichimec	VI
19	CEMPOALA	MX	Mexicano	I.1
			Otomi	II.1
			Chichimec	VI
	A. Epazoyuca		Mexicano	I.1
			Otomi	II.1
			Chichimec	VI
	B. Tetlistaca		Mexicano	I.1
			Otomi	II.1
20	CHANCENOTE	Y	?[Maya]	III.1
21	CHICHICAPA	A	Zapotec	II.4
	A. Amatlan		Zapotec	II.4
	B. Miaguatlan		Zapotec	II.4
	C. Coatlan		Zapotec	II.4
	D. Ozelotepec		Zapotec	II.4
22	CHICONAUTLA	MX	Mexicano	I.1
			Otomi	II.1
22 bis	CHILAPA	T	Mexicano	I.1
23	CHILCHOTLA	MN	Tarascan	IV
24	CHINANTLA	A	Chinantec	II.5
25	CHOLULA	T	Mexicano	I.1
26	CHUBULNA	Y	Maya	III.1
27	CHUNCHUCHU	Y	Maya	III.1
28	CITLALTOMAGUA	MX	Mexicano	I.1
			Tepuztec	VI
	A. Anecuilco		Tepuztec	VI
	X - Tepetistla		different from Tepuztec	VI
	X - Xahualtepec		Mexicano	I.1
			Tepuztec	VI
29	COATEPEC	MX	Mexicano	I.1
			Otomi	II.1
	A. Chimalhuacan Toyac		Mexicano	I.1
	B. Chicoaloapa		Mexicano	I.1
	X - Sta. Ana Tetitlan		Otomi (subjects)	II.1
	X - S. Miguel Tepetlapa		Otomi (estancia)	II.1
	X - S. Fco. Aquautla		?	
	X - Stgo. Quatlapanaca		?	
30	COATZOCOALCO	A	Mexicano	I.1
			Popoluca	III.3
			Mixtec	II.2
			Zapotec	II.4

*Diocese and archdiocese abbreviations: A, Antequera; G, Guatemala; MN, Michoacan; MX, Mexico; NG, Guadalajara (Nueva Galicia); T, Tlaxcala; Y, Yucatan. Census numbers are from Article 8. Communities with prefix "X" are not in the Census; they were added by the author.

(Table 2, continued)

Census No.*	Communities	Diocese	Languages	Group and Subgroup
31	COMPOSTELA	NG	Mexicano	I.1
			Tecoxquin	I
32	CUAUHQUILPAN	MX	Mexicano	I.1
			Otomi	II.1
33	CUAHUITLAN	A	Mixtec	II.2
34	CUAUTLA	A	Mixtec	II.2
	A. Xocoticpac		Mixtec	II.2
	B. Xaltepetongo		Mixtec	II.2
	C. Tutupetongo		Cuicatec	II.2
	D. Tanatepec		Cuicatec	II.2
35	CUICATLAN	A	Cuicatec	II.2
			Mexicano	I.1
36	CUICUIL	Y	?[Maya]	III.1
37	CUILAPA	A	Mixtec	II.2
38	CUISEO DE LA LAGUNA	MN	Tarascan	IV
39	CUITELCUM	Y	Maya	III.1
40	CUIZIL	Y	Maya	III.1
41	CULHUACAN	MX	Mexicano	I.1
42-43	CUZCATLAN	T	Mexicano	I.1
			Chocho	II.3
			Mazatec	II.3
44	FRESNILLO	NG	Guachichil	I
			Zacatec	I.1(?)
			Others	VI
45	GUATULCO	A	Mexicano	I.1
	A. Pochutla		Mexicano	I.1
	B. Tonameca		Mexicano	I.1
46	GUAXOLOTITLAN	A	Mixtec	II.2
			Zapotec	II.4
47	GUAXTEPEC	MX	Mexicano	I.1
48	GUAYMA	Y	?[Maya]	III.1
49	GUEYTLALPA	T	Totonac	III.2
			Mexicano	I.1
	A. Zacatlan		Mexicano	I.1
			Totonac	III.2
	B. Jujupango		Mexicano	I.1
			Totonac	III.2
	C. Matatlan-Chila		Totonac	III.2
	D. Papantla		Totonac	III.2
50	HOCABA	Y	?[Maya]	III.1
51	HUEXOTLA	MX	Mexicano	I.1
			Tepehua	III.2
52	ICHCATEOPAN	MX	Mexicano	I.1
			Tuztec (formerly)	VI
			Chontal	VI
	A. Tzicaputzalco		Mazatec	VI
	B. Alaustlan		Chontal	VI

*Diocese and archdiocese abbreviations: A, Antequera; G, Guatemala; MN, Michoacan; MX, Mexico; NG, Guadalajara (Nueva Galicia); T, Tlaxcala; Y, Yucatan. Census numbers are from Article 8. Communities with prefix "X" are not in the Census; they were added by the author.

(*Table 2, continued*)

Census No.*	Communities	Diocese	Languages	Group and Subgroup
	C. Ostuma		Mexicano	I.1
			Chontal	VI
	D. Acapetlaguaya		Mexicano	I.1
	E. Cuatepec		Chontal	VI
	F. Tlacotepec		Tepustec	VI
	G. Utatlan		Tepustec	VI
	H. Tetela del Rio		Cuitlatec	VI
	I. Cuezala		Mexicano	I.1
	J. Apastla		Chontal	VI
	K. Tenepatlan		?	
	L. Teloloapan		Iscuca	VI
			Chontal	VI
			Mexicano	I.1
	M. Tutultepec		Chontal	VI
53	IGUALA	MX	Cuisca	I
			Chontal (Tustec)	VI
	A. Cocula		Cuisca	I.1
			Matlatzinca	II.1
	B. Tepecuacuilco		Mexicano	I.1
			Cuisca	I.1
			Chontal	VI
	C. Mayanala		Cuisca	I.1
			Mexicano	I.1
	D. Hoapa		?	
	E. Tasmaloca		Cuisca	I.1
	F. Izuco		?	
54	IXCATLAN	A	Chocho	II.3
			Mexicano	I.1
	A. Quiotepec		Quioteca (Cuicatec)	II.2
	B. Tecomabaca		Pinoles	II(?)
55	IXMUL	Y	?[Maya]	III.1
56	IXTAPALAPA	MX	Mexicano	I.1
57	IXTEPEXIC	A	Zapotec	II.4
			Mexicano	I.1
58	IZAMAL	Y	Maya	III.1
59	IZTEPEC	A	Zapotec	II.4
60	JILQUILPAN	MN	Mexicano	I.1
			Tarascan	IV
			Sayultec	I.1(?)
	A. Chocondiran		Tarascan	IV
	B. Tarecuato		Tarascan	IV
	C. Perivan		Tarascan	IV
61	JUSTLAVACA	A	Mixtec	II.2
			Mexicano	I.1

*Diocese and archdiocese abbreviations: A, Antequera; G, Guatemala; MN, Michoacan; MX, Mexico; NG, Guadalajara (Nueva Galicia); T, Tlaxcala; Y, Yucatan. Census numbers are from Article 8. Communities with prefix "X" are not in the Census; they were added by the author.

(*Table 2, continued*)

Census No.*	Communities	Diocese	Languages	Group and Subgroup
	A. Tecomastlauaca		Mixtec	II.2
			Mexicano	I.1
	B. Mistepec		Mixtec	II.2
			Mexicano	I.1
	C. Ayusuchiquilazala		Mixtec	II.2
			Amusgo	II.2
	D. Xicayan de Tovar		Amusgo	II.2
			Mixtec	II.2
	E. Puctla		Mixtec	II.2
			Mexicano	I.1
	F. Zacatepec		Mixtec	II.2
			Mexicano	I.1
			Amusgo	II.2
62	MACUILSUCHIL	A	Zapotec	II.4
	A. Teotitlan del Valle		Zapotec	II.4
63	MAMA	Y	?[Maya]	III.1
64	MERIDA	Y	Maya	III.1
65	MEXICATZINGO	MX	Mexicano	I.1
66	MEZTITLAN	MX	Mexicano	I.1
67	MISANTLA	T	Totonac	III.2
	X - Nanacatlan		Totonac	III.2
	X - Pilopa		Totonac	III.2
	X - Poztectlan		Totonac	III.2
68	MOTINES	MN		
	A. Cualcolman		Mexicano	I.1
			Quacumec (Tlaotli)	VI
	B. Maquili		Mexicano	I.1
			"muchas lenguas"	VI
	C. Motin		?	
	D. Pomar		?	
69	MOTUL	Y	Maya	III.1
70	MOXOPIPE	Y	Maya	III.1
71	NABALON	Y	?[Maya]	III.1
72	NECOTLAN	MN	Otomi	II.1
			Tarascan	IV
73	NEXAPA	A	Zapotec	II.4
	X -Quesatepec		Mixe	III.3
	X - Xilotepec		Mixe	III.3
	X - Nanacatepec		Chontal (de Oaxaca)	V.2
			Mexican interpreters in all parts	
74	NOCHIZTLAN	A	Mixtec	II.2
75	NUCHISTLAN	NG	Cazcan	I.1(?)
			Mexicano	I.1
76	OCOPETLAYUCA	MX	Mexicano	I.1
77	OSCUZCAS	Y	?[Maya]	III.1

*Diocese and archdiocese abbreviations: A, Antequera; G, Guatemala; MN, Michoacan; MX, Mexico; NG, Guadalajara (Nueva Galicia); T, Tlaxcala; Y, Yucatan. Census numbers are from Article 8. Communities with prefix "X" are not in the Census; they were added by the author.

(Table 2, continued)

Census No.*	Communities	Diocese	Languages	Group and Subgroup
78	PAPALOTICPAC	A	Cuicatec	II.2
	A. Tepeucila		Cuicatec	II.2
79	PATZCUARO	MN	Tarascan	IV
80	PEÑOLES, LOS	A		
	A. Eztitla		Mixtec	II.2
	B. Huiztepec		Mixtec	II.2
	C. Itzcuintepec		Mixtec	II.2
	D. Cuauxoloticpac		Mixtec	II.2
	E. Elotepec		Zapotec	II.4
	F. Totomachapa		Zapotec	II.4
81	PIJOY	Y	?[Maya]	III.1
82	PONCITLAN	NG	Coca	I
			Mexicano	I.1
	A. Cuiseo del Rio		Coca	I
83	POPOLA	Y	Maya ("achmaya")	III.1
84	PURIFICACION, Villa	NG	Mexicano	I.1
			Culiaretes	VI
			Mazatec	VI
			Izteca	VI
			Pocotec	VI
			Melaguese	VI
			Tomatec	VI
			Cuacumanes	VI
	[Reported that each of 23 Indian settlements spoke different languages, for which they had no local names.]			
85	QUATLATLAUCA	T	Mexicano	I.1
	A. Gueguetlan		Mexicano	I.1
86	QUERETARO	MN	Otomi	II.1
			Mexicano	I.1
	X - Xilotepec		Otomi	II.1
			Mexicano	I.1
87	SAN MARTIN, Villa	NG	Zacatec	I.1(?)
88	SUCHITEPEC	A	Zapotec	II.4
			Mexicano (old people)	I.1
	A. Tlacotepec		Chontal (de Oaxaca)	V.2
	B. Zozopastepec		Chontal (de Oaxaca)	V.2
	C. Tamaspaltepec		Chontal (de Oaxaca)	V.2
	D. Macupilco		Chontal (de Oaxaca)	V.2
89-91	TABASCO	Y	Mexicano	I.1
			Zoque	III.3
			Chontal	III.1
92	TAHZIB	Y	Maya	III.1
93	TAIMEO	MN	Otomi	II.1
94	TALISTACA	A	Zapotec	II.4

*Diocese and archdiocese abbreviations: A, Antequera; G, Guatemala; MN, Michoacan; MX, Mexico; NG, Guadalajara (Nueva Galicia); T, Tlaxcala; Y, Yucatan. Census numbers are from Article 8. Communities with prefix "X" are not in the Census; they were added by the author.

(*Table 2, continued*)

Census No.°	Communities	Diocese	Languages	Group and Subgroup
95	TANCITARO	MN	Tarascan	IV
			Mexicano	I.1
	A. Tlapalcatepec		Tarascan	IV
	X - Sta. Ana Tetlaman		Mexicano	I.1
	X - Stgo. Acauat		Tarascan	IV
			Mexicano	I.1
96	TAXCO, MINAS	MX	Mexicano	I.1
			Tarascan	IV
			Mazatec	VI
			Chontal	VI
97	TEABO	Y	Maya	III.1
98	TECAL	Y	Maya	III.1
99	TECANTO	Y	Maya	III.1
100	TECON	Y	?[Maya]	III.1
101	TECUICUILCO	A	Zapotec	II.4
	A. Atepec		Zapotec	II.4
	B. Zoquiapa		Zapotec	II.4
	C. Xaltianguis		Zapotec	II.4
102	TEHUANTEPEC	A	Zapotec	II.4
			Mexicano	I.1
			Mixe	III.3
			Mixtec	II.2
	A. Xalapa		Zapotec	II.4
			Mixe	III.3
			Mixtec	II.2
	B. Tequezistlan		Zapotec	II.4
			Chontal	V.2
	X - Coast towns		Guazontec (Huave)	III.4
103	TEMAZCALTEPEC, MINAS	MX	Mexicano	I.1
			Matlatzinca	II.1
	A. Tescaltitlan		Matlatzinca	II.1
			Mexicano	I.1
	B. Texupilco		Matlatzinca	II.1
			Mexicano	I.1
	C. Temazcaltepec, pueblo		Matlatzinca	II.1
			Mazahua	II.1
			Mexicano	I.1
	D. Tuzantla	MN	Tarascan	IV
			Mazahua	II.1
104	Temul	Y	?[Maya]	III.1
105	TENANMAZTLAN	NG	Mexicano	I.1
			Unidentified	VI
			Unidentified	VI
106	TENUM	Y	?[Maya]	III.1
107	TEOTITLAN DEL CAMINO	A	Mexicano	I.1
	A. Matzatlan		Mazatec	II.3
			Mexicano	I.1

°Diocese and archdiocese abbreviations: A, Antequera; G, Guatemala; MN, Michoacan; MX, Mexico; NG, Guadalajara (Nueva Galicia); T, Tlaxcala; Y, Yucatan. Census numbers are from Article 8. Communities with prefix "X" are not in the Census; they were added by the author.

(*Table 2, continued*)

Census No.*	Communities	Diocese	Languages	Group and Subgroup
	B. Huautla		Mexicano	I.1
			Mazatec	II.3
	C. Nextepec		Mexicano	I.1
			Mazatec	II.3
	D. Nanahuatepec		Mazatec	II.3
			Mexicano	I.1
	E. Tecolutla		Mexicano	I.1
			Mazatec	II.3
108	TEOZACOALCO	A	Mixtec	II.2
	A. Amoltepec		[Mixtec]	II.2
109	TEOZAPOTLAN	A	Zapotec	II.4
	A. Cuylapa		Mixtec	II.2
110	TEPEACA	T	Mexicano	I.1
			Otomi	II.1
	A. Tecamachalco		Mexicano (nobles)	I.1
			Otomi	II.1
			Popoloca	II.3
	B. Cachula		Mexicano,	I.1
			Popoloca	II.3
			Otomi	II.1
	C. Tecali		?	
111	TEPEAPULCO	MX	Mexicano	I.1
			Otomi	II.1
			Chichimec	VI
112	TEPUZTLAN	MX	Mexicano	I.1
113	TEQUALTICHE	NG	Cazcan	I.1(?)
			Mexicano	I.1
114	TEQUISQUIAC	MX	Mexicano	I.1
			Otomi	II.1
	A. Citlaltepec		Mexicano	I.1
			Otomi	II.1
	B. Xilocingo		Mexicano	I.1
			Otomi	II.1
115	TEQUITE	Y	Maya	III.1
116	TEQUIZISTLAN	MX	Mexicano	I.1
	A. Tepexpa		Mexicano	I.1
			Otomi	II.1
	B. Aculma		Mexicano	I. 1
			Otomi	II.1
	C. San Juan Teotihuacan		Mexicano	I. 1
			Otomi	II.1
			Popoloca	II.3
117	TETELA DEL VOLCAN	MX	Mexicano	I.1
118	TETELA-XONOTLA	T		
	A. Xonotla		Mexicano	I.1
			Totonac	III.2
	X - San Martin Tutzamapa		Totonac	III.2
			Mexicano	I.1

*Diocese and archdiocese abbreviations: A, Antequera; G, Guatemala; MN, Michoacan; MX, Mexico; NG, Guadalajara (Nueva Galicia); T, Tlaxcala; Y, Yucatan. Census numbers are from Article 8. Communities with prefix "X" are not in the Census; they were added by the author.

(*Table 2, continued*)

Census No.*	Communities	Diocese	Languages	Group and Subgroup
	X - San Francisco		Mexicano	I.1
			Totonac	III.2
	X - San Estevan		Mexicano	I.1
	X - Stgo. Ecatlan		Totonac	III.2
			Mexicano	I.1
	X - San Miguel Capulalapa		Mexicano	I.1
	X - S. F. Cucumba		Mexicano	I.1
	X - San Juan Tututla		Mexicano	I.1
119	TETICPAC	A	Zapotec	II.4
120	TETIQUIPA–RIO HONDO	A	Zapotec	II.4
	A. Cozautepec		Zapotec	II.4
			Mexicano	I.1
121	TETZAL	Y	Chontal [Tzeltal?]	III.1
122	TEUTENANGO	MX	Mexicano	I.1
			Matlatzinca	II.1
123	TEXCOCO	MX	Mexicano	I.1
124	TEXUPA	A	Mixtec	II.2
			Chocho	II.3
125	TEZEMI	Y	?[Maya]	III.1
126	TEZOCO	Y	?[Maya]	III.1
127	TILANTONGO	A	Mixtec	II.2
	A. Mitlantongo		Mixtec	II.2
	B. Tamazula		Mixtec	II.2
128	TINGUINDIN	MN	Tarascan	IV
			Mexicano (women)	I.1
129	TIQUIBALON	Y	?[Maya]	III.1
130	TIRIPITIO	MN	Tarascan	IV
131	TISHOTZUCO	Y	?[Maya]	III.1
132	TISTLA	T	Mexicano	I.1
			Matlatzinca	II.1
			Tustec	VI
133	TLACOLULA	A	Zapotec	II.4
	A. Miquitla		Zapotec	II.4
134	TLACOTALPA	T	Mexicano	I.1
	A. Cotastla		Mexicano	I.1
	B. Tuztla		Mexicano	I.1
135	TORNACUSTLA, MINAS	MX		
	A. Axocupan		Otomi	II.1
			Mexicano	I.1
	B. Yetecomac		Otomi	II.1
	C. Tornacustla, pueblo		Otomi	II.1
			Mexicano	I.1
	D. Gueypuchtla		Otomi	II.1
			Mexicano	I.1

*Diocese and archdiocese abbreviations: A, Antequera; G, Guatemala; MN, Michoacan; MX, Mexico; NG, Guadalajara (Nueva Galicia); T, Tlaxcala; Y, Yucatan. Census numbers are from Article 8. Communities with prefix "X" are not in the Census; they were added by the author.

(*Table 2, continued*)

Census No.[*]	Communities	Diocese	Languages	Group and Subgroup
	E. Tezcatepec		Otomi	II.1
	F. Teopatepec		Otomi	II.1
			Mexicano	I.1
136	TOTOLAPA	MX	Mexicano	I.1
137	TUXPAN	MN	Mexicano	I.1
			Tiam	VI
			Cochin	VI
	A. Zapotlan		Mexicano	I.1
			Tarascan	IV
			Sayultec	1.1(?)
			Zapotec (local)	VI
	B. Tamatzula		Mexicano	I.1
			Tarascan	IV
			Tamatzultec	VI
138	USILA	A	Chinantec	II.5
			Mexicano (principales)	I.1
139	VALLADOLID, VILLA	Y	Maya	III.1
140	VERACRUZ	T	Mexicano	I.1
141	XALAPA DE LA VERA CRUZ	T	Mexicano	I.1
	A. Xilotepec		Totonac	III.2
			Mexicano	I.1
	B. Tlaculula		Totonac	III.2
			Mexicano	I.1
	C. Cuacuazintla		?	
	D. Chepultepec		Totonac	III.2
			Mexicano	I.1
	E. Naolingo		Totonac	III.2
			Mexicano	I.1
	F. Acatlan		?	
	G. Miaguatlan		Totonac	III.2
			Mexicano	I.1
	H. Chiconquiyauca		Totonac	III.2
			Mexicano	I.1
	I. Colipa		Totonac	III.2
	J. Ciguacoatlan		Totonac	III.2
			Mexicano	I.1
	K. Tepetlan		Totonac	III.2
	L. Almoloncan		Totonac	III.2
			Mexicano	I.1
	M. Maxtlatlan		?	
	N. Chiltoyac		Totonac	III.2
			Mexicano	I.1
	O. Atescac		Mexicano	I.1
	P. Xalcomulco		?	
	Q. Cuatepec		?	
	R. Xicochimalco		?	
	S. Izguacan		Mexicano	I.1

[*]Diocese and archdiocese abbreviations: A, Antequera; G, Guatemala; MN, Michoacan; MX, Mexico; NG, Guadalajara (Nueva Galicia); T, Tlaxcala; Y, Yucatan. Census numbers are from Article 8. Communities with prefix "X" are not in the Census; they were added by the author.

(*Table 2, continued*)

Census No.*	Communities	Diocese	Languages	Group and Subgroup
142	XALAPA-CINTLA-ACA-TLAN	T/A		
	A. Xicayan	A	Amusgo	II.2
			Mixtec	II.2
	B. Ayozinapa	A	Amusgo	II.2
	C. Ometepec	A	Amusgo	II.2
			Ayacastec	VI
	D. Suchistlauca	A	Amusgo	II.2
	E. Tlaculula	A	Mexicano	I.1
	F. Huehuetlan	A	Huehuetec	VI
			Mexicano	I.1
	G. Ihualapa	A	Amusgo	II.2
			Ayacaztec	VI
	H. Cintla	T	Tlapanec	V.1
			Cintec	VI
			Mexicano	I.1
	I. Tepetlapa	T	Tlapanec	V.1
			Mexicano	I.1
	J. Copalitas	T	Mexicano	I.1
	K. Xalapa	T	Mexicano	I.1
	L. Nespa	T	Mexicano	I.1
	M. Cuahutepec	T	Mexicano	I.1
	N. Tototepec	T	Mexicano	I.1
	O. Ayutla	T	Tlapanec	V.1
	P. Suchitonala	T	Tlapanec	V.1
	Q. Acatlan	T	Tlapanec	V.1
	R. Cuacoyolichan	T	Tlapanec	V.1
	S. Colutla	T	Tlapanec	V.1
	T. Azoyuque	A	Tlapanec	V.1
	U. Cuahuitlan	A	Quahutec	VI
			Mexicano	I.1
	V. Cuahuzapotla	A	Zapotec	II.4
143	XEREZ, VILLA	NG	Zacatec	I.1(?)
	A. Taltenango		Mexicano	I.1
			Cazcan	I.1(?)
144	XOCOTLAN, MINAS	NG	Xocotec	VI
			Mexicano	I.1
145	XOQUEN	Y	?[Maya]	III.1
146	YALCON	Y	?[Maya]	III.1
147	YUCATAN	Y	Maya	III.1
148	ZACATULA	MN	Mexicano	I.1
	A. Teccomatan		Cuitlatec	VI
			Tepuztec	VI
	B. Azuchitlan		Cuitlatec	VI
			Tepuztec	VI
	C. Tamalacan		Cuitlatec	VI
			Tepuztec	VI

*Diocese and archdiocese abbreviations: A, Antequera; G, Guatemala; MN, Michoacan; MX, Mexico; NG, Guadalajara (Nueva Galicia); T, Tlaxcala; Y, Yucatan. Census numbers are from Article 8. Communities with prefix "X" are not in the Census; they were added by the author.

(*Table 2, continued*)

Census No.[*]	Communities	Diocese	Languages	Group and Subgroup
	D. Pantla		Panteca	VI
	E. Iztapan		Panteca	VI
	F. Tamaluacan		Tarascan	IV
	G. Vitaluta		Chunbia	VI
	H. Guauayutla		Chunbia	VI
	I. Coyuquila		Chunbia	VI
	J. Pochutla		Tolimeca	VI
	K. Chepila		Tolimeca	VI
	L. Toliman		Tolimeca	VI
	M. Suchitlan		Tolimeca	VI
	N. Zacualpa		Mexicano	I.1
149	ZAMA	Y	?[Maya]	III.1
150	ZAMAHIL	Y	?[Maya]	III.1
151	ZAN	Y	Maya	III.1
152	ZAPOTITLAN	G	Achi	III.1
			Mam	III.1
			Mexicano	I.1
153	ZAYULA	MX	Otomi	II.1
			Mexicano	I.1
154	ZICAB	Y	?[Maya]	III.1
155	ZIMAPAN, MINAS	MX	Otomi	II.1
			Mexicano	I.1
			Chichimec	VI
156	ZINAGUA	MN	?	
157	ZIRANDARO	MN	Tarascan	IV
	A. Guaymeo		Tarascan	IV
			Apanec	VI
	B. Cusco		Tarascan	IV
	C. Guetamo		Matlatzinca	II.1
158	ZISMOPO	Y	?[Maya]	III.1
159	ZIZINTUM	Y	?[Maya]	III.1
160	ZONOT	Y	?[Maya]	III.1
161	ZOTUTA	Y	Maya	III.1
162	ZOZIL	Y	?[Maya] [Tzotzil?]	III.1
163	ZULTEPEC, MINAS	MX	Mexicano	I.1
			Matlatzinca	II.1
			Mazatec	VI
			Tarascan	IV
164	ZUMPANGO, MINAS	MX	Mexicano	I.1
165	ZUSOPO	Y	?[Maya]	III.1
166	ZUZAL	Y	Maya	III.1

[*]Diocese and archdiocese abbreviations: A, Antequera; G, Guatemala; MN, Michoacan; MX, Mexico; NG, Guadalajara (Nueva Galicia); T, Tlaxcala; Y, Yucatan. Census numbers are from Article 8. Communities with prefix "X" are not in the Census; they were added by the author.

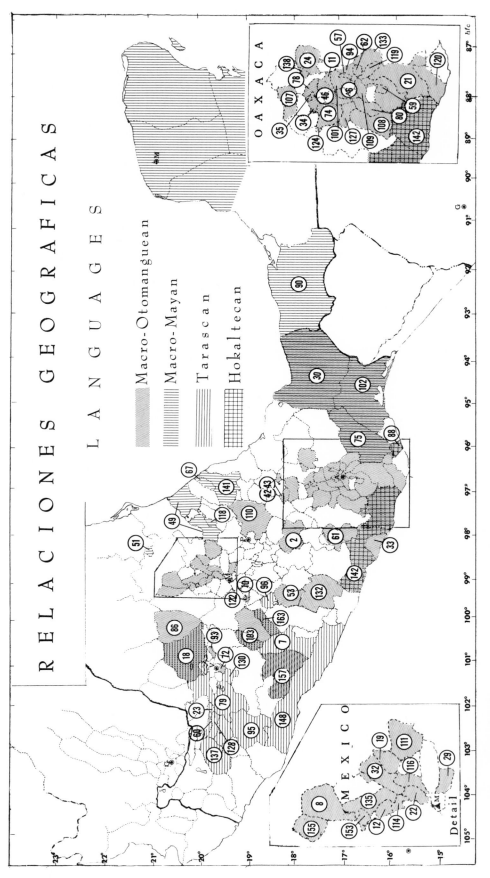

Fig. 2—DISTRIBUTION OF MACRO-OTOMANGUEAN, MACRO-MAYAN, TARASCAN, AND HOKALTECAN
Numbers refer to Table 2.

TABLE 3—LANGUAGE INDEX TO RELACIONES GEOGRÁFICAS, BY LANGUAGES

Language	Group	Subgroup	Symbol	Number of Communities
Achi (Cakchiquel?)	MACRO-MAYAN	Mayan	III.1	2
Amusgo	MACRO-OTOMANGUEAN	Mixtecan	II.2	8
Apanec	UNCLASSIFIED		VI	1
Ayacastec	UNCLASSIFIED		VI	2
Cakchiquel (see Achi)				
Cazcan	UTO-AZTECAN	Nahua	I.1(?)	4
Chichimec	UNCLASSIFIED		VI	6
Chinantec	MACRO-OTOMANGUEAN	Chinantecan	II.5	3
Chocho	MACRO-OTOMANGUEAN	Popolocan	II.3	3
Chontal de Guerrero	UNCLASSIFIED		VI	10
Chontal (Oaxaca)	HOKALTECAN	Tequistlatecan	V.2	6
Chontal	MACRO-MAYAN	Mayan	III.1	2
Chunbia	UNCLASSIFIED		VI	3
Cintec	UNCLASSIFIED		VI	1
Coca	UTO-AZTECAN	Related	I	2
Cochin	UNCLASSIFIED		VI	1
Cuacumanes	UNCLASSIFIED		VI	1
Cuicatec	MACRO-OTOMANGUEAN	Mixtecan	II.2	7
Cuisca	UTO-AZTECAN	Nahua	I.1	5
Cuitlatec	UNCLASSIFIED		VI	5
Culiaretes	UNCLASSIFIED		VI	1
Guachichil	UTO-AZTECAN	Related	I	1
Guazontec	MACRO-MAYAN	Huave	III.4	1
Huave (see Guazontec)				
Huehuetec	UNCLASSIFIED		VI	1
Iscuca	UNCLASSIFIED		VI	1
Izteca	UNCLASSIFIED		VI	1
Mam	MACRO-MAYAN	Mayan	III.1	1
Matlatzinca	MACRO-OTOMANGUEAN	Pame-Otomian	II.1	9
Maya (Yucatec)	MACRO-MAYAN	Mayan	III.1	50
Mazahua	MACRO-OTOMANGUEAN	Pame-Otomian	II.1	3
Mazatec	MACRO-OTOMANGUEAN	Popolocan	II.3	6
Mazatec de Guerrero	UNCLASSIFIED		VI	3
Mazatec de Jalisco	UNCLASSIFIED		VI	1
Melaguese	UNCLASSIFIED		VI	1
Mexicano (exclusively)	UTO-AZTECAN	Nahua	I.1	53
Mexicano (+ other)				108
Mexicano (total)				161
Mixe	MACRO-MAYAN	Mixe-Zoquean	III.3	4
Mixtec	MACRO-OTOMANGUEAN	Mixtecan	II.2	34
Otomi	MACRO-OTOMANGUEAN	Pame-Otomian	II.1	33
Otomi (de Jalisco)	UNCLASSIFIED		VI	3
Panteca	UNCLASSIFIED		VI	2
Pinoles	MACRO-OTOMANGUEAN	(?)	II	1
Pipil	UTO-AZTECAN	Nahua	I.1	1
Pocotec	UNCLASSIFIED		VI	1

(*Table 3, continued*)

Language	Group	Subgroup	Symbol	Number of Communities
Popoloca	MACRO-OTOMANGUEAN	Popolocan	II.3	3
Popoluca	MACRO-MAYAN	Mixe-Zoquean	III.3	1
Quacumec (*see* Tlaotli)	UNCLASSIFIED		VI	1
Quahutec	UNCLASSIFIED		VI	1
Quiche (*see* Uhtlatec)				
Quioteca (*see* Cuicatec)				
Sayultec	UTO-AZTECAN	Nahua	I.1(?)	2
Tamazultec	UNCLASSIFIED		VI	1
Tarascan	TARASCAN		IV	26
Tecoxquin	UTO-AZTECAN	Related	I	1
Tepehua	MACRO-MAYAN	Totonacan	III.2	1
Tepuztec	UNCLASSIFIED		VI	8
Tiam	UNCLASSIFIED		VI	1
Tlaotli (*see* Quacume)				
Tlapanec	HOKALTECAN	Tlapanecan	V.1	8
Tolimec	UNCLASSIFIED		VI	4
Tomatec	UNCLASSIFIED		VI	1
Totonac	MACRO-MAYAN	Totonacan	III.2	24
Totonac (local)	UNCLASSIFIED		VI	1
Tuztec	UNCLASSIFIED		VI	2
Tzeltal (*see* Chontal)				
Uhtlatec	MACRO-MAYAN	Mayan	III.1	1
Xocotec	UNCLASSIFIED		VI	1
Zacatec	UTO-AZTECAN	Nahua	I.1(?)	3
Zapotec	MACRO-OTOMANGUEAN	Zapotecan	II.4	31
Zapotec (local)	UNCLASSIFIED		VI	1
Zoque	MACRO-MAYAN	Mixe-Zoquean	III.3	1
Zutuhil	MACRO-MAYAN	Mayan	III.1	1

cludes: 1. Mayan; 2. Totonacan; 3. Mixe-Zoquean; 4. Huave. This group conforms in its composition to what McQuown has called Macro-Mayan (McQuown, 1942, pp. 37–38).[2] Group IV is Tarascan. Group V consists of: 1. Tlapanecan; and 2. Tequistlatecan. Both were included by Mason (1940) in his Hokaltecan (fig. 2). Group VI contains the unclassified languages (fig. 3). Table 1 lists the languages and dialects by these groups; Table 2 lists the languages by jurisdictions as they are reported in the RG's.

[2] For an evaluation of McQuown's hypothesis, see Wonderly, 1953.

The data from Table 2 have been regrouped in Table 3 to provide an alphabetical index to the languages and dialects mentioned in the RG's. It should be noted that there is considerable disparity in the size of communities noted under "Number of Communities," ranging from a large area like Tabasco, an alcaldía mayor, for example, to a small subject community of a minor cabecera. However, even this rough measure gives some impression of the distribution of languages around 1580. The largest number of communities is represented by Mexicano, with 53 reporting it as the only language and with another 108 reporting Mexicano together with some other language(s), totaling 161 Nahua-speaking settlements. This is followed by Yucatec Maya with 50. Mixtec and Otomi, with 33 and 34 respectively, and Zapotec with 31, follow at considerable distance. Totonac and Tarascan, with 24 and 26 respectively, mark the other main tongues, as all others in Table 3 show less than 10 communities reporting that language or dialect. Appendix B provides details on the specific places for which the languages listed on Table 3 were noted.

Group I: Uto-Aztecan Languages

Mexicano (I.1)

The most widespread language reported in the RG's was Mexicano. The term, still popular, was applied to the many dialects of Nahua, although differences were often noted. The standard was Mexihca or Nahuatl as spoken in the cities of the Valley of Mexico, and, as noted above, was well known and widely used by the Spaniards. In contrast to some Indian languages, such as Otomi which one report describes as "barbaric," Nahuatl seems to have been highly respected and was considered to be a "refined" language. Dialect differences provoked comment, and were sometimes viewed with disdain when they departed from the Mexihca norm.

There are many adjectives used to describe local Nahua dialects—crude, corrupt, unpolished, coarse, mutilated or jumbled. In Cholula, for example, they

all speak the Mexican language somewhat more crudely than those of Mexico and Texcoco. They lack six letters of our alphabet which are b, d, f, g, r, s. In place of the b and f, the natives use p; and for d, t. They substitute x for g and s. They substitute l for r, and for the s, x, and z. As can be seen by the pronunciation that we make of these names and words: Santa Maria, Santiago, San Pedro, Gabriel, Bartolome, Francisco, Diego, Hernandez, aforroxanta malia, xantiago, xan petolo, capiliel, paltolome, palacisco, tieco, helnantez, apolo. It

might be noted that in this language two l's are never pronounced together as in Castilian, but are pronounced as in Latin—nullus, nulla, nullum, and so on [Gómez de Orozco, 1927a, p. 159].

According to Brand (1960, p. 125), "it now seems clear that Mexicano Corrupto (perhaps everywhere and certainly in Colima and Zacatula) was the term used for Mexicano of the Valley of Mexico as it was used by non-Nahuatlans who adopted it perforce as the language of intercourse with the conquerers and with the missionary-priests." Although Brand's observation doubtlessly applies in some instances, there is no question that such terms as "corrupt" and "crude," were generally used to describe any or all dialects of Nahua that differed from that of the Valley of Mexico at any level—phonological, morphological, syntactical.

Table 4 contains a sample of terms from selected Nahua speech communities that received attention in the RG's. Mexihca may be considered the norm or standard against which other Nahua dialects were judged. As this material, brief as it is, implies, there are considerable differences in the local dialects of Nahua. The percentage of shared basic vocabulary ranged between 69 per cent and 92 per cent in a comparison of 10 localities (Swadesh, 1954–55). In this group, Mexihca and Pochutla were the most divergent dialects. As far as the evidence in the RG's is concerned, it is generally possible to distinguish clearly only two types of Nahua: Nahuatl or Mexihca as it was spoken in the Valley of Mexico, as opposed to all other Nahua dialects. To determine the identity of other dialects, it is necessary to rely on other sources.

Nahua Bilingualism

Nahua is the only major Indian language that significantly expanded in proportion to some other languages following the Spanish conquest. In the RG's it is reported spoken in 83 major jurisdictions. In 18 of these,

298

TABLE 4—TERMS FROM SELECTED NAHUA SPEECH COMMUNITIES

	Mexihca	Mecayapan	Pipil	Los Tuxtlas	Oapan	Tuxtepec	Zacapoaxtla	Pomaro	Pochutla
I	ne?wa	neh	naja	ne	nexwa	neju	nehwa	nehual	nen
who	aak	a?kon	ka	ak	akin	angi	aakoni	akʷi	ak
what	λe	tee	tey	ta, onon	tlinon	—	tooni	len	te
not	a?mo	aya?	ma, inte	amo	kayuwa	ajni	amo	amo	as
two	ome	oome	ume	ume	ome	omi	oome	ome	omem
woman	siwaaλ	siwat	cihguat	sibat	siwaw	siwat	siwaat	sihual	klast
bird	tootooλ	totot	tútuč	totot	wilatl	—	tootootsiin	tutul	—
ear	nakastli	nakas	nakaz	nagas	rakas	numagat	nakaas	nakas	nekest
mouth	kamaλ	ten	ten	móten	tokamak	bogamat	teen	kamak	ten
eat	kʷa	kʷaa	takʷa	tabatij	tlakʷa	—	kʷaa	lakua	kʷa
die	miki	miki	miki	miguis	yexwamik	miškatsi	miki	miki	mok
give	maka	maga	maka	maga	timakas	čimaga	maka	meka	kʷimaka
sun	toonatiw	tonatin	túnal	tonati	tona	tunati	toonal	tunali	tunel
white	istaak	istak	iztac	istak	ista·k	istat	istaak	istak	čupek
water	aaλ	aat	at	at	atl	at	aat	al	at

Sources: Mexihca, Mecayapan, Pochutla, and Zacapoaxtla from Swadesh, 1954–55. Others from unpublished vocabulary lists: Tuxtepec, Oaxaca, collected by Roberto Weitlaner; Pomaro, Michoacan, by Ignacio Manuel del Castillo; San Augustín Oapan, Gro., by J. Ékstrom; Nahuizalco Pipil, El Salvador, by J. G. Todd; Los Tuxtlas, Veracruz, by Juan Hasler. Original orthography has been retained.

it is the only native language reported. For those where more than one language is reported spoken, bilingualism is clearly indicated in several documents, and implied in many others. In Citlaltomagua (Census, 58), for example, "They commonly speak the Tepuztec language, which is their language, although all understand and speak the Mexican language which is the language through which they are ruled and governed . . ." (PNE, 6: 156). In contrast to full-scale bilingualism, limited bilingualism is also very widely reported. In Gueytlalpan (Census, 49), where Totonac speech prevailed, the leaders and important people all spoke Nahua. In Cuicatlan (Census, 35) the oldest and "most honorable" Indians were sought as informants—and they spoke Mexicano. Indeed, there were probably few localities throughout the whole region from Nueva Galicia to Guatemala where the Mexican language would not serve (fig. 1).

The reasons for the expansion of Nahua following the Conquest are readily apparent. Much of the population of Central Mexico was already either Nahua-speaking or else under the control of Nahua-speakers. Beyond its home territory, the trade routes were dotted with Nahua-speaking colonies as far south as Costa Rica in Central America. It was an established language of commerce, of political administration, a *lingua franca* for an enormous expanse of territory. Small wonder that the Spaniards readily adopted it and actively promoted it. Furthermore, its acceptance received support from the situation. Population was declining, and, to administer the remnants, peoples of disparate origin were often brought together and purposefully resettled into more manageable units. In some areas, in particular, a *lingua franca* became a practical necessity for existence. As Brand has suggested, such conditions of acceptance and use can account for the "rustic" qualities of the speech of some localities that the Spaniards observed.

Regional Dialects and Extinct Uto-Aztecan Languages

The dialects of Nahua that are known to any degree either from modern data or historical descriptions seem all to be mutually intelligible. Doubtlessly, all dialects listed as Mexicano in the RG's were or they would not have been so called.

In addition, there was Coisca, a Nahua dialect centering in the area of Tlalcozauhtitlan, Guerrero (Census, 53C). Coisca is described as being similar to Nahuatl, but simply less refined. Furthermore, it was noted to have been written like Mexicano and Coixca texts have been preserved (Ruiz de Alarcon, 1892). Calling it Coisca rather than Mexicano perhaps followed local usage. In the Relación of Atitlan (Census, 9), for example, corrupt Mexicano is reported, but the respondent noted that it was locally known as Pipil.

Several other languages of probable Uto-Aztecan affinity are also reported in the RG's: Zacatec (Census, 44, 87, 143), Cazcan (Census, 4, 75, 113, 143A), Coca (Census, 82, 82A), Guachichil (Census, 44), Tecoxquin (Census, 31), and Sayultec (Census, 60, 137A). These are all long extinct, and information on them is very scant.

Cazcan seems to have been closely related to the Nahua group. It was located in Jalisco and Zacatecas. A few terms assembled by Dávila Garibi (1935), which he considered to be Cazcan, would indicate the latter to be a dialect of Nahua. Cazcan is distinguished from Mexicano in the reports, but each of the jurisdictions in which it

occurs is described as being fully bilingual. Its apparent closeness helps to explain why Mexicano might have been so widely adopted by the Cazcanos after the Spanish Conquest. What little is known of Tecoxquin, reported from Compostela, Nayarit (Census, 31) would also suggest its close affinities to Nahua.

To the north and east of the Cazcan area were Zacatec and Guachichil, respectively. Zacatec seems unquestionably to have been a Nahua language. It is equated with Cazcan by Mota Padilla (1870), and place names in the region are Nahua. The affinities of Guachichil, however, are much less certain. Its relation to Huichol has been suggested.[3]

Coca is reported from Jalisco, from Poncitlan and Cuiseo del Rio (Census, 82). This jurisdiction was also bilingual Coca-Mexicano in 1585. Dávila Garibi (1935) has assembled a brief vocabulary which he identifies as Coca, in which case the latter was clearly a Uto-Aztecan language. Sayul-

---

[3] A Huichol informant of Hrdlička stated that Guachichil was the old name for the Huichols. Quoted in Thomas and Swanton, 1911, p. 41.

In 1940 Pedro Hendrichs recorded a short vocabulary from two traveling musicians, who said they were from Peña Colorada, Zacatecas. Roberto Weitlaner kindly made the vocabulary available, and from it I have taken the following terms, preserving the orthography of Hendrichs.

name of the language:	z'apa
body:	ku'āza
nose:	?z'uri
mouth:	t'ēni
bone:	um'ɛ
rabbit:	t'ač<u
moon:	m'ɛȼə
corn:	i?k̓u?
metate:	maťa?
tortilla:	pa?ᵃp'a

In comparison with Cora, Huicol, Tepehuan, and Nahua, the greatest similarities are with Huichol, although some terms are distinct from the latter. The informants insisted that their language was none of the above, including Huichol, but was Zacatec. It is distinct enough to have been called another language in the 16th century, although a modern linguist would recognize its obvious affinities to Huichol. This particular dialect could well represent a relic of Guachichil or some other language in the area that was simply noted as "diffferent" or "obscure" in the 16th century.

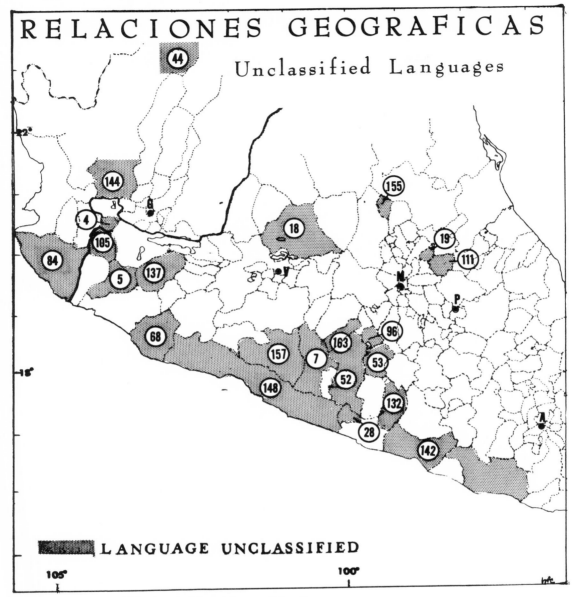

Fɪɢ. 3—UNCLASSIFIED LANGUAGES, ABOUT 1580

tec is reported from Jilquilpan, Michoacan, and Zapotlan, Jalisco (Census, 60, 137A). Here again Mexicano, in both places, was generally spoken, but not by the Tarascan-speakers of Jilquilpan's subject towns. Although the evidence is meager, Sayultec appears to have been a Nahua dialect.

GROUP II: MACRO-OTOMANGUEAN LANGUAGES

Otomi (II.1)

At the time of the Conquest, Otomi was second only to Nahua in importance on the Central Plateau. It was spoken over a wide area that included most of the modern states of Mexico, Hidalgo, Queretaro, and San Luis Potosi, and there were also enclaves of Otomi-speakers in Puebla, Tlaxcala, and Michoacan. Throughout the area it occupied, it was interspersed with other languages. In only one relación, Atengo (Census, 8), was Otomi the exclusive language reported.

Like the Mexicans before them, the Spaniards viewed the Otomi as a rather crude, barbaric lot. Despite the large number of speakers situated in the heart of New Spain, the Otomi language proved difficult for the Spaniards and does not seem to have been well known until toward the end of the 16th century. The Relación of Queretaro (Census, 86) comments that

. . . although the ministers of the holy gospel have worked very inquisitively in it, they have not been able to print books about our Holy Faith as they have in the other languages of this land because of the difficulty of writing it as it is spoken. Saying something fast or slow, high or low, each one of these has its own meaning and each one says something different. They have, however, endeavored to print a *doctrina christiana* that could be understood by the natives. Thus, they are a poor people whom the Spaniards find more difficult to communicate with and manage than the other nations.

In 1579 the Jesuits established themselves in Huixquilucan for the purpose of learning Otomi, and after three months of intensive study found they could explain the *doctrina* in it (Alegre, 1956, 1: 242).

Despite the transcription problem, many of the Otomi were reported to have been bilingual. Along the Tarascan frontier, where they had been permitted to settle in a buffer zone between the Mexican and Tarascan states, they also spoke Tarascan. In and around the Valley of Mexico, many spoke Nahuatl. Thus, communication between the Spaniards and the Otomi was conducted for many years after the Conquest by means of a *lingua franca*, Nahuatl or Tarascan.

302

Mazahua (II.1)

Mazahua speech, closely related to Otomi, is reported from two main jurisdictions (Census, 18, 103). Though widely separated, they are both in the Tarascan frontier zone. Unfortunately, the main area of Mazahua occupation, the Valley of Toluca, was not the subject of reports at this time, although it is described in other 16th-century documents.

Matlatzinca (II.1)

Both Otomi and Mazahua speech have survived in a substantial portion of their traditional areas, but Matlatzinca (II.1) has become nearly extinct. It is spoken today only in San Francisco Oxtotilpan, state of Mexico. In the 1580's enclaves of Matlatzinca-speakers were reported from Michoacan, Guerrero, and the state of Mexico; but again, there were very few reports from within the principal Matlatzinca zone of occupation. Actually, in the 16th century well over 40 towns are known to have been Matlatzinca-speaking to some extent. The majority of these were situated in the southern part of the state of Mexico, from Toluca to near the Guerrero border (García Payón, 1941).

While the Matlatzinca seem to have been relatively populous in the 16th century, García Payón has observed (1942, p. 74) that "if the Spanish Conquest had come at the end of the 16th century, the conquerers and missionaries would not even have found traces of the Matlatzinca." Situated as they were, between two expanding empires, the Matlatzinca had suffered severe losses in the decades preceding the Spanish Conquest. Displeased with Mexican encroachment into their territory, one group had sought asylum and relocated within Tarascan territory in the mid-15th century. These became known as Pirindas. Another group actively allied themselves with the Mexicans; a third group attempted to remain independent. In the succession

FIG. 4—DISTRIBUTION OF LANGUAGES: NORTHERN AND EASTERN OAXACA.

of wars which followed, Matlatzinca fought Matlatzinca. There was little effect on the boundary shared by the Tarascan and Mexican states, but in the process the Matlatzinca were gradually decimated. Notwithstanding, they opposed the Spanish entry into their territory with a remarkable display of strength, but their resistance was quickly crushed in a costly battle and their domain fell into Spanish hands.

The gradual disappearance of Matlatzinca speech since the end of the 16th century is somewhat puzzling, especially when a language such as Ocuiltec, which had a very limited distribution within the same zone, continues to survive.[4] Moreover, on the northern border of their former territory, where Matlatzinca speech was interspersed with Otomi, Mazahua, and Nahuatl, the latter have continued as important languages to the present, while Matlatzinca has all but disappeared.[5] Since the same historical factors in post-Conquest times presumably affected all groups, at least within the northern zone of contact more or less similarly, another explanation of their disappearance has to be sought. The most plausible at present, as will be discussed

[4] It is still spoken in the town of San Juan Acingo located a few kilometers from Ocuila. Although this is the heart of Ocuiltec country, Ocuiltec is also mentioned as one of three languages spoken in Tlachinolticpac, which was located in modern Hidalgo (PNE, 3: 130).

[5] It is still (1967) spoken in San Francisco Oztotilpan, state of Mexico.

303

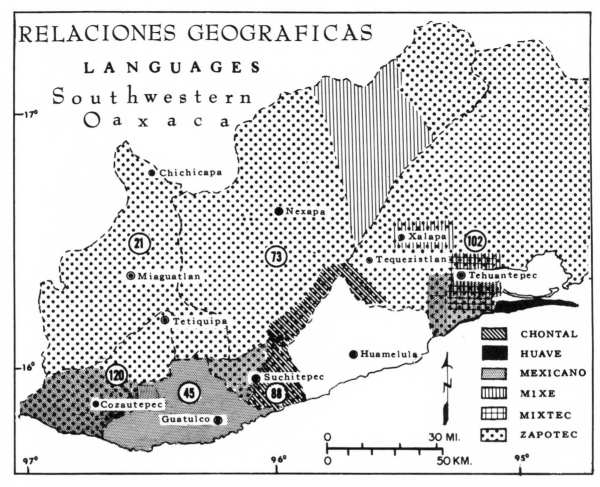

Fɪɢ. 5—DISTRIBUTION OF LANGUAGES: SOUTHWESTERN OAXACA

further on, is the possibility of large-scale pre-Hispanic bilingualism, and its effect on post-Hispanic linguistic acculturation.

Chichimec (VI) (II?)

Chichimec is reported from four jurisdictions. That of Cempoala (Census, 19) and of Tepepulco (Census, 111) were doubtlessly the same, but possibly different from that of Acambaro and Yuririapundaro (Census, 18A, 18B). Chichimec is also reported for Zimapan (Census, 155), in conjunction with Mexicano and Otomi. The term itself is of little help since it was generically applied to any people of low culture, bar-

barians, without ethnic or linguistic connotations. The particular Chichimecs mentioned in these reports were most likely related linguistically to the Pamean groups, but for lack of linguistic evidence, they are best left unclassified.

Oaxaca

Representatives of all linguistic subgroups reported in the RG's for Oaxaca have survived to the present. As shown on most linguistic maps of the area, Oaxaca appears to be about equally divided between Mixtec (II.2) and Zapotec (II.4) with Mixtec located in the upper half of the state, spilling over into Guerrero and Puebla; and Zapotec in the lower half, extending into the coastal lowlands of the Isthmus of Tehuantepec. Pockets of other languages are situated primarily in the northeastern sector, and in the west and southwest, occupying territories that stretched inland from the Pacific coast (figs. 4 and 5).

Mixtec (II.2)

The Mixtec region can be divided into three geo-cultural areas: high, low, and coastal. When the Spaniards arrived, the Mixteca Alta and Baja were partitioned into tribute paying provinces of the Triple Alliance. In the Mixteca Baja, although Mixtec (Group II.2) is the dominant language, it is interspersed with Nahua (I.1) and Amuzgo (II.2). Trique, which is also situated in this region, was unfortunately not mentioned in the RG's. Both the Mixteca Alta and the coast, however, are relatively homogeneous as far as Mixtec speech is concerned. It is mainly on the borders of their territory that other languages are encountered. For example, in Guaxolotitlan (Census, 46) "they speak two languages in this village because it is on the edge of two provinces, which are Mixtec and Zapotec." Outside the Mixteca, colonies of Mixtec-speakers are quite widespread. In the RG's barrios of Mixtec are reported in the province of Coatzacoalco (Census, 30) and in Tehuantepec (Census, 102).

Cuicatec (II.2)

The Cuicatec area lies northeast of the Mixteca. Although generally recognized as a distinct language, in more than one account it is reported as "corrupt Mixtec." The language of Quiotepec (Census, 54A) is called "Quioteca," something similar but yet quite distinct from Mixtec, that is, Cuicatec. Atlatlauca (Census, 11) was then Cuicatec-speaking and was reliably reported as Zapotec-speaking in the 18th century (Villaseñor y Sánchez, 1952, 2: 144), but is now Chinantec.

Amuzgo (II.2)

Amuzgo was considered to be a language "muy oscura." It is doubtful if there were many clerics who spoke it at the time. Of the eight towns of the Mixteca Baja where it was reported, however, in only two of these does Amuzgo appear to have been the exclusive language. In four, Mixtec is also reported, and in another two, Ayacasteca.

Popolocan: Chocho, Popoloca, Mazatec (II.3)

The Popolocan group is in Oaxaca and adjacent parts of Puebla. Chocho, Popoloca, and Mazatec are all reported in the RG's, but Ixcatec is not. This is especially curious since the cabecera of the province is none other than Santa Maria Ixcatlan (Census, 54), the principal center of Ixcatec speech. Chocho is likewise one of the languages reported for Coxcatlan (Census, 42, 43) rather than Popoloca. It seems, therefore, that the three languages (which are closely related, and which would have displayed even less difference four centuries ago) were not generally distinguished (see Fernández de Miranda, 1956). When the distinction was made, for example Popoloca of Tepeaca (Census, 110), the basic consideration may have been cultural or political. Outside the home territory, Popoloca is reported as one of the languages spoken in San Juan Teotihuacan (Census, 116C), a relic perhaps from earlier times when Teotihuacan was a flourishing, cosmopolitan city.

Mazatec was considered, along with Chocho or Popoloca, to be unpleasant to hear. Immediately south of the Mazatec area is Tecomabaca (Census, 54B). Here, the "language of the pinoles" was spoken. In the 18th century Mazatec is reported for Tecomabaca (Villaseñor y Sánchez, 1952, 2: 139). Although it may also have been Mazatec in 1579, there is another possible interpretation: considering 16th-century orthography, "pinoles" might refer to "los peñoles," in which case the language could have been Mixtec, Papabuco, or Zapotec. Within the Mazatec area today, Mixtec is spoken in the village of San Juan Coatzospan (fig. 4).

Zapotec (II.4)

Zapotec was well known in the 16th century and was a *lingua franca* in Oaxaca. Its boundaries with other language groups were well defined. Outside the main zone, a Zapotec town, Quahuzapotla, is reported (Census, 142-V) in the extreme southwestern corner of Guerrero, not far from the ocean or the Oaxaca border. Since Zapotec was so well known, there seems little reason to question the identification (Barlow, 1944a,b). In the Los Peñoles province, corrupt Zapotec is reported for Elotepec and Totomachapa (Census, 80E, F). The dialects of these towns may be identified as Papabuco, a language related to, but not, Zapotec. Papabuco appears to have closer affinities with Chatino (Upson and Longacre, 1965). A corrupt Zapotec is also reported from Cozautepec (Census, 120A) but in this case, it may refer to Chatino, which is concentrated at present slightly north of this locality.

Chinantec (II.5)

Chinantec was considered very difficult to learn, but among the clergy a few spoke it. It is also concentrated in northeastern Oaxaca, wedged between Zapotec on the south and Cuicatec and Mazatec on the north. It is the only language reported in two of the RG's (Census, 24, 138).

GROUP III: MACRO-MAYAN LANGUAGES

Group III languages are concentrated in eastern and southern Mesoamerica from the Rio Panuco on the north through Honduras on the south (fig. 2). An otherwise continuous distribution of these languages is in-

terrupted only by wedges of Nahua in central Veracruz and Tabasco.

More than a third of the RG's emanate from the Maya area. Two of these are from Guatemala, but the rest (54) come from the bishopric of Yucatan. In all, five Mayan (Group III.1) languages are mentioned.

Yucatec Maya (III.1)

The most extensive is what is now called Yucatec Maya, or what was then called Mayathan. Not all the reports specify the language spoken within the jurisdiction, but several reports (e.g., Census, 147) from the Yucatan Peninsula state that "in all these provinces there is only one language. . . ." Some minor dialect differences are noted in that "some towns of the coast differ in some sounds" and that the people of Chiquinchel, for example, have a more refined speech (Census, 139). The latter called the speech of their neighbors in Popola and Sinsimato "achamaya," because they considered them to be people "of vile and low understanding."

Chontal (III.1)

Chontal is reported to have been a major language of Tabasco (Census, 91) and is described as a "very ample" language with "abundant sounds." Chontal is also reported from Tetzal and Temax (Census, 121), unidentifiable localities. In this instance, what is called Chontal is probably Tzeltal, a language of highland Chiapas.

The people of Zozil and Tecay (Census, 162) spoke a language which was "general in all the province." These places have not been identified either. "Zozil" suggests Tzotzil but, in any case, a Mayan language.

Guatemalan Mayance Dialects (III.1)

In two accounts from the Lake Atitlan area of Guatemala, five languages are mentioned. The reported jurisdictions overlap to some extent, and, unfortunately, the reports are not specific as to which languages were spoken in what towns. In the jurisdiction of Santiago Atitlan, Zutuhil is noted to be the parent tongue, but some also spoke Mexicano or Pipil. In addition, they understood Uhtlatec (Quiche) and Achi. In the adjoining and somewhat overlapping jurisdiction of Zapotitlan, however, Mexicano (Pipil) seems to have been the principal tongue, whereas Achi was the mother language. Mam was also spoken, but neither it nor Achi was used with perfection. Achi probably referred to Cakchiquel, but the equation between the two is by no means certain.

Zoque (III.3), Mixe, Huave (III.4)

Zoque is reported for the sierra region of the Tabasco province (Census, 89–92) and adjacent parts of the Chiapas province; Popoluca is reported in Coatzacoalcos (Census, 30). Across the isthmus, in Tehuantepec (Census, 102) Mixe was spoken in some of its subject towns, in the sierra to the north, and in barrios of Xalapa. Huave, which is called Guaçonteca in the relación, is reported from nearby communities on the coast.

Totonac (III.2)

Totonac was spoken over a wide area in the 16th century. It stretched from the Sierra de Puebla to the coast, where it extended from the Rio Cazones on the north to the Rio de la Antigua on the south (distribution of 16th-century Totonac and its Nahua bilingualism appears in Kelly and Palerm, 1952). There were no extensive areas within its entire zone of distribution of exclusively Totonac speech. In the Sierra it was interspersed with Otomi and Mexicano. On the coast it was interspersed with Mexicano. The jurisdiction of Misantla (Census, 67) seems to be the most extensive area of Totonac speech and the RG reports only Totonac. Another source indicates that Mexicano was at least spoken in the cabecera, not in its subjects (ENE,

1940, 14: 80). Three of the four RG's from the Totonac area (Census, 49, 118, 141) imply or directly indicate that Totonac-Mexicano bilingualism was extremely widespread, especially on the coast. Tepehua, related to Totonac, is reported from Huexotla (Census, 51).

GROUP IV: TARASCAN

Tarascan is concentrated in the state of Michoacan and was occasionally referred to as the language of Michoacan, or simply "mechoacan." The Tarascans themselves called it Purepecha, which is reported to have meant "language of working men" (Census, 38). The name Tarascan, according to some sources, was applied by the Spaniards.

The Tarascan language was well known in the 16th century and was an important *lingua franca*, since, like Mexicano, one language served a large area. Studies of modern Tarascan indicate only the slightest dialect differences. The linguistic situation suggests a relatively late and rapid expansion of the language, and this is in accord with historical accounts of the formation and expansion of the Tarascan empire. As one of the major languages of Middle America, Tarascan is somewhat of an enigma since it bears no demonstrable affinities with other language groups. However, western Mexico seems to have been an area of extreme linguistic diversity in pre-Hispanic times. Tarascan is not the only orphan in the region.

GROUP V: HOKALTECAN
Tlapanec (V.1)

Group V languages are reported from southwestern Guerrero and southern Oaxaca (fig. 2). Tlapanec was spoken immediately west of the Mixteca Baja, from the region of modern Tlapa, south to the coast. The RG's cover only the coastal area. There, Tlapanec is reported from a cluster of towns in the Ayutla-Azoyu vicinity, including both the latter. Tlapanec has survived in Azoyu until modern times, and its speakers refer to their language as Tlapaneca. In the region of Tlapa, it is called Tlapaneco, and Radin (1933, p. 45) has pointed out that "the differences between these two dialects are quite marked." Although it seems perhaps all too obvious that the Tlapanec reported in the Relación of Xalapa should be equated with the Tlapaneca dialect, it should also be noted that the other dialect does extend into the northern fringe of the Ayutla-Azoyu vicinity. It is reported spoken in the town of Iliatengo. Immediately west of Ayutla lay the boundary of Yopitzingo, territory of the Yopes, who were Tlapanec-speaking according to Sahagún (1938, 3: 133). It is not unlikely that the same dialect prevailed throughout the coastal province, which is a relatively restricted and ecologically homogeneous area.

Chontal of Oaxaca (Tequistlatecan, V.2)

The Chontal of Oaxaca are situated in rugged terrain between Pochutla and Tehuantepec on the southern coast. Tequicistlan, one of their principal towns, which was in the eastern end of their area, seems to have been thoroughly bilingual Zapotec-Chontal in 1580. Suchitepec, toward the western end of the region, was a Zapotec-speaking cabecera, whose estancias spoke Chontal. Although the Zapotec, therefore, appear to have dominated the fringes of Chontal territory, linguistically (if not politically) most of the Chontal region appears to have not been part of a major pre-Hispanic tribute province. The RG's, nevertheless, indicate that a significant amount of Nahua was spoken throughout the Chontal area, amongst old people as well as the nobility. This would suggest that their Nahua neighbors in and around Pochutla had formerly exerted a much greater influence in the affairs of the region than they had in late pre-Conquest times (fig. 5).

308

GROUP VI: UNCLASSIFIED AND EXTINCT LANGUAGES

Cuitlatec

Cuitlatec was an important language in the 16th century, but is now all but extinct. Fortunately, it survived long enough to have commanded some attention from linguists. All the descriptive material on it, however, derives from one locality, San Miguel Totolapan, Guerrero (Escalante Hernández, 1962; Hendrichs Pérez, 1947; McQuown, 1941). Based on these data, collected in modern times, its affinities with other language groups have been suggested, but no clearcut or definitive relationship still has been demonstrated (Mason, 1940, p. 77). Cuitlatec does share certain characteristics of other Middle American language groups, but it yet remains unclassified.

In the RG's the Cuitlatec are reported to have occupied two distinct areas of Guerrero. One group was located along the Rio Balsas, from Changata in Tarascan-held territory, east to Acatlan del Rio. The other was on the Costa Grande, between Acapulco and Petatlan. The principal town of the coastal Cuitlatec was Mexcaltepec, situated in the mountains, above modern Atoyac. By 1580 Mexcaltepec had been abandoned and its inhabitants had been relocated by the Spaniards nearer the coast.

Tepuztec (Tlacotepehua)

Between the coastal Cuitlatec and those on the Rio Balsas were the Tepehua whose language was called Tepuztec or Tlacotepehua. The RG's are the principal source of information on this extinct group, whose main centers were the towns of Citlaltomahua, Anecuilco, Xahualtepec, Utatlan, and Tlacotepec. On the coast, in the Teccomatan-Azuchitlan-Tamalacan area, it is interspersed with Cuitlatec, and around Acapulco, with the latter and other languages. In these areas specifically, as well as Xahualtepec, the reports note that everyone also spoke Mexicano. Mexicano was

FIG. 6—DISTRIBUTION OF LANGUAGES: COSTA GRANDE OF GUERRERO

probably widely spoken throughout the Tepuztec area. As to the nature of Tepuztec, nothing is known of the language.

Costa Grande Languages

As described in the 16th century, the Costa Grande was a hodgepodge so far as languages were concerned. Around modern Acapulco, Yope was spoken; 8 leagues southeast, in Naguala, Tuztec. In Acamalutla, Tlatzihuizteca was spoken, but in its three estancias Tepuztec was spoken in Otlahuiztla, both Coyutumatec and Tepuztec in Atoyac, Tistec in Tiztla. West of Acamalutla, the language of Texcatlan was Texcatec; of Amatla, Camotec. Up the coast toward Zacatula, there were Cuitlatec and a few enclaves of Tepuztec, as described. Above them, in Pantla and Iztapan, the language was different and called Panteca. The next group of towns, Pochutla, Toliman, and Suchitlan, spoke Tolimeca, and the Tolimec territory was bordered on the north by Chunbia, the language of Vitaluta and its subjects. Finally, Mexicano was spoken in Zacatula itself. In addition to all these languages, the Relación of Sirandaro states that Apanec, which was spoken in Guaymeo, a barrio of Sirandaro, had formerly come from the province of Zacatula. The key to this linguistic tangle was a "corrupt" Mexicano, *lingua franca* for the whole coast.

Most of the old towns reported in the Relación of Zacatula have disappeared. All along the coast, the native population had suffered a severe decline by 1580, a situation that probably fostered large-scale bi-

309

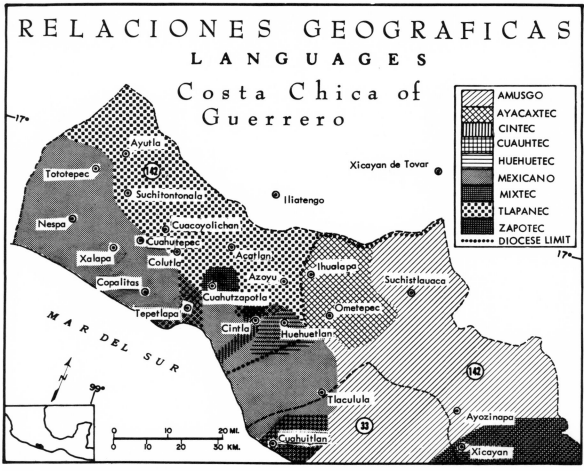

FIG. 7—DISTRIBUTION OF LANGUAGES: COSTA CHICA OF GUERRERO

lingualism, but here, as in some other parts of Guerrero, Nahua must have been deeply entrenched from earlier times. Apart from Cuitlatec, Nahua or Mexicano, and Yope, there remains no shred of evidence other than the names as reported in the RG's to relate these extinct languages to presently known tongues (fig. 6).

Costa Chica Languages

The linguistic situation on Guerrero's lower coast is comparable. Below Naguala there was a zone of Tlapanec, as described. Between it and the Oaxaca border, where Mixtec began, were Cintec, Huehuetec,

Quahutec, Zapotec, Amuzgo, Mexicano, and Ayacastec. All these have disappeared, except for Mexicano, Amuzgo in Ometepec, and Tlapanec in Azoyu.

Cintla was a trilingual community with the mysterious Cintec, Mexicano, and Tlapanec. Huehuetec was the language of Huehuetlan; Quahutec, of Quahuitlan. What survived of both towns by 1582 also spoke Mexicano. Ayacastec is the more interesting of any of those that have since disappeared in this area. In the relación, it is reported from Ometepec and Ygualapa, both of which were also centers for Amuzgo. The relación notes that the Huehuetec

310

had applied the name to Ygualapa, which hints that the two may have been kindred. In addition to Ygualapa and Ometepec the province of the Ayacastecs included Quahuitlan, the Mexicano town of Tlacolula, and the Tlapanec town of Azoyu (García Pimentel, 1904, p. 65). Were Ayacastec related to Mexicano, it probably would have been noted. If indeed related to any of the known languages, more than likely it would have been Tlapanec.

Chontal and Tuxtec of Guerrero

North of the Rio Balsas and west of the Coixca were the Chontal. Like their neighbors to the north, the Matlatzinca, the Chontal of Guerrero had unsuccessfully resisted Mexican domination in the decades immediately preceding the Spanish Conquest. Their principal towns in the late 16th century were Ixcateopan, Alahuistlan, Ostuma, Coatepec, Toltoltepec, Teloloapan, and Apastla. Important as the language was, in terms of geographical distribution and number of speakers, no description of it is known. One report (Census, 53) observed that it was spoken in the throat and that *it wasn't written because it wasn't pronounced*. The same report relates it to Tuxtec, but elsewhere a distinction is made between the two. Ixcateopan, for example, was noted to have once been Tuxtec, but by 1579 was Chontal. Tuxtec (or Chontal) is reported (Census, 53) from Iguala, Mayanala, Tlalcozauhtitlan, and Oapan, towns located well to the east of the Chontal area. The two may simply have been dialects of the same language, with Chontal on the west and Tuxtec on the east. On the coast, Naguala was Tuxtec-speaking, as noted, and Tuxtec was also one of the languages reported from the Tistla (Census, 132) vicinity. Both Tuxtec and Chontal are extinct and their linguistic affinities unknown.

The array of languages learned and used by the missionary-priests of the 16th century is quite impressive, as was their linguistic strategy. Among them are not only Nahuatl, Tarascan, Matlatzinca, Totonac, and Maya but most of the languages of Oaxaca, as well. Included are not only important languages in terms of geographical distribution and numbers of speakers, but also languages and dialects of very limited distribution. It is all the more puzzling, therefore, that an important language such as Chontal of Guerrero was ignored. One source reported that there was "no minister in New Spain who understands" Chontal (García Pimentel, 1897, p. 125). Although Chontal-Nahua bilingualism is explicitly mentioned for only one community in the RG's, Nahua-speaking communities were interspersed among the Chontal, and most of the rest of the Chontal must have been bilingual, thus enabling the Spanish clergy to bypass the Chontal language.

The Chontal region had been subjugated by the Mexicans, and it was an important tribute province at the time of the Spanish Conquest. There are interesting accounts in the chronicles of the Chontal-Mexican wars. Apart from this experience, the Chontal had intimate contact with an earlier wave of Nahua-speakers, who had settled in and around their area. To the east were the Coixca; to the southeast were the Cuezala Nahua. Both are associated in legends with the *peregrinación*, which would date their appearance in Guerrero at about A.D. 1250 (if taken literally), but one or both may have entered and settled much earlier, perhaps during the early days of Toltec expansion. The nature of that expansion is not known, but there are suggestions that it was not peaceful. Both the Cuezala Nahua and the Apastla Chontal had similar accounts of the strife between them surrounding the Cuezala settlement. Unfortunately, the relationship of these early Nahua groups to the Chontal prior to Aztec expansion into Guerrero is not detailed in known historical accounts. Most importantly, the conditions for Nahuatization were present for at least three centuries prior to the Spanish Conquest and perhaps much

311

longer. The absence of an explicit report of bilingualism in the late 16th century, therefore, is probably more of an inadvertent omission than a denial. And the same probably holds true for the Cuitlatec.

Guerrero Mazatec and Ixcuca

Within the Chontal area, two other extinct languages are reported. Tzicapuzalco and its subjects spoke Mazatec, a language also reported in the nearby jurisdiction of Zultepec. Whether Guerrero Mazatec was related to Oaxaca Mazatec is an open question. The latter were trading salt for use in the mines near Taxco, a fact which suggests an old commercial link between the two regions and therefore tempts the equation of the two. By 1580 Mazatec of Oaxaca was well enough known to have been properly identified wherever it appeared.

The other language, Ixcuca, is only reported from one locality: a barrio of Teloloapan. Again, nothing more is known of the language than its name. Insofar as the area may have been linked in trade with northeast Oaxaca and southern Puebla, however, a relationship with Itzucan should not be ruled out. Itzucan appears in the Conquest lists of Montezuma I, and was Nahua-speaking in historic times. Formerly, it could well have been a center for Popoloca or Mixtec. Thus, while the affinities of Guerrero Mazatec and Izcuca are doubtful, the one might have been Mazatec (i.e., of Oaxaca), the other, Popoloca or Mixtec.[6]

Coastal Michoacan

Coastal Michoacan was an area of great activity from the mid-1520's through the mid-1530's. The province of Motines was the center of gold production in New Spain during these years. According to the relación which covers this area, there were many languages in the province, but Mexicano was generally used. Quauhcomeca, for example, was reported from Coalcoman (Census, 68A) and described simply as a "very obscure language." Mexicano survives today in Coire, Pomara and Ostula, but the other languages have disappeared without a trace.

Jalisco

Like Guerrero and Coastal Michoacan, Jalisco also contained a host of vanished languages. Around Tuxpan, besides Mexicano, Tarascan, and Sayultec, there were also Tiam, Cochin, Tamacultec, and Zapotec. At least one historian has considered Jalisco Zapotec to have been related to Oaxaca Zapotec, but there is no demonstrable evidence (Dávila Garibi, 1947, quoting Guevara, 1919, and Santoscoy). In the jurisdiction of Ameca, Totonac is reported along with Cazcan and Mexicano. Again, there is no reason other than the name itself to connect it with Totonac of the Gulf Coast. In Xocotlan there was an unidentified language reported. In Tenamastlan there were two unidentified languages. In both localities, however, Mexicano was also spoken. Finally, Otomi is reported from the jurisdiction of Amula (Census, 5). It is highly probable that this enclave could have represented colonies of Otomi-speakers from the plateau area, but linguistic evidence on these Amula groups is lacking. For the present, the language is best left unclassified. Were it Otomi (II.1), it would have been the westernmost extension of it.

Within the jurisdiction of Purificacion (Census, 84) the relación states that there were seven or eight languages which were called "Culiaretes, maçatecas y iztecas, pocotecas, melaguesas, tomatecas, cuacumanes." It goes on, however, to list 17 subcabeceras and implies that each had its own language. One of these is noted to have

---

[6] The name might also suggest its affinities with Izuco, a town in the jurisdiction of Iguala. The Relación of Iguala (Census, 53) does not state the language of that town. It was probably Coixca or Tuxtec.

been bilingual, the second language being described as a very corrupt Mexicano. Although little can be gleaned from the report beyond the obvious implied linguistic diversity of the province, if "cuacumanes" is the same Cuacuman as that in the Motines area, an extensive distribution is implied for at least one of these extinct languages.

LINGUISTIC ACCULTURATION

Mesoamerica was an area of extreme linguistic complexity at the time of the Spanish Conquest. Many of the native languages have survived and are spoken by substantial numbers of people. A few have become extinct in modern times, but the majority of those that have disappeared did so relatively early and little or nothing is known of them except some information on their distribution. There is no question that were something more known of these many languages, the implied diversity would be greatly reduced. Many or most of them would turn out to be dialects or languages of known groups. Even so, the diversity in western Mexico cannot be minimized. Simply the known languages of Guerrero— Tlapanec, Cuitlatec, Tarascan, Nahua, Amuzgo, and Matlatzinca—attest to this.

It is apparent in the RG's and other sources that both Guerrero and Jalisco were heavily Nahuatized, with Nahua as the principal language, or as a most important second language in what appears to have been bilingual populations. Because Nahua had been so widely adopted by the Spaniards and its use actively encouraged by them, the Spaniards are often considered responsible for the bilingual situation that prevailed in these areas in the final quarter of the 16th century. In fact, however, most of the groups that were bilingual in the late 16th century had probably been largely bilingual for a long time, certainly antedating the Spanish Conquest. The situation is similar to what Palerm has inferred for Totonacapan (Kelly and Palerm, 1952).

Viewed in such perspective, it becomes quite apparent why linguistic acculturation proceeded so effectively in some areas, and with regard to some languages, but not in others. Through the combination of population decline and Spanish promotion of Nahua, its use increased in some areas after the Conquest at the expense of the mother tongues. In the Matlatzinca area in the state of Mexico, for example, all the languages reported from different localities still persist, whereas Matlatzinca itself barely survives. In Guerrero the Cuitlatec enclave that persisted the longest, San Miguel Totolapan, was within Tarascan-dominated territory in late pre-Conquest times, thus insulating it from the Nahuatizing influences felt by other Cuitlatecs.

Those areas that were the most linguistically diverse, but bilingual, are the areas which have undergone the greatest change. Post-Hispanic linguistic acculturation, in other words, was only an intensification of a process already well under way at the time of the Spanish Conquest. In Guerrero and southern Nueva Galicia it resulted in the replacement of the native languages by Nahua. On the other hand, in large, linguistically homogeneous areas such as the Chontal, Maya, Zoque, and Totonac, where Nahua was widely spoken as a second language but not fostered by the early missionary-priests, it disappeared, whereas the mother languages survived.

EXTENT AND DISTRIBUTION OF NAHUA

Unfortunately, a detailed linguistic census for the period of initial Spanish contact is not available, but the order of magnitude of Nahua speech for this point in time can be inferred with reasonable certainty. There are, in fact, a multitude of firsthand reports of the 16th century in addition to the RG's that contain linguistic references.

Almost all jurisdictions where Nahua was the mother tongue can be reasonably well established. In general, the sources are more

313

TABLE 5—ESTIMATED NAHUA-SPEAKING POPU-
LATION, CENTRAL MEXICO, 1519

Region		Total Population (millions)	Nahua percentage (estimated)	Total Nahua (estimated millions)
I	Central Plateau	10.9	95	10.355
II	Valles–Panuco	2.8	...	...
IIA-III	Veracruz–Jalapa	1.9	95	1.805
IV	Northwest Oaxaca	1.7	30	.51
V	Central Oaxaca	.75	...	...
VI-VII	Oaxaca Coast–Zacatula, Guerrero	4.6	60	2.76
VIII	Michoacan	1.3	...	...
IX-X	Jalisco–Zacatecas Colima, Nayarit	1.2	80	.96
	TOTAL	25.15	65.84	16.39

explicit about describing the mother tongue of a locality than they are in reporting secondary languages. In those jurisdictions where Nahua was not the mother language but was reported, the problem becomes one of determining the extent of Nahua bilingualism in that jurisdiction. Many reports are explicit in stating that although Nahua is not the indigenous language, everyone speaks and understands it. Such localities, in other words, seem to have been fully bilingual in the sense that all their inhabitants knew and used Nahua. When it is not explicitly reported, there are often good indirect hints as to its presence. The presence and relative importance of Nahua is strongly suggested, for example, when it can be established that the clergy were administering to their Indians in Nahua in preference to the mother language. Finally, for some localities, the absence of Nahua

seems to have struck the observer as so extraordinary that he explicitly noted it.

In totaling the evidence, jurisdiction by jurisdiction, we can have little doubt that over 90 per cent of the population in the region in which the Triple Alliance held sway was Nahua-speaking. There were, of course, some non-Nahua-speaking enclaves within this area, but for the most part these were located in the more remote backwash areas with relatively low population densities.

Although the sources are not as ample as for the nuclear area, Nahua was extensively spoken in Jalisco and other parts of Nueva Galicia. There, some of the indigenous languages, at least, were closely related to Nahua, perhaps mutually intelligible dialects. Here as in most of Guerrero and Totonacapan, Nahua was too widespread, too entrenched, to be wholly attributable to post-Hispanic introduction. Conservatively, at least 80 per cent of this region can be estimated to have spoken Nahua and closely related dialects at the time of the Spanish Conquest.

Borah and Cook (1963) have estimated that central Mexico contained a native population of approximately 25 million people on the eve of the Spanish Conquest. This estimate provides one basis by which the frequency of native languages spoken at the time of the Conquest can be expressed in terms of an absolute number of speakers. In total, a minimum of 16½ million people appear to have spoken Nahua either as their mother tongue or as a second language in central Mexico.

The main region in which Nahua predominated includes the following demographic provinces of Borah and Cook: Central Plateau, Region I; Jalapa-Veracruz, Regions IIA-III; Coastal Guerrero, Region VII; and the contiguous portions of Region IV, Northwest Oaxaca. By their estimates, these four regions alone contained a total of approximately 19 million people, of

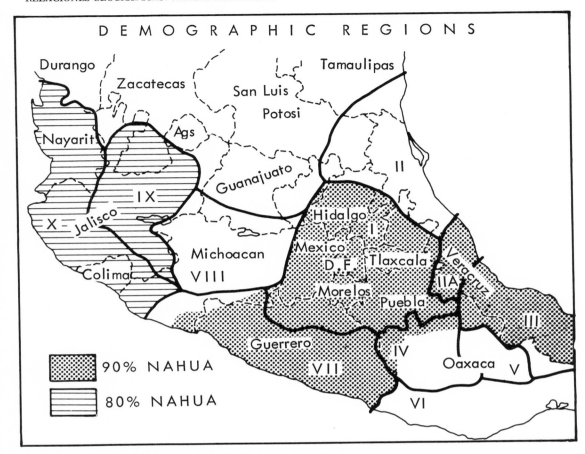

Fig. 8—PREDOMINANTLY NAHUA AREAS, 16TH CENTURY
(after Borah and Cook, 1963, adapted)

which 15½ were Nahua-speakers. These calculations are presented in Table 5 and are based on an average estimate for each of the preceding four regions of 95 per cent ± 5 per cent—representing a figure greater than 90 per cent, but less than 100 per cent.

To the population of the main area estimated to have spoken Nahua may be added nearly a million more speakers from Borah and Cook's Regions IX-X, Colima-Nayarit-Jalisco-Zacatecas. This calculation is based on an estimated 80 per cent Nahua-speaking population for these two demographic provinces (fig. 8).

Nahua was also spoken in each of the other regions, but there is very little empirical basis for determining its importance relative to the total population of these regions. No separate regional estimate, therefore, has been included in Table 5 for Regions II (Valles-Panuco), V (Central Oaxaca), VI (Coastal Oaxaca), VIII (Michoacan, and the balance of Region IV (Northwest Oaxaca), but their omission is not to deny their importance. Even allowing from 5 to 10 per cent for these regions combined, which the direct evidence will readily support, the total Nahua-speaking population for central Mexico on the eve of the Spanish Conquest approached 19 million.

315

REFERENCES

Alegre, 1956
Barlow, 1944a, 1944b
Borah and Cook, 1963
Brand and others, 1960
Cline, 1964a
Cook and Borah, 1960
Dávila Garibi, 1935, 1947
Escalante Hernández, 1962
Fernández de Miranda, 1956
———— and Weitlaner, 1961
García Icazbalceta, 1954
García Payón, 1941, 1942
García Pimentel, 1897, 1904
Gómez de Orozco, 1927a
Gudschinsky, 1959
Henrichs Pérez, 1947
Kelly and Palerm, 1952

Ledesma, 1905
Longacre, 1957, 1961
McQuown, 1941, 1942
Mason, 1940
Mota Padilla, 1870
Orozco y Berra, 1864
Papeles de Nueva España, 1905–06
Paso y Troncoso, 1940
Radin, 1933
Ruiz de Alarcon, 1892
Sahagún, 1938
Swadesh, 1954–55, 1960
Thomas and Swanton, 1911
Upson and Longacre, 1965
Villaseñor y Sánchez, 1952
Wonderly, 1953

APPENDIX A. A BIBLIOGRAPHICAL NOTE ON 16TH-CENTURY LINGUISTIC PUBLICATIONS CONCERNING NEW SPAIN

The publishing industry in New Spain was launched with the publication of a *Doctrina Christiana* in the Mexican language, printed by order of Fray Juan de Zumárraga in 1539. Publications relating to native languages continued throughout the 16th century to be one of the most popular subjects treated by the press. A total of 88 items is known or thought to have been published before the beginning of the 17th century. Doubtless there were more, but they have not been preserved. These 88 titles represent 28 per cent of the total number of titles known to have been produced in 16th-century Mexico.

The most complete treatment of 16th-century Mexican publications is Joaquín García Icazbalceta's *Bibliografía Mexicana del Siglo XVI*, recently revised by Millares Carlo (García Icazbalceta, 1954). The following bibliography of 16th-century native language titles is taken from this publication. In some instances, the lengthy full title has been shortened, with details as to place of publication and publisher omitted. The number in parentheses beside each title is the Icazbalceta entry number, included to facilitate location of the full citation in that work.

As in the Icazbalceta bibliography, the following bibliography is divided into three sections: I, extant publications; II, publications of which no copies are known to exist; III, publications that exist only in fragmentary form and those thought to have been published, but which are not extant and which are somewhat conjectural.

I: EXTANT PUBLICATIONS

1539
Fray Juan de Zamárraga, *Breve y mas compendiosa doctrina christiana en lengua mexicana y castellana* (no. 1).

1546
Fray Alonso de Molina, *Doctrina christiana breve traduzida en lengua Mexicana* (no. 10).

ca. 1547
Fray P. de Gante, *Doctrina christiana en lengua Mexicana* (no. 14).

1548
Doctrina christiana en lengua Española y Mexicana: hecha por los religiosos de la orden de Sancto Domingo (no. 15).

Fray Juan de Guevara, *Doctrina christiana en lengua Huasteca* (no. 17).

1550
Doctrina christiana en lengua Española y Mexicana: hecha por los religiosos de la orden de Sancto Domingo, agora nuevamente corregida y enmendada (no. 19).

1553
Fray Pedro de Gante, *Doctrina christiana en lengua Mexicana* (no. 20).

1555
Fray Alonso de Molina, *Vocabulario en la lengua Castellana y Mexicana* (no. 24).

1556
Illmo. Sr. D. Francisco Marroquin, Obispo de Guatemala, *Catecismo y Doctrina Cristiana en idioma Utlateco* (no. 29).

1558
Fray Maturino Gylberti, *Arte de la lengua de Michuacan* (no. 32).

Fray Maturino Gilberti, *Thesoro spiritual en lengua de Mechuacan* (no. 33).

1559
Fray Maturino Gylberti, *Dialogo de Doctrina Christiana, en la lengua de Mechuacan* (no. 34).

Fray Maturino Gilberti, *Vocabulario en lengua de Mechuacan* (no. 35).

317

Fray Maturino Gilberti, *Cartilla para los niños, en lengua tarasca* (no. 36).

1560
Fray Francisco de Cepeda, *Artes de los idiomas Chiapaneco, Zoque, Tzendal y Chinanteco* (no. 41).

1565
Fray Alonso de Molina, *Confessionario breve, en lengua Mexicana y Castellana* (no. 44).

Fray Alonso de Molina, *Confessionario mayor, en lengua Mexicana y Castellana* (no. 45).

Fray Domingo de la Anunciacion, *Doctrina Christiana breve y compendiosa por via de dialogo entre un maestro y un discipulo, sacada en lengua castellana y mexicana* (no. 46).

1567
Fray Pedro de Feria, *Doctrina christiana en lengua Castellana y çapoteca* (no. 49).

Fray Benito Fernández, *Doctrina misteca* (no. 54).

1568
Fray Benito Fernández, *Doctrina christiana en lengua Misteca* (no. 55).

1569
Fray Alonso de Molina, *Confessionario breve, en lengua Mexicana y Castellana* (no. 62).

Fray Alonso de Molina, *Confessionario mayor en la lengua Mexicana y Castellana* (no. 63).

1571
Fray Alonso de Molina, *Arte de la lengua Mexicana y Castellana* (no. 65).

Fray Alonso de Molina, *Doctrina breve en lengua mexicana* (no. 66).

Fray Alonso de Molina, *Vocabulario en lengua Castellana y Mexicana* (no. 68).

Fray Juan de la Cruz, *Doctrina christiana en la lengua Guasteca con la lengua Castellana* (no. 69).

1574
Fray Juan Baptista de Lagunas, *Arte y Diccionario; con otras obras, en lengua Michuacana* (no. 71).

1575
Fray Maturino Gilberti, *Thesoro spiritual de pobres en lengua de Michuacan* (no. 73).

Fray Juan de la Anunciacion, *Doctrina christiana muy cumplida compuesta en lengua Castellana y Mexicana* (no. 74).

Fray Juan de la Anunciacion, *Sermones para publicar y despedir la Bulla de la sancta cruzada: compuestos y traduzidos en lengua Mexicana y Castellana* (no. 75).

Fray Juan de Medina, *Doctrinalis fidei in Michuacanensium Indorum linguam* (no. 77).

1576
Fray Alonso de Molina, *Arte de la lengua Mexicana y Castellana* (no. 78).

Fray Melchior de Vargas, *Doctrina christiana, muy util, y necessaria en Castellano, Mexicana y Otomi* (no. 79).

1577
Fray Juan de la Anunciacion, *Sermonario en lengua Mexicana* (no. 85).

Fray Alonso de Molina, *Confessionario breve, en lengua Mexicana y Castellana* (no. 86).

1577–78
Fray Juan de Medina, *Doctrinalis fidei in Mechuacanensium Indorum Lengua* (no. 87).

1578
Fray Alonso de Molina, *Confessionario mayor, en la lengua Mexicana y Castellana* (no. 88).

Fray Alonso de Molina, *Doctrina christiana, en lengua Mexicana* (no. 89).

Fray Juan de Cordova, *Arte en lengua Zapoteca* (no. 90).

Fray Juan de Cordova, *Vocabulario en lengua Çapoteca* (no. 91).

1580
Fray Bartholome Roldan, *Cartilla y doctrina christiana, en la lengua Chuchona del pueblo de Tepexic de la Seda* (no. 100).

1582
Fray Juan de Gaona, *Colloquios de la paz, y tranquilidad Christiana, en lengua Mexicana* (no. 101).

1583
Fray Bernardino de Sahagún, *Psalmodia christiana, y sermonario de los Sanctos del Año, en lengua Mexicana* (no. 105).

II: PUBLICATIONS OF WHICH NO COPIES ARE KNOWN TO EXIST

n.d.
Pedro de Betanzos, *Cartilla de oraciones en las lenguas guatemalteca, utlateca y tzutigil* (no. I.5).

n.d.
Diego de Carranza, *Doctrina christiana en lengua chontla* (no. I.7).

157–?

Andrés de Castro, *Arte de aprender las lenguas mexicana y matlazinga* (no. I.9).

n.d.

Francisco Cepeda, *Arte de los idiomas chiapaneco, zoque, etc.* (no. I.11).

157–?

Juan de Córdoba, *Confessionario breve en lengua zapoteca* (no. I.13).

n.d.

Felipe Díaz, *Sermones en lengua mexicana* (no. I.14).

n.d.

Doctrina cristiana en lengua mexicana (no. I.16).

1552

Doctrina christiana en lengua de Michoacan, por los religiosos de la Orden de San Francisco (no. I.17).

156–?

Doctrina christiana en lengua de los indios de Tepuzculula (no. I.18).

n.d.

Pedro de Feria, *Confessionario en lengua zapoteca* (no. I.21).

n.d.

Benigno Fernández, *Epístolas y Evangelios en lengua misteca* (no. I.22).

1550

Benito Fernández, Doctrina en lengua misteca (no. I.23).

1557

Maturino Gilberti, *Vocabulario de la lengua de Michoacán* (no. I.25).

1553

Maturino Gilberti, *Oraciones devotas y santas en lengua tarasca* (no. I.26).

1559

Maturino Gilberti, *Cartilla para los niños en lengua tarasca* (no. I.27).

n.d.

Maturino Gilberti, *Confesionario en lengua tarasca* (no. I.28).

n.d.

Maturino Gilberti, *Sermones de doctrina cristiana en lengua tarasca* (no. I.29).

n.d.

Maturino Gilberti, *Doctrina cristiana en tarasco* (no. I.30).

1548

Juan de Guevara, *Doctrina cristiana en lengua huasteca* (no. I.31).

n.d.

Juan Bautista de Lagunas, *Doctrina cristiana en tarasco* (no. I.37).

1574–75

Diego de Landa, *Doctrina cristiana en lengua maya* (no. I.38).

n.d.

Alonso de Molina, *Doctrina cristiana breve en legua mexicana* (no. I.44).

157–?

Alonso de Molina, *Vocabulario en lengua mexicana y castellana* (no. I.45).

n.d.

Alonso de Molina, *Evangelios de todo el año en lengua mexicana* (no. I.47).

n.d.

Toribio de Benavente Motolinia, *Doctrina cristiana en lengua mexicana y castellana* (no. I.50).

n.d.

Andrés de Olmos, *Arte de la lengua mexicana* (no. I.52).

n.d.

Pedro de Oroz, *Gramática en lengua otomí* (no. I.55).

n.d.

Pedro de Palacios, *Arte en lengua otomí* (no. I.60.

n.d.

Juan de Ribas, *Catecismo mexicano* (no. I.63).

n.d.

Juan de Ribas, *Respuestas de la vida cristiana en mexicano* (no. I.64).

n.d.

Sebastián Ribero, *Vocabulario en otomí* (no. I.65).

n.d.

Antonio Rincón, *Arte Mexicana* (no. I.66).

1598

Elías de San Juan Bautista, *Diálogos en lengua mexicana* (no. I.69).

n.d.

Sumario de las indulgencias de Nuestra Señora del Rosario en mexicano (no. I.70).

n.d.

Francisco Toral, *Arte, vocabulario y doctrina cristiana en popoloca* (no. I.76).

1573?

Juan de Tovar, *Diálogos y Catecismo de la lengua espanola, traducidos al mexicano* (no. I.77).

319

III: Publications Existing in Fragmentary Form and Those Thought to Have Been Published but Not Extant

n.d.

Cartilla para la enseñanza de la doctrina cristiana en lengua zotzil, latina y castellana (no. II.5).

154–?

Doctrina cristiana en lengua mexicana (no. II.9).

155–?

Doctrina cristiana en lengua mexicana y castellana (no. II.10).

1546?

Doctrina cristiana en lengua mexicana (no. II.11).

1539?

Pedro de Gante, *Doctrina cristiana en lengua mexicana* (no. II.28).

n.d.

Pedro de Gante, *Doctrina cristiana en mexicana* (no. II.29).

n.d.

Pedro de Gante, *Doctrina cristiana en lengua mexicana* (no. II.30).

n.d.

Alonso de Molina, *Confesionario breve en lengua mexicana y castellana* (no. II.42).

Appendix B. LANGUAGES LISTED IN THE RELACIONES GEOGRÁFICAS: DISTRIBUTION BY COMMUNITIES

Numbers refer to the RG Census (Article 8). Where not included in the Census, a community is given "x" suffix, indicating it is listed in Table 2. Extinct languages are marked by an asterisk.

Achi (Cakchiquel?). MACRO-MAYAN. Mayan, III.1. ATITLAN (9); ZAPOTITLAN (152).

Amusgo. MACRO-OTOMANGUEAN. Mixtecan. II.2. Ayusuchiquilazala (61C), Xicayan de Tovar (61D), Zacatepec (61F), Xicayan (142A), Ayozinapa (142B), Ometepec (142C), Suchistlauca (142D), Ihualapa (142G).

Apanec.° UNCLASSIFIED. VI. Guaymeo (157A).

Ayacastec.° UNCLASSIFIED. VI. Ometepec (142C), Ihualapa (142G).

Cakchiquel. *See* Achi.

Cazcan.° UTO-AZTECAN. NAHUA. I.1 AMECA (4), NUCHISTLAN (75), TEQUALTICHE (113), Taltenango (143A).

Chichimec.° UNCLASSIFIED. VI. Acambaro (18A), Yurirpundaro (18B), CEMPOALA (19), Epazoyuca (19A), TEPEAPULCO (111), ZIMAPAN (155).

Chinantec. MACRO-OTOMANGUEAN. Chinantecan. II.5. Malinaltepec (11A), CHINANTLA (24), USILA (138).

Chocho. MACRO-OTOMANGUEAN. Popolocan. II.3. CUZCATLAN (42–43), IXCATLAN (54), TEXUPA (124).

Chontal. UNCLASSIFIED. VI. ICHCATEOPAN (52), Alaustlan (52B), Ostuma (52C), Cuatepec (52E), Apastla (52J), Teloloapa (52L), Tutultepec (52M), IGUALA (53), Tepecuacuilco (53B), TAXCO (96).

Chontal (Oaxaca). HOKALTECAN. Tequistlatecan. V.2. Nanacatepec (73), Tlacotepec (88A), Zozopastepec (88B), Tamaspaltepec (88C), Macupilco (88D), Tequesistlan (102B).

Chontal. MACRO-MAYAN. Mayan. III.1. TABASCO (89–91), TETZAL (121).

Chunbia.° UNCLASSIFIED. VI. Vitaluta (148G), Guauayutla (148H), Coyuquila (148I).

Cintec.° UNCLASSIFIED. VI. Cintla (142H).

Coca.° UTO-AZTECAN. Related language. I. PONCITLAN (82), Cuiseo del Rio (82A).

Cochin.° UNCLASSIFIED. VI. TUXPAN (137).

Cuacumanes.° UNCLASSIFIED. VI. PURIFICACION (84).

Cuicatec. MACRO-OTOMANGUEAN. Mixtecan. II.2. ATLATLAUCA (11), Tutupetongo (34C), Tanatepec (34D), CUICATLAN (35), Quiotepec ("Quiotecas," 54A), PAPALOTICPAC (78), Tepeucila (78A).

Cuisca. UTO-AZTECAN. Nahua. I.1. IGUALA. (53), Cocula (53A), Tepecuacuilco

320

(53B), Mayanala (53C), Tasmaloca (53E).

Cuitlatec. UNCLASSIFIED. VI. ASUCHITLAN (7), Tetela del Rio (52H), Teccomatan (148A), Azuchitlan (148B), Tamalacan (148C).

Culiartes.° UNCLASSIFIED. VI. PURIFICACION (84).

GUACHICHIL.° UTO-AZTECAN. Related language. I. FRESNILLO (44).

Guazontec (Huave). MACRO-MAYAN. Huave. III.4. TEHUANTEPEC coast towns (102X).

Huave. *See* Guazontec.

Huehuetec.° UNCLASSIFIED. VI. Huehuetlan (142F).

Iscuca.° UNCLASSIFIED. VI. Teloloapa (52L).

Izteca.°UNCLASSIFIED. VI. PURIFICACION (84).

Mam. MACRO-MAYAN. Mayan. III.1. ZAPOTITLAN (152).

Matlatzinca. MACRO-OTOMANGUEAN. Pame-Otomian. II.1. ATLATLAUCA (10), Cocula (53A), TEMAZCALTEPEC, MINAS (103), Tescaltitlan (103A), Temazcaltepec, pueblo. (103C), TEUTENANGO (122), TISTLA (132), Guetamo (157C), ZULTEPEC (163).

Maya (Yucatec). MACRO-MAYAN. Mayan. III.1. CACALAC (13), CACALCHEN (14), CAMPOCOLCHE (15), CANACHE (16), CANZACABO (17), CHANCENOTE (20), CHUBULNA (26), CHUNCHUCHU (27), CUICUIL (36), CUITELCUM (39), CUIZIL (40), GUAYMA (48), HOCABA (50), IXMUL (55), IZAMAL (58), MAMA (63), MERIDA (64), MOTUL (69), MOXOPIPE (70), NABALON (71), OSCUZCAS (77), PIJOY (81), POPOLA (83), TAHZIB, (92), TEABO (97), TECAL (98), TECANTO (99), TECON (100), TEMUL (104), TENUM (106), TEQUITE (115), TEZEMI (125), TEZOCO (126), TIQUIBALON (129), TISHOTZUCO (131), VALLADOLID (139), XOQUEN (145), YALCON (146), YUCATAN (147), ZAMA (149), ZAMAHIL (150), ZAN (151), ZICAB (154), ZISMOPO (158), ZIZINTUM (159), ZONOT (160), ZOTUTA (161), ZOZIL (162), ZUSOPO (165), ZUZAL (166).

Mazahua. MACRO-OTOMANGUEAN. Pame-Otomian. II.1. Acambaro (18A), Temazcaltepec, pueblo (103C), Tuzantla (103D).

Mazatec. MACRO-OTOMANGUEAN. Popolocan. II.3. CUZCATLAN (42–43), Matzatlan (107A), Huautla (107B), Nextepec (107C), Nanahuatepec (107D), Tecolutla (107E).

Mazatec° (de Guerrero). UNCLASSIFIED. Tzicapuzalco (52A), TAXCO (96), ZULTEPEC (163).

Mazatec° (de Jalisco). UNCLASSIFIED. VI. PURIFICACION (84).

Melaguese.° UNCLASSIFIED. VI. PURIFICACION (84).

Mexicano (only). UTO-AZTECAN. Nahua. I.1. ACAPISTLA (1), Piastla (2D), AHUATLAN (3), Texaluca (3A), Zoyatitlanapa (3B), Coatzinco (3C), Tetela (7), Capulalcoculco (7), CHILAPA (22 bis), CHOLULA (25), Chimalhuacan Toyac (29A), Chicoaloapa (29B), CULHUACAN (41), GUATULCO (45), Pochutla (45B), Tonameca (45C), GUAXTEPEC (47), Acapetlaguaya (52D), Cuezala (52I), IXTAPALAPA (56), MEXICATZINGO (65), MEZTITLAN (66), OCOPETLAYUCA (76), QUATLATLAUCA (85), Gueguetlan (85A), Santa Ana Tetlaman (95x), TEOTITLAN DEL CAMINO (107), TEPUZTLAN (112), TEQUIZISTLAN (116), TETELA DEL VOLCAN (117), TETELA (118), San Estevan (118x), San Miguel Capulapa (118x), S. F. Cucumba (118x), San Juan Tututla (118x), TEXCOCO (123), TLACOTALPA (134), Cotastla (134A), Tuztla (134B), TOTOLAPA (136), VERACRUZ (140), XALAPA DE LA VERA CRUZ (141), Atesac (141O), Izguacan (141S), Tlaculula (142E), Copalitas (142J), Xalapa (142K), Nespa (142L), Cuahutepec (142M), Tototepec (142N), Zacatula (148), Zacualpa (148N), ZUMPANGO (164).

Mexicano (plus some other). UTO-AZTECAN. Nahua. I.1. AMECA (4), Cusalapa (5A), Tuscaquesco (5B), Zapotitlan (5C); ANTEQUERA (6), ATITLAN (9), ATLATLAUCA (10), ATITLALQUIA (12), CEMPOALA (19), Epazoyuca (19A), Tetlistaca (19B), CHICONAUTLA (22), CITLALTOMAGUA (28), Xahulatepec (28x), COATEPEC (29), COATZOCOALCO (30), COMPOSTELA (31); CUAUHQUILPAN (32), CUICATLAN (35), CUZCATLAN (42–

321

43); GUEYTLAPA (49), Zacatlan (49A), Jujupango (49B); HUEXOTLA (51), ICHCATEOPAN (52), Ostuma (52C), Teloloapan (52L), Tepecuacuilco (53B), Mayanala (53C), IZCATLAN (54), IZTEPEXIC (57), JILQUILPAN (60), JUSTLAVACA (61), Tecomastlauca (61A), Mistepec (61B), Puctla (61E), Zacatepec (61F), Cualcolman (68A), Maquili (68B), Nexapa (interpreters) (73), NUCHISTLAN (75), PONCITLAN (82), PURIFICACION (84), QUERETARO (86), Xilotepec (86x), SUCHITEPEC (88); TABASCO (89–91), TANCITARO (95); Stgo. Acauat (95x); TAXCO (96); TEHUANTEPEC (102), TEMAZCALTEPEC (103), Tescaltitlan (103A), Texupilco (103B); Temazcaltepec, pueblo 103C), TENAMAZTLAN (105), Matzatlan (107A), Huautla (107B), Nextepec (107C), Nanahuatepec (107D), Tecolutla (107E), TEPEACA (110), Tecamachalco (110A), Cachula (110B), Tecali (110C), TEPEAPULCO (111), TEQUALTICHE (113), TEQUISQUIAC (114), Citlaltepec (114A), Xilocingo (114B), Tepexpa (116A), Aculma (116B), San Juan Teotihuacan (116C), Xonotla (118A), San Martin Tutzamapa (118x), San Francisco (118x), Santiago Ecatlan (118x), Cozautepec (120A), TEUTENANGO (122), TINGUINDIN (128), TISTLA (132), Axocupan (135A), Tornacustla (135C), Gueypuchtla (135D), Tecpatepec (135F), TUXPAN (137), Zapotlan (137A), Tamatzula (137B), USILA (138), Xilotepec (141A), Tlaculula (141B), Chepultepec (141D), Naolingo (141E), Miaguatlan (141G), Chiconquiyauca (141H), Ciguacoatlan (141J), Almoloncan (141L), Chiltoyac (141N), Huehuetlan (142F), Cintla (142H), Tepetlapa (142I), Cuahuitlan (142U), Taltenango (143A), XOCOTLAN (144), ZAPOTITLAN (152), ZAYULA (153), ZIMAPAN (155), ZULTEPEC (163).

Mixe. MACRO-MAYAN. Mixe-Zoquean. III.3. Quesatepec (73x), Xilotepec (73x), TEHUANTEPEC (102), Xalapa (102A).

Mixtec. MACRO-OTOMANGUEAN. Mixtecan. II.2. ACATLAN (2), Chila (2A), Petlalzinco (2B), Icxitlan (2C), ANTEQUERA (6), COATZOCOALCO (30), CUAHUITLAN (33), CUAUTLA (34), Xocoticpac (34A), Xaltepetongo (34B), CUILAPA (37), GUAXOLOTITLAN (46), JUSTLAVACA (61), Tecomastlauca (61A), Mistepec (61B), Ayusuchiquilazala (61C), Xicayan (61D), Puctla ((61E), Zacatepec (61F), NOCHIZTLAN (74), Eztitla (80A), Huiztepec (80B), Itzcuintepec (80C), Cuauxoloticpac (80D), TEHUANTEPEC (102), Xalapa (102A), TEOZACOALCO (108), Amoltepec (108A), Cuylapa (109A), TEXUPA (124), TILANTONGO (127), Mitlantongo (127A), Tamazula (127B), Xicayan de Tovar (142A).

Otomi. MACRO-OTOMANGUEAN. Pame-Otomian. II.1. ATENGO (8), ATLITLALAQUIA (12), Acambaro (18A), CEMPOALA (19), Epazoyuca (19A), Tetlistaca (19B), CHICONAUTLA (22), COATEPEC (29), Santa Ana Tetitlan (29x), San Miguel Tepetlapa (29x), CUAUHQUILPAN (32), NECOTLAN (72), QUERETARO (86), Xilotepec (86x), TAIMEO (93), TEPEACA (110), Tecamachalco (110A), Cachula (110B), TEPEAPULCO (111), TESQUISQUIAC (114), Citlaltepec (114A), Xilocingo (114B), Tepexpa (116A), Aculma (116B), San Juan Teotihuacan (116C), Axocupan (135A), Yetecomac (135B), Tornacustla (135C), Gueypuchtla (135D), Tezcatepec (135E), Tecpatepec (135F), ZAYULA (153), ZIMAPAN (155).

Otomi (de Jalisco). UNCLASSIFIED. VI. Cusalapa (5A), Tuscaquesco (5B), Zapotitlan (5C).

Panteca. UNCLASSIFIED. VI. Pantla (151D), Iztupan (151E).

Pinoles. MACRO-OTOMANGUEAN (?). II. Tecomabaca.

Pipil. UTO-AZTECAN. Nahua. I.1. Aguatepec (9A).

Pocotec.° UNCLASSIFIED. VI. PURIFICACION (84).

Popoloca. MACRO-OTOMANGUEAN. Popolocan. II.3. Tecamachalco (110A), Cachula (110B), San Juan Teotihuacan (116C).

Popoluca. MACRO-MAYAN. III.3. COATZACOALCO (30).

Quacumec (Tlaotli). UNCLASSIFIED. VI. Cualcoman (68A).

Quahutec.° UNCLASSIFIED. VI. Cuahuitlan (142U).

Quiche. See Uhtlateca.

Quiotec. *See* Cuicatec.

Sayultec.° UTO-AZTECAN. Nahua. I.1 (?). JILQUILPAN (60), Zapotlan (137A).

Tamazultec.° UNCLASSIFIED. VI. Tamazula (137B).

Tarascan. TARASCAN. IV. Pungaravato (7B), Cuzamala (7C), Acambaro (18A), Yurirpundaro (18B), CHILCHOTLA (23), CUISEO DE LA LAGUNA (38), JILQUILPAN (60), Chocondiran (60A), Tarecuato (60B), Perivan (60C), NECOTLAN (72), PATZCUARO (79), TANCITARO (95), Tlapalcatepec (95A), Santiago Acauat (95x), TAXCO (96), Tuzantla (103D), TINGUINDIN (128), TIRIPITIO (130), Zapotlan (137A), Tamatzula (137B), Tamaluacan (148F), ZIRANDARO (157), Guaymeo (157A), Cuseo (157B), ZULTEPEC (163).

Tecoxquin.° UTO-AZTECAN. Related language. I. COMPOSTELA (31).

Tepehua. MACRO-MAYAN. Totonacan. III.2. HUEXOTLA (51).

Tepuztec.° UNCLASSIFIED. VI. CITLALTOMAGUA (28), Anecuilco (28A), Xahualtepec (28x), Tlacotepec (52F), Utatlan (52G), Teccomatan (148A), Azuchitlan (148B), Tamalacan (148C).

Tiam.° UNCLASSIFIED. VI. TUXPAN (137).

Tlaotli. *See* Quacumec.

Tlapanec. HOKALTECAN. Tlapanecan. V.1. Cintla (142H), Tepetlapa (142I), Ayutla (142O), Suchitonala (142P), Acatlan (142Q), Cuacoyolichan (142R), Colutla 142S), Azoyuque (142T).

Tomatec.° UNCLASSIFIED. VI. PURIFICACION (84).

Totonac° (de Jalisco). UNCLASSIFIED. VI. AMECA (4).

Totonac. MACRO-MAYAN. Totonacan. III.2. GUEYTLAPA (49), Zacatlan (49A), Jujupango (49B), Matatlan-Chila (49C), Papantla (49D), MISANTLA (67), Nanacatlan (67x), Pilopa (67x), Poztectlan (67x),

Xonotla (118A), San Martin Tutzamapa (118x), San Francisco (118x), Santiago Ecatlan (118x), Xilotepec (141A), Tlaculula (141B), Chepultepec (141D), Naolingo (141E), Miaguatlan (141G), Chiconquiyauca (141H), Colipa (141I), Ciguacoatlan (141J), Tepetlan (141K), Almoloncan (141L), Chiltoyac (141N).

Tuztec.° UNCLASSIFIED. VI. ICHCATEOPAN (52), TISTLA (132).

Tzeltal. *See* Chontal.

Uhtlatec. MACRO-MAYAN. Mayan. III.1. ATITLAN (9).

Xocotec.° UNCLASSIFIED. VI. XOCOTLAN (144).

Popoluca. MACRO-MAYAN. 111.3. COATZACOALCO (30).

Zacatec.° UTO-AZTECAN. Nahua. I.1. FRESNILLO (44), SAN MARTIN (87), XEREZ (143).

Zapotec. MACRO-OTOMANGUEAN. Zapotecan. II.4. ANTEQUERA (6), CHICHICAPA (21), Amatlan (21A), Miaguatlan (21B), Coatlan (21C), Ozelotepec (21D), COATZACOALCO (30), GUAXOLOTITLAN (46), IXTEPEXIC (57), IZTEPEC (59), MACUILSUCHIL (62), Teotitlan del Valle (62A), NEXAPA (73), Elotepec (80E), Totomachapa (80F), SUCHITEPEC (88), TALISTACA (94), TECUICUILCO (101), Atepec (101A), Zoquiapa (101B), Xaltianguis (101C), TEHUANTEPEC (102), Xalapa (102A), Tequesistlan (102B), TEOZAPOTLAN (109), TETICPAC (119), TETIQUIPA–RIO HONDO (120), Cozautepec (120A), TLACOLULA (133), Miquitla (133A), Cuahuzapotla (142V).

Zapotec° (local). UNCLASSIFIED. VI. Zapotlan (137A).

Zoque. MACRO-MAYAN. Mixe-Zoquean. III.3. TABASCO (89–91).

Zutuhil. MACRO-MAYAN. Mayan. III.1. ATITLAN (9).

323

8. A Census of the Relaciones Geográficas of New Spain, 1579–1612

HOWARD F. CLINE

THIS CENSUS lists and describes the *Relaciones Geográficas* prepared in New Spain during the 16th and 17th centuries. The listing is restricted for the 16th century to reports prepared in response to the Royal Cédula of May 25, 1577 (see Article 5, Appendices A–C), but all such documents, whether presently extant or lost, are included. Omitted are numerous reports somewhat similar to RG's but not in the specific 1579–85 series. Many such are listed in Jiménez de la Espada, 1881.

For the 17th century, the Census lists only documents related to the 1604 questionnaire. These take numbers beginning with 301, whereas extant RG's from the 16th century are numbered consecutively from 1 to 166; "lost" items from 201.

ELEMENTS OF THE ENTRIES

So far as information has been available through May, 1971, each Census entry has been standardized. Nearly all contain the following data:

a. *Census Number of Principal Document.* For extant documents of the 1579–85

series, Census numbers are consecutive, with two exceptions. After the basic numeration was established and published in Cline, 1964a, it was determined that CHILAPA merited separate notice; it was assigned the awkward number of 22bis. In similar fashion, XONOTLA was inadvertently omitted, but later was restored as 118bis. To have renumbered the many cross-references at a late point in the process would have produced chaos, hence the lesser of two evils.

b. *Principal Settlement.* The town or settlement used in the title for the document is frequently an arbitrary choice. It appears in capital letters. Spellings of places within any given document are quite variant, hence again the form used here may well represent a subjective decision among equally valid alternatives. No attempt has been made to correlate the place names in the Census with those used by Gerhard and others in their respective articles.

c. *Archbishopric or Bishopric.*

d. *Province or Area.* In addition to more formal jurisdictional names, compilers often added a local or popular name to the general region. Where thus supplied, these are included after the bishopric.

e. *Class or Type*. As explained in Article 5, nearly all RG's can be categorized as "simple," "composite," or "complex." Such classification appears in brackets as the final element of the first line of an entry.

f. *Synonyms*. Variants of the name, or synonyms found in the RG, are generally included on a separate line, where available. Many RG's do not include synonyms.

g. *Compiler*. The name and title of the principal compiler are furnished. The numerous native aides, scribes, and others often named at the beginning or end of the RG have not been included.

h. *Dates*. The dates when the document was compiled are given, usually as stated in the RG or its cover.

i. *Indicia*. As outlined in Article 5, the various archival indicia and note of the document in listings are provided. Many of these were kindly provided by Dr. Adele Kibre for documents in AGI. Not all RG's have all indicia. Where ascertainable, the following are employed:

DyP—Descripción y Población. Legajo/ document number, usually on cover.

JGI —Joaquín García Icazbalceta Collection, University of Texas. The Latin American Collection at UTX has retained the original volume/document numbers given his materials by JGI.

JLV—Juan López de Velasco Inventory of 1583. Article 5, Appendix D. Legajo number, and document number within legajo.

MP —Memoria by Pinelo, reproduced as Appendix E, Article 5.

RM —Received by Muñoz, 1783. From Muñoz, 1783.

SIM—Simancas number. From Larrañaga, 1783, and also often independently noted on RG.

See "Abbreviations" at the front of this volume for further explanations.

j. *Repository*. The repository (UTX, University of Texas; AGI, Archivo General de Indias; RAH, Royal Academy of History) is indicated, together with local indentification number(s). If known, foliation is provided, plus data on whether a *pintura* (map) is extant and published or unpublished.

k. *Publication Status*. Published versions of text materials are provided in chronological order, the citations being to the Annotated Bibliography, Article 9. Map publication refers to the Robertson Catalog, Article 6, which provides further details.

l. *Locational Data*. "Mod" refers to the modern community as it appears in the official 1950 Mexican census. Most of these data were supplied by Peter Gerhard, supplemented by data from Clinton Edwards and Howard Cline. "Map" directs the reader to state/municipio maps in Article 1, appendix. Figure numbers there are followed by the coordinates at which the locality will be found; this is then followed by the number assigned that municipio in the table accompanying each state map in that appendix. For reasons given in Article 1, communities in Oaxaca (no. 20) are first cited by ex-distrito, plus municipio number in that ex-distrito listing.

m. *Language*. From Herbert Harvey's Table 2 (Article 7), the language(s) there reported have been excerpted and repeated. Further data on these languages will be found in that article.

n. *Jurisdictional History*. Changes before and after the RG compilation are provided by Peter Gerhard in Article 2. As places considered "Principal" in this Census are not always entered as such in his summaries, references have been provided to the section/entry of Article 2.

o. *Related* [communities]. This is a generic, shorthand term to indicate sizable communities but lesser than the principal one, covered in the RG. Such subentries follow the preceding form, where applicable. Excluded are mention of many smaller "subjects" (*sujetos*), or very minor communities attached either to a principal place or to a sizable community listed as "Related."

1. ACAPISTLA (V). Mexico. [Cuatro Villas.] Prov. Marquesado del Valle. [Simple].
Ayacapistla, Yacapichtla, Yacapiztla, Xihutzacapitzalan.
Juan Gutiérrez de Liebana, alcalde mayor.
Oct. 10, 1580.
JLV, 1/11. DyP, 1009/8. SIM, 183. RM 27. JGI, XXIII-8.
UTX. CDG, 318. 6 ff. Map.
Text: (1) García Pimentel, 1906. (2) VR, 1956k.
Map: Unpublished. Catalog, 2.
Mod: Yecapixtla, Morelos. Map: fig. 21-M/15-28.*
Lang: Mexicano. Article 2: I-21.
See also GUAXTEPEC, 47; TEPUZTLAN, 112; OCUITUCO, 210; YAUTEPEC, 221.

2. ACATLAN. Tlaxcala. Prov. Mixteca Baja. [Composite].
Juan de Vera, alcalde mayor.
Jan. 2–3, 1581. Crown.
JLV, 2/12. DyP, 623/6. SIM, 140. RM, 62.
RAH. 9-25.4/4663-XXXVIII. 19 ff.; Acatlan, ff. 1–7r. No map.
Text: (1) PNE, 5: 55–65. (2) González Obregón, 1907.
Mod: Acatlan de Osorio, Puebla. Map: fig. 26-N/16-198.
Lang: Mixtec. Article 2: I-2.

Related

A. CHILA. Encomendera: Ana Pérez de Zamora.
RAH. ff. 7r–10r, f. 9 blank.
Text: (1) PNE, 5: 65–69. (2) González Obregón, 1907, pp. 106–09.

*Figures refer to Article 1, appendix. Coordinates at which locality is found are letter/number combinations (M/15); the final number is the listing of that municipio in the key accompanying the figure in Article 1, appendix.

326

Mod: Chila, Puebla. Map: fig. 26-N/16-195.
Lang: Mixtec.
B. PETLALTZINGO. Encomendero: Francisco Hernández Guerrero.
RAH. ff. 10r–12v.
Text: PNE, 5: 69–74.
Mod: Petlalcingo, Puebla. Map: fig. 26-N/16-197.
Lang: Mixtec.
C. ICXITLAN. Encomendero: Luis Velázquez de Lara.
RAH. ff. 13r–14v.
Text: PNE, 5: 74–77.
Mod: S. Miguel Ixtlan, Puebla. Map: fig. 26-0/16-196.
Lang: Mixtec.
D. PIASTLA. Prov. de los Totoltecas. Encomendero (1/2): Heirs of Francisco de Olmos; Crown (1/2).
RAH. ff. 15r–17v.
Text: PNE, 5: 77–80.
Mod: Piaxtla, Puebla. Map: fig. 26-N/16-190.
Lang: Mexicano.

3. AHUATLAN. Tlaxcala. Prov. Izucar. [Composite].
Aguatlan.
Salvador de Cárdenas, corregidor.
Aug. 19, 1581. Crown.
JLV, 1/18. DyP, 622/6. SIM, 139. RM, 66.
RAH. 9-25-4/4663-XXXIX. 10 ff. Ahuatlan, ff. 1–2r. No map.
Text: PNE, 5: 81–84.
Mod: Ahuatlan, Puebla. Map: fig. 26-N/15-151.
Lang: Mexicano. Article 2: I-28.

Related

A. TEXALUCA
Aug. 21, 1581. Crown.
RAH. ff. 3r–5r. ff. 5v, 6r, 6v blank.
Text: PNE 5: 84–88.
Mod: S. Lucas Tejaluca, M. Ahuatlan, Puebla. Map: fig. 26-N/15-151.
Lang: Mexicano.
B. ZOYATITLANAPA
Aug. 22, 1581. Crown.
RAH. ff. 7r–8v.

Text: PNE, 5: 89–93.

Mod: Zoyatitlanapa, M. Huatlatlauca, Puebla. Map: fig. 26-M/16-155.

Lang: Mexicano.

C. COATZINCO

Aug. 24, 1581. Encomendero: Diego de Quesada.

RAH. ff 9r–10v.

Text: PNE, 5: 94–97.

Mod: Coatzingo, Puebla. Map: fig. 26-M/16-152.

Lang: Mexicano.

4. AMECA. Guadalajara. Prov. Amula. [Simple].

Antonio de Leyva, alcalde mayor.

Oct. 2, 1579–Dec. 15, 1579.

JLV, 4/18. DyP, 646/6. SIM, 143. RM, 39. JGI, XXIII-10.

UTX. CDG, 343. 14 ff. Map. Drawing, Catalog, Appendix, 1.

Text: (1) Hernández y Dávalos, 1870. (2) Pérez Hernández, 1874–75. (3) NV, 1878. (4) Palomino y Cañedo, 1947. (5) Amaya, 1951. (6) VR, 1951.

Map: Published. Catalog, 3.

Mod: Ameca, Jalisco. Map: fig. 19-J/6-98.

Lang: Mexicano, Cazcan, Totonac (de Jalisco). Article 2: I-9.

5. AMULA. Guadalajara. [Composite].

Francisco de Agüero, corregidor.

Sept. 4, 1579.

JLV, 1/14. DyP, 979/8. SIM, 195. RM, 128. JGI, XXIII-9.

UTX. CDG, 1857. 8 ff. No map.

Text: (1) NV, 1878, pp. 282–321. (2) VR, 1952a,b.

Mod: See Related. Article 2: I-1.

Related

A. *Cusalapa*

Text: (1) NV, 1878, pp. 282–302. (2) VR, 1952b.

Mod: Cuzalapa, M. Cuautitlan, Jalisco. Map: fig. 19-L/6-112.

Lang: Mexicano, Otomi (de Jalisco).

B. TUSCAQUESCO [Tusacuesco]

Text: (1) NV, 1878, pp. 302–12. (2) VR, 1952b.

Mod: Tuxcacuesco, Jalisco. Map: fig. 19-L/6-93.

Lang: Mexicano, Otomi (de Jalisco).

C. ZAPOTITLAN

Text: (1) NV, 1878, pp. 283–302. (2) VR, 1952a.

Mod: Zapotitlan, Jalisco. Map: fig. 19-L/6-91.

Lang: Mexicano, Otomi (de Jalisco).

6. ANTEQUERA. Ciudad. Antequera. [Simple].

Guaxaca.

Pedro Franco, clérigo presbitero.

Jan. 8–9, 1580.

JLV, 4/12. SIM, 31. RM, 72. JGI, XXIII-11.

UTX. CDG, 1428. 5 ff. No map.

Text: (1) Barlow, 1946. (2) VR, 1957c.

Mod: Oaxaca de Juarez, Oaxaca. Map: fig. 25-P/19-1/8.

Lang: Mexicano, Mixtec, Zapotec. Article 2: I-5.

7. ASUCHITLAN. Michoacan. [Complex].

Ajuchitlan. Tthichuc.

Diego Garcés, corregidor.

Oct. 10, 1579. Crown.

JLV, 1/27. DyP, 230/3. SIM, 114. RM, 118.

RAH. 9-25-4/4663-V. Instr., 8 ff. No map.

Text: (1) VR/PNE, 7/5: 7–50. (2) RGM, 1: 61–82.

Mod: Ajuchitlan de Progreso, Guerrero. Map: fig. 17-O/12-21.

Lang: Cuitlatec. Article 2: I-94.

Related

A. COYUCA

Mod: Coyuca de Catalan, Guerrero. Map: fig. 17-O/11-22.

B. PUNGARAVATO

Mod: Cd. Altamirano, M. Pungarabato, Guerrero. Map: fig. 17-N/12-2.

Lang: Tarascan.

327

C. CUZAMALA
    Mod: Cutzamala de Pinzon, Guerrero.
        Map: fig. 17-N/12-1.
    Lang: Tarascan.

8. ATENGO. Mexico. Prov. Teutlalpa. [Complex].
    Juan de Padilla, corregidor.
        Oct. 8, 1579. Crown.
    JLV, 1/26. DyP, 243/3 (text), 297/3 (map). SIM 109. RM, 37. JGI, XXIII-12.
    UTX. CDG, 397. 4 ff.
    Text: VR, 1957a.
    Map: Original unpublished. Copy published. Catalog, 38.
    Mod: Atengo, M. Tezontepec de Aldama, Hidalgo. Map: fig. 18-K/14-79.
    Lang: Otomi. Article 2: I-96.

Related

A. TEUTLALPA [and CUITLALPA]
    Mod: unidentified.
B. MISQUIAHUALA [Misquiguala]
    1/2 Crown; encomendero, Melchior de Contreras, 1/2.
    Map: Original unpublished; copy published. Catalog, 38.
    Mod: Mixquihuala, Hidalgo. Map: fig. 18-K/14-41.
C. TESONTEPEC (Tathobo [Otomi])
    Encomendero: Hijo de Alonso Pérez.
    Mod: Tezontepec de Aldama, Hidalgo. Map: fig. 18-K/14-79.

9. ATITLAN. Santiago. Guatemala. Prov. Zapotitlan (AM). [Composite].
    Tecpan Atitlan, Nra. Sra de la Asuncion de Solola, Tecpancitlan.
    Alonso Páez de Betancor, corregidor, and Fray Pedro de Arboleda.
    Feb. 8–9, 1585. Crown, and encomendero: Sancho Barabona.
    SIM, 47. RM, 138. JGI, XX-10a.
    UTX. CDG, 179. Instr., 44 ff. Atitlan, ff. 1–11. Map.
    Text: Relación, 1964. *See* Broussard, 1952.
    Map: Published. Catalog, 5.

Mod: Santiago Atitlan, Dept. Solola (Guatemala).
Lang: Zutuhil, Achi, Uhtlatec, Pipil. Article 2: XVI-7,9.

Related

A. S. BARTOLOME AGUACTEPEC (AHUATEPEC)
    Feb. 23, 1585.
    JGI, XX-10b.
    UTX. ff. 12–20.
    Text: Descripción, 1965.
B. SAN ANDRES [SEMETABAJ]
    Feb. 26, 1585.
    JGI, XX-10c.
    UTX. ff. 21–29.
    Text: Unpublished.
    Mod: M. San Andres Semetabaj, Dept. Solola.
C. SAN FRANCISCO [ZAPOTITLAN]
    Feb. 27, 1585.
    JGI, XX-10d.
    UTX. ff. 30–38.
    Text: Unpublished.
    Mod: M. S. Francisco Zapotitlan, Dept. Suchitepequez.
See also ZAPOTITLAN, 152.

10. ATLATLAUCA. Mexico. [Composite].
    Gaspar de Solís, corregidor.
    Sept. 17, 1580.
    JLV, 4/5. DyP, 299/3. SIM, 209. RM, 55. JGI, XXIII-13.
    UTX. CDG, 398. 7 ff. Map.
    Text: VR, 1956j.
    Map: Published. Catalog, 7.
    Mod: Atlatlahuca, M. Tenango del Valle, Mexico. Map: fig. 14-M/13-48.
    Lang: Mexicano, Matlatzinca. Article 2: I-88.

Related

A. SUCHIACA
    Mod: Xochiaca, M. Tenancingo, Mexico. Map: fig. 14-M/13-49.

11. ATLATLAUCA. Antequera. [Complex].
    Francisco de la Mezquita, corregidor.
    Sept. 8, 1580. Crown.
    JLV, 3/18. SIM, 25. RM, 96.

RAH. 9-25-4/4663-XXVI.   Map.
Text: PNE, 4: 163–76.
Map: Published.   Catalog, 6.
Mod: S. Juan Bautista Atatlahuca, Oaxaca.   Map: fig. 25-O/18-6/1.
Lang: Cuicatec.   Article 2: I-7.

Related

A. MALINALTEPEC
   Mod: Maninaltepec, M. S. Juan Quiotepec, Oaxaca.   Map: fig. 25-O/19-8/1.
   Lang: Chinantec.

12. ATLITLALAQUIA.   Mexico.   [Complex].
   Atitalquia?
   Valentin de Jaso, corregidor.
      Feb. 22, 1580.
   JLV, P-4, 1/9.   DyP, 1022/8.   SIM, 177.
      RM, 47.
   AGI, IG 1529.   No. 389.   Instr., 9 ff.
      Map lost.
   Text: PNE, 6: 199–208.
   Map: Lost.   Catalog, 8.
   Mod: Atitalaquia, Hidalgo. Map: fig. 18-K/14-76.
   Lang: Otomi, Mexicano.   Article 2: I-96.

Related

A. TLAMACO
   Mod: Tlemaco, M. Atitalaquia, Hidalgo.
      Map: fig. 18-K/14-76.
B. ATOTONILCO
   Mod: Atotonilco Grande, Hidalgo.   Map:
      fig. 18-K/15-30.
C. APAZCO
   Mod: Apaxco de Ocampo, Mexico.   Map:
      fig. 18-K/14-84
D. TETLAPANALOYA
   Mod: Tlapanaloya, M. Tequixquiac, Mexico.   Map: fig. 18-K/14-83.

13. CACALAC (V).   Yucatan.   Prov. Cupules.   [Complex].
   Zacalac.
   Pedro de Valencia, vezino.
   May 6, 1579. Encomendero: (1/2) Heirs
      of Estéban & Juan de la Cruz; (1/2)
      Pedro de Valencia.
   SIM, 214.   RM, 135.
   AGI, IG 1530.   No. 378.   No map.

Text: RY, 2-XVI; DIU, 13: 142–48.
Mod: Sacalaca, M. Felipe Carrillo Puerto,
   Quintana Roo.   Map: fig. 28-J/32-3.
Lang: ? [Maya]. Article 2: XV.

Related

A. TAMUY
   Mod: Tahmuy, M. Valladolid, Yucatan.
      Map: fig. 35-I/32-58.

14. CACALCHEN (M).   Yucatan.   Prov.
Quepech.   [Composite].
   Francisco Tamayo Pacheco, vezino.
   Feb. 20–21, 1581.   Encomendero: Francisco Tamayo Pacheco.
   SIM, 214.   RM, 135.
   AGI, IG 1530.   No. 378.   No map.
   Text: RY, 1-VII; DIU, 11: 126–32 [Related to p. 136].
   Mod: Cacalchen, Yucatan.   Map: fig. 35-H/30-45.
   Lang: ? [Maya].   Article 2: XV.

Related

A. YAXA
   Mod: Yaxha.   Map: fig. 35-I/30-97.
B. ZINHUNCHEN

15. CAMPOCOLCHE   (V).   Yucatan.
Prov. Cochoah.   [Complex].
   Juan Farfán el Viejo, vezino y encomendero.
   n.d. [1579].
   SIM, 214.   RM, 135.
   AGI, IG 1530.   No. 378.   No map.
   Text: (1) RY, 2-XXII: DIU, 13: 176–95.
      (2) Barrera Vásquez, 1938.
   Mod: Kampokolche, M. Felipe Carrillo
      Puerto, Quintana Roo.   Map: fig. 28-J/32-3.
   Lang: ? [Maya].   Article 2: XV.

Related

A. CHOCHOLA
   Mod: Chochola.   Map: fig. 35-I/29-36.

16. CANACHE [CINANCHE] (M).   Yucatan.   [Complex].
   Juan de la Cámara, encomendero.
   Feb. 30 [sic], 1580.
   SIM, 214.   RM, 135.

AGI, IG 1530. No. 378. No map.
Text: RY, 1-VIII; DIU, 11: 137–41.
Mod: Sinanche, Yucatan. Map: fig. 35-H/30-5.
Lang: ? [Maya]. Article 2: XV.

Related

A. EGUM

17. CANZACABO (M). Yucatan. [Simple].
Cristóbal de San Martín, encomendero.
Feb. 20, 1579.
SIM, 214. RM, 135.
AGI, IG 1530. No. 378. No map.
Text: RY, 1-XIV; DIU, 11: 190–98.
Mod: Cansahcab, Yucatan. Map: fig. 35-H/30-17.
Lang: Maya. Article 2: XV.

18. CELAYA. Nuestra Señora de la Concepcion, Villa. Michoacan. [Composite].
Zalaya, Salaya.
Cristóbal de Vargas Valades, alcalde mayor.
June 15, 1580.
JLV, 4/23. DyP, 224/3 (text), 305/3 (map). SIM, 101. RM, 111.
RAH. 9-25-4/4663-X. Instr., 5 ff. Map: RAH.
Text: (1) VR/PNE, 7/4: 115–56. (2) RGM, 2: 50–69.
Map: Published. Catalog, 1.
Mod: Celaya, Guanajuato. Map: fig. 16-J/11-26.
Lang: Spanish. Article 2: I-11.

Related

A. ACAMBARO. Prov. Xilotepec.
Encomendero: Nuño de Chaves.
Text: (1) VR/PNE, 7/4: 124–46. (2) RGM, 2: 55–66.
Map: Published. Catalog, 1.
Mod: Acambaro, Guanajuato. Map: fig. 16-K/11-42.
Lang: Tarascan, Otomi, Mazahua, Chichimec.
B. YURIRPUNDARO. Crown.
Maps: AGI. DyP, 236/3. 1 published, 1 unpublished. Originally in AGI, IG 1529, file folder 274. Catalog, 85, 86.

330

Text: RGM, 2: 66–70.
Mod: Yuriria, Guanajuato. Map: fig. 16-K/10-35.
Lang: Tarascan, Chichimec.

19. CEMPOALA. Mexico. [Composite].
Zempoala, Zempala.
Luís Obregón, corregidor.
Nov. 1, 1580.
DyP, 238/3. SIM, 104. RM, 24. JGI, XXV-10.
UTX. CDG, 522. 3 ff. 3 maps.
Text: Barlow, 1949b.
Map: Published. Catalog, 10.
Mod: Zempoala, Hidalgo. Map: fig. 18-K/15-66.
Lang: Mexicano, Otomi, Chichimec. Article 2: I-12.
See also Tlalquilpa, 218.

Related

A. EPAZOYUCA
Nov. 1, 1580.
JGI, XXV-11. CDG, 701. 3 ff.
Map: Published. Catalog, 22.
Mod: Epazoyucan, Hidalgo. Map: fig. 18-K/15-67.
Lang: Mexicano, Otomi, Chichimec.
B. TETLISTACA (Tletlistaca, Atlixtaca)
Nov. 15, 1581.
JGI, XXV-12. CDG, 1778. 2 ff.
Map: Published. Catalog, 67.
Mod: Atlixtaca, M. Metepec, Hidalgo (?). Map: fig. 18-K/15-55.
Lang: Mexicano, Otomi.

20. CHANCENOTE (V). Yucatan. Prov. Tasees. [Composite].
Juan de Urrutia, encomendero.
May 4, 1579.
SIM, 214. RM, 135.
AGI, IG 1530. No. 378. No map.
Text: (1) RY, 2-IVa. DIU, 13: 61–76. (2) RNE, 1920b, pp. 69–79.
Mod: Chancenote, M. Tizimin, Yucatan. Map: fig. 35-G/33-12.
Lang: ? [Maya]. Article 2: XV.

Related

A. CHUACA

B. Chichimila
   Mod: Chichimila, Yucatan.   Map: fig. 35–I/32-83.

21. CHICHICAPA.   Antequera.   [Composite].
   Nicolas Espindola, corregidor y justicia mayor.
   May 15, 1580.
   JLV, 1/19.   SIM, 26.   RM, 78.
   AGI, IG 1529.   No. 387.   Instr., 24 ff. Chichicapa, ff. 1–4.   No map.
   Text: PNE, 4: 115–19.
   Mod: S. Baltasar Chichicapan, Oaxaca. Map: fig. 25-P/18-16/18.
   Lang: Zapotec.   Article 2: I-58.

Related

A. Amatlan
   Crown.
   AGI.   ff. 4–6v.
   Text: PNE, 4: 119–23.
   Mod: S. Luis Amatlan, Oaxaca.   Map: fig. 25-Q/19-13/3.
   Lang: Zapotec.
B. Miaguatlan
   Encomenderos: (1/2) Mateo de Monjaraz, (1/2) Alonso de Loaysa.
   AGI.   ff. 7–11v.
   Text: PNE, 4: 123–31.
   Mod: Miahuatlan de Porfirio Díaz, Oaxaca.   Map: 25-Q/19-13/2.
   Lang: Zapotec.
C. Coatlan
   Encomenderos: (1/2) Mateo de Monjaraz, (1/2) Alonso de Loaysa.
   AGI.   ff. 12–15v.
   Text: PNE, 4: 131–37.
   Mod: S. Pablo Coatlan, Oaxaca.   Map: fig. 25-Q/18-13/13.
   Lang: Zapotec.
D. Ozelotepeque
   Encomendero: Andrés Ruíz.
   AGI.   ff. 15v–19v.
   Text: PNE, 4: 137–43.
   Mod: Santa Maria Ozoltepec, Oaxaca. Map: fig. 25-R/19-13/29.
   Lang: Zapotec.

22. CHICONAUTLA.   Mexico.   [Complex].

Chiconauhtla, San Cristobal Ecatepec.
Pedro López de Ribera, corregidor.
Jan. 21, 1580.   Crown.
JLV, 2/27.   DyP, 655/6.   SIM, 153.   RM, 46.
AGI, IG 1529.   No. 392.   Instr., 6 ff.   No map.
Text: PNE, 6: 167–77.
Mod: Santa Maria Chiconautla, M. Ecatepec, Mexico.   Map: fig. 14-L/14-89.
Lang: Mexicano, Otomi.   Article 2: I-71.

Related

A. Tecama
   Mod: Santa Cruz Tecamac, M. Tecamac de FN, Mexico.   Map: fig. 14-L/14-86.
B. Xaltocan
   Mod: S. Miguel Jaltocan, M. Nextlalpan, Mexico.   Map: fig. 14-L/14-87.
C. San Cristobal Ecatepec
   Mod: Ecatepec Morelos, Mexico. Map: fig. 14-L/14-89.

22bis. CHILAPA.   Tlaxcala.   [Simple].
   Fray Juan Nuñez, prior, and Gonzalo Bazan, alcalde mayor.
   Feb. 21, 1582.   Encomendero: Antonio de Ordas Villagómez.
   JLV, P-2, 4/38.   DyP, 617/6.   SIM, 134. RM, 69.
   RAH.   9-25-4/4663-XXXVI.   ff. 1–4v. Map lost.
   Text: PNE, 5: 174–82.
   Map: Lost.   Catalog, 12.
   Mod: Chilapa de Alvarez, Guerrero. Map: fig. 17-O/14-49.
   Lang: Mexicano.   Article 2: I-29.
   See also TISTLA, 132; ZUMPANGO, 164; Map, Catalog, 91.

23. CHILCHOTLA. Michoacan. [Simple].
   Zirapo (Tarascan).
   Pedro de Villelas, corregidor.
   Oct. 15–28, 1579.
   JLV, 4/22.   DyP, 221/3.   SIM, 119.   RM, 123.
   RAH.   9-25-4/4663-VI.   Instr., 18 ff.   No map.

Text: (1) VR/PNE, 7/5: 7–56. (2) RGM, 2: 7–38.

Mod: Chilchota, Michoacan. Map: fig. 20-K/9-27.

Lang: Tarascan. Article 2: I-113.

24. CHINANTLA. Antequera. [Simple].
Diego de Esquibel, corregidor.
Nov. 1, 1579. Crown.
JLV, 1/17. SIM, 12. RM, 85.
RAH. 9-25-4/4663-XX. 10 ff. No map.
Text: (1) PNE, 4: 58–68. (2) Bevan, 1938 (English trans.).
Mod: S. Juan Bautista Valle Nacional, Oaxaca. Map: fig. 25-O/19-26/10.
Lang: Chinantec. Article 2: I-97.

25. CHOLULA. Tlaxcala. [Simple].
Gabriel de Rojas, corregidor.
1581.
JLV, 1/20. SIM, 79. RM, 61. JGI, XXIV-1.
UTX. CDG, 532. 10 ff. Map.
Text: (1) García Icazbalceta, 1875. (2) Gómez de Orozco, 1927a.
Map: Published. Catalog, 14.
Mod: Cholula de Rivadabia, M. S. Pedro Cholula, Puebla. Map: fig. 26-M/16-104.
Lang: Mexicano. Article 2: I-30.
Bibliog: Kubler, 1968a, 1968b.

26. CHUBULNA (M). Yucatan. Prov. Chacun. [Composite].
Diego de Santillán, encomendero.
n.d. [Feb., 1581].
SIM, 214. RM, 135.
AGI, IG 1530. No. 378. No map.
Text: (1) RY, 1-XXIII; DIU, 11: 277–83. (2) Barrera Vásquez, 1938.
Mod: Chuburna de Hidalgo, M. Merida, Yucatan. Map: fig. 35-H/30-25.
Lang: Maya. Article 2: XV.

Related

A. HUNACAMA
Mod: Hunucma, Yucatan. Map: fig. 35-H/29-27.

B. TIXCOCOB
Mod: Tixkokob, Yucatan. Map: fig. 35-H/30-44.
C. NOLO
Mod: Nolo, M. Tixkokob, Yucatan.
D. MOCOCHO
Mod: Mococho.
E. TABUCOZ

27. CHUNCHUCHU (M). Yucatan.
Prov. Mani (Cochuvas). [Complex].
Pedro García, encomendero, aided by Gaspar Antonio Chi.
Jan. 20, 1581.
SIM, 214. RM, 135.
AGI, IG 1530. No. 378. No map.
Text: RY, 1-IX; DIU, 11: 142–53.
Mod: Chunhubu, M. Felipe Carrillo Puerto, Quintana Roo. Map: fig. 28-J/32-3.
Lang: Maya. Article 2: XV.

Related

A. TABI
Mod: Tabi, M. Sotuta, Yucatan. Map: fig. 35-I/30-77.

28. CITLALTOMAGUA. Mexico. Prov. Costa de la Mar del Sur. [Complex].
Juan de Tolosa Olea, corregidor.
Jan. 12, 1580. Crown.
JLV, 4/33. DyP, 652/6. SIM, 148. RM, 34.
AGI, IG 1529. No. 382. Instr. missing, 10 ff. No map.
Text: PNE, 6: 153–66.
Mod: Zitlala? Guerrero. Map: fig. 17-O/14-43.
Lang: Mexicano, Tepuztec. Article 2: I-1.

Related

A. ANECUILCO (Zeuctla)

29. COATEPEC. Mexico. Chalco. [Composite].
Cristóbal de Salazar, corregidor.
Nov. 16, 1579. Crown.
JLV, 2/22. SIM, 191. RM, 54.
AGI, IG 1529. No. 376. Instr., 26 ff.

[Document filed in map section] Coatepec, ff. 6-18. 3 maps (bound with text and numbered as folios)

Text: PNE, 6: 39–86.

Map: Published. Catalog, 15.

Mod: Coatepec, M. Ixtapaluxa, Mexico. Map: fig. 14-L/14-107.

Lang: Mexicano, Otomi. Article 2: I-16.

Related

A. CHIMALHUACAN TOYAC

Dec. 1, 1579. Encomendero: Gerónimo de Bustamente.

Map: Published. Catalog, 13.

Mod: Sta. Maria Chimalhuacan, Mexico. Map: fig. 14-L/14-104?

Lang: Mexicano.

B. CHICOALOAPA

Dec. 3, 1579. Encomendero: Gaspar López.

Map: Published. Catalog, 11.

Mod: Chicoloapan de Juarez, Mexico. Map: fig. 14-15-L/14-106?

Lang: Mexicano.

30. COATZOCOALCO. Espiritu Santo, Villa. Antequera. [Simple].

Quetlascolapa, Guazacualco.

Suero de Cangas y Quiñones, alcalde mayor.

Apr. 29, 1580.

JLV, 1/5. DyP, 657/6. SIM, 155. RM, 74. JGI, XXIV-2.

UTX. CDG, 706. 5 ff. Map.

Text: (1) FPT, 1880. (2) Caso, 1928c. (3) VR, 1956b.

Map: Unpublished. Catalog, 16.

Mod: Nr. Tuzandepetl, M. Chapopotla, Veracruz. Map: fig. 34-N/22-191.

Lang: Mexicano, Popoluca, Mixtec, Zapotec. Article 2: I-38.

31. COMPOSTELA, Minas. Guadalajara. [Simple].

Caquetlan. [Tepic].

Lázaro Blanco, teniente alcalde mayor.

Nov. 26, 1584.

DyP, 974/8. SIM, 198. RM, 127.

RAH. 9-25-4/4662-III. Item 1. 8 ff., 8v blank. Map.

Text: VR/PNE, 8/1: 11–32.

Map: Published. Catalog, 17.

Mod: Compostela, Nayarit. Map: fig. 22-I/4-12.

Lang: Mexicano, Tecoxquin. Article 2: II-25.

32. CUAUHQUILPAN. Mexico. Prov. Tolcayuca. [Simple].

Quauhquilpan, Guaquilpa.

Pedro de Monjaraz Zamorano, corregidor.

Oct. 9, 1581.

JLV, 2/24. DyP, 1006/8. SIM, 186. RM, 50.

AGI, IG 1529. No. 393. Instr., 4 ff. No map.

Text: PNE, 6: 306–12.

Mod: S. Pedro Huauquilpan, M. Zapotlan de Juarez, Hidalgo. Map: fig. 18-K/14-72.

Lang: Mexicano, Otomi. Article 2: I-66.

33. CUAHUITLAN. Antequera. Prov. Tututepec, Costa del Mar del Sur. [Complex].

Yonoyuto [Mixtec].

Cosme de Cangas, corregidor.

Aug. 14, 1580.

JLV, 4/37. SIM, 37. RM, 80.

RAH. 9-25-4/4663-XXXI. 9 ff. Map.

Text: PNE, 4: 155–62.

Map: Published. Catalog, 18.

Mod: Cahuitan, M. Stgo. Tapextla, Oaxaca. Map: fig. 25-Q/15-9/15.

Lang: Mixtec. Article 2: I-43, 121.

Related

A. PINOTECPA

Mod: Stgo. Pinotepa Nacional, Oaxaca. Map: fig. 25-Q/16-9/18.

B. POTUTLA

Mod: Collantes, M. Stgo. Pinotepa Nacional, Oaxaca. Map: 25-Q/16-9/18.

C. ICPATEPEC, Mixteca, Baja Tlaxcala.

Mod: ?, M. Silacayoapan, Oaxaca. Map: fig. 25-O/16-9/16.

34. CUAUTLA. Antequera. Prov. Mixteca Alta. [Composite].

Guautla, Huautla.

Melchor Suárez, corregidor.
Feb. 26, 1580. Crown.
JLV, 4/34. SIM, 36. RM, 102. JGI,
XXIV-4.
UTX. CDG, 623. 6 ff. No map.
Text: Bernal, 1962.
Mod: S. Miguel Huautla Nochixtlan,
Oaxaca. Map: fig. 25-O/18-15/1.
Lang: Mixtec. Article 2: I-62.

Related

A. XOCOTICPAC
Feb. 26, 1580. Encomendero: García de
Robles.
Mod: S. Pedro Jocoticpac, Oaxaca. Map:
fig. 25-O/18-3/14.
Lang: Mixtec.

B. XALTEPETONGO (Papalotlayagua)
Mar. 1, 1580. Encomendero: Agustín de
Salinas.
Mod: S. Pedro Jaltepetongo, Oaxaca. Map:
fig. 25–O/18-15/2.
Lang: Mixtec.

C. TUTUPETONGO (Yada)
Mar. 3, 1580. Crown.
Mod: S. Francisco Tutepetongo, M. S. Juan
Bta. Cuicatlan, Oaxaca. Map: fig. 25-O/
18-3/10.
Lang: Cuicatec.

D. TANATEPEC
Mar. 5, 1580. Crown.
Mod: S. Juan Tonaltepec, M. Stgo. Nacal-
tepec, Oaxaca.
Map: fig. 25-O/18-3/18.
Lang: Cuicatec.

35. CUICATLAN. Antequera. [Simple].
Juan Gallegos, corregidor.
Sept. 15, 1580.
JLV, 2/14. SIM, 13. RM, 86.
RAH. 9-25-4/4663-XXI. 5 ff. No map.
Text: PNE, 4: 183–89.
Mod: S. Juan Bautista Cuicatlan, Oaxaca.
Map: fig. 25-O/18-3/10.
Lang: Cuicatec; Mexicano. Article 2:
I-5, 98.

36. CUICUIL (V). Yucatan. Prov. Cu-
pules. [Simple].
Quiquil.
Francisco de Cárdenas, vezino.

May 6, 1579.
SIM, 214. RM, 135.
AGI, IG 1530. No. 378. No map.
Text: RY, 2-VI; DIU, 13: 85–87.
Mod: Kikil, M. Tizimin, Yucatan. Map:
fig. 35-H/32-12.
Lang: ? [Maya]. Article 2: XV.

37. CUILAPA. Antequera. [Simple].
Yuchaca (Mixteco).
Fr. Agustín de Salazar.
Nov. 20, 1580.
JLV, 4/11. SIM, 23. RM, 94. JGI,
XXIV-10.
UTX. CDG, 629. 4 ff. No map.
Text: (1) Barlow, 1945. (2) Butter-
worth, 1962 (English trans.).
Mod: Cuilapan de Guerrero, Oaxaca.
Map: fig. 25-P/1-1/16.
Lang: Mixtec. Article 2: I-20.

38. CUISEO DE LA LAGUNA. Michoa-
can. [Simple].
Pedro Gutiérrez de Cuevas, corregidor.
Aug. 28–Sept. 1, 1579. Crown.
JLV, 4/30. DyP, 227/3. SIM, 111. RM,
115.
RAH. 9-25-4/4663-IV. 6 ff. No map.
Text: (1) VR/PNE, 7/7: 32–40. (2)
RGM, 1: 44–61.
Mod: Cuitzeo del Porvenir, Michoacan.
Map: fig. 20-K/11-82.
Lang: Tarascan. Article 2: I-23.

39. CUITELCUM (M). Yucatan. [Com-
plex].
Quitelcum.
Iñigo Nieto, encomendero, aided by Gas-
par Antonio Chi.
Feb. 13, 1581.
SIM, 214. RM, 135.
AGI, IG 1530. No. 378. No map.
Text: RY, 1-XVII; DIU, 11: 220–31.
Mod: Citilcun, M. Izamal, Yucatan. Map:
35-I/31-65.
Lang: Maya. Article 2: XV.

Related

A. CABICHE

40. CUIZIL (M) Yucatan. [Complex].
Quizil.
Juan de Paredes, encomendero, aided by
  Gaspar Antonio Chi.
Feb. 13, 1581.
SIM, 214. RM, 135.
AGI, IG 1530. No. 378. No map.
Text: RY, 1-XVI; DIU, 11: 209–20.
Mod: Kikil?, Yucatan. Map: fig. 35-G/
  33-12.
Lang: Maya. Article 2: XV.

Related

A. ZITIPECHE
  Mod: Sitpach, M. Merida, Yucatan. Map:
    fig. 35-H/30-25. *Or*: Sitilpech, M. Iza-
    mal, Yucatan. Map: fig. 35-H/31-65.

41. CULHUACAN. Mexico. Prov. Chu-
rubusco. [Simple].
Gonzalo Gallegos, corregidor.
Jan. 17, 1580.
JLV, none. DyP, 1002/8. SIM, 189.
  JGI, XXIII-14.
UTX. CDG, 628. 2 ff. Map.
Text: (1) Gómez de Orozco, 1927b. (2)
  VR. 1956g.
Map: Published. Catalog, 19.
Mod: Culhuacan, Ixtapalapa, D.F. Map:
  fig. 14-L/14-VI.
Lang: Mexicano. Article 2: I-55.
See also IXTAPALAPA, 56; MEXICA-
  TZINGO, 65; CHURUBUSCO, 204.

42. CUZCATLAN. *Version 1.* Tlaxcala.
[Simple].
Juan de Castañeda León, corregidor.
Oct. 26, 1580.
JLV, 3/9. DyP, 176/3. SIM, 126. RM,
  64.
AGI, IG 1529. No. 383. Instr. missing,
  6 ff. Map.
Text: (1) PNE, 5: 46–54. (2) BCE,
  1920. (3) RNE, 1920: 8–16.
Map: Published. Catalog, 20.
Mod: Coxcatlan, Puebla. Map: fig. 26
  N/18-216.
Lang: Mexicano, Chocho, Mazatec. Ar-
  ticle 2: I-85.

43. CUZCATLAN. *Version 2.* Tlaxcala.
[Simple].
Juan de Castañeda León, corregidor.
Oct. 26, 1580.
JGI, XXIII-15.
UTX. CDG, 630. 6 ff. Map.
Text: Unpublished.
Map: Published. Catalog, 21.
Mod: Coxcatlan, Puebla. Map: fig. 26-
  N/18-216.
Lang: Mexicano, Chocho, Mazatec. Ar-
  ticle 2: I-38.

44. FRESNILLO, Minas. Guadalajara.
[Composite].
Alonso Alcaraz, alcalde mayor.
Jan. 1, 1585. Crown.
DyP, 978/8. SIM, 196. RM, 133.
RAH. 9-25-4/4662-X. Instr., 21 ff. (6 re-
  ports). No map.
Text: VR/PNE, 8/5: 263–336.
Mod: Fresnillo de González Echeverría,
  Zacatecas. Map: fig. 36-E/8-9.
Lang: Guachichil, Zacatec, others. Ar-
  ticle 2: II-10.
Note: This report includes 5 supplemen-
  tary reports:

A. FRESNILLO
  Pedro de Medina, minero.
  Jan., 1585.
  RAH. Xa. 3 ff.
  Text: VR/PNE, 8/5: 263–79.
B. FRESNILLO
  Francisco Ruíz, minero.
  Jan., 1585.
  RAH. Xb. 3 ff.
  Text: VR/PNE, 8/5: 281–91.
C. FRESNILLO
  Alonso Tabuyo, vezino y minero.
  Feb. 17, 1585.
  RAH. Xc. 2 ff.
  Text: VR/PNE, 8/5: 293–304.
D. FRESNILLO
  Juan de Huidobro, vezino y minero.
  Jan. 20, 1585.
  RAH. Xd. 3 ff.
  Text: VR/PNE, 8/6: 305–24.
E. FRESNILLO
  Pedro Gaitán.
  Feb. 7, 1585.

335

RAH. Xe. 3 ff.
Text: VR/PNE, 8/6: 325–36.

45. GUATULCO. (AM). Antequera.
Prov. Costa del Sur. [Composite].
Gaspar de Vargas, alcalde mayor.
n.d. [ca. 1580]. Crown.
JLV, 2/6. SIM, 30. RM, 73.
RAH. 9-25-4/4663-XXXIII. Instr., 23 ff.
No map.
Text: PNE, 4: 232–33.
Lang: Mexicano. Article 2: I-33.

Related

A. PUERTO DE GUATULCO
Text: PNE, 4: 233–38. Crown.
Mod: Bahia de Sta. Cruz, Oaxaca. Map:
fig. 25-R/20-17/13.
B. POCHUTLA
Text: PNE, 4: 238–42. Crown.
Mod: S. Pedro Pochutla, Oaxaca. Map: fig.
25-R/19-17/12.
Lang: Mexicano.
C. TONAMECA
Text: PNE, 243–47. Crown.
Mod: Sta. Maria Tonameca, Oaxaca. Map:
fig. 25-R/19-17/7.
Lang: Mexicano.
D. PUEBLO DE GUATULCO
Text: PNE, 4: 247–51. Encomendero:
Bernardino López.
Mod: Sta. Maria Huatulco, Oaxaca. Map:
fig. 25-R/20-17/13.

46. GUAXOLOTITLAN. Antequera.
[Simple]
Huexolotitlan.
Bartolomé de Zarate, corregidor.
Mar. 10, 1581.
JLV, 4/20. SIM, 17. RM, 90.
RAH. 9-25-4/4663-XXXIII. Instr., 3 ff.
No map.
Text: PNE, 4: 196–205.
Mod: S. Pablo Huitzo, Oaxaca. Map:
fig. 25-P/18-6/6.
Lang: Mixtec; Zapotec. Article 2: I-5.

**47. GUAXTEPEC (V). Mexico. [Cuatro
Villas.] Prov. Marquesado del Valle.
[Simple].**

336

Guastepec, Huastepec, Oaxtepec.
Juan Gutiérrez de Liebana, alcalde mayor.
Sept. 24, 1580.
JLV, 4/3. DyP, 14/1 (text), 150/2
(map). SIM, 200. RM, 25. JGI,
XXIV-3.
UTX. CDG, 865. 7 ff. Map.
Text: (1) García Pimentel, 1908. (2)
Palacios, 1930.
Map: Unpublished. Catalog, 23.
Mod: Oaxtepec, M. Yautepec, Morelos.
Map: fig. 21-M/14-17.
Lang: Mexicano. Article 2: I-21.
See also ACAPISTLA, 1; TEPUZTLAN,
112; OCUITUCO, 210; YAUTEPEC,
221.

48. GUAYMA (V). Yucatan. [Complex].
Juan Vellido, alcalde ordinario.
Mar. 20, 1579. Encomendero: Juan
Vellido.
SIM, 214. RM, 135.
AGI, IG 1530. No. 378. No map.
Text: RY, 2-V; DIU, 13: 77–84.
Mod: Uayma, Yucatan. Map: fig. 35-I/
32-59.
Lang: ? [Maya]. Article 2: XV.

Related

A. CANTANIQUI
Mod: Kantunil-Kin, Quintana Roo.

**49. GUEYTLALPA. Tlaxcala. [Compos-
ite].**
Guytlalpay, Teutalpa [JLV, RM], Izte-
pec, Guitlapa.
Juan de Carrión, corregidor, and José
Velázquez.
May 30, 1581. (Signed July 20, 1581).
JLV, 2/8. DyP, 621/6. SIM, 138. RM,
67. JGI, XXIV-5.
UTX. CDG, 848. 18 ff. 7 maps. [Guey-
tlalpa, ff. 1-4].
Text: García Payón, 1965.
Map: Published. Catalog, 25.
Mod: Hueytlalpan, Puebla. Map: fig. 26-
K/17-34.

Lang: Totonac, Mexicano.   Article 2: I-125.

Related

A. ZACATLAN
ff. 4v-6v.
Encomendero: Antonio de Carvajal.
Text: García Payón, 1965.
Map: Published. Catalog, 87.
Mod: Zacatlan, Puebla. Map: fig. 26-K/16-12.
Lang: Mexicano, Totonac.

B. JUJUPANGO
ff. 7-8v.
Encomenderos: Diego de Villa Paderna, Gonzalo Salazar.
Text: García Payón, 1965.
Map: Published. Catalog, 31.
Mod: Jojupango, M. S. Felipe Tepatan, Puebla. Map: fig. 26-K/16-26.
Lang: Mexicano, Totonac.

C. MATATLAN-CHILA
ff. 9-11.
Encomendera: Catalina de Montejo.
Text: García Payón, 1965.
Map: Published. Catalog, 34.
Mod: Chila, Puebla. Map: fig. 26-O/16-195.
Lang: Totonac.

D. PAPANTLA
ff. 12-16.
Encomendero: Cristóbal de Tapía.
Text: García Payón, 1965.
Map: Published. Catalog, 44.
Mod: Papantla de Olarte, Veracruz. Map: fig. 34-J/17-43.
Lang: Totonac.

E. TECOLUTLA
No text.
Map only: Published. Catalog, 53.
Mod: Tecolutla, Veracruz. Map: fig. 34-K/18-45.

F. TENAMPULCO-MATLACTONATICO
Encomendero: Francisco Valadés (Tenampulco), Gonzalo de Salazar (Matlachnatico).
No text.
Map only: Published. Catalog, 58.
Mod: Tenampulco, Puebla. Map: fig. 26-K/17-45.

50. HOCABA (M). Yucatan. [Simple].

Melchor Pacheco, vezino [y encomendero].
Jan. 1, 1581.
SIM, 214. RM, 135.
AGI, IG 1530. No. 378. No map.
Text: (1) RY, 1-III; DIU, 11: 88–93.
(2) RNE, 1920b, pp. 65–68.
Mod: Hocaba, Yucatan. Map: fig. 35-I/31-72.
Lang: ? [Maya]. Article 2: XV.

51. HUEXOTLA. Mexico. Panuco. [Simple].
Huaxutla, Guaxutla, Uexultla.
Cristóbal Pérez Puebla, corregidor.
Feb. 3–4, 1580.
JLV, 2/1. DyP, 650/6 (map). SIM, 146. RM, 42.
AGI, IG 1529. No. 385. Instr., 7 ff. Map.
Text: PNE, 6: 183–92.
Map: Published. Catalog, 26.
Mod: Huejutla de Reyes, Hidalgo. Map: fig. 18-I/15-8.
Lang: Mexicano, Tepehua. Article 2: I-41.

52. ICHCATEOPAN. Mexico. [Composite].
Iscateupa, Yzcateupa.
Capitán Lucas Pinto, corregidor.
Oct. 15, 1579.
JLV, 4/29. DyP, 1023/8. SIM, 176. RM, 22.
AGI, IG 1529. No. 377. Instr., 38 ff. Ichcateopan, ff. 1v-4. No map.
Text: PNE, 6: 87–93.
Mod: Ixcateopan, Guerrero. Map: fig. 17-N/13-8.
Lang: Mexicano, Tuztec (formerly), Chontal. Article 2: I-44.

Related

A. TZICAPUTZALCO
Oct. 20, 1579. PNE, 6: 93–100.
Mod: Ixcapuzalco, M. Pedro Asencio Alquisiras, Guerrero. Map: fig. 17-N/13-7.
Lang: Mazatec.

B. ALAUSTLAN

n.d. PNE, 6: 100–05.

Mod: Alahuistlan, M. Teloloapan, Guerrero. Map: fig. 17-N/12-6.

Lang: Chontal. "llamase la lengua chontal por ablar todos chontal" [PNE, 6: 100].

C. OSTUMA

Oct. 12, 1579. PNE, 6: 105–15.

Mod: S. Simon Ostumba, M. Teloloapan, Guerrero. Map: 17-N/12-6.

Lang: Mexicano, Chontal.

D. ACAPETLAGUAYA

n.d. PNE, 6: 115–17.

Lang: Mexicano.

E. CUATEPEC (Quatepec)

Oct. 15, 1579. PNE, 6: 117–22.

Mod: Coatepec Costales, M. Teloloapan, Guerrero. Map: fig. 17-N/13-6.

Lang: Chontal.

F. TLACOTEPEC

Nov. 8, 1579. PNE, 6: 122–27.

Mod: Tlacotepec, M. Gral. Heliodoro Castillo, Guerrero. Map: fig. 17-P/12-31.

Lang: Tepustec.

G. UTATLAN

Nov. 12, 1579. PNE, 6: 127–31.

Mod: Otatlan, M. S. Miguel Totolapan, Guerrero. Map: fig. 17-O/12-20.

Lang: Tepustec.

H. TETELA [DEL RIO]

Nov. 16, 1579. PNE, 6: 131–37.

Mod: Tetela del Rio, M. Gral. Heliodoro Castillo, Guerrero. Map: fig. 17-O/12-31.

Lang: Cuitlatec.

I. CUEZALA (Cozala)

n.d. PNE, 6: 137–43.

Mod: Cuetzala del Progreso, Guerrero. Map: fig. 17-O/13-18.

Lang: Mexicano. [see J]

J. Apastla

n.d. PNE, 6: 143–44.

Mod: [?], M. Cuetzala del Progreso, Guerrero. Map: fig. 17-O/13-18.

Lang: Chontal.

K. TENEPATLAN

n.d. PNE, 6: 144

Mod: [?] Guerrero.

L. TELOLOAPA

Dec. 1, 1579. PNE, 6: 144–48.

Mod: Teloloapan, Guerrero. Map: fig. 17-N/12-6.

Lang: Iscuca, Chontal, Mexicano.

M. TUTULTEPEC

Dec. 1, 1579. PNE, 6: 148–52.

Mod: Totoltepec, M. Teloloapan, Guerrero. Map: fig. 17-N/12-6.

Lang: Chontal.

53. IGUALA. Mexico. [Composite].

Capitán Fernando Alfonso de Estrada, corregidor.

Sept., 1579.

JLV, 4/19. DyP, 649/6. SIM, 149. RM, 44. JGI, XXIV-6.

UTX. CDG, 868. 12 ff. No map.

Text: Toussaint, 1931.

Mod: Iguala, Guerrero. Map: fig. 17-N/13-13.

Lang: Cuisca, Chontal (Tuesteco). Article 2: I-42.

Related

A. COCULA

Mod: Cocula, Guerrero. Map: fig. 17-N/13-17.

Lang: Cuisca, Matlazinca.

B. TEPECUACUILCO

Mod: Tepecuacuilco de Trujano, Guerrero. Map: fig. 17-N/15-16.

Lang: Mexicano, Cuisca, Chontal.

C. MAYANALA

Mod: Mayanalan, M. Tepecoacuilco, Guerrero. Map: fig. 17-N/13-16.

Lang: Cuisca, Mexicano.

D. HOAPA

Mod: S. Agustin Oapan, M. Tepecoacuilco, Guerrero. Map: fig. 17-N/13-16.

E. TASMALOCA

Mod: Tlaxmalac, M. Huitzuco, Guerrero. Map: fig. 17-N/13-16.

Lang: Cuisca.

F. IZUCO

Mod: Huitzuco de los Figueroa, Guerrero. Map: 17-N/14-14.

54. IXCATLAN, Sta. Maria. Antequera.

Prov. Mixteca. [Composite].

Gonzalo Velázquez de Lara, corregidor.

Oct. 13, 1579.

JLV, 2/13. DyP, 656/6. SIM, 154. RM, 77. JGI, XXIV-7.

UTX. CDG, 955. 3 ff. 2 maps.

Text: Unpublished.

Maps: Published. Catalog, 27, 28.

Mod: Sta. Maria Ixcatlan, Oaxaca. Map: fig. 25-O/18-15?

Lang: Chocho, Mexicano. Article 2: I, 98.

Related

A. QUIOTEPEC

Mod: Stgo. Quiotepec, M. S. Juan Bta. Cuicatlan, Oaxaca. Map: fig. 25-O/18-3/10.

Lang: Quioteca (Cuicatec).

B. TECOABACA

Mod: Sta. Maria Tecomavaca, Oaxaca. Map: fig. 25-H/18-22/24.

Lang: Pinoles.

55. IXMUL (V). Yucatan. Prov. Cochua. [Complex].

Blas Gonzáles, vezino y regidor perpetuo [encomendero].

May 12, 1579.

SIM, 214. RM, 135.

AGI, IG 1530. No. 378. No map.

Text: RY, 2-x, DIU; 13: 110–18.

Mod: Ichmul, M. Felipe Carillo Puerto, Quintana Roo. Map: 28-I/33-3.

Lang: ? [Maya]. Article 2: XV.

Related

A. TECUCHE

56. IXTAPALAPA. Mexico. Prov. Churubusco. [Simple].

Iztapalzetl, Istapalapa.

Gonzalo Gallegos, corregidor.

Jan. 31, 1580.

DyP, 651/6. SIM, 147. RM, 43. JGI, XXIV-8.

UTX. CDG, 957. 3 ff. Map.

Text: VR, 1957b.

Map: Unpublished. Catalog, 29.

Mod: Ixtapalapa, D. F. Map: fig. 14-L/14-VI.

Lang: Mexicano. Article 2: I-55.

See also CULHUACAN, 41; MEXICATZINGO, 65; CHURUBUSCO, 204.

57. IXTEPEXIC. Antequera. Prov. Zapo-

tecas. [Simple].

Yaxitza (Zapotec), Iztepexi.

Juan Ximénez Ortiz, corregidor.

Aug. 27–30, 1579.

JLV, 4/28. DyP, erased. SIM, 20. RM, 92.

RAH. 9-25-4/4663-XIV. Instr., 14 ff. Map.

Text: PNE, 4: 9–23.

Map: Published. Catalog, 30.

Mod: Sta. Catrina Ixtepeji, Oaxaca. Map: fig. 25-P/19-8/17.

Lang: Zapotec, Mexicano. Article 2: I-47.

58. IZAMAL (M). Yucatan. Prov. Quinchel. [Complex].

Cachupuy.

Juan Cueva Santillán, encomendero.

Feb. 20, 1581.

SIM, 214. RM, 135.

AGI, IG 1530. No. 378. No map.

Text: (1) RY, 1-XXI; DIU, 11: 265–75. (2) Barrera Vásquez, 1938.

Mod: Izamal, Yucatan. Map: fig. 35-H/31-65.

Lang: Maya. Article 2: XV.

Related

A. SANTA MARIA

Mod: Sta. Maria de Mexquita, M. Izamal, Yucatan. Map: 35-H/31-65.

59. IZTEPEC, Sta. Cruz. Antequera. [Complex].

Quialoo [Zap].

Fr. Andrés Mendes, Vicario, for Lic. Ledesma, alcalde mayor.

Jan. 10–12, 1581. (Signed by alcalde mayor, Jan. 23, 1581).

JLV, 4/9. SIM, 21. RM, 93. JGI, XXIV-9.

UTX. CDG, 958. 3 ff. No map.

Text: (1) Caso, 1928d. (2) VR, 1955.

Mod: Sta. Cruz Mixtepec, Oaxaca. Map: fig. 25-P/18-30/8.

Lang: Zapotec. Article 2: I-5.

Related

A. STA. ANA TACOLABACOYA

Mod: Sta. Ana Tlapacoyan, Oaxaca. Map: fig. 25-f/18-30/8.

B. AYOCUEXCO

Mod: Sta. Maria Ayoquezco, Oaxaca. Map: fig. 25-Q/18-30/11.

C. S. BERNARDO TEPEZIMATLAN

Mod: S. Bernardo Mixtepec, Oaxaca. Map: fig. 25-P/18-29/7.

D. STA. MARIA MAGDALENA TEPEZIMATLAN

Mod: Magdalena Mixtepec, Oaxaca.

60. JILQUILPAN. Michoacan. [Composite].

Xiquilpan, Guaninba (Tarascan).

Francisco de Medinilla Alvarado, corregidor.

June 1, 1579. Crown.

JLV, 1/10. DyP, 222/3. SIM, 118. RM, 122.

RAH. 9-25-4/4663-I. 12 ff. Jilquilpan, ff. 1r-5v. No map.

Text: (1) Barlow, 1944. (2) VR/PNE, 7/1: 29-45. (3) RGM, 1: 7-36.

Mod: Jiquilpan de Juarez, Michoacan. Map: fig. 20-K/8-2.

Lang: Mexicano, Tarascan, Sayultec. Article 2: I-101.

Related

A. CHOCONDIRAN (Tingüindin, Tingüendin, Dingüindin)

(2) VR/PNE, 7/2: 65-74. (3) RGM, 1: 16-22.

Mod: Tingüindin, Michoacan. Map: fig. 20-L/9-14.

Lang: Tarascan.

B. TARECUATO

(2) VR/PNE, 7/2: 75-84. (2) RGM, 1: 22-28.

Mod: Tarecuato, M. Tangamandapio, Michoacan. Map: fig. 20-L/9-15.

Lang: Tarascan.

C. PERIVAN

(2) VR/PNE, 7/3: 85-98. (2) RGM, 1: 29-36.

Mod: Periban de Ramos, Michoacan. Map: fig. 20-L/9-30.

Lang: Tarascan.

61. JUSTLAVACA. Antequera. Prov. Mixteca. [Composite].

Instlauca, Justlaguaca, Yozocuyya [Mix.].

Andrés Aznar de Cozar, corregidor.

Jan. 3, 1580. Crown.

JLV, 3/15. SIM, 35. RM, 101. JGI, XXIV-11.

UTX. CDG, 973. 4 ff. No map.

Text: (1) Caso, 1928a. (2) VR, 1956c.

Mod: Stgo. Juxtlahuaca, Oaxaca. Map: fig. 25-P/16-12/7.

Lang: Mixtec, Mexicano. Article 2: I-49.

Related

A. TECOMASTLAUCA

Jan. 3, 1580. VR, 1956c. Crown.

Mod: S. Sebastian Tecomaxtlahuaca, Oaxaca. Map: fig. 25-O/16-12/3.

Lang: Mixtec; Mexicano.

B. MISTEPEC (Tlaxcala)

Jan. 7, 1580. VR, 1956d. Crown.

Mod: S. Juan Mixtepec Juxtlahuaca, Oaxaca. Map: fig. 25-P/16-12/8.

Lang: Mixtec, Mexicano.

C. AYUSUCHIQUILAZALA

Jan. 12, 1580. VR, 1956e. Encomenderos: Felipe de Arellano, Francisco de Terrazas.

Mod: Zochiquilazala, M. Stgo. Juxtlahuaca, Oaxaca. Map: 25-P/16-12/7.

Lang: Mixtec, Amusgo.

D. XICAYAN

Jan. 14, 1580. VR, 1956f. Encomenderos: Cristóbal Guillén (1/2), Juan Hypólito Tovar (1/2).

Mod: Jicayan de Tovar. M. Tlacoachixtlahuaca Guerrero. Map: fig. 17-Q/17-69.

Lang: Amusgo, Mixtec.

E. PUCTLA

Jan. 22, 1580. VR, 1956g. Crown.

Mod: Putla de Guerrero, Oaxaca. Map: fig. 25-P/16-18/1.

Lang: Mixtec, Mexicano.

F. ZACATEPEC

Feb. 17, 1580. VR, 1956h. Encomendero: Rafael de Trejo.

Mod: Sta. Maria Zacatepec, Oaxaca. Map: fig. 25-P/16-18/4.

Lang: Mixtec, Mexicano, Amusgo.

62. MACUILSUCHIL. Antequera. Prov. Zapotecas. [Composite].

Gaspar Asensio, corregidor.

Apr. 9, 1580. Crown.

JLV, 2/17. DyP, 307/3. SIM, 11. RM, 84.

RAH. 9-25-4/4663-XIX. Instr., ff. 1-3. Map.

Text: PNE, 4: 100–04.

Map: Published. Catalog, 32.

Mod: S. Mateo Macuilxochitl, M. Tlacochahuaya, Oaxaca. Map: fig. 25-P/19-24/5.

Lang: Zapotec. Article 2: I-59.

Related

A. TEOTITLAN DEL VALLE

Apr. 11, 1580. PNE, 4: 104–08.

Mod: Teotitlan del Valle, Oaxaca. Map: fig. 25-P/19-24/1.

Lang: Zapotec.

63. MAMA. (M). Yucatan. Prov. Mani. [Composite].

Juan de Aguilar, regidor [encomendero]. Jan. 20, 1580.

SIM, 214. RM, 135.

AGI, IG 1530. No. 378. No map.

Text: RY, 1-XI; DIU, 11: 159–74.

Mod: Mama, Yucatan. Map: fig. 35-I/30-92.

Lang: ? [Maya]. Article 2: XV.

Related

A. PETO

Mod: Peto, Yucatan. Map: fig. 35-J/31-85.

64. MERIDA, Ciudad and Prov. (M). Yucatan. [Simple].

Tiho.

Martín de Palomar, regidor, aided by Gaspar Antonio Chi.

Feb. 18, 1579. Crown.

SIM, 214. RM, 135.

AGI, IG 1530. No. 378. No map.

Text: (1) RY, 1-I; DIU, 11: 37–75. (2) Barrera Vásquez, 1938.

Mod: Merida, Yucatan. Map: fig. 35-H/30-25.

Lang: Maya. Article 2: XV.

65. MEXICATZINGO. Mexico. Prov. Churubusco. [Simple].

Mexicaltzinco, Mexicatzinco.

Gonzalo Gallegos, corregidor.

Feb. 7, 1580.

JLV, 1/21. DyP, 1007/8. SIM, 185. RM, 49.

AGI, IG 1529. No. 380. Instr. missing, 4 ff. Map lost.

Text: PNE, 6: 193–98.

Map: Lost. Catalog, 35.

Mod: Mexicaltzingo, Ixtapalapa, D. F. Map: fig. 14-L/14-VI.

Lang: Mexicano. Article 2: I-55.

See also CULHUACAN, 41; IXTAPALAPA, 56; CHURUBUSCO, 204.

66. MEZTITLAN. Mexico. [Complex].

Gabriel de Chaves, corregidor.

Oct. 1, 1579. Crown.

JLV, 4/17. DyP, 1004/8. SIM, 232. RM, 23. JGI, XXIV-12.

UTX. CDG, 1285. 14 ff. Map. Calendarical drawing. [Catalog, Appendix, 2].

Text: (1) Ternaux Compans, 1840 (French trans.). (2) DII, 4: 530–55. (3) Gómez de Orozco, 1924. (4) Cantú Treviño, 1953.

Map: Copy published. Catalog, 37.

Mod: Metztitlan, Hidalgo. Map: fig. 18-J/15-27.

Lang: Mexicano. Article 2: I-57.

Related

A. CHAPULHUACAN

Mod: Chapulhuacan, Hidalgo. Map: fig. 18-I/14-2.

B. CHICONTEPEC

Mod: Chicontepec, Veracruz. Map: fig. 34-I/16-20.

C. GUAZALINGO

Encomendero: Diego de Aguilera.

Mod: Huazalingo, Hidalgo. Map: fig. 18-J/15-13.

D. ILAMATLAN

Encomendero: Leon de Cervantes.

Mod: Ilamatlan, Veracruz. Map: fig. 34-J/16-23.

E. MALILA

Crown.

Mod: M. Molango, Hidalgo. Map: fig. 18-
J/15-17.

F. MOLANGO
Crown.
Mod: Molango, Hidalgo. Map: fig. 18-J/
15-17.

G. SUCHICOATLAN
Crown.
Mod: Xochicoatlan, Hidalgo. Map: fig. 18-
J/15-16.

H. TIANQUESCO
Encomendero: Francisco de Teminde.
Mod: Tianguistengo, Hidalgo. Map: fig.
18-J/15-15.

I. TLANCHINOLTICPAC
Encomenderos: Alonso Ortiz de Zúñiga
(1/2), Juan Maldonado (1/2).
Mod: Tlanchinol, Hidalgo. Map: fig. 18-I/
15-5.

J. XELITLA
Crown.
Mod: Xilitla, San Luis Potosi. Map: fig.
29-1/15-43.

K. YAGUALICA
Crown.
Mod: Yahualica, Hidalgo. Map: fig. 18-J/
15-11.

67. MIZANTLA. Tlaxcala. [Simple].
Mazantla.
Diego Pérez de Arteaga, corregidor.
Oct. 1, 1579.
JLV, 3/19. DyP, 616/6. SIM, 136. RM,
63. JGI, XXIV-13.
UTX. CDG, 1339. 4 ff. Map.
Text: Ramírez Lavoignet, 1962.
Map: Published. Catalog, 39.
Mod: Misantla, Veracruz. Map: fig. 34-
K/18-48.
Lang: Totonac.

68. MOTINES, Provincia. Michoacan.
[Composite].
Baltasar Dávila Quiñones, corregidor,
and others.
March–June, 1580.
JLV, 4/14. DyP, 228/3. SIM, 112. RM,
116.
RAH. 9-25-4/4663-IX. 26 ff. No map.
Mod: See Related. Article 2: I-60.

Related
A. CUALCOLMAN (Cuacoman, Quacoman)
Baltasar Dávila Quiñones, corregidor.
June 3, 1580.
RAH. ff. 1–6.
Text: (1) VR, 1952c. VR, 1954.
Mod: Coalcoman de Matamoros, Michoa-
can. Map: fig. 20-M/8-35.
Lang: Mexicano, Quacumec (Tlaotli).

B. MAQUILI
Sebastián Romano, corregidor.
Mar. 15, 1580.
RAH. ff. 10–14.
Text: (1) VR, 1952d. (2) VR, 1953.
Mod: Mauili, M. Aquila, Michoacan. Map:
fig. 20-N/7-38.
Lang: Mexicano; "muchas lenguas."

C. MOTIN
Juan Allende de Rueda, corregidor.
May 10–27, 1580.
RAH. ff. 16-26v. (Includes complex treat-
ment of Pomaro.)
Text: Unpublished.
Mod: [?], M. Aquila, Michoacan. Map:
fig. 20-N/7-38.

D. POMARO
Same as Motin
Mod: Pomaro, M. Auila, Michoacan.
Map: fig. 20-N/7-38.

69. MOTUL, San Juan Bautista (M). Yu-
catan. [Simple].
Martín de Palomar, vezino.
Feb. 20, 1581.
Encomendero: Francisco Bracamonte.
SIM, 214. RM, 135.
AGI, IG 1530. No. 378. Map.
Text: RY, 1-II; DIU, 11: 75–88.
Map: Published. Catalog, 40.
Mod: Motul de Felipe Carrillo Puerto,
Yucatan. Map: fig. 35-H/30-20.
Lang: Maya. Article 2: XV.

70. MOXOPIPE (M). Yucatan. Prov.
Quepech. [Simple].
Quinacana (ancient).
Pedro de Santillana, encomendero, aided
by Gaspar Antonio Chi.
Feb. 22, 1581.
SIM, 214. RM, 135.

AGI, IG 1530. No. 378. No map.

Text: (1) RY, 1-XX; DIU, 11: 251–65. (2) Barrera Vásquez, 1938.

Mod: Muxupip, Yucatan. Map: fig. 35-H/30-21.

Lang: Maya. Article 2: XV.

71. NABALON (V). Yucatan. Prov. Cupul. [Complex].

Diego de Contreras, encomendero.

Mar. 23, 1579.

SIM, 214. RM, 135.

AGI, IG 1530. No. 378. No map.

Text: (1) RY, 2-III; DIU, 13: 50–60. (2) Barrera Vásquez, 1938.

Mod: Nabalam, M. Tizimin, Yucatan. Map: fig. 35-H/32-12.

Lang: ? [Maya]. Article 2: XV.

Related

A. TAHCABO

Mod: Tancah (?), M. Conzumel, Quintana Roo. Map: fig. 28-J/33-2.

B. ISLA DE COZUMEL

Mod: Cozumel, Quintana Roo. Map: fig. 28-J/34-2.

72. NECOTLAN. Michoacan. Prov. Charo-Matalzingo. [Simple].

Undameo (Santiago).

Pedro Moreno Gallego, corregidor.

Sept. 1, 1579. Crown.

JLV, 4/6. DyP, 241/3. SIM, 107. RM, 65.

RAH. 9-25-4/4663-III. Instr., 1 f., 1 blank f. No map.

Text: (1) VR/PNE, 7/3: 107–12. (2) RGM, 1: 40–44.

Mod: Stgo. Undameo, M. Morelia, Michoacan. Map: fig. 20-L/10-77.

Lang: Otomi; Tarascan. Article 2: I-113.

Bibliog: Brand, 1948.

73. NEXAPA. Santiago del Valle de. Antequera. [Simple].

Juan Díaz Canseco, alcalde mayor, and Fr. Bernardo de Santamaria, vicario.

Sept. 12, 1579–Apr. 20, 1580.

JLV, 4/7. DyP, 654/6. SIM, 152. RM, 26.

AGI, IG 1529. No. 373. Instr. missing, 12 ff. Map lost.

Text: PNE, 4: 29–44.

Map: Lost. Catalog, 42.

Mod: Nejapa de Madero, Oaxaca. Map: fig. 28-O/20-28/3.

Lang: Zapotec. Article 2: I-61.

74. NOCHIZTLAN. Antequera. Prov. Mixteca Alta. Comarca Yanguitlan. [Simple].

Nochistlan, Atuco (Mixteco).

Rodrigo Pacho, corregidor.

Apr. 9–11, 1581. Crown.

JLV, 3/20. SIM, 38. RM, 103.

RAH. 9–25-4/4663-XXXIII. Instr., 4 ff. Map: f. 7.

Text: PNE, 4: 206–12.

Map: Published. Catalog, 43.

Mod: Asuncion Nochixtlan, Oaxaca. Map: 25-O/18-15/25.

Lang: Mixtec. Article 2: I-62.

See also Nochistlan, 220H.

75. NUCHISTLAN. Guadalajara. Prov. Minas de Tepec. [Complex].

Franco de Placa, alcalde mayor.

Dec. 2, 1584.

DyP, 974/8. SIM, 198. RM, 127.

RAH. 9-25-4/4662-V. Item 3. 4 ff., f. 4v blank. No map.

Text: VR/PNE, 8/1: 59–74.

Mod: Nochistlan, Zacatecas. Map: fig. 36-I/8-51.

Lang: Cazcan, Mexicano. Article 2: II-16.

Related

A. SUCHIPILA

Mod: Juchipila, Zacatecas. Map: fig. 36-I/7-49.

Note: Despite inclusion of Suchipila in title, RG does not give data on it.

76. OCOPETLAYUCA, Sta. Maria Asuncion. Mexico. [Simple].

Tochimilco.

Juan de la Vega, corregidor.
Oct. 6, 1580.
JLV, 3/21. DyP, 648/6. SIM, 145. RM, 41.
AGI, IG 1529. No. 384. Instr. missing, 6 ff. No map.
Text: PNE, 6: 251–62.
Mod: Tochimilco, Puebla. Map: fig. 26-M/15-110.
Lang: Mexicano. Article 2: I-107.

77. OSCUZCAS (M). Yucatan. Prov. Mani. [Simple].
Hernando Muñoz Zapata, encomendero.
Feb. 21, 1581.
SIM, 214. RM, 135.
AGI, IG 1530. No. 378. No map.
Text: RY, 1-XVIII; DIU, 11: 231–40.
Mod: Oxkutzcab, Yucatan. Map: fig. 35-J/30-99.
Lang: ? [Maya]. Article 2: XV.

78. PAPALOTICPAC. Antequera. Prov. Teotila. [Composite].
Pedro de Navarrete, corregidor.
Dec. 7, 1579. Crown.
JLV, 4/15. SIM, 33. RM, 100.
RAH. 9-25-4/4663-XX. ff. 1-5r. No map.
Text: PNE, 4: 88–93.
Mod: Santos Reyes Papalo, Oaxaca. Map: fig. 25-O/18-3/13.
Lang: Cuicatec. Article 2: I-97.

Related

A. TEPEUCILA
Dec. 11, 1579. PNE, 4: 93–99.
Mod: S. Juan Tepeuxila, Oaxaca. Map: fig. 25-O/18-3/16.
Lang: Cuicatec.

79. PATZCUARO. Michoacan. [Simple].
Mechoacan, Ciudad de.
Bachiller Juan Martínez, teniente de alcalde mayor.
Apr. 8, 1581. Crown.
JLV, 3/16. DyP, 27/1. SIM, 201. RM, 108. JGI, XXIV-14.
UTX. CDG, 1492. 4 ff. No map.

Text: (1) León, 1889. (2) VR/PNE, 7/7: ?–60. (3) RGM, 2: 107–117.
Mod: Patzcuaro, Michoacan. Map: fig. 20-L/10-64.
Lang: Tarascan. Article 2: I-113.

80. PEÑOLES, LOS. Antequera. [Complex].
Juan López de Zarate, corregidor.
Aug. 20–Oct. 3, 1579.
JLV, 4/27. SIM, 18. RM, 91. JGI, XXIV-15.
UTX, CDG, 1448. 8 ff. Map.
Text: (1) Caso, 1928e. (2) VR, 1956i.
Map: Unpublished. Catalog, 45.
Article 2: I-5, 62.

Related

A. EZTITLA
Mod: Sta. Catarina Estetla, M. Sta. Maria Peñoles, Oaxaca. Map: fig. 25-P/18-6/22.
Lang: Mixtec.
B. HUIZTEPEC (Yucuyatha)
Mod: S. Antonio Huitepec, Oaxaca. Map: fig. 25-P/18-15/32.
Lang: Mixtec.
C. ITZCUINTEPEC
Mod: Sta. Maria Peñoles, Oaxaca. Map: fig. 25-P/18-6/22.
Lang: Mixtec.
D. CUAUXOLOTICPAC (Guauxoloticpac, Quauxoloticpac)
Mod: Stgo. Huajolotipac, M. S. Antonio Huitepec, Oaxaca. Map: fig. 25-P/18-15/32.
Lang: Mixtec.
E. ELOTEPEC (Telotepec)
Mod: S. Juan Elotepec, M. S. Miguel Sola de Vega, Oaxaca. Map: fig. 25-P/18-20/10.
Lang: Zapotec.
F. TOTOMACHAPA
Mod: S. Pedro Totomachapan. M. Zimatlan de Alvarez, Oaxaca.
Lang: Zapotec.

81. PIJOY (V). Yucatan. Prov. Cupules. [Simple].
Pizoy, Pisoy.

Esteben González de Najera, encomendero.

Feb. 15, 1579.

SIM, 214. RM, 135.

AGI, IG 1530. No. 378. No map.

Text: RY, 2-XV; DIU, 13: 139–41.

Mod: Pixoy, M. Valladolid, Yucatan.
   Map: fig. 35-I/32-58.

Lang: ? [Maya]. Article 2: XV.

82. PONCITLAN. Guadalajara. [Composite].

Antonio de Medina, corregidor.

Mar. 9, 1585. Crown.

DyP, 977/8.

RAH. 9-25-4/4662-IX. Instr., 8 ff. No
   map.

Text: VR/PNE, 8/4: 221–60.

Mod: Poncitlan, Jalisco. Map: fig. 19-
   K/8-45.

Lang: Coca, Mexicano. Article 2: II-4.

Related

A. Cuiseo del Rio
   (Coatlan [ancient]; Tasnahui [Coca]).
   Mod: Cuitzeo, M. Poncitlan, Jalisco. Map:
      fig. 19-K/8-45.
   Lang: Coca.

83. POPOLA (V). Yucatan. [Composite].
   Diego Sarmiento de Figueroa, alcalde
      mayor.

Apr. 8, 1579. Encomenderos: Diego Sarmiento de Figueroa, Catalina de Chaves.

SIM, 214. RM, 135.

AGI, IG 1530. No. 378. No map.

Text: (1) RY, 2-II; DIU, 13: 41–49. (2)
   RNE, 1920b, pp. 90–95.

Mod: Popola, M. Valladolid, Yucatan.
   Map: fig. 35-I/32-58.

Lang: Maya ("achmaya"). Article 2:
   XV.

Related

A. Sinsimato

B. Zamiol

84. PURIFICACION (V). Guadalajara.
[Composite].

Luis Gómez de Alvarado, cura beneficiado.

Jan. 12–19, 1585.

DyP, 974/8. SIM, 198. RM, 127.

RAH. 9-25-4/4662-VI. Item 4. 9 ff.
   No map.

Text: VR/PNE, 8/2: 78–130.

Mod: Villa Vieja, M. Purificacion, Jalisco.
   Map: fig. 19-L/5-115.

Lang: Mexicano, Culiaretes, Mazatec, Izteca, Pocotec, Melaguese, Tomatec, Cuacumanes. Article 2: II-19.

Note: Reported that each of 23 Indian
   settlements spoke different languages,
   for which they had no local names.
   Most settlements cannot be identified
   with a modern community.

Related

A. Panputzin
   Text: VR/PNE, 8/2: 96–97.

B. Copono, Crown
   Text: VR/PNE, 8/2: 97–99.

C. Cocohol, encomendero
   Text: VR/PNE, 8/2: 99–100.

D. Mazatlan [with Acatlan], encomendero
   Text: VR/PNE, 3/2: 100–03.

E. Acatlan [with Mazatlan, q.v.]

F. Cuamihitlan [with Chamela]
   Text: VR/PNE, 8/2: 103–04.

G. Chamela [with Cuamihitlan, q.v.]

H. Taltempa [with Ocotitlan]
   Text: VR/PNE, 8/2: 104–06.

I. Ocotitlan [with Taltempa, q.v.]

J. Contla, Crown
   Text: VR/PNE, 8/2: 106–08.

K. Jocotlan, encomendero
   Text: VR/PNE, 82: 108–10.
   Mod: Jocotlan, M. Purificacion, Jalisco (?).

L. Zapotlan, Crown
   Text: VR/PNE, 8/2: 110–12.
   Mod: Zopotan, M. Purificacion, Jalisco.

M. Tene, encomendero
   Text: VR/PNE, 8/2: 112–13.

N. Melagua (Jala [ancient]), encomendero
   Text: VR/PNE: 8/2: 113–15

O. Tuito (Los Frailes [from native headdress
shape]), encomendero
   Text: VR/PNE, 8/2: 115–17.
   Mod: El Tuito, Jal.

P. Alengo [with Piloto]

345

Text: VR/PNE, 8/2: 118–20.

Q. Piloto [with Alengo, q.v.]
Mod: Piloto, M. Tomatlan, Jalisco.

R. Cabrayel, encomendero: Benito Florz
Text: VR/PNE, 8/2: 120–22.
Mod: Cabrel, M. Tomatlan, Jalisco.

S. Tomatan, encomendero: Juan Fernández de Ijar
Text: VR/PNE, 8/2: 122–23.
Mod: Tomatlan, Jalisco.

T. Malabaco, encomendero
Text: VR/PNE, 8/2: 123–24.

U. Coyatlan
Text: VR/PNE, 8/2: 124–26.

V. Ayutla [with Cacoman], encomendero: Cristobal Ordoñez
Text: VR/PNE, 8/2: 126–29.

W. Cacoman [with Ayutla, q.v.]

85. QUATLATLAUCA. Tlaxcala. [Composite].

Guatlatlauca.

Antonio de Vargas, corregidor.

Sept. 2, 1579.

JLV, 4/39. DyP, 1012/8. SIM, 179. RM, 104. JGI, XXIV-6.

UTX. CDG, 1564. 3 ff. 2 maps.

Text: Unpublished.

Maps: Unpublished. Catalog, 46.

Mod: Huatlatlauca, Puebla. Map: fig. 26-M/16-155

Lang: Mexicano. Article 2: I-92.

Related

A. Gueguetlan
Francisco de Najera, presbitero vicario, for Antonio de Vargas.
Sept. 15, 1579.
Map: Unpublished. Catalog, 24.
Mod: Sto. Domingo Huehuetlan, Puebla. Map: fig. 26-M/16-134.
Lang: Mexicano.

86. QUERETARO. Michoacan. Prov. Xilotepec. [Complex].

Nopala, Querenda.

Hernando de Vargas, alcalde mayor, and Francisco Ramos de Cárdenas.

Jan. 20–Mar. 30, 1582.

JLV, P-7, 2/29. DyP, 975/8. SIM, 202. RM, 32. JGI, XXIV-17.

UTX. CDG, 1566. 19 ff. Map lost.

Text: (1) Orozco y Berra, 1864. (2) Velásquez, 1897. (3) Frías, 1906.

Map: Lost. Catalog, 47.

Mod: Queretaro, Queretaro. Map: fig. 27-J/12-13.

Lang: Otomi, Mexicano. Article 2: I-70.

Related

A. San Juan del Rio, Mexico
Mod: San Juan del Rio, Queretaro. Map: fig. 27-K/13-17.

87. SAN MARTIN (V). Guadalajara. [Complex].

Rodrigo de Belcazar, alcalde mayor.

Feb. 6, 1585.

DyP, 974/8. SIM, 198. RM, 127.

RAH. 9-25-4/4662-VII. Item 5. 17 ff. [Contemporary copy submitted by Gutierre de Segura.] No map.

Text: VR/PNE, 8/3: 135–90.

Mod: San Martin, M. Sombrerete, Zacatecas. Map: 36-E/7-11.

Lang: Zacatec. Article 2: II-22.

Related

A. Llerena
Mod: Sombrerete, Zacatecas.

B. Sombrerete, Minas de
Mod: Sombrerete, Zacatecas.

88. SUCHITEPEC. Antequera. [Complex].

Xuchitepec, Xochitepec.

Gutierre Diez de Miranda, corregidor.

Aug. 23–29, 1579.

JLV, 2/2. DyP, 308/3. SIM, 14. RM, 87.

Text: RAH. 9-25-4/4663-XVI. Instr., 4 ff.

Maps: AGI, IG 1529. 5 maps [now in map section].

Text: PNE, 4: 24–28.

Map: Published. Catalog, 49.

Mod: Sta. Maria Xadan, M. S. Miguel del Puerto, Oaxaca. Map: fig. 25-R/20-17/14.

Lang: Zapotec: Mexicano (old people). Article 2: I-33, 118.

Note: Related communities cannot be identified.

Related

A. SAN SEBASTIAN TLACOTEPEC
Map: Published. Catalog, 74.
Lang: Chontal (de Oaxaca).

B. SANTA MARIA ZOZOPASTEPEC
Map: Published. Catalog, 90.
Lang: Chontal (de Oaxaca).

C. SAN BARTOLOME TAMASPALTEPEC (Tlamasgastepec, Tamazgastepec)
Map: Published. Catalog, 51.
Lang: Chontal (de Oaxaca).

D. SAN MIGUEL MACUPILCO (Mancupilco, Macopilco)
Map: Published. Catalog, 33.
Lang: Chontal (de Oaxaca).

89. TABASCO (AM). Yucatan. [Complex].
Vasco Rodríguez, alcalde mayor.
Mar. 6, 1579.
SIM, 214. RM, 135.
AGI, IG 1530. No. 378. No map.
Text: RT, Ib, DIU, 11: 311–17.
Mod: Not located in detail.
Lang: Mexicano, Zoque, Chontal. Article 2: XIII, XIV.
Note: This is not formally a RG. It is found in ff. 167–69 of the bound volume, entitled "Mandamiento del Sr. Governador." Data from A. Kibre, personal communication.

90. TABASCO. Yucatan. [Complex].
Melchor de Alfaro Santa Cruz, vezino y encomendero.
May 2, 1579.
SIM, 214. RM, 135.
AGI, IG 1530. No. 378. Map.
Text: RT, IIa; DIU, 11: 318–41.
Map: Published. Catalog, 50.
Mod: Not located in detail.
Lang: Mexicano, Zoque, Chontal. Article 2: XIII, XIV.
Note: Dated at Gueimango de los Naguatatos. Pages 327–30 constitute a "Memoria. Teapa, Mochitín, Casados," a listing of Spaniards of Teapa, fol-

lowed by a listing of tributary Indians (pp. 330–41). Data from A. Kibre, personal communication.

91. [TABASCO] VICTORIA, STA. MARIA DE LA (V). Yucatan. [Complex].
Diego Alver de Soria and others.
May 12, 1579.
SIM, 214. RM, 135.
AGI, IG 1530. No. 378. No map.
Text: RT, III; DIU, 11: 341–74.
Mod: La Victoria, M. Centla, Tabasco. Map: fig. 31-M/25-8.
Lang: Mexicano, Zoque, Chontal. Article 2: XIII, XIV.
Note: The province is Tabasco, with S. M. Victoria as cabecera, here out of alphabetical order.

92. TAHZIB (M). Yucatan. Prov. Mani. [Simple]
Hunpiczib.
Juan de Magaña Arroyo, encomendero.
Mar. 28, 1580.
SIM, 214. RM, 135.
AGI, IG 1530. No. 378. No map.
Text: RY, 1-XIII; DIU, 11: 185–90.
Mod: Tahdziu, Yucatan. Map: fig. 35-J/31-86.
Lang: Maya. Article 2: XV.

93. TAIMEO. Michoacan. [Simple].
Tarimeo, Taymeo.
Juan Martínez Verduzco, corregidor.
Aug. 29–Sept. 2, 1579. Crown.
JLV, 3/23. DyP, 223/3. SIM, 116. RM, 120.
RAH. 9-25-4/4663-II. 2 ff. No map.
Text: (1) VR/PNE, 7/3: 99–105. (2) RGM, 1: 36–40.
Mod: Taimeo, M. Zinepecuaro, Michoacan. Map: fig. 20-K/11-88.
Lang: Otomi. Article 2: I-113.

94. TALISTACA. Antequera. Prov. Valle de Tlacolula. [Simple].
Taliztaca, Yatiqui (Zapotec).
Juan del Rio, corregidor.

Sept. 12, 1580. Crown.

JLV, 1/15. DyP, 309/3. SIM, 16. RM, 89.

RAH. 9-25-4/4663-XXII. 2 ff. No map.

Text: PNE, 4: 177–82.

Mod: Tlalixtac de Cabrera, Oaxaca. Map: fig. 25-P/19-1/11.

Lang: Zapotec. Article 2: I-5.

95. TANCITARO. Michoacan. [Composite].

Tantaro.

Sebastián Macarro, corregidor.

Sept. 27, 1580. Encomendero: Diego Enríquez (1/2); Crown (1/2).

JLV, 1/13. DyP, 244/3. SIM, 110. RM, 114. JGI, XXIV-18.

UTX. CDG, 1763. 11 ff. No map.

Text: Bernal, 1952.

Mod: Tancitaro, Michoacan. Map: fig. 20-M/9-32.

Lang: Tarascan, Mexicano. Article 2: I-80.

Related

A. TLAPALCATEPEC. Crown
Mod: Tepalcatepec, Michoacan. Map: fig. 20-M/8-34.
Lang: Tarascan.

[B. COLIMA, VILLA]
Mod: Colima, Colima. Map: fig. 13–M/7-7.
Note: No data on this included in RG.

C. PINZANDARO ARIMEO. Crown
Mod: Pinzandaro, M. Buenavista, Michoacan. Map: fig. 20-M/8-33.
Note: Adds extra materials on the habits of large ants in area.

[D. TAMAZULAPA]
Note: No data on this in RG.

96. TAXCO, Minas de. Mexico. [Complex].

Tasco, Tlacho.

Pedro de Ledesma, alcalde mayor.

Jan. 1–Mar. 6, 1581.

JLV, 4/24. DyP, 653/6. SIM, 150. RM, 35.

AGI, IG 1529. No. 396. Instr., 17 ff. No map. Document missing.

Text: PNE, 6: 263–82.

Mod: Taxco de Alarcón, Guerrero. Map: fig. 17-N/13-9.

Lang: Mexicano, Tarascan, Mazatec, Chontal. Article 2: I-81.

Related

A. HUEZTACA (Teultistaca)
Mod: Huixtac, M. Taxco, Guerrero.

B. TENANGO
Mod: Cacalotenango, M. Taxco, Guerrero.

97. TEABO (M). Yucatan. Prov. Mani (Tutulxiu). [Complex].

Teav, Tiev.

Juan Bote, regidor and encomendero, aided by Gaspar Antonio Chi.

Feb. 20, 1581.

SIM, 214. RM, 135.

AGI, IG 1530. No. 378. No map.

Text: RY, 1-XXIV; DIU, 11: 284–92.

Mod: Teabo, Yucatan. Map: fig. 35-I/30-102.

Lang: Maya. Article 2: XV.

Related

A. TECH
Mod: Tekit? Yucatan. Map: fig. 35-I/30-90.

98. TECAL (M). Yucatan. Prov. Aquinchel. [Simple].

Tiral.

Diego Briceño, encomendero, aided by Gaspar Antonio Chi.

n.d. [1581].

SIM, 214. RM, 135.

AGI, IG 1530. No. 378. No map.

Text: RY, 1-XII; DIU, 11: 174–85.

Mod: Tekal de Venegas, Yucatan. Map: fig. 35-H/31-51.

Lang: Maya. Article 2: XV.

99. TECANTO (M). Yucatan. [Complex].

Tecauto.

Cristóbal Sánchez, encomendero, aided by Gaspar Antonio Chi.

Feb. 15, 1581.

SIM, 214. RM, 135.

AGI, IG 1530. No. 378. No map.
Text: RY, 1-VI; DIU, 11: 115–26.
Mod: Tekanto, Yucatan. Map: fig. 35-H/31-47.
Lang: Maya. Article 2: XV.

Related

A. TEPECAN
Mod: Tepakan, Yucatan.

100. TECON (V). Yucatan. [Composite].
Juan de Cárdenas, encomendero.
May 1, 1579.
SIM, 214. RM, 135.
AGI, IG 1530. No. 378. No map.
Text: RY, 2-XXI; DIU, 13: 172–75.
Mod: Tekom, Yucatan. Map: fig. 35-I/33-82.
Lang: ? [Maya]. Article 2: XV.

Related

A. ECABO

101. TECUICUILCO. Antequera. Prov. Valle de Oaxaca. [Complex].
Teoquillo [FGO], Teoquilco, Tecoquilco.
Francisco de Villegas, corregidor.
Oct. 2, 1580.
JLV, 4/26. DyP, 980/8. SIM, 194. RM, 106. JGI, XXIV-19.
UTX. CDG, 1766. 8 ff. Map.
Text: Gómez de Orozco, 1928b.
Map: Published. Catalog, 54.
Mod: Teococuilco, Oaxaca. Map: fig. 25-O/19-8/12.
Lang: Zapotec. Article 2: I-84.

Related

A. ATEPEC
Mod: S. Juan Atepec, Oaxaca. Map: fig. 25-O/19-8/9.
Lang: Zapotec.
B. ZOQUIAPA
Mod: Stgo. Zoquiapan, Oaxaca. Map: fig. 25-O/19-3/16.
Lang: Zapotec.
C. XALTIANGUIS (co)
Mod: Sta. Maria Jaltianguis, Oaxaca. Map: fig. 25-O/19-8/14.
Lang: Zapotec.

102. TEHUANTEPEC. Antequera. [Complex].
Teguantepec.
Juan de Torre de Lagunas, alcalde mayor.
Sept. 20–Oct. 5, 1580.
JLV, 2/16. DyP, 310/3. SIM, 29. RM, 76. JGI, XXV-4.
UTX. CDG, 1767. 16 ff. 1 map, 1 chart.
Text: (1) Caso, 1928b. (2) Cajigas Langner, 1953. (3) VR, 1958.
Map: Partially published. Catalog, 55. Chart unpublished; Catalog, 56.
Mod: Sto. Domingo Tehuantepec, Oaxaca. Map: 25-Q/21-21/15.
Lang: Zapotec, Mexicano, Mixe, Mixtec. Article 2: I-86.

Related

A. XALAPA
Mod: Sta. Maria Jalapa del Marques, Oaxaca. Map: 25-Q/21-21/8.
Lang: Zapotec, Mixe, Mixtec.
B. TEQUEZISTLAN
Mod: Magdalena Tequisitlan, Oaxaca. Map: fig. 25-Q/21-21/7.
Lang: Zapotec, Chontal.

103. TEMAZCALTEPEC, Minas de. Mexico. Prov. Matalcinga. [Complex–Composite].
Cacaloztoc, Real de los Rios.
Gaspar de Covarrubias, alcalde mayor and corregidor of Tuzantla.
Dec. 1, 1579–Jan. 1, 1580.
JLV, 1/23.
AGI, PR 238, no. 2, ramo 1. Instr. 24 ff. [Last 3 blank. Document filed in map section. Minas de Temazcaltepec, ff. 6-8r]. 5 maps; 2 drawings [Catalog, Appendix, 3].
Text: (1) De la Puente y Olea, 1890. (2) PNE, 7: 15–29.
Map: Published. Catalog, 57.
Mod: Real de Arriba, M. Temascaltepec, Mexico. Map: fig. 14-M/13-21.
Lang: Mexicano, Matlatzinca. Article 2: I-87.
Note: Minas de Temazcaltepec, plus Tescaltitlan, Tepuxpilco, and pueblo of

349

Temazcaltepec, form a complex RG; Tuzantla follows this material as added composite item.

Related

A. TESCALTITLLAN
AGI, ff. 8v–16r, (covers A, B, C).
Map: Published. Catalog, 65.
Mod: Stgo. Texcaltitlan, Mexico. Map: fig. 14-M/13-19.
Lang: Matlatzinca, Mexicano.

B. TEXUPILCO
Map: Published. Catalog, 70.
Mod: Tejupilco de Hidalgo, Mexico. Map: fig. 14-M/12-15.
Lang: Matlatzinca, Mexicano.

C. TEMAZCALTEPEC, Pueblo (Cacaloztoc, Tamazcaltepec)
Map: Published. Catalog, 9.
Mod: Temascaltepec, Mexico. Map: fig. 14-M/13-21.
Lang: Matlatzinca, Mazahua, Mexicano.

D. TUZANTLA, Michoacan
Diego de las Roelas, teniente.
Oct. 20, 1579.
AGI, ff. 16v–21r.
Text: Cline, 1965.
Map: Published. Catalog, 76.
Mod: Tuzantla, Michoacan. Map: fig. 20-M/12-91.
Lang: Tarascan, Mazahua. Article 2: I-53.

104. TEMUL (V). Yucatan. Prov. Tizimin. [Simple].
Juan de Benavides, alguacil mayor (and encomendero).
Feb. 19, 1579.
SIM, 214. RM, 135.
AGI, IG 1530, no. 378. No map.
Text: RY, 2-XI; DIU, 13: 119–26.
Mod: Dzemul, Yucatan. Map: fig. 35-H/30-19.
Lang: ? [Maya]. Article 2: XV.

105. TENAMAZTLAN. Guadalajara. Prov. Avalos. [Simple].
Pedro de Avila, corregidor.
Nov. 28, 1579. Encomenderos: Martín Monge de Leon (1/2), Francisco de Aguallo (1/2).

JLV, 3/24. DyP, 242/3. SIM, 108. RM, 129. JGI, XXV-1.
UTX. CDG, 1769. 7 ff. No map.
Text: (1) NV, 1878, pp. 321–46. (2) VR, 1952e.
Mod: Tenamaxtlan. Jalisco. Map: fig. 19-K/6-106.
Lang: Mexicano. Article 2: I-9.

106. TENUM (V). Yucatan. [Complex].
Juan Cano el Viejo, encomendero.
Mar. 12, 1579.
SIM, 214. RM, 135.
AGI, IG 1530. No. 378. No map.
Text: RY, 2-XIII; DIU, 13: 130–34.
Mod: Tinum, Yucatan. Map: fig. 35-I/32-60.
Lang: ? [Maya]. Article 2: XV.

Related

A. TEMOZON
Mod: Temozon, Yucatan.

107. TEOTITLAN. Antequera. [Composite].
Francisco de Castañeda, corregidor.
Sept. 15, 1581.
JLV, 1/12. SIM, 27. RM, 97.
RAH. 9-25-4/4663-XXVII. Instr., 8 ff. Map.
Text: (1) PNE, 4: 213–31. (2) VR, 1957d.
Map: Published. Catalog, 59.
Mod: Teotitlan del Camino, Oaxaca. Map: fig. 25-N/18-22/2.
Lang: Mexicano. Article 2: I-98.

Related

A. MATZATLAN
Sept. 16, 1581. Crown.
Mod: Mazatlan de Flores, Oaxaca. Map: fig. 25-N/18-22/22.
Lang: Mazatec, Mexicano.

B. HUAUTLA (Guauhtla)
Sept. 18, 1581. Crown.
Mod: Huautla de Jimenez, Oaxaca. Map: fig. 25-N/18-22/19.
Lang: Mexicano, Mazatec.

C. NEXTEPEC
Sept. 19, 1581. Crown.

Mod: S. Gabriel Casa Blanca, Oaxaca.
Map: fig. 25-N/18-22/1?
Lang: Mexicano, Mazatec.

D. NANAHUATEPEC
Sept. 20, 1581. Crown.
Mod: S. Antonio Nanahuatipan, Oaxaca.
Map: fig. 25-N/18-22/1.
Lang: Mazatec, Mexicano.

E. TECOLUTLA
Sept. 22, 1581. Crown.
Mod: S. Juan los Cues, Oaxaca. Map: fig.
25-N/18-22/23.
Lang: Mexicano, Mazatec.

108. TEOZACOALCO. Antequera. Prov.
Mixteca Alta. [Composite].
Hernando de Cervantes, corregidor, and
Juan Ruiz Zuazco, cura.
Jan. 9, 1580.
JLV, 2/20 (Teozacoalco). DyP, 312/3.
SIM, 34. RM, 81. JGI, XXV-3.
UTX. CDG, 1770. 8 ff. 2 maps.
Text: (1) Gómez de Orozco, 1927c. (2)
Caso, 1949a. (3) VR, 1956a.
Map: Published (copy). Catalog, 60.
Mod: S. Pedro Teozacoalco, Oaxaca.
Map: fig. 25-P/18-15/27.
Lang: Mixtec. Article 2: I-90.
Note: The two RG's were separate when
listed by JLV. Subsequently they were
united, as RM, 81, lists "Teozacualco i
Amoltepeque." Data from A. Kibre.

Related

A. AMOLTEPEC (Yacunama [Mixtec])
JLV, 2/21.
Jan. 21, 1580.
Text: Gómez de Orozco, 1927c.
Map: Published. Catalog, 4.
Mod: Stgo. Amoltepec, Oaxaca. Map: fig.
25-Q/17-11/1.
Lang: [Mixtec].

109. TEOZAPOTLAN. Antequera. [Simple].
Zaachila (Zapotec).
Fray Juan de Mata, vicario.
Nov. 11, 1580.
JLV, 4/8. SIM, 24. RM, 95.

RAH. 9-25-4/4663-XXV. Instr., 3 ff. No
map.
Text: PNE, 4: 190–95.
Mod: Zaachila, Oaxaca. Map: fig. 25-
P/18-29/3.
Lang: Zapotec. Article 2: I-5.

110. TEPEACA, Ciudad. Tlaxcala. Prov.
Tepeyaca. [Complex].
Jorge Cerón Carvajal, alcalde mayor.
Feb. 4 and 20, 1580.
JLV, 2/23. DyP, 976/8. SIM, 193. RM,
60.
AGI, IG 1529. No. 381. Instr., 30 ff.
No map.
Text: PNE, 5:12–45.
Mod: Tepeaca, Puebla. Map: fig. 26-
M/16-116.
Lang: Mexicano, Otomi. Article 2: I-91.

Related

A. TECAMACHALCO
Encomenderos: Rodrigo de Vivero and wife
Melchora de Averruzia.
Mod: Tecamachalco, Puebla. Map: fig.
26-M/17-125.
Lang: Mexicano (nobles), Otomi, Popoloca.

B. CACHULA (Quechola)
Encomenderos: Gonzalo Coronado (1/2),
Nicolas de Villanueva (1/2).
Mod: Quecholac, Puebla. Map: fig. 26-
M/17-124.
Lang: Mexicano, Popoloca.

C. SANTIAGO TECALI
Encomendero: Joseph de Orduña.
Mod: Tecali de Herrera, Puebla. Map: fig.
26-M/16-131.
Lang: ? Otomi.

111. TEPEAPULCO. Mexico. [Simple].
Tepepulco.
Juan López Cacho, corregidor.
Apr. 15, 1581.
JLV, P-3, 4/21. DyP, 1008/8. SIM, 184.
RM, 48.
AGI, IG 1529. No. 394. Instr., 10 ff.
Map lost.
Text: PNE, 6: 291–305.
Map: Lost. Catalog, 61.

Mod: Tepeapulco, Hidalgo. Map: fig. 18-L/15-63.

Lang: Mexicano, Otomi, Chichimec. Article 2: I-6.

112. TEPUZTLAN (V). Mexico. [Cuatro Villas]. Prov. Marquesado del Valle. [Simple].

Tepoztlan.

Juan Gutiérrez de Liebana, alcalde mayor.

Sept. 19, 1580. Marquesado.

JLV, 2/28. DyP, 152/2. SIM, 215. RM, 28.

AGI, IG 1529. No. 390. Instr. missing, 5 ff. Map lost.

Text: (1) PNE, 6: 237–50. (2) García Pimentel, 1909a.

Map: Lost. Catalog, 62.

Mod: Tepoztlan, Morelos. Map: fig. 21-M/14-13.

Lang: Mexicano. Article 2: I-21.

See also ACAPISTLA, 1; GUAXTEPEC, 47; YAUTEPEC, 221; OCUITUCO, 210.

113. TEQUALTICHE. Guadalajara. [Simple].

Hernando Gallegos, teniente del alcalde mayor.

Dec. 30, 1585.

DyP, leg. 7. SIM, 199. RM, 131. JGI, XXV-2.

UTX. CDG, 1773. 6 ff. Map lost.

Text: NV, 1878, pp. 346–60.

Map: Lost. Catalog, 63.

Mod: Teocaltiche, Jalisco. Map: fig. 19-I/8-20.

Lang: Cazcan, Mexicano. Article 2: II-17.

114. TEQUISQUIAC. Mexico. [Composite].

Alonso de Galdo, corregidor.

Sept. 10, 1579.

JLV, 4/32. DyP, 1003/8. SIM, 190. RM, 53. JGI, XXV-5.

UTX. CDG, 1774. 4 ff. No. map.

Text: Bernal, 1957, pp. 290–96.

Mod: Tequizquiac, Mexico. Map: fig. 14-K/14-83.

Lang: Mexicano, Otomi. Article 2: I-89.

Related

A. CITLALTEPEC, Crown
Text: Bernal, 1957, pp. 296–303.
Mod: S. Juan Zitlaltepec, M. Zumpango, Mexico. Map: fig. 14-K/14-82.
Lang: Mexicano, Otomi.

B. XILOCINGO
Text: Bernal, 1957, pp. 303–08.
Mod: Jilotzingo, M. Hueypoxtla, Mexico. Map: fig. 14-K/14-85.
Lang: Mexicano, Otomi.

115. TEQUITE (M). Yucatan. [Simple].

Hernando de Bracamonte, encomendero.

Feb. 20, 1581.

SIM, 214. RM, 135.

AGI, IG 1530. No. 378. No map.

Text: RY, I-V; DIU, 11: 103–115.

Mod: Tekit, Yucatan. Map: fig. 35-I/30-90.

Lang: Maya. Article 2: XV.

116. TEQUIZISTLAN. Mexico. Prov. Texcoco. [Composite].

Francisco de Castañeda, corregidor.

Feb. 22, 1580.

JLV, 3/17. DyP, 1005/8 (text), 999/8 map). SIM, 188. RM, 33.

AGI, IG 1529. No. 386. Instr. missing, 16 ff. Map.

Text: (1) PNE, 6: 209–36. (2) Nuttall, 1926 (English trans.).

Map: Published. Catalog, 64.

Mod: Tequisistlan, M. Tezoyuca, Mexico. Map: fig. 14-L/14-91.

Lang: Mexicano. Article 2: I-89.

Related

A. TEPEXPA
Feb. 23, 1580.
Mod: Tepexpan, M. Acolman, Mexico. Map: fig. 14-L/14-92.
Lang: Mexicano, Otomi.

B. ACULMA
Feb. 26, 1580.

Mod: El Calvario Acolman, Mexico. Map: fig. 14-L/14-92.

Lang: Mexicano, Otomi.

C. S. Juan Teotihuacan

Mar. 1, 1580.

Mod: S. Juan Teotihuacan, Mexico. Map: fig. 14-L/14-93.

Lang: Mexicano, Otomi, Popoloca.

117. TETELA [DEL VOLCAN]. Mexico. Prov. Suchimilco. [Complex].

Cristóbal Godinez Maldonado, corregidor.

June 20, 1581. (Signed: Gueyapa, July 9, 1581.)

JLV, 4/35. DyP, 645/6. SIM, 142. RM, 38.

AGI, IG 1529. No. 395. Instr., 6 ff. No map.

Text: (1) PNE, 6: 283–90. (2) García Pimentel, 1909b. (3) BCE, 1920a. (4) RNE, 1920b, pp. 29–36.

Mod: Tetela del Volcan, Morelos. Map: fig. 21-M/15-32.

Lang: Mexicano. Article 2: I-93.

Related

A. Gueyapa (Ueyapan)

Mod: Hueyapan, M. Tetela, Morelos. Map: fig. 21-M/15-32.

118. TETELA and XONOTLA. Tlaxcala. [Composite].

Note: Xonotla and Tetela were co-equal cabeceras, each with related dependencies. In various revisions of this Census, TETELA was inadvertently substituted for XONOTLA, which appears first in the document. Herewith the entry for TETELA. Data for XONOTLA, 118bis, follow entry for XOCOTLAN, Minas de, 144.

Juan Gonzáles, corregidor.

Oct. 29, 1581. Crown.

JLV, 2/19. DyP, 1010/8. SIM, 182. RM, 57.

AGI, IG 1529. No. 397. Instr., 31 ff. [Document filed in map section.] 2 maps.

Text: PNE, 5: 143–50.

Map: Published. Catalog, 66.

Mod: Tetela de Ocampo, Puebla. Map: fig. 26-K/15-16.

Lang: Mexicano. Article 2: I-124.

Related to Tetela

A. Guytlentla, San Pedro
PNE, 5: 151.
Mod: Hueytentan, M. Cuautempan, Puebla.

B. Tonalapa, Santiago
PNE, 5: 151.
Mod: Tonalapa, M. Tetela, Puebla.

C. San Estevan [Tzanaquatla] Tehoquateno.
PNE, 5: 151–57.
Mod: S. Esteban Cuautempa, Puebla.
Lang: Mexicano.

D. Capulapa, San Miguel
PNE, 5: 157–63.
Mod: Capuluaque, barrio, M. Tetela, Puebla (?)
Lang: Mexicano.

E. Zuzumba, San Francisco
PNE, 5: 163–67.
Lang: Mexicano.

F. Tututla, San Juan
PNE, 5: 167–73.
Mod: Totutla, M. Huitzilan, Puebla.
Lang: Mexicano.

119. TETICPAC. Antequera. [Simple]. Zetoba (Zapotec).

Pedro Pérez de Zamora Abarca, corregidor.

Apr. 15, 1580.

JLV, 2/9. SIM, 10. RM, 83.

RAH. 9-25-4/4663-XVIII. Instr., 3 ff. No map.

Text: PNE, 4: 109–14.

Mod: S. Sebastian Teitipac, Oaxaca. Map: fig. 25-P/19-24/10.

Lang: Zapotec. Article 2: I-5, 14.

120. TETIQUIPA–RIO HONDO. Antequera. [Composite]. Yegoyuxi (Zapotec).

Cristóbal de Salas, corregidor.

n.d. [1580?]

JLV, 3/10. SIM, 15. RM, 88. JGI, XXV-6.

UTX. CDG, 1777. 3 ff. No map.

Text: (1) Gómez de Orozco, 1928a. (2) VR, 1955.

Mod: S. Sebastian Rio Hondo, Oaxaca. Map: fig. 25-P/19-13/24.

Lang: Zapotec. Article 2: I-14.

Related

A. Cozautepec

Text: (1) Gómez de Orozco, 1928a. (2) VR, 1956a.

Mod: S. Francisco Cozoaltepec, M. Sta. Maria Tonameca, Oaxaca. Map: fig. 25-R/19-17/7.

Lang: Zapotec, Mexicano.

121. TETZAL (M). Yucatan. Prov. Peto. [Complex].

Alonso Julián, encomendero.

Feb. 19, 1581.

SIM, 214. RM, 135.

AGI, IG 1530. No. 378. No map. 1 drawing [Catalog, Appendix 4].

Text: RY, 1-XXV; DIU, 11: 292–307.

Mod: Unlocated, Yucatan.

Lang: Chontal [Tecltal?]. Article 2: XV.

Related

A. Ixtual

122. TEUTENANGO. Mexico. Prov. Valle de Matalzingo. [Simple].

Francisco Dávila, corregidor.

Mar. 12, 1582.

JLV, 2/18. DyP, 240/3. SIM, 106. RM, 36.

AGI, IG 1529. No. 401? [No file folder at present]. Instr., 6 ff. Map.

Text: (1) PNE, 7: 1–7. (2) BCE, 1920a. (3) RNE, 1920b, pp. 23–28. (4) Gómez de Orozco, 1923. (5) Romero Quiroz, 1963.

Map: Published. Catalog, 68.

Mod: Tenango de Arista, M. Tenango del Valle, Mexico. Map: fig. 14-M/13-48.

Lang: Mexicano, Matlatzinca. Article 2: I-88.

123. TEXCOCO. Mexico. [Complex]. Tezcuco.

Juan Bautista Pomar, for Juan Velázquez de Salazar, alcalde mayor.

Mar. 9, 1582.

JGI, XII-16 (copy).

Original lost. Copy, JGI, UTX. CDG, 1517; another, CDG, 1518. Illustrations lost [Catalog, Appendix: 5].

Text: (1) García Icazbalceta, 1891. (2) Garibay, 1964.

Mod: Texcoco de Mora, Mexico. Map: fig. 14-L/14-103.

Lang: Mexicano. Article 2: I-100.

Related

A. Huexotlan

Mod: Huexotla, M. Texcoco, Mexico.

B. Cohuatlinchan

Mod: S. Miguel Coatlinchan, M. Texcoco, Mexico.

C. Chiauhtla

Mod: S. Andres Chiautla, Mexico. Map: fig. 14-L/15-101.

D. Tetzoyucan

Mod: Tezoyuca, Mexico. Map: fig. 14-L/14-91.

124. TEXUPA. Antequera. Prov. Mixteca Alta. [Simple].

Diego de Avendaño, corregidor.

Oct. 20, 1579.

JLV, 4/10. DyP, 1013/8. SIM, 180. RM, 105.

RAH. 9-25-4/4663-XVII. Instr., 3 ff. Map.

Text: (1) PNE, 4: 53–57. (2) León, 1933.

Map: Published. Catalog, 69.

Mod: Stgo. Tejupan, Oaxaca. Map: fig. 25-O/17-23/7.

Lang: Mixtec, Chocho. Article 2: I-93.

Bibliog: De Blois, 1963.

125. TEZEMI (V). Yucatan. Prov. Tezemin. [Complex].

Temozon, Tizimin.

Diego de Burgos Cansino, encomendero.

May 8, 1579.

SIM, 214. RM, 135.

AGI, IG 1530. No. 378. No map.

Text: (1) RY, 2-XIX; DIU, 13: 164–68.
(2) Barrera Vásquez, 1938.

Mod: Tizimin, Yucatan. Map: fig. 35-H/32-12.

Lang: ? [Maya]. Article 2: XV.

Related

A. ATEQUEAC

B. CACALCHEN
   Mod: Cacalchen, Yucatan. Map: 35-H/30-45.

C. CENOTE TEPIPE

D. CAGUAN
   Mod: Kaua, Yucatan. Map: fig. 35-I/32-79.

E. CANXOCO

126. TEZOCO (V). Yucatan. Prov. Tezemin. [Complex].

Diego Osorio, vezino.

May 4, 1579. Encomenderos: Diego Osorio (1/2); Juan Ruizdaves, menor, (1/2).

SIM, 214. RM, 135.

AGI, IG 1530. No. 378. No map.

Text: RY, 2-VII; DIU, 13: 88–92.

Mod: Tesoco, M. Valladolid, Yucatan. Map: fig. 35-I/33-58.

Lang: ? [Maya]. Article 2: XV.

Related

A. TECAY

B. COZIL

127. TILANTONGO. Antequera. Prov. Mixteca Alta. [Composite].

Nutuco (Mixteco).

Juan de Bazán, corregidor, and Fray Pedro de las Eras, vicario.

Nov. 5, 1579. (Signed Nov. 20, 1579.) Crown.

JLV, P-6, 6A, 11; 4/16. SIM, 32. RM, 99.

RAH. 9-25-4/4663-XXIX. 13 ff. Tilantongo, ff. 1–6r. Maps lost.

Text: PNE, 4: 69–77.

Map: Lost. Catalog, 71.

Mod: Stgo. Tilantongo, Oaxaca. Map: fig. 25-P/17-15/22.

Lang: Mixtec. Article 2: I-93.

Related

A. STA. CRUZ AND SANTIAGO MITLANTONGO (2 places) (Sandaya [Mixtec])
   Nov. 12, 1579. Crown.
   Text: PNE, 4: 77–82.
   Map: Lost. Catalog, 72.
   Mod: Sta. Cruz Mitlantongo, Oaxaca; Stgo. Mitlatongo, Oaxaca. Map: fig. 25-P/18-15/?.
   Lang: Mixtec.

B. SAN JOSE TAMAZULA (Yaqui [Mixtec])
   Nov. 16, 1579. Crown.
   Text: PNE, 4: 82–87.
   Map: Lost. Catalog, 52?.
   Mod: San Juan Tamazola, Oaxaca. Map: fig. 25-P/18-15/31.
   Lang: Mixtec.

128. TINGÜINDIN. Michoacan. [Simple].

Chocandiran, Dingüindin, Tinhuindin.

Gonzalo Galván, corregidor, and Francisco Dolmos, español.

Apr. 17, 1581.

JLV, 4/25. DyP, 224/3. SIM, 117. RM, 121.

RAH. 9-25-4/4663-XI. Instr., 4 ff. No map.

Text: (1) VR/PNE, 7/8: 73–90. (2) RGM, 2: 74–83.

Mod: Tingüindin, Michoacan. Map: fig. 20-K/9-14.

Lang: Tarascan, Mexicano (women). Article 2: I-101.

129. TIQUIBALON (V). Yucatan. Prov. Cupules. [Simple].

Chuaca?

Juan Gutiérrez Picón, vezino and encomendero.

Mar. 4, 1579.

SIM, 214. RM, 135.

AGI, IG 1530. No. 378. No map.

Text: (1) RY, 2-XVIII, DIU, 13: 153–63.
(2) Barrera Vásquez, 1938.

Mod: Unlocated, Yucatan.

Lang: ? [Maya]. Article 2: XV.

Note: Much historical information was given compiler by an unidentified aged Maya who wrote the "historias" for him [DIU, 13: 159–62].

130. TIRIPITIO. Michoacan. [Simple].
Pedro de Montes de Oca, corregidor.
Sept. 15, 1580.
JLV, 4/13. DyP, 229/3. SIM, 113. RM, 117. JGI, XXV-7.
UTX. CDG, 1781. 7 ff. No map. 2 drawings [Catalog, Appendix, 6].
Text: Unpublished.
Mod: Tiripetio, M. Morelia, Michoacan. Map: fig. 20-L/11-72.
Lang: Tarascan. Article 2: I-113.
Note: At close is letter, October 16, 1580, from Fray Guillermo de Santa María to Fray Alonso de Albarado, concerning "Guerra justa contra los Chichimecas."

131. TISHOTZUCO (V). Yucatan. Prov. Cochoah. [Complex].
Antonio Méndez, vezino and encomendero.
Mar. 25, 1579.
SIM, 214. RM, 135.
AGI, IG 1530. No. 378. No map.
Text: RY, 2-VIII; DIU, 13: 93–97.
Mod: Chikindzonot (?), M. Tekom, Yucatan. Map: fig. 35-I/32-82.
Lang: ? [Maya]. Article 2: XV.

Related

A. CHIQUINCENOTE
Mod: Chikindzonot, M. Tekom, Yucatan. Map: fig. 35-I/32-82.

132. TISTLA. Tlaxcala. Prov. Minas de Zumpango. [Composite].
Tetzahuapa (ancient).
Gonzalo Bazán, alcalde mayor, and Francisco Martínez, beneficiado.
Mar. 7, 1582. Encomendero: Luis de Velasco.
JLV, 1/16. DyP, 1011/8. SIM, 181. RM, 70. JGI, XXV-13.

UTX. CDG, 1875. 7 ff. [Tistla, ff. 1-3v]. Map [Muchitlan].
Text: Unpublished.
Mod: Tixtla de Guerrero, Guerrero. Map: fig. 17-O/14-44.
Lang: Mexicano, Matlatzinca, Tutec. Article 2: I-29, 102.
Note: Text material nearly exclusively on Tistla, although map is labeled "Muchitlan." Closely related to two other reports by same alcalde mayor and religious co-authors. *See also* CHILAPA, 22bis; ZUMPANGO 164.

Related

A. MUCHITLAN (TETZAHUAPA)
UTX. ff. 3v-7.
Encomendero: Luis de Velasco.
Text: Unpublished.
Map: Unpublished. Catalog, 41.
Mod: Mochitlan, Guerrero. Map: fig. 17-P/14-48.

133. TLACOLULA. Antequera. [Composite].
Paza (Zapotec).
Alonso de Canseco, corregidor.
Aug. 12–13, 1580. Crown.
JLV, 2/7. SIM, 22. RM, 79.
RAH. 9-25-4/4663-XXIV. Instr., 2 ff. No map.
Text: (1) PNE, 4: 144–47. (2) Horcasitas and George, 1955.
Mod: Tlacolula de Matamoros, Oaxaca. Map: fig. 25-P/19-24/13.
Lang: Zapotec. Article 2: I-59.

Related

A. MIQUITLA (Mitla, Lioba [Zapotec])
Aug. 23, 1580. Crown.
Text: PNE, 4: 147–54.
Mod: S. Pablo Mitla, Oaxaca. Map: fig. 25-P/19-24/18.
Lang: Zapotec.

134. TLACOTLALPA. Tlaxcala. [Composite].
Cotastla.
Juan de Medina, alcalde mayor

Feb. 18, 1580. Crown.

JLV, 1/22. DyP, 239/3. SIM, 105. RM, 68.

RAH. 9-25-4/4663-XXXVII. Instr., 7 ff. Tlacotlalpan, ff. 1–2v. Map.

Text: PNE, 5: 1–4.

Map: Published. Catalog, 73.

Mod: Tlacotalpan, Veracruz. Map: fig. 34-M/20-168.

Lang: Mexicano. Article 2: I-112, 114.

Related

A. COTASTLA (Cuextlaxtlan)

Feb. 20, 1580. Marquesado del Valle.

Text: PNE, 5: 9–11.

Mod: Pueblo Viejo, M. Cotaxtla, Veracruz. Map: 34-M/19-152.

Lang: Mexicano.

B. TUZTLA, VILLA

Feb. 22, 1580. Marquesado del Valle.

Text: PNE, 5: 4–9.

Mod: Stgo. Tuxtla, Veracruz. Map: fig. 34-N/20-172.

Lang: Mexicano.

135. TORNACUSTLA, Minas de (AM). Mexico. Prov. Teutlalpa. [Composite]. Tolnacuchtla [Tetepango. Hueypostla]. Alonso de Contreras Figueroa, alcalde mayor.

Oct. 10, 1579–Mar. 24, 1580.

JLV, 1/8. DyP, 1000/8. SIM, 192. RM, 31.

AGI, IG 1529. No. 375. Instr., 16 ff. No map.

Text: PNE, 6: 12–38.

Lang: Article 2: I-96.

Related

A. AXOCUPAN (Axacuba)

Mod: Ajacuba, Hidalgo. Map: fig. 18-K/ 14-74.

Lang: Otomi, Mexicano.

B. YETECOMAC, Prov. Apazco

Mod: ? Hidalgo.

Lang: Otomi.

C. TORNACUSTLA, PUEBLA

Mod: Tornacuxtla, M. S. Agustin Tlaxiaca, Hidalgo. Map: fig. 18-K/15-73.

Lang: Otomi, Mexicano.

D. GUEYPUCHTLA

Mod: Hueypoxtla, Mexico. Map: fig. 14-K/14-85.

Lang: Otomi, Mexicano.

E. TEZCATEPEC

Mod: Texatepec, M. Chilcuautla, Hidalgo. Map: fig. 18-K/14-40.

Lang: Otomi.

F. TECPATEPEC

Mod: Texatepec, M. Francisco I. Madero, Hidalgo. Map: fig. 18-K/14-42.

Lang: Otomi, Mexicano.

G. TETEPANGO

Mod: Tetepango, Hidalgo. Map: fig. 18-K/14-78.

136. TOTOLAPA. Mexico. [Complex]. Andrés de Curiel, corregidor.

Sept. 4, 1579.

JLV, 1/3. DyP, 614/6. SIM, 81. RM, 82.

RAH. 9-25-4/4663-XXXIV. Instr., 1 f. blank, 2 ff. No map.

Text: PNE, 6: 6–11.

Mod: Totolapan, Morelos. Map: fig. 21-M/15-15.

Lang: Mexicano. Article 2: I-25.

Related

A. TLAYACAPA

Mod: Tlayacapan, Morelos. Map: fig. 21-M/14-16.

B. ATATLAUCA

Mod: Atlatlahucan, Morelos. Map: fig. 21-M/15-29.

137. TUXPAN. Michoacan. [Composite]. Tuspa. Gerónimo Flores, corregidor.

Feb. 20, 1580.

JLV, 2/3. DyP, 226/3. SIM, 115. RM, 119.

RAH. 9-25-4/4663-VIII. Instr. missing, 12 ff. No map.

Text: (1) VR/PNE, 7/8: 93–130. (2) RGM, 2: 83–92.

Mod: Tuxpan, Jalisco. Map: fig. 19-L/17-69.

Lang: Mexicano, Tiam, Cochin. Article 2: I-111.

Related

A. ZAPOTLAN (Tlayula)
Mod: Cd. Guzman, Jalisco. Map: fig. 19-L/17-72.
Lang: Mexicano, Tarascan, Sayultec, Zapotec (local).

B. TAMATZULA
Mod: Tamazula de Gordiano, Jalisco. Map: fig. 19-L/8-64.
Lang: Mexicano, Tarascan, Tamatzultec.
See also TAMAZULA, 213.

138. USILA. Antequera. [Simple].
Ucila.
Hernando Quijada, corregidor.
Oct. 2, 1579. Crown.
JLV, P-5, 1/2. SIM, 28. RM, 98.
RAH. 9-25-4/4663-XXVIII. Instr., 3 ff. Map lost.
Text: (1) PNE, 4: 45–52. (2) Bevan, 1938 (English trans.).
Map: Lost. Catalog, 77.
Mod: S. Felipe Usila, Oaxaca. Map: fig. 25-N/19-26/9.
Lang: Chinantec, Mexicano (principales). Article 2: I-97.

139. VALLADOLID (V). Yucatan. Prov. Chiquichel. [Complex].
Zaquiva, Zaki, Chuaca.
Diego Sarmiento de Figueroa, alcalde mayor.
Apr. 8–9, 1579.
SIM, 214. RM, 135.
AGI, IG 1530. No. 378. 2 maps.
Text: (1) Marimón, 1884. (2) RY, 2-I; DIU, 13: 3–40. (3) Barrera Vásquez, 1938. (4) Mimenza Castillo, 1943.
Map: Published. Catalog, 79, 80.
Mod: Valladolid, Yucatan. Map: fig. 35-I/32-58.
Lang: Maya. Article 2: XV.
Note: Contains data on some 39 communities within general Valladolid jurisdiction; concerned principally with old site of Chuaca, from which Valladolid was founded in 1545 by 39 Spanish encomenderos.

140. VERA CRUZ. Tlaxcala. [Complex].
Alvaro Patiño de Avila, alcalde mayor, by Lic. Alonso Hernandez Diosdado.
Mar. 15, 1580 (transmitted Nov. 7, 1580).
JLV, 3/25. DyP, 300/3 [996/8?]. SIM, 210. RM, 58. JGI, XXV-8.
UTX. CDG, 1829. 17 ff. 2 maps.
Text: (1) Ramírez Cabañas, 1943. (2) Pasquel, 1958.
Maps: Published. Catalog, 81, 82.
Mod: La Antigua Veracruz, M. La Antigua, Veracruz. Map: fig. 34-L/19-91.
Lang: Mexicano. Article 2: I-117.
Bibliog: Cline, 1959 (identifies about 100 places shown on pinturas).

141. XALAPA DE LA VERA CRUZ. Tlaxcala. [Composite].
Xalapa de la Feria.
Constantine Bravo de Lagunas, alcalde mayor.
Oct. 20, 1580. Crown.
JLV, 4/2. DyP, 624/6 (map). SIM, 80. RM, 59.
AGI, IG 1529. No. 388. Instr., 24 ff. [Text now missing.] Map.
Text: PNE, 5: 99–123.
Map: Published. Catalog, 83.
Mod: Jalapa Enríquez, Veracruz. Map: fig. 34-L/18-78.
Lang: Mexicano. Article 2: I-119.

Related

A. XILOTEPEC, Crown
Mod: Jilotepec, Veracruz. Map: fig. 34-L/18-73.
Lang: Totonac, Mexicano.

B. TLACULULA, Crown
Mod: Tlacolula. Veracruz. Map: fig. 34-L/18-58.
Lang: Totonac, Mexicano.

C. CUACUAZINTLA (Quaquazintlan)
Encomendero: Domingo Gallego.
Mod: Coacoatzintla, Veracruz. Map: fig. 34-L/18-72.

D. CHEPULTEPEC, Crown
Mod: Chapultepec, M. Coacaozintla, Veracruz. Map: fig. 34-L/18-72.
Lang: Totonac, Mexicano.

E. Naolingo, Crown
Mod: Naolinco de la Victoria, Veracruz.
Map: fig. 34-L/18-71.
Lang: Totonac, Mexicano.

F. Acatlan
Encomendero: Martin de Mafla.
Mod: Acatlan, Veracruz. Map: fig. 34-L/
18-63.

G. Miaguatlan
Encomendero: Juan Valiente.
Mod: Miahuatlan, Veracruz. Map: fig. 34-
L/18-62.
Lang: Totonac, Mexicano.

H. Chiconquiyauca
Encomendero: Juan Valiente.
Mod: Chiconquiaco, Veracruz. Map: fig.
34-L/18-62.
Lang: Totonac, Mexicano.

I. Colipa, Crown
Mod: Colipa, Veracruz. Map: fig. 34–K/
18-66.
Lang: Totonac.

J. Ciguacoatlan, Crown
Mod: Juchique de Forrer, Veracruz. Map:
fig. 34-L/18-68.
Lang: Totonac, Mexicano.

K. Tepetlan, Crown
Mod: Tepetlan, Veracruz. Map: fig. 34-L/
18-70.
Lang: Totonac.

L. Almoloncan, Crown
Mod: Almolonga, M. Naolinco, Veracruz.
Map: fig. 34-L/18-71.
Lang: Totonac, Mexicano.

M. Maxtlatlan, Crown
Mod: Mesa de Maxtlatlan, Veracruz [un-
located].

N. Chiltoyac, Crown
Mod: Chiltoyac, M. Jalapa, Veracruz. Map:
fig. 34-L/18-78.
Lang: Totonac, Mexicano.

O. Atescac, Crown
Mod: Atexca, M. Actopan, Veracruz. Map:
fig. 34-L/19-89.
Lang: Mexicano.

P. Xalcomulco, Crown
Mod: Jalcomulco, Veracruz. Map: fig. 34-
L/18-86.

Q. Cuatepec (Guatepec), Crown
Mod: Coatepec, Veracruz. Map: fig. 34-
L/18-79.

R. Xicochimalco, Crown
Mod: Jico Viejo, M. Jico, Veracruz. Map:
fig. 34-L/18-80.

S. Izguacan
Encomendero: Francisco de Reinoso.
Mod: Ixhuacan de los Reyes, Veracruz.
Map: fig. 34-L/18-82.
Lang: Mexicano.

142. XALAPA-CINTLA-ACATLAN (AM).

Tlaxcala-Antequera. Prov. Costa del Sur.
[Composite].
Note: For cabeceras, *see below*: H, K, Q.
Antonio de Sedaño, alcalde mayor.
Jan. 1–Feb. 7, 1582. Crown.
JLV, 2/4. DyP, 282/3. SIM, 211. RM,
75.
RAH. 9-25-4/4663-XV. Instr., 1 blank,
8 ff. No map.
Text: PNE, 4: 252–66.
Article 2: I-43.

Related

A. Xicayan, Antequera
Mod: S. Pedro Jicayan, Oaxaca. Map: fig.
25-Q/16-9/9.
Lang: Amusgo, Mixtec.

B. Ayozinapa, Antequera
Lang: Amusgo.

C. Ometepec, Antequera
Mod: Ometepec, Guerrero. Map: fig. 17-
Q/15-71.
Lang: Amusgo, Ayacastec.

D. Suchistlauca, Antequera
Mod: S. Cristobal Suchixtlahuaca, Oaxaca.
Map: fig. 25-O/17-2/11.
Lang: Amusgo.

E. Tlaculula, Antequera
Lang: Mexicano.

F. Huehuetlan, Antequera
Mod: S. Francisco Huehuetlan, Oaxaca.
Map: fig. 25-N/19-26/4.
Lang: Huehuetec, Mexicano.

G. Ihualapa, Antequera
Mod: Igualapa, Guerrero. Map: fig. 17-
P/15-67.
Lang: Amusgo, Ayacaztec.

H. Cintla (Cabecera), Tlaxcala
Lang: Tlapanec, Cintec, Mexicano.

I. Tepetlapa, Tlaxcala
Lang: Tlapanec, Mexicano.

J. Copalitas (Copalitech), Tlaxcala
Lang: Mexicano.

K. Xalapa (Cabecera), Tlaxcala
Mod: Jalapa, M. Cuautepec, Guerrero.
Map: fig. 17-Q/14-64.
Lang: Mexicano.

L. Nespa, Tlaxcala
Lang: Mexicano.

M. Cuahutepec, Tlaxcala
Mod: Cuautepec, Guerrero. Map: fig. 17-
Q/14-64.
Lang: Mexicano.

N. Tototepec, Tlaxcala
Mod: Ayutla de los Libres, Guerrero. Map:
fig. 17-P/14-61.
Lang: Mexicano.

O. Ayutla, Tlaxcala
Mod: Ayutla de los Libres, Guerrero. Map:
fig. 17-P/14-61.
Lang: Mexicano.

P. Suchitonala, Tlaxcala
Lang: Tlapanec.

Q. Acatlan (Cabecera), Tlaxcala
Mod: S. Luis Acatlan, Guerrero. Map: fig.
17-P/15-60.
Lang: Tlapanec.

R. Cuacoyolichan, Tlaxcala
Lang: Tlapanec.

S. Colutla (Cuylutla), Tlaxcala
Lang: Tlapanec.

T. Azoyu[que], Antequera
Mod: Azoyu, Guerrero. Map: fig. 17-Q/
15-66.
Lang: Tlapanec.

U. Cuahuitlan, Antequera
Mod: Cahuitan, M. Stgo. Tapextla, Oaxaca.
Map: fig. 25-Q/15-9/15.
Lang: Quahutec, Mexicano.

V. Cuahuzapotla, Antequera
Lang: Zapotec.

143. XEREZ (V). Guadalajara. [Composite].
Diego Nieto Maldonado, juez de comisión
y justicia mayor.
Oct. 13–21, 1584.
DyP, 974/8. SIM, 198. RM, 127.
RAH. 9-25-4/4662-VIII. Item 8. Instr.,
6 ff. No map.
Text: VR/PNE, 8/4: 192–206.

Mod: Cd. Garcia Salinas, M. Jerez, Zacatecas. Map: fig. 36-G/7-18.
Lang: Zacatec. Article 2: II-15.

Related
A. Taltenango (Xaltenango)
Oct. 21, 1584.
Text: VR/PNE, 8/4: 208–19.
Mod: Sanchez Roman. Zacatecas.
Lang: Mexicano, Cazcan.

144. XOCOTLAN, Minas de. Guadalajara.
Provincia Coanos. [Simple].
Diego Cornejo Temiño, alcalde mayor.
Oct. 15, 1584.
DyP, 974/8. SIM, 198. RM, 127.
RAH. 9-25-4/4662-IV. Item. 2. 7 ff.,
f. 7v. blank. No map.
Text: VR/PNE, 8/1: 35–57.
Mod: Jocotlan, M. Hostotipaquilla, Jalisco. Map: fig. 19-I/6-11.
Lang: Xocotec, Mexicano. Article 2: II-14.

118bis. XONOTLA and TETELA. Tlaxcala. [Composite].
Note: See note to TETELA and XONOTLA. Herewith entry for co-cabecera,
XONOTLA and its dependencies.
Juan Gonzáles, corregidor.
Oct. 20, 1581. Crown.
JLV, 2/19. DyP, 1010/8. SIM, 182.
RM, 57.
AGI, IG 1529. No. 397. Instr., 31 ff.
[document filed in map section]. 2
maps.
Text: PNE, 5: 124–31.
Map: Published. Catalog, 84.
Mod: Jonotla, Puebla. Map: fig. 26-K/
17-43.
Lang: Mexicano, Totonac. Art. 2: I-124.

Related
A. Tutzamapa, San Martin
PNE, 5: 131–35.
Mod: Tuzamapa de Galeana, Puebla.
Lang: Mexicano, Totonac.
B. Ayotusco, San Francisco
PNE, 5: 135–38.
Mod: Zoquiapan, Puebla.

Lang: Mexicano, Totonac.

C. ECATLAN, SANTIAGO
PNE: 5: 138–43.
Mod: Ecatlan, M. Jonotla, Puebla.
Lang: Totonac, Mexicano.

145. XOQUEN (V). Yucatan. [Simple].
Salvador Corzo, vezino and encomendero.
Apr. 20, 1579.
SIM, 214. RM, 135.
AGI, IG 1530. No. 378. No map.
Text: RY, 2-XIV; DIU, 13: 135–38.
Mod: Xocen, M. Valladolid, Yucatan.
Map: fig. 35-I/33-58.
Lang: ? [Maya]. Article 2: XV.

146. YALCON (V). Yucatan. [Simple].
Juan Farfán el Mozo, encomendero.
n.d. [1579].
SIM, 214. RM, 135.
AGI, IG 1530. No. 378. No map.
Text: RY, 2-XX; DIU, 13: 169-71.
Mod: Yalcon, M. Valladolid, Yucatan.
Map: fig. 35-H/32-58.
Lang: ? [Maya]. Article 2: XV.

147. YUCATAN, Provincia. Yucatan.
[Simple].
Gaspar Antonio Chi.
Mar. 20, 1582.
No provenance data.
AGI [section not stated]. No map.
Text: Tozzer, 1941 (English trans.).
Lang: Maya. Article 2: XV.
Note: Text badly damaged; partial re-
construction by Ralph L. Roys from
MS located by France V. Scholes, for
Tozzer, 1941; material exclusively con-
cerning ancient customs. Does not
follow order of standard 1577 question-
naire. Not included in parchment-
bound volume with other Yucatan
RG's [AGI, IG, 1530]. Here included
because of Chi's close connection with
composition of historical sections of
other Yucatan RG's.

148. ZACATULA, VILLA DE LA CON-
CEPCION. Michoacán. [Simple].

Hernando de Vascones, alcalde mayor.
Nov. 25–Dec. 10, 1580.
JLV, 3/22. DyP, 303/3. SIM, 206. RM,
110. JGI, XXV-9.
UTX. CDG, 1855. 6 ff. No map.
Text: Barlow, 1947.
Mod: Nr. Melchor Ocampo de Balsas,
Michoacan. Map: fig. 20-N/9-39.
Lang: Mexicano. Article 2: 126.
Note: Report was prepared by Juan Ruíz
de Mendoza, alcalde of the Villa, and
Baltasar de Trujillo, Andrés Gómez,
and Melchor de Vargas, regidores. Re-
ply to Question 11 lists many subject
and subsubject places, but gives few
data on them. Most information relates
to languages, shown on Table 2, Article
7.

149. ZAMA (V). Yucatan. [Simple].
Juan de Reigosa, tutor y curador.
Mar. 9, 1579. Encomendero: Juan Mar-
tín (menor).
SIM, 214. RM, 135.
AGI, IG 1530. No. 378. No map.
Text: RY, 2-XXIII; DIU, 13; 196–200.
Mod: Tulum, M. Cozumel, Quintana
Roo. Map: fig. 28-J/33-2.
Lang: ? [Maya]. Article 2: XV.

150. ZAMAHIL (M). Yucatan. [Com-
plex].
Rodrigo Alvarez, encomendero.
Feb. 21, 1581.
SIM, 214. RM, 135.
AGI, IG 1530. No. 378. No map.
Text: RY, 1-XXII; DIU, 11: 275–77.
Mod: Samahil, Yucatan. Map: fig. 35-
I/29-31.
Lang: ? [Maya]. Article 2: XV.

Related

A. CALAMUL
Mod: Calotmul, Yucatan. Map: fig. 35-
H/32–55.

151. ZAN (M). Yucatan. Prov. Mani.
[Complex].

Alonso Rosado, encomendero, aided by Gaspar Antonio Chi.

Feb. 20, 1581.

SIM, 214. RM, 135.

AGI, IG 1530. No. 378. No map.

Text: RY, 1-X; DIU, 11: 153–59.

Mod: Dzan, Yucatan. Map: fig. 35-I/30-94.

Lang: Maya. Article 2: XV.

Related

A. PANABACHEN
   Mod: Panaba, Yucatan. Map: fig. 35-H/32-13.
B. MONA
   Mod: Muna, Yucatan. Map: fig. 35-I/30-97.

152. ZAPOTITLAN (AM). Guatemala. [Complex].

Capitán Juan de Estrada, alcalde mayor.

Nov. 22, 1579.

DyP, leg. 1. SIM, 230. RM, 139. JGI, XX-9.

UTX. CDG, 1503b. 13 ff. Map.

Text: Descripción, 1955.

Map: Published. Catalog, 88. Probably made by Fernando de Niebla, scribe.

Lang: Achi, Mam, Mexicano. Article 2: XVI-9.

Note: Following RG is genealogy "De los Señores antiguos de esta tierra," text and chart (Catalog appendix, 7) answering Questions 14 and 15. (Published: Descripción, 1965, pp. 82–84.)

Related

A. S. FRANCISCO ZAPOTITLAN
   Mod: M. S. Francisco Zapotitlan, Dept. Suchitepequez.
B. S. ANTONIO SUCHITEPEC
   Nov. 26, 1579.
   Mod: M. San Antonio Suchitepequez, Dept. Suchitepequez.
C. STGO. ATITLAN
   Mod: M. Stgo. Atitlan, Dept. Solola.
   See ATITLAN, 9.
D. TECPANCITLAN
   Mod: M. Asuncion de Solola, Dept. Solola.

E. TULIMAN
   Mod: M. S. Lucas Toliman, Dept. Solola.
F. PATOLUL
   Mod: M. Patulul, M. Suchitepequez.
G. S. BARTOLME AGUACATEPEC
H. S. JUAN DE NAHUALPA (Nagualapa)
   Mod: M. Nahuala, Dept. Solola.
I. ZAMAYAC (Samayaque)
   Mod: M. Samayac, Dept. Suchitepequez.
J. XICALAPA, Costa de Zapotitlan
   Nov. 22, 1579. Encomendero: Juan Rodríguez Cabrillo de Medrano.
   Mod: ? [1 1/2 leagues from sea].

153. ZAYULA. Mexico. [Simple].

Alonso de Coria, corregidor.

Feb. 3, 1580.

JLV, 4/4. DyP, 654/6. SIM, 151. RM, 45.

AGI, IG 1529. No. 391. Instr., 4 ff. No map.

Text: PNE, 6: 178–82.

Mod: Sayula, M. Tepetitlan, Hidalgo. Map: fig. 18-K/14-80.

Lang: Otomi, Mexicano. Article 2: I-55, 109.

Note: Has same DyP signature as NEXAPA, 73.

154. ZICAB (V). Yucatan. [Simple].

Alonso de Villanueva, tutor y curador.

Mar. 28, 1579. Encomendero: Baltasar de Montenegro (menor).

SIM, 214. RM, 135.

AGI, IG 1530. No. 378. No map.

Text: RY, 2-XXIV; DIU, 13: 201–03.

Mod: Part of Valladolid, Yucatan. Map: fig. 35-I/32-58.

Lang: ? [Maya]. Article 2: XV.

155. ZIMAPAN, Minas de. Mexico. Prov. Xilotepec. [Simple].

Cimapan.

Alexo de Murguia, juez repartidor.

Aug. 11, 1579.

JLV, 2/26. DyP, 647/6. SIM, 144. RM, 40.

AGI, IG 1529. No. 400? [Presently no file folder.] Instr., 6 ff. Map.

Text: (1) PNE 6: 1–5. (2) BCE, 1920a. (3) RNE, 1920b, pp. 17–22.
Map: Published. Catalog, 89.
Mod: Zimapan, Hidalgo. Map: fig. 18-J/14-23.
Lang: Otomi, Mexicano, Chichimec. Article 2: I-113.

156. ZINAGUA. Michoacan. [Simple].
Zinguacingo, Sinagua.
Fernando de Padilla Varaona, corregidor.
Dec. 8, 1581.
JLV, 2/11. DyP, 231/3. SIM, 99. RM, 113.
RAH. 9-25-4/4663-XII. Instr., 2 ff. No map.
Text: (1) VR/PNE, 7/7: 61–67. (2) RGM, 2: 70–74.
Mod: Sinagua, M. Churumuco, Michoacan. Map: fig. 20-N/10-71.
Lang: ?. Article 2: I-115.

157. ZIRANDARO. Michoacan. Prov. Minas de Espiritu Santo. [Composite-Complex].
Sirandaro.
Hernando de Coria, alcalde mayor.
Nov. 1, 1579–Jan. 6, 1580. Crown.
JLV, 2/5. DyP, 232/3. SIM, 98. RM, 112.
RAH. 9-25-4/4663-VII. Instr., 1 blank, 5 ff. No map.
Text: (1) VR/PNE, 7/7: 9–31. (2) RGM, 2: 38–46.
Mod: Zirandaro, Guerrero. Map: fig. 25-N/10-23.
Lang: Tarascan. Article 2: I-37.

Related

A. GUAYMEO (with Zirandaro) barrio
Nov. 1, 1580.
Mod: S. Agustin Güimeo, M. Huetamo, Michoacan. Map: fig. 28-M/11-72.
Lang: Tarascan, Apanec.
B. CUSEO (with Güetamo)
Jan. 6, 1580. Encomendero: Luis de Velasco.
Text: RGM, 2: 46–50.

Mod: Cutzio, M. Huetamo, Michoacan. Map: fig. 28-M/11-72.
Lang: Tarascan.
C. GÜETAMO (described with Cuseo)
Jan. 6, 1580. Encomendero: Luis de Velasco.
Mod: Huetamo de Núñez, Michoacan. Map: fig. 28-N/11-72.
Lang: Matlatzinca.

158. ZISMOPO (V). Yucatan. Prov. Cupul. [Simple].
Juan de Benavides, encomendero.
Feb. 18, 1579.
SIM, 214. RM, 135.
AGI, IG 1530. No. 378. No map.
Text: (1) RY, 2-XII; DIU, 13: 127–29. (2) RNE, 1920b, pp. 88–89.
Mod: Dzitnup, M. Valladolid, Yucatan. Map: fig. 35-I/32-58.
Lang: ? [Maya]. Article 2: XV.

159. ZIZONTUM (M). Yucatan. Prov. Quinche. [Simple].
Martín Sánchez, encomendero, aided by Gaspar Antonio Chi.
n.d. [Feb., 1581].
SIM, 214. RM, 135.
AGI, IG 1530. No. 378. No map.
Text: RY, 1-XV; DIU, 11: 199–209.
Mod: Dzidzantun, Yucatan. Map: fig. 35-H/31-7.
Lang: ? [Maya]. Article 2: XV.

160. ZONOT (V). Yucatan. Prov. Tezemin. [Simple].
Giraldo Díaz de Alpuche, vezino and encomendero.
Feb. 18, 1579.
SIM, 214. RM, 135.
AGI, IG 1530. No. 378. No map.
Text: RY, 2-XXV; DIU, 13: 204–23.
Mod: Tizimin, Yucatan. Map: fig. 35-H/33-12.
Lang: ? [Maya]. Article 2: XV.

161. ZOTUTA (M) Yucatan. [Complex].
Zututha.

Juan de Magaña, encomendero.
Jan. 1, 1581.
SIM, 214. RM, 135.
AGI, IG 1530. No. 378. No map.
Text: (1) RY, 1-IV; DIU, 11: 93–103.
(2) Barrera Vásquez, 1938.
Mod: Sotuta, Yucatan. Map: fig. 35-I/31-77.
Lang: Maya. Article 2: XV.

Related

A. TIBOLON
Mod: Tibolon, M. Sotuta, Yucatan. Map: fig. 35-I/31-77.

162. ZOZIL (V). Yucatan. Prov. Tezemin. [Complex].
Zezil.
Juan de Reigosa, tutor y curador.
Mar. 2, 1579. Encomendero: Juan [Ruiz] Darce, menor.
SIM, 214. RM, 135.
AGI, IG 1530. No. 378. No map.
Text: RY, 2-XVII; DIU, 13: 149–52.
Mod: Unlocated, Yucatan.
Lang: ? [Maya]; [Teoteil?]. Article 2: XV.

Related

A. TECAY

163. ZULTEPEC, Minas de. Mexico. [Complex].
Rodrigo Davila, alcalde mayor.
Mar. 5, 1582.
JLV, 2/10. DyP, 235/3. SIM, 102. RM, 30.
AGI, IG 1529. No. 379. Instr., 6 ff. No map.
Text: PNE, 7: 8–14.
Mod: Sultepec de Pedro Ascencio, Mexico. Map: fig. 14-N/13-18.
Lang: Mexicano, Matlatzinca, Mazatec, Tarascan. Article 2: I-87.

Related

A. ALMOLOYA
Mod: Almoloya de Alquisiras, Mexico. Map: fig. 14-M/13-37.

364

B. AMATEPEC
Mod: Amatepec, Mexico. Map: fig. 14-N/12-16.
C. TLATLAYA
Mod: Tlatlaya, Mexico. Map: fig. 14-N/12-17.
D. PUEBLO DE ZULTEPEC
Mod: Sultepequito, M. Sultepec, Mexico. Map: fig. 14-N/13-18.

164. ZUMPANGO, Minas de (AM). Mexico. [Simple].
Gonzalo Bazán, alcalde mayor, and others.
Mar. 10, 1582.
JLV, I/23. SIM 213. RM, 29.
RAH. 9-25-4/4663/XXXVI. 7 ff. 1 blank f. Map.
Text: PNE, 6: 313–22.
Map: Unpublished. Catalog, 91.
Mod: Zumpango del Rio, Guerrero. Map: fig. 17-O/13-33.
Lang: Mexicano. Article 2: I-29.
Note: The Provincia included Chilapa, Zumpango [pueblo], Tistla, Mochitlan, Huiziltepec. This RG covers the pueblo of Zumpango, cabecera of the A.M.
See also CHILAPA, 22bis; TISTLA, 132.

165. ZUSOPO (V). Yucatan. Prov. Tezemin. [Simple].
Sucopo.
Juan Rodríguez el Viejo, vezino and encomendero.
Mar. 2, 1579.
SIM, 214. RM, 135.
AGI, IG 1530. No. 378. No map.
Text: (1) RY, 2-IX; DIU, 13: 98–109.
(2) RNE, 1920b, pp. 80–87.
Mod: Sucopo, M. Tizimin, Yucatan. Map: fig. 35-H/32-12.
Lang: ? [Maya]. Article 2: XV.

166. ZUZAL (M). Yucatan. Prov. Quinchil. [Complex].
Alonso de Rojas, encomendero, aided by Gaspar Antonio Chi.
n.d. [Feb., 1581].
SIM, 214. RM, 135.

AGI, IG 1530. No. 378. No map.
Text: (1) RY, I-XIX; DIU, 11: 240–51.
(2) RNE, 1920b, pp. 58–64.
Mod: Sudzal, Yucatan. Map: fig.. 35-I/
31-64.

Lang: Maya. Article 2: XV.

Related

A. CHALANTE
   Mod: Chalante, M. Sudzal, Yucatan. Map:
   fig. 35-I/31-64.

DOCUMENTS CONSIDERED "LOST"

201. ACAPULCO. Mexico.
JLV, 2/15.
LOST.
Mod: Acapulco de Juarez, Guerrero.
   Map: fig. 17-P/13-46.
Article 2: I-1.

202. CAPOLA. Michoacan.
JLV, 3/11.
LOST.
Mod: Capula, M. Morelia, Michoacan.
   Map: fig. 20-L/11-77.
Article 2: I-113.

203. CHICHIMECAS, S. Miguel y San Fe-
lipe. Michoacan.
1582?
JLV, 1/1. MP, 21. DyP, 225/3 (text
   [Instr. only]), 302/3 (map).
AGI, PR 18, no. 16, ramo 2. Text lost;
   printed Instr. only.
RAH. Map. 9-25-4/4663-XIII.
Text: Lost.
Map: Published. Catalog, 48.
Mod: S. Miguel de Allende, Guanajuato.
   Map: fig. 16-J/11-12.
Article 2: I-75.

204. CHURUBUSCO. Mexico.
Huichilobusco, Huichulupuzco, Uitzilu-
   puchco, etc.
LOST.
Mod: Churubusco, D. F. Map: fig. 14-
   L/14-V.
Article 2: I-25, 55.
Note: RG prepared by Gonzalez Galle-
   gos, corregidor, ca. Jan. 31, 1580. He
   also prepared similar reports on de-
   pendencies of CHURUBUSCO, viz.,

CULHUACAN, 41; IXTAPALAPA, 56;
and MEXICATZINCO, 65. *See* PNE,
6: 193, n. 1; 195–96, n. 2.

205. GUASPALTEPEC. Antequera. Prov.
Rio de Alvarados.
Alonso de Pineda, corregidor.
1580.
JLV, 2/25. MP, 7.
LOST.
Mod: Guaxpala, M. Playa Vicente, Vera-
   cruz. Map: 34-O/20-174.
Article 2: I-19.

Related

A. OXITLAN
   Mod: S. Lucas Ojitlan Oaxaca. Map: fig.
   25-N/19-26/8.

206. HUAMELULA. Antequera. Prov.
Mixteca.
1580.
JLV, 3/2. MP, 96.
LOST.
Mod: S. Pedro Huamelula, Oaxaca. Map:
   fig. 25-R/20-21/13.
Article 2: I-33.

207. ISMIQUILPA. Mexico.
1579.
JLV, 3/7. MP, 97.
LOST.
Mod: Ixmiquilpan, Hidalgo. Map: fig.
   18-J/14-33.
Article 2: I-45.

208. LEON, Villa. Michoacan.
1582.
JLV, 3/26. MP, 13.
LOST.

Mod: Leon, Guanajuato. Map: fig. 16-I/10-16.
Article 2: I-50.

Related

A. Silao, Llanos de
   Mod: Silao, Guanajuato. Map: fig. 16-J/10-15.

209. MEXICO, Ciudad. Mexico.
   Lic. Aviles.
   1580.
   JLV, P-1, 4/1. MP, 18.
   LOST.
   Map: Lost. Catalog, 36.
   Mod: Mexico, D.F. Map: fig. 14-L/14.
   Article 2: I-56.

210. OCUITUCO. Mexico. Prov. Marquesado del Valle.
   [Juan Gutiérrez de Liebana, alcalde mayor del marquesado, corregidor de Ocuituco].
   [Sept., 1580?]
   JLV, 1/4.
   LOST.
   Mod: Ocuituco, Morelos. Map: fig. 21-M/15-30.
   Article 2: I-21.
   See also ACAPISTLA, 1; GUAXTEPEC, 47; TEPUZTLAN, 112; YAUTEPEC, 210.

211. SICHU. Michoacan. Prov. Xilotepec.
   [San Luis de la Paz.]
   JLV, 3/5. MP, 105.
   LOST.
   Mod: Xichu, Guanajuato. Map: fig. 16-I/12-6.
   Article 2: I-73, 113.

Related

A. Puzcinquia
   Mod: Puginguia, M. Amoles, Queretaro. Map: fig. 27-I/13-4.

212. TALASCO. Mexico.
   1580.
   JLV, 1/25. MP, 98.
   LOST.

Mod: S. Mateo Atarasquillo? M. Lerma, Mexico. Map: fig. 14-L/13-62.
Article 2: I-51.

213. TAMAZULA. Obispado unidentified.
   JLV, 2/3.
   LOST.
   Map lost. [Catalog, 52?]
   See also 137B.
   Note: Data are now lacking, in Cline's view, for identification of the lost text and map with San Jose Tamazula (127B) or Tamatzula (137B), despite such identification stated in Catalog, 52.

214. TAZAZALCA. Michoacan.
   1580.
   JLV, 3/6. MP, 99.
   LOST.
   Mod: Tlazazalca, Michoacan. Map: fig. 20-K/9-24.
   Article 2: I-113.

215. TEPEZI DE LA SEDA. Tlaxcala.
   JLV, 4/36.
   LOST.
   Mod: Tepexi de Rodriguez, Puebla. Map: fig. 26-N/16-172.
   Article 2: I-92.

216. TEPOSCOLULA. Antequera. Prov. Mixteca.
   1580.
   JLV, 3/1. MP, 101.
   LOST.
   Mod: S. Pedro y S. Pablo Teposcolula, Oaxaca. Map: fig. 25-O/17-23/14.
   Article 2: I-93.

217. TEUTILA (AM). Antequera. Prov. Rio de Alvarados.
   1580.
   JLV, 3/3. MP, 94.
   LOST.
   Mod: S. Pedro Teutila, Oaxaca. Map: fig. 25-N/19-3/4.
   Article 2: I-97.

218. TLAQUILPA. Arzobispado Mexico. Guaquilpa?
JLV, 4/31.
Mod: S. Pedro Huauquilpan, M. Zapotlan de Juarez, Hidalgo. Map: fig. 21-13-H/14-72.
Note: This refers to Cempoala (Census, 19). The MS is headed "Tlaquilpa y Zempoala," of which JLV copied only the first part. Tlaquilpa was a sujeto. Data from Peter Gerhard, personal communication, 8/29/67.

219. VALLADOLID. Michoacan.
1581
JLV, P-8, 3/14. MP, 95.
LOST.
Map: Lost. Catalog, 78.
Mod: Morelia, Michoacan. Map: fig. 20-L/11-77.
Article 2: I-113.

220. YANGUITLAN. Antequera. Prov. Mixteca.
1579.
JLV, 3/8. MP, 3.
LOST.
Mod: Sto. Domingo Yanhuitlan, Oaxaca. Map: fig. 25-O/17-15/6.
Article 2: I-62.

Related

A. Tonaltepec
Mod: Sto. Domingo Tonaltepec, Oaxaca. Map: fig. 25-O/17-23/5.
B. Coyaltepec
Mod: S. Bartolo Soyatepec, Oaxaca. Map: fig. 25-O/17-23/16.
C. Coixtlahuaca
Mod: S. Juan Bautista Coixtlahuaca, Oaxaca. Map: fig. 25-O/17-2/13.
D. Tequicistepec
Mod: San Miguel Tequixtepec, Oaxaca. Map: fig. 25-O/17-2/10.
E. Apoala
Mod: Stgo. Apoala, Oaxaca. Map: fig. 25-O/17-15/4.
F. Istactepec
Mod: S. Juan Ixtaltepec, M. S. Pedro Cán-

taros, Oaxaca. Map: fig. 25-O/18-15/11.
G. Chichuaztepec
Mod: S. Miguel Chicahua(xtepec), Oaxaca. Map: fig. 25-O/18-15/4.
H. Nochistlan
Mod: Asuncion Nochixtlan, Oaxaca. Map: fig. 25-P/18-15/25.

221. YAUTEPEC (V). Mexico. [Cuatro Villas.] Prov. Marquesado del Valle.
[Juan Gutiérrez de Liebana, alcalde mayor].
[Sept.] 1580.
JLV, 3/4. MP, 103.
LOST.
Mod: Yautepec, Morelos. Map: fig. 21-M/14-17.
Article 2: I-21.
See also ACAPISTLA, 1; GUAXTEPEC, 47; TEPUZTLAN, 112; OCUITUCO, 210.

222. ZACUALPA. Mexico.
JLV, 1/6.
LOST.
Mod: Zacualpan, Mexico. Map: fig. 14-N/13-38.
Article 2: I-127.

223. ZAPOTECAS, Villa de S. Ildefonso de. Antequera. Prov. Zapotecas.
JLV, 1/7. MP, 102.
LOST.
Mod: S. Ildefonso Villa Alta, Oaxaca. Map: fig. 25-O/20-27/10.
Article 2: I-118.

224. ZAYULA. Guadalajara. Prov. Avalos.
Sayula.
1580.
JLV, 3/13. MP, 92.
LOST.
Mod: Sayula, Jalisco. Map: fig. 19-L/7-89.
Article 2: I-76.

Related

A. Atoyac
    Mod: Atoyac.   Map: fig. 19-K/7-74.

225. ZIMATLAN.   Antequera.   Prov. Antequera.
    1580.
    JLV, 3/12.   MP, 93.

LOST.
Mod: Zimatlan de Alvarez, Oaxaca.
    Map: fig. 25-P/18-30/1.
Article 2: I-14.

Related

A. Tepezimatlan

RELACIONES GEOGRÁFICAS OF THE 1604 SERIES

NOTE: No originals of these documents are extant. The only known copies are in MS 3064, BNM.

301. AMATLAN, PUEBLO.   Antequera.
    Distrito Miaguatlan.
    Estéban Gutiérrez.
    Mar., 1609.
    MP, 72.   JDE, 8.
    Copy: BNM, MS 3064 [old J–42], ff. 263–40.
    Text: (1) DII, 9:309.   (2) PNE, 4:314–19.
    Mod: S. Luis Amatlan, Oaxaca.
    See also Census, 21A, 302, 306, 308.

302. COATLAN, PUEBLO.   Antequera.
    Distrito Miaguatlan.
    Estéban Gutiérrez.
    Apr., 1609.
    MP, 72.   JDE, 42.
    Copy: BNM, MS 3064 [old J-42], ff. 232–34.
    Text: (1) DII, 9:386.   (2) PNE, 4: 308–13.
    Mod: S. Pablo Coatlan, Oaxaca.
    See also Census, 21A, 301, 306, 308.

303. COLIMA, VILLA DE.   Michoacan.
    Melchor de Colindres Puerta.
    MP, 69.   JDE, 45.
    LOST.
    Mod: Colima, Colima.

304. GUACHINANGO and TAMIAGUA.
    Tlaxcala.
    May 13, 1609.

MP, 63.   JDE, 110.
Copy: BNM, MS 3064 [old J-42].
Text: DII, 9:133.
Mod: Huauchinango, Puebla.

305. GUAXUAPA, PUEBLO PROVINCIA
    1608.
    MP, 64.   JDE, 117.
    LOST.
    Mod: Huajuapan de Leon, Oaxaca.

306. MIAGUATLAN, PARTIDO.   Antequera.
    Estéban Gutiérrez.
    MP, 72.   JDE, 170–172.
    Copy: BNM, MS 3064 [old J-42], ff. 99–106.
    Text: (1) DII, 9: 210. (2) PNE, 4: 289–300.
    Mod: Miahuatlan de Porfirio Diaz, Oaxaca.
    See also Census, 21B, 301, 302, 308.

307. NOMBRE DE DIOS, VILLA.   NUEVA VIZCAYA.   Guadalajara.
    May, 1608.
    MP, 74.   JDE, 182, 184.
    Copy: BNM, MS 3064 [old J-42].
    Text: DII, 9: 211.
    Mod: Nombre de Dios, Durango.

308. OCELOTEQUE, PUEBLO.   DISTRITO DE MIAGUATLAN.   Antequera.
    Estéban Gutiérrez.
    Mar., 1609.
    MP, 72.   JDE, 228–229.

Copy: BNM, MS 3064 [old J-42], ff. 109–13.

Text: (1) DII, 9:223. (2) PNE, 4: 301–07.

Mod: Sta. Maria Ozolotepec, Oaxaca.

See also Census, 21D, 301, 302, 306.

309. PACHUCA, MINAS. Mexico.
Diego de Ovalle y Guzman.
1608.
MP, 71. JDE, 234.
Copy: BNM, MS 3064 [old J-42].
Text: DII, 9: 192.
Mod: Pachuca de Soto, Hidalgo.

310. PANUCO and TAMPICO. Mexico.
Pedro Martínez de Loaysa, capitán y alcalde mayor.
1612.
MP, 66. JDE, 247–249, 251.
Copy: BNM, MS 3064 [old J-42].
Text: DII, 9: 150.
See also Census, 312.

311. SULTEPEQUE, MINAS. Mexico.
Geronimo de Salinas Salazar.
1609.
MP, 73. JDE, 335.
LOST.
Mod: Sultepec de Pedro Ascencio, Mexico.
See also Census, 163.

312. TAMPICO, VILLA DE. DISTRITO TAMPICO. Mexico.
Pedro Martínez de Loaysa, capitán y alcalde mayor.
1612.
MP, 66. JDE, 340–341.
Copy: BNM, MS 3064 [old J-42].
Text: DII, 9: 167.

Mod: Tampico, Tamaulipas.
See also Census, 310.

313. TEPEXI DE LA SEDA, PUEBLO.
Tlaxcala.
1608.
MP, 65. JDE, 354.
LOST.
Mod: Tepexi de Rodriguez, Puebla.
See also Census, 215.

314. TEPOZCOLULA, ALCALDIA MAYOR. Antequera.
Francisco Ruano.
1608.
MP, 67. JDE, 356.
LOST.
Mod: S. Pedro y S. Pablo Tepescolula, Oaxaca.

315. ZACATECAS, CIUDAD. Guadalajara.
1608.
MP, 70. JDE, 431–433.
Copy: BNM, MS 3064 [old J-42].
Text: DII, 9: 179.
Mod: Zacatecas, Zacatecas.

316. ZAGUALPA, MINAS. Mexico.
1608.
MP, 75. JDE, 435.
LOST.
Mod: Zacualpan, Mexico.
See also Census, 222.

317. ZUMPANGO, MINAS. Mexico.
1608.
MP, 68. JDE, 447.
LOST.
Mod: Zumpango del Rio, Guerrero.
See also Census, 132, 164.

9. The Relaciones Geográficas of Spain, New Spain, and the Spanish Indies: An Annotated Bibliography

HOWARD F. CLINE

As the title suggests, this listing includes work on *Relaciones Geográficas* outside the Middle American area. Although probably less comprehensive for Spain, the Caribbean, and South America than for New Spain, no titles for those regions were purposely omitted. A conscientious effort was made to include all titles related to New Spain, but in the disordered bibliographical literature on that viceroyalty possibly some fugitive works have inadvertently escaped notice.

The main emphasis has been on the bibliography of the RG's for the 1578–86 series, discussed at length in Article 5. All citations in that treatment are included in this bibliography, as are references in the Census (Article 8) and citations to RG's in Article 7. The bibliography for Robertson's Article 6 has been incorporated into this bibliography with the exception of special items dealing with artistic style not specifically related to the RG's. The literature on the 18th-century reports discussed by Robert West (Article 10) tends to be rather distinct, hence all of his references are not included here. Occasionally where a title might suggest inclusion of 16th- or 17-century documents, it appears in this bibliography, with negative information in the annotation.

Academia (Madrid)

1821 Catálogo alfabético de los pueblos descritos en las relaciones topográficas formadas de order de Felipe II, que existían en la biblioteca del Escorial, y de que posee copia la Academia de la Historia. Memorias RAH, 6: 614–17.

Early listing of RG's of Spain; superseded later. *See also* Real Academia de la Historia.

Acosta Saignes, Miguel, ed.

1946 Bernardino de Sahagún. Historia general de las cosas de la Nueva España. 3 vols. Mexico, D.F.

Listing of various RG's 3: 195–96, with inadequate citations.

Alba, Duque de

1951 Mapas españoles de América, siglos XV–XVII. Madrid.

Reproduces (pl. 33) colored maps of Macuilsuchil and San Miguel y San Felipe Chichimecas. [Census, 62, 203; Catalog, 32, 48.]

ALTOLAGUIRRE Y DUVALE, ANGEL DE, ed.

1909 Relaciones Geográficas de la Gobernación de Venezuela (1767–68) con prólogo y notas. Real Sociedad Geográfica (Col. geográfica, 24) [1908, i.e., 1909]. Madrid.

Separate publication of earlier Real Sociedad Geográfica *Boletín* materials. No 1577–1586 documents.

1954 Relaciones Geográficas de la Gobernación de Venezuela (1767–68) con prólogo y notas. Madrid.

Reissue of Altolaguirre, 1909.

AMAYA, JESÚS

1944 La "Fundasion" de Ameka: para una istoria lokal. *Renovigo (Renobasion)*, Jaro 10, no. 65 (Nov. 15, 1944), pp. 6–8.

Article in Esperanto commenting on RG of Ameca [Census, 4], and reproducing pintura [Catalog, 3] from 1858 copy.

1951 Ameca: protofundación mexicana. Historia de la propriedad del Valle de Ameca, Jalisco, y circumvecinidad. Mexico, D.F.

From UTX photocopy reproduces RG of Ameca, with transcription and map, pp. 23–75; map facing p. 76. [Census, 4].

AMERICAN HERITAGE BOOK OF INDIANS
See Brandon, 1961.

ANONYMOUS

1878 Noticias varias de Nueva Galicia, Intendencia de Guadalajara, Ed. de "El Estado de Jalisco." Guadalajara. Abbreviation: NV.

From unidentified texts, publishes RG's of Ameca, Amula, Zapotitlan, Tuscaquesco, Cusalapa (pp. 282–321); Tenamaztlan (pp. 321–46); and Tequaltiche (pp. 346–60). [Census 4, 5, 5A, 5B, 5C, 105, 113.] No maps.

1936? Catálogo de libros y manuscritos del Sr. Joaquín García Icazbalceta. MS in UTX. Photocopy in Library of Congress.

Inventory, including RG's now in UTX.

ARELLANO MORENO, ANTONIO, ed.

1964 Relaciones Geográficas de Venezuela. Recopilación, estudio preliminar y notas por Antonio Arellano Moreno. *Biblioteca de la Academia Nacional de la Historia*, 70. Caracas.

Carefully edited materials from 16th to 18th century, republishing from earlier scattered sources. For 1577 questionnaire has 5 RG's: Santiago de Leon (1578), pp. 113–37; El Tocuyo (1578), pp. 143–60; Cd. de Trujillo, pp. 163–70; Cd. de la Nueva Segovia (1579), pp. 175–98; Cd. de Nueva Zamora (1579), pp. 203–12. Footnotes to each indicate previous publication (usually local journals), citations not here repeated. These come from AGI, Patronato, sec. 1a, ramo 12, leg. 294, except Trujillo, in UTX and first published 1942. Zamora is in AGI, Indiferente General, 1528. Seemingly lost are RG's for Coro, Nirgua, Espiritu Santo de la Grita, S. Cristobal y Merida, and Cumana.

ASENSIO, JOSÉ MARÍA, ed.

1898, Relaciones de Yucatán. Colección
1900 de documentos inéditos relativos al descubrimiento, conquista y organización de las antiguas posesiones españolas de Ultramar. 2a ser. publicada por la Real Academia de la Historia. Vols. 11, 13. Madrid. Abbreviation: DIU, RY 1, 2.

RG's carelessly edited, with numerous paleographical mistakes. The introductory matter to each volume is superficial and of little scholarly value, derived mainly from Marcos Jiménez de la Espada. [Census 13, 14, 15, 16, 17, 20, 26, 27, 36, 39, 40, 48, 50, 55, 58, 63, 64, 69, 70, 71, 81, 83, 89, 90, 91, 92, 97, 98, 99, 100, 104, 106, 115, 121, 125, 126, 129, 131, 139, 145, 146, 149, 150, 154, 158, 159, 160, 161, 162, 165, 166.]

BAILEY, J. W.
See De Blois, 1963.

BALLESTEROS Y BERETTA, ANTONIO
See Real Academia de la Historia.

BALLESTEROS-GAIBROIS, MANUEL

1955 Manuscritos hispano-indígenas (mapas Mejicanos). 31st International Congress of Americanists (São Paulo, 1954), *Acta*, 2: 1099–1108.

Notes on 9 colored RG maps in RAH: Celaya [Catalog, 1], S. Miguel [Catalog, 48], Ixtepexic [Catalog, 30], Texupa [Catalog, 69], Teotitlan [Catalog, 59], Cuahuitlan [Catalog, 18], Zumpango [Catalog, 91], Tlacotalpa [Catalog, 73], Macuilsuchil [Catalog, 32].

BANDELIER, ADOLPH F.

1884 Report of an archaeological tour in Mexico in 1881. *Papers Archaeological Institute of America, American Series*, 2. Boston.

RG of Cholula, discussed, pp. 110–251; map, pl. XV between pp. 230 and 231. [Census, 25.]

BARLOW, ROBERT H., ed.

1944 Relación de Xiquilpan y su partido, 1579. *Tlalocan*, 1/4: 278–306.

Covers Xiquilpan, Chocandiran, Tarequato, and Perivan, from photo of RAH original furnished from University of California (Berkeley), Department of Geography Collection. [Census, 60].

1945 Dos relaciones antiguas del pueblo de Cuilapa, Estado de Oaxaca. *Tlalocan*, 2/1: 18–28.

RG by Fr. Agustín de Salazar, 1580, pp. 22–26, from JGI transcripts, via FGO. The other relación is 1777–78. [Census, 37.]

1946 Descripción de la Ciudad de Antequera. *Tlalocan*, 2/2: 134–37.

Text from JGI transcripts furnished by FGO. [Census, 6.]

1947 Relación de Zacatula, 1580. *Tlalocan*, 2/3: 258–68.

RG from JGI transcripts, FGO collection, MNA. [Census, 148.]

1949a The extent of the empire of Culhua Mexica. *Ibero-Americana*, 28. University of California. Berkeley and Los Angeles.

Data for this volume largely from RG's; Barlow used MS JGI transcripts, plus published versions.

1949b Relación de Zempoala y su partido, 1580. *Tlalocan*, 3/1: 29–41.

From photo of original in UTX, with maps (facing p. 40): pl. V, Epazoyuca; pl. VI, Cempoala, Hidalgo y su comarca; pl. VII, Tetliztaca. [Census, 19, 19A, 19B.]

——, GEORGE T. SMISOR, IGNACIO BERNAL, FERNANDO HORCASITAS, eds.

1943– Tlalocan: a journal of source materials on the native cultures of Mexico.

Often from imperfect texts, this journal published RG's from Antequera, 2/2: 134–37 (1946); Cuilapa, 2/1: 18–28 (1945); Tancitaro, 3/3: 205–35 (1952); Tesquisiac, 3/4: 289–308 (1957); Jiquilpan, 1/4: 278–306 (1944); Zacatula, 2/3: 258–68 (1947); Cempoala, 3/1: 29–41 (1949); Cuautla, 4/1: 3–16 (1962); Tuzantla, 5/1: 58–73 (1965); Valladolid, Yuc. [pinturas], 5/3: 220–221 (1967). These are entered under individual editor in this Bibliography. [Census, 6, 19, 34, 37, 60, 95, 103D, 114, 139, 148.]

BARRERA VÁSQUEZ, ALFREDO, ed.

1938 Reimpresión de diez relaciones de los encomenderos de la Provincia de Yucatán, escritas en el año de 1579. *In* Diego de Landa, Relación de las cosas de Yucatán. . . . Primera edición yucateca, Mérida, Yuc., Apéndice, pp. 150–289.

Reprinted, without editorial changes, from DIU. Includes the following (Census nos. added): CAMPOCOLCHE, pp. 249–60 [Census, 15]; CHUNCHUCHU, pp. 205–12 [Census, 27]; IZAMAL, pp. 187–93 [Census, 58]; MERIDA, pp. 163–86 [Census, 64]; MOXOPIPE, pp. 195–203 [Census, 70]; NABALON, pp. 261–68 [Census, 71]; TEZEMI, pp. 278–89 [Census, 125]; TIQUIBALON, pp. 241–47 [Census, 129]; VALLADOLID, pp. 213–40 [Census, 139]; ZOTUTA, pp. 269–75 [Census, 161].

BAUDOT, GEORGES

1968 La *Memoria* de Antonio de León Pinelo: unos títulos de historiografía mexicana. *Historia Mexicana*, 18: 227–43.

Discussion and reproduction of León Pinelo, 1624?, with identification of some non-RG titles.

BECKER, JERÓNIMO

1917 Los estudios geográficos en España (ensayo de una historia de la geografía). Madrid.

Basic pioneering monograph, with many data on 16th-century developments; chap. 8 (pp. 97–111) devoted to RG's of Spain and the Indies.

BENÍTEZ, FERNANDO

1967 Los Indios de México. Mexico, D.F.

Reproduces RG pintura of Teozacoalco from the original [Catalog, 60], in color, pl. XI (foldout) facing p. 320.

BERNAL, IGNACIO, ed.

1952 Relación de Tancítaro (Arimeo y Tepalcatepec). *Tlalocan*, 3/3: 205–35.

From JGI transcripts, FGO collection; no map. [Census, 95.]

1957 Relaciones de Tequisquiac, Citaltepec y Xilocingo. *Tlalocan*, 3/4: 289–308.

From JGI transcripts, FGO collection; no map. [Census, 114.]

1962 Relación de Guautla. *Tlalocan*, 4/1: 3–16.

From JGI transcript, but with 1 page of original MS reproduced. RG, composite, by Melchor Suarez, corregidor, Feb. 1580. Guautla, Feb. 26, pp. 3–7; Xocoticpaque, pp. 7–9; Xaltepetongo, Mar. 1, pp. 9–11; Tutupetongo, Mar. 3, pp. 11–14; Tanatepec, Mar. 5, pp. 14–16. Pl. I (facing p. 16) fol. 1r; pl. II, Mapa [sketch map]; pl. III, an informant from Tetelcingo; pl. IV, stela, from Tlaxiaco, Oaxaca. [Census, 34.]

BEVAN, BERNARD, trans.

1938 The Chinantec: report on the central and south-eastern Chinantec region. PAIGH, Pub. 24. Mexico, D.F.

English translations, from PNE, of RG's

of Usila (pp. 129–34) and Chinantla pp. 135–44), with minor notes. [Census, 24, 138.]

BIBLIÓFILOS ESPAÑOLES
See Serrano y Sanz.

BLACKER, IRWIN R.

1965 Cortés and the Aztec conquest. New York.

RG pinturas of Xonotla (p. 46) and Tetela (p. 53) [Catalog, 84, 66], margins cropped.

BLÁZQUEZ Y DELGADO-AGUILERA, ANTONIO

1904 El itinerario de don Fernando Colón y las relaciones topográficas. *Revista de Archivos, Bibliotecas y Museos*, 10: 83–105 (February–March).

Detailed discussion of Biblioteca Nacional (Spain) MS 7,855, listing 390 towns, and relationships to Colon's 1518–23 similar attempt, as prototypes of RG's. Also discusses RG inquiries in Spain of 1591, 1610, 1623, 1624.

1909 Geografía de España en el siglo xvi. Discursos leídos ante la Real Academia de la Historia en la recepción pública . . . el día 16 de Mayo de 1909. Madrid.

Pamphlet containing speech, outlining history of geography in Spain, with much stress on Spanish RG's.

BLOM, FRANS

1928 Gaspar Antonio Chi, interpreter. *American Anthropologist*, n.s., 30: 250–62.

Data on a Europeanized Maya who aided in compilation of several RG's from Yucatan.

BRAND, DONALD D.

1944 An historical sketch of geography and anthropology in the Tarascan region. Part. I. *New Mexico Anthropologist*, 6–7/2: 37–108.

Useful discussion of RG's of the area (pp. 75–81) and map of main centers.

1948 Place-name problems in Mexico, as illustrated by Necotlán. *Papers*

Michigan Academy of Science, Art, and Letters, 24: 241–52.

RG data summarized (pp. 245–47) identifying colonial Necotlan with modern Santiago Undameo, with map of area. [Census, 72.]

—— AND OTHERS

1960 Coalcoman and Motines del Oro, an ex-Distrito of Michoacan, Mexico. University of Texas, Institute of Latin American Studies. The Hague.

Detailed study, with Brand as author of "History and Government" (pp. 54–216), relying heavily on RG's for 1580 data; identifies many places mentioned in them.

BRANDON, WILLIAM

1961 The American Heritage Book of Indians. New York.

RG pintura of Tescaltitlan [Catalog, 65], pp. 106–07.

BROUSSARD, RAY F., ed. and trans.

1952 Description of Atitlán and its dependencies, 1585: a translation, with introduction and notes [of the transcription of an unpublished 16th-century MS in the Latin American Collection of the University of Texas Library]. Unpublished M.A. thesis, Univ. Texas.

Not seen; apparently a translation of the RG of Atitlan, Guatemala, [Census, 9], from transcription made in 1950 by Luis F. Muro Arias. Local call no. T 1952 B 799.

BUTTERWORTH, DOUGLAS, ed. and trans.

1962 Relaciones of Oaxaca of the 16th and 18th centuries. *Boletín de Estudios Oaxaqueños,* 21–23: 35–55 (August). Maps.

English translation of the 1581 RG of Cuilapa, from Barlow, 1945. Also includes answer to Question 14 of the 1577 questionnaire for RG of Chicapa (1580) and of Antequera (1580). [Census, 6, 21, 37.]

CABALLERO, FERMÍN

1866 Las Relaciones Topográficas de España. Discurso leido ante la Real Academia de la Historia en su recepción pública [Dec. 9]. Madrid.

Rare 84-page pamphlet which first systematically discussed the RG's of Spain and of the Indies, and their value for historical and other studies. Caballero argued for a primacy of the Spanish documents over the New World ones, a view challenged by Jiménez de la Espada and others, and no longer considered valid. Apparently the Library of Congress has the unique copy of this title in the United States (call no. DP 1.A17). Presentation by Fermín Caballero (pp. 5–53), with documentary appendices (pp. 55–64) that include the 1578 questionnaire and materials relating to transfer of RG's from and returned to the Escorial. "Discurso de D. Cayetano Rosell en contestación al precedente" (pp. 66–84) gives bio-bibliographical data on Caballero, then discusses earlier related materials (Itinerario of Colon, 1517, etc.), as well as the Spanish RG's.

CABRERO FERNANDO, LEONCIO

1959 Historia de las Relaciones Geográficas de Indias: Nueva España, siglo XVI. Unpublished Ph.D. dissertation, Univ. Madrid. 3 vols.

Vol. 1, text; vol. 2, documents; vol. 3, graphic materials. Unfortunately this study remains unpublished; it seems to be the only full-length, scholarly investigation of the RG's.

1960 La economía básica de los indios de la región mixteca. 34th International Congress of Americanists (Vienna, 1960), *Acta,* p. 688.

Based on RG materials.

1964a La flora y fauna de la Mixteca a través de las Relaciones Geográficas de Indias. 6th International Congress of Anthropological and Ethnological Sciences (Paris, 1960). 2 tomes in 3 vols.; tome 2, part 2, pp. 15–19.

1964b Descripción física de la Mixteca en las Relaciones Geográficas del siglo XVI. *In* Homenaje a Fernando Márquez Miranda, pp. 129–37. Madrid.

374

Based on RG's, list of which for Mixteca is appended.

CAJIGAS LANGNER, ALBERTO

1954 Monografía de Tehuantepec. Mexico.

RG text of Tehuantepec; no map. Source of text not given, but probably Caso, 1928b. [Census, 102.]

CANTÚ TREVIÑO, SARA

1953 La Vega de Metztitlan en el Estado de Hidalgo. *Boletín SMGE* 75: 9–284 (January–June).

On pp. 247–61 are reprints RG of Metztitlan (from DII, 4: 530–55); map b/w, 1857 copy, facing p. 248; schematic drawing of calendar wheel p. 260. [Census, 66.]

CARRASCO PIZANA, PEDRO

1950 Los otomies. Cultura e historia prehispánica de los pueblos mesoamericanos de habla otomiana. UNAM, Instituto de Historia. Mexico, D.F.

List of RG's, p. 319, including some in FGO collection (JGI transcripts). Discussion of day and month names of the Meztitlan calendar wheel, pp. 193–95.

CARRERA STAMPA, MANUEL

1949 Misiones mexicanas en archivos europeos. PAIGH, Pub. 93. Mexico, D.F.

FPT RG transcripts, pp. 17–18, for PNE, vols. 3, 7, 8, utilized by Luis Vargas Rea. RG and other maps listed, pp. 39–44.

1968 Relaciones geográficas de Nueva España, siglos xvi y xviii. *Estudios de Historia Novohispana*, 2: 233–61.

Summary discussion of published RG's. Incomplete, with some factual errors, but still useful.

CASO, ALFONSO, ed.

1928a Relación del pueblo de Instlauca [*sic*] que está puesto en corregimiento con la jurisdicción del pueblo de Teomastlahuala. *RMEH*, vol. 2, suplemento, pp. 135–63.

JGI transcript. Composite RG, Jan.–Feb., 1580, Aznar de Cozar, corregidor. No map. Instlauaca, Jan. 3, pp. 135–42; Mistepeque, Jan. 7, pp. 142–46; Ayusuchiquilzala, Jan. 12, pp. 147–51; Xicayan [de Tovar], Jan. 14, pp. 151–55; Puctla, Jan. 22, pp. 156–59; Zacatepeque, Feb. 17, pp. 159–63. [Census, 61.]

1928b Tehuantepec. *RMEH*, vol. 2, suplemento, pp. 164–75.

JGI transcripts. Complex RG for Tehuantepec, Xalapa, Tequesistlan, Sept. 20, 1580, by Juan de Torres de Lagunas, alcalde mayor; no maps. [Census, 102.]

1928c Descripción de la Villa de Espiritu Santo. *RMEH*, vol. 2, suplemento, pp. 176–80.

RG for Coatzocoalco [Guazqualco], Apr. 29, 1580, by Suero de Cangas by Quiñones, alcalde mayor de la Villa y de la Provincia. No map. [Census, 30.]

1928d Relación de la vicaria y partido de Santa Cruz que en mexicano se dize Iztepec y en zapoteco Quialoo. *RHEM*, vol. 2, suplemento, pp. 180–84.

Composite RG, Jan. 10, 1581, by Fray Andres Mendez, vicar; no map. Primarily RG of Santa Cruz Iztepec, but with summary paragraphs at end on its main dependencies: Santa Ana Tocolobacoya (p. 183), Ayocuexco (p. 183), San Bernardo Tepezimatlan (pp. 183–84), and Santa Maria Madalena Tepezimatlan (p. 184). [Census, 59.]

1928e Relación de los pueblos Peñoles del Obispado de Antequera. *RMEH*, vol. 2, suplemento, pp. 185–91.

Complex RG, Oct. 3, 1579, by Juan Lopez, corregidor and Diosdado y Treviño, cura beneficiado; no map. Data on Itzquintepec, Eztetla, Quauxolticpac, Huiztepec, Totomachapa, and Jilotepec, in that order under each question. [Census, 80.]

1949a El mapa de Teozacoalco. *Cuadernos Americanos*, año 8, 47/5: 145–81 (September–October).

Reprints RG from RMEH, with colored map facing p. 176, from 1858 copy; text is detailed, major reconstruction of Mixtec history from materials from RG and other sources. [Census, 108.]

1949b El mapa de Teozacoalco. Reprinted from 29th International Congress of Americanists (New York, 1949). Mexico, D.F.

Reprint of 1949a but paged differently (i.e., pp. 3–40). Map copy reprinted facing p. 40.

CASTAÑEDA, CARLOS E., AND JACK AUTREY DABBS, comps.

1939 Guide to the Latin American manuscripts in the University of Texas Library. ACLS Committee on Latin American Studies, Misc. Pub. 1. Cambridge. Abbreviation: CDG.

Lists, among other MSS, the RG's from JGI collection, acquired 1937. Some minor errors and omissions.

CATALINA GARCÍA, JUAN, AND MANUEL PÉREZ VILLAMIL, eds.

1903–15 Relaciones Topográficas de España. Relaciones de pueblos que pertenecen hoy a la Provincia de Guadalajara, con notas y aumentos. 6 vols. Madrid. Memorial Histórico Español: Colección de documentos, opúsculos y antigüedades que publica de Real Academia de la Historia, 41 (1903), 42 (1903), 43 (1905), 45 (1912), 46 (1914), 47 (1915).

Vols. 1–3 edited by Catalina García; vols. 4–6 issued posthumously with additional notes by Pérez Villamil. Texts from RAH are deficient, but antiquarian notes by editors are important.

CERVANTES DE SALAZAR, FRANCISCO
See García Icazbalceta, 1875.

CHEVALIER, FRANÇOIS

1956 La formación de los grandes latifundios en México: tierra y sociedad en los siglos XVI y XVII. *Problemas Agrícolas e Industriales de México*, 8/1. Mexico, D.F.

Translation of French text, 1952, but

added graphic material (not in original) includes RG maps of Yurirpundaro, Ameca, Cholula. [Census, 4, 18B, 25.]

1963 Land and society in colonial Mexico, the great hacienda. Alvin Eustis, trans. Edited with a foreword by Lesley Byrd Simpson. Berkeley, University of California Press.

English version of Chevalier, 1956; reproduces RG map of Ameca only.

CLINE, HOWARD F.

1959 The Patiño maps of 1580 and related documents: analysis of 16th century cartographic sources for the Gulf Coast of Mexico. *Mexico Antiguo*, 9: 633–92.

Publishes and analyzes the 2 RG maps for Vera Cruz, localizing communities (102) shown on them; also reproduces RG map of Tlacotalpan, identifying places; same, Xalapa (reoriented). Extensive bibliography. [Census, 134, 140, 141.]

1961a Apuntes históricos de las tribus Chinantecas, Mazatecas y Popolucas (1910) por Mariano Espinosa. Reedición con notas y apéndices. MNA, Serie Científica, 7; Papeles de la Chinantla, 3. Mexico, D.F.

Pages 200–05 discuss the RG of Chinantla and related contemporary documents. [Census, 24.]

1961b Mapas and lienzos of the colonial Chinantla, Oaxaca, Mexico. *In* A William Cameron Townsend, B. F. Elson, ed., pp. 49–77. Instituto Lingüístico de Verano. Cuernavaca.

Table 2 correlates communities listed in RG of Chinantla with other sources, and localizes them, pl. 7. Pl. 6b reproduces, from PNE, RG map of Atatlauca-Malinaltepec, noting Chinantec communities. [Census, 11, 24.]

1964a The Relaciones Geográficas of the Spanish Indies, 1577–1586. *HAHR*, 44: 341–74.

Summary synthesis. Appendix I translates the Instruction; Appendix II gives listing of 166 Principal Documents, with repository and other information. Revision and enlargement of article appears in this volume of the *Handbook* as Article 5.

1964b Lienzos y comunidades mazatecos de la época colonial, Oaxaca, México. 35th International Congress of Americanists (Mexico, 1962), *Acta*, 1: 397–424.

Fig. 4 (p. 411) reproduces reoriented map of the 1581 RG of Teotitlan del Camino [Census, 107], and fig. 5 (p. 419) locates and bounds communities shown on it.

1965 The Relación Geográfica of Tuzantla, Michoacan, 1579. *Tlalocan*, 5/1: 58–73.

Transcription from photograph of original, with pintura, modern maps; editorial notes and introductory commentary; bibliography. [Census, 103D.]

1966a Colonial Mazatec lienzos and communities. *In* Ancient Oaxaca: discoveries in Mexican archeology and history, J. Paddock, ed., pp. 270–97. Stanford, California.

Adapted from Cline, 1964b. Map 4 (p. 275) reorients and locates communities on pintura of Teotitlan del Camino (after PNE) [Catalog, 59; Census, 107]; Map 5 (p. 276) locates them as of 1581; Map 9 (p. 290) plots places on modern map.

1966b Native pictorial documents of eastern Oaxaca, Mexico. *In* Summa Anthropologica en homenaje a Roberto J. Weitlaner, Antonio Pompa y Pompa, ed., pp. 101–30. INAH. Mexico, D.F.

Fig. 5 (p. 113), reproduces in b/w hitherto unpublished map of RG of Tecuicuilco, from original. [Census, 101.]

1967 Figuras of the Relación Geográfica of Valladolid, Yucatán, 1579: a note, with illustrations. *Tlalocan*, 5/3: 220–21.

Plate 1 (facing p. 220) reproduces unpublished drawings in RG [Catalog, 79, 80], with brief notes.

COOK, SHERBURNE F., AND WOODROW BORAH
1966 On the credibility of contemporary testimony on the population on [*sic*; i.e., of] Mexico in the sixteenth century. *In* Summa Anthropologica en homenaje a Roberto J. Weitlaner, Antonio Pompa y Pompa, ed., pp. 229–39. INAH. Mexico, D.F.

Use RG demographic data to support other 16th-century demographic materials; detailed analysis summarized in final table.

CORONA NÚÑEZ, JOSÉ, ed.
1958 Relaciones Geográficas de la diócesis de Michoacán, 1579–1580. 2 vols. Colección Siglo XVI. Guadalajara.

From INAH FPT transcripts, leg. 103 (and one printed source) provides RG texts (no maps) of Michoacan which FPT intended for PNE, 7. Vol. 1 includes Asuchitlan [Census, 7], Cuiseo de la Laguna [Census, 38], Jilquilpan [Census, 60], Necotlan [Census, 72], Taimeo [Census, 93]. Vol. 2 includes Celaya [Census, 18], Chilchotla [Census, 23], Patzcuaro [Census, 79, from León, 1889], Tingüindin [Census, 128], Tuxpan [Census, 137], Zinagua [Census, 156], Zirandaro [Census, 157]. Abbreviation: RGM.

COVARRUBIAS, MIGUEL
1946 Mexico South: Isthmus of Tehuantepec. New York.

On title page is glyph sign from RG Map 1 of Tehuantepec; p. 212 reproduces (b/w) much-reduced portion of same from UTX original. [Census, 102.]

DAHLGREN DE JORDÁN, BARBRO
1954 La Mixteca: su cultura e historia prehispánicas. UNAM. Mexico, D.F.

Map IIIa, based on published RG's attempts to fix boundaries of various Mixtex communities. Text utilizes RG's very systematically under topical headings.

DE BLOIS, JOYCE WADDELL BAILEY
1963 An interpretation of the map and Relación of Texupa in Oaxaca,

377

Mexico, and an analysis of the style of the map. Unpublished M.A. thesis, Tulane Univ.

Interlinear translation of the RG text, pp. 64–71. [Census, 124.]

DE LA PUENTE Y OLEA, MANUEL

1890 Relación de la comarca y minas de Temascaltepec, hecha en 1579 por D. Gaspar de Covarrubias, Alcalde Mayor de dichas minas y corregidor por S. M. de la Provincia de Tuzantla, extractada por el Sr. Ingeniero de Minas D. . . . *Memorias Sociedad Científica "Antonio Alzate,"* 3: 203–14 (March–April).

Extracts, RG of Temascaltepec, pp. 205–11; extracts, RG of Tuzantla, pp. 211–13; no maps. Introduction, pp. 203–04, adds nothing. [Census, 103.]

DESCRIPCIÓN

1955 Descripción de la Provincia de Zapotitlán y Suchitepéquez, año de 1579. . . . *Anales Sociedad de Geografía e Historia de Guatemala,* 28: 68–84 (March–December).

Text of RG, with accompanying genealogical text and chart, no map, from UTX photostat. *See* Mapa, 1966. [Census, 152.]

DESCRIPCIÓN

1965 Descripción de San Bartolomé del Partido de Atitlán, año 1585. *Anales Sociedad de Geografía e Historia de Guatemala,* 38: 262–76.

Reproduces pintura of Santiago Atitlàn (p. 263) which belongs with RG text published in Relación, 1964. Also publishes RG text for S. Bartolome [Census, 9A], dependency of Santiago Atitlan.

DUQUE DE ALBA

See Alba, Duque de, 1951.

EDWARDS, CLINTON R.

1969 Mapping by questionnaire: an early Spanish attempt to determine New World geographical positions. *Imago Mundi,* 23: 17–28.

Based in part on RG's from New Spain and South America.

EXPOSICIÓN AMERICANISTA

See International Congress of Americanists, 1881.

EXPOSICIÓN HISTÓRICO-AMERICANA

See Madrid, 1892a; Paso y Troncoso, 1892–93.

FISCHER SALE CATALOG

See Puttick and Simpson, 1869.

FERNÁNDEZ DURO, CESÁREO

1899 Los orígenes de la carta o mapa geográfica de España. *Boletín RAH,* 35: 502–25.

Spanish summary and comments on Marcel, 1899; on pp. 516–17 discussion of Spanish RG's.

FRÍAS Y FRÍAS, VALENTÍN [pseud.]

1906 La conquista de Querétaro: obra ilustrada con grabados que contiene lo que hasta hoy se ha escrito. . . . Queretaro.

Author's note dated 1901. RG, Queretaro, pp. 9–60, from JGI collection, copy furnished by García Pimentel, "Descripción de Querétaro, por su alcalde mayor Hernando de Cargas, 20 de enero de 1582." [Census, 86.]

GAMIO, MANUEL, ed.

1922 La población del Valle de Teotihuacan. 3 vols. Mexico, D.F.

RG map, Tequistlan-Teotihuacan, vol. 1, pl. 138, after PNE. [Census, 116.]

GARCÍA-BADELL Y ABADIA, GABRIEL

1963 Introducción a la historia de la agricultura española. Madrid.

Appendix 4 (p. 211 ff.) "Felipe II y los estudios geográficos y estadísticos de los pueblos de España (relaciones topográficas de los pueblos de España)," a somewhat rambling speech he gave in 1947; few new data. Biographical sketch of Fermín Caballero Mirogay (1800–76), pp. 162–64; *see* Caballero, 1866.

GARCÍA ICAZBALCETA, JOAQUÍN, comp.

1858? Relaciones historicas estadísticas. MS. 2 vols.

JGI handcopies of original RG's in his collection (vols. 23, 24, 25), not sold to Texas with other JGI MSS. Owned by FGO, who put them in MNA. These transcripts were much utilized by Gómez de Orozco, Barlow, and others for published versions of RG's. There seem to be major or minor divergences from originals in UTX. The original RG's were apparently obtained by JGI in 1853. A second set of JGI MS copies is in the private library of Ignacio Bernal. Neither set contains maps.

1875   [ed. and trans.] Cervantes de Salazar. Mexico en 1554: tres diálogos latinos traducidos. Mexico, D.F. [2d ed. 1939.]

Partial publication, RG of Cholula, pp. 227–28. [Census, 25.]

1891   [ed.] Relación que se envió a su majestad. *Nueva Colección de Documentos para la Historia de Mexico*, 3: 1–69. Mexico, D.F.

RG of Texcoco by Juan Bautista Pomar, Mar. 9, 1582, from unique but defective contemporary copy, now in UTX. [Census, 126.]

GARCÍA PAYÓN, JOSÉ, ed.

1965   Descripción del pueblo de Gueytlalpan (Zacatlan, Juxupango, Matlatan y Chila, Papantla) 30 de mayo de 1581. Alcalde Mayor Juan de Carrion. Con aclaraciones y notas histórico-arqueológicas. Universidad veracruzana, Cuadernos de la Facultad de Filosofía, Letras y Ciencias, 20. Xalapa, Ver.

Cédula of May 25, 1577 (pp. 13–18); Gueytlalpan (text, pp. 19–36; pintura, p. 35); Zacatlan (text, pp. 37–42; pintura, p. 45); Juxupango (text, pp. 43–48; pintura, p. 51); Matlatlan y Chila (text, pp. 49–54; pintura, p. 57); Papantla (text, pp. 55–71; pintura, p. 68); Tenanpulco y Matlactonatico (pintura, p. 59, also in color on book cover); mouth of Rio San Pedro y San Pablo o Tecolutla (pintura, p. 67). After PNE, also pinturas of Xonotla (p. 85), and Tetela (p. 86). [Census, 49, 49A–F.]

GARCÍA PIMENTEL, LUIS, ed.

1906   Relación de Yecapiztla. *OBBORE*, 7: 395–97, 8: 408–13.

From JGI collection. RG of Acapistla, 1580, without map. [Census, 1.]

1908   Relación de Oaxtepec, por Juan Gutiérrez de Liévana, 1580. *OBBORE*, 9: 315–19, 332–34, 350–57.

From JGI collection. RG of Guaxtepec, 1580, without map. [Census, 47.]

1909a   Relación de Tepoztlan, por Juan Gutiérrez de Liévana, 1580. *OBBORE*, 10: 313–17, 326–31, 348–52.

RG of Tepuztlan, 1580. [Census, 112.]

1909b   Relación de Tetela y Hueyapan por Cristóbal Godínez, 1580. *OBBORE*, 10: 428–34.

RG of Tetela del Volcan, 1581. [Census, 117.]

GARIBAY K., ANGEL M., ed.

1964   Poesía náhuatl. I: Romances de los señores de la Nueva España. Manuscrito de Juan Bautista de Pomar, Texcoco, 1582. Fuentes indígenas de la cultura náhuatl. UNAM, Instituto de Historia; Seminario de cultura náhuatl. Mexico, D.F.

Notes and transcription of RG of Texcoco, from photos of UTX original, pp. 149–228. [Census, 123.]

GATES, WILLIAM E.

[1924]   The William Gates collection. American Art Association. [n.d.] New York.

1937   The Maya Society and its work. The Maya Society, Pub. 19. Baltimore.

[1940]   The Gates collection of Middle American literature. [Section A printed; sections B–G mimeographed]. n.p., n.d. [Baltimore].

Listings of materials owned or photocopied by Gates; very minor RG listings.

GENET, JEAN, ed.

1928–29 Relation des choses de Yucatan: Diego de Landa. Texte espagnol et traduction française. Edition complète annotée par.... Paris. 2 vols. Collection de textes relatifs aux anciennes civilizations du Mexique et de l'Amérique Centrale.

Numerous footnote references to Yucatecan RG's. Hypothesizes that Gaspar Antonio Chi [Xiu], who compiled many of them, was a major contributor to Landa's work.

GERHARD, PETER

1968 Descripciones geográficas (pistas para investigadores). *Historia Mexicana*, 17: 618–27.

Summarizes various colonial programs that produced RG's and related documents, with notes on lost materials.

GLASS, JOHN B.

1964 Catálogo de la colección de códices. INAH/MNA. Mexico, D.F.

As pl. 17 this reproduces 1892 copy of Misquiahuala [Census, 8B] mapa, cataloged as MNA 35-15 (p. 56) and, as pl. 24, another 1892 copy of the Mapa of RG de Cholula [Census, 25], cataloged as MNA 35-23. Both originals are in UTX.

GÓMEZ DE OROZCO, FEDERICO, ed.

1923 Relación de Teutenango. *Boletín MNA*, ep. 4, 2: 85–90.

From PNE transcripts [Census, 122]; map, p. 87.

1924 Relación de la provincia de Meztitlan. *Boletín MNA*, ep. 4, 2: 109–20.

From DII, 4: 530–55; variant calendar wheel (p. 118). No map [Census, 66]. Original in JGI collection.

1927a Descripción de Cholula. *RMEH*, vol. 1/6, suplemento, pp. 158–70.

RG of Cholula, 1581, text from JGI transcripts, but small and badly printed map (p. 170), from MNA copy. [Census, 25.]

1927b Culhuacan. *RMEH*, vol. 1/6, suplemento, pp. 171–73.

RG text, from JGI transcripts, without map [Census, 41].

1927c Descripción de Teotzacualco y de Amoltepeque. *RMEH*, vol. 1/6, suplemento, pp. 174–78.

RG of Teozacoalco (pp. 174–76), and of Amoltepec (pp. 176–78) from JGI transcripts, without map [Census, 108].

1927d Catálogo de la colección de manuscritos de Joaquín García Icazbalceta relativos a la historia de América. Ministerio de Relaciones Exteriores (Mexico), *Monografías Bibliográficas Mexicanas*, 9. Mexico, D.F.

Inventory made by JGI for Nicolás León, with much added note material by FGO. RG's listed (pp. 20–21, 34–42) with notes (pp. 138–50), giving publication data. FGO also reproduces RG maps: Cuzcatlan (facing p. 148), AGI after PNE, and MNA copy of Cholula (facing p. 150). [Census, 25, 42.]

1927e Relación de las descripciones y pinturas de las provincias del distrito de Nueva España que se an traydo al Consejo y se entregan a Juan López de Velasco. *Anales MNA*, ep. 4, 5: 365–66.

JLV 1583 list, incorrectly dated 1573, from FPT transcript; this text is full of typographical errors, and quite corrupt. For trustworthy version, see Article 5, Appendix D, in this volume of the *Handbook*.

1928a Descripción de Tetiquipa Rio Hondo, hecha por el Señor Cristóbal de Salas. *RMEH*, vol. 2, suplemento, pp. 114–20.

From JGI transcripts. RG text for Tetiquipa–Rio Hondo, pp. 114–17; Cozautepeque, pp. 117–20. [Census, 120.]

1928b Relación de los pueblos de Tecuicuilco, Atepq, Zoquiapa, Xaltianguez. *RMEH*, vol. 2, suplemento, pp. 121–32.

From JGI transcripts. RG map is not included. [Census, 101.]

1931 Relaciones historico-geográficas de Nueva España. *Mexico Antiguo*, 3: 43–51 (September).

Brief discussion of RG's, with defective reproduction of Juan de Velasco list of 1583, and some attempt to indicate which items were then published.

GONZÁLEZ OBREGÓN, LUIS, ed.
1907 Relación de los pueblos de Acatlan, Chila, Petlatzingo, Icxitlan y Piaztla (Real Academia de la Historia en Madrid). R.M. 62 (136) [Nota de Ximénez de la Espada]. *Anales MNA*, ep. 2, 4/2: 97–118.

Ed. note (p. 118) indicates text from MS copy made for Nicolás León by JDE. RG's: Acatlan, pp. 97–106; Chila, pp. 106–109; Petlalzingo, pp. 109–112; Icxitlan, pp. 115–18. [Census, 2.]

GORBEA TRUEBA, JOSÉ
1959 Culhuacán, Mexico. INAH. Dirección de Monumentos Coloniales, 6. Mexico.

RG map, from copy in OyB Mapoteca, DGMH, no. 1187, p. 8. [Census, 41.]

GUZMÁN, EULALIA
1948 Colección de Papeles del Paso y Troncoso: Relaciones de Michoacán, siglos XVI y XVIII. *In* Occidente de Mexico, pp. 158–59.

Listing of FPT transcripts.

HERNÁNDEZ Y DÁVALOS, JUAN E., ed.
1870 Materiales para un diccionario geográfico, estadístico, histórico y biográfico del Estado de Jalisco. *Boletín SMGE*, ep. 2, 2: 453–84 (June).

RG of Ameca (pp. 464–78) from unknown MS copy, preceded by Instrucción and Memoria (pp. 460–64); no map. This MS copy apparently not recorded in calendar of Hernández y Dávalos Manuscript Collection, UTX. [Census, 4.]

INTERNATIONAL CONGRESS OF AMERICANISTS (4TH)
1881 Lista de los objetos que compren-

de la exposición americanista. Madrid.

Large exhibition of RG's and pinturas from the Spanish collections.

HORCASITAS, FERNANDO, AND RICHARD GEORGE
1955 Relación de Tlacolula y Mitla. Mexico City College, *Mesoamerican Notes*, 4: 13–14.

Reissue of RG [Census, 133], from PNE.

JAKEMAN, M. WELLS
1945 The origins and history of the Mayas, a general reconstruction in the light of the basic documentary sources and latest archaeological discoveries. Part I: Introductory investigations. Los Angeles.

Based in part on RG's of Yucatan.

1952 The "historical recollections" of Gaspar Antonio Chi, an early source-account of ancient Yucatán. *Brigham Young University, Publications in Archaeology and Early History*, 3. Provo.

Translated excerpts, from DIU, vols. 11, 13.

1954 The Relación de Motul: a sixteenth century account of some of the history, customs, and religious beliefs of the ancient Maya. *Brigham Young University. Bulletin University Archaeological Society*, 5: 22–29 (October). Provo.

Translated excerpts from RG, taken from DIU, 11: 75–88 (RG no. 11, 1898). [Census, 69.]

JIMÉNÉZ DE LA ESPADA, MARCOS, comp.
1881 Catálogo alfabético de las relaciones y descripciones geográficas, geográfico-históricas y geográfico-estadísticas, hechas por interreogatorio, memoria, instrucción u otro formulario semejante y de órden del Consejo de Indias. . . . In his 1881–97, 1: cxxi–cliv. Abbreviation: JDE.

Listing of about 450 items, including RG's. Still the most comprehensive single treatment. Many items he lists were known through imperfect bibliographical citations.

1881–97 [ed.] Relaciones Geográficas de Indias. 4 vols. Madrid.

The RG's he published relate solely to South America. The long "antecedentes" in vol. 1, and continued through vol. 4, is the single most detailed history of the background of the RG's; the main essay is in vol. 1. All subsequent writers on RG's draw heavily on this pioneering and still basic treatment. The catalog included in these "antecedentes" is separately entered in this Bibliography.

1965 Relaciones Geográficas de Indias. Peru. Edición y estudio preliminar por José Urbano Martínez Carreras. 4 vols. Madrid. Biblioteca de Autores Españoles desde la formación del lenguaje hasta nuestros días (continuación), vols. 183–86.

Reissue of 1881–97 materials, preceded by useful introduction. One chapter provides detailed biobibliographical materials of Jiménez de la Espada; the other discusses at length the RG's of the Indies and of Spain, relationships, and similar matters, with helpful bibliographical notes and listing.

JIMÉNEZ MORENO, WIGBERTO
1944 La colonización y evangelización de Guanajuato en el siglo XVI. Cuadernos Americanos, año 3, no. 13: 125–44.

"Mapa de las villas de San Miguel y San Felipe, que data, probablemente, de 1580," b/w, facing p. 144. No map source or other data given. [Census, 203.]

1958 Estudios de historia colonial. Mexico, D.F.

RG map of "villas de San Miguel y San Felipe" [Chichimecas], facing p. 90. No provenance data. [Census, 203.]

KELLY, ISABEL T., AND ANGEL PALERM
1952 The Tajin Totonac. Part 1: History, subsistence, shelter and technology. Smithsonian Institution, Institute of Social Anthropology, Pub. 13. Washington.

List of RG's for Tajin and Totonac area, including copies in MNA, pp. 359–60.

KUBLER, GEORGE
1948 Mexican architecture of the sixteenth century. Yale Historical Publications, History of Art, 5. 2 vols. New Haven.

From PNE reproduces 9 RG maps (vol. 1, figs. 19–28) with RG map of Cholula from MNA copy.

—— AND CHARLES GIBSON
1951 The Tovar calendar, an illustrated Mexican manuscript ca. 1585, reproduced with a commentary and handlist of sources on the Mexican 365-day year. Memoirs Connecticut Academy of Sciences, 11 (January). New Haven.

Brief discussion of calendars in Meztitlan RG, from DII, 4: 555, RG of Tezcoco (Pomar, 1891) and RG of Teotitlan del Camino, PNE, 4: 217–20, on p. 71. [Census, 66, 107, 123.]

LANGMAN, IDA K.
1955 The flora of Mexico as described in the 16th century relaciones. University of Michigan, Asa Gray Bulletin, 3: 59–63 (spring).

Translation of Questions 22–26, and translated answers from RG of Ameca [Census, 4], with brief bibliography.

LARRAÑAGA, [first name unknown], archivo en Simancas
1783 Papeles que están separados para don J. M. Muñoz, Cosmógrafo de Indias . . . y que se le remiten en un cajón de Simancas. December 22. RAH, MS no. 1711 of Muñoz Collection, vol. 75, fols. 143–45. Abbreviation: LPM.

Unpublished list of actual documents shipped; see Muñoz, 1783, for those requested.

LATORRE, GERMÁN, ed.

1919 Relaciones de Indias (contenidas en el Archivo General de Indias de Sevilla). La Hispano-Americano del siglo XVI. Colombia, Venezuela, Puerto Rico, República Argentina. Publicaciones del Centro Oficial de Estudios Americanistas de Sevilla, Biblioteca Colonial Americana, 3. Seville.

RG of May 25, 1577, pp. 3–8. RG of Puerto Rico (Jan. 1, 1582), pp. 37–55, with remainder from South America. Some useful notes.

1920a Relaciones Geográficas de Nueva España. *Boletin Centro Oficial de Estudios Americanistas de Sevilla,* 7, passim. Seville. Abbreviation: BCE.

Later collected and reprinted in Latorre, 1920b, where listed in detail.

1920b Relaciones Geográficas de Indias (contenidas en el Archivo General de Indias de Sevilla). La Hispano-América del siglo XVI. Virreinato de Nueva España. (Mexico. Censos de población). *Centro Oficial de Estudios Americanistas de Sevilla, Biblioteca Colonial Americana,* 4. Seville. Abbreviation: RNE.

Various RG's from AGI, some maps (after PNE). Contents, with Census numbers: CHANCENOTE, pp. 69–79 [Census, 20]; CUZCATLAN, pp. 8–16, map, p. 13 [Census, 42]; HOCABA, pp 65–68 [Census, 50]; POPOLA, pp. 90–95 [Census, 83]; TETELA DEL VOL-CAN, pp. 29–36, map, p. 33 [Census, 117]; TEUTENANGO, pp. 23–28, map, p. 25 [Census, 122]; ZIMAPAN, pp. 17–22, map, p. 21 [Census, 155]; ZISMO-PO, pp. 88–89 [Census, 158]; ZUSOPO, pp. 80–87 [Census, 165; ZUZAL, pp. 58–64. In addition, volume includes a Relación of Vera Cruz, dated 1571, pp. 37–52, by Arias Hernandez, cura, with 2 maps (pp. 45, 49). On pp. 53–57 Latorre briefly discusses RG's of Yucatan, providing minor bibliography. On p. 77 is the map of the Province of Tabasco, drawn by Melchor Alfaro de Santa Cruz; discussed on p. 54.

LEÓN, NICOLÁS, ed.

1889 Relación de Patzcuaro. *Anales Museo Michoacano,* 2: 41–48. Morelia.

From MS copy especially made by JGI for publication by León. [Census, 79.]

1904 Los tarascos. Primera parte. Mexico, D.F.

For RG of Tiripitio León mentions unpublished drawings (pp. 39, n. 56; 156) in a copy made for him of RG by JGI. Other RG's copied from JGI for León mentioned in Teixidor, 1937, pp. 79, 207, 304–05.

1933 Códice Sierra. Traducción al español de su texto nahuatl y explicación de sus pinturas jeroglíficas. MNA. Mexico, D.F.

RG map of Texupan, facing p. 10, adding to text the FPT notes from PNE, 4: 53–57. [Census, 124.]

LEÓN PINELO, ANTONIO DE

1624? Memoria de los papeles que tengo para la descripción de las Indias. BNMA, MS 3064, 2 fols.

MS listing of 105 MS items, including 15 RG's, all of which are now lost. Text reproduced in Article 5, Appendix E. See also Baudot, 1968.

LÓPEZ, JOSÉ EUCARIO, ed.

1958 Descripción del partido y jurisdicción de Tlaltenango hecha en 1650 por Don Francisco Manuel de Salcedo y Herrera. Colección Nueva Galicia, 1. Mexico, D.F.

Sole published response to an RG questionnaire of 1648, from a MS in episcopal archives in Guadalajara.

LÓPEZ DE VELASCO, JUAN

1583 Relación de las descripciones y pinturas de las provincias del distrito de Nueva España que se an traydo al Consejo y se entrega a Juan López de Velasco, 21 de noviembre 1583. MS, AGI, Patronato Real, leg. 171, doc. 1, ramo 16, fols. 11–14v. [Old, 2-1-2/19 No. 1, R-16.] Abbreviation: JLV.

Basic contemporary inventory. List re-arranged and published, without JLV legajo numbers, in Jiménez de la Espada, 2:xxxvii–xxxviii; printed (faulty paleography), Gómez de Orozco, 1927e, 1931. Reproduced in Article 5, Appendix D, in this volume of the *Handbook*.

MCANDREW, JOHN

1965   The open air churches of sixteenth century Mexico: atrios, posas, open chapels, and other studies. Cambridge, Mass.

Reproduces various RG's, maps and parts of texts related to his topic.

MADRID

1892a   Exposición histórico-americana: catálogo de los documentos históricos de Indias presentados por la nación española. . . . [Vol. Q.] Madrid.

Possibly missing RG map of Tequaltiche [Catalog, 63] appears as Item 883, p. 129.

1892b   *See* Paso y Troncoso, 1892–93.

MAPA

1966   Mapa de la costa de Suchitepéquez y Zapotitlán, 1579. *Anales Sociedad de Geografía e Historia de Guatemala*, 39: 96–99.

Reproduces pintura of Zapotlan and Suchitepec (p. [97]) which belongs with RG text published in Descripción, 1955; also publishes extensive inscription at bottom of pintura.

MARCEL, GABRIEL

1899   Les origines de la Carte d'Espagne. *Revue Hispanique*, 18: 163–98.

Erudite discussion of attempts to depict Spain cartographically, from 15th century. Underscores importance of the Spanish 1575–78 RG's as sources (pp. 177–80), lamenting their unpublished state.

MARIMÓN, SEBASTIAN, ed.

1884   Relación de la villa de Valladolid, escrita por el Cabildo de aquella ciudad . . . abril de 1579. 4th International Congress of American-

ists (Madrid, 1881) *Acta*, 2: 166–95.

RG text of Valladolid, Yucatan. No map. [Census, 139.]

MARTÍNEZ CARRERAS, JOSÉ URBANO

1965   Estudio preliminar. *See* Jiménez de la Espada, 1965.

MAUDSLAY, A. P., ed. and trans.

1908–16   Bernal Díaz del Castillo. The true history of the Conquest of New Spain. . . . Hakluyt Society Publications, 2d ser., nos. 23–25, 30, 40. 5 vols. London.

Vol. 5 (no. 40, 1916) has color reproduction of RG map of Tabasco, based on certified copy of original, in end pocket. [Census, 90.]

MAZA, FRANCISCO DE LA

1959   La ciudad de Cholula y sus iglesias. UNAM. *Instituto de Investigaciones Estéticas, Estudios y fuentes*, 9. Mexico, D.F.

RG map of Cholula, pl. 5. [Census, 25.]

MELÓN Y RUIZ DE GORDOJUELA, AMANDO

1943   España en la historia de la Geografía. *Estudios Geográficos*, 4: 195–232 (May). Madrid.

Includes brief discussion of the RG's of Spain, pp. 216–17.

MIGUÉLEZ, MANUEL

1917   Relaciones histórico-geográficas de los pueblos de España. *In* his Catálogo de los códices españoles de la Biblioteca de El Escorial, 1: 249–332. Madrid.

Detailed index and analysis, with full listing of RG materials in the 8 vols. of Spanish RG's in El Escorial. Reproduces the 57/59-question Memoria of 1575 (pp. 262–68) and the 1578 (45-question) Memoria (pp. 271–76). Basic research tool for the Spanish materials.

MIMENZA CASTILLO, RICARDO

1937   El cronista yucateco, Gaspar Antonio Xiu. *Anales Sociedad de Geografía e Historia de Guatemala*, 13: 388–90.

Biographical data on compiler of several Yucatecan RG's.

1943 Fundación de Valladolid, Yucatán. *Boletín Archivo General Nación*, 14: 75–84.

Reprint of RG [Census, 139], from DIU, without drawings.

MORENO DE TOSCANO, ALEJANDRA
1969 Geografía económica de Nueva España, siglo XVI: un estudio de las Relaciones Geográficas de 1580. Colegio de Mexico.

MOTA Y ESCOBAR, ALONSO DE LA
1930, 1940 *See* Ramírez Cabañas, Joaquín

MUÑOZ, JUAN BAUTISTA
1783 Relación de los papeles geográficos y algunos otros que don Juan Bautista Muñoz deja separados en Simancas, los cuales suplicó a S. M. se mandasen traer para tenerlos presentes al tiempo de escribir la Historia General de América. RAH, MS 1710, Muñoz Collection, vol. 75, fols. 121–42. Abbreviation: RM.

Unpublished list of approximately 224 MSS, many RG's, in Simancas, seen there by Muñoz.

MUÑOZ COLLECTION
See Real Academia de la Historia.

NICHOLS, MADALINE W.
1944 An old questionnaire for modern use. *Agricultural History*, 18/4: 150–60.

Summary of 1577 RG questionnaire.

NOTICIAS VARIAS
See Anonymous, 1878.

NUNEMAKER, J. HORACE
1948 The Biblioteca *Aportación Histórica* Publications, 1943–1947. *HAHR*, 28: 316–34.

A pioneering attempt to unravel mysteries of the Luis Vargas Rea publications. Valuable to date of appearance, giving data on the VR/PNE materials in which several RG's are included, from FPT transcripts, first and only such publication of them.

NUTTALL, ZELIA
1926 Official reports on the towns of Tequizistlan, Tepechpan, Acolman, and San Juan Teotihuacan, sent by Francisco de Castañeda to His Majesty, Philip II, and the Council of the Indies, in 1580. Translated and edited, with an introduction and notes. *Papers Peabody Museum of Archaeology and Ethnology*, Harvard University, 11/2: 41–84. Cambridge.

Translation into English of RG of Tequizistlan; material regrouped by Nuttall, who also published RG map. [Census, 116.]

1929 The causes of physical degeneracy of Mexican Indians after the Spanish conquest as set forth by Mexican informants in 1580. *Journal of Hygiene*, 27: 40–43.

Reprints from Nuttall, 1926, translated answers to Questions 5, 15, of the 1577 questionnaire, with minimal comment.

OLVERA, JORGE
1964 Ciudad Sahagún y sus alrededores. UNAM. *Artes de México*, 12/56–57.

From OyB copy, RG map of Cempoala [Catalog, 10] in color on cover, b/w in plate; Epazoyuca [Catalog, 22] (copy), with bottom cut off, in plates; Tetlistaca, line drawing of main church [Catalog, 67].

ORENSTEIN, A. GHISLAINE PLEASONTON
1967 Late sixteenth century Mexican paintings: an analysis of the style of early colonial map paintings executed in the region of the Mixtec Indians. Unpublished M.A. thesis, Tulane Univ.

RG pinturas from the Mixteca.

385

OROZCO Y BERRA, MANUEL

1864 Geografía de las lenguas y carta etnográfica de México. Mexico, D.F.

From JGI collection utilizes and lists RG's, pp. 240–55; partial publication of RG of Queretaro, pp. 258–62. [Census, 86.]

1871 Materiales para una cartografía mexicana. Mexico, D.F.

A listing of various materials; Items 5–23, 860–62, 926–27, 3043–44 include RG's then in JGI collection.

1881 Apuntes para la historia de la geografía de México. Mexico, D.F.

List of RG's in JGI collection, also printed in Ministerio de Fomento (Mexico), *Anales*, 6: 5–48 (1881), and reprinted in Jiménez de la Espada, 2: xxxviii–xlvi (1885), rearranged alphabetically and keyed to his "Catálogo."

ORTEGA RUBIO, JUAN, comp.

1918 Relaciones Topográficas de los pueblos de España. Lo más interesante de ellos escogidos. Madrid.

Alphabetically arranged summaries of data in Spanish RG's for places covered by the 1574–78 RG series. Reproduces cédulas, instrucciones of Oct. 27, 1575 (59 questions) and Aug. 7, 1578 (45 questions), pp. 12–28.

PACHECO, JOAQUÍN F., FRANCISCO DE CÁRDENAS, AND LUIS TORRES DE MENDOZA, eds.

1864–84 Colección de documentos inéditos relativos al descubrimiento, conquista y organización de las antiguas posesiones españolas de América y Oceanía, sacados de los archivos del Reino, y muy especialmente del de Indias. 42 vols. Madrid. Abbreviation: DII.

Corrupt and badly edited texts, including some RG's from Muñoz copies; mostly 1604 series, vol. 9 (1868).

PALACIOS, ENRIQUE JUAN

1930 Huaxtepec y sus reliquias arqueológicos. Contribución al XXIV Congreso de Americanistas, Hamburgo, 1930. Anexo a la Guía de las ruinas arqueológicas del Estado de Morelos. SEP, Sección de Arquelogía. Mexico, D.F.

RG Text of Guaxtepec, 1580. Reprinted from OBBORE, 9: 315–19, 332–35, 350–57, "Oaxtepec: Descripción del Guastepeque por el Alcalde Mayor Juan Gutierrez de Lievana, 24 de setiembre de 1580," pp. 33–43. [Census, 47.]

PALOMINO Y CAÑEDO, JORGE

1947 La casa y mayorazgo de Cañedo de Nueva Galicia. 2 vols. Mexico, D.F.

Ameca RG [Census, 4] and pintura [Catalog, 3] reproduced, 2: 469–78.

PASO Y TRONCOSO, FRANCISCO DEL, ed.

1880 Descripción de la Villa del Espiritu Santo por el Alcalde Mayor, Suero de Cangas, en 29 abril, 1580, con notas. *Revista Mexicana* (?), 3, no. 7: 55–56, 70–72.

RG of Coazocoalco, without map, from JGI copy. FPT mentions publishing this in *Economista Mexicana* (Zavala, 1939: 49, n. 1), but CDG, 706, gives *Revista Mexicana*. [Unlocated by HFC.]

1892–93 Exposición histórico-americana. Catálogo de los objetos que presenta la República de México. 2 vols. Madrid.

In vol. 1 he discusses MNA copies of RG maps of Cholula (p. 53) [Census, 25], and Misquiahuala (p. 62) [Census, 8B].

1905–06 Papeles de Nueva España. Segunda Serie. Geografía y Estadística. 8 vols. Madrid and Paris. Abbreviation: PNE.

Only 5 vols. published by FPT: vols. 4, 5, 6, 7 contain exclusively RG's from RAH and AGI. Vols. 2, 7 Suplemento, 8, not published by FPT, were later issued in separate parts from his transcripts by Luis Vargas Rea, in poorly edited, limited, flimsy editions. By Census numbers, RG's published by FPT are as follows, preceded by the Instructions (PNE, 4: 1–7):
ACATLAN, 5: 55–80 [Census, 2];
AHUATLAN, 5: 81–98 [Census, 3];

ATLATLAUCA, 4: 163–76, map, 4: 163 [Census, 11]; ATLITLALQUIA, 6: 199–208 [Census, 12]; CHICHICAPA, 4: 115–43 [Census, 21]; CHICONAUTLA, 6: 167–77 [Census, 22]; Chilapa (ZUMPANGO), 5: 174–82 [Census, 164A]; CHINANTLA, 4: 58–68 [Census, 24]; CITLALTOMAGUA, 6: 153–66 [Census, 28]; COATEPEC, 6: 39–86, 3 maps [Census, 29]; CUAUHQUILPA, 6: 306–12 [Census, 32]; CUAHUITLAN, 4: 155–62, map, 4: 155 [Census, 33]; CUICATLAN, 4: 183–89 [Census, 35]; CUZCATLAN, 5: 46–54, map, 5: 46 [Census, 42]; GUATULCO, 4: 232–51 [Census, 45]; GUAXOLOTITLAN, 4: 196–205 [Census, 46]; HUEXOTLA, 6: 183–92 [Census, 51]; ICHCATEOPAN, 6: 87–152 [Census, 52]; IXTEPEXIC, 4: 9–23, map, 4: 10 [Census, 57]; MACUILSUCHIL, 4: 100–108, map, 4: 100 [Census, 62]; MEXICATZINGO, 6: 193–98 [Census, 65]; NEXAPA, 4: 29–44 [Census, 73]; NOCHIZTLAN, 4: 206–12, plan, 4: 206 [Census, 74]; OCOPETLAYUCA, 6: 251–62 [Census, 76]; PAPALOTICPAC, 4: 88–99 [Census, 78]; SUCHITEPEC, 4: 24–28, 5 maps [Census, 88]; TALISTACA, 4: 177–82 [Census, 94]; TAXCO, 6: 263–82 [Census, 96]; TEMAZCALTEPEC, 7: 15–29, 4 maps [Census, 103]; TEOTITLAN, 4: 213–31, map, 4: 213 [Census, 107]; TEOZAPOTLAN, 4: 190–95 [Census, 109]; TEPEACA, 5: 12–45 [Census, 110]; TEPEAPULCO, 6: 291–305 [Census, 111]; TEPUZTLAN, 6: 237–50 [Census, 112]; TEQUIZISTLAN, 6: 209–36, maps, 6: 209 [Census, 116]; TETELA DEL VOLCAN, 6: 283–90 [Census, 117]; TETELA, S.M.A., 5: 124–73, maps, 5: 127, 146 [Census, 118]; TETICPAC, 4: 109–114 [Census, 119]; TEUTENANGO 7: 1–7, map, 7: 1 [Census, 122]; TEXUPA, 4: 53–57, map, 4: 53 [Census, 124]; TILANTONGO, 4: 69–87 [Census, 127]; TLACOLULA, 4: 144–54 [Census, 133]; TZACOTALPA, 5: 1–11, map, 5: 1 [Census, 134]; TORNACUSTLA, 6: 12–38 [Census, 135]; TOTOLAPA, 6: 6–11 [Census, 136]; USILA, 4: 45–52 [Census, 138]; XALAPA, 5: 99–123, map, 5: 99 [Census, 141]; XALAPACINTLA, 4: 252–66 [Census, 142]; ZAYULA, 6: 178–82 [Census, 153]; ZIMAPAN, 6: 1–5, map, 6: 1 [Census, 155]; ZULTEPEC, 7: 8–14 [Census, 163]; ZUMPANGO, 6: 313–22 [Census, 164].

PASQUEL, LEONARDO, ed.

1958 La ciudad de Veracruz. Vol. 1.

Colección Suma veracruzana: serie historiografía. Mexico, D.F.

Text of RG of Veracruz [Census, 140], pp. 179–208 (source not given). No maps.

PERALTA, MANUEL M. DE, comp.

1883 Costa Rica, Nicaragua y Panamá en el siglo XVI. Su historia y sus limites según los documentos del Archivo de Indias de Sevilla, del Simancas, etc. Madrid and Paris.

No RG's of 1577 questionnaire, but many useful "Descripción y Población" items.

PÉREZ BUSTAMENTE, CIRIACO

1928a Don Antonio de Mendoza, primer virrey de la Nueva España. *Anales Universidad de Santiago* (Chile), 3.

Reproduces from PNE RG maps of Cuzcatlan [Census, 42], Teutenango [Census, 122], Telela [Census, 118], and Zimapan [Census, 155].

1928b Los orígenes del gobierno virreinal en las Indias españolas, Don Antonio de Mendoza, primer virrey de la Nueva España (1535–1550). Santiago de Compostela, Chile.

Reproduces same RG pinturas as his 1928a.

PÉREZ [Y] HERNÁNDEZ, JOSÉ MARÍA, comp.

1874–75 Diccionario . . . geográfico de la República Mexicana. 4 vols. Mexico, D.F.

Vol. 1: 381–95, has RG of Ameca, based on handcopy furnished by García Icazbalceta. Instructions, pp. 381–82; Questionnaire, 1577, pp. 382–84; RG, pp. 384–95. [Census, 4.]

PLANCARTE Y NAVARRETE, FRANCISCO, ed.

1906–09 Boletín Oficial y Revista Eclesiástica del Obispado de Cuernavaca. Cuernavaca. Abbreviation: OBBORE.

Founded and edited by Plancarte. Nos. 8–10 contain RG's from JGI collection, edited by JGI's son, Luis García Pimentel (q.v., for listing).

387

PLEASONTON, A. G.

See Orenstein, A. Ghislaine Pleasonton.

POMAR, JUAN BAUTISTA

1891 Relación que se envió a su majestad [1582]. *In* Nueva colección de documentos para la historia de México, Joaquín García Icazbalceta, ed., 3: 1–69.

RG text of Texcoco [Census, 123], from contemporary copy. *See also* Garibay K., 1964.

POWELL, PHILIP WAYNE

1952 Soldier, Indians and silver. Berkeley.

RG map of Chichimecas, endpaper drawing. [Census, 203.]

PUTTICK AND SIMPSON, auctioneers

1869 Bibliotheca Mejicana . . . To be sold by auction. London.

Fischer Sale Catalog; Item 1849 (p. 204) lists several MS RG's, provenance and present location of which are not known.

RAMÍREZ CABAÑAS, JOAQUÍN, ed.

1930 Descripción geográfica de los Reinos de Galicia, Vizcaya, y León, por D. Alonso de la Mota y Escobar. Bibliófilos Mexicanos. Mexico, D.F.

Limited, noncommercial edition, from MSS Add. 13,964, Item 7, fols. 72–128, British Museum; material gathered 1602, and answers questionnaire of 1604. Facing p. 80, however, is RG map of Compostela, in answer to 1577 questionnaire. [Census, 31.]

1940 Descripción geográfica de los Reinos de Nueva Galicia, Nueva Vizcaya y Nuevo León [por D. Alonso de la Mota y Escobar]. 2d ed. Mexico, D.F.

Reprint of Ramírez Cabañas, 1930, for public sale. RG map of Compostela, facing p. 80. [Census, 31.]

1943 La ciudad de Veracruz en el siglo XVI. UNAM. Mexico, D.F.

RG of Vera Cruz, from JGI/UTX, pp. 15–41, RG Map 2 (copy) facing p. 18 [Census, 140.]

RAMÍREZ LAVOIGNET, DAVID

1952 Notas históricas de Misantla. *Revista Mexicana de Estudios Antropológicas*, 13: 315–31.

Liberal extracts from RG of Mizantla, from unidentified copy. [Census, 67.]

1962 [ed.] Relación de Misantla. Revisión y notas de Ramírez Lavoignet. *Universidad Veracruzana, Cuadernos de la Facultad de Filosofía y Letras*, 8. Xalapa, Ver.

RG, MIZANTLA, by Diego Pérez de Arteaga, Oct. 1, 1579. Poor reproduction of map, p. 16 (line drawing). [Census, 67.]

REAL ACADEMIA DE LA HISTORIA

1954–56 Catálogo de la Colección de don Juan Bautista Muñoz. Antonio Ballesteros y Beretta, ed. 3 vols. Madrid.

Notes (1: 114–17) on Muñoz copies of RG's of Meztitlan [Census, 66], and Zapotitlan y Suchitepec [Census, 152]. *See also* Academia (Madrid).

REAL DÍAZ, JOSÉ JOAQUÍN

1959a Las ferias de Jalapa. *Anuario de Estudios Americanos*, 16: 167–314. Seville.

Pl. 1 reproduces RG map of Xalapa de la Vera Cruz, detail, upper center [Census, 141].

1959b Las ferias de Jalapa. *Escuela de Estudios Hispano-Americanos*, Pub. 128. Seville.

Same as 1959a.

RECINOS, ADRIAN, ed. and trans.

1950 Memorial de Sololá. Anales de los Cakchiquels. Traducción directa del original, introducción y notas de Adrian Recinos. Fondo de Cultura Económica. Mexico, D.F.

"Papel del orígen de los señores," Anexo A (pp. 245–47) reproduces with diagram the historical-genealogical material at end of RG of ZAPOTITLAN [Census, 152]. This is not included in English translation, published by University of Oklahoma Press (Norman, 1953).

RELACION

1964 Relación de Santiago Atitlán, año de 1585, por Alonso Paez Betancor y Fray Pedro de Arboleda. *Anales Sociedad de Geografía e Historia de Guatemala*, 37: 87–106.

Text of RG of Santiago Atitlan [Census 9, but not 9A, 9B, or 9C]; *see* Descripción, 1965. Reproduction of fol. 1 from UTX photostat, no map.

RELACIONES DE YUCATAN

See Asensio, José María.

[RENOUARD, ANTOINE AUGUSTIN]

1839 Catalogue de la Bibliothèque d'un amateur, avec notes bibliographiques, critiques, et littéraires. Vol. 4: Histoire.

Notes "Histoires et Relations des Indes occidentales," a folio volume of MSS, 376 fols. in Spanish, most of them original documents, reporting in 16th century on natural history, antiquities, etc., illustrated with "positions géographiques," and more than 400 Mexican drawings related to history, religion, etc. Present location of these materials (possibly "lost" RG's?) unknown.

REVISTA MEXICANA DE ESTUDIOS HISTÓRICOS

1927–28 Suplementos, 1, 2. Abbreviation: RMEH.

Under editorship of Federico Gómez de Orozco, aided by Alfonso Caso, published RG's of Cholula, Culhuacan, Teotzacualco-Amoltepeque, Ixtlahuaca, Tehuantepec, Coatzocoalco, Cozautepec, Peñoles, and Santa Cruz Iztepec, from JGI transcripts. Entered separately here under Gómez de Orozco, and Alfonso Caso.

ROBERTSON, DONALD

1959a Mexican manuscript painting of the early colonial period: the Metropolitan schools. *Yale Historical Publications, History of Art*, 12. New Haven.

Discussion and bibliography of maps,

with various reproductions of RG maps.

1959b The Relaciones Geográficas of Mexico. 33d International Congress of Americanists (San Jose, 1958), *Acta*, 2: 540–47. San Jose, Costa Rica.

From art historian's point of view discusses maps of RG's, reproducing (b/w) from UTX materials several RG maps.

1963 The style of the Borgia group of Mexican pre-conquest manuscripts. *In* Millard Meiss and others, eds., Studies in Western Art: Acts of the Twentieth International Congress of the History of Art. Vol. 3: Latin American art and the Baroque Period in Europe, pp. 148–64, pls. XLIX–LII. Princeton Univ. Press.

Marginally related to RG's. Incorrectly states RG pintura of Amoltepec [Catalog, 4] painted on skin.

1968 Provincial town plans from late sixteenth century Mexico. 38th International Congress of Americanists (Stuttgart, 1968). Unpublished.

Analysis of RG pinturas for variations of grid plans.

ROMERO QUIROZ, JAVIER

1963 Teotenanco y Matalatzinco (Calixtlahuaca). Toluca.

RG of Teutenango, pp. 12–13. [Census, 122.]

ROSELL, CAYETANO

See Caballero, 1866.

ROYS, RALPH L.

1943 The Indian background of colonial Yucatan. *Carnegie Institution of Washington*, Pub. 548. Washington.

Brief discussion of RG's of Yucatan, pp. 123–24.

RUBIO MAÑÉ, JORGE IGNACIO

1956 El cronista Maya Gaspar Antonio

389

Chi, 1531–1610. *Memorias Academia Mexicana de la Historia*, 15: 102–08.

Data on a Maya who aided preparation of several RG's from Yucatan.

SALCEDO Y HERRERA, FRANCISCO MANUEL DE
1958 Descripción del partido y jurisdicción de Tlaltenango hecha en 1650. *Col. Nueva Galicia*, 1. Mexico, D.F.

Only published response to questionnaire of 1648. Original in the Archivo Arquiepiscopal de Guadalajara.

SALOMON, NOËL
1964 La campagne de Nouvelle Castille a la fin du xvie siècle. École Pratique des Hautes Études. VIe Section, Centre de Recherches Historiques, Les Hommes et la Terre, 9. Paris.

Marxian analysis of agricultural conditions in Castile, based on materials in Spanish RG's.

SCHOLES, FRANCE V., AND RALPH L. ROYS
1948 The Maya Chontal Indians of Acalan-Tixchel: a contribution to the history and ethnography of the Yucatan Peninsula. *Carnegie Institution of Washington*, Pub. 560. Washington.

Redrawn RG map of Tabasco, with English translation of place names; based on versions published in DIU and Maudslay, 1916. [Census, 90.]

1968 The Maya Chontal Indians of Acalan-Tixchel: a contribution to the history and ethnography of the Yucatan Peninsula. 2d ed. Univ. Oklahoma Press.

Reprint of 1948.

SERRANO Y SANZ, MANUEL, ed.
1908 Relaciones históricas y geográficas de América Central. *Colección de Libros de Historia de América*, 8. Madrid.

No RG's responding to 1577 questionnaire in this 510-page volume. The introduction gives erudite review of literature on Central America, and reproduces many valuable ethnohistorical sources.

1916 Relaciones históricas de América. Primera mitad del siglo XVI. Bibliófilos Españoles. Madrid.

Ten documents, concerning trips and voyages, chiefly Panama, Nicaragua. No 1577 questionnaire RG's.

SMITH, BUCKINGHAM, copyist
1857 Relación de la provincia de Meztitlan [1579]. MS copy, 20 fols., photocopied by W. E. Gates. Gates copy in Tulane University.

Copied by Smith "from the XXXIXth vol. of the collection of Muñoz in the Royal Academy of History, Madrid: 29 March 1857" [Census, 66]. This item is mentioned in the W. E. Gates catalogs, 1924, Item 622, 1937, Item 506; 1940, p. 15. Has calendar wheel but no map.

SPAIN, MINISTERIO DE FOMENTO
See Jiménez de la Espada, 1881–97, 1965.

TAMAYO, JORGE L.
1949 Geografía general de México. 2 vols. Mexico, D.F.

RG map of Teozacoalco, 1: 48, and of Amoltepec, 1: 50, from Orozco y Berra Mapoteca 19th-century copies. [Census, 108, 108A.]

1950 Geografía de Oaxaca. Mexico.

RG map of Amoltepec, b/w, p. 11, from Orozco y Berra Mapoteca 19th-century copy. [Census, 108A.]

1962 Geografía general de México. 2d ed. *Instituto Mexicano de Investigaciones Económicas*. 4 vols. Mexico, D.F.

RG Map of Teozcoalco, 1: 52 [Census, 108], and Amoltepec, 1: 54 [Census, 108A].

—— AND RAMÓN ALCORTA G.
1941 Catálogo de la exposición de cartografía mexicana. PAIGH, Pub. 59. Mexico.

Brief and sometimes incorrect descriptions of RG maps in Orozco y Berra

390

Mapoteca, pp. 16–22. Include Mizquia-huala, Teozacoalco, Culhuacan, Cempo-ala, Amoltepec Atlixtac [Tetlistaca], Te-huantepec, on display for the Assembly of the Institute.

TEIXIDOR, FELIPE, comp. and ed.

1937 Cartas de Joaquín García Icazbal-ceta. Mexico, D.F.

Contain passing references to JGI col-lection of MS RG's; does not reveal de-tails of original acquisition.

TERNAUX COMPANS, HENRI

1840 Voyages, relations et mémoires originaux pour servir a l'histoire de la découverte de l'Amérique, 16: 293–331. Paris.

RG of Meztitlan, apparently from Muñoz collection copy, without map or calendar, translated into French. [Census, 66.]

THOMPSON, J. ERIC S.

1941 The missing illustrations of the Pomar Relación. *Carnegie Insti-tution of Washington, Notes on Middle American Archaeology and Ethnology,* no. 4. Washing-ton.

RG of Texcoco. Indicates that Ixtlilxo-chitl had either the original Pomar docu-ment, or a better copy than JGI found and published; emphasis on graphic ma-terials mentioned, and extant in Codex Ixtlilxochitl and Codex Veytia. [Cen-sus, 123.]

TLALOCAN

See Barlow, Robert H., and others, 1943.

TORRE VILLAR, ERNESTO DE LA, AND GRACE METCALF

1948 Las Relaciones Geográficas de la diócesis de Oaxaca, siglo XVI. *Bo-letín Archivo General de la Na-ción* 20: 71–130. Mexico.

A subject index to RG's published in PNE and RMEH.

TORRES DE MENDOZA, LUIS

See Pacheco, Joaquín F., and oth-ers, 1864–84.

TORRES LANZAS, PEDRO

1900 Relación descriptiva de los mapas, planos, etc. de México y Floridas, existentes en el Archivo General de Indias. 2 vols. Seville. Ab-breviation: TL.

In vol. 1 lists RG maps.

TOUSSAINT, MANUEL

1931 Tasco: su historia, sus monumen-tos . . . Mexico, D.F.

RG of Iguala, pp. 221–25, from JGI transcript. [Census, 53.]

1942 Patzcuaro. UNAM. Mexico, D.F.

Discussion of RG of Patzcuaro, p. 47. Reprints from León, 1889 (JGI hand-copy), RG, pp. 231–35, with related documents. [Census, 79.]

1948a Arte colonial en México. UNAM. Mexico, D.F.

RG map of Teutenango reproduced on p. 13, fig. 10, after PNE (?) [Census, 122.]

1948b La conquista de Pánuco. Colegio Nacional, Mexico, D.F.

In documentary appendices reproduces from DII, 9, the 1604 RG series for Panuco [Census, 310] (pp. 261–81); Tampico [Census, 312] (pp. 284–91); and Guachinango [Census, 304] (pp. 293–301).

1962 Arte colonial en México. 2d ed. UNAM, Instituto de Investigacio-nes Estéticas. Mexico, D.F.

RG map of Teutenango, pl. 11, after PNE (?). [Census, 122.]

1967 Colonial art in Mexico. Elizabeth Wilder Weismann, trans. and ed. Univ. Texas Press. Austin and London.

RG map of Teutenango reproduced on p. 13, fig. 10, after PNE (?) [Census, 122].

TOZZER, ALFRED M.

1941 Landa's Relación de las Cosas de Yucatan, edited with notes. *Pa-pers Peabody Museum of Archae-ology and Ethnology,* Harvard University, 18. Cambridge.

RG on Yucatan, by Gaspar Antonio Chi, translated, pp. 230–32; discussion of Chi, note 219 (pp. 44–46). [Census, 147.]

TRENS, MANUEL B.
1947 Historia de Veracruz. Tomo 2. Jalapa.

From Ramírez Cabañas, 1943, reproduces copy of Map 2 of Veracruz RG.

UHAGÓN Y GUARDAMINO, FRANCISCO RAFAEL DE [Marqués de Laurencino]
1896 Relaciones históricas de los siglos XVI y XVII. Bibliófilos Españoles. Madrid.

Various MSS, chiefly from Col. de Jesuítas, RAH, and BNM, dealing with Peninsular Spain; no RG's of 1577 questionnaire for America.

VARGAS REA, LUIS, ed.
1943–58

This editor has produced more than 500 titles, privately printed, in very limited editions, on poor paper, and with texts full of typographical errors. His series and subseries are the cataloger's nightmare, the bibliographer's horror, and the investigator's despair. Among his titles are numerous RG's, listed below chronologically. For earlier treatment of Vargas Rea publications, see Nunemaker, 1948.

1944–46 Papeles de Nueva España colecionados por Francisco del Paso y Troncoso. Segunda Serie, Geografía y Estadística. Tomo VII. Suplemento. BAH, 5 vols. Mexico, D.F. Cited: VR/PNE, 7 [volume: pages].

From FPT transcripts in MNA, VR issued the materials destined for PNE, 7, in 5 small volumes, continuously paginated. VR/PNE, 7/1 (1944); VR/PNE, 7/2 (1945); VR/PNE, 7/3 (1945); VR/PNE, 7/4 (1945); VR/PNE, 7/5 (1946). Included, PNE, 7/2: 47–64, is cédula of May 25, 1577, the Instruction and Memoria re RG's. The RG's published are as follows, all without maps, except Celaya and Yurirpundaro: ASUCHITLAN, 5: 7–50 [Census, 7]; CELAYA, 4: 115–23, [Census, 18]; Acambaro (CELAYA), 4: 124–46 (map fac-

ing p. 115) [Census, 18A]; Yurirpundaro (CELAYA), 4: 147–56 (map facing p. 146) [Census, 18B]; JILQUILPAN, 1: 29–45 [Census, 60]; Chocandaro (JILQUILPAN), 2: 65–74 [Census, 60A] 1 Tarecuato (JUILQUILPAN), 2: 75–84 [Census, 60B]; Perivan (JUILQUILPAN), 3: 85–98 [Census, 60C] TAIMEO, 3: 99–105 [Census, 93]; NECOLTAN, 3: 107–12 [Census, 72].

1947 Papeles de Nueva España coleccionados por Francisco del Paso y Troncoso. Segunda Serie, Geografía y Estadística. Tomo VIII. Relación de Minas [sic]. BAH, 6 vols. Mexico, D.F. Cited: VR/PNE, 8 [volume: pages].

From FPT transcripts in MNA, VR issued materials intended for PNE, 8, in 6 small volumes, generally paged continuously. No RG maps appear. The RG texts include the following: COMPOSTELA, 1: 11–32 [Census, 31]; FRESNILLO, 5: 263–336 (main RG and 5 supplementary accounts) [Census, 44]; NUCHISTLÁN, 1: 59–74 [Census, 75]; PONCITLAN, 4: 221–60 [Census, 82]; PURIFICACION, 2: 78–130 [Census, 84]; SAN MARTIN, 3: 135–85 [Census, 87]; XEREZ, 4: 192–219 [Census, 143]; XOCOTLAN, 1: 33–57 [Census, 144].

1951 Relaciones de los pueblos de la Provincia de Amula. Ameca. 2 vols. Mexico, D.F. Dec. 6.

RG, AMECA from FPT/MNA, leg. 99. [Census, 4.]

1952a Relaciones de los Pueblos de la Provincia de Amula. Zapotitlan. Mexico, D.F. Jan. 3.

RG, Zapotitlan (AMULA), from FPT/MNA, leg. 99. [Census, 5C.]

1952b Relaciones de los Pueblos de la Provincia de Amula. Tuscaquesco y Cusalapa. Mexico, D.F. Feb. 8.

From FPT/MNA, leg. 99, RG of Tuscaquero (AMULA) [Census, 5A], and of Cusalapa (AMULA) [Census, 5B].

1952c Relación de Quacoman. Anónimo

encontrado por don Francisco del Paso y Troncoso. BHM. Mexico, D.F. Dec. 20.

RG of Cuacolman (MOTINES), from FPT/MNA, leg. 3, exp. 94. [Census, 68A.]

1952d Relación de Maquili, Alimanci, Cuxquaquatla y Epatlan. Anónimo encontrado por don F. del Paso y Troncoso. BHM. Mexico, D.F. Dec. 27.

From FPT/MNA, leg. 3, exp. 94, RG for Maquili (MOTINES). [Census, 68B.]

1952e Relación de Tenamastlan. Mexico, D.F.

RG for TENAMAZTLAN. [Census, 105.]

1953 Relación de Maquili y otros pueblos. BHM. Mexico, D.F. Dec. 24.

Reissue of VR 1952d, with slightly altered title page.

1954 Relación de Cualcoman. BHM. Mexico, D.F. June 26.

Reissue of VR 1952c, with slightly altered title page.

1955 Relación de Santa Cruz Tequipa. Mexico, D.F. Dec. 30.

RG, IZTEPEC [Census, 59], apparently reprinted from Caso, 1928d; also RG, TETIQUIPA [Census, 120], reprinted from Gómez de Orozco, 1928a.

1956a Relación de los Pueblos: Cocau-·tepec, Teotzacualco y de Amoltepeque. Mexico, D.F. Feb. 4.

RG, Cozautepec (TETIQUIPA) [Census, 120A], apparently reprinted from Gómez de Orozco, 1928a; RG, TEOZA-COALCO [Census, 108] and Amoltepec (TEOZACOALCO) [Census, 108A], reprinted from Gómez de Orozco, 1927c.

1956b Descripción de la Villa del Espíritu Santo. Mexico, D.F. Feb. 18.

RG, COATZOCOALCO [Census, 30], reprinted from Caso, 1928c.

1956c Relación de Instlahuaca. Mexico, D.F. Aug. 17.

RG of JUSTLAVACA and Tecomastlauca (JUSTLAVACA) [Census, 61, 61A], reprinted from Caso, 1928a.

1956d Relación de Mistepeque. Mexico, D.F. Aug. 17.

RG, Mistepec (JUSTLAVACA) [Census, 61B] reprinted from Caso, 1928a.

1956e Relación de Aysuchiquilazala Mexico, D.F. Aug. 17.

RG, Ayusuchiquilazala (JUSTLAVACA) [Census, 61C], reprinted from Caso, 1928a.

1956f Relación de Puebla de Xicalayan. Mexico, D.F. Aug. 17.

RG, Xicayan (JUSTLAVACA) [Census, 61D], reprinted from Caso, 1928a.

1956g Relación de Puctla y Relación de Culhuacan. Mexico, D.F. Aug. 17.

RG, Puctla (JUSTLAVACA) [Census, 61E], reprinted from Caso, 1928a. Also, RG, CULHUACAN [Census, 41], reprinted from Gómez de Orozco, 1927b.

1956h Relación de Zacatepec. Mexico, D.F. Aug. 17.

RG, Zacatepec (JUSTLAVACA) [Census, 61F], reprinted from Caso, 1928a.

1956i Relación de los Pueblos de Peñoles. Mexico, D.F. Aug. 24.

RG, PENOLES [Census, 80], reprinted from Caso, 1928a.

1956j Descripción de Atlatlauca. Mexico, D.F. Sept. 14.

RG, ATLATLAUCA [Census, 10], source unknown, but probably JGI/MNA transcript.

1956k Relación de Acapistla. Mexico, D.F.

RG, ACAPISTLA [Census, 1] from unknown source, but probably JGI/MNA transcript.

1957a Relación de Atenco, Misquiahuala. Mexico, D.F. May 17.

RG, ATENGO and its sub-cabecera, Misquiahuala [Census, 8, 8B], from unknown source, probably JGI/MNA transcripts. RG's from Teutlalpa and Tesontepec (both sub-cabeceras of ATENGO) not published.

1957b Relación de Iztapalapa. Mexico, D.F. Oct. 11.

RG, IXTAPALAPA [Census, 56] from unknown source, probably JGI/MNA transcript.

1957c Descripción de Antequera. Mexico, D.F.

RG, ANTEQUERA [Census, 6], from unknown source, probably JGI/MNA transcript.

1957d Relación de Teutitlán. Mexico, D.F.

RG, TEOTITLAN and sub-cabeceras [Census, 107], from unknown source, probably PNE.

1958 Descripción de Teguantepec. Mexico, D.F. Feb. 21.

RG, TEHUANTEPEC [Census, 102], probably reprinted from Caso, 1928b.

VÁZQUEZ, JOSEFINA ZORAIDA

1962 La imagen del indio en el español del siglo XVI. Universidad veracruzana. Xalapa.

Using extracts from Oviedo and materials from RG's provides Spanish view of natives of New Spain and Peru. Incorrectly states (p. 22) that "Relaciones Geográficas de la Nueva España se encuentra inéditas en la Biblioteca de la Real Academia de la Historia de Madrid, en el legajo 855 de su sala perteneciente a la Colección Muñoz." Chap. 3 (pp. 73–100) utilizes RG's (MSS, RAH) and JDE: "Basic themes" also use RG's (pp. 112–22). Appendix, pp. 159–68, includes Cédula, Memoria, May 25, 1577, from JDE, 1: cxiii–cxix.

VÁZQUEZ VÁZQUEZ, ELENA

1965 Distribución geográfica de las órdenes religiosas en la Nueva Espana [siglo XVI]. UNAM. Mexico, D.F.

Cover carries copy of RG pintura of Cuzcatlan, AGI version. [Catalog, 20.]

VELÁSQUEZ, PRIMO FELICIANO, ed.

1897 Colección de documentos para la historia de San Luis Potosí. 4 vols. San Luis Potosi.

RG of Queretaro, 1: 1–48. [Census, 86.]

VIÑAS Y MEY, CARMELO

1951 Las relaciones de Felipe II y su publicación. Estudios Geográficos (Spain), 42: 131–36.

Briefly outlines publication plans for 8 MS vols. of Escorial RG's of Spain (see Viñas y Mey and Paz, 1949–63), indicating that he expects to issue separately in the series a monographic study of the origins of the RG's. The article summarizes points he expects to elaborate. The study has not yet appeared.

—— AND RAMÓN PAZ, eds.

1949–63 Relaciones histórico-geográfico-estadísticas de los pueblos de España, hechas por iniciativa de Felipe II. 2 vols. (4 tomos) to date. Instituto Balmés de Sociología. Madrid.

Scholarly publication of the Spanish RG's. A continuing enterprise (see Viñas y Mey, 1951). Vol. 1, Madrid; vol. 2 (3 partes, each a separate tomo), Toledo; next scheduled are Cuenca and Guadalajara (Spain).

VIVÓ, JORGE A.

1942 Cotejos etnográficos. Las Relaciones Geográficas y una encuesta del Departamento de Asuntos Indígenas de México. Anales Instituto de Etnografía Americana, 3: 23–60. Mendoza, Argentina.

Reproduces 1577 questionnaire, comparing it with similar one produced in Mexico, 1939. Compares data for Huauhtla de Jiménez, Oax., from each. [Census, 107B.]

WAGNER, HENRY R.

1944 The rise of Fernando Cortés. Cortés Society, Documents and Narratives concerning the Discovery *and Conquest of America*, n.s., 3. Los Angeles.

RG map 1 of Vera Cruz, pl. 6 [Census, 140.]

ZARCO CUEVAS, EUSEBIO JULIÁN

1927 Relaciones de pueblos del obispado de Cuenca, hechas por orden Felipe II. 2 vols. Cuenca, Spain.

From Escorial original, reproduces texts (vol. 1), with discussion and analytical indexes (vol. 2). Reproduces 1575 and 1578 questionnaires (2: 345–57), and briefly mentions other Spanish series of 1621, 1634, 1712 (1: xxii).

ZAVALA, SILVIO

1938 Francisco del Paso y Troncoso: su misión en Europa, 1892–1916. Mexico, D.F.

List of JGI RG's known to FPT, pp. 43–49; list of maps published by FPT, pp. 601–04, with notes by Zavala.

10. The Relaciones Geográficas of Mexico and Central America, 1740–1792

ROBERT C. WEST

Dᴜʀɪɴɢ ᴛʜᴇ 18ᴛʜ ᴄᴇɴᴛᴜʀʏ, the Spanish Crown made several attempts to revive the tradition of the 1578–89 Geographical Relations that so well described the lands and peoples of New Spain and other parts of its American possessions a half-century after European conquest and settlement.[1] Yet, despite the positive influence that the Bourbon kings exerted on administrative, economic, and intellectual reforms both at home and in the colonies, the various geographical surveys carried out in New Spain during the 18th century rarely measured up to those of the 16th in areal and topical coverage, quality, or usefulness. Nonetheless, the 18th-century relations contain sufficient basic geographical and anthropological information to make their study worthwhile. Moreover, they describe many areas, especially in central and southern Mexico, that were covered 150 to 200 years earlier by the 16th-century survey. The 16th- and 18th century RG's thus afford comparative data for two widely separated periods. On the other hand, the 18th-century descriptions are today little known and rarely used by scholars; comparatively few have been published; many of the various surveys are fragmentary in geographical coverage; and the extant original documents or copies thereof lie scattered in many archives and libraries in Europe, Mexico, and Central America.[2] Fortunately, within

[1] I wish to acknowledge the valuable aid that Dr. Howard F. Cline, Dr. Adele Kibre, and Mr. Peter Gerhard have given me in the preparation of this article. Through Dr. Cline and by personal communication, Mr. Gerhard furnished abundant basic data on the 18th-century geographical relations obtained from the Archivo General de Indias, Seville; the Archivo General de la Nación, Mexico City; and the Bibliothèque Nationale, Paris. Mr. Gerhard aided me especially with the various complex relations of the late 18th century, found in the Mexico City archives. The colonial political boundaries shown on the accompanying maps were taken from charts prepared by Mr. Gerhard. Dr. Kibre, again through Dr. Cline, was most helpful in obtaining typescripts, photographs, and microfilm of key documents from the Archivo General De Indias. I am grateful to the Council on Research, Louisiana State University, for a grant-in-aid that enabled me to consult documents for this study in various archives and libraries in Mexico City.

[2] Designations of the various archival and library repositories mentioned herein are listed in "Abbreviations" at the front of this volume.

396

TABLE 1—SUMMARY OF 18TH-CENTURY RELACIONES GEOGRÁFICAS FOR MEXICO AND CENTRAL AMERICA

Date (range of submittal date)	Agency and/or Main Personality Involved In Survey	Repository of MS Original or Unique Copy	Number of RC's Known To Be Extant	Number of RC's Known To Be Published	Administrative Unit Covered by RG	Geographical Coverage
			Major Surveys			
1743–46	Crown; José Antonio Villaseñor y Sánchez	AGI, AGG	87	3	Alcaldía Mayor	Central and southern Mexico (Nueva España); Central America
1777–78	Crown; Antonio de Ulloa	BNMA, BNP, BNMex, UTX	132	40	Curacy	Spotty; best coverage: Oaxaca, Nayarit, northwestern Mexico
1789–92	Crown; Gazeta de México	BNMA, AGN	26	8	Alcaldía Mayor, Curacy	Spotty; chiefly central Mexico
			Minor Surveys			
1740–41	Crown; Pedro Rivera	AGG, ANCR	14	7	Alcaldía Mayor	Central America
1754	Tribunal del Santo Oficio de la Inquisición	AGN	43	1	Comisaría Regional	Spotty; chiefly central Mexico; northern Central America
1772–79	Crown; Eusebio Sánchez Pareja, gov. of Nueva Galicia	AGI	23 (?)	none	Alcaldía Mayor	Western Mexico (Nueva Galicia)
1788–89	("Revenue Series") Intendant Governor and treasury officials	AGI	27 (lists)	none	Alcaldía Mayor (subdelegación)	Intendancy of Guadalajara
1788–89	("Indian Pueblo Series") José Antonio Calderon	AGN	9	1	Alcaldía Mayor (subdelegación) or portions thereof	Parts of Intendency of Valladolid (present state of Michoacan)
1791*	Crown; Antonio de Pineda y Ramírez	ACM	?	?	?	Mexico
1791–94	("Padrones Series") Viceroy Conde de Revilla Gigedo II	AGN	72 (lists and RG's)	none	Alcaldía Mayor (subdelegación)	Spotty; chiefly central Mexico
1792–94	("Toponym Series") Viceroy Conde de Revilla Gigedo II	AGN, UTX	95 (lists and RG's)	none	Alcaldía Mayor (subdelegación)	Spotty; chiefly central and western Mexico

* The 1791 Pineda relations are mentioned by Wilson (1963), who, unfortunately, does not give the number of RG's extant or their coverage. I have not examined the Pineda collection in the Archivo Central de la Marina, Museo Naval, Madrid.

the last few years, photocopies of many of these documents have been acquired by the Hispanic Foundation, Library of Congress, Washington, D.C., where they are now readily available for scholarly use.

In this article the treatment of each of the geographical surveys will follow in general the scheme used by Cline in Articles 5 and 8 of this volume: (1) administrative history of the survey; (2) the nature of the reports and their geographical coverage; (3) present repositories of the documents and their publication status. Appendices contain English translations of pertinent documents.

During the 18th century, the Spanish government initiated at least 11 different geographical surveys of all or parts of Mexico and Central America. These surveys are here classified as three major and eight minor ones. Some of their pertinent characteristics are given in Table 1. Discussion of each of the surveys follows.

RELACIONES GEOGRÁFICAS OF 1743–46

The first general attempt to gather geographical information on the Spanish colonies after the ineffectual surveys of the 17th century was not made until 1741. At that time Felipe V, the first of the enlightened Bourbon kings, had occupied the Spanish throne for more than 40 years. Until the mid-18th century, he and his Council of the Indies appear to have been abysmally ignorant even of the political divisions and jurisdictions within their American colonies (Rubio Mañé, 1946, p. 463; 1955, 1: 42). To rectify the lack of knowledge, on July 19, 1741, the king issued a royal cédula in which he frankly admitted the ignorance on the part of the royal officials in Spain of natural and human conditions within the colonies, and forthwith ordered the collection of geographical data from the viceroyalties of Mexico, Peru, and New Granada (Appendix A).[3] These data, to be collected by alcaldes mayores and their subordinates within their respective territorial jurisdictions, were to give information on the "names, numbers, and qualities of settlements," with special attention paid to missions and missionaries among the Indian inhabitants. In Mexico the viceroy Conde de Fuenclara, on December 22, 1742, acknowledged receipt of the RC and informed the king that he had commissioned the cleric and Royal Chronicler, Juan Sahagún de Arévalo, and the General Auditor of the Azogues (quicksilver) Office and Royal Cosmographer of New Spain, José Antonio Villaseñor y Sánchez, to compile a questionnaire as a basis for the geographical survey. The questionnaire was to be dispatched to officials within all alcaldías majores and corregimientos of New Spain, the answers collected, and from them the two men were to formulate a succinct descriptive summary of the viceroyalty for the use of the king and the Council of the Indies (AGN, Reales Cédulas 61, exp. 60, fol. 229v). As Sahagún de Arévalo was overburdened by his ecclesiastical and other duties, most of the work of assembling the RG's and reducing them to a presentable report fell to Villaseñor y Sánchez (González de Cossío, 1952). Thus, the results of the 1743–46 geographical survey formed the major source of raw material for the famous *Theatro Americano*, written by Villaseñor y Sánchez and published in two volumes (1746–48) in Mexico City. This work served as the "descriptive summary" of the geographical survey of the viceroyalty of Mexico that had been requested by the king in 1741.[4]

[3] Printed copies of this Real Cédula are extant in AGI, Indiferente de Nueva España 107, fols. 103–103v and in AGN, Reales Cédulas 61, exp. 60, fols. 228–229. See discussion of a possible 18th-century precursor to the survey ordered in 1741, p. 423 below.

[4] The complete title of the work is *Theatro Americano, descripción general de los reynos y provincias de la Nueva-España, y sus jurisdicciones.* Volume 1 appeared in 1746, volume 2 in 1748. The description of New Spain presented therein is organized by bishoprics. This work is sometimes said to be the best general description of Mexico during

Questionnaire

The questionnaire that Sahugún de Aré-valo and Villaseñor formulated left much to be desired (Appendix B). It is in no way comparable to the comprehensive 50-point instruction of 1577. It consists of some dozen unnumbered, ambiguously worded points to be covered in the reports made by the alcaldes mayores or other local officials. These points include such things as location of settlements in relation to the local administrative seat and to Mexico City; natural conditions (chiefly climate); number of people: Spaniards, Indians, and other castes; the products of the area; its commerce and the decline thereof and reasons therefore and the best ways to increase it; minerals and nature of mineral deposits of the area; number of priests administering the area; the nature and origin of miraculous images with the church; status of the missions, the number of missionaries and their ability to speak Indian languages; need to establish new settlements in areas where there were great distances between present towns.

The printed questionnaire, signed by both Sahagún de Arévalo and Villaseñor, carries the date March 6, 1743. It can be assumed that soon thereafter these instructions were dispatched to the various local officials for answers.[5]

Replies

Like the RG's of the 16th century, those

the 18th century. In 1952, 500 copies of a facsimile edition of the original were published in Mexico City by the Editora Nacional, S.A. Volume 1 of this edition contains an informative introduction by Francisco González de Cossío. The original edition is rare, and during the colonial period its public distribution was curbed by the Spanish government. A royal cédula of October 30, 1748, prohibited its public sale and reserved its use for members of the Council of the Indies (AGN, Reales Cédulas 68, exp. 39, fols. 154–55).

[5] A printed copy of the questionnaire is in AGI, Indiferente de Nueva España 107, fols. 105–105v; copies are also frequently attached to the RG.

of the 1743–46 series are highly variable in length, structure, completeness, and utility. Nevertheless, in view of the poor quality of the questionnaire, some of the replies form surprisingly detailed and valuable descriptions of a given alcaldía mayor or corregimiento. All the structural arrangements of replies that Cline has tabulated for the 16th century RG's (simple, complex, compound) are found in the 1743–46 series. In addition, many of the replies consist of courtroom-type questions and answers taken from various witnesses chosen by the alcalde mayor. This arrangement has led to much repetition of data within a given report (e.g., Census 15, 17, 52, 67). The RG's vary in length from one folio page (Census, 16, Guajolotitlan in Oaxaca) to nearly 100 (Census 24, Igualapa in Guerrero). Information for two RG's (Census 18, 76) is in table form. Others include detailed population matrículas, or censuses of the settlements within the administrative unit. Especially valuable for the anthropologist are the RG's that enumerate the Indian population and the languages spoken within given communities. Nearly every RG gives valuable data on agricultural production and the prevailing commerce of the area; Indian crafts are often enumerated for each settlement. As might be expected, many of the replies go overboard on the question concerning miraculous images attached to the local church. Lack of numbered questions and the varying order of subject matter, however, make these RG's much less easy to use for comparative studies than those of the 16th century. Unfortunately, a few of the documents are badly damaged and some folio pages are unusable (especially Census, 14, 28).

Corpus and Geographical Coverage

Table 2 lists 87 of the 1743–46 RG's known to be extant. Only six were originally accompanied by maps, all of which Torres Lanzas (1900, vol. 2) describes. Two

TABLE 2—SUMMARY LISTING OF 1743–46 RELACIONES GEOGRÁFICAS

Alcaldía Mayor or Corregimiento	Bishopric	Date	Length (folio pages)	Repository	Modern State
1 Acapulco	Mexico & Tlaxcala	1743	66	AGI	Guerrero
2 Amula	Guadalajara	1743	2½	AGI	Jalisco
3 Antequera	Antequera	1746	2	AGI	Oaxaca
4 Autlan	Guadalajara	1743	7	AGI	Jalisco
5 Chalco	Mexico	1743	12	AGI	Mexico
6 Chilapa (with Acapulco MS)	Tlaxcala & Mexico	1743		AGI	Guerrero
7 Cholula (I)	Tlaxcala	1743	39	AGI	Puebla
7a Cholula (II)	Tlaxcala	1744	6½	AGI	Puebla
8 Colima	Michoacan	1744	8	AGI	Colima
9 Cordoba	Tlaxcala	1744	19	AGI	Veracruz
10 Cozamaloapan y Chinantla-Usila (I)	Antequera & Tlaxcala	1743	14	AGI	Veracruz
10a Cozamaloapan-Chinantla (II)	Antequera & Tlaxcala	1743	2	AGI	Veracruz
11 Cuatro Villas (Oaxaca) (with map)	Antequera	1743	10	AGI	Oaxaca
12 Cuautla-Amilpas (with map)	Mexico	1743	21	AGI	Morelos
13 Cuernavaca (with map)	Mexico	1743	13	AGI	Morelos
14 Cuitzeo de la Laguna	Michoacan	1743	6½	AGI	Michoacan
15 Guadalcazar (San Luis Potosi)	Michoacan	1743	7	AGI	San Luis Potosi
16 Guajolotitlan	Antequera	1745	1	AGI	Oaxaca
17 Guanajuato	Michoacan	1744	36	AGI	Guanajuato
18 Guatulco y Guamelula	Antequera	1745	(table)	AGI	Oaxaca
19 Guauchinango	Tlaxcala & Mexico	1743	4½	AGI	Puebla & Veracruz
20 Guaymeo y Zirandiro (I)	Michoacan	1743	45	AGI	Michoacan & Guerrero
20a Guaymeo y Zirandiro (II)	Michoacan	1743	3	AGI	Michoacan
21 Guazacualco	Antequera	1743	8½	AGI	Veracruz
22 Huejotzingo	Tlaxcala	1743	23	AGI	Puebla
23 Huejutla	Mexico	1743	11	AGI	Hidalgo
24 Igualapa	Tlaxcala & Antequera	1743	99	AGI	Guerrero
25 Ixmilquipan (*with map*)	Mexico	1743–44	57	AGI	Hidalgo
26 Izatlan y la Magdalena	Guadalajara	1744	7	AGI	Jalisco
27 Iztepexi	Antequera	1745	2	AGI	Oaxaca
28 Izucar	Tlaxcala	1743	4	AGI	Puebla

(*Table 2, continued*)

	Alcaldía Mayor or Corregimiento	Bishopric	Date	Length (folio pages)	Repository	Modern State
29	Justlahuaca	Antequera & Tlaxcala	1745	2½	AGI	Oaxaca
30	Leon (with map of Penjamo)	Michoacan	1743	8	AGI	Guanajuato
31	Lerma	Mexico	1743	20	AGI	Mexico
32	Malinalco	Mexico	1743	52	AGI	Mexico
33	Maravatio	Michoacan	1743	49	AGI	Michoacan
34	Mexicalzingo	Mexico	1743	5	AGI	Distrito Federal
35	Miahuatlan	Antequera	1745	4	AGI	Oaxaca
36	Michoacan (Valladolid) (with map)	Michoacan	1745	56	AGI	Michoacan
37	Nexapa	Antequera	n.d. (1743)	1½	AGI	Oaxaca
38	Nuevo Mexico	Durango	1744	10	AGI	
39	Orizaba	Tlaxcala	1743	8½	AGI	Veracruz
40	Panuco y Tampico	Mexico	1744	30	AGI	Tamaulipas
41	Papantla	Tlaxcala	1743	3	AGI	Veracruz
42	Puebla	Tlaxcala	1746	50	AGI	Puebla
43	Queretaro	Mexico	1743	47	AGI	Queretaro
44	San Luis de la Paz	Michoacan & Mexico	1743	68	AGI	Guanajuato
45	San Luis Potosi	Michoacan	1744	9	AGI	San Luis Potosi
46	Sayula	Guadalajara	1743	20	AGI	Jalisco
47	Sinaloa	Durango	n.d. (1743)	8	AGI	Sinaloa
48	Sochicoastlan	Mexico	1743	9	AGI	Hidalgo
49	Sombrerete	Durango	1746	5	AGI	Zacatecas
50	Tabasco	Yucatan	1743	15½	AGI	Tabasco
51	Tancitaro y Pinzandaro	Michoacan	1743	16	AGI	Michoacan
52	Tecali	Tlaxcala	1743	31	AGI	Puebla
53	Temascaltepec y Sultepec	Mexico	1744	30	AGI	Mexico
54	Teotlalco	Tlaxcala	1743	7	AGI	Puebla
55	Teotihuacan	Mexico	1743	18	AGI	Mexico
56	Teozacualco	Antequera	1745	1	AGI	Oaxaca
57	Tepeaca	Tlaxcala	1743	13½	AGI	Puebla
58	Teposcolula	Antequera	1745	7	AGI	Oaxaca
59	Tetela del Rio	Michoacan & Mexico	1743	91	AGI	Guerrero
60	Tetela del Volcan (I)	Mexico	1743	4½	AGI	Morelos
60a	Tetela del Volcan (II)	Mexico	1743	5	AGI	Morelos
61	Tetela y Jonotla	Tlaxcala	1743	9	AGI	Puebla
62	Texas	Guadalajara	1746	6	AGI	

Alcaldía Mayor or Corregimiento	Bishopric	Date	Length (folio pages)	Repository	Modern State
63 Tezcoco	Mexico	1744	14	AGI	Mexico & Tlaxcala
64 Teziutlan	Tlaxcala	1743	65	AGI	Puebla
65 Tistla (with Acapulco MS)	Mexico & Tlaxcala	1743		AGI	Guerrero
66 Tlapa	Tlaxcala	1743	10	AGI	Guerrero
67 Tlayacapa (Chalco)	Mexico	1743	3½	AGI	Morelos
68 Tlazazalca	Michoacan	1743	73	AGI	Michoacan
69 Tochimilco	Mexico	1743	6	AGI	Puebla
70 Toluca	Mexico	1743	30	AGI	Mexico
71 Valles	Mexico	1743	12	AGI	San Luis Potosi
72 Veracruz Nueva	Tlaxcala	1744	81	AGI	Veracruz
73 Villa Alta	Antequera	n.d. (1743)	3½	AGI	Oaxaca
74 Xacona y Zamora	Michoacan	1743	12	AGI	Michoacan
75 Xalapa de la Feria	Tlaxcala	1743	18	AGI	Veracruz
76 Xicayan	Antequera	n.d. (1743)	(table)	AGI	Oaxaca
77 Xiquilpan, Periban, y Tingüindin	Michoacan	1743	15	AGI	Michoacan
78 Zacatlan de las Manzanas	Tlaxcala	n.d. (1743)	12	AGI	Puebla
79 Zinagua y la Guacana	Michoacan	1744	13	AGl	Michoacan
80 Zumpango de la Laguna	Mexico	1743	7	AGI	Mexico
Captaincy of Guatemala (see fig. 5)					
9 Leon or Subtiaba	Leon	1743	?	AGG	Nicaragua
23 Tegucigalpa	Guatemala	1743	?	AGG	Honduras
24 Totonicapan	Guatemala	1743	?	AGG	Guatemala

of the RG's (Census, 6, 65) represent AM's that are included in the Acapulco report (Census, 1). Several AM's are represented by two separate reports of different dates (Census, 7a, 10a, 20a, 60a).

Although the RC of 1741 ordered geographical surveys to be made in the viceroyalties of Peru and New Granada, I am unaware of the existence of RG's from areas outside Mexico and the captaincy-general of Guatemala for this period. The 1741 RC, however, was definitely received in Peru, but, according to a letter written in the Council of the Indies May 11, 1750, at that time none of the RG's from the viceroyalty

had been received in Spain (González de Cossío, 1952, p. vi).[6]

From the captaincy of Guatemala I know of only three extant RG's that stemmed from the RC of 1741; they are here classed as part of the 1743–46 series. Dated 1743, they cover the AM's of Leon or Subtiaba

[6] Close approximations to the 1743–46 RG's for South America are (1) *Relación del estado político y militar de las provincias, ciudades, villas y lugares de la Audiencia de Quito dada por su Presidente el Marqués de Selva-alegre al Virrey de Nueva Granada en 1754*, published in Pardo y Barreda (1905); (2) *Relaciones Geográficas de la Gobernación de Venezuela, 1767–68*, the originals of which are in ACM (MSS 574, 564, 566) and were published by Altolaguirre in 1908.

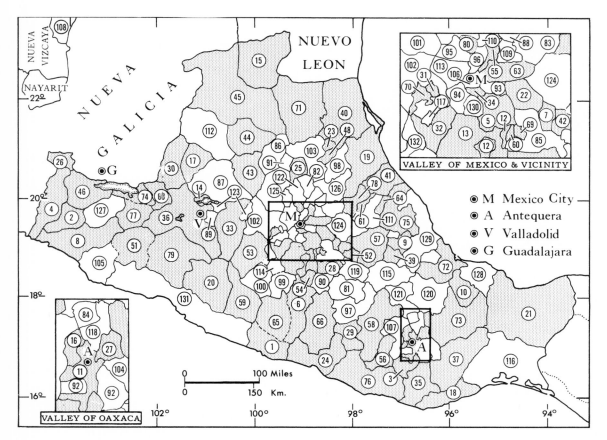

Fig. 1—DISTRIBUTION OF 1743–46 RG'S IN MEXICO
Alcaldías Mayores for which RG's exist are shaded. Numbers refer to places listed in Tables 2 and 3.

(Nicaragua), Tegucigalpa (Honduras), and Totonicapan (Guatemala). Apparently they are based on a questionnaire different from that used in Mexico.

The 1743–46 RG's for the viceroyalty of Mexico cover mainly the political area known as New Spain (fig. 1). Only five reports fall outside this area. These include Sombrerete (the only AM represented in Nueva Galicia), Tabasco, Nuevo Mexico, Texas, and Sinaloa (which includes reports on the provinces of Chametla, Maloya, Copala, Culiacan, Sinaloa, Ostimuri, and Sonora), or much of northwestern Mexico. In his *Theatro Americano* Villaseñor y Sánchez treats the entire viceroyalty of Mexico, save most of the bishopric of Yucatan. Thus, either the remaining RG's of the areas included within the jurisdictions of

Nueva Galicia, Nueva Vizcaya, and Nuevo Leon have been lost, or they were never made and other source material was utilized by Villaseñor to complete his summary description.

Within the territorial jurisdiction of Nueva España, reports are lacking for 52 of the total of 130 alcaldías mayores and corregimientos in existence at the time of the survey. As figure 1 indicates, the major areas for which we have no or few RG's are (1) the Valley of Mexico and the surrounding Otomi-speaking area to the north within the present states of Hidalgo and Mexico; (2) the middle and upper Balsas, including much of the Mixteca Baja; and (3) the Costa Grande of Guerrero and Michoacan. Within Nueva España, the AM's that lack RG's are listed in Table 3.

403

Census No.	Alcaldía Mayor or Corregimiento	Bishopric	Modern State
81	Acatlan y Piastla	Tlaxcala	Puebla
82	Actopan	Mexico	Hidalgo
83	Apan y Tepeapulco	Mexico	Hidalgo
84	Atlatlauca	Antequera	Oaxaca
85	Atlixco	Tlaxcala	Puebla
86	Cadereyta	Mexico	Queretaro
87	Celaya	Michoacan	Guanajuato
88	Cempoala	Mexico	Hidalgo
89	Charo	Michoacan	Michoacan
90	Chiautla de la Sal	Tlaxcala	Puebla
91	Cimapan	Mexico	Hidalgo
92	Cimatlan y Chichicapa	Antequera	Oaxaca
93	Coatepec	Mexico	Mexico
94	Coyoacan	Mexico	Distrito Federal
95	Cuautitlan	Mexico	Mexico
96	Ecatepec, San Cristobal	Mexico	Mexico
97	Guaxuapa (Huajuapan)	Tlaxcala	Oaxaca
98	Guayacocotla	Mexico & Tlaxcala	Veracruz
99	Iguala	Mexico	Guerrero
100	Ixcuteupa	Mexico	Mexico
101	Jilotepec	Mexico	Mexico
102	Metepec	Mexico	Mexico
103	Meztitlan	Mexico	Hidalgo
104	Mitla y Tlacolula	Antequera	Oaxaca
105	Motines	Michoacan	Michoacan
106	Mexico City	Mexico	Distrito Federal
107	Nochistlan	Antequera	Oaxaca
108	Nombre de Dios	Durango	Durango
109	Otumba	Mexico	Hidalgo
110	Pachuca	Mexico	Hidalgo
111	San Juan de los Llanos	Tlaxcala	Puebla
112	San Miguel el Grande	Michoacan	Guanajuato
113	Tacuba	Mexico	Distrito Federal & Mexico
114	Taxco	Mexico	Guerrero
115	Tehuacan	Tlaxcala	Puebla
116	Tehuantepec	Antequera	Oaxaca
117	Tenango del Valle	Mexico	Mexico
118	Teocuicuilco	Antequera	Oaxaca
119	Tepeji de la Seda	Tlaxcala	Puebla
120	Teutila	Antequera	Oaxaca
121	Teutitlan del Camino	Antequera	Oaxaca
122	Tetepango Hueypostla	Mexico	Mexico & Hidalgo
123	Tlalpuxajua	Michoacan	Michoacan
124	Tlaxcala	Tlaxcala	Tlaxcala
125	Tula	Mexico	Hidalgo
126	Tulancingo	Mexico & Tlaxcala	Hidalgo
127	Tuspa	Michoacan	Jalisco
128	Tuxtla y Cotaxtla	Antequera & Tlaxcala	Veracruz
129	Veracruz Vieja	Tlaxcala	Veracruz
129a	Xalapa del Marques	Antequera	Oaxaca
130	Xochimilco	Mexico	Distrito Federal
131	Zacatula	Michoacan	Guerrero
132	Zacualpa	Mexico	Mexico

Repository

All the original manuscripts of the known Mexican 1743–46 RG's are found in the AGI, where they are filed in two legajos (Indiferente de Nueva España 107, 108) in the form of five bound volumes. The disposition of these documents has an interesting history. While he was viceroy of Mexico (1746–55), the first Conde de Revillagigedo apparently acquired the documents as part of his personal library. This was shipped to Spain, where it was eventually broken up and sold at auction by his heirs. Six bound volumes which contained the geographical reports and other documents fell into the hands of a Madrileño bookdealer, one Elias Ranz. In 1800 officials of the Council of the Indies got wind of the existence of these documents on sale in the Ranz collection, and, fearing that such detailed descriptions of the colonies might fall into foreign hands, purchased the set for the Council's secretarial archive. As part of the official records of the Council of the Indies, these documents were later sent to the Archivo de Indias in Seville.[7]

Volume six of the original collection, which, among other documents, contained a lengthy treatise on schemes for the draining of the Valley of Mexico, has either been misplaced or lost. The few maps that once accompanied the RG's have been removed from the volumes and placed in AGI, Mapas y Planos de México. Only one RG of this series from Mexico has been published: that of Cuernavaca (1909).[8]

The original documents of the three RG's from the captaincy of Guatemala are in the AGG (Guatemala City) and two of these have been published in the *Boletín* of that archive (vol. 1 [1935], pp. 25–26 [Totonicapan]; pp. 29–39 [Tegucigalpa]). The RG's of the remaining minor political divisions of the captaincy are either lost or are perhaps in some of the local archives of Central America or in some unknown ramo of the AGI.

Summary

Despite incomplete geographical coverage and irregular quality, the 1743–46 RG's form a valuable corpus of descriptive material that is little known and apparently unused by modern scholars. It is a pity that Sahagún de Arévalo and Villaseñor y Sánchez did not have before them a copy of the 16th-century questionnaire that was so effectively used more than 160 years previously. Nonetheless, the more useful documents of this series deserve publication.

RELACIONES GEOGRÁFICAS OF 1777–78

About 30 years after the publication of Villaseñor's *Theatro Americano*, the second major 18th-century geographical survey of New Spain was undertaken during the reign of the ablest of the Bourbon kings, Carlos III. By that time, José de Gálvez had completed his general visitation of New Spain (1765–71), which resulted in fundamental administrative reforms in the colony, and the visitador had subsequently been appointed to the powerful position of Universal Minister of the Indies in Madrid. García Ruiz (1947, p. 349) suggested that Gálvez, cognizant of the need for precise geographical information on the colonies, was instrumental in starting the survey of 1777–78. In part this is true, but a more direct reason for its initiation appears to lie in the Crown's desire to expand the Gabinete Real de Historia Natural, a natural history museum established in Madrid by Carlos III in 1771 (Murray, 1904, 3: 5).

Throughout western Europe, and espe-

[7] This information was extracted from typescript copies of correspondence concerning the negotiations for purchase of the documents, which is found in the first bound volume of leg. 107. The material was kindly copied by Dr. Adele Kibre.

[8] This appeared in the obscure and not easily available journal, *Boletín Oficial y Revista Eclesiástica del Obispado de Cuernavaca*, año X, pp. 451–56, 469–78 (Cuernavaca, 1909).

cially in France, the last half of the 18th century saw a rapid advance in the natural and physical sciences. During this period scientific expeditions sent out by various countries returned with shiploads of mineral, plant, animal, and ethnographic specimens. On the basis of these collections a rash of natural history museums broke out in western Europe after 1750. In Madrid, Fernando IV established the Gabinete Real de Historia Natural de las Minas in 1752, and through a royal order called for the collection of mineral specimens from mines in all of the American colonies (AGN, Bandos y Ordenanzas 4, exp. 28). It is not known how faithfully the colonial officials fulfilled this order, but with the material received and that later purchased from other sources, Spain acquired one of the best mineralogical collections in Europe (Ferrer del Río, 1856, 4: 495).

With the founding of the new Gabinete de Historia Natural in 1771, Carlos III wished to expand the collection to include not only mineralogical specimens, but also plant, animal, and ethnographic materials. Accordingly, a royal order issued May 10, 1776, and signed by José de Gálvez, requested the collection of such objects from all parts of the overseas possessions and their dispatch to the Gabinete in Madrid. The order was accompanied by a detailed 24-page printed instruction on what materials to collect and how to prepare them for shipment to Spain (AGN, Reales Cédulas 107, exp. 106, fols. 383–383v; Bandos y Ordenanzas 9, exp. 27, fols. 231–242v).[9]

Closely following these instructions, on October 20, 1776, the Ministro Universal de Indias, José de Gálvez, issued a second royal order that requested the collection of data from New Spain on ". . . the aspects of Geography, Physics [meaning chiefly weather and climate], Antiquities, Mineralogy and Metallurgy," for the Gabinete de Historia Natural (AGI, Indiferente 1549). The data that resulted from this request formed the 1777–78 RG's with which we

are now concerned. To formulate a questionnaire and to supervise this survey, the king, through José de Gálvez, selected Antonio de Ulloa, who was then rear admiral of the fleet at Veracruz and had previously won fame from his *Noticias Secretas* (coauthored with Jorge Juan), the renowned exposé of administrative irregularities in Peru. In addition to his engineering and naval abilities, Ulloa was a respectable natural scientist, having published several notable geographical treatises on the Americas.[10] He may have had a hand in the establishment of the Gabinete de Historia Natural in Madrid (Ballesteros y Beretta, 1918–41, 6: 343; Whitaker, 1935, p. 192).

Questionnaire

Antonio de Ulloa's wide experience in administration, mining economy, and natural history of the Spanish colonies made him a logical choice to supervise the 1777–78 geographical survey of New Spain. In January, 1777, he completed a long, detailed questionnaire of some 60 points, divided

[9] The instructions were divided into the following subjects: (1) minerals, (2) animals, (3) plants, (4) fossils, and (5) art objects (including samples of native dress, arms, agricultural instruments, furniture, idols, "and other things that the ancient Indians or other people used." Then follows an interesting section on the methods of preparing and preserving animal and plant specimens for shipment.

[10] Examples are the widely read *Relación histórica del viage a la América Meridional* (4 vols., Madrid, 1748) and *Noticias americanas: entretenimientos phísicos-históricos sobre la América Meridional y la Septentrional Oriental* . . . (Madrid, 1772). The latter is especially notable, since its organization apparently served as Ulloa's model in constructing the questionnaire for the 1777–78 survey. In 1785 he wrote "Descripción geográfica-física de una parte de la Nueva España" and, of unknown date, "Noticia y descripción de los paises que median entre la ciudad y puerto de Veracruz en el reino de Nueva España hasta los asientos de Minas de Guanajuato, Pachuca, y Real del Monte, de sus territorios, clima y producciones," neither of which was ever published. Copies of the latter work are in the Muñoz Collection, Real Academia de la Historia, Madrid, and in the University of Texas Library, Austin.

into seven parts (Appendix C): (1) *Geography* (distances of inhabited places from Mexico City and from the local administrative seat; methods of measuring distances; description of mountains, rivers, lakes); (2) *Physics* (temperatures; methods of measuring degree of frost; character of winds, storms, volcanoes); (3) *Natural History* (cultivated crops and domestic animals; wild plants and animals and their uses; mineral springs); (4) *Antiquities* (archaeological ruins; native Indian tools and weapons; idols formerly worshipped; old Indian graves; modern Indian dress); (5) *Mineralogy* (types of minerals present in mines; precious metals mined); (6) *Metallurgy* (fineness of metals refined; methods of refinement); (7) *Fossils and Shells* (types of fossils and shells found in mines and quarries).[11] Such an outline was familiar to Ulloa, for he used a similar one in writing his *Noticias Americanas* in 1772 (see note 10). Moreover, many of the points in the questionnaire paralleled those of the previous instructions for the acquisition of museum specimens. The difficulty of using Ulloa's questionnaire, however, lay not in its lack of clarity or logic, but in its length and complexity, especially in view of the untrained personnel who were to compile the answers. To explain methods of measuring as clearly as possible, Ulloa described quaint but effective ways of estimating distance in leagues by mule travel and of calculating the degree of frost by observing the thickness of ice formed on water bodies. The questionnaire was printed in Mexico City February 22, 1777, and bears the signature of Melchor de Peramas, secretary to the viceroy.

Replies

In contrast to the 1743–46 RG's, which were organized by alcaldías mayores, those of the 1777–78 series were by curacies or by mission settlements. Once Ulloa had compiled the questionnaire, the entire survey appears to have been handled by the clergy. It is not clear why the survey was conducted in this way. The prefaces to some RG's indicate that copies of the printed questionnaire were sent from Mexico City to the bishops of the various dioceses within the viceroyalty; the bishops in turn dispatched the forms to the priests in charge of the curacies and missions within the diocesan jurisdiction. Most of these RG's, then, are descriptions of relatively small areas. They were compiled and returned to Mexico City through the bishops during 1777 and 1778.

In their replies most of the priests followed closely the sevenfold organization of the questionnaire, but many of the points within each section were ignored or cursorily answered. The length of the reports vary from half a folio page to 57 folio pages; one (Census, 94) is in table form; although not specifically requested, maps accompany at least six RG's (Census, 25, 27, 39, 94, 109, 110; see Table 4). A frequent lament voiced by the priests was their inability to do justice to the questionnaire owing to ignorance of the natural history within their curacy. Only priests recently arrived in their area, however, could be excused on such grounds. In general, the reports of the missionaries in Nayarit and in the northwestern frontier areas are more complete and conscientiously done than those made by the regular clergy in the long-settled sections of central and southern Mexico.

The replies are consistently good on descriptions of native agriculture, of wild plants and animals, and, in mining areas, of minerals and metallurgy. They contain a wealth of data, for example, on the cochineal industry within the Mixteca of Oaxaca. They likewise afford much interesting information on 18th-century Indian dress, thanks to one of the questions listed under

[11] The printed questionnaire is in various archives: AGI, Mexico 1239; AGI, Indiferente 1549; AGN, Bandos y Ordenanzas 10, exp. 9: BNMex, MS 356 [1383], fols. 447–460v.

TABLE 4—SUMMARY LISTING 1777–78 RELACIONES GEOGRÁFICAS

	Curacy	Alcaldía Mayor	Bishopric	Date	Repository	Length (folio pages)	Publication Text	Publication Map	Modern State
1	Acatlan	Nexapa	Antequera	n.d.	BNMA	7	unpub	none	Oaxaca
2	Acatzingo	Tepeaca	Puebla	1777	BNMA	3½	unpub	none	Puebla
3	Amacueca	Sayula	Guadalajara	1778	BNP	3	unpub	none	Jalisco
4	Amatlan de Jora	Hostotipaquillo	Guadalajara	1777	BNMA	11	pub	none	Nayarit
5	Amusgos	Xicayan	Antequera	n.d.	BNMA	9	unpub	none	Oaxaca
6	Apoala	Teposcolula	Antequera	1777	BNMA	9	unpub	none	Oaxaca
7	Atoyac (San Pedro)	Xicayan	Antequera	1778	BNMA	4	unpub	none	Oaxaca
8	Atoyac	Sayula	Guadalajara	1778	BPEJ	4	pub	none	Jalisco
9	Atlatlacua	Oaxaca	Antequera	1777	BNMA	3	unpub	none	Oaxaca
10	Autlan	Autlan	Guadalajara	1777	BNMA	10½	pub	none	Jalisco
11	Ayapango	Chalco	Mexico	1777	BNMA	3	unpub	none	Mexico
12	Ayoquezco	Oaxaca	Antequera	1777	BNMA	3½	unpub	none	Oaxaca
13	Bacerac	Sonora	Durango	1777	BNP	2	unpub	none	Sonora
13a	Bacerac	Sonora	Durango	1777	BNMex	57	pub	none	Sonora
14	Bacoachic	Cusihuiriachic	Durango	1778	BNMA	4½	unpub	none	Chihuahua
15	Baborigame	Batopilas	Durango	1777	BNP	1½	unpub	none	Chihuahua
16	Baroyeca	Ostimuri	Durango	1777	BNP	1½	unpub	none	Sonora
17	Basis	Basis	Durango	1778	BNMA	8½	unpub	none	Durango
18	Batopilillas	Cusihuiriachic	Durango	1778	BNMA	4½	unpub	none	Chihuahua
19	Capulhuac	Tenango del Valle	Mexico	n.d.	BNMA	3½	unpub	none	Mexico
20	Casas Viejas (Iturbide)	San Luis de la Paz	Mexico	1777	BNMA	7½	unpub	none	Guanajuato
21	Cerocahui	Batopilas	Durango	1777	BNMA	3½	pub	none	Chihuahua
22	Chacaltianguiz	Cosamaloapan	Antequera	1777	BNMA	11	unpub	none	Veracruz
23	Chalchihuites	Sombrerete	Durango	1777	BNMA	3½	pub	none	Zacatecas
24	Chapulco	Tehuacan	Puebla	1777	BNMA	6	unpub	none	Puebla
25	Charo	Charo	Michoacan	n.d.	BNMA	3½	pub	map,unpub	Michoacan
26	Chazumba	Guajuapan	Puebla	1778	BNMA	7	unpub	none	Oaxaca
27	Chicahuaxtla	Teposcolula	Antequera	1777	BNMA	9	pub	map,unpub	Oaxaca
28	Chicomezuchitl	Ixtepeji	Antequera	1777	BNMA	9	unpub	none	Oaxaca
29	Chiepetlan	Tlapan	Puebla	1777	BNMA	13½	pub	none	Guerrero
30	Chilapa	Teposcolula	Antequera	1777	BNMA	4½	unpub	none	Oaxaca
31	Chinameca	Coatzacoalcos	Antequera	1777	BNMA	7½	pub	none	Veracruz
32	Chinipas	Botopilas	Durango	1777	BNMA	5½	unpub	none	Chihuahua
33	Coatlan	Miahuatlan	Antequera	1777	BNMA	6½	unpub	none	Oaxaca
34	Cocula	Sayula	Guadalajara	1778	BNP	3½	unpub	none	Jalisco
35	Coixtlahuaca	Teposcolula	Antequera	1778	BNMA	14	unpub	none	Oaxaca
36	Comaltepec	Villa Alta	Antequera	1778	BNMA	5	unpub	none	Oaxaca
37	Coscatlan	Tehuacan	Puebla	1777	BNMA	8	unpub	none	Puebla

No.	Place	Jurisdiction	Diocese	Year	Archive	Leaves	Text	Map	State
38	Cuicatlan	Teotitlan del Camino	Antequera	1777	BNMA	4	unpub	none	Oaxaca
39	Cuilapa	Cuatro Villas	Antequera	n.d.	BNMA	3½	pub	pub	Oaxaca
40	Cuitzeo de la Laguna	Cuitzeo de la Laguna	Michoacan	1777	BNMA	4	pub	none	Michoacan
41	Cusihuiriachic	Cusihuiriachic	Durango	1778	BNMA	6½	unpub	none	Chihuahua
42	El Oro	El Oro	Durango	1777	BNP	1½	unpub	none	Durango
43	Elotepec	Nochistlan	Antequera	1777	BNMA	1½	unpub	none	Oaxaca
44	Eloxochitlan	Tehuacan	Puebla	1777	BNMA	4½	unpub	none	Puebla
45	Guadalcazar	San Luis Potosi	Michoacan	1778	BNMA	2½	unpub	none	San Luis Potosi
46	Guaguachic	Batopilas	Durango	1777	BNMA	13½	pub	none	Chihuahua
47	Guajolotitlan (San Pablo)	Guaxolotitlan	Antequera	1777	BNMA	3½	unpub	none	Oaxaca
48	Guajolotitlan (Santa Maria Asumpcion)	Xicayan	Antequera	n.d.	BNMA	4	unpub	none	Oaxaca
49	Guanajuato (Santa Ana)	Guanajuato	Michoacan	1778	BNMA	3½	unpub	none	Guanajuato
50	Guazapares	Batopilas	Durango	1777	BNMA	5	pub	none	Chihuahua
51	Guichicovi	Tehuantepec	Antequera	1777	BNMA	4½	unpub	none	Oaxaca
52	Huaximic	Hostotipaquillo	Guadalajara	1777	BNP	½	unpub	none	Nayarit
53	Huaynamota	Nayarit	Guadalajara	1777	BNP	1½	pub	none	Nayarit
54	Inde	Santa Maria del Oro	Durango	1777	BNMA	9½	unpub	none	Durango
55	Ixcatan	Nayarit	Guadalajara	1777	BNP	½	pub	none	Nayarit
56	Ixtapan de la Sal	Zacualpan	Mexico	1778	BNMA	3	unpub	none	Mexico
57	Ixtlahuacan	Colima	Michoacan	1778	BNMA	18	pub	none	Colima
58	Jalapa del Marques	Jalapa	Antequera	1777	BNMA	6	unpub	none	Oaxaca
59	Jalatlaco	Oaxaca	Antequera	1777	BNMA	7½	unpub	none	Oaxaca
60	Jaltepec	Nochistlan	Antequera	1777	BNMA	6	unpub	none	Oaxaca
61	Jamiltepec	Xicayan	Antequera	1777	BNMA	4	unpub	none	Oaxaca
62	Jesus Maria y Jose	Nayarit	Guadalajara	1777	BNP	3½	pub	none	Nayarit
62a	Suplemento to #62, Provincia de Nayarit	Nayarit	Guadalajara	1777	BNP	5	pub	none	Nayarit
63	Jilotepec	Nexapa	Antequera	1777	BNMA	3½	pub	none	Oaxaca
64	Jolalpan	Chiautla de la Sal	Puebla	1777	BNMA	2½	pub	none	Puebla
65	Justlahuaca	Justlahuaca	Antequera	1777	BNMA	9½	pub	none	Oaxaca
66	Lachixio	Oaxaca	Antequera	1777	BNMA	6½	unpub	none	Oaxaca
67	Lapaguia	Nexapa	Antequera	1777	BNMA	4½	unpub	none	Oaxaca
68	Malinalco	Malinalco	Mexico	n.d.	BNMA	1	unpub	none	Mexico
69	Mapimi	Cuencame	Durango	1777	BNP	½	unpub	none	Durango
70	Mazatepec	Cuernavaca	Mexico	1777	BNMA	6	unpub	none	Morelos

(*Table 4, continued*)

	Curacy	Alcaldía Mayor	Bishopric	Date	Repository	Length (folio pages)	Publication Text	Publication Map	Modern State
71	Mesa del Nayar (Mesa de Tonati)	Nayarit	Guadalajara	1777	BNP	½	pub	none	Nayarit
72	Miahuatlan	Miahuatlan	Antequera	1777	BNMA	5	unpub	none	Oaxaca
73	Mixtepec	Oaxaca	Antequera	1777	BNMA	5	unpub	none	Oaxaca
74	Moris	Cusihuiriachic	Durango	1778	BNMA	3½	unpub	none	Chihuahua
75	Nabogame	Batopilas	Durango	1777	BNMA	3½	unpub	none	Chihuahua
76	Nieves	Sombrerete	Durango	1777	BNMA	11	unpub	none	Zacatecas
77	Nombre de Dios	Nombre de Dios	Durango	1777	BNMA	9	pub	none	Durango
78	Oaxaca (Villa de)	Cuatro Villas	Antequera	1777	BNMA	6	unpub	none	Oaxaca
79	Papalo	Teotitlan del Camino	Antequera	1778	BNMA	1½	unpub	none	Oaxaca
80	Peyotan	Nayarit	Guadalajara	1777	BNP	½	pub	none	Nayarit
81	Piastla (San Ignacio)	Copala	Durango	1777	BNMA	2½	pub	none	Sinaloa
82	Pozos	San Luis de la Paz	Michoacan	1778	BNMA	2	unpub	none	Guanajuato
83	Pueblo Nuevo	Guarisamey	Durango	1777	BNP	2	unpub	none	Durango
84	Puruandiro	Valladolid	Michoacan	1778	BNMA	4½	pub	none	Michoacan
85	Puxmetecan	Villa Alta	Antequera	n.d.	BNMA	5½	unpub	none	Oaxaca
86	Quetzaltepec	Nexapa	Antequera	1777	BNMA	7½	unpub	none	Oaxaca
87	Quiatoni	Teotitlan del Valle	Antequera	1777	BNMA	3½	unpub	none	Oaxaca
88	Quiechapa	Nexapa	Antequera	1777	BNMA	14	unpub	none	Oaxaca
89	Quiegolani	Nexapa	Antequera	1777	BNMA	5	unpub	none	Oaxaca
90	Rio Chico	Ostimuri	Durango	1778	BNMA	8	unpub	none	Sonora
91	Rosario	Rosario	Durango	1778	BNMA	5	pub	none	Sinaloa
92	Rosario, El	Nayarit	Guadalajara	1777	BNP	½	pub	none	Nayarit
93	Sahuaripa	Sonora	Durango	1778	BPEJ	20	pub	none	Sonora
94	San Buenaventura	Chihuahua	Durango	1777	BNMA	7 (table illus.)	unpub	unpub	Chihuahua
95	San Francisco de los Huaves	Tehuantepec	Antequera	1777	BNMA	14	unpub	none	Oaxaca
96	San Miguel el Grande	San Miguel el Grande	Michoacan	1777	BNP	2½	pub	none	Guanajuato
97	San Miguel de las Bocas	El Oro	Durango	1777	BNMA	2	unpub	none	Durango
98	San Pedro del Gallo	Cuencame	Durango	1777	BNP	1	unpub	none	Durango
99	San Sebastian	Copala	Durango	1777	BNP	1½	unpub	none	Sinaloa
100	Santa Ana	Batopilas	Durango	1777	BNP	2½	unpub	none	Chihuahua

No.									
101	Santa Barbara	Santa Barbara	Durango	1777	BNP	1½	unpub	none	Chihuahua
102	Santa Eulalia	Chihuahua	Durango	1778	BNMA	11	pub	none	Chihuahua
103	Santa Lucia	Miahuatlan	Antequera	1777	BNMex	½	pub	none	Oaxaca
104	Santa Teresa	Nayarit	Guadalajara	1777	BNP	1½	pub	none	Nayarit
105	Sianori	Sianori	Durango	1777	BNP	1½	unpub	none	Durango
106	Sinaloa (Villa)	Sinaloa	Durango	1777	BNP	3½	unpub	none	Sinaloa
107	Tabaa	Villa Alta	Antequera	1778	BNMA	1½	unpub	none	Oaxaca
108	Tamazula	Sianori	Durango	1777	BNMA	4½	unpub	none	Durango
109	Tanetze	Villa Alta	Antequera	1777	BNMA	1½	unpub	unpub	Oaxaca
110	Tejupan	Teposcolula	Antequera	1777	BNMA	4½	unpub	unpub	Oaxaca
111	Teococuilco	Teococuilco	Antequera	1778	BNMA	4	pub	none	Oaxaca
112	Teotitlan del Valle	Teotitlan del Valle	Antequera	1777	BNMA	3½	unpub	none	Oaxaca
113	Teozacualco	Teozacualco	Antequera	1777	BNMA	6	unpub	none	Oaxaca
114	Tepalcaltepec	Nexapa	Antequera	1777	BNMex	13	pub	none	Oaxaca
115	Teticpac	Cimatlan	Antequera	1777	BNMA	2	unpub	none	Oaxaca
116	Tilcajete	Oaxaca	Antequera	1777	BNMA	6	unpub	none	Oaxaca
117	Tlajomulco	Tlajomulco	Guadalajara	1778	BPEJ	2½	pub	none	Jalisco
118	Tlalixtac	Oaxaca	Antequera	1777	BNMA	5	unpub	none	Oaxaca
119	Tlalnepantla	Chalco	Mexico	1777	BNMA	5½	unpub	none	Morelos
120	Tlalocozuatitlan	Chilapa	Puebla	1777	BNMA	2	pub	none	Guerrero
121	Tomochic	Cusihuiriachic	Durango	1777	BNMA	2½	pub	none	Chihuahua
122	Tonachic	Cienega de Olivos	Durango	1777	BNMA		pub	none	Chihuahua
123	Totolapa	Nexapan	Antequera	1778	BNMA	3½	unpub	none	Oaxaca
124	Tupares (San Miguel)	Batopilas	Durango	1778	BNP	½	unpub	none	Chihuahua
125	Tupares (Purisima Concepcion)	Batopilas	Durango	1777	BNP	2½	unpub	none	Chihuahua
126	Tutuaca	Cusihuiriachic	Durango	1777	BNMA	4½	pub	none	Chihuahua
127	Yagavita	Villa Alta	Antequera	1777	BNMA	5	unpub	none	Oaxaca
128	Yahuive	Villa Alta	Antequera	1777	BNMA	9½	unpub	none	Oaxaca
129	Zapotlan el Grande	Tuspa	Michoacan	1778	BNMA	5½	pub	none	Jalisco
130	Missions of Tarahumara Alta y Baja		Durango	n.d. (c. 1777)	AGN		unpub	none	Chihuahua, Sonora, Durango
131	Acayucan (AM) a. Acayucan b. Tenatitlan Chinameca c. Ocoapan d. Santiago Moloacan	Acayucan	Antequera	1777	UTX	7	unpub	none	Veracruz (S.E.) Tabasco (W.)

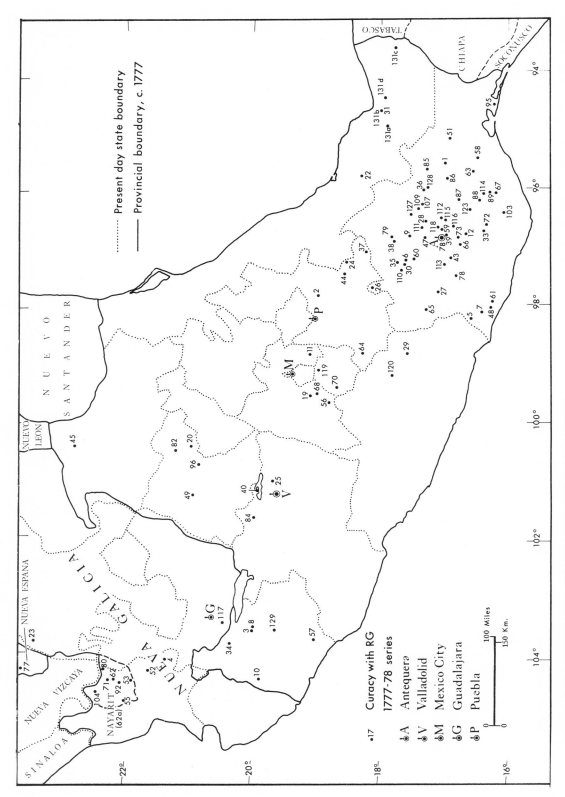

Fig. 2—DISTRIBUTION OF 1777–78 RG'S IN CENTRAL MEXICO
Numbers refer to places listed in Tables 4, 5, 6, and 7.

Antiquities. But there are few data on Indian population, aboriginal languages spoken, or dwelling types.

Corpus and Geographical Coverage

Of all the 18th-century geographical surveys of New Spain, the 1777–78 series contains the largest number of RG's (132 known originals or copies), is the best known by scholars, and has the largest number of published reports (40). Table 4 gives the general status of this set of documents. Nearly all the RG's in the table have been listed or cited in print during the present century. Although incomplete, the most extensive listings are those by Robert Barlow (1943, 1944c); others are listed in García Ruiz (1947), Núñez y Domínguez (1939), Carrera Stampa (1949), and Boban (1891).

As figures 2 and 3 indicate, the geographical coverage of the RG's is extremely irregular. Only two large areas are covered by a sizable number of reports: the bishopric of Oaxaca and northwestern Mexico, the latter encompassing mainly the mission settlements of the Alta and Baja Tarahumara within the bishopric of Durango. A third, but smaller, area that is well represented is the Huichol-Cora Indian redoubt of Nayarit (Nuevo Reino de Toledo), missionized by the Franciscans. The geographical pattern of the coverage is puzzling. Could the curacies and missions within other bishoprics have been described but the documents lost? Could the bishops of only the dioceses of Antequera and Durango have been diligent in supervising the survey within their respective jurisdictions? Was there insufficient viceregal authority behind the survey? Regardless of the causes, the poor geographical coverage of this survey is indeed disappointing to the modern researcher.

Since the geographical area of the curacies and mission settlements is small, the distribution of the places having RG's has been depicted on figures 2 and 3 by dots with respective census numbers given in Table 4. Each curacy contained an administrative seat (cabecera) and several subject towns, but most of the RG's describe the curacy as a whole. One report (Census, 131) covers four curacies within the AM of Acayucan (formerly Coatzacoalcos). There exist two generalized reports covering a large area in addition to the individual RG's on missions therein: that of the Tarahumara Alta (Census, 130) and that of the Provincia de Nayarit (Census, 62a).

Repositories

The present disposition of the originals and copies of the 1777–78 RG's is quite complex, as Table 5 indicates.

TABLE 5—PRESENT DISPOSITION OF THE ORIGINALS AND UNIQUE COPIES OF THE 1777–78 RELACIONES GEOGRÁFICAS

No. of RG's	Repository	MS Reference
99	BNMA	MSS 2449 and 2450
26	BNP	MSS Fonds Mexicains 201 and 202
3	BNMex	MS 1762
3	BPEJ	MS 50, vol. 3
1	AGN	Historia 72
1 (4)	UTX	WBS-320

Most of the extant original documents (99) are bound in two volumes in the Biblioteca Nacional de Madrid. I have been unable to trace the route by which these papers found their way to that repository. These originals have been copied several times and both manuscript and photographic copies are now in many libraries. During his extended stay in Europe at the end of the 19th century, Francisco del Paso y Troncoso (1842–1916) handcopied both volumes of the 1777–78 RG's in Madrid. These copies now form MSS 99 and 100 in the Archivo de Historia, Museo Nacional de Antropología, Mexico, D.F. The Madrid

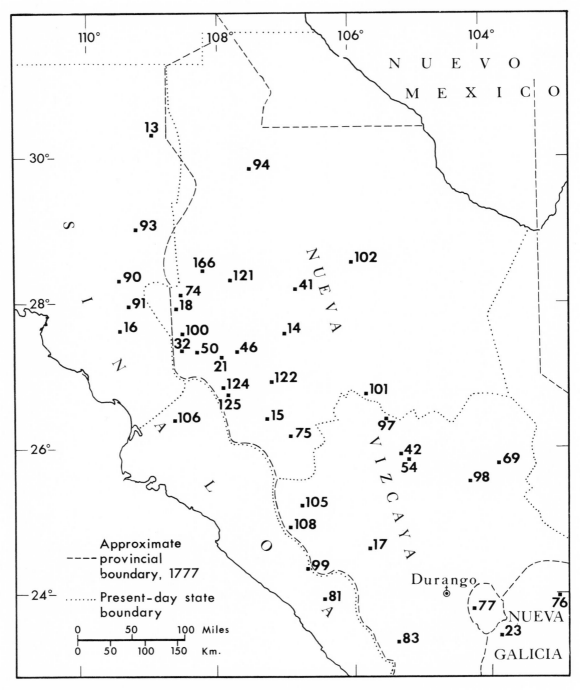

Fig. 3—DISTRIBUTION OF 1777–78 RG'S IN NORTHWESTERN MEXICO
Numbers refer to places listed in Tables 4, 5, 6, and 7.

TABLE 6—LISTING OF 1777–78 RELACIONES GEOGRÁFICAS IN BNP

Census No.	Curacy or Mission	Location of Original	Location of Other Copies
3	Amacueca	lost?	none
4	Amatlan de Jora	BNMA	AMNA
10	Autlan	BNMA	AMNA, BNMex
13a	Bacerac (abstract of no. 13)	——	(no. 13 in BNMex)
14	Bacoachic	BNMA	AMNA
15	Bagorigame	lost?	none
16	Baroyeca	lost?	none
17	Basis	BNMA	AMNA
18	Batopilillas	BNMA	AMNA
23	Chalchihuites	BNMA	AMNA
25	Charo	BNMA	AMNA
32	Chinipas	BNMA	AMNA
34	Cocula	lost?	none
40	Cuitzeo de la Laguna	BNMA	AMNA
41	Cusihuiriachic	BNMA	AMNA
42	El Oro (Santa Maria)	lost?	none
45	Guadalcazar	BNMA (incomplete)	AMNA (incomplete)
46	Guaguachic	BNMA	AMNA
49	Guanajuato	BNMA	AMNA
50	Guazapares	BNMA	AMNA
52	Huaximic	lost?	BNMex
53	Huanamota	lost?	none
55	Ixcatan	lost?	BNMex
57	Ixtlahuacan	BNMA	BNMex
62	Jesus Maria y Jose	lost?	AMNA
62a	Suplemento on Nayarit missions	lost?	BNMex
69	Mapimi	lost?	none
71	Mesa del Nayar	lost?	BNMex
74	Moris	BNMA	AMNA
75	Nabogame	BNMA	AMNA
76	Nieves	BNMA	AMNA
77	Nombre de Dios	lost?	BNMex
80	Peyotan	lost?	BNMex
81	Piastla	BNMA	AMNA
82	Pozos	BNMA	AMNA
83	Pueblo Nuevo	lost?	none
84	Puruandiro	BNMA	AMNA
90	Rio Chico	BNMA	AMNA
91	Rosario	BNMA	AMNA
92	Rosario, El	lost?	BNMex
94	San Buenaventura	BNMA	AMNA
96	San Miguel el Grande	lost?	BNMex
97	San Miguel de las Bocas	BNMA	AMNA
98	San Pedro del Gallo	lost?	none
99	San Sebastian	lost?	none
100	Santa Ana	lost?	none
101	Santa Barbara	lost?	none
102	Santa Eulalia	BNMA	AMNA
104	Santa Teresa	lost?	BNMex
105	Sianori	lost?	none
106	Sinaloa	lost?	none
108	Tamazula	BNMA	AMNA
121	Tomochic	BNMA	AMNA
122	Tonachic	BNMA	AMNA
124	Tupares (San Miguel)	lost?	none
125	Tupares (Purisima Concepcion)	lost?	none
126	Tutuaca	BNMA	AMNA
129	Zapotlan el Grande	BNMA	AMNA

TABLE 7—PUBLISHED RELACIONES GEOGRÁFICAS OF THE 1777–78 SURVEY

Census No.	Relacion Geográfica	Year of Publication	Publication	Editor
4	Amatlan de Jora	1945	San Juan Bautista de Amatlan de Xora	Vargas Rea
8	Atoyac	1878	Descripción . . . de la topografía del Curato y Pueblo de Atoyac. Noticias varias de Nueva Galicia pp. 170–82	
10	Autlan	1905	Bol. Biblio. Nac. México, 1 (10): 150–58	
		1945	Autlan	Vargas Rea
13	Bacerac	1905	Bol. Biblio. Nac. México, 1 (13): 198–208; 1 (14): 214–24; 2 (15): 231–34	
21	Cerocahui	1950	Sorocahui y otros pueblos	
		1953, 1954	Sorocahui y Tomochic	Vargas Rea
23	Chalchihuites	1945	Real de Minas del Señor San Pedro de los Chalchihuites	Vargas Rea
25	Charo	1945	Charo y pueblo de Santa Maria de Cuitzeo de la Laguna	Vargas Rea
		1946	La Relación Geográfica del Pueblo de Charo. An. Museo Michoacano, 4: 97–106	Antonio Arriaga
27	Chicahuaxtla	1905	Bol. Biblio. Nac. México, 2 (16): 235–56, 2 (17): 263	
29	Chiepetlan	1946	Memorias Acad. Mex. Historia, 3: 239–56	Barlow
31	Chinameca	1950, 1955	Relaciones de Chinameca	Vargas Rea
39	Cuilapan	1945	Dos relaciones antiguas del pueblo de Cuilapa, Oaxaca. Tlalocan, 2 (1): 18–28	Barlow
40	Cuitzeo de la Laguna	1945	Charo y el pueblo de Santa Maria de Cuitzeo de la Laguna	Vargas Rea
46	Guaguachic	1954	Misión de Guaguachic	Vargas Rea
50	Guazapares	1954	Descripción geografica de Guazapares	Vargas Rea
		1950	Guazapares y otros pueblos	Vargas Rea
53	Huaynamota	1905	Bol. Biblio. Nac. México, 1 (9): 138–41	
55	Ixcatan	1905	Bol. Biblio. Nac. México, 2 (18): 281–84	
57	Ixtlahuacan	1949	Iztlahuacán y sus pueblos	Vargas Rea
62	Jesus Maria y Jose (suplemento on Nayarit missions)	1905	Bol. Biblio. Nac. México, 2 (18): 284–88;	
		1906	2 (19–20): 303–04; 2 (21–22): 318–20; 2 (27–28): 350–52, 366–68	
63	Jilotepec	1950, 1954	Relación de Xilotepec	Vargas Rea
65	Justlahuaca	1950	Xustlahuacan	Vargas Rea
71	Mesa del Nayar	1905	Bol. Biblio. Nac. México, 1 (9): 136–38	
77	Nombre de Dios	1943	Nombre de Dios, Durango, pp. 73–80	Barlow Smisor
80	Peyotan	1905	Bol. Biblio. Nac. México, 1 (8): 122–25	

(*Table 7, continued*)

Census No.	Relacion Geográfica	Year of Publication	Publication	Editor
81	Piastla	1950	Piaxtla	Vargas Rea
84	Puruandiro	1945	Puruandiro y Urecho	Vargas Rea
91	Rosario	1945	El Rosario; Real de Minas del Señor San Pedro de los Chalchihuites	Vargas Rea
92	Rosario, El	1905	*Bol. Biblio. Nac. México*, 1 (8): 125–28	
93	Sahuaripa	1947	Real de Sahuaripa de 1778, *Memorias Acad. Mex. Historia*, 6: 60–89	Barlow
96	San Miguel el Grande	1905	*Bol. Biblio. Nac. México*, 1 (11): 167–79; 1 (12): 190–92	
		1950	San Miguel el Grande	Vargas Rea
102	Santa Eulalia	1950, 1954	Santa Eulalia Chihuahua	Vargas Rea
103	Santa Lucia	1905	*Bol. Biblio. Nac. México*, 2 (16): 250–53	
104	Santa Teresa	1905	*Bol. Biblio. Nac. México*, 2 (18): 279–80	
114	Tepalcaltepec	1905	*Bol. Biblio. Nac. México*, 2 (17): 263–68; 2 (18): 279	
111	Teococuilco	1950	Teocuilco [sic] *in* Ocuapan y otros pueblos	Vargas Rea
117	Tlajomulco	1878	Topografía del curato de Tlaxomulco . . . Noticias Varias de Nueva Galicia, pp. 183–224	
120	Tlalcozuatitlan	1947	*El México Antiguo*, 4: 383–91	
121	Tomochic	1950, 1954	Tomochic y otros pueblos	Vargas Rea
122	Tonachic	1950, 1954	Tonachic y otros pueblos. Descripción de Tonachic con sus anexos	Vargas Rea
126	Tutuaca	1954	Tutaca y otros pueblos	Vargas Rea
129	Zapotlan el Grande	1945	Zapotlan y Teguepespan	Vargas Rea

volumes also have been microfilmed, probably several times.[12]

The most celebrated copies of the original 1777–78 RG's are those that are now found in the Bibliothèque Nationale de Paris. Near the close of the 18th century, the Mexican scientist Antonio León y Gama (1735–1802) had copied those RG's of this series that pertained to northern Mexico, Nayarit, and Nueva Galicia (Cline, personal communication). These found their way into the Aubin-Goupil collection of Mexican manuscripts, which were later acquired by the Bibliothèque Nationale and now form MSS 201 and 202 of the Fonds Mexicains of that repository. León y Gama apparently copied a total of 54 original RG's, 26 of which are unique in that the originals have since disappeared from the Madrid collection. Moreover, some RG's that are now incomplete in the Madrid collection are found to be intact in the copied Paris document (e.g., the RG of Guadalcazar, Census, 45). A complete list of the Paris holdings is given in Table 6. MSS

[12] Sanford Mosk microfilmed them in 1934. His film is now deposited in the Geography Department, University of California, Berkeley. In 1956, R. C. West obtained microfilm of the same documents; this film is now in the Hispanic Foundation, Library of Congress, Washington, D.C.

417

201 and 202 have been microfilmed at least twice.[13]

Another collection of 13 handcopied 1777–78 RG's is found in the Biblioteca Nacional de México in the form of a small volume entitled *Noticias de Varias Misiones* (MS 1762). These consist of the Nayarit reports as well as the only known complete manuscript of the Bacerac (Sonora) RG, the longest (57 folio pages) and most detailed of the series. The collection contains two additional unique copies (Census, 103, 114). The BNMex RG's are listed in Table 7. All have been published (see next section).

Finally, three original RG's of this series are housed in the Biblioteca Pública del Estado de Jalisco (Census, 8, 93, 117); one original, a summary description of the Tarahumara Alta missions (Census, 130) occurs in the Archivo General de la Nación, Mexico City; and one covering four curacies in Acayucan AM is in The University of Texas Library, Austin. Possibly other 1777–78 RG's lie hidden in local archives in Mexico and in the Archivo General de Indias, Seville.

Published Relaciones Geográficas

Forty of the 1777–78 reports have been published, usually in quite obscure publications that are often more difficult to obtain than the original documents (Table 7). Most of the published RG's appear in the atrociously edited and poorly printed series of booklets issued by Vargas Rea of Mexico City during the past 20 years. All the Biblioteca Nacional RG holdings have appeared in that library's *Boletín* (vols. 1–3). Robert Barlow was responsible for the editing of four other published accounts (Census, 29, 39, 77, 93).

[13] In 1939 by José de Jesús Núñez y Domínguez, whose film is now deposited in the Biblioteca del Museo National de Antropología, México, D.F. (Carrera Stampa, 1949, p. 92); in 1965 for Peter Gerhard, the film now in the Library of Congress, Washington, D.C.

Summary

The spotty geographical coverage and the haphazard disposition of the extant documents of the 1777–78 series might indicate that the survey was a failure. Apparently insufficient territory was covered to make the results worthwhile for the needs of the Natural History Museum, for which they were originally intended. Nevertheless, the extant 1777–78 RG's contain a wealth of geographical and anthropological data that scholars working on Oaxaca, Nayarit, or northwestern Mexico can ill afford to overlook.

RELACIONES GEOGRÁFICAS OF 1789–92

The third major 18th-century geographical survey of New Spain took place between 1789 and 1792. Because many of these reports are bound with the 1777–78 series in the Madrid collection, they have often been confused with the latter (for example, see Barlow, 1943). The 1789–92 series consists of a disappointingly small collection of RG's; only 26 originals and copies are known to be extant, and the entire survey, like the 1777–78 one, appears to have been something less than successful (Table 8).

The history of the later series is closely related to the publication of the *Gazeta de México*, the semiofficial viceregal newspaper that ran from 1784 through 1809. Viceroy Matías de Gálvez suggested the founding of such a newspaper in Mexico City in imitation of that of Madrid and those of other European courts, and in 1783 issued an order to that effect, the publication to be under the editorship of the printer and literateur Manuel Antonio Valdés (AGN, Bandos y Ordenanzas 12, exp. 70, fol. 390). The first number of the *Gazeta* was printed in January, 1784. Royal approval of the project came from Madrid the following year, but with the proviso (suggested by the Minister of the Indies, José de Gálvez) that geographical descriptions of various

TABLE 8—SUMMARY LISTING OF 1789-92 RELACIONES GEOGRÁFICAS, GAZETA SERIES

Census No.	Political Area	Alcaldía Mayor	Bishopric	Date	Reposi-tory	Length	Publication Text	Publication Map	
1	Alahuistlan	Zacualpan	Mexico	1789	BNMA	2½	pub	none	Guerrero
2	Cadereyta	Cadereyta	Mexico	1789	AGN	4	unpub	unpub	Queretaro
3	Chilapa	Chilapa	Mexico & Tlaxala	1792	AGN	4	unpub	none	Guerrero
4	Colima (I)	Colima	Michoacan	1789	BNMA	33½	unpub	2 maps, unpub	Colima
5	Colima (II)	Colima	Michoacan	1787	BNMA	3	pub	none	Colima
6	Elotepec	Nochistlan	Antequera	1791	BNMA	1½	unpub	none	Oaxaca
7	Guauchinango	Guauchinango	Tlaxcala & Mexico	1791	BNMA	6½	unpub	none	Puebla
8	Huatulco y Huamelula	Huatulco y Huamelula	Antequera	1789	BNMA	5	unpub	none	Oaxaca
9	Igualapa	Igualapa	Antequera & Tlaxcala	1789	AGN	1	unpub	none	Guerrero
10	Isla del Carmen	?	Yucatan	1790	AGI	6	unpub	none	Campeche
11	Malinalco	Malinalco	Mexico	1791	BNMA	5	unpub	unpub	Mexico
12	Mexicalcingo	Mexicalcingo	Mexico	n.d.	BNMA	2	unpub	none	Distrito Federal
13	Montesclaros (El Fuerte)	Sinaloa	Sonora	n.d.	BNMA	11	unpub	unpub	Sonora
14	Motines del Oro	Motines	Michoacan	1791	BNMA	2	pub	none	Michoacan
15	Nochistlan	Nochistlan	Antequera	1791	BNMA	7	unpub	none	Oaxaca
16	Ocuapan	Acayucan	Antequera	1792	BNMA	5	pub	none	Tabasco
17	Santa Maria del Oro	Tequepespan	Guadalajara	1791	BNMA	1½	pub	unpub	Nayarit
18	Sayula	Sayula	Guadalajara	1791	BNMA	5½	pub	none	Jalisco
19	Teotitlan del Camino	Teotitlan del Camino	Antequera	n.d.	BNMA	3½	unpub	none	Oaxaca
20	Tetela	Tetela	Mexico	1791	BNMA	3	unpub	none	Puebla
21	Tlaxiaco	Teposcolula	Antequera	1791	BNMA	4	unpub	none	Oaxaca
22	Tochimilco (I)	Tochimilco	Mexico	1789	BNMA	13½	unpub	none	Puebla
23	Tochimilco (II)	Tochimilco	Mexico	1789	BNMA	4	unpub	none	Puebla
24	Urecho	Sinagua	Michoacan	1789	BNMA	3	pub	none	Michoacan
25	Yolotepec	Actopan	Mexico	1789	BNMA	1	unpub	none	Hidalgo
26	Zimapan	Zimapan	Mexico	1789	UTX	4	unpub	2 maps, unpub	Hidalgo

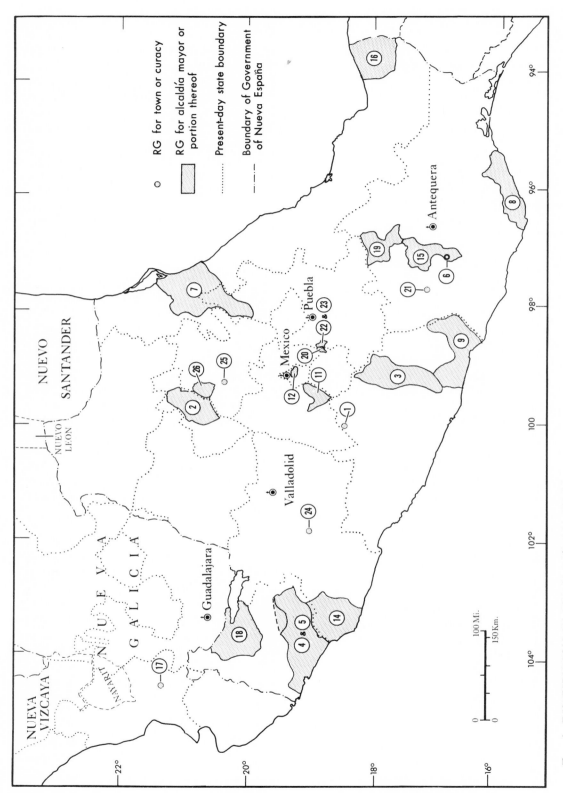

Fig. 4—DISTRIBUTION OF 1789-92 RG'S IN MEXICO
Numbers refer to places listed in Tables 8 and 9.

parts of the viceroyalty be published in the *Gazeta* from time to time (AGN, Reales Cédulas 130, exp. 41, February 4, 1785; Fisher, 1926, p. 237). To fulfill this royal order, in 1788, the new viceroy, Manuel Antonio Flores, commanded Valdés to compile a questionnaire to be sent to all "governors, intendants and other officials . . . for the formation of Notices on Geography and Civil and Natural History of the Kingdom of New Spain, which his Majesty wishes to be inserted and published in the *Gazeta* that is printed in the City of Mexico," the first reports to be published early in 1789 (AGN, Bandos y Ordenanzas 14, exp. 132). Once compiled, the questionnaire and accompanying instructions were dispatched to provincial authorities within alcaldías mayores and subdelegaciones of intendancies. A shortened version of the questionnaire was printed in the *Gazeta* (prologue, vol. 3, 1788).

But for reasons as yet unclear, none of these geographical relations was ever printed in the *Gazeta*. Apparently few reports were ever made or received in Mexico City. In 1791 viceroy Conde de Revilla Gigedo again urged the provincial authorities to send in their geographical reports, following the detailed instructions sent out three years previously (AGN, Bandos y Ordenanzas 16, exp. 19, fols. 31–31v). As late as 1802, Valdés printed in the *Gazeta* a letter he had written to viceroy José de Iturrigaray, lamenting the local officials' lack of cooperation in fulfilling the royal request for geographical reports (*Gazeta de México*, prologue, vol. 11, 1802–03). Here was a splendid opportunity lost for the compilation of a vast amount of geographical information on the viceroyalty.

Questionnaire (Appendix D)

The set of instructions that Valdés compiled consisted of 23 points, grouped under eight major headings (AGN, Bandos y Ordenanzas 14, exp. 133, fols. 406–09). These dealt with distance and direction of local places from Mexico City and from the capital of the diocese; the meaning of local place names and the number of settlements within minor civil divisions; the population in terms of race (Spaniards, Indians, and other castes) and their languages; the climate and other physical features of the area; the main products and manufactures; ecclesiastical units and settlements; natural resources (minerals, plants, animals); and travel facilities. The questionnaire was accompanied by an example of a hypothetical report with 11 additional explanatory notes. Little was left to the imagination of the local officials.

Replies

Like the RG's of previous surveys, the 1789–92 reports vary in length and quality. In length they range from one folio page (Census, 9, 25) to 33½ folio pages (Census, 4). That of Colima I (Census, 4) is rich in ethnographic detail. Nearly all RG's were written either in 1789 or 1791, the latter ones apparently in response to Revilla Gigedo's order. That of Colima II (Census, 5) is dated 1787 and may not belong to the series under discussion; that of Ocuapan (Census, 16) was compiled in 1792. Although the instruction specified that a map should accompany the reports, only six are so illustrated.

Geographical Coverage

Figure 4 shows the scattered distribution of the 1789–92 RG's. Most of the RG's cover alcaldías mayores or subdelegaciones de intendencias, a new minor civil division name introduced with the intendency system (1786); a few come from the much smaller curacies (Census, 1, 17, 21, 24, 25). In two cases (Census, 4 and 5; 22 and 23) two reports of different dates were made for the same place.

Repositories

Twenty-one of the RG's of this series are bound with those of 1777–78 in either

TABLE 9—PUBLISHED RELACIONES GEOGRÁFICAS OF THE 1789–92 SURVEY

Census No.	RG	Year of Publication	Publication	Editor
1	Alahuistlan	1946	La descripción de Alahuistlan, 1789. *Tlalocan*, 2 (2): 106–09	Barlow
5	Colima (II)	1946	Real de Santa Maria de Guadalupe de Tecalitan (Colima)	Vargas Rea
14	Motines del Oro	1945	Real de minas del Señor San Pedro de Chalchiuites; Motines del Oro	Vargas Rea
16	Ocuapan	1950	Ocuapan y otros pueblos	Vargas Rea
17	Santa Maria del Oro	1945	Zapotlan y Tequepespan	Vargas Rea
18	Sayula	1954	Provincia de Sayula	Vargas Rea
24	Urecho	1945	Puruandiro y Urecho	Vargas Rea

TABLE 10—SUMMARY LISTING OF EXTANT 1740–41 RELACIONES GEOGRÁFICAS FOR THE CAPTAINCY OF GUATEMALA*

Census No.	Political Division†	Bishopric	Date	Repository	Publication	Modern Country
3	Chiquimula (C)	Guatemala	1740	AGG	unpub	Guatemala
5	Costa Rica (P)	Leon	1741	AGG, ANCR	pub	Costa Rica
6	Escuintla (AM)	Guatemala	1740	AGG	pub	Guatemala
10	Matagalpa (C)	Leon	1740	AGG	unpub	Nicaragua
14	Quetzaltenango (AM)	Guatemala	1741	AGG	unpub	Guatemala
15	Realejo, El (villa y puerto)	Leon	1740	AGG	unpub	Nicaragua
17	San Salvador (AM)	Guatemala	1740	AGG	pub	El Salvador
18	Sebaco y Chontales (C)	Leon	1740	AGG	pub	Nicaragua
19	Soconusco (P)	Chiapa	1740	AGG	unpub	Mexico (Chiapas)
20	Solola (AM)	Guatemala	1740	AGG	pub	Guatemala
24	Totonicapan (AM) (Partido de Huehuetenango)	Guatemala	1740	AGG	pub	Guatemala
25	Valle de Guatemala (C)	Guatemala	1740	AGG	pub	Guatemala
26	Verapaz (AM)	Guatemala	1740	AGG	unpub	Guatemala
S	Salama (pueblo) (in Verapaz, AM)	Guatemala	1740	AGG	unpub	Guatemala

* Taken from *Indice de los documentos existentes en el Archivo General del Gobierno* (Guatemala City), 1 (n.d.): 267–68.

† C=Corregimiento; AM=Alcaldía Mayor; P=Province.

MSS 2449 or 2450 in the Biblioteca Nacional de Madrid. Three (Census, 2, 3, 9) occur in AGN, Historia 578-B; that of Isla del Carmen is in AGI, Indiferente 1527; that of Mexicalcingo in BNMA 20058; and that of Zimapan in UTX, G-248. Just how some found their way to Spain and got mixed with those of the earlier survey remains a mystery. The Paso y Troncoso copies of these papers are found in the 1777–78 series in AMNA, MSS 99 and 100. Likely, additional unidentified reports of the 1789–92 series may be scattered in some sections of the AGN. Seven of the extant

RG's have been published; they are listed in Table 9.

MINOR 18TH-CENTURY SURVEYS

The eight geographical surveys of Mexico and Central America that are here considered to be minor ones range in time from the earliest known series of the 18th century (1740–41) to the last one (1792–94). They are deemed minor because, variously, they applied to only a particular part of Mexico and Central America, or they were undertaken by an agency other than the Spanish Crown, or the limited range of data presented precludes their classification as true geographical relations.

Survey of Central America, 1740–41

This series of RG's may have been the forerunner of the major general geographical survey of 1743–46 described above. In an RC dated July 28, 1739, sent to Pedro Rivera, the captain-general of Guatemala, Felipe V ordered that the governors of the provinces

. . . remit a report of the greatest possible accuracy on the cities, villas, and towns that each Province contains, and what corregimientos and alcaldías mayores there are, their names and those of the towns within their respective jurisdictions, expressing by class, the number of inhabitants within each, Spaniards as well as mulattoes, mestizos, and Negroes; what fruits, harvests, gold and silver mines, manufactures that might be in said Provinces, and the distances from the capital, under whose jurisdiction they are found; the quality of the lands, the healthfulness and temperatures thereof, and anything else that might lead to an exact and prompt geographical relation. . . .[14]

This order resulted in geographical reports on a number of provinces, alcaldías mayores, corregimientos, partidos, and towns

[14] Taken from Rivera's instructions to the provincial governors (April 2, 1740), published in "Relación geográfica de la Provincia de San Salvador," *Boletín del Archivo General del Gobierno,* 2 (1936): 20–34. The disposition of the original RC is unknown.

within the captaincy of Guatemala during 1740 and 1741. The 14 RG's known to be extant are listed in Table 10 and their distribution is shown in figure 5. Half of them have been published in the *Boletín del Archivo del Gobierno* (Guatemala), volumes 1 (1935) and 2 (1936). The RC of 1739 may have been sent only to Guatemala as a trial run, for there appears to have been no RG's made for other parts of the colonies during 1740–41. If the survey was a test case, it appears to have been successful, for the RC of 1741 requesting similar reports from all the Spanish Americas followed shortly thereafter. Moreover, some of the RG's of the Central American series are even better in quality and coverage than many of those of 1743–46 on Mexico.

TABLE 11—SUMMARY LISTING OF MISSING 1740–41 RELACIONES GEOGRÁFICAS FOR CAPTAINCY OF GUATEMALA

Census No.	Political Division[*]	Modern Country
1	Chiapa (P)	Mexico
2	Chimaltenango (AM)	Guatemala
4	Comayagua	Honduras
7	Gracias a Dios	Honduras
8	Granada	Nicaragua
9	Leon (Subtiaba)	Nicaragua
11	Nicoya (C)	Costa Rica
12	Nueva Segovia	Nicaragua
13	Olancho	Honduras
16	San Pedro Sula	Honduras
21	Sonsonate (AM)	El Salvador
22	Suchitepeques (AM)	Guatemala
23	Tegucigalpa (AM)	Honduras
27	Yoro (partido)	Honduras

[*] C=Corregimiento; AM=Alcaldía Mayor; P=Province.

Survey by the Inquisition, 1754

The Holy Office of the Inquisition in Mexico occasionally issued circulars requesting various kinds of information from regional commissaries under its jurisdiction, which included the viceroyalty of New Spain and the captaincy-general of Guatemala. In 1754 the Office sent to its com-

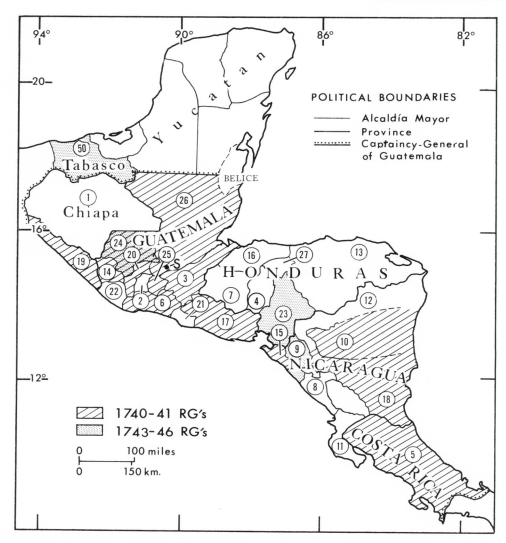

FIG. 5—DISTRIBUTION OF 1740–41 AND 1743–46 RG'S IN CAPTAINCY-GENERAL OF GUATEMALA AND SOUTHEASTERN MEXICO. Numbers and letters refer to places listed in Tables 10 and 11.

missaries an instruction that requested, among other things, data of a geographical nature: the names of settlements, their distances and directions from their respective administrative seats; population numbers and racial composition; brief description of the area. The instruction and extant replies are found in AGN, Inquisición 937, fols. 226–421. Table 12 lists the regional commissaries (which approximated the ex-

isting alcaldías mayores and corregimientos) for which there are reports. Most of these are short and contain little information of value to anthropologists or geographers. But some, such as that of Patzcuaro (Census, 19), Atlixco (4), and Tehuacan (31), give sufficient data on settlement and population to justify calling them true geographical relations. That of Patzcuaro is the sole RG of this series that has been

TABLE 12—SUMMARY LISTING OF 1754 RELACIONES GEOGRÁFICAS OF THE INQUISITION

Census No.	Comisario Regional	Length (folio pages)	Modern State
1	Acambaro	1	Guanajuato
2	Acayucan	6½	Veracruz
3	Agualulco	(w/Tabasco MS)	Veracruz, Tabasco
4	Atlixco	12	Puebla
5	Celaya	3½	Guanajuato
6	Ciudad Real	1	Chiapas
7	Cordoba	4	Veracruz
8	Chihuahua	1	Chihuahua
9	Cholula	1	Puebla
10	Durango	14	Durango
11	Guanajuato (map)	5	Guanajuato
12	Izucar	7	Puebla
13	La Piedad y Tlazazalca	1½	Guanajuato, Michoacan
14	Leon	1	Guanajuato
15	Mazapil	3½	Zacatecas
16	Oaxaca	2½	Oaxaca
17	Orizaba	2½	Veracruz
18	Pachuca (map)	4½	Hidalgo
19	Patzcuaro	16	Michoacan
20	Puebla	4½	Puebla
21	Queretaro	2½	Queretaro
22	Salamanca	6½	Guanajuato
23	Salvatierra	3	Guanajuato
24	San Juan Teotihuacan	1	Mexico
25	San Luis de la Paz	1	Guanajuato
26	San Miguel el Grande	1½	Guanajuato
27	Silao	1½	Guanajuato
28	Sombrerete	1½	Zacatecas
29	Sultepec	6½	Mexico
30	Tabasco	4½	Tabasco
31	Tehuacan	13	Puebla
32	Toluca	3	Mexico
	(10 fols. missing)		
33	Valladolid	1½	Michoacan
34	Veracruz	6½	Veracruz
35	Xalapa de la Feria	3	Veracruz
36	Zacatecas	2	Zacatecas
37	Zichu	1	Guanajuato

Captaincy-General of Guatemala

38	Chiquimula	—	Guatemala
39	Nicaragua	3½	Nicaragua
40	San Luis Xilotepeque	1	Guatemala
41	San Salvador	4	El Salvador
42	Santiago Esquipulas	4	Guatemala
43	San Vicente	6	El Salvador

published (Lemoine Villicaña, 1963). This series also includes reports on places within the captaincy of Guatemala.

TABLE 13—SUMMARY LISTING OF 1772–79 RELACIONES GEOGRÁFICAS FOR NUEVA GALICIA
(Based on map listings by Torres Lanzas, 1900)

Census No.	Cabecera of Alcaldía Mayor	Bishopric	Modern State
1	Acaponeta	Guadalajara	Nayarit
2	Aguacatlan	Guadalajara	Nayarit
4	La Barca	Michoacan & Guadalajara	Jalisco
6	Centipac	Guadalajara	Nayarit
8	Cuquio	Guadalajara	Jalisco
9	Charcas	Guadalajara	San Luis Potosi
12	Guauchinango	Guadalajara	Jalisco
14	Hostotipaquillo	Guadalajara	Jalisco
15	Jerez	Guadalajara	Zacatecas
17	Lagos	Guadalajara	Jalisco
18	Mazapil	Guadalajara	Zacatecas
19	Purificacion	Guadalajara	Jalisco
20	San Cristobal de la Barranca	Guadalajara	Jalisco
21	Sierra de Pinos	Guadalajara	Zacatecas
23	Tala	Guadalajara	Jalisco
25	Tepic	Guadalajara	Nayarit
26	Tequepespan	Guadalajara	Nayarit
27	Tequila	Guadalajara	Jalisco
28	Tlajomulco	Guadalajara	Jalisco
29	Tlaltenango	Guadalajara	Zacatecas
30	Tonala	Guadalajara	Jalisco

Alcaldías Mayores Not Represented by Maps
(according to Torres Lanzas' listing)

3	Aguascalientes	Guadalajara	Aguascalientes
5	Cajititlan	Guadalajara	Jalisco
7	Colotlan	Guadalajara	Jalisco
10	Fresnillo	Guadalajara	Zacatecas
11	Guadalajara	Guadalajara	Jalisco
13	Hostotipac	Guadalajara	Jalisco
16	Juchipila	Guadalajara	Zacatecas
22	Sombrerete	Durango	Zacatecas
24	Tecpatitlan	Guadalajara	Jalisco
31	Zacatecas	Guadalajara	Zacatecas

Survey of Nueva Galicia, 1772–79

According to Peter Gerhard, a set of geographical relations dated from 1772 to 1779 on various pueblos and curacies of Nueva Galicia exists in AGI, Guadalajara 348. These reports were accompanied by maps which have been placed in AGI, Mapas y Planos de Mexico, 279–299 and 339–345. The maps were listed by Torres Lanzas (1900, vol. 1), from whose data Table 13 was compiled. As I have not ex-

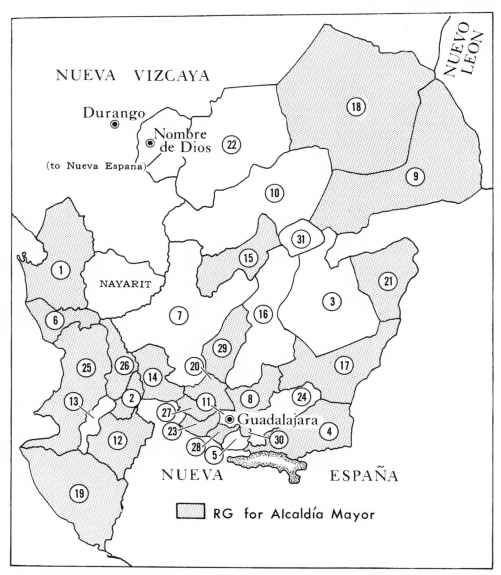

Fɪɢ. 6—DISTRIBUTION OF 1772–79 RG'S OF NUEVA GALICIA. Numbers refer to places listed in Table 13.

amined the AGI reports, the table may be faulty. The names listed refer to administrative seats (cabeceras) or sometimes curacies within an alcaldía mayor or corregimiento of the same name. Figure 6 was compiled from this listing, but, although an entire alcaldía mayor is shaded on the map, the associated RG does not necessarily cover the entire political area.

Torres Lanzas gave the title of the survey: "Plan de Curatos de la Diócesis de la Nueva Galicia," and quotes (1: 39) a lengthy title of a map, which reads to the effect that the survey ". . . was formed by Don Domingo Anastacio Ponce, by virtue of a mandate by the very Illustrious Regent and President, Governor and Captain General of this said Kingdom [of Nueva Ga-

426

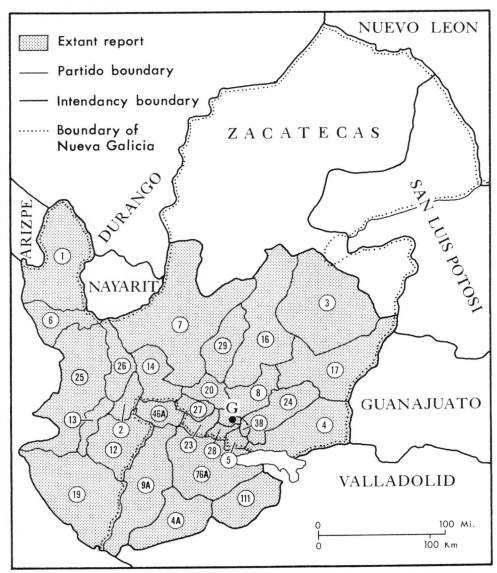

FIG. 7—DISTRIBUTION OF 1788–89 "REVENUE SERIES," GUADALAJARA INTEND-ANCY. Numbers refer to places listed on Table 14.

licia], Don Eusebio Sánchez Pareja, through consequence of the Royal Order of 21 January 1772. Guadalajara, June 1780."

From the Torres Lanzas listing I have arrived at 30 RG's of Nueva Galicia that had accompanying maps, whereas Gerhard states that only 23 are extant in AGI, Guadalajara 348. Evaluation of these seemingly valuable RG's awaits further study.

"Revenue" Series 1788–89

Another survey of a portion of Nueva Galicia was made after the establishment of the intendancies (1786). Reports are extant only for the intendancy of Guadalajara (Table 14, fig. 7). These appear in a single document (AGI, Mexico, 1675, fols. 1–15) as a résumé in tabular form com-

427

TABLE 14—SUMMARY LISTING OF 1788–89 "REVENUE SERIES," GUADALAJARA INDENDANCY

Census No.	Partido	Bishopric	Modern State	Date
		Former Gobierno de Nueva Galicia		
1	Acaponeta	Guadalajara	Nayarit	n.d.
2	Aguacatlan y Jala	Guadalajara	Nayarit	n.d.
3	Aguascalientes	Guadalajara	Aguascalientes	n.d.
4	Barca, La	Michoacan & Guadalajara	Jalisco	n.d.
5	Cajititlan	Guadalajara	Jalisco	1788
6	Centipac	Guadalajara	Nayarit	n.d.
7	Colotlan (Bolaños)	Guadalajara	Jalisco	n.d.
8	Cuquio	Guadalajara	Jalisco	1788
12	Guauchinango	Guadalajara	Jalisco	1788
13	Hostotipac	Guadalajara	Jalisco	n.d.
14	Hostotopaquillo	Guadalajara	Jalisco & Nayarit	n.d.
16	Juchipila	Guadalajara	Zacatecas	n.d.
17	Lagos	Guadalajara	Jalisco	n.d.
19	Purificacion, La	Guadalajara	Jalisco	1789
20	San Cristobal de la Barranca	Guadalajara	Jalisco	n.d.
23	Tala	Guadalajara	Jalisco	n.d.
24	Tecpatitlan	Guadalajara	Jalisco	n.d.
25	Tepic	Guadalajara	Nayarit	n.d.
26	Tequepespan	Guadalajara	Nayarit	n.d.
27	Tequila	Guadalajara	Jalisco	n.d.
28	Tlajomulco	Guadalajara	Jalisco	n.d.
30	Tonala	Guadalajara	Jalisco	1788
		Former Gobierno de Nueva España		
4A	Amula (Tuscacuesco)	Guadalajara	Jalisco	1788
9A	Autlan	Guadalajara	Jalisco	n.d.
46A	Izatlan (Etzatlan)	Guadalajara	Jalisco	1788
76A	Sayula	Guadalajara	Jalisco	n.d.
111A	Tuspa (Zapotitlan el Grande)	Michoacan	Jalisco	n.d.

piled by a treasury official in Guadalajara from longer reports submitted by the sub-delegados (local officials of the former AM's).[15] Dated March 28, 1789, the résumé was made to comply with a vice-regal order issued September 30, 1788, but indicates the submittal dates of only seven of the original reports.

Apparently, this survey was made expressly to ascertain the amount of tribute

and taxes due the Crown from each inhabited place within the intendancy. In addition to fiscal information, the extant summaries indicate the names and types of all settlements within a given partido (AM), the distances in leagues from one settlement to the next, and the population of each settlement in terms of numbers of Indian and Spanish inhabitants. A brief description of economic and social conditions within the partido concludes some of the summaries. The data on Indian popula-

[15] Peter Gerhard kindly lent me microfilm of this AGI document.

TABLE 15—SUMMARY LISTING OF 1788–89 MICHOACAN PUEBLO SERIES

Census No.	Partido	Bishopric	Date	AGN Ramo	Length (folio pages)	Modern State
15	Sinagua y la Guacana	Michoacan	n.d.	Historia 73	11½	Michoacan
37	Guaymeo y Sirandiro	Michoacan	n.d.	Historia 73	27	Michoacan & Guerrero
60	Motines	Michoacan	1789	Historia 73	14	Michoacan
80	Tancitaro	Michoacan	n.d.	Historia 73	20½	Michoacan
101	Tingüindin	Michoacan	1789	Historia 73	9½	Michoacan
103	Tlalpujagua	Michoacan	1788–89	Historia 73	34	Michoacan
113	Valladolid	Michoacan	n.d.	Historia 73	89	Michoacan
123	Xiquilpan	Michoacan	1789	Historia 73	14½	Michoacan
128	Zamora y Xacona	Michoacan	1789	Historia 73	22½	Michoacan

tion would be especially useful to anthropologists. Since the survey was ordered by the viceroy, possibly similar reports of the same period were made for other intendencies of Mexico. These documents may now lie buried somewhere within the AGI in Seville.

"Indian Pueblo" Series of Michoacan, 1788–89

A valuable collection of geographical descriptions of Indian villages within the intendancy of Valladolid is found in AGN, Historia 73 (Table 15). Each report gives a lengthy account of the population, economy, government, town property, communal lands, hospitals, cofradías, and other aspects of Indian and some Mestizo settlements within a given partido (AM). Insufficient documentation accompanies this series to ascertain at whose instigation or by whom the reports were made; however, at least one—that of Valladolid partido—was done under the direction of one José Antonio Calderón. I was unable to find the questionnaire which must have been drawn up for these reports, nor do I know that the survey was conducted for areas outside the intendancy of Valladolid.[16]

This survey includes reports of all the partidos (AM's) of Valladolid intendancy, save those of Maravatio, Tlazcazala, Charo, and Colima, and thus covers most of the present state of Michoacan and part of Guerrero. For the student of Tarascan culture, the material contained in this series is invaluable.

Pineda Survey, 1791

The Pineda RG's have been only partially investigated (Wilson, 1963). Antonio de Pineda y Ramírez was put in charge of natural history on the Malaspina expedition around the world (1789–94), underwritten by the Spanish government (Novo y Colson, 1885). He spent most of 1791 in New Spain, during which time he formulated a geographical questionnaire of 35 points that was circulated to the local officials of the viceroyalty. The questions dealt with the mining industry, economic species of trees, conditions of the roads, agriculture, and manufactures within the provinces. According to Wilson (1963), in December of 1791 Pineda gave the results of his investigations to the viceroy, Conde de Revilla Gigedo, for their remission to Madrid. Some of these papers are now in the Archivo de

[16] According to Peter Gerhard (personal communication), a report on the Indian towns within the jurisdictions of Zacualpan and Ixcateopan, intendancy of Mexico, found in the Archivo Histórico de Hacienda, Mexico, D.F., MS 391-3, may belong to this series.

TABLE 16—SUMMARY LISTING OF 1791-94 REPORTS, PADRONES SERIES

Census No.	Alcaldía Mayor (Subdelegación)	Intendancy	Bishopric	Date	AGN Ramo	Nature of Report		Map	Modern State
						List	Essay (RG)		
	Former Gobierno de Nueva España								
1	Acapulco	Mexico	Mexico & Tlaxcala	1792	Padrones 16	X	9 f.	—	Guerrero
3	Actopan	Mexico	Mexico	1791	Padrones 3	X	2 f.	X	Puebla
5	Antequera	Oaxaca	Antequera	1792	Padrones 13	X	[city only]	—	Oaxaca
6	Apam y Tepeapulco	Mexico	Mexico	n.d.	Padrones 5	X	1 f.	X	Hidalgo
8	Atlixco	Puebla	Tlaxcala	1792	Padrones 25	X	5½ f.	—	Puebla
11	Celaya	Guanajuato	Michoacan	1792	Padrones 23, 26	X	—	—	Guanajuato
12	Cempoala	Mexico	Mexico	n.d.	Padrones 20	X	2 f.	X	Hidalgo
15	Cinagua y la Huacana	Valladolid	Michoacan	n.d.	Historia 72	X	—	—	Michoacan
16	Coatepec	Mexico	Mexico	1791	Padrones 3	X	—	X	Mexico
17	Colima	Valladolid	Michoacan	1793	Padrones 11	X	17 f.	X	Colima
21	Cuautla Amilpas	Puebla	Mexico	n.d.	Padrones 8	X	—	X	Morelos
22	Cuernavaca	Mexico	Mexico	n.d.	Padrones 8	X	—	X	Morelos
23	Cuiseo de la Laguna	Valladolid	Michoacan	n.d.	Padrones 1-B	X	—	—	Michoacan
24	Cuyoacan	Mexico	Mexico	n.d.	Historia 72	X	—	X	Distrito Federal
26	Charo	Valladolid	Michoacan	n.d.	Padrones 1-B	X	—	—	Michoacan
28	Chietla	Puebla	Tlaxcala	1792	Padrones 28	X	1½ f.	—	Puebla
29	Chilapa	Mexico	Mexico & Tlaxcala	1791	Padrones 16	X	—	—	Guerrero
31	Guachinango	Puebla & Veracruz	Mexico & Tlaxcala	1791	Padrones 18	X	2 f.	—	Puebla & Veracruz
32	Guanajuato	Guanajuato	Michoacan	1791–94	Padrones 30–33, 37, 42	X	—	—	Guanajuato
33	Guatulco y Guamelula	Oaxaca	Antequera	1792	Padrones 12	X	—	—	Oaxaca
34	Guautitlan	Mexico	Mexico	1792	Padrones 4	—	—	X	Mexico
36	Guayacocotla	Puebla & Veracruz	Mexico & Tlaxcala	1791	Padrones 12	X	—	X	Veracruz
37	Guaymeo y Sirindaro	Valladolid	Michoacan	n.d.	Historia 72	X	—	—	Michoacan & Guerrero
39	Huejocingo	Puebla	Tlaxcala	1791	Padrones 27	X	7 f.	—	Puebla
41	Huejutla	Mexico	Mexico	1791	Padrones 3	X	1½ f.	—	Hidalgo

43	Igualapa	Mexico	Antequera & Tlaxcala	1791	Padrones 18	X	—	X	—	Guerrero
45	Ixmiquilpan	Mexico	Mexico	n.d.	Padrones 2	X	2 f.	X	X	Hidalgo
48	Izucar	Puebla	Tlaxcala	1791	Padrones 28	X	4 f.	X	—	Puebla
49	Justlahuaca	Oaxaca	Antequera & Tlaxcala	1792	Historia 72	X	—	X	—	Oaxaca
50	Leon	Guanajuato	Michoacan	n.d.	Padrones 41	X	[Penjamo]	X	—	Guanajuato
51	Lerma	Mexico	Mexico	1791	Padrones 12	X	2½ f.	X	—	Mexico
57	Maravatio	Valladolid	Michoacan	n.d.	Historia 72	X	—	X	—	Michoacan
60	Motines	Valladolid	Michoacan	1792	Padrones 21	X	4½ f.	X	—	Michoacan
64	Orizaba	Veracruz	Tlaxcala	n.d.	Padrones 19	X	—	X	X	Veracruz
65	Otumba	Mexico	Mexico	1791	Padrones 12	X	—	X	X	Mexico
66	Pachuca	Mexico	Mexico	n.d.	Padrones 2	X	5 f.	X	X	Hidalgo
70	Queretaro	Mexico	Mexico	1794	Historia 72 Padrones 35, 39, 40	—	33 f.	X	—	Queretaro
71	San Cristobal Ecatepec	Mexico	Mexico	n.d.	Padrones B	X	3½ f.	X	—	Mexico
72	San Juan de los Llanos	Puebla	Tlaxcala	1791	Padrones 7	X	10 f.	X	X	Puebla
74	San Luis Potosi	San Luis Potosi	Michoacan	1792	Historia 72	X	—	X	—	San Luis Potosi
75	San Miguel el Grande	Guanajuato	Michoacan	1791–94	Padrones 24 34, 36	X	—	X	—	Guanajuato
78	Sochimilco (Xochimilco)	Mexico	Mexico	n.d.	Padrones 29	X	—	X	X	Distrito Federal
79	Tacuba	Mexico	Mexico	n.d. (inc. no. 21)	Padrones 6	X	1 f.	X	X	Mexico & Distrito Federal
80	Tancitaro	Valladolid	Michoacan	n.d.	Historia 72	X	—	X	—	Michoacan
83	Teciutlan y Atempa	Puebla	Tlaxcala	1791	Padrones 2	X	—	X	X	Puebla
85	Tehuacan	Puebla	Tlaxcala	1791	Padrones 3	X	13 f.	X	X	Puebla
89	Teotihuacan	Mexico	Mexico	n.d.	Padrones 18	X	1½ f.	X	X	Mexico
91	Tepeaca	Puebla	Tlaxcala	1791	Padrones 38	X	4 f.	X	—	Puebla
95	Tetela del Volcan	Puebla	Mexico	n.d.	Padrones 8	X	—	X	X	Morelos
96	Tetepango y Hueypustla	Mexico	Mexico	n.d.	Padrones 18	X	1 f.	X	X	Mexico & Hidalgo
100	Tezcoco	Mexico	Mexico	n.d.	Padrones 14	X	—	X	—	Mexico & Tlaxcala
101	Tingüindin	Valladolid	Michoacan	n.d.	Historia 72	X	—	X	—	Michoacan
102	Tistla	Mexico	Mexico & Tlaxcala	1792	Padrones 17	X	—	X	—	Guerrero

Census No.	Alcaldía Mayor (Subdelegación)	Intendancy	Bishopric	Date	AGN Ramo	Nature of Report			
						List	Essay (RG)	Map	
103	Tlapujahua	Valladolid	Michoacan	n.d.	Historia 72	X	—	—	Michoacan
104	Tlapa	Mexico	Mexico	1791	Padrones 21	X	—	—	Guerrero
105	Tlaxcala	Puebla	Tlaxcala	1791	Padrones 22	—	8½ f.	—	Tlaxcala
106	Tlazazalca	Valladolid	Michoacan	n.d.	Historia 72	X	—	X	Michoacan
107	Tochimilco	Puebla	Mexico	1791	Padrones 12	X	—	—	Puebla
108	Toluca	Mexico	Mexico	1791	Padrones 21	X	—	—	Mexico
109	Tula	Mexico	Mexico	n.d.	Padrones 7	—	1 f.	X	Hidalgo
110	Tulancingo	Mexico	Mexico & Tlaxcala	1792	Padrones 1	X	6 f.	X	Hidalgo
113	Valladolid	Valladolid	Michoacan	n.d.	Historia 72	X	—	—	Michoacan
114	Valles	San Luis Potosi	Mexico	1792	Historia 72	—	8 f.	—	San Luis Potosi
115	Venado y Hedionda	San Luis Potosi	Michoacan	1792	Historia 72	X	—	—	San Luis Potosi
119	Xalapa de la Feria	Veracruz	Tlaxcala	n.d.	Padrones 20	X	10 f.	—	Veracruz
123	Xiquilpan	Valladolid	Michoacan	n.d.	Historia 72	X	—	—	Michoacan
128	Zamora	Valladolid	Michoacan	n.d.	Historia 72	X	—	—	Michoacan
129	Zumpango de la Laguna	Mexico	Mexico	n.d.	Historia 72	X	1½ f.	X	Mexico
	Former Gobierno de Nueva Galicia								
2A	Aguacatlan y Jala	Guadalajara	Guadalajara	1793	Padrones 14	X	2 f.	—	Nayarit
3A	Aguascalientes	Guadalajara	Guadalajara	1792	Padrones 5	X	5½ f.	X	Aguascalientes
9A	Charcas	San Luis Potosi	Guadalajara	1792	Historia 72	—	3½ f.	—	San Luis Potosi
	Provincias Internas								
	Sonora	Arizpe	Sonora	1792	Historia 72	X	43 f.	—	Sonora

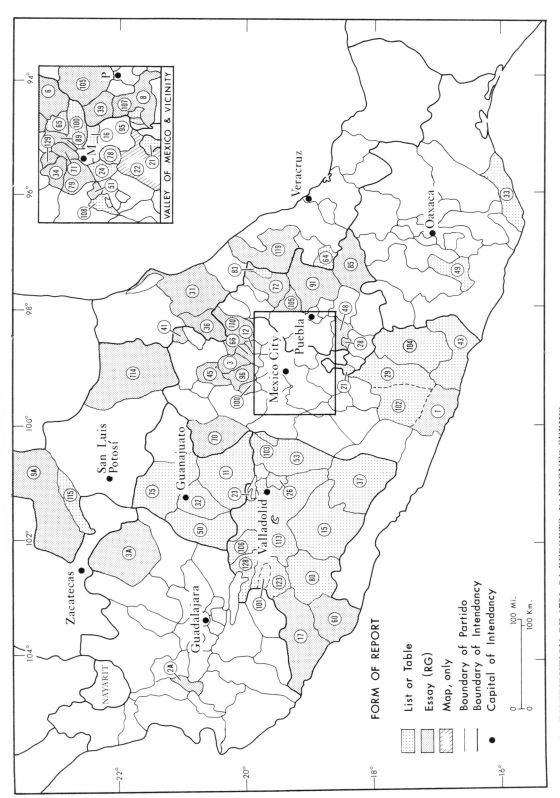

FORM OF REPORT

List or Table

Essay (RG)

Map, only

———— Boundary of Partido

———— Boundary of Intendancy

• Capital of Intendancy

100 Mi.

100 Km.

FIG. 8—DISTRIBUTION OF 1791–94 REPORTS, PADRONES SERIES
Numbers refer to places listed in Table 16.

TABLE 17—SUMMARY LISTING OF 1792–94 REPORTS, TOPONYM SERIES

Census No.	Partido (Alcaldía Mayor)	Intendancy	Bishopric	Date	AGN Ramo	Nature of Report List	Essay (RG)	Modern State
			Former Gobierno de Nueva España					
1	Acapulco	Mexico	Mexico & Tlaxcala	1792	Historia 578-B	X	—	Guerrero
2	Acatlan y Piastla	Puebla	Tlaxcala	n.d.	Historia 73	X	—	Puebla
4	Amula	Guadalajara	Guadalajara	1792	Historia 72	X	—	Jalisco
6	Apam y Tepeapulco	Mexico	Mexico	1794	Historia 578-B	X	—	Hidalgo
8	Atlisco	Puebla	Tlaxcala	n.d.	Historia 73	X	—	Puebla
9	Autlan	Gaudalajara	Guadalajara	1793	Historia 72	X	—	Jalisco
11	Celaya	Guanajuato	Michoacan	1792	Historia 72	X	—	Guanajuato
12	Cempoala	Mexico	Mexico	1794	Historia 578-B	X	—	Hidalgo
13	Cimapan (Zimapan)	Mexico	Mexico	1792	Historia 578-B	X	—	Hidalgo
16	Coatepec	Mexico	Mexico	1792	Historia 578-B	—	1½ f.	Mexico
21	Cuautla Amilpas	Puebla	Mexico	n.d.	Historia 73	X	—	Morelos
22	Cuernavaca	Mexico	Mexico	1792	Historia 578-B	X	1 f.	Morelos
24	Cuyuacan	Mexico	Mexico	1794	Historia 578-B	—	2 f.	Distrito Federal
25	Chalco	Mexico	Mexico	n.d.	Historia 578-B	X	1 f.	Mexico & Morelos
27	Chiautla	Puebla	Tlaxcala	n.d.	Historia 73	X	—	Puebla
28	Chietla	Puebla	Tlaxcala	n.d.	Historia 73	X	—	Puebla
29	Chilapa	Mexico	Mexico & Tlaxcala	1792	Historia 578-B	X	—	Guerrero
30	Cholula	Puebla	Tlaxcala	n.d.	Historia 73	X	—	Puebla
31	Guachinango	Puebla & Veracruz	Mexico & Tlaxcala	n.d.	Historia 73	X	—	Puebla & Veracruz
32	Guanajuato	Guanajuato	Michoacan	1792	Historia 72	X	—	Guanajuato
34	Guautitlan (Cuautitlan)	Mexico	Mexico	1792	Historia 578-B	—	2 f.	Mexico
36	Guayacocotla	Puebla & Veracruz	Mexico & Tlaxcala	n.d.	Historia 73	X	—	Veracruz
39	Huexocingo	Puebla	Tlaxcala	n.d.	Historia 73	X	—	Puebla
41	Huexutla	Mexico	Mexico	1794	Historia 578-B	—	4 f.	Hidalgo
42	Iguala	Mexico	Mexico	1794	Historia 578-B	X	—	Guerrero
43	Igualapa	Mexico	Antequera & Tlaxcala	1792	Historia 578-B	—	1½ f.	Guerrero
44	Iscateupa	Mexico	Mexico	1794	Historia 578-B	X	—	Guerrero
45	Ixmiquilpan	Mexico	Mexico	1792	Historia 578-B	—	2½ f.	Hidalgo
46	Iztlan	Guadalajara	Guadalajara	1792	Historia 72	X	—	Jalisco
48	Izucar	Puebla	Tlaxcala	n.d.	Historia 73	X	—	Puebla

No.								
50	Leon	Guanajuato	Michoacan	1792	Historia 72	X	—	Guanajuato
51	Lerma	Mexico	Mexico	1792	Historia 578-B	—	1 f.	Mexico
52	Malinalco	Mexico	Mexico	1792	Historia 578-B	X	—	Mexico
54	Metepec	Mexico	Mexico	1792	Historia 578-B	X	1 f.	Mexico
55	Mexicalcingo	Mexico	Mexico	1792	Historia 578-B	X	—	Distrito Federal
65	Otumba	Mexico	Mexico	1792	Historia 578-B	X	—	Mexico
69	Puebla	Puebla	Tlaxcala	n.d.	Historia 73	X	—	Puebla
70	Queretaro	Mexico	Mexico	1794	Historia 578-B	X	7 f.	Queretaro
72	San Juan de los Llanos	Puebla	Tlaxcala	n.d.	Historia 73	X	—	Puebla
73	San Luis de la Paz	Guanajuato	Michoacan & Tlaxcala	1792	Historia 72	X	—	Guanajuato
74	San Luis Potosi	San Luis Potosi	Michoacan	1793	Historia 72	X	—	San Luis Potosi
75	San Miguel el Grande	Guanajuato	Michoacan	1792	Historia 72	X	—	Guanajuato
76	Sayula	Guadalajara	Guadalajara	n.d.	Historia 72	X	6½ f.	Jalisco
77	Sochicoatlan	Mexico	Mexico	1794	Historia 578-B	—	6½ f.	Hidalgo
78	Sochimilco (Xochimilco)	Mexico	Mexico	1794	Historia 578-B	—	2½ f.	Distrito Federal
79	Tacuba	Mexico	Mexico	1793	Historia 578-B	—	9 f.	Mexico & Distrito Federal
81	Tasco	Mexico	Mexico	1794	Historia 578-B	—	9 f.	Guerrero
82	Tecali	Puebla	Tlaxcala	n.d.	Historia 73	X	—	Puebla
83	Teciutlan y Atempa	Puebla	Tlaxcala	n.d.	Historia 73	X	—	Puebla
85	Teguacan	Puebla	Tlaxcala	n.d.	Historia 73	X	—	Puebla
89	Teotihuacan	Mexico	Mexico	1792	Historia 578-B	—	1 f.	Mexico
91	Tepeaca	Puebla	Tlaxcala	n.d.	Historia 73	X	—	Puebla
92	Tepeji de la Seda	Puebla	Tlaxcala	n.d.	Historia 73	X	5 f.	Puebla
94	Tetela del Rio	Mexico	Mexico & Michoacan	1792	Historia 578-B	—	5 f.	Guerrero
95	Tetela del Volcan	Puebla	Mexico	n.d.	Historia 73	X	—	Morelos
96	Tetepango y Hueypustla	Mexico	Mexico	1792	Historia 578-B	—	2 f.	Mexico & Hidalgo
99	Teutlalco	Puebla	Mexico	n.d.	Historia 73	X	—	Puebla
102	Tistla	Mexico	Mexico & Tlaxcala	1793	Historia 578-B	—	2½ f.	Guerrero
105	Tlaxcala	Puebla	Tlaxcala	n.d.	Historia 73	X	—	Tlaxcala
107	Tochimilco	Puebla	Mexico	n.d.	Historia 73	X	—	Puebla
109	Tula	Mexico	Mexico	1794	Historia 578-B	X	—	Mexico
111	Tuspa	Guadalajara	Michoacan	1792	Historia 72	X	—	Jalisco
114	Valles	San Luis Potosi	Mexico	1793	Historia 72	X	—	San Luis Potosi
115	Venado y la Hedionda	San Luis Potosi	Michoacan	1793	Historia 72	X	—	San Luis Potosi
122	Xilotepec	Mexico	Mexico	1794	Historia 578-B	—	8 f.	Mexico & Hidalgo

(*Table 17, continued*)

Census No.	Partido (Alcaldía Mayor)	Intendancy	Bishopric	Date	AGN Ramo	Nature of Report List	Essay (RG)	Modern State
124	Xonotla y Tetela	Puebla	Tlaxcala	n.d.	Historia 73	X	—	Puebla
125	Zacatlan de las Manzanas	Puebla	Tlaxcala	n.d.	Historia 73	X	—	Puebla
126	Zacatula	Mexico	Michoacan	1794	Historia 578-B	X	3 f.	Guerrero
127	Zacualpa	Mexico	Mexico	1794	Historia 578-B	X	—	Mexico & Guerrero
129	Zumpango de la Laguna	Mexico	Mexico	1792	Historia 578-B	—	½ f.	Mexico

Former Gobierno de Nueva Galicia

Census No.	Partido (Alcaldía Mayor)	Intendancy	Bishopric	Date	AGN Ramo	Nature of Report List	Essay (RG)	Modern State
1A	Acaponeta	Guadalajara	Guadalajara	n.d.	Historia 72	X	—	Nayarit
2A	Aguacatlan y Jala	Guadalajara	Guadalajara	1792	Historia 72	X	—	Nayarit
3A	Aguascalientes	Guadalajara	Guadalajara	1793	Historia 72	X	—	Aguascalientes
4A	Barca, La	Guadalajara	Michoacan & Guadalajara	n.d.	Historia 72	X	—	Jalisco
5A	Cajititlan	Guadalajara	Guadalajara	n.d.	Historia 72	X	—	Jalisco
6A	Centipac	Guadalajara	Guadalajara	n.d.	Historia 72	X	—	Nayarit
7A	Colotlan (Bolaños)	Guadalajara	Guadalajara	1793	Historia 72	X	—	Jalisco
8A	Cuquio	Guadalajara	Guadalajara	n.d.	Historia 72	X	—	Jalisco
9A	Charcas	San Luis Potosi	Guadalajara	1793	Historia 72	X	—	San Luis Potosi
12A	Guauchinango	Guadalajara	Guadalajara	n.d.	Historia 72	X	—	Jalisco
13A	Hostotipac	Guadalajara	Guadalajara	n.d.	Historia 72	X	—	Jalisco
14A	Hostotopaquillo	Guadalajara	Guadalajara	1792	Historia 72	X	2½ f.	Jalisco & Nayarit
16A	Juchipila	Guadalajara	Guadalajara	1792	Historia 72	X	—	Zacatecas
17A	Lagos	Guadalajara	Guadalajara	n.d.	Historia 72	X	—	Jalisco
19A	Purificacion	Guadalajara	Guadalajara	1793	Historia 72	X	—	Jalisco
20A	San Cristobal de la Barranca	Guadalajara	Guadalajara	1794	Historia 72	X	—	Jalisco
23A	Tala	Guadalajara	Guadalajara	n.d.	Historia 72	X	—	Jalisco
24A	Tecpatitlan	Guadalajara	Guadalajara	n.d.	Historia 72	X	—	Jalisco
25A	Tepic	Guadalajara	Guadalajara	1792	Historia 72	X	—	Nayarit
26A	Tequepespan	Guadalajara	Guadalajara	1792	Historia 72	X	—	Nayarit
27A	Tequila	Guadalajara	Guadalajara	n.d.	Historia 72	X	—	Jalisco
28A	Tlajomulco	Guadalajara	Guadalajara	1793	Historia 72	X	—	Jalisco
30A	Tonala	Guadalajara	Guadalajara	n.d.	Historia 72	X	—	Jalisco

entire collection consists of 94 reports, 23 of which are in essay form, ranging from a half-folio to 9 folios in length. Some, such as that of Tasco (Census, 81), give economic data on the subdelegación in addition to the specific information requested. Although these documents cannot be considered true RG's, they contain substantial geographic data on Mexico that are rarely obtainable elsewhere for this period.[17]

Conclusion

Compared to the single, well-organized geographic survey of New Spain in 1577–85, the numerous 18th-century surveys form a complex array of source material, the scholarly use of which is often frustrating. Whereas most of the 16th-century relations

[17] One additional report which can be considered a true RG describes the villa of Santiago Papasquiaro and its jurisdiction within the intendancy of Durango. This valuable essay, dated 1793, was published in the *Boletín de la Sociedad Mexicana de Geografía y Estadística*, ser. 2, vol. 2, 1870, pp. 333–43. The RG appears to belong to a series entirely separate from those described above. It is an answer to a 16-point questionnaire, signed by the provisional intendant governor of Durango, in response to a viceregal order of October 12, 1793. The disposition of the original document is unknown.

are available in printed form, less than a fifth of the 18th-century material has been published, and except for the recently acquired microfilm collections in the Library of Congress, the manuscripts of the later surveys are difficult of access. To be sure, there are several good published 18th-century descriptions of various parts of Mexico and Central America that were not associated with the systematic geographical surveys and, consequently, were not mentioned in this article.

It is surprising that under the Bourbon rule better geographical surveys of the colonies were not forthcoming during the 18th century. Perhaps local administration, on which the compilation of the reports had to rest, had become so inefficient that no amount of attempted reform was sufficient to alter the clumsy bureaucratic system until the last years of the century. But however complex and difficult of use the 18-century RG's may be, they form a valuable corpus of information on population, ethnography, and economy of Mexico and Central America taken near the close of the colonial period, some 250 years after European contact.

REFERENCES

Altolaguirre y Duvale, 1908
Arriaga, 1946
Ballesteros y Beretta, 1918–41
Barlow, 1943, 1944c, 1945, 1946a, 1946b, 1947
———— and Smisor, 1943
Boban, 1891
Carrera Stampa, 1949
Ferrer del Río, 1856
Fisher, 1926
García Ruiz, 1947
González de Cossío, 1952
Humboldt, 1825

Lemoine Villicaña, 1963
Murray, 1904
Novo y Colson, 1885
Núñez y Domínguez, 1939
Pardo y Barreda, 1905
Rubio Mañé, 1946, 1955
Torres Lanzas, 1900
Ulloa, 1772
Villaseñor y Sánchez, 1746–48
Whitaker, 1935
Wilson, 1963

APPENDIX A. ROYAL CÉDULA AUTHORIZING THE GEOGRAPHICAL SURVEY OF 1743–46 IN MEXICO

Don Pedro Cebrian y Augustín, Conde de Fuen-Clara, grandee of Spain of the first class, (etc. . . .) Viceroy, Governor, and Captain-General of this New Spain, and President of its Royal Audiencia, etc.

Whereas His Majesty (God save Him) was pleased to issue the following Royal Order: =THE KING= Whereas experience having proved the grave inconveniences and detriments that result from the lack, within My Council of the Indies, of detailed data on the true state of those [the overseas] Provinces: and realizing that persons in charge of the Government can easily make inquiries and, thru such reports, can formulate all that is necessary, it has seemed, that these tasks may generally be effected precisely and in detail at the present time as in the future, as provided in the Laws and Ordinances of those my Kingdoms: Therefore, I command the Viceroys of New Spain, Peru, and the New Kingdom of Granada; the Presidents of my Royal Audiencias, and the Governors and Captain-Generals of the Provinces included within each of the three Viceroyalties, to apply their entire attention and effort to the acquisition, through reports of the Alcaldes Mayores and officials of the minor civil divisions, and through any other possible means, the detailed data that are needed for the correct knowledge of the names, number, and quality of the settlements within their jurisdiction and vicinity; of the nature, status and progress of the missions, of the live conversions, and of the new reductions; and, precisely given, not only the present conditions, but also those occurrences which may come about in the future and that might lead to a fuller knowledge of this important matter, according to the pub-

lished Laws and Ordinances of the said Kingdoms; for any omission or negligence in the punctual compliance of this matter, would be much to my Royal displeasure. And I especially charge the said Viceroys to take note of the form in which the missionaries fulfill the obligations of their office and ministry; and especially whether or not they are learned and skillful in the use of the languages of the Indians, to whose conversion and instruction they are dedicated, to fit the service of God, and mine; and may [the said Viceroys] acknowledge receipt and fulfillment of this Order at their earliest convenience. Dated at el Buen Retiro, July 19, 1741. == I THE KING == By the order of the King, our master == D. FERNANDO TRIVIÑO == affixed with three signatures == And having been seen and obeyed by me for its exact and punctual fulfillment: For the present I command all the Governors, Alcaldes Mayores, and district judges of this Government, being aware of what His Majesty orders in the attached Royal Order, to carry out the necessary proceedings and take the most exact data of importance regarding this requested and desired end (forming, thus, reports and relations; and once finished, they will remit them accompanied by a clear summary of all that they contain; being aware that for the best expedition of this grave matter, I have duly commissioned Lic. don Juan Francisco Sahagún de Arévalo Ladrón de Guevara, cleric of this archbishopric and General Chronicler of these Kingdoms, etc. and the purser don Joseph Sánchez Villa Señor to direct the dispatches that will be carried out in the jurisdictions of this Government; and once the reports that are made are collected, they should examine

440

of Manila, which are outside the continent, should not be included within this [survey].

6. The episcopal seats will serve as centers for measuring the distances and directions of other subordinate [towns], which are seats of governments and of alcaldías.

7. The seats of governments and of alcaldías serve as centers for the determination of the towns that are seats of curacies, and with respect to these, [the location] of the dependent annexes, as well as other notable places that make up the district will be particularized.

8. The geographical report of each Audiencia should explain the extension of the jurisdiction by means of the four cardinal directions and with the intermediate directions; and the same [should apply] for the bishoprics, the governments, the alcaldías, and the curacies, and the places confined within them.

9. These distances should be indicated in common leagues of one hour's walk of an unburdened animal [mule or horse], as this is the easiest way; but the calculation should be made in a straight line, or as the crow flies, and this will be done in the following manner.

10. In flat country, which is not interrupted by canyons or by moderate elevations, the time elapsed in walking should be reduced by one quarter, and the remaining three-quarters in hours represent leagues, because of the sinuosities that always characterize the road.

11. In those [areas] characterized by canyons or elevations that must be ascended and descended, [the time] should be reduced by one-third.

12. In those that have a roundabout course, because of river fords or because of mountainous conditions, through good

judgment [the time] should be reduced by one-half; and if the roundabout course, is great, by three-fifths, and on occasions, by two-thirds, all of which is made by arbitrary judgment, aided by the observation of time spent on the road, with attention to the various directions taken.

13. Having made the determination of distances, there follows the description of the mountains that occupy the province, the territory of the gobierno, alcaldía, curacy, or town, the direction of them and the distance over which they extend.

14. The same is done for the rivers that drain the mountains, with an explanation of their volume; those that carry gently flowing water by certain places, and those that flow precipitously in the form of torrents.

15. The bridges that are along the way are to be described, as are the detours made to cross them.

16. Also the lakes, their extent, the direction of their longest portion, any information on depths, the quality of the water, fresh or salty.

17. In this way the geographic description of all the Kingdom, by provinces or Audiencias; bishoprics, gobiernos, and alcaldías; curacies and towns, will be made.

PHYSICS

1. This subject should begin with a report on temperatures; to do this well, it would be necessary to take them from observations with the thermometer during each season of the year: wherever there might be some intelligent person who may have done so [surely] he will not refuse to furnish his data; in the absence of this, the following procedure will serve.

2. The degree of cold is known from [the occurrence] of ice and by [the amount]

443

of time that it remains without melting, after the end of winter; equally so by the thickness that [the ice] acquires: having recorded this, the frost that appears in the mornings on the grass and disappears after sunrise, is called congelation, or the beginning of ice: when the water of pools is frozen in the mornings and the crust has but the thickness of a peso [coin], it is considered a degree of ice: when it has a thickness double that, it is estimated at 2 degrees: when it remains frozen until midday and at this hour with the sun's heat it is melted, it is estimated at 3 degrees: when it remains throughout the day, even though the sun may be bright, and on the following day is recognized as being thicker, it is estimated at four degrees; and from there on up, it is not possible to determine colder degrees without a thermometer.

3. The degree of heat can be computed by the effect it has on one's own body: when woolen clothing does not feel uncomfortable and that of summer does not cause coldness, it is 15 to 17 [degrees]: when summer clothing feels better than that of wool, it is 18 to 20: when one feels like shedding even summer clothing, it is 21 to 22: when one begins to perspire with some exercise, it is from 23 to 24; when one perspires freely and abundantly, it is around 25 degrees, this being considered in the shade.

4. The products of the land also reflect a measure of cold or heat of temperatures: the areas where wheat is grown and matures well are cold until the end of freezing time: where wheat does not mature well but barley does, it freezes as low as 3 degrees: where barley grows but does not mature perfectly, it is because the freezes come early and are heavy from 2 to 5 or 6

degrees. Where fruits of the hot country, such as aguacates, chirimoyas, plantains, etc., are grown, the degree of heat is from 26 to 28; the same happens where sugar cane is grown. Oranges and limes grown in medium climates, the heat of which is from 24 to 25 degrees in summer: maize is of the same temperature, and also that of sugar cane.

5. With that which has been said, the reporting of temperatures experienced by each place will be eased, by distinguishing the four seasons of the year and the large or small differences that is noted between one and the other.

6. The position of the settlements should be explained in [terms of] altitude, plains or valleys in which they are situated.

7. The prevailing winds, explaining whether or not they are strong or weak; their duration, and the effects that they cause on health, as well as on plants and planted fields.

8. The storms and tempests that take place; the winds that characterize them, and the season of the year in which they occur regularly.

9. The snow-covered mountains that there are in each province or district; explaining if the snow is permanent without melting completely in summer.

10. The volcanoes, and those that are erupting fire, cinders, and lava, the accounts [of] past eruptions and the damage that they caused or are causing, if they continue to erupt fire.

NATURAL HISTORY

1. Information on the [cultivated] trees and the minor plants that occur in each area, their species, wood, fruits that they produce, and time [of year] when they yield.

2. Similar information on the wild plants,

and on cultivated grains, of all kinds, time of planting and ripening.

3. On medicinal herbs, roots, and seeds, as well as those that are poisonous; the uses of the former according to experience.

4. On the domesticated animals, and the wild ones; their abundance, and utility that comes from the latter in terms of their hides such as deer skins or those of other hide- or wool-bearing animals.

5. On birds of all species, domesticated ones and wild ones, song birds and those of brilliant plumage; their numbers and any particulars that may give them note.

6. On reptiles and vermin, with reports on their abundance; on the poisonous ones and on those that have some particular characteristic.

7. On the insects of all kinds; on those that customarily cause damage to plants, fruits, and grains, and on those that are useful such as cochineal bug, of which it would be convenient to make a complete description, including the various species.

8. On thermal springs, saline or bituminous, and those useful for taking baths for certain illnesses, explaining the degree of heat for some and the alkalinity, bituminous quality, or salinity of others.

9. On the waters that petrify wood, plants, and other objects that they affect.

10. On the noxious gases that customarily exude from the ground.

On Antiquities

1. Antiquities throw light on the character of areas in remote times, and through them one can gain knowledge of the increase or decrease that has taken place; with this motive [in mind, one should] endeavor to investigate the leading to their discovery, reporting on the vestiges that remain in various places.

2. These reports will be [on] the ruins of ancient buildings of the Indians, of whatever material they may be, concerning the interior walls, enclosures, exterior walls, canals or ditches, burials or graves, of shrines and temples; of houses or huts that they inhabited, with description of their outlines, entrances, and interior rooms.

3. Of common pots for all kinds of uses, of clay or other material.

4. Of the tools used for cultivating the land, made of stone, copper, animal bones, or hard wood.

5. Of the weapons, such as bows, arrows, lances, darts, slings, etc., with their names, according to that conserved in the Indian language.

6. Of the amulets, or idols, of various materials, and of all kinds of common objects.

7. Of the ornaments, emblems, or insignia that the ancient Indians used, and which were encountered in their graves and tombs.

8. Generally, of everything that is indicative of antiquity, for it is not unusual to find in the same graves other kinds of things, and even some shreds of pita cloth which indicates that it was used for clothing.

9. Also reports will be given on the modern dress that the Indians use, men as well as women, and the material of which it is made.

Mineralogy

1. Under the subject of mines are included not only those of metals known as gold, silver, copper, tin, etc., but also those of the precious and semi-precious stones; those of marble, jaspar, and

those of the semi-metals and the various salts, including common salt: it is desirable to give a detailed report of their location, directional trend of the principal veins, and minor veins; the depth, thickness, and width that they have, and the metals that are found combined with the principal one; their richness in terms of abundance, and the facility or difficulty of extracting them, and the profit from their extraction.

2. In regard to the mines of precious metals, it should be explained how much can be extracted, according to common measurement; the kind of refining treatment that is given them, and the quantity of quicksilver needed for those that require amalgamation, and the amount of quicksilver consumed.

3. The same should be done for the gold mines explaining the temperatures within all of them, and [the quantity of] water that they contain, and the facility or difficulty of draining it according to the conditions [of the mines] by making drainage adits, or to use machinery if there is knowledge of it, when the richness of the mine is such to allay the great cost that [this] would incur.

4. Customarily there are difficulties in operating profitably some kinds of mines of precious metals; such mines consist of certain cores of extremely hard rock, and in some parts are called "toros"; it would be desirable to explain this in the report made on them.

5. Deposits of shells, or of other material that are recognized to have an aquatic origin.

METALLURGY

1. In this section should be given information on the fineness of the metals after smelting them; the amount of metal the ores produce, the ease of

their refinement, and the ingredients used to refine them.

2. Fineness of metals includes their tractability, and although silver is rarely found mixed with gold, if on the contrary it does occur, it should be anticipated, inasmuch as this lends to the knowledge of the metals in question, as well as of other metals.

3. Copper mines should be explained in a similar manner; in these the ores usually contain some gold, and it should be explained if a separation of [gold and copper] is made, or if they contain gold in sufficient quantity to make the expense of extracting it worth while.

FOSSILS AND SHELLS

1. Information of petrified objects [fossils] of whatever kinds, and on the places where they are found. On this subject it should be noted that in mines, particularly in quarries, figures of fish are found impressed into the very rocks, shells sculptured upon them, corals, and other objects that are recognized as having been water plants in their primitive state, or sea animals.

2. Regarding these things, not only should the report or description be given, but also samples that can be found should be remitted.

3. Also there are figured stones, which, like a painting, represent trees, as distinguished from those with sculptured branches and other various figures: a report should be given of them and of the places where they are found, accompanied by a few samples of the same stones.

4. Also of mineral crystals that are found in mines; of precipitates, and other rarities of nature.

5. These reports are to be prepared on separate sheets of paper, by subject so that persons can complete and remit

certain sections with which they are familiar without having to wait until the entire survey is completed. They are to be remitted to the Chamber Secretary of his excellency, the Viceroy, with the name of the place in which the author resides, the date, and his signature. It will not be necessary to send a letter with them, for there they will be processed according to his Majesty's orders.

Veracruz, January 22, 1777 = D. Antonio de Ulloa =

This document is a copy of the original. Mexico, February 22, 1777

Melchor de Peramás

Appendix D. QUESTIONNAIRE FOR 1789–92 RG'S

INSTRUCTION

to which the governors, intendants, and other officials should address themselves for the formation of Notices on Geography and Civil and Natural History of the Kingdom of New Spain, which his Majesty wishes to be inserted and published in the Gazeta that is printed in the City of Mexico.

As our main object should be to aid the persons commissioned to remit these Notices in the manner of forming them; for, although most will understand the geographical aspects of the instruction, others will not be so well informed: thus, we shall proceed with the greatest simplicity and clarity and uniform manner, so that they may duly adjust themselves without difficulty; leaving those of high intelligence sufficient leeway so that they may form and direct the Notices according to the laws of this most useful branch of Mathematics and accompany [the data] with the corresponding topographic map, giving precisely the points of longitude and latitude and anything else that may seem to them to lead to perfection.

Considering Mexico [City] as the principal point and center to which all lines should be drawn, distances in leagues to it will be given, according to common knowledge, from the city, or town or place described, assigning the direction that it may be in respect to [Mexico City]; and in the same manner the distances from the capital of the Bishopric should be expressed, when [the places] do not belong to the Archbishopric of Mexico; assigning as well the corresponding directions, for which an exact compass is indispensable.

The meaning of the name of the principal place and its surroundings will be given in our common language [Spanish]: how many such names are there: which of them are ecclesiastical seats: which are curacies and vicarages; and how many families compose each town, of Spaniards as well as of Indians and other castes, with their peculiar languages.

Indicate the climate of the countryside: the main fruits that it may produce: what does its main commerce consist of, and which are its peculiar manufactures.

Indicate the extent of the jurisdiction in each direction: what are its borders in each direction: what mountains, volcanoes, rivers, lakes, spas, mines, haciendas, ranches, etc. belong to it; whether the rivers are gentle or torrential; how are they forded: and whether they contain some kinds of fish.

When there is in the place some convent or convents, monasteries or church schools, indicate the people in charge and to what

447

province, religion or church does each correspond; not omitting the number of individuals that compose each, and the secular churchmen that there may be, although these may be comparatively few.

If in some of the convents, monasteries or church schools there might be some celebrated image, tell of its advocation, and given the opportunity, tell what may be true of its order, be [the information] from written history or from accepted tradition.

Describe briefly anything extraordinary that may be in the area, be it within the realm of minerals, to which the land, mines, salt deposits, tar seeps, and mineral dyes belong; or be it in the animal kingdom, which encompasses the creatures that populate the land, water and air; or be it in the plant kingdom, which extends to trees, plants, wood, roots, leaves, flowers, fruits, seeds, gums, oils, and balsams.

Finally, express the regular number of days in travel by horse or coaches to Mexico City, with the distance of each day's journey, although it be a rough estimate; whether there is along the way a river, mountain, incline, or dangerous barranca; what inn, way station or hostelry is there along each day's journey; and by the same token those that should be established on the way within the bishopric to which the road belongs; indicating also the inns or stations along each.

So that all may be easier, it has been deemed appropriate to illustrate [the scheme] with an example; indicating with a small letter what should be inserted for each place [described].

[There follows an example and eleven additional explanatory notes for the compilation of the geographic relations.]

[Undated and unsigned, but this document follows a second viceregal order to carry out the survey, dated 9 December 1788 and signed by Manuel Antonio Flores.]

448

Epilogue
by *Howard F. Cline*

After the foregoing treatment of the 18th-century inquiries had been submitted by Dr. West, Professor Sylvia Vilar published an important survey of the Relaciones Geográficas from the 1577 series through a final colonial effort made in 1812. As the latter is nearly unknown, a summary of her findings is presented here. I have made no extensive effort to locate documents for New Spain that may have been prepared in response to the 1812 questionnaire. That document is reproduced in Professor Vilar's article, "Une vision indigéniste de l'Amérique en 1812," published in *Mélanges de la Casa de Velázquez*, vol. 7 (1971).

When the Spanish Cortes was acting as regent for Ferdinand VII, it reorganized the Spanish government. For governance of the overseas realms it created the Gobernación de Ultramar. In the reformist spirit of the times Ciriaco González Carvajal, for the Gobernación, outlined a series of administrative changes, which were to be based on factual information acquired through the intendants and bishops in the New World. He was especially interested in obtaining exact demographic statistics, as well as historical, cultural, and sociological information. In addition to statistics and these socio-cultural data, the reformers also wanted scientific data, to be provided by local scientists who would visit given areas and take measurements with instruments which were to be furnished them. A separate questionnaire was formulated for this purpose. One is reminded of the vain efforts made by Velasco to obtain similar data in the 16th century by requesting local savants to record eclipses and the summer solstice to provide a scientific cartographic base for the 1577 documents (Edwards, 1969).

The 1812 inquiry devotes the first six questions to geography of the American provinces. The reformers wanted, in addition to descriptions, a set of charts and plans. They stressed the need for exact tabulations.

Article 9 in this volume of the *Handbook* reflects the great interest developed by physiocrats and others during the 18th century in scientific agriculture and land utilization. Like previous similar inquiries, the early 19th-century bureaucrats wanted information on metals, fossils, volcanoes, and other natural phenomena. However, they were equally insistent on acquiring data concerning government, educational institutions, libraries, the press, and especially the state of Indian education. They were little concerned with religion. Bourbon emphasis on economic development is also seen in the 1812 inquiry. Commerce and industry, particularly working conditions and utilization of prime local resources, were of special interest.

Professor Vilar remarks that this questionnaire in a sense provides a Utopian view of the future of America. Scientific data were to be obtained, necessary reforms were to be put into effect, to free the New World to develop ideal societies.

Unfortunately, it is not known what response this document elicited. The only reply I know about comes from Yucatan. There a local priest did give enormously useful information about the Maya on the eve of Mexican Independence. Perhaps if search of other archives would bring to light similar reports, they would be invaluable for comparative studies, as well as for this important moment in Mexican history.

449

REFERENCES

REFERENCES

ADAMS, R. N.
1962 Ethnohistoric research methods: some Latin American features. *Anthr. Linguistics*, 9: 179–205.

AITON, A. S.
1927 Antonio de Mendoza: first viceroy of New Spain. Duke Univ. Press.

AJOFRÍN, F.
1959 Diario del viaje que . . . hizo a la América septentrional en el siglo XVIII el P. Fray Francisco Ajofrín Capuchino. 2 vols. Madrid.

ALCEDO, A. DE
1786–89 Diccionario geográfico-histórico de las Indias occidentales ó América. 5 vols. Madrid.

ALEGRE, F. J.
1956 Historia de la provincia de la Compañía de Jesús de Nueva España. Vol. 1. Rome.

ALESSIO ROBLES, V.
1938 Coahuila y Texas en la época colonial. Mexico, D. F.

ALTOLAGUIRRE Y DUVALE, A. DE, ed.
1908 Relaciones geográficas de la gobernación de Venezuela (1767–68). Madrid.

ANGULO IÑÍGUEZ, D.
1954 Pintura del Renacimiento. *Ars Hispaniae*, vol. 12. Madrid.

ARÉVALO, J. J.
1936 Geografía elemental de Guatemala. Guatemala.

ARREGUI, D. L. DE
1946 Descripción de la Nueva Galicia. Seville.

ARRIAGA, A.
1946 La relación geográfica del pueblo de Charo. *An. Mus. Michoacano*, 4: 97–106.

BALLESTEROS Y BERETTA, A.
1918–41 Historia de España y su influencia en la historia universal. 10 vols. Barcelona. (Vol. 6, 1932.)

BANCROFT, H. H.
1883–86 History of Mexico. 5 vols. San Francisco.
1884–89 History of the North American states and Texas. 2 vols. San Francisco.
1886–87 History of Central America. 3 vols. San Francisco.

BARLOW, R. H.
1943 The 18th century relaciones geográficas: a bibliography. *Tlalocan*, 1: 54–70.
1944a A western extension of Zapotec. *Ibid.*, 1:267–68.
1944b A western extension of Zapotec: further remarks. *Ibid.*, 1: 359–61.
1944c The 18th century relaciones geográficas: further notes. *Ibid.*, 1: 362–63.
1945 Dos relaciones antiguas del pueblo de Cuilapa, estado de Oaxaca. *Ibid.*, 2: 18–28.
1946a Chiepetlán. . . . *Mem. Acad. Mex. Hist.*, 3: 239–56.
1946b La descripción de Alahuiztlán, 1789. *Tlalocan*, 2: 106–09.
1947 Real de Sahuaripa de 1778. *Mem. Acad. Mex. Hist.*, 6: 60–89.
—— AND G. T. SMISOR
1943 Nombre de Dios, Durango. Sacramento, Calif.

BARÓN CASTRO, R.
1942 La población de El Salvador. Madrid.

BARROCO, J. V.
1960 An ethnohistory program for the Chiapas project. Man-in-Nature Project, Dept. Anthropology, Univ. Chicago.

BAYLE, C.
1933 Historia de los descubrimientos y colonización de los padres de la Compañía de Jesús en la Baja California. Madrid.

BELEÑA, E. B.
1787 Recopilación sumaria de todos los autos acordados de la real audiencia y sala del crimen de esta Nueva España. . . . Mexico.

BENESCH, O.
1945 The art of the Renaissance in northern Europe. Harvard Univ. Press. Other eds.: 1964, Archon Books, Hamden,

Conn.; 1965, Phaidon Pub., New York Graphic Soc., Greenwich, Conn.

BERNAL, I.
1962 Archeology and written sources. *34th Int. Cong. Amer.* (Vienna, 1960), *Acta*, pp. 219–25.

BERNSTEIN, H. L.
1944 Regionalism in the national history of Mexico. *Acta Amer.*, 2: 305–14.

BOBAN, E.
1891 Documents pour servir à l'histoire du Mexique. Catalogue raisonné. 2 vols. Paris.

BOLTON, H. E.
1917 The mission as a frontier institution in the Spanish American colonies. *Amer. Hist. Rev.*, 23: 42–61.

BORAH, W.
1955 Francisco de Urdiñola's census of the Spanish settlements in Nueva Vizcaya, 1604. *Hisp. Amer. Hist. Rev.*, 35: 398–401.

1964 Un gobierno provincial de frontera. *Hist. Mex.*, 52: 532–50.

—— and S. F. COOK
1963 The aboriginal population of central Mexico on the eve of the Spanish conquest. *Ibero-Amer.*, 45.

BRAND, D. D.
1944 An historical sketch of geography and anthropology in the Tarascan region. Part 1. *New Mexico Anthr.*, 6–7: 37–108.

1951 Quiroga: a Mexican municipio. *Smithsonian Inst., Inst. Social Anthr.*, Pub. 11.

—— and others
1960 Coalcoman and Motines del Oro: an ex-distrito of Michoacan, Mexico. Univ. Texas, Inst. Latin American Studies. The Hague.

BRAVO UGARTE, J.
1965 Diócesis y obispos de la iglesia mexicana (1519–1965). Mexico, D. F.

BURRUS, E. J.
1955 An introduction to the bibliographical tools in Spanish archives and manuscript collections relating to Latin America. *Hisp. Amer. Hist. Rev.*, 25: 443–83.

CALNEK, E. E.
1961a Ethnohistory of the tribal groups of Chiapas. MS. Doctoral dissertation, Dept. Anthropology, Univ. Chicago.

1961b Distribution and location of the Tzeltal and Tzotzil pueblos of the highlands of Chiapas from earliest times to the present. Mimeographed. Man-in-Nature Project, Dept. Anthropology, Univ. Chicago.

CARBIA, R. D.
1940 La crónica oficial de las Indias occidentales: estudio histórico y crítico acerca de la historiografía, mayor de Hispano-América en los siglos XVI a XVIII. 2d ed. [1st ed. 1934]. Buenos Aires.

CARRASCO, PEDRO
1966 La etnohistoria en Meso-américa. *36th Int. Cong. Amer.* (Barcelona, 1964), *Acta*, 2: 109–10.

CARRERA STAMPA, M.
1949 Misiones mexicanas en archivos europeos. *Inst. Panamer. Geog. Hist.*, Pub. 93.

CARTAS DE INDIAS
1877 Cartas de Indias. . . . Madrid.

CASTAÑEDA, C. E.
1929 The corregidor in Spanish colonial administration. *Hisp. Amer. Hist. Rev.*, 9: 446–70.

CHAMBERLAIN, R. S.
1953 The conquest and colonization of Honduras. *Carnegie Inst. Washington*, Pub. 598.

CHAPMAN, A. M.
1960 Los Nicarao y los Chorotega según las fuentes históricas. *Univ. Costa Rica, History and Geography Ser.*, 4. San Jose.

CHAPMAN, C. E.
1939 A history of California: the Spanish period. New York.

CHEVALIER, F.
1952 La formation des grands domaines au Mexique. Paris.

CLEGERN, W. M.
1967 British Honduras: colonial dead end, 1859–1900. Louisiana State Univ. Press.

CLINE, H. F.
1946 The terragueros of Guelatao, Oaxaca, Mexico. *Acta Amer.*, 4: 161–84.

1947 Background of the War of the Castes in nineteenth century Yucatan. Doctoral dissertation, Dept. History, Harvard Univ. [Included in his 1952b.]

1949 Civil congregations of the Indians in New Spain, 1598–1606. *Hisp. Amer. Hist. Rev.*, 29: 349–69. [See also translation, with added material, *Bol. Archivo General Nación*, 16: 195–235.]

1952a Mexican community studies. *Hisp. Amer. Hist. Rev.*, 33: 212–42.

1952b Related studies in early nineteenth century Yucatecan social history. 2 vols. *Univ. Chicago, Micro. Coll. MSS Middle Amer. Cult. Anthr.*, no. 32.

1953 The United States and Mexico. Harvard Univ. Press. [Rev. ed. 1967.]

1955 Civil congregations of the western Chinantla, New Spain, 1599–1603. *The Americas*, 12: 115–37.

1957 Problems of ethno-history: the ancient Chinantla, a case study. *Hisp. Amer. Hist. Rev.*, 37: 273–95.

1960a Ethnohistory: a progress report on the Handbook of Middle American Indians. *Ibid.*, 50: 224–29.

1960b Ethnohistory of Middle America: historian's view. Unpublished paper delivered at 4th Int. Cong. Anthr. Ethnol. Sci., Paris.

1961 Imperial perspectives on the borderlands. *In* Probing the American West, K. R. Toole and others, eds., pp. 168–74.

1962 Mexico: revolution to evolution, 1940–60. Oxford Univ. Press.

1964a The Relaciones Geográficas of the Spanish Indies, 1577–1586. *Hisp. Amer. Hist. Rev.*, 44: 341–74.

1964b *See* Art. 9.

1966a Guide to ethnohistorical sources: a progress report. *36th Int. Cong. Amer.* (Barcelona, 1964), *Acta*, 2: 133–43.

1966b Native pictorial documents of eastern Oaxaca, Mexico. *In* Pompa y Pompa, 1966, pp. 101–30.

Colección de Documentos Inéditos
1864–84 Colección de documentos inéditos, relativos al descubrimiento, conquista y organización de las antiguas posesiones españolas de América y Oceanía, sacados de los archivos del reino, y muy especialmente del de Indias. 42 vols. Madrid.

Comas, J.
1950 Bosquejo histórico de la antropología en Mexico. *Rev. Mex. Estud. Antr.*, 10: 97–191.

1953 Algunos datos para la historia de indigenismo en México. *In* his Ensayos sobre indigenismo, pp. 63–108. Inst. Indigenista Interamer. Mexico. [From *América Indígena*, 8: 181–218 (1948).]

1956 La vida y obra de Manuel Gamio. *In* Estudios antropológicos publicados en homenaje al doctor Manuel Gamio, pp. 1–26.

Cook, S. F.
1949a The historical demography and ecology of the Teotlalpan. *Ibero-Amer.*, 33.

1949b Soil erosion and population in central Mexico. *Ibid.*, 34.

1958 Santa María Ixcatlán: habitat, population, subsistence. *Ibid.*, 41.

——— and W. Borah
1960 The Indian population of central Mexico, 1531–1610. *Ibid.*, 44.

Cortés, H.
1963 Cartas y documentos. Mexico.

Cosío Villegas, D.
1967 History and the social sciences in Latin America. *In* Social science in Latin America, M. Diégues Júnior and B. Wood, eds., pp. 121–37.

Cowgill, G. L.
1963 Postclassic period culture in the vicinity of Flores, Peten, Guatemala. Doctoral dissertation, Harvard Univ.

Cuevas, M., ed.
1944 Descripción de la Nueva España en el siglo XVI. Mexico.

Dávila Garibi, J. I.
1935 Recopilación de datos acerca del idioma coca y su posible influencia en el lenguaje folklórico de Jalisco. *Investigaciones Lingüísticas*, 3: 248–302.

1947 ¿Un interesante manuscrito en una de las lenguas indígenas, desaparecidas de Jalisco? *27th Int. Cong. Amer.* (Mexico, 1939, 1st sess.), *Acta*, 2: 337–53.

Dávila Padilla, A.
1625 Historia de la fundación y discurso de la provincia de Santiago de México. Brussels.

Díez de la Calle, J.
1646 Memorial, y noticias sacras, y reales del imperio de las Indias occidentales. . . . Madrid.

Dirección General
1961–62 Diccionario geográfico de Guatemala. 2 vols. Dirección General de Cartografía. Guatemala.

Documentos para la Historia de Yucatan
See Scholes and others, 1936–38

Durán Ochoa, J.
1955 Población: estructura económica y social de México. Fondo de Cultura Económica. Mexico, D. F.

EDWARDS, C. R.
1969 Mapping by questionnaire: an early Spanish attempt to determine New World geographical positions. *Imago Mundi*, 23: 17–28.

ENCINAS, D. DE
1945–46 Cedulario Indiano. . . . 4 vols. Madrid.

EPISTOLARIO DE NUEVA ESPAÑA
1939–42 Epistolario de Nueva España, 1505–1818. 16 vols. Mexico, D. F.

ESCALANTE HERNÁNDEZ, R.
1962 El Cuitlateco. *Inst. Nac. Antr. Hist., Depto. Invest. Antr.*, Pub. 9. Mexico, D. F.

FENTON, W. N.
1952 The training of historical ethnologists in America. *Amer. Anthr.*, 54: 328–39.

FERNÁNDEZ DE MIRANDA, M. T.
1956 Glotocronología de la familia popoloca. *Inst. Nac. Antr. Hist., Ser. Cien. Museo Antr.*, 4. Mexico, D. F.

—— AND R. J. WEITLANER
1961 Sobre algunas relaciones de la familia mangue. *Anthr. Linguistics*, 3 (7): 1–99.

FERRER DEL RÍO, A.
1856 Historia del reinado de Carlos III en España. 4 vols. Madrid.

FISHER, L. E.
1926 Viceregal administration in America. *Univ. California Pub. Hist.*, 15. Berkeley.
1928 The intendant system in Spanish-America. *Hisp. Amer. Hist. Rev.*, 8: 3–13.
1929 The intendant system in Spanish America. Univ. California Press.

GARCÍA ICAZBALCETA, J.
1954 Bibliografía mexicana del siglo XVI. 2d ed. Mexico, D. F.

GARCÍA PAYÓN, J.
1941 Matlatzincas o Pirindas. Mexico, D. F.
1942 Interpretación de la vida de los pueblos matlatzincas. *El Mex. Antiguo*, 6:47–60.

GARCÍA PIMENTEL, L., ed.
1897 Descripción del arzobispado de México hecha en 1570 y otros documentos. Mexico, D. F.
1904 Relación de los obispados de Tlaxcala, Michoacán, Oaxaca, y otros lugares en el siglo XVI. Mexico, Paris, and Madrid.

GARCÍA RUIZ, A.
1947 La misión del historiador José de Jesús Núñez y Domínguez en archivos de Europa (1937–1939). *An. Inst. Nac. Antr. Hist.*, n.s., 2: 321–71.

GAY, J. A.
1950 Historia de Oaxaca. 2d ed. Mexico, D. F.

GIBSON, C.
1952 Tlaxcala in the sixteenth century. *Yale Hist. Pub., Miscellany*, 56.
1961 Consideraciones sobre la etnohistoria. *Estud. Amer.*, 21 (108): 279–84.
1964 The Aztecs under Spanish rule: a history of the Indians of the Valley of Mexico, 1519–1810. Stanford Univ. Press.
1966 Spain in America. New York.

GIL Y SÁENZ, M.
1872 Compendio histórico, geográfico y estadístico del estado de Tabasco. Tabasco.

GLASS, J. B.
1964 Catálogo de los códices. Mus. Nac. Antr. Mexico.

GÓMEZ CANEDO, L.
1961 Los archivos de la historia de América. *Panamer. Inst. Geog. Hist.*, Pub. 225. Mexico, D. F.

GÓMEZ DE OROZCO, F., ed.
1927a Descripción de Cholula. *Rev. Mex. Estud. Hist.*, vol. 1, no. 6, suppl., pp. 158–70.
For other titles of this date *see* Art. 9.

GONZÁLEZ DE COSSÍO, F.
1952 Prólogo. *In* Villaseñor y Sánchez, 1952.

GONZÁLEZ NAVARRO, M.
1953 Repartimiento de indios en Nueva Galicia. Mexico, D. F.
1954 Instituciones indígenas en México independiente. *In* A. Caso, Métodos y resultados de la política indigenista en México, pp. 113–69. *Mem. Inst. Nac. Indigenista*, 6. Mexico, D. F.

GRIFFIN, C. C., ed.
1971 Latin America: a guide to the historical literature. *Conference on Latin American History Pub.*, 3. Univ. Texas Press.

GUDSCHINSKY, S. C.
1959 Proto-popotecan. *Int. Jour. Amer. Linguistics*, vol. 25, no. 2 (whole).

GUNNERSON, J. H.
1958 A survey of ethnohistoric sources. *Kroeber Anthr. Soc. Papers*, 18: 49–65.

HACKETT, C. W.
1918 The delimitation of political jurisdictions in Spanish North America to 1535. *Hisp. Amer. Hist. Rev.*, 1: 40–69.

HANDBOOK OF AMERICAN INDIANS NORTH OF MEXICO
1907–10 Handbook of American Indians north of Mexico. F. W. Hodge, ed. 2 vols. *Smithsonian Inst., Bur. Amer. Ethnol.*, Bull. 30.

HANDBOOK OF LATIN AMERICAN STUDIES
1936– Handbook of Latin American studies: a selective and annotated guide to recent publications . . . prepared by a number of scholars for the Hispanic Foundation in the Library of Congress. Various editors. 32 vols. to date (1970), annually.

HANDBOOK OF SOUTH AMERICAN INDIANS
1946–59 Handbook of South American Indians. J. H. Steward, ed. 7 vols. *Smithsonian Inst., Bur. Amer. Ethnol.*, Bull. 143.

HARING, C. H.
1947 The Spanish empire in America. New York.
1963 *Idem*, 2d ed.

HARTSHORNE, R.
1939 The nature of geography: a critical survey of current thought in the light of the past. Assoc. Amer. Geographers. Lancaster.

HENDRICHS PÉREZ, P.
1947 Por tierras ignotas. 2 vols. Mexico, D. F.

HEXTER, J. H.
1968 Historiography: the rhetoric of history. *In* International Encyclopedia of the Social Sciences, 6: 368–94.

HUASTECOS, TOTONACOS Y SUS VECINOS
1953 Huastecos, Totonacos y sus vecinos. I. Bernal and E. Dávalos Hurtado, eds. *Rev. Mex. Estud. Antr.*, vol. 13, nos. 2 and 3.

HUMBOLDT, A. VON
1811 Essai politique sur le royaume de la Nouvelle-Espagne. 5 vols. Paris.
1825 *Idem*, another edition.

HUMPHREYS, R. A.
1961 The diplomatic history of British Honduras, 1638–1901. Oxford Univ. Press.

JIMÉNEZ MORENO, W.
1958 Estudios de historia colonial. Inst. Nac. Antr. Hist. Mexico, D. F.

JUARROS, D.
1809 Compendio de la historia de la ciudad de Guatemala. 2 vols. Guatemala.

KELLY, I. T., AND A. PALERM
1952 The Tajin Totonac. Part 1: History, subsistence, shelter, and technology. *Smithsonian Inst., Inst. Social Anthr.*, Pub. 13.

KIRCHHOFF, P.
1943 Mesoamérica. *Acta Amer.*, 1: 92–107.
1966 Los estudios mesoamericanos, hoy y mañana. *In* Pompa y Pompa, 1966, pp. 205–08.

KUBLER, G.
1946 The Quechua in the colonial world. *In* Handbook of South American Indians, 2: 331–410.
1961 On the colonial extinction of the motifs of pre-Columbian art. *In* S. K. Lothrop and others, Essays in pre-Columbian art and archaeology, pp. 14–34. Harvard Univ. Press.

—— AND M. SORIA
1959 Art and architecture in Spain and Portugal and their American dominions, 1500 to 1800. Pelican History of Art, Z17. Penguin Books.

LAFORA, N. DE
1958 The frontiers of New Spain: Nicolás de Lafora's description, 1766–1768. Berkeley.

LAFUENTE FERRARI, E.
1953 Breve historia de la pintura española. Colección Síntesis de Arte. Madrid.

LEDESMA, B. DE
1905 Descripción del arzobispado de México. *In* Paso y Troncoso, Papeles de Nueva España, vol. 3. Madrid.

LEMOINE VILLICAÑA, E.
1954 Ensayo de división municipal del estado de Oaxaca en 1950. *Yan*, no. 3, pp. 69–74.
1963 Relación de Pátzcuaro y su distrito en 1754. *Bol. Archivo General Nación*, n.s., 4: 57–92.
1964 Miscelánea zacatecana: documentos histórico-geográficos de los siglos XVII al XIX. *Ibid.*, 5: 243–331.

LEÓN–PORTILLA, M., AND A. M. GARIBAY K., eds. and trans.
1959 Visión de los vencidos: relaciones indígenas de la conquista. Univ. Nac. Autónoma Mex., Biblioteca estudiante universitario, 81.

LEWIS, O.
1942 The effects of White contact upon

457

Blackfoot culture. *Amer. Ethnol. Soc.*, Monogr. 6.
1951 Life in a Mexican village: Tepoztlán restudied. Univ. Illinois Press.

LIBRO DE TASACIONES
1952 El libro de las tasaciones de pueblos de la Nueva España, siglo XVI. Archivo General de la Nación. Mexico, D. F.

LOHMANN VILLENA, G.
1957 El corregidor de indios en el Perú bajo los Austrias. Cultura Hispánica. Madrid.

LONGACRE, R. E.
1957 Proto-mixteca. *Int. Jour. Amer. Linguistics*, vol. 23, no. 4, part 3.
1961 Swadesh's Macro-Mixtecan hypothesis. *Ibid.*, 27: 9–29.

LÓPEZ DE VELASCO, J.
1894 Geografía y descripción universal de las Indias. *Bol. Soc. Geog. Madrid*, vol. 12. Madrid.

McQUOWN, N. A.
1941 La fonémica del cuitlateco. *El Mex. Antiguo*, 5: 239–54.
1942 Una posible síntesis lingüística Macro-Mayance. *In* Mayas y Olmecas, 2: 37–38.

MAGDALENO, R., ed.
1954 Títulos de Indias. Valladolid.

MANRIQUE, J. A., ed.
1966 Veintecinco años de investigación histórica en México. El Colegio de México, Edición especial de historia mexicana.

MANRIQUE, L., AND Y. LESUR
1966 Historia prehispánica. *In* J. A. Manrique, 1966, pp. 375–403.

MARTÍNEZ, M. G.
1947 Don Joaquín García Icazbalceta: his place in Mexican historiography. *Catholic Univ. Amer., Studies in Hispanic American History*, 4. Washington.
1951 Don Joaquín García Icazbalceta, su lugar en la historiografía mexicana. Traducción, notas, y apéndice de Luis García Pimentel y Elguero. *Rev. Interamer. Bibliografía*, 1: 81–88. Mexico, D. F.

MASON, J. A.
1940 The native languages of Middle America. *In* The Maya and their neighbors, pp. 52–87. New York.

MAYA AND THEIR NEIGHBORS, THE
1940 The Maya and their neighbors. C. L. Hay and others, eds. New York.

MAYER, A. L.
1949 La pintura española. Barcelona.

MECHAM, J. L.
1927 The *real de minas* as a political institution. *Hisp. Amer. Hist. Rev.*, 7: 45–83.

MEIGS, P.
1935 The Dominican mission frontier of Lower California. Berkeley.

MEJÍA, J. V.
1927 Geografía de la Republica de Guatemala. 2d ed. Guatemala.

MINK, L. O.
1968 Collingwood's dialetic of history. *History and Theory*, 7: 3–37. Wesleyan Univ. Press.

MIRANDA, J.
1952 Las ideas y las instituciones políticas mexicanas. . . . Mexico, D. F.

MOLINA ARGÜELLO, C.
1960 Gobernaciones, alcaldías mayores y corregimientos en el reino de Guatemala. *Anuario Estud. Amer.*, 17: 105–32. Seville.

MOTA PADILLA, M. DE LA
1870 Historia de la conquista de la provincia de la Nueva Galicia. Mexico, D. F.

MOTA Y ESCOBAR, A. DE LA
1940 Descripción geográfica de los reinos de Nueva Galicia, Nueva Vizcaya y Nuevo León. Mexico, D. F.

MURO OREJÓN, A., ed.
1957 Las ordenanzas de 1571 del Real y Supremo Consejo de las Indias. *Anuario Estud. Amer.*, 14: 363–423. Seville.

MURRA, J. V.
1967 Ethnohistory: South America. *In* Handbook of Latin American Studies, 29:200–13.

MURRAY, D.
1904 Museums, their history and their use. 3 vols. Glasgow.

NAVARRO GARCÍA, L.
1959 Intendencias en Indias. *Escuela estud. hispano-amer. de Sevilla*, Pub. 118. Seville.
1964 Don José de Gálvez y la comandancia general de las Provincias Internas del norte de Nueva España [1765–1783]. *Ibid.*, Pub. 148.

NICHOLSON, H. B.
1955 Native historical traditions of nuclear America and the problem of their archeological correlation. *Amer. Anthr.*, 57: 594–613.

1960–67 Ethnohistory: Mesoamerica. *In* Handbook of Latin American studies, 22: 30–42 (1960); 23: 57–70 (1961); 24: 56–66 (1962); 25: 50–61 (1963); 27: 75–96 (1965); 29: 156–99 (1967).

1962 The Mesoamerican pictorial manuscripts: research, past and present. *34th Int. Cong. Amer.* (Vienna, 1960), *Acta*, pp. 199–215.

NOVO Y COLSON, P. DE
1885 Viaje político-científico alrededor del mundo. Madrid.

NÚÑEZ Y DOMÍNGUEZ, J.
1939 Documentos existentes en la Biblioteca Nacional de Paris, relativos a Chihuahua y Durango. *Bol. Chihuahuense Estud. Históricos*, 2: 128–30, 133.

NUTTALL, Z.
1921–22 Royal ordinances concerning the laying out of new towns. *Hisp. Amer. Hist. Rev.*, 4: 743–53 (1921); 5: 249–54 (1922).

OCARANZA, F.
1937–39 Crónicas y relaciones del occidente de México. 2 vols. Mexico, D. F.

O'GORMAN, E.
1966 Historia de las divisiones territoriales de México. 3d ed. [1st ed. 1937]. Mexico, D. F.

OROZCO Y BERRA, M.
1864 Geografía de las lenguas y carta etnográfica de México. Mexico, D. F.
1881 Apuntes para la historia de la geografía en México. Mexico, D. F.

PADDEN, R. C.
1967 The hummingbird and the hawk: conquest and sovereignty in the Valley of Mexico, 1503–1541. Ohio State Univ. Press.

PADDOCK, J., ed.
1966 Ancient Oaxaca: discoveries in Mexican archeology and history. Stanford Univ. Press.

PADGETT, L. V.
1966 The Mexican political system. Boston.

PÁEZ BROTCHIE, L.
1940 La Nueva Galicia a través de su viejo archivo judicial. Mexico, D. F.

PAPELES DE NUEVA ESPAÑA
1905–06 Papeles de Nueva España. F. del Paso y Troncoso, ed. 7 vols. Madrid.

PARDO Y BARREDA, J.
1905 Arbitraje de límites entre Perú y el Ecuador. Madrid.

PARRY, J. H.
1948 The audiencia of Nueva Galicia in the sixteenth century. Cambridge Univ. Press.
1953 The sale of public office in the Spanish Indies under the Hapsburgs. *Ibero-Amer.*, 37.

PASO Y TRONCOSO, F. DEL, comp.
1940 Epistolario de Nueva España. Vol. 14. Mexico, D. F.

PASSMORE, J. A.
1958 History and sociology. *Australian Jour. Politics and Hist.*, 3: 218–28.

PERALTA, M. M. DE
1883 Costa-Rica, Nicaragua y Panamá en el siglo XVI. . . . Madrid.

PÉREZ DE RIBAS, A.
1645 Historia de los triumphos de nuestra santa fee. . . . Madrid.

PHELAN, J. L.
1959 The Hispanization of the Philippines: Spanish aims and Filipino responses. Univ. Wisconsin Press.

POMPA Y POMPA, A., ed.
1960 Estudios históricos de Sinaloa. Mexico, D. F.
1966 Summa anthropologica: en homenaje a Roberto J. Weitlaner. Mexico, D. F.

PONCE, A.
1873 Relación breve y verdadera. . . . 2 vols. Madrid.

PORTILLO Y DÍEZ DE SOLLANO, A. DEL
1947 Descubrimientos y exploraciones en las costas de California. Madrid.

POTASH, R. A.
1960 Historiography of Mexico since 1821. *Hisp. Amer. Hist. Rev.*, 40: 383–424.

POWELL, T. G.
1968 Mexican intellectuals and the Indian question. *Ibid.*, 43: 19–36.

PRIESTLEY, H. I.
1916 José de Gálvez, visitor-general of New Spain, 1765–1771. Univ. California Press.

PUGA, V. DE
1563 Prouisiões, cedulas, instruciones [*sic*] de su magestad. . . . Mexico, D. F.

RADIN, P.
1933 Notes on the Tlappanecan languages of Guerrero. *Int. Jour. Amer. Linguistics*, 8: 45–72.

REED, N.
1964 The Caste War of Yucatan, with a

foreword by H. F. Cline. Stanford Univ. Press.

REYES M., J. L.
1960 Bibliografía de los estudios geográficos de la República de Guatemala desde 1574 hasta nuestros días. Guatemala.

RICO GONZÁLEZ, V.
1953 Hacia un concepto de la conquista de México. *Univ. Nac. Autónoma Mex., Inst. Historia*, ser. 1, no. 29.

RIVERA, P. DE
1736 Diario ye derrotero de lo caminado, visto, y obcervado en el discurso de la visita general . . . que de orden de su magestad executó D. Pedro de Rivera. . . . Guatemala.

ROBERTSON, D.
1964 Los manuscritos religiosos mixtecos. *35th Int. Cong. Amer.* (Mexico, 1962), *Acta*, 1: 425–35.
1966 The Mixtec religious manuscripts. *In* Paddock, pp. 298–312.

RODRÍGUEZ ZETINA, A.
1956 Jacona y Zamora. Mexico, D. F.

ROWE, J. H.
1946 Inca culture at the time of Spanish conquest. *In* Handbook of South American Indians, 2: 183–330.

ROYS, R. L.
1943 The Indian background of colonial Yucatan. *Carnegie Inst. Washington*, Pub. 548.
1957 The political geography of the Yucatan Maya. *Ibid.*, Pub. 613.
1962 Literary sources for the history of Mayapan. *In* H. E. D. Pollock and others, Mayapan, Yucatan, Mexico, pp. 24–86. *Ibid.*, Pub. 619.

RUBIO MAÑÉ, J. I.
1946 Jurisdicciones del virreinato de Nueva España en la primera mitad del siglo XVIII. *Rev. de Indias*, 7: 463–502.
1955 Introducción al estudio de los virreyes de Nueva España, 1535–1746. Vol. 1: Orígenes y jurisdicciones, y dinámica social de los virreyes. Mexico, D. F.

RUIZ DE ALARCON, H.
1892 Tratado de las idolatrías, supersticiones, dioses, ritos. . . . *An. Mus. Nac. Antr.*, ep. 1, 6: 123–223.

SAHAGÚN, B. DE
1938 Historia general de las cosas de Nueva España. 5 vols. Mexico, D. F.

SAMAYOA GUEVERA, H. H.
1960 Implantación del régimen de intendancias en el reino de Guatemala. Guatemala.

SAPIR, E.
1916 Time perspectives in aboriginal American culture: a study in method. *Mem. Canadian Dept. Mines*, 90. Ottawa.

SARAVIA, A. G.
1930 Apuntes para la historia de la Nueva Vizcaya. Vol. 1. Mexico, D. F.

SAUER, C. O.
1932 The road to Cíbola. *Ibero-Amer.*, 3.
1948 Colima of New Spain in the sixteenth century. *Ibid.*, 29.

SCHÄFER, E.
1935–47 El Consejo Real y Supremo de las Indias. 2 vols. Seville.

SCHOLES, F. V., AND R. L. ROYS
1948 The Maya Chontal Indians of Acalan-Tixchel: a contribution to the history and ethnography of the Yucatan peninsula. *Carnegie Inst. Washington*, Pub. 560.

——, C. R. MENÉNDEZ, J. I. RUBIO MAÑÉ, AND E. B. ADAMS, eds.
1936–38 Documentos para la historia de Yucatán. 3 vols. Merida.

SEPÚLVEDA, C.
1958 Historia y problemas de los límites de México. II: La frontera sur. *Hist. Mex.*, 30: 145–74.

SERRANO Y SANZ, M., ed.
1908 Relaciones históricas y geográficas de América Central. Madrid.

SOMOLINOS D'ARDOIS, G., ed.
1960 Vida y obra de Francisco Hernández. *Obras Completas de Francisco Hernández*, vol. 1. Mexico, D. F.

SPARKS, E. E.
1908 Report of a conference on the relations of geography to history. *Amer. Hist. Assoc.*, ann. rept. for 1908, pp. 57–61.

STABB, M. S.
1959 Indigenism and racism in Mexican thought: 1857–1911. *Jour. Inter-Amer. Studies*, 50: 405–23.

STURTEVANT, W. C.
1957 The problems of historical ethnology.